Voice, Slavery, and Race in Seventeenth-Century Florence

Voice, Slavery, and Race in Seventeenth-Century Florence

EMILY WILBOURNE

Oxford University Press is a department of the University of Oxford. It furthers
the University's objective of excellence in research, scholarship, and education
by publishing worldwide. Oxford is a registered trade mark of Oxford University
Press in the UK and certain other countries.

Published in the United States of America by Oxford University Press
198 Madison Avenue, New York, NY 10016, United States of America.

© Oxford University Press 2023

OUP gratefully acknowledges support from the Margarita M. Hanson Fund of the
American Musicological Society, supported in part by the National Endowment for the
Humanities and the Andrew W. Mellon Foundation.

All rights reserved. No part of this publication may be reproduced, stored in
a retrieval system, or transmitted, in any form or by any means, without the
prior permission in writing of Oxford University Press, or as expressly permitted
by law, by license, or under terms agreed with the appropriate reproduction
rights organization. Inquiries concerning reproduction outside the scope of the
above should be sent to the Rights Department, Oxford University Press, at the
address above.

You must not circulate this work in any other form
and you must impose this same condition on any acquirer.

Library of Congress Cataloging-in-Publication Data
Names: Wilbourne, Emily, author.
Title: Voice, slavery, and race in seventeenth-century Florence /
Emily Wilbourne.
Description: [1.] | New York : Oxford University Press, 2023. |
Includes bibliographical references and index.
Identifiers: LCCN 2023011414 (print) | LCCN 2023011415 (ebook) |
ISBN 9780197646915 (hardback) | ISBN 9780197646939 (epub)
Subjects: LCSH: Music—Italy—Florence—17th century—History and criticism. |
Orientalism in music—Italy—Florence—History—17th century. |
Music—Social aspects—Italy—Florence—History—17th century. |
Music—Political aspects—Italy—Florence—History—17th century. |
Enslaved persons—Social conditions—Italy—Florence—History—17th century. |
Music and race—Italy—Florence—History—17th century. |
Buonaccorsi, Giovannino, -1674. | Singers—Italy—Florence—Biography.
Classification: LCC ML290.2.W55 2023 (print) | LCC ML290.2 (ebook) |
DDC 780.945/51109032—dc23/eng/20230317
LC record available at https://lccn.loc.gov/2023011414
LC ebook record available at https://lccn.loc.gov/2023011415

DOI: 10.1093/oso/9780197646915.001.0001

Printed by Integrated Books International, United States of America

I dedicate this book to my undergraduate students at the Aaron Copland School of Music: may they find themselves in music history.

In memoriam
Roma Carmel Hoskin Cresp (July 12, 1929–August 10, 2022)

Contents

Acknowledgments ix
Abbreviations xiii
Notes on Sources xv
Prologo xvii

Introduction 1

ACT I 41

Scene 1. Songs to Entertain Foreign Royalty 43

Scene 2. Comic Songs Imitating Foreign Voices 64

Scene 3. Music *all'Usanza Loro* (Performed in a Foreign Way) 84

Scene 4. "Turkish Music" in Italy 104

Scene 5. Trumpets and Drums Played by Enslaved Musicians 120

Scene 6. Scholarly Transcriptions of Foreign Musical Sounds 135

Scene 7. Music Proper to Enslaved Singers 146

Intermezzo Primo: Thinking from Enslaved Lives 162

ACT II 169

Scene 8. Introducing Giovannino Buonaccorsi 171

Scene 9. Buonaccorsi Sings on the Florentine Stage 193

Scene 10. Buonaccorsi as Court Jester 208

Scene 11. Buonaccorsi as a Black Gypsy 232

Scene 12. Buonaccorsi as a Soprano 238

Scene 13. Buonaccorsi Sings on the Venetian Stage 254

Intermezzo Secondo: Thinking from Giovannino
 Buonaccorsi's Life   283

Epilogo (Axiomatic)   289
*Appendix: Archival References to Enslaved, Moorish, and
 "Turkish" ("Non-Christian") Individuals*   317
Bibliography   465
Index   485

Acknowledgments

The writing of books requires time, resources, access to archives and sources, reliable childcare, and a legion of friends and accomplices to cheer the spirits, read drafts, make food, make art, listen to complaints, and help in all the ways that human beings need one another every day. To finish a book during a pandemic is a rather forceful reminder of how important, how precarious, and how mutually dependent we are on one another. This book would not exist if the bulk of my research had not happened in the before times, when international travel and archive access were a question of schedules and travel budgets, not of closed borders and contagion avoidance. Likewise, the final writing process of this book would not—could not—have happened if the public schools had not reopened, welcoming my (grateful) children to a safe place outside the home for several hours most days of the week. In the placid, quiet hours of their absence, I managed to finally get this book done, though I am most grateful for the noisy, companionable hours of their presence. In academic acknowledgments, it is traditional to thank one's immediate family last; however, under current circumstance, the last needs to be first. Luki, Anastasia, Rex: you are a shining, powerful, energizing joy. I never thought that we would spend quite as much time together, just us four, as we have the last few years, but what a delight to know that my most trenchant critics, biggest advocates, and three dearest people in the world are one and the same; to know that my three nearest and dearest make entertaining and caring companions, even under long, drawn-out, and trying circumstances. I love each of you—so much—and I couldn't have done this, or much else, to be honest, without you.

Professionally and personally, the last two years have been long and lonely: as of January 2022, I have yet to return to the physical classroom; conference after conference has postponed or "moved" online; and so many people have left New York that at times, our busy, vibrant city has seemed like a ghost town. I have missed the presence of friends, colleagues, and students and the serendipity of chance interactions. I miss the way ideas bounce in space and am heartily sick of Zoom anything. I therefore want to celebrate those who have managed to be present, even in absence; those who mailed coffee, wine, or cards or picked up the phone; those who visited on my stoop; those who sat with me at outdoor concerts or in cold, outdoor coffee shops, walked briskly round the block or the park or the Chelsea piers, or knitted in solidarity while seated six feet apart on the stairs. Here—in a jumble of family, friends, colleagues, students, and those border crossers who fit more than one category—are those who have gotten me through: María Edurne Zuazu (cited first, so that the Z doesn't make her last); Gael Cresp; Stephen Wilbourne; Elizabeth Wilbourne; Rebecca Wilbourne; Yun Emily Wang; Suzanne G. Cusick; Karen Henson and Anne Stone (the best of friends and best of colleagues); Elizabeth Fleming; Elizabeth Weinfield; Elizabeth Clayton (the Elizabeths in my life are multiplying); Sara James; LJ Jellinek; Terese Wadden; Francesca Fantappiè; Nanika Coors; Serena Parker (those birthday balloons make me smile every time I think of them); Teddy Hunter; Greg Costanzo; Marsha Stephanie Blake; Michael Stevens; Amy Brosius; my AMS mentees Daniel Castro Pantoja, Anne Levitsky, Samantha Ege, and Alecia Barbour; Laura, Kelly, Jasper, and Piper Moffat; Kevin Ferguson (and his car); my summer boot camp writing group Yun Emily Wang (again), Iantheia Calhoun, and Clara Hunter Latham; Michelle Yom; Samuel Teeple; Chelsea Lane; Ana Beatriz Mujica Lafuente; Kristopher Konigin; Tod Hedrick; Jennifer Roderer (those fruit cakes!); and of course, my wild visitor Cooper.

I want to thank, too, all those whom I have missed during lockdown but were vibrant parts of my life in the before times: everyone at conferences who has questioned or prodded me on parts of the argument given here, those whose brilliance and whose company lights up the AMS, and the many members of my department whose presence enlivens the corridors and classrooms of the Aaron Copland School of Music and the Graduate Center. In particular, thanks to my I Tatti cohort and those in the Acoustemologies project (Patricia Akimie, Olivia Bloechl, Ireri Chavez Barcenas, Suzanne G. Cusick, Glenda Goodman, Lester Hu, Danielle Skeehan, Nina Treadwell, Jane Tylus). Kate van Orden, Bonnie Gordon, Martha Feldman, and Suzanne G. Cusick: you are shining lights of scholarship and inspiration; I wouldn't think about the seventeenth century and musical sound the way I do if I hadn't encountered your writings, nor would I think as coherently or have made it this far without your constructive criticism and your support. Thanks, too, to the graduate students in my doctoral seminars, "Critical Approaches to Race and Musicology" (Spring 2019) and "Early Modern Voice" (Spring 2021); your provocations and your enthusiasms have shaped and fueled this project in important ways: Stephen Ai, Evangeline Athanasiou, Luca Battioni, Hayle Briggles, Nafest Chenib, Ana Beatriz Mujica Lafuente, Diana Maron Mendonce, Jennifer Roderer, Elaine Sandoval, Aidan Selmer, Sandow Sinai, Samuel Teeple, Matthew Timmermans, Robert Wrigley, and Michelle Yom. To my truly excellent research assistants I remain extremely grateful: Rebecca Coale, Ana Beatriz Mujica Lafuente, and Samuel Teeple, who helped look through the baptismal records; Tod Hedrick and Danielle Bonaiuto, for their work on the musical examples; and Emily Addis, for the index. Lucia Marchi was the first to read this manuscript through from start to finish, and her help correcting and proofing my Italian translations was very much appreciated.

Thank you to fellow travelers, archivists, and academics who have answered my (many) questions or responded to emails with generosity and insight and those who have shared materials or drafts of their work, particularly Paul Kaplan, Jennifer Williams Brown, Jessica Goethals, Lucia Sandri, Lucia Ricciardi of the Innocenti archives, Arne Spohr, Nathan Reeves, Lucia Frattarelli-Fisher, E. Natalie Rothman, Adela Gjata of the Pergola archives, Stephanie Nadalo, Mustafà Avci and Jonathan Shannon for their exemplary Turkish translations and advice, Özden Mercan, Pier Mattia Tommasino, Alessio Assonitis, Roger Frietas, Stephan Wolohojian and Patrice Mattia of the Metropolitan Museum, Letizia Treves of the National Gallery in London, and Elisabetta Bettio and Andrea Ossani of the Archivio di Stato di Firenze.

Thank you, too, to everyone at Oxford University Press, among them Norman Hirschy, Laura Santo, and Wendy Keebler (I fear that copyediting that appendix may have taken years of your life! Thank you immensely).

In last-but-not-least place, I want to return to the question of time. I remain immensely grateful to the institutions that saw fit to fund time spent on this book: my university, Queens College in the City University of New York, supported me with both a Fellowship Leave and a Research Incentive Award, as well as assistance with travel expenses; Villa I Tatti, the Harvard University Center for Italian Renaissance Studies, funded a magical year in Florence; the PSC-CUNY funded a research trip in the summer of 2019; and the CUNY Office of Research provided a book completion grant that enabled the inclusion of so many beautiful color prints.

Earlier versions of material published here were presented at many conferences and colloquium talks. Some material has previously appeared in print. See Emily Wilbourne, "*Four Servants of the Medici Court, Anton Domenico Gabbiani (1686),*" in *On Being Present: Images of Black Africans in the Galleria degli Uffizi*, in collaboration with Black History

Month Florence, https://www.uffizi.it/mostre-virtuali/on-being-present (March 2020); Emily Wilbourne, "Music, Race, Representation: Three Scenes of Performance at the Medici Court (1608–1616)," *Il Saggiatore Musicale* 27, no. 1 (2020): 5–45; Emily Wilbourne, "Little Black Giovanni's Dream: Black Authorship and the 'Turks, Dwarves, and Bad Christians' of the Medici Court," in *Acoustemologies in Contact: Sounding Subjects and Modes of Listening in Early Modernity*, ed. Emily Wilbourne and Suzanne G. Cusick (Cambridge: Open Book, 2021), 135–165; and Emily Wilbourne, "'. . . La Curiosità del Personaggio': 'Il Moro' on the Mid-Century Operatic Stage," in *Seachanges: Music in the Mediterranean and Atlantic Worlds, 1550–1880*, ed. Kate van Orden, I Tatti Research Series 2 (Cambridge, MA: Harvard University Press, 2022), 133–148. See also Emily Wilbourne, "Gio: Buonaccorsi 'the Moor': An Enslaved Black Singer at the Medici Court," in *Teaching Race in the European Renaissance: A Classroom Guide*, edited by Matthieu Chapman and Anna Wainwright, 267–287. Tempe: Arizona Center of Medieval and Renaissance Studies Press, 2023.

Abbreviations

b.	*busta*, archival box
c.	*carta*, sheet (recto, verso)
c.n.n.	*carte non numerate*, unnumbered sheets
f.	*filza*, archival file
fol.	folio
fg.	*fotogramma*, photogram
I-Fas	Florence, Archivio di Stato
I-FAoi	Florence, Archivio Storico dell'Istituto degli Innocenti
I-FcasaB	Florence, Archivio Buonarroti
I-Fca	Florence, Curia Arcivescovile, Archivio Storico
I-Fd	Florence, Opera del Duomo, Archivio
I-FImmobili	Florence, Archivio dell'Accademia degli Immobili
I-Fl	Florence, Biblioteca Medicea Laurenziana
I-Fn	Florence, Biblioteca Nazionale Centrale
I-MAa	Mantua, Archivio di Stato
imm.	image
ins.	insert
I-Ras	Archivio di Stato, Rome
I-Ru	Rome, Biblioteca Universitaria Alessandrinia
I-Vas	Venice, Archivio di Stato
m., mm.	measure, measures
reg.	*registro*, register
SA	*Sua Altezza*, His/Her Highness
SAS	*Sua Altezza Serenissima*, Your/His/Her Serene Highness

For libraries and archives, the RISM (Répertoire International des Sources Musicales) sigla have been used where possible; where RISM sigla do not exist, abbreviations have been constructed using the sigla as models.

Notes on Sources

The musical examples used in this book are transcribed from contemporary sources, whether manuscript or early printed edition. With very few exceptions, original note values and barring have been maintained.

Where Italian lyrics, play texts, or archival sources are cited, I have maintained the spelling and punctuation of the original text. Where abbreviations are expanded for clarity, the added letters are rendered in italics.

Sua Altezza si contenta che si battezzino, ma sappino che restano in ogni modo stiavi.

His Highness [Ferdinando I de' Medici] gives permission that they can be baptized, but they must know that in every way they will remain slaves.
                    I-Fca, *Pia Casa dei Catecumini*, f. 1, 1617, c.n.n.

Prologo

Artemisia Gentileschi's *Esther before Ahasuerus* hangs at the Metropolitan Museum of Art, up on Fifth Avenue, just south of the Egyptian playground where my children love to run through tunnels and up pyramids, screaming with laughter. The story in the painting is biblical (see Figure P.1, reproduced after page 240). Esther (the secretly Jewish wife of the Persian monarch Ahasuerus) is (rightly) horrified by a recent decree that all Jews are to be slaughtered. She resolves to take action and enters the throne room in order to supplicate her husband, even though to approach the throne without permission is punishable by death. As she enters, she swoons. Viewers familiar with the Old Testament story would have known what is to happen next: Ahasuerus, moved by his love for Esther and her evident distress, spares her life. Esther pleads for the lives of her coreligionists, and Ahasuerus grants her request.

The scene depicted is, more properly, a depicted scene, for, unlike Paolo Veronese's treatment of the same subject (shown as Figure P.2, reproduced after page 240), Gentileschi eschews the pomp and exotic detail of the biblical palace in favor of an intimate theatrical performance; she paints a commedia dell'arte troupe in theatrical costume performing a dramatic rendering of the tale. A clear reference to the earlier Veronese work can be seen in the position of the women and their location in relation to Ahasuerus and his elevated throne.

Gentileschi's citation of Veronese has distracted art historians, who have largely adjudicated the comparison in Veronese's favor, lauding his "large-scale *istoria*, full of figures and incidental details," attributing to Gentileschi a desire for similar effect, and finding her "ill-equipped to do so entirely successfully."[1] In the absence of biblical detail, Gentileschi's *Esther* has been found wanting—there are no watching courtiers, the room itself is plain rather than ostentatious, and the king is youthful and somewhat overwhelmed by

---

[1] Jesse M. Locker, *Artemisia Gentileschi: The Language of Painting* (New Haven, CT: Yale University Press, 2015), 75. Shelia Barker is an outlier, interpreting the work as an allegory of religious conflict and female political power reflecting the role of Henrietta Maria (wife of Charles I) at the English court; see Shelia Barker, *Artemisia Gentileschi* (Los Angeles: Getty Publications, 2022), 107–115.

his situation. The female painter's presumed inadequacy is underscored by pentimenti that are now (re)visible to the eye: emerging through the paint as it fades are a young Black boy and a dog on the steps between the king and his fainting wife. The boy was complete before the decision was made to remove him, with even the lights in his eyes fixed in paint (see Figure P.3, reproduced after page 240); the precise rendering of the covering paint, and particularly the distinctively Artemisian floor tiles, imply that the repainting happened before the work left Gentileschi's studio.[2]

Jesse Locker, writing in 2015, has come closest to seeing Gentileschi's painting on its own terms, identifying the outfit of the monarch Ahasuerus as that of a commedia dell'arte *innamorato* (a "lover," or young male lead),[3] though he misreads the conventions of commedia dell'arte performance and fails to note that the women, too, are in commedia costumes—indeed, the actress playing Esther is identifiable as Virginia Ramponi Andreini (1583–1630/1631), familiar perhaps to my readers from the Domenico Fetti portrait of Andreini-as-Arianna that graced the cover of my previous book (see Figure P.4, reproduced after page 240).[4] For Locker, the association of the king with the commedia dell'arte was an association with comedy, though traditionally the *innamorati* and *innamorate* are serious figures within the drama. The youth of the *innamorato* was a convention of commedia and Italian drama more broadly, drawing lines of allegiance between the youthful heroes of the Italian novella and the castrato leads of the operatic stage and symbolizing an adolescent vulnerability to love[5]—precisely the affect and dramatic crux of the story as depicted by Gentileschi. Yet Locker reads the king's youth as an elevation of Esther's female authority and a means to insert the painting into Venetian academic discourses on the relative value of men and women. To recognize Ahasuerus as an *innamorato*, however, is to see the painting as a record of performance, with much to tell us about theatrical

---

[2] I am grateful to Stefan Wolohojian for access to the object file at the Metropolitan Museum and to Shelia Barker for discussing the pentimenti over drinks at the Palazzo Strozzi in Florence.

[3] Locker, *Artemisia Gentileschi*, 73–83. Locker also mentions the influence of the commedia dell'arte in Jesse M. Locker, "Artemisia Gentileschi: The Literary Formation of an Unlearned Artist," in *Artemisia Gentileschi: Interpreting New Evidence, Assessing New Attributions*, ed. Shelia Barker (Turnhout: Brepols, 2017), 89–101.

[4] I have written elsewhere about Gentileschi's depictions of Andreini, though I did not discuss this painting of Esther. See Emily Wilbourne, "A Question of Character: Virginia Ramponi Andreini and Artemisia Gentileschi," *Italian Studies* 71, no. 3 (2016): 335–355.

[5] On the prevalence of ephebic heroes in Italian literature and drama and their representation by castrati on the operatic stage, see Roger Freitas, "The Eroticism of Emasculation: Confronting the Baroque Body of the Castrato," *Journal of Musicology* 20, no. 2 (2003): 196–249; Roger Freitas, *Portrait of a Castrato: Politics, Patronage, and Music in the Life of Atto Melani* (Cambridge: Cambridge University Press, 2009).

practice and contemporary reception. Rather than a failed history painting, Gentileschi's *Esther* is a successful depiction of the contemporary theater, deliberately crafted to represent the performance of a traveling commedia dell'arte troupe who have set up stage, perhaps in a recognizable room of the original patron's house. Gentileschi's work allows the viewer/patron to imagine the performance, to luxuriate in the allure of the actress, and to indulge in the fantasy of a command performance, perpetually available to view.[6]

Here the bare architecture of the room is itself theatrical. Rather than an exotic Persian palace or regal throne, we see a rather more mundane and thoroughly European room, paneled with dark wood. Doorway architraves and skirting boards mark out this space as a specific interior locale and not merely a *scuro* background against which Gentileschi could contrast her human forms. Instead of a throne, we have a chair. Instead of a dais, we have a set of internal stairs, with the doorway behind concealed by a scrap of curtain—see, as a point of comparison, the internal stairs in the library at Villa I Tatti (shown in Figure P.5, reproduced after page 240), where I spent many hours working on this book. Paintings such as this provide priceless testimony for theater scholars eager to recover the stagecraft of the baroque theater: the costumes, the blocking, the forty-five-degree turn of the "throne," the drapes behind the "dais." As a commedia dell'arte scene, Esther's approach to Ahasuerus is less invested in the intricacies of political etiquette (on which the drama of the biblical story relies) and instead invokes the quintessential love affair of commedia's *prima donna* and *primo uomo*, played out over countless scenarios and dramatic permutations, night after night.

The three women are sharply differentiated through costume. The *prima donna innamorata* is dressed in costly gold, the voluminous sleeves flaunting her social and dramatic status. To the viewer's left, the *seconda donna* performs a supporting role, in similar but less elaborate dress. Behind Esther, the duller-colored, more workable outfit of the *fantesca* (servant girl) fleshes out the three available female performers of the standard commedia troupe, all called into service in their Veronese tableau. All four actors rely on their standard costumes. Only the long folds of the king's purple scarf, which hangs around his neck and drapes behind him over the arm of his chair/throne, hint at an Oriental milieu. This length of fabric, with its elaborate trim, is superfluous to the somewhat dated finery of the commedia dell'arte

---

[6] On the way in which portraits of musicians functioned as a means to imagine performance and possession, see Amy Brosius, "'Il Suon, lo Sguardo, il Canto': The Function of Portraits of Mid-Seventeenth-Century *Virtuose* In Rome," *Italian Studies* 63, no. 1 (2013): 17–39.

courtier and was presumably sufficient to identify the role as "Persian," standing in metonymically for the turban and robes of the iconographically familiar East. Andreini-as-Esther performs an impressively physical rendition of the ideal feminine: the gestural weight of her swoon is reminiscent of other images of Andreini performing similar moments of emotional intensity.[7] In the exposed breasts, slumping shoulders, limp arms, and heavily lidded (though still attentive) eyes of such images, we can see a consistent repertoire of theatrical gesture associated with the giving over or giving up of the body in supplication, prayer, or despair.

In theatrical context, the reference to the Veronese is particularly clever, providing multiple layers through which the viewer could identify with the image and the depicted performance. Importantly, we cannot know whether Gentileschi chose to pose the actors in order to invoke the earlier picture or whether the actors themselves already did so, perhaps sparking her decision to immortalize the scene.[8] Certainly, the Andreini were no strangers to Venice, having performed on the lagoon regularly from the earliest years of the seventeenth century, and would have had ample opportunity to have seen and studied the original painting.[9] Theatrical practitioners worked in close quarters with painters and artisans; indeed, Andreini's only son, Pietro Enrico Andreini, studied and worked as a painter. Virginia Andreini is known to have posed for several portraits; alongside extant works by Fetti and Gentileschi, poetry by Giambattista Marino describes a lost work by Bronzino;[10] in the words of her husband, Giovan Battista Andreini,

---

[7] Interested readers could look at the images illustrating Siro Ferrone, "Pose sceniche di una famiglia d'attori," in *Domenico Fetti (1588/89–1623)*, ed. Eduard A. Safarik (Milan: Electra, 1996), 51–58.

[8] Notably, the dating of this painting has been contested by scholars, with estimates ranging from the early 1620s to as late as 1640. Most scholars have assumed the production of the work to postdate Gentileschi's presence in Venice (in order to have seen the Veronese herself); Locker cites Gentileschi's *Esther* as the only surviving painting from her Venetian sojourn. Jesse M. Locker, "Gli anni dimenticati: Artemisia Gentileschi a Venezia, 1626–1629," in *Artemisia Gentileschi e il suo tempo, exh. cat. Palazzo Braschi, Rome*, ed. Nicola Spinosa and Francesca Baldassari (Milan: Skira, 2016), 43. Virginia Andreini died in 1630 or 1631, providing a terminus ante quem for the production of the painting.

[9] A timeline of Virginia Andreini's movements can be inferred from the documents cited regarding her husband's movements, given in Claudia Burattelli, Domenica Landolfi, and Anna Zinanni, eds., *Comici dell'arte: Corrispondenze, G. B. Andreini, N. Barbieri, P. M. Cecchini, S. Fiorillo, T. Martinelli, F. Scala*, Vol. 2 (Florence: Le Lettere, 1993).

[10] Bronzino in this instance is almost certainly Cristofano Allori, not the more famous artist from whom he inherited the name. The poem is titled *Florinda comica*: "Bronzin, mentre ritraggi/questo Fior di beltà, beltà gentile,/che co' detti e co' raggi/degli occhi vaghi e del facondo stile,/spetra i duri pensier, doma i selvaggi,/se non ardi d'amore,/hai ben di bronzo il core." See Giambattista Marino, *Galeria poetica*, ed. Marzio Pieri (Padua: Liviana, 1979), 239.

There are many who, in galleries and in the most rare places, have wanted painted images of actors in the guise of various gods, not only to glorify the spaces with the colors of the most talented painters, but also to say: "That was the affectionate and learned Vittoria, this Orazio, the wise and gracious," and so forth.[11]

Gentileschi's *Esther* holds out the tantalizing possibility that the stagecraft of commedia theater explicitly drew upon the posed and framed bodies of baroque painting, much as painting regularly relied upon actors as models and subjects.

Notably, for art historians, the pentimento figures—boy and dog alike—are also inspired by the Veronese.[12] Keith Christiansen notes that "Artemisia initially painted an African boy restraining a dog—another motif interpolated from Veronese's work, in which a dwarf and a dog appear, though the dog is resting rather than growling at the queen in the Veronese composition."[13] Locker elaborates:

> The inclusion of the dog and servant indicates how much Veronese was on the artist's mind in the early stages of this painting. Artemisia evidently kept these Veronesian figures in the composition until a very late stage in the pictorial process: the African boy, for example, is so fully finished that even the final highlights, such as the reflected light in the whites of his eyes, are visible. Clearly she did not find this first attempt at creating an *istoria* satisfactory and decided to resolve the problems by composing a concentrated dramatic contrapposto of the two primary figural groups—a formula that had previously proven successful (and at which she would later excel).[14]

I wish to consider an alternative hypothesis, presuming instead an originary theatrical performance of the Esther story on which this painting

---

[11] Giovan Battista Andreini, "La ferza: Ragionamento secondo contra l'accuse date alla Commedia (Paris, 1625)," in *La commedia dell'arte e la società barocca: La professione del teatro*, ed. Ferruccio Marotti and Giovanna Romei (Rome: Bulzoni, 1994), 521. All translations from Italian are mine unless otherwise indicated.

[12] Mary D. Garrard, *Artemisia Gentileschi: The Image of the Female Hero in Italian Baroque Art* (Princeton, NJ: Princeton University Press, 1989); R. Ward Bissell, *Artemisia Gentileschi and the Authority of Art: Critical Reading and Catalogue Raisonné* (University Park: Pennsylvania State University Press, 1999).

[13] Keith Christiansen, "Artemisia Gentileschi: Esther before Ahasuerus," Metropolitan Museum of Art, https://www.metmuseum.org/art/collection/search/436453 (accessed 2020).

[14] Locker, *Artemisia Gentileschi*, 76.

is based. Under such circumstances, there is little about the depicted staging that is purely decorative. The costumes, while elaborate, are clearly generic in nature (reused for each performance, even for wildly different dramatic material). The props are minimal. Ahasuerus doesn't even have his scepter (prominently featured in biblical accounts). In the professional theater, there was little call for extraneous characters.[15] Thus, if we take this painting seriously as a representation of performance, we have to assume that the Black boy also performed. This assumption—that Black individuals formed an integral part of the Italian theater and of Italian courtly life—is one of the central claims of this book. Indeed, the presence, subsequent erasure, and recent—ghostly—re-emergence of this child provide a forceful illustration of my thesis. What does it mean to take his presence seriously? What work do we need to do to hear his voice? To listen to this image is to follow Tina Campt toward representations of Black individuals that were never intended "to figure Black subjects, but to delineate instead differential or degraded forms of personhood or subjection."[16] Her description, aimed at the mug shots of Black incarcerations, prison registers, and passport photos, is an equally valid account of the young Black pages of Italian court portraiture, whose very objectification as possession is intended as foil to the possessiveness of the white sitter. Listening in this situation, then, is to recognize that the young Black boy in Gentileschi's *Esther* is also a reference to court portraiture (as well as to Veronese), for the theatricality of the boy (with his dog) is sufficient to represent the court as a whole. Ahasuerus's throne room (in Veronese's account, a conclave of busy-looking bearded men, hard at work governing the kingdom) is, in Gentileschi's commedia dell'arte performance, a Black page entertaining the white sovereign.

That such a scene could stand as emblematic of Italian court culture in general is an important observation, but pragmatically, when we think about this scene in performance, it becomes clear that the entertainment provided by the young Black boy—his wit, actions, or song—served as the scene into which Esther's intrusion registered as interruption. His astonished silence at her arrival, his eyes wide and turned toward her face, was preceded by sound. How this scene of entertainment would have sounded is the question at the heart of this book.

---

[15] This is in contrast with court theater, where there were often many extras and wildly elaborate sets.
[16] Tina M. Campt, *Listening to Images* (Durham, NC: Duke University Press, 2017), 3.

Tentatively, entirely speculatively, we could associate the young Black boy depicted in this painting with the "Moro" who served the commedia dell'arte actor Girolamo Caraffa *detto* Gonnella. Caraffa was active as a *secondo zanni* between 1615 and 1630, performing for at least one Venetian season with the Andreini during 1623–1624 and active with the Confidenti acting troupe during the later 1620s.[17] During this period, Caraffa-Gonnella appears in the accounts of the Camera del Granduca with some regularity, as does his son, Giovanni, who had several children baptized in the city of Florence.[18] In June 1630, a "Moro" was given "one scudo to give to his master, Gonnella."[19] This rare citation—the only one I know of that links a Black African directly to the household of a commedia dell'arte performer—is suggestive;[20] were he the same Black boy represented in Gentileschi's painting, he may have been a regular participant in commedia performances. It is also possible that the patron whose room appears in the painting supplied his or her own enslaved page as subject.

In Gentileschi's hand, this young boy is—to cite Campt once again—"posed to produce particular 'types' of regulated and regulatable subjects."[21] In the pages that follow, I heed Campt's injunction to "refuse to accept the 'truth' of such images and archives," seeking the "fissures, gaps, and interstices that emerge" when we listen for voice and its relation to race and slavery in seventeenth-century Florence.[22]

---

[17] Francesca Fantappiè, "Girolamo Caraffa *detto* Gonnella," amati.fupress.net.

[18] For example, in 1627, the Confidenti were paid 100 scudi, to be carried by Beltrame (Nicolò Barbieri) and Gonnella: "Alla Compag*n*ia de Comedianti sc. cento portò Beltrame e Gonnella," I-Fas, Camera del Granduca, f. 8, c. 11r. Caraffa was evidently quite talented, as in December 1628, the Grand Duke rewarded him with two necklaces, weighing three ounces in total and valued at 30 scudi: "All'orefici *per* due collanine che SA donò a Gonnella Zanni pesarono tre oncie in tu*t*to, s*c*udi 30," I-Fas, Camera del Granduca, f. 10, c. 14v. I found reference to two of Caraffa's grandchildren, one in January 1628: "Al Battesimo d'un fig*u*olo del Caraffa scudi quindici," I-Fas, Camera del Granduca, f. 8, c. 16r; the baptismal record for "Francesco son of Giovanni son of Girolamo Caraffa and of Margherita daughter of Domenico Bonseri" can be found at I-Fd, Registri Battesimali, Maschi, reg. 36, fg. 101. Then, in September 1630: "Al Bettesimo del Caraffa quindici piastre disse SA," I-Fas, Camera del Granduca, f. 12, c. 3v; the baptismal record for "Ferdinando son of Giovanni son of Girolamo Caraffa" can be found at I-Fd, Registri Battesimali, Maschi, reg. 38, fg. 37.

[19] "Al Moro uno scudo p*er* dare al Gonnella suo m*aes*tro," I-Fas, Camera del Granduca, f. 12, c. 45v.

[20] Notably, several opera singers from the late seventeenth and early eighteenth centuries kept Black individuals in servile positions, a phenomenon briefly discussed in the Epilogo.

[21] Campt, *Listening to Images*, 8.

[22] Campt, *Listening to Images*, 8.

Faccio fede come Auzza di Macometto Mora stiava di Bona d'Anni 25 fu presa nella presa di Bona dalle Galere di S.A.S. et condotta in questo Arzenale, et sotto il dì 29 di 9bre 1607 fu conduta dal Signor Francesco Salviati Priore dell'Arzenale di Pisa a Jacopo Simonelli per ducati cento di moneta, et per essere cosi la verita si è fatto la presente fede quale sara sotto scritta, et siggillata secondo il solito dell'Arzenale di Pisa . . . d. 100-

I swear and attest that Auzza, daughter of Macometto, Moorish slave from Bona, aged 25, was taken in the sack of Bona by the galleys of the Grand Duke and conducted to this Arsenal, and on the 29th of November 1607 was sold by Signore Francesco Salviati, Prior of the Pisa Arsenal, to Jacopo Simonelli for 100 ducats in coins, and this being the truth, the present document will be underwritten and sealed with the seal of the Pisa Arsenal, as is customary . . . d[ucats] 100-

I-Fca, Pia Casa dei Catecumini, f. 1, December 26, 1609, c.n.n. [ins. 26]

Introduction

This is a book about voice and race in the seventeenth century. My work is predicated on the persistence of what Roland Barthes called the "grain" of the voice: "the body in the voice as it sings."[1] Note that I am not claiming that race manifests in the voice but that Western culture has long assumed that it does.[2] Thus, I argue that in the voices scripted for racialized others, we can hear a history of race as an embodied and physical element. Such scripted voices include those of theatrical characters and historical persons.

Words in the mouth have pitch, timbre, rhythm, and intensity; spoken or sung, they take their shape from the warm interior spaces of the body, and the sounds that voices make carry markers promising access to internal bodily truths.[3] From the sounding voice, modern listeners regularly cull information of three different types: (1) literal physical traces, such as age, sex or gender, and good health; (2) historical residue, such as regional accent, linguistic fluency, social class, and education; and (3) emotional indices such as sorrow, joy, confidence,

---

[1] Roland Barthes, "The Grain of the Voice," in *Image, Music, Text* (London: Flamingo, 1977), 188.

[2] The racialization of voice has begun to draw considerable attention from music scholars, including Katherine Meizel, *Multivocality: Singing on the Borders of Identity* (Oxford: Oxford University Press, 2020); Nina Sun Eidsheim, *The Race of Sound: Listening, Timbre, and Vocality in African American Music* (Durham, NC: Duke University Press, 2019); Jennifer Lynn Stoever, *The Sonic Color Line: Race and the Cultural Politics of Listening* (New York: New York University Press, 2016). See also earlier work on national vocal styles, such as Sally A. Sanford, "A Comparison of French and Italian Singing in the Seventeenth Century," *Journal of Seventeenth-Century Music* 1, no. 1 (1995), https://sscm-jscm.org/v1/no1/sanford.html. Increased attention has been paid to the varied ways in which race has been mapped beyond the visible. See Richard Cullen Rath, *How Early America Sounded* (Ithaca, NY: Cornell University Press, 2003); Mark M. Smith, *How Race Is Made: Slavery, Segregation, and the Senses* (Chapel Hill: University of North Carolina Press, 2006). With particular relevance for the study of early modern racial formations and the voice, see also Robert Hornback, *Racism and Early Blackface Comic Traditions: From the Old World to the New*, Palgrave Studies in Theatre and Performance History (Cham, Switzerland: Palgrave Macmillan, 2018); Nicholas Jones, *Staging Habla de Negros: Radical Performances of the African Diaspora in Early Modern Spain* (University Park: Pennsylvania State University Press, 2019). More broadly, the burgeoning importance of race within musicology is evidenced by several recent special issues: *Women & Music: A Journal of Gender and Culture*, ed. Emily Wilbourne, vol. 22, special issue on Race-ing Queer Music Scholarship (2018); *Journal of the American Musicological Society*, ed. George E. Lewis, vol. 72, no. 3, special issue on Music, Race and Ethnicity (2019).

[3] There are strong psychoanalytic assumptions that underlie contemporary models of vocality and embodiment; such assumptions are manifest when scholars of subjectivity touch on the voice, often prioritizing a voice that betrays (involuntarily) the (sexual) history of the body. See, for example, Judith Butler, "Bodily Confessions," in *Undoing Gender* (New York: Routledge, 2004), 161–173.

and sincerity.[4] Even as we know that the voice can be trained, manipulated, and modulated, the slippery slope between acting and lying, performance and deceit, natural and affected speech betrays our trust in epistemologies of voice.[5] We want to believe in voice even as we doubt empty words.

Amanda Weidman has argued that in modernity, voice itself is a crucial site of knowledge: "both a set of sonic, material, and literary practices shaped by culturally and historically specific moments and a category invoked in discourse about personal agency, communication and representation, and political power."[6] This slippery intersection between the tangible body and the referential power of words as they sound in space has made the voice a foundational metaphor for agency and politics. Exploiting the nexus of body, sound, and linguistic content, we "speak up," "find our voice," "sound off," and "hear each other out." Crucially, the continued valence of vocal epistemologies has largely naturalized their presence: we need to work to remind ourselves that the voice has a history.

Voice

In 1600, the idea that vocal music should represent the voice and the body, the present and the past of a character was relatively new. With the "invention" of opera or, more specifically, the invention of recitative—a responsive text setting for the solo voice designed to imitate, in music, the flexible rhythms and declamatory impact of the spoken word—radically new musical priorities found notational form. Florentine court chroniclers, commentators, and composers recount a remarkably consistent narrative of academic experimentation: select circles in which noble amateurs and professional musicians rubbed shoulders and where the felicitous combination of Medici patronage, individual talent, and the close study of ancient Greek theatrical practice culminated in the dramatically effective genre that we now call opera.[7] The

---

Forthcoming work by Jessica Gabriel Peritz considers the way in which such readings of voice (and particularly its moments of rupture) consolidate around concepts of authentic expression during the late eighteenth century.

[4] Emily Wilbourne, *Seventeenth-Century Opera and the Sound of the Commedia dell'Arte* (Chicago: University of Chicago Press, 2016).
[5] Emily Wilbourne, "Demo's Stutter, Subjectivity, and the Virtuosity of Vocal Failure," *Journal of the American Musicological Society* 68, no. 3 (2015): 659–663.
[6] Amanda Weidman, "Anthropology and Voice," *Annual Review of Anthropology* 43 (2014): 38.
[7] Claude Palisca, "The Florentine Camerata," in *The Florentine Camerata: Documentary Studies and Translations* (New Haven, CT: Yale University Press, 1989), 1–12; Warren Kirkendale,

coherence of this story, the delightfully round number of 1600, and the speed with which the notational and stylistic difference of the "new music" spread throughout Europe have proved a boon to music history teachers, allowing this moment and the invention of this music to serve as the musical end of the Renaissance and the dramatic beginning of the baroque; Gary Tomlinson (borrowing an analytic vocabulary from Michel Foucault) famously referred to this break as an epistemic shift from a model of knowledge production based on "Resemblance" to one of "Representation."[8] Even as more recent scholarship has worked, productively, to blur period boundaries—dismantling the mythology of creation ex nihilo and tracing the prehistories of operatic song through the music and the listening practices associated with the *concerto delle donne*;[9] the madrigal, the pastorale, and the commedia dell'arte;[10] extant practices of dramatic declamation and improvisation;[11] and the performance practice of plainchant[12]—I want to re-emphasize the difference of operatic eloquence.[13]

"The Myth of the 'Birth of Opera' in the Florentine Camerata Debunked by Emilio de' Cavalieri: A Commemorative Lecture," *Opera Quarterly* 19 (2003): 631–643; Tim Carter, ed. and trans., *Composing Opera: From "Dafne" to "Ulisse errante"* (Kraków: Musica Iagellonica, 1994); Tim Carter, "Music and Patronage in Late Sixteenth-Century Florence: The Case of Jacopo Corsi (1561–1602)," *I Tatti Studies in the Italian Renaissance* 1 (1985): 57–104.

[8] Gary Tomlinson, *Music in Renaissance Magic: Toward a Historiography of Others* (Chicago: University of Chicago Press, 1993).

[9] Anthony Newcomb, *The Madrigal at Ferrara, 1579–1597* (Princeton, NJ: Princeton University Press, 1980); Laurie Stras, *Women and Music in Sixteenth-Century Ferrara* (Cambridge: Cambridge University Press, 2018); Andrew Dell'Antonio, *Listening as Spiritual Practice in Early Modern Italy* (Berkeley: University of California Press, 2011).

[10] Massimo Ossi, *Divining the Oracle: Monteverdi's Seconda Prattica* (Chicago: University of Chicago Press, 2003); Mauro P. Calcagno, "'Imitar col canto chi parla': Monteverdi and the Creation of a Language for Musical Theater," *Journal of the American Musicological Society* 55, no. 3 (2002): 383–431; Mauro P. Calcagno, "Dramatizing Discourse in Seventeenth-Century Opera: Music as Illocutionary Force in Francesco Cavalli's *Giasone* (1649)," in *Word, Image, and Song*, Vol. 1: *Essays on Early Modern Italy*, ed. Rebecca Cypess, Beth Glixon, and Nathan Link, Eastman Studies in Music (Rochester, NY: University of Rochester Press, 2013), 318–343; Paolo Fabbri, *Il secolo cantante: Per una storia del libretto d'opera in Italia nel seicento* (Bologna: Il Mulino, 1990); Giuseppe Gerbino, *Music and the Myth of Arcadia in Renaissance Italy* (Cambridge: Cambridge University Press, 2009); Wilbourne, *Seventeenth-Century Opera*.

[11] Elena Abramov-van Rijk, *Singing Dante: The Literary Origins of Cinquecento Monody* (Farnham, UK: Ashgate, 2014); John Walter Hill, *Roman Monody, Cantata and Opera from the Circles around Cardinal Montalto*, 2 vols. (Oxford: Clarendon Press, 1997).

[12] Barbara Swanson, "Old Chant, New Songs: Plainchant and Monody in Sixteenth-Century Rome," in *Chant Old and New/Plain-chant: L'ancien et le nouveau*, ed. William Renwick (Ottawa: Institute of Medieval Music, 2012), 215–224; Barbara Swanson, "Plainchant Psalmody in the Prologues of Early Opera," in *Chant and Culture/Plain-chant et culture*, ed. Armin Karim and Barbara Swanson (Ottawa: Institute of Medieval Music, 2014), 151–160.

[13] I am aware of the pitfalls of claiming a moment of rupture, which tends to paper over the continuities that persist through moments of historical change; see Paul N. Edwards et al., "AHR Conversation: Historical Perspectives on the Circulation of Information," *American Historical Review* 116, no. 5 (2011): 1393–1435.

The success of early opera, the *nuove musiche*, and the *seconda prattica* lay not merely in the use of music to accompany drama but in the influential conviction that (musical) sound could itself *narrate* the theatrical work more effectively than words alone. Freed from formal repetitions and from the metrical regularity required by elaborate polyphony, monodic voice and basso continuo accompaniment could respond to and embody each word, phrase, or emotion. There is a genuine drama—an acting out—inherent in the way this "new music" is put together. Furthermore, the European-wide craze for the Italian operatic sound served to institutionalize in song the convergence of literal and metaphoric agency that we now take for granted, as operatic vocal music emerged throughout Europe as a privileged mode with which to represent emotional affect.[14] I will argue throughout this book that the coagulation of body and sound allows us to read the sonic materiality of music and narrativized sounds (in particular, but not only, theatrical vocal music) in order to rethink historiographies of race. In what follows, I consider various contexts in which the voice and specifically its musical sounds (epitomized by but not limited to opera) were able to carry meanings and to convincingly represent subjectivity. Some of the "voices" I discuss are not literally vocal but instantiate sound as a means to communicate presence and identity. Such sounds, in Carolyn Abbate's work, are called "unsung voices,"[15] and to listen for them on- and offstage, I mobilize strategies from musicology and from the emergent genre of historical sound studies.[16]

Importantly, I am not interested in the voice as a natural or unmediated phenomenon but in the ways that the voice was assumed to work and the extent to which the scripted and improvised theatrics of the Italian stage deployed the voice as a means to stage the body. Such stagings relied

---

[14] The monodic texture of recitative and the representational focus of the *nuove musiche* encouraged a large-scale shift from amateur to professional musical performance and a concomitant turn toward the virtuosic in both vocal music and instrumental practice. The notational forms of the basso continuo accompaniment marked a shift to a harmonic way of conceptualizing musical construction.

[15] Carolyn Abbate, *Unsung Voices: Opera and Musical Narrative in the Nineteenth Century* (Princeton, NJ: Princeton University Press, 1991).

[16] See, for example, Rath, *How Early America Sounded*; Bruce R. Smith, *The Acoustic World of Early Modern England: Attending to the O-Factor* (Chicago: University of Chicago Press, 1999); Deborah Howard and Laura Moretti, *Sound and Space in Renaissance Venice* (New Haven, CT: Yale University Press, 2009); Niall Atkinson, *The Noisy Renaissance: Sound, Architecture, and Florentine Urban Life* (University Park: Pennsylvania State University Press, 2016); Sarah Eyerly, *Moravian Soundscapes: A Sonic History of the Moravian Missions in Early Pennsylvania* (Bloomington: Indiana University Press, 2020).

upon and exploited the sonicized interpretive power of offstage interaction, mobilizing presumptions about bodies and their appropriate noises to dramatic (and communicative) effect. In my previous book, I referred to the dramatic and communicative power of sound as *sonic epistemology*; others, borrowing a term from Steven Feld, have called such listening cultures *acoustemologies*; Murray Schafer writes of *soundscapes* and *acoustic ecologies*.[17] I am interested in the ways in which sounds—made by bodies, (musical) instruments, and noise makers of all types, including weaponry, clothing, and architectural spaces—narrate information about bodies, race, and power.

The use of the term "race" to describe early modern identity formation has been contested by some scholars, particularly those who consider religious difference as the key axis of cultural identification or those who conclude that an absence of biological science within early modernity precludes an understanding of racial belonging, yet a burgeoning literature grounded in postcolonial and Black feminist theory insists on the utility of "race" as a heuristic to understand the period. This change has been relatively recent.[18] Indeed, Ayanna Thompson begins the introduction to the 2021 edited collection *The Cambridge Companion to Shakespeare and Race* with the observation, "When I was in university over thirty years ago, the answer to the question—did the concept of race exist during Shakespeare's lifetime—was an emphatic no."[19] On the following page, she elaborates:

> If you ask today in the 2020s if the concept of race existed for Shakespeare and his contemporaries, the answer is an emphatic yes. Yes, the concept of race existed. Yes, racialized epistemologies existed and were employed and deployed. And, yes, Shakespeare himself engages in both the symbolic and

---

[17] Steven Feld derived the term "acoustemology" (combining "acoustics" and "epistemology") to describe the use of sound and listening practices in knowledge production. See Steven Feld, "Voices of the Rainforest: Politics of Music," *Arena* 99–100 (1992): 164–177. He provides a clear definition and explores the ramifications of the term in Steven Feld, "Acoustemology," in *Keywords in Sound*, ed. David Novak and Matt Sakakeeny (Durham, NC: Duke University Press, 2015), 12–21.

[18] The field of race and early modern studies is burgeoning, and in the eighteen months since this book first went to press, a considerable number of books and articles have appeared. Two notable examples are Noémie Ndiaye, *Scripts of Blackness: Early Modern Performance Culture and the Making of Race* (Philadelphia: University of Pennsylvania Press, 2022), and *Renaissance Quarterly* vol. 74, no.4 (2022), special issue on race in early modernity.

[19] Ayanna Thompson, "Did the Concept of Race Exist for Shakespeare and His Contemporaries? An Introduction," in *The Cambridge Companion to Shakespeare and Race*, ed. Ayanna Thompson (Cambridge: Cambridge University Press, 2021), 1.

materialistic elements that comprise race-making. Yes, Shakespeare and race are coeval; they grew up as contemporaries.[20]

In this book, I take the relevance of race as a given, though I do not presume that race in seventeenth-century Florence was coterminous with the modern filiation of the term. Religious, linguistic, and national affiliations created complex relationships between locals and foreigners, distant—voluntarily or involuntarily—from their homes. In 1444, Portuguese ships landed in West Africa (in what is now Senegal); in 1492, the Italian navigator Christopher Columbus made landfall on the continent that would come to be called America (named after the Florentine navigator Amerigo Vespucci, who visited the "New World" at least twice between 1497 and 1504); in the early 1500s, Bartolomé de las Casas advocated for the liberation of enslaved indigenous Americans in New Spain, suggesting the substitution of enslaved Africans in their place;[21] in 1619, enslaved Black laborers were recorded in North American colonies for the first time. By the end of the seventeenth century, race-based slavery was endemic, though the concept of slavery was not itself new.[22] Sylvia Wynter has argued that the enormous geographical and mercantile changes of early modernity instantiated a shift in Western subjectivity from what she calls the "Christian" to "Man_1," or man "as political subject" (to be replaced, in turn, during the Enlightenment by "Man_2," or man "as bioeconomic subject"):

> It was here [during the late sixteenth and early seventeenth centuries] that the modern phenomenon of race, as a new extrahumanly determined classificatory principle and mechanism of domination was first invented, if still in its first religio-secular form.[23]

In the humanist logics of the Italian Renaissance, Wynter locates "a model for the invention of a by-nature difference between 'natural masters' and 'natural slaves,' one able to replace the Christian/Enemies-of-Christ legitimating

---

[20] Thompson, "Did the Concept?," 2–3.
[21] Wynter makes much of Las Casas's arguments in an article that has been vastly formative for my thinking about race. See Sylvia Wynter, "Unsettling the Coloniality of Being/Power/Truth/Freedom: Towards the Human, after Man, Its Overrepresentation—An Argument," *CR: New Centennial Review* 3, no. 3 (2003): 257–337.
[22] For a powerful articulation of the relationship between transatlantic slavery and capitalism, see Jennifer L. Morgan, *Reckoning with Slavery: Gender, Kinship, and Capitalism in the Early Black Atlantic* (Durham, NC: Duke University Press, 2021).
[23] Wynter, "Unsettling," 296.

difference."[24] The emergence of race was—as I argue in this book—facilitated and legitimized by the narrativized, expressive voice of the Italian baroque, which consolidated—in representational form—the idea of natural aptitude, reinforcing strict categorical divisions between types of people.

Where possible, I have identified and listened to the voices of real "Others" who were present in Florence during the seventeenth century, searching the archives for traces of visitors, trafficked humans, and immigrants to better understand the relationship between the scripted voices that theatrical vocal music transcribes and thus records and the lived, embodied experiences of markedly foreign bodies. This is thus a "history" book in a very real sense, pivoting on the presence of actual people—their lives and their labor (their lives, their "works"). To find foreign or othered characters on the theatrical stage is relatively easy: Middle Easterners, Turks, Indians, Black Africans, "Gypsies" (Rom), Jews, dwarves, the enslaved, differently able and non-elite bodies understood as "different" in early modern Europe proliferate in the theater. The work that needs to be done in order to recover the voices of historical foreigners from the Western archive, however, remains in a formative stage. Where archive sources do exist, they are partial and incomplete, transcribed by Western pens and articulated in Western terms. Still, what I have uncovered suggests that the presence of these "Others" at the Florentine court was surprisingly numerous; though I discuss many individuals and sources in the pages that follow (with a particular focus on moments illuminating the intersection of enslaved individuals with musical and theatrical performance), hundreds more examples and people contextualize my choice of examples and archival citations, and this plenitude undergirds my insistence on the integral impact of slavery and foreign presence within Medici Florence. I have attempted to document the extent of the foreign presence in two ways. First, in the appendix, I have listed the full range of references to enslaved, Moorish, and "Turkish" ("non-Christian") individuals that I encountered in the archive. This list makes no attempt to document these individuals in any comprehensive way but is intended—in its sheer length—to demonstrate the emblematic (rather than exemplary) status of those I have discussed in the text and will—I hope—encourage other researchers to turn their attention to the archive in future research projects. Second, I have reproduced a selection of archival mentions as interleaved quotes prefacing each chapter of the book. These quotes appear without commentary, testifying to the humanity

[24] Wynter, "Unsettling," 297.

of the individuals concerned and to the many ways in which social forces constrained their lives and freedoms. These quotes make explicit the fragmentary nature of the archive and the many lives that were caught up with the Medici court. Among all the possible categories of social "Other" that were present in Florence, I have focused on enslaved people and theatrical representations of the enslaved for three reasons: first, for the clarity with which questions of both race and agency pertain to enslaved people; second, because the sources I found in the archive facilitated such a focus; and third, because European slavery is underrepresented in both European history and histories of slavery more broadly. The Medici court and the city of Florence have deep, disturbing, and infrequently acknowledged connections to the traffic and trade in human bodies.

This study covers the period 1600–1670, and as such, it overlaps with three different Medici Grand Dukes: Ferdinando I (ruled 1587–1609), Cosimo II (1609–1621), and Ferdinando II (1621–1670), as well as the regency (1621–1631) during which Christine of Lorraine (wife of Ferdinando I) and Maria Maddalena of Austria (wife of Cosimo II) shared political power in anticipation of Ferdinando II's maturity. Each of these rulers had a different personality and different political priorities; however, the practice of court, domestic, and galley slavery persisted relatively unchanged. Only recently has early modern Italian slavery begun to receive sustained attention, as part of a renewed interest in the Mediterranean and in conditions of unfreedom. As increasing amounts of information and documentation emerge emphasizing the prevalence and ubiquity of enslavement of various kinds (including the predations of pirates and corsairs), common literary and dramatic tropes of imprisonment, conversion, escape, and ransom have attracted attention as reflections on contemporary lived experience rather than as imaginative or fantastical literary fictions.[25] The dramatized representations I discuss in this book give voice to experiences of agency, slavery, and unfreedom and to perceptions of racialized difference as experienced within the Italian city state. Heard alongside archival voices, race emerges as an integral element of early modern society and the racialized voice as a foundational component of vocality and musical sound.

[25] See, for example, E. Natalie Rothman, *Brokering Empire: Trans-Imperial Subjects between Venice and Istanbul* (Ithaca, NY: Cornell University Press, 2012); Erith Jaffe-Berg, *Commedia dell'Arte and the Mediterranean: Charting Journeys and Mapping "Others"* Transculturalisms, 1400–1700 (London: Routledge, 2016); Daniel Hershenzon, *The Captive Sea: Slavery, Communication, and Commerce in Early Modern Spain and the Mediterranean* (Philadelphia: University of Pennsylvania Press, 2018); Jones, *Staging Habla de Negros*.

Slavery

In 1614, the English Protestant William Davies published a popular travel narrative under an expansive title: *A true relation of the travailes and most miserable captiuitie of William Dauies, barber-surgion of London, under the Duke of Florence. Wherein is truly set downe the manner of his taking, the long time of his slauerie, and meanes of his deliuerie, after eight yeeres, and ten monoths captiuitie in the gallies. Discouering many manye landes, ilandes, riuers, cities, and townes, of the Christians and infidels, the condition of the people, and the manner of their contrey: with many more strange things, as in the booke is briefely and planely expressed.* For his intended audience of armchair travelers, Davies provided a riveting account of the affective consequences of his adventures; along with geographical and proto-ethnographic observations, he offered titillating details of what it felt like to endure military defeat, capture, and the conditions of enslavement.[26] Archival documents confirm many of the pragmatic details of Davies's account:[27]

> Now leave we Tunys [Tunisia] in the same Ship that I came out of England in, named the Francis of Saltash, being bound to Syo [Chios] within the Arches of Archipelago, and fraighted with Turkish goods by Turkes, and some Turks abord with us, for wee traded as well with the Turke as the Christian: but we had not sailed above foure leagues out of our Port in the night season, but that we were most fiercely set upon by fire of the Duke of

---

[26] Davies's emotional text is in sharp contrast with that of Aurelio Scetti, a late-sixteenth-century Florentine musician who was condemned to life on the galleys after bludgeoning his wife to death with a candlestick. Scetti compiled a manuscript account of his travels with the Florentine fleet. His text is addressed to the Grand Duke (not a general readership) and is suffused throughout with a proto-nationalist pride in the achievements of the granducal fleet. It is difficult to know how "authentically" Scetti lived such political sentiments or how crafted they were for his intended audience. Scetti hoped that his account would move the Grand Duke to give him a full pardon, and he appeals to a sense of having served his sovereign well and having atoned for his errors through his years of galley service. Not once does he elaborate on the miseries he feels as a "forzato" (a convict), nor does he critique the harsh labor required to propel the galley ships or the goals or aspirations of the Florentine state. Unfortunately, he also does not discuss musical sounds. Scetti's manuscript has been published in a modern edition and in an English translation. See Luigi Monga, ed., *Galee toscane e corsari barbareschi: Il diario di Aurelio Scetti galeotto fiorentino 1565–1577* (Fornacette: CDL, 1999); Aurelio Scetti, *The Journal of Aurelio Scetti: A Florentine Galley Slave at Lepanto (1565–1577)*, trans. Luigi Monga (Tempe: Arizona Center for Medieval and Renassance Studies, 2004).

[27] The original print is widely available digitally. A modern facsimile edition, with translation into Italian and a scholarly introduction (including transcription of a number of contemporary sources), was published in 2000. See Algerina Neri, *Uno schiavo inglese nella Livorno dei Medici* (Pisa: ETS, 2000).

Florence his Gallies, (who being in continuall warre with the Turke, tooke us as a Turkish prize) which spit fire like divels, to our great discomfort, but at length couraging of our selves in Gods mercies, we continued fight with them, to the losse of many a mans life of each side, but all in vaine for us, for they were fortie for one of us, and our S[h]ip torne downe to the water with their Ordinance, our mayne Mast, and missen Mast, shot by the boord, the one end of the Mast with all the sayles lying in the Sea, the other end aboord: thus were we taken, and stript everyman starke naked, and then were we distributed, some into one Gallie, and some into another, where we had as many Irons knocked upon us, and more, than then we were able to beare. Our Ship presently sent to Ligorne [Livorno], being mended as well as they could, but we in the Gallies continued a moenth before we came thither, to the losse of many of our lives: but at length comming thither, as many of us as were left alive were thus intertained. We were all shaven both head and beard, and every man had given him a red coate, and a red cap, telling of us that the Duke had made us all Slaves, to our great woe and griefe: where I continued eight yeares and ten moneths in this slaverie.[28]

Davies's story—in all of its "planely expressed" detail—differs from most extant Mediterranean slavery narratives in that the author (a white Christian) was enslaved by other (white Christian) Europeans, not by the Ottoman Turks. Thus, Davies sidesteps some of the exoticizing stereotypes typically associated with the Turks as slave masters, providing a more nuanced understanding of the role of slavery in early modern Europe and of the ways in which cultural, religious, and racial difference was conceived in relation to enslavement. Davies foregrounds the brutal and characteristic use of enslaved labor to power Mediterranean galley ships and the ongoing naval skirmishes and piracy that characterized the littoral region. Entrance into the state of unfreedom that Davies endured is marked by humiliating physical rituals: he is stripped naked, his hair and beard are shaved off, and he is knocked into more chains than any man can bear.[29] Repeatedly, he

---

[28] William Davies, *True Relation of the Travails and Most Miserable Captivite of William Davies, Barber-Surgion of London, under the Duke of Florence* (London: Nicholas Bourne, 1614), n.p. [15].

[29] The military historian Anna Agostini claims that the process of stripping and shaving captured prisoners was as much about infection as it was about demoralization: "I prigionieri catturati venivano completamente spogliati e lavati così come gli oggetti prelevati dai vascelli nemici." Anna Agostini, *Istantanee dal seicento: L'album di disegni del cavaliere pistoiese Ignazio Fabroni* (Florence: Polistampa, 2017), 78. Agostini also cites a contemporary manuscript describing the practice, which seems to

emphasizes his unwilling submission to the condition of enslavement—not least by his careful count and precise iteration of the "eight yeers and ten moneths" spent under slavery's yoke.

Galley slavery was one of the most visible and widely acknowledged forms of early modern European slavery, though in the popular modern imaginary, the practice is more widely associated with the medieval and early Roman eras. As witness to specifically Florentine practices, Davies provides useful testimony regarding conditions on the galleys and in Livorno, where, in the years between 1598 and 1604, the Medici constructed (using enslaved labor) the so-called slave *bagno*—infamous as the largest independent structure for the housing of enslaved people on European soil.[30] The *bagno* was a symptom of Grand Duke Ferdinando I's expansionist political and military aims; it housed the galley slaves of the Medici fleet along with Italian-born convicts who also labored at oar and the *benevoglie* (impoverished "volunteers" who worked on the galleys in order to pay off their debts). In 1616, according to the contemporary observer Vincenzo Pitti, there were around three thousand enslaved individuals in Livorno alone—approximating 35 percent of the city's population.[31] Historian Franco Angiolini estimates that between 1563 and 1700, the Tuscan fleet captured around fifteen thousand "infidels," largely from North Africa and the eastern Mediterranean.[32] Importantly, not all of these enslaved laborers worked on the galleys, nor were all of them men.[33] An archival list from Florence in 1604 sums the number of state-owned enslaved and convict laborers active in the galleys and armories, along with those in hospital, totaling 1,302 convicts and 1,304 state-owned enslaved workers.[34] That significant numbers of men and women were in service within domestic households, both at court and in wealthy mercantile families, is attested by documents within the same *busta*. One document from 1605 lists 285 enslaved people who were captured the previous year

---

have been common: "si imbarcavano gli schiavi 'come la Natura gl'Ha generati, cioè ignudi, con farli ben lavare, come si usa alle genti sospette,'"; BNCF, Ms. 400, *Del modo di fare l'impositura . . . per la Galera*, c. 43. Cited in Agostini, *Istantanee dal seicento*, 103.

[30] Stephanie Nadalo, "Negotiating Slavery in a Tolerant Frontier: Livorno's Turkish *Bagno* (1547–1747)," *Mediaevalia* 32 (2011): 275–324.
[31] Franco Angiolini, "Slaves and Slavery in Early Modern Tuscany," *Italian History and Culture* 3 (1997): 73.
[32] Angiolini, "Slaves and Slavery," 70.
[33] Samuela Marconcini, "Una presenza nascosta: Battesimi di 'turchi' a Firenze in età moderna," *Annali di Storia di Firenze* 7 (2012): 97–121. See also *Quaderni storici* 42, no. 3, special issue on Slavery in the Mediterranean (2007).
[34] I-Fas, Carte strozziane, I, f. 148, c. 382r.

during a raid on the city of Bona (now Annaba), on the coast of Algeria, and put up for sale. Whole families are included. The list, which stretches to seven and a half pages, details their names, relationships, ages, skin color, any other identifying features, the prices paid, and the names of the new owners.[35]

Rarely are galley slavery and the more dispersed forms of enslaved domestic labor thought together, since the conditions of servitude differed so widely, yet in some ways the various forms of unfree labor were mutually reinforcing. While galley warfare necessitated a steady supply of able-bodied male slaves, generating a market for enslaved workers and motivating many skirmishes and attacks, raids on merchant vessels captured passengers as well as sailors and oarsmen, and those on coastal towns rounded up men, women, and children of a variety of social levels and occupations. Wealthy or politically valuable captives could hope to be ransomed, but less well-connected individuals had few options. In the sixteenth and seventeenth centuries, most enslaved people arrived in Europe via maritime routes, though in addition, enslaved workers—particularly women—were trafficked out of northern and eastern Europe.[36] There were substantial slave markets in Livorno, Venice, Genoa, Naples, and Palermo, and the Italian-based Knights of Malta ran a significant slaving operation in Malta; the enslaved percentage of the Italian population varied dramatically between cities.[37] Enslaved retainers were often carried back to Italy by travelers or purchased from slave markets in other European countries, including Portugal, which began transporting, selling, and exploiting large numbers of enslaved sub-Saharan Africans in the early sixteenth century. Unfree labor was an aspect of the European economy that has been underrecognized in all but the literature devoted explicitly to the phenomenon, and importantly, the Mediterranean slave trade differed substantially from the transatlantic trade. Early modern slavery provided an intimate connection to notions of the foreign and of the kinds of categorical thinking that underpin modern racial formulations.

---

[35] I-Fas, Carte stozziane, I, f. 148, cc. 226r–229v.

[36] Salvatore Bono, "Slave Histories and Memoirs in the Mediterranean World," in *Trade and Cultural Exchange in the Early Modern Mediterranean: Braudel's Maritime Legacy*, ed. Maria Fusaro, Colin Heywood, and Mohamed-Salah Omri (London: I.B. Taurus, 2010), 97–116; Salvatore Bono, "Schiavi in Europa nell'età moderna: Varietà di forme e di aspetti," in *Schiavitù e servaggio nell'economia europea secc. XI–XVIII/Serfdom and Slavery in the European Economy 11th–18th Centuries*, ed. Simonetta Cavaciocchi (Florence: Firenze University Press, 2014), 309–335; Iris Origo, "The Domestic Enemy: The Eastern Slaves in Tuscany in the Fourteenth and Fifteenth Centuries," *Speculum* 30 (1955): 321–366.

[37] See Angiolini, "Slaves and Slavery." See also a discussion of purchases of galley slaves in Livorno during the seventeenth century in Paul Walden Bamford, "The Procurement of Oarsmen for French Galleys, 1660–1748," *American Historical Review* 65, no. 1 (1959): 31–48.

To contextualize slavery in Florence, I draw upon archival sources, including financial and clerical documents, and the growing literature on Mediterranean and Italian slavery during early modernity.[38] I first visited Florence as an undergraduate exchange student in the year 2000 and have been working on Italian music and theater consistently ever since, but it wasn't until after I began this project that I learned that many of the Medici buildings I had admired and parts of the beautiful Boboli gardens were built using enslaved labor.[39] In this book, I argue that the music itself—its form, function, and the ways in which it signifies—was also shaped by enslaved labor; understanding how widespread the practice was and the specific meanings of enslavement in early modern Florence are crucial to this project.

In the late sixteenth century and on throughout the seventeenth, the previously dominant military powers in the Mediterranean waned or withdrew to concentrate their forces elsewhere. Spain and the Ottoman Empire—the two largest naval powers in the Mediterranean Sea—called an end to ongoing hostilities in 1581 when they both found themselves fighting wars on two fronts.[40] The timing coincided with the decline of the Venetian merchant marine. One consequence was a sharp rise in piracy, particularly that originating from the Barbary Coast, though numerous European ships were also involved. The vacuum left behind by the departure of strong naval powers also provided an opportunity for the Florentines to increase their seafaring fleet. To support his expansionist agenda, Grand Duke Ferdinando I had the port at Livorno rebuilt (using, as was previously noted, enslaved labor); the silting up of the mouth of the Arno had made the port at Pisa impractical for seafaring vessels. During the same period, large numbers of English, Dutch, and French merchants (the so-called Northern

---

[38] The field of Mediterranean studies could be said to begin with Fernand Braudel, *La Méditerranée et le monde méditerranéen à l'époque de Philippe II* (Paris: Librairie Armand Colin, 1949). More recent examples include Molly Greene, *Catholic Pirates and Greek Merchants: A Maritime History of the Early Modern Mediterranean* (Princeton, NJ: Princeton University Press, 2010); Rothman, *Brokering Empire*; Hershenzon, *Captive Sea*. For a summary and critique of recent trends, see Daniel Hershenzon, "Towards a Connected History of Bondage in the Mediterranean: Recent Trends in the Field," *History Compass* 15 (2016): 1–13.

[39] Bonnie Gordon has given a similar account about the construction of the Piazza Navona statues in Rome.

[40] Some scholars date this treaty to 1580. At this point, Spain had recently taken control of Portugal, while the Spanish war with the Netherlands reached new levels of intensity after the English threw their support behind the Dutch. The Ottomans, for their part, were involved with a war against the Safid Empire (in what is modern-day Iran). A more detailed account is given in Hershenzon, *Captive Sea*.

Invasion) flooded the Mediterranean trade routes;[41] their ships also served to make piracy more profitable for corsairs of various nations—including, as Davies's account above makes clear, the Florentines, who did not hesitate to attack any ship whose financial and political interests ran counter to the Grand Duchy. Daniel Hershenzon has noted the impact of this political and mercantile fragmentation on the structures of Mediterranean enslavement during the early seventeenth century: while the naval warfare of the ongoing Spanish-Ottoman war had utilized enemy ships—and their crews—as the primary source for the procurement of enslaved labor, the shift to smaller circulating forces and increased piracy led to a rise in shore raids and attacks on merchant vessels, increasing the numbers of ordinary citizens who ended up in forced servitude.[42] Soldiers and sailors remained highly vulnerable to capture, as did coastal inhabitants all around the Mediterranean Sea.

Mediterranean slavery was reciprocal, with huge, roughly equivalent numbers of Europeans enslaved in northern Africa and the Near and Middle East and Muslims and non-Catholics (including Jews, various Protestant denominations, and other "infidels") enslaved by Christian forces. Recent estimates for the period 1530 to 1780 put the regional number of the enslaved somewhere between 3 million and 5 million people, spread throughout the Mediterranean basin.[43] The long history and wide extent of this trade in foreign captives gave Mediterranean slavery a familiarity that differed substantially from transatlantic slavery, which is not to claim that the experience of enslavement was easy or non-traumatic for the individuals involved. Hershenzon writes:

---

[41] The notion of the "Northern Invasion" can be traced to Ferdinand Braudel. For a critique and an excellent summary of the political and mercantile conditions in the Mediterranean Sea basin during the seventeenth century, see Molly Greene, "Beyond the Northern Invasion: The Mediterranean in the Seventeenth Century," *Past & Present* 174, no. 1 (2002): 42–71.

[42] Hershenzon writes, "When corsairs took the place of imperial fleets, the number of captives increased and the patterns of their circulation across time and space changed. In earlier periods, dramatic maritime battles like Lepanto (1571) had seen thousands of captives lose their liberty, but some had regained it quickly, often within a few short hours, while many captives had changed hands in the cease-fire and peace treaties that followed such large-scale and violent encounters. After 1581, seldom did more than a few hundred soldiers or sailors aboard ship lose or regain their liberty within such short intervals. Most incidents involved the seizure, by corsairs, of small numbers of captives—a few fishermen or peasants, or dozens of travelers. In other words, piracy transformed the circulation of captives across the imperial map, producing a longer-lasting and more stable population of captives than had large-scale naval battles before 1581." Hershenzon, *Captive Sea*, 8–9.

[43] The largest number cited here, Salvatore Bono's 5 million, includes Black Africans who were enslaved by the Ottomans. See Bono, "Slave Histories," 105. Hershenzon cites several other estimates. See Hershenzon, *Captive Sea*, 2.

Captivity and enslavement were undoubtedly among the worst experiences of the early modern Mediterranean; numerous texts recount the hellish living conditions captives-turned-authors suffered. Yet the mechanisms of captivity, enslavement, and ransom prevented the full alienation or social isolation of enslaved captives in the Mediterranean.[44]

Most early modern inhabitants of the Mediterranean had personal connections to compatriots, coreligionists, or family members who had been taken into slavery and, in some cases, returned home afterward. The estimated percentage of enslaved Christians who were ransomed, were manumitted, or escaped to freedom vary widely; Robert Davies has argued that only 2 percent to 4 percent of enslaved Christians held in North Africa regained their freedom and returned to Europe, though Hershenzon suggests that number must have been higher.[45]

Stories of enslavement and return are ubiquitous in Italian and European drama—with good reason. The celebrated Spanish author Miguel de Cervantes Saavedra (author, among other texts, of *Don Quijote*) spent five years enslaved in Algeria; he wrote several plays set under similar circumstances.[46] Francesco Andreini, patriarch of the famous Andreini family of commedia dell'arte performers and writers, was reputedly enslaved to the Turks for eight years, an experience that his son, Giovan Battista Andreini, linked to Francesco's decision to leave the military and take to the stage.[47] While both Cervantes and Andreini were soldiers at the time of their capture, the very real possibility of enslavement existed for all those who ventured near shore or boarded a boat: Michel de Montaigne, describing his travel through Italy, reports that in Pisa on July 22, 1581, "at dawn, three ships of Turkish corsairs arrived at the nearby shore, and took away fifteen or twenty prisoners of fishermen and poor shepherds."[48] Letters to and by enslaved individuals circulated widely; Mediterranean distances are relatively small,

---

[44] Hershenzon, *Captive Sea*, 4.

[45] Robert C. Davis, *Christian Slaves, Muslim Masters: White Slavery in the Mediterranean, the Barbary Coast, and Italy, 1500–1800* (New York: Palgrave Macmillan, 2003), 19–21; Hershenzon, *Captive Sea*, 193n2.

[46] Ottmar Hegyi, *Cervantes and the Turks: Historical Reality versus Literary Fiction in* La Gran Sultana *and* El Amante Liberal (Newark, DE: Juan de la Cuesta, 1992).

[47] This story is repeated in most biographical treatments of the actor. See, for example, Burattelli, Landolfi, and Zinanni, *Comici dell'arte*, 97–98.

[48] "[A] l'alba, arrivarono tre legni di corsari turcheschi al lito vicino, e levarono via quindici o venti prigioni pescatori e poveri pastori." Michel de Montaigne, *Viaggio in Italia* (Milan: Rizzoli, 2008), 368; cited in Maria Alberti, "Battaglie navali, scorrerie corsare e politica dello spettacolo: Le naumachie medicee del 1589," *California Italian Studies* 1, no. 1 (2010): 7.

and ships crisscrossed the sea.[49] To some extent, the reciprocal, multivalent nature of the Mediterranean trade in human beings protected the enslaved from large-scale physical and religious abuses; Hershenzon documents several incidents in which Christian authorities provided concessions to Muslim slaves as an explicit gesture designed to ensure similar treatment for enslaved Christians in Ottoman territory.[50]

The individual experience of enslavement varied widely. Domestic, court, and galley slaves could be given or purchased, with many enslaved people changing hands multiple times. The Florentine archives provide some examples. In 1646, when Mustafà di Amat Moro (lit. Mustafà son of Amat the Moor, or Black Mustafà son of Amat), originally from Rodos, filed for baptism at the age of approximately twenty years, he recounted that he had been sold first by Spanish slavers, then again in the slave market in Malta, where he was purchased by the French ambassador, who eventually gifted him to the Grand Duke in early 1645.[51] In 1661, the approximately ten-year-old Zaffira d'Orace Turca (Zaffira, daughter of Orace, a Turk or Muslim), who was owned by the Most Serene Princess of Tuscany and living in the Palazzo Pitti, had spent two previous years living with the senator Giovanni Federighi; years before that, she had been taken by slavers, then sold in Bari to Paolo Federighi, who sent her to his sister-in-law, who in turn gifted her to the ducal couple, who put her in service to the princess.[52] Every time an individual was sold or gifted, Hershenzon notes, "entailed not only new masters or employers and altered labor conditions but also a reframing of bondage by both its perpetrator and its object in terms of future sale, enslavement for life, conversion and adoption, or ransom and liberty."[53]

No published accounts of European enslavement written by non-Europeans survive from this period. Details about the movements of Mustafà and Zaffira were preserved only because they chose to convert to Christianity. Under such circumstances, religious authorities were keen to "demonstrate that they did not proceed without due diligence in the matter of slave baptisms."[54]

---

[49] Hershenzon talks specifically about the Mediterranean as a place of writing, passim, but particularly *Captive Sea*, 5, 9.
[50] See, for example, events from 1663 as described in Hershenzon, *Captive Sea*, 29.
[51] I-Fca, Pia Casa dei Catecumini, f. 1, c.n.n.
[52] I-Fca, Pia Casa dei Catecumini, f. 2, c.n.n.
[53] Hershenzon, *Captive Sea*, 24.
[54] "[M]ostrare che non si proceda senza diligentia al battezzare schiavi," requiring "testimonianza in scrittura di quali di persona d'autorità, come sarebbero capitani di nave, o Ministri di Livorno, o di Corte, di dove sia stato preso lo schiavo, che l'habbi condotto in Livorno, e da chi sia stato qui principalmente consegnato o venduto." I-Fca, Pia Casa dei Catecumini, f. 1, c.n.n. [ins. 30].

Such clerical fervor was motivated by both mercenary and doctrinal concerns. On the one hand, the clergy made sure that a given slave had the permission of their owner to seek baptism and was not converting in a (vain) attempt to secure their freedom; only then could the authorities feel certain that the volition toward Christianity was motivated by a proper desire for eternal salvation (rather than the more pragmatic comforts of the earthly life). Conversion, it should be noted, did not necessarily result in manumission; in 1617, when Asano, Hassardino, and Salemme—three enslaved laborers in the granducal stables—requested permission to convert from Grand Duke Cosimo II, the Grand Duke granted their request yet added the caveat that "they are to know that in every way they shall remain slaves."[55] In contrast, when Maometi, a Turk from Cairo who served in Cardinal Prince Giovan Carlo's stables, decided to convert to Christianity in 1630 (taking the name Carlo after his owner), he immediately began earning a salary (of thirty lire a month), though it is not clear whether the act of conversion freed Maometi-Carlo from slavery (the question of enslavement and payment is discussed further below).[56] While technically, Christians could not own Christian slaves, papal opinion exempted the class of those who had been enslaved prior to conversion—only thus, the logic held, could the clergy feel confident that conversion was genuine. Slightly different circumstances held for converted Christians who were enslaved to Jewish or Muslim owners: in such cases, the Christian authorities stepped in immediately, and conversion to Christianity was understood to compel their release. Notably, converts regularly took the surnames (and sometimes also the given names) of their sponsors (of the godfather in the case of male converts and of the godmother in the case of female converts). For those who stayed in Italy and those who had Italian-born children, it took only a few short generations before descendants became fully integrated into Italian society.[57] Often the archival sources make reference to familial relationships spanning several generations: in August 1633, for example, the Grand Duke tipped "Ferdinando Battezzato" (lit. "Ferdinando who has been baptized") ten scudi on the baptism of his son;[58] in August 1652,

---

[55] "S[ua] A[ltezza] si contenta che si battezzino, ma sappino che restano in ogni modo stiavi." I-Fca, Pia Casa dei Catecumini, f. 1, c.n.n.

[56] I-Fas, Mediceo del Principato, f. 5178, c. 20–21.

[57] Bono writes, "The separation of slaves from their geographical and social origins, together with their return or their integration within the new society, gave rise to inter-breeding and multiculturalism which are characteristic of the Mediterranean area, and which needs to be researched in relation to the phenomenon of slavery." Bono, "Slave Histories," 104.

[58] "Al Battesimo del figuolo di Ferdinando Battezzato che sta al Condotto dieci [scudi]." I-Fas, Camera del Granduca, f. 15, c. 52v.

"Mattio son of Giorgio the Moor" was tipped seven scudi;[59] in July 1656, "the sister of the Moor" was tipped two scudi;[60] that August, "the wife of the Moor who was a footman" received four scudi;[61] in March 1657, "the little Moor who married off a daughter" was tipped four scudi,[62] and a few days later, the daughter herself received six scudi on the direct recommendation of the Grand Duke.[63] Other examples can be seen in the appendix.

Most of the archival details I cite about conversion come from a series of first-person narratives preserved by the Pia Casa dei Catecumeni (the Holy House of Religious Converts). The records of the Pia Casa are particularly fascinating because, prior to baptism, *catecumeni* received religious instruction and were interviewed several times to ensure that the conversion was willingly and legitimately made. Scribes took notes, transcribing first-person accounts of birth name, age, parentage, and birthplace, as well as descriptions of how converts came to be in Florence, which often included details of how converts were taken and sold as slaves. Few Jews converted in Florence, since nearby Livorno was a free city, where Jews (and merchants of any creed) were welcomed in return for their investment in the city. The rights of Jews in Livorno were enshrined in the "Livornina," signed by Grand Duke Ferdinando I in 1593; the Livornina famously begins, "To all merchants of whatsoever Nation: Levantines, Western Jews, Spanish, Portuguese, Greeks, Germans, Italians, Jews, Turks, Moors, Armenians, Persians, to each of you good health"[64]—the irony of housing the Medici slave *bagno* in the "free" city is not lost.

In Florence and Livorno, state-owned, able-bodied male captives were put to work in physically demanding tasks. The labor that Davies was forced to provide, for example, was relentless, back-breaking work, not only at oar on the galleys but also laboring to build the city and port:

> three yeeres of this time I lived in this manner, from Sunne rising to Sunne set, chained in a Cart like a horse, recefuing more blowes then any Cart-horse in England, our diet being Bread and Water, and not so much Bread in three daies as we might have eaten at once, thus we were used to go fortie

---

[59] "A Mattio figlio di Giorgio moro, 7.-.-.-." I-Fas, Camera del Granduca f. 14, c. 52v.
[60] "Alla sorella del Moro due scudi." I-Fas, Camera del Granduca f. 27, c. 74v.
[61] "Alla moglie del Moro già staffiere quattro scudi." I-Fas, Camera del Granduca f. 27, c. 83r.
[62] "Al Morino che marita una figlia quattro scudi." I-Fas, Camera del Granduca f. 28, c. 57v.
[63] "Alla Mora che si marita sei scudi disse SA." I-Fas, Camera del Granduca f. 28, c. 63v.
[64] The full text of the Livornina is widely available online. See, for example, www.liberliber.it/online/autori/autori-m/ferdinando-i-de-medici/costituzione-livornina/. "A tutti voi mercanti di qualsivoglia Nazione, Levantini, Ponentini, Spagnuoli, Portoghesi, Greci, Tedeschi, Italiani, Hebrei, Turchi, Mori, Armeni, Persiani, dicendo ad ognuno di essi salute."

or fiftie Carts together, being all slaves: our lading would be Sand, or Lyme, or bricke, or some such like, and to draw it whither the Officers appointed us, for their buildings.[65]

Jacques Callot's print "The Fortification of the Gate of Livorno by Order of the Grand Duke," part of his series on the *Life of Ferdinando I de' Medici*, shows the kind of work Davies describes (see Figure I.1). In this image, the luxurious status of the Grand Duke is foregrounded. He is seated in an advantageous position, lavishly dressed, and attended by a host of courtiers; a young boy holds an *ombrellone* to shade him from the sun, and the weaponry of his private guard of German *lanze* is visible at the far right of the image. The artisan who is there to provide a report on the progress of the fortifications bows deferentially over a model. In the middle ground, a group of masons are busy chiseling stone; in the background, a line of enslaved laborers carry the cut stone up a series of rather perilous-looking ramps. Early in his tenure as Grand Duke, Ferdinando I had attracted criticism for the abusive conditions under which peasants had been forced to work on improving and constructing his property; the use of enslaved labor achieved similar results and incited less critique.[66] Archival documents show that the Medici regularly had recourse to the labor forces stockpiled at Livorno, whether for stablehands, gardeners, or court retainers.

After several years spent working on capital improvements in Livorno, Davies and his coreligionists were reassigned:

Three yeeres being spent in this manner: all we Englishmen were called as many as were left alive, making choise of the ablest of us to goe into the Gallies, of which I was one chosen, then did my miserie increase manyfold, for then I was made a Gally-slave to row at an Oare, where our former diet lessened, but blowes increased, to the losse of many of our lives. We were shaven Head and Beard every eight or tenth day, being alwaies naked, but onely a payre of linnen breeches and chaines continually.[67]

On and off ship, the lives of those obliged to work rowing the galleys were medieval in metaphorical and literal terms, with conditions at oar largely

[65] Davies, *True Relation*, n.p.
[66] Agostini, *Istantanee dal seicento*.
[67] Davies, *True Relation*, n.p.

Figure I.1. Jacques Callot after Matteo Rosselli, "The Grand Duke Fortifies the Port of Livorno," from *Life of Ferdinando I de' Medici* (1616). The Joseph Brooks Fair Collection at the Art Institute of Chicago. 1976.16. Used with permission.

unchanged over hundreds of years. "The miserie of the Gallies," writes Davies, "doth surpasse any mans iudgement or imagination, neyther would any man thinke that such torture, or torment were used in the world, but onely they that feele it." Chained night and day to an oar and exposed to the elements,

> the extremitie of miserie causeth many a slave to kill themselves, or else seeke to kill their Officers; but we were not suffered to have so much as a knife about us, yea if we had gotten one by any extrordinarie meanes, and offered any violence to any Officer, we should presently have lost our nose and eares, and received a hundred blowes on our bare backe, and a hundred on our belly with a double rope, or a Buls pisse, continuing a slave still.[68]

The bread consumed on the galleys was a hard *biscotto*, produced in the *bagno* in enormous quantities and valued for its long shelf life. In addition to thirty ounces per day of *biscotto*, *galeotti* were fed a "vegetable soup, generally made with beans or chickpeas, drizzled with olive oil and blended with rice. Typically this soup and a ration of wine were dispensed on Sunday, Wednesday, and Friday."[69] Meat was served four times a year.

Ignazio Fabroni, a Pistoiese nobleman who served as a knight of San Stefano, voyaging on the Florentine galleys between 1664 and 1687, left behind a portfolio of images, largely sketched in situ. Fabroni's images are available online in high resolution, and a considerable selection was recently published with accompanying essays by the naval historian Anna Agostini.[70] Fabroni's drawings include numerous images of the *galeotti* (representative examples are shown as Figures I.2 and I.3, reproduced after page 240). *Galeotti* rowed, ate, and slept chained in place. As Davies notes, they wore minimal clothes. Agostini elaborates: "During the [summer] season, when they were at oar, the slaves stayed bare-chested, but they also had at their disposal a shirt of strong cotton, a jacket made of cloth and, for the winter

---

[68] Davies, *True Relation*, n.p.

[69] Agostini, a naval historian of the San Stefano knights, is an unapologetic enthusiast of the Tuscan forces; she goes on to assert, "Questa che sembra essere una dieta molto povera era in realtà una dieta ben calcolata, che un medico moderno consiglierebbe volentieri ai suoi pazienti, una dieta in grado di fornire calorie senza eccessivi grassi e proteine." Agostini, *Istantanee dal seicento*, 82.

[70] For a full, high-resolution facsimile of the Fabroni images, see I-Fn, Rossi Cassigioli 199, https://archive.org/details/rossi-cassigoli-199-images. See also Agostini, *Istantanee dal seicento*.

season, an overcoat of wool furnished with a hood, a long cloak that also served them as a blanket with which to sleep."[71]

During periods of inactivity, the enslaved were encouraged in small money-making ventures (Figure I.3, for example, shows an enslaved man knitting a stocking to be sold to merchants in port). Not only did such activities distract enslaved populations from rebellious activity, but most money earned by such tasks went to supplement their meager food rations—with appreciable strength and labor benefits to the slave owners at no additional cost. Such activities continued on land as well as on the galleys themselves. Stephanie Nadalo, describing conditions in the *bagno*, notes that "slaves in Livorno were employed as barbers and vendors of water, wine, tobacco, and used clothing."[72] Luigi Monga, relying heavily on Jean-Jacques Bouchard's description of a galley voyage undertaken in 1630, writes:

> Galley slaves enjoyed a certain freedom in some ports, particularly during the winter months [when galley ships were confined to shore]. In Toulon, for example, they were allowed to move about the city, chained two by two, and sell the articles they made in their free time: handbags, leather belts, toothpicks, silk or wool socks. Often, they were given permission to work for private employers or to play musical instruments in the local inns for pocket money.[73]

For my purposes, the reference to music here is particularly intriguing. A similar observation is echoed by Agostini, who notes that when noble guests were received on board the Tuscan galleys, it was "common to liven up the atmosphere with small orchestras of musicians drawn from the [enslaved] crew."[74] The music making of the galley slaves and the extent to

---

[71] "Gli schiavi, quando stavano al banco, nella buona stagione rimanevano a torso nudo, ma potevano disporre anche di una camica di fustagno, di un giacchetto di panno e, per la stagione invernale, di un gabbano di lana munito di cappuccio, un lungo cappotto che serviva loro anche come coperta per dormire." Agostini, *Istantanee dal seicento*, 75.

[72] Nadalo, "Negotiating Slavery," 296.

[73] Introduction to Scetti, *Journal*, 17. Monga cites Jean-Jacques Bouchard, "Voyage de Paris à Rome," in *Oeuvres complètes*, ed. E. Kanceff (Turin: Giappichelli, 1976), I:39–135, here 80–83, 99–117. Monga's choice of English words is not always entirely felicitous; here, for example, "freedom" of movement and "free time" are unfortunate.

[74] "Quando poi venivano ricevuti a bordo ospiti di riguardo come ambasciatori, o gli stessi granduchi o le principesse regnanti, accompagnati da un ricco seguito di dame e cavalieri, le galere si trasformavano in ambienti più raffinati, erano allestite tavole imbandite con ogni genere di rinfreschi e spesso si rallegrava l'atmosfera con orchestrine di musici tratti dalla stessa ciurma." Agostini, *Istantanee dal seicento*, 88.

which their performances were heard and appreciated by European auditors are questions I take up in more detail in the fourth chapter. As a form of labor, music making was vastly preferable to rowing or carting building supplies; either as a means to earn a supplemental income or as an opportunity to escape from more physically demanding tasks, enslaved laborers had every incentive to reveal or develop their music-making skills.

The "hustle" economy of Mediterranean slavery impacted the lives of privately held enslaved individuals as well as those held by large institutions such as the Florentine state *bagno*. Some enslaved individuals were effectively rented out by their owners; in some cases, they were permitted a share of the profits.[75] Others drew a salary commensurate with those earned by free laborers completing the same work, though tracking such circumstances is difficult. In Florence in 1642, for example, "Filippo moro schiavo" (lit. "the Black slave Filippo") applied for (and was accepted into) the position of footman to Prince Giovan Carlo de' Medici; a secretarial note on his petition indicates that he (like the white Italian noblemen who requested the same position) was inscribed into the rolls "with the usual salary."[76] Some other Black retainers were paid for their service; for example, in a list of footmen to the Grand Duke from ca. 1620, both "Pietro Moro" and "Giovanni Mezzo Moro" (lit. "Half Black"; given the context, Giovanni's *sopranome* is plausibly a reference to biracial heritage) were paid at the rate of sixty-eight scudi and four lire, precisely the same amount as the other seventeen men listed in the document.[77] Such payments have complicated the question of whether court "slaves" were in fact enslaved or whether they should be better understood as racially marked or foreign-born servants. The question is rendered even more complicated by the limited autonomy of servants under sovereign rule. Neither slaves nor servants were free to leave the service of their patrons without explicit (usually written) permission. Many servants led mean, miserable lives, with little opportunity to ameliorate their circumstances or to claim agency over their biographical trajectory. That some enslaved people within Europe found themselves in circumstances similar to those of paid servitude, however, is not to argue that the institution of slavery was benign. Indeed, on the contrary, it should be taken as a condemnation of the many ways in which class injustices were manifest and as a trenchant critique of the

---

[75] See, for example, Hershenzon, *Captive Sea*, 28–29. Several similar examples are cited in Bono, "Slave Histories."
[76] I-Fas, Mediceo del Principato, f. 5279b, insert 3, c. 16r.
[77] I-Fas, Mediceo del Principato, f. 5385, c. 90v.

ways in which modern slavery continues, not only through racist structures and cultural norms within Western democracies but also through the exploitation of migrant labor, particularly undocumented or underdocumented people of color in agricultural, manufacturing, and domestic contexts. Such inequalities persist: in July 2022, the Black British athlete Sir Mo Farah revealed that he was trafficked into the United Kingdom as a child and forced into domestic servitude.[78]

Irrespective of a salary or other income, foreigners were dependent on their patrons (owners) to a degree far greater than were local servants, who could count on familial and cultural ties. Enslaved individuals, including trafficked women and those taken prisoner by galley piracy, were resource poor: "Slaves had no family of their own but were inserted into the households of their owners in the lowest-status position."[79]

The lives of women enslaved within the domestic sphere were less generalizable than the lives of those on the galleys, and almost certainly more mundane, probably not that dissimilar to the grinding reality of many trafficked women and migrant laborers today. The sense of community potentially experienced on a galley may or may not have translated to domestic slaves, who were typically isolated within private households. The opportunity for such women (and men) to socialize with other enslaved individuals varied widely, dependent largely on individual circumstances, including location (those enslaved within larger cities and households would have had more opportunities to encounter other enslaved people). Notably, the documents in the Pia Casa mention the spouses of converts with some regularity. In 1610, Fatilena (baptized as Lisabetta), who was enslaved in the granducal household, explained that she wanted to convert in order to follow in the footsteps of her husband, "Sulfiare, who was a Turk, and now is a Christian named Simone."[80] Others mention siblings, children, and other family members who were taken into slavery with them. Such sources suggest that in Florence, the sizable enslaved population provided significant opportunities for community.

---

[78] See, for example, Ashitha Nagesh, "Sir Mo Farah Reveals He Was Trafficked to the UK as a Child," BBC News, https://www.bbc.com/news/uk-62123886.

[79] Kate Lowe, "Visible Lives: Black Gondoliers and Other Black Africans in Renaissance Venice," *Renaissance Quarterly* 66 (2013): 445. Lowe also makes the point that manumission did not remove a dependency upon the (ex-)owner: "If their path to a new life was not smoothed by their former masters through money or contacts, and if they had no trade by which they could earn money, freedom could have been a bitter blessing" (422).

[80] I-Fca, Pia Casa dei Catecumini, f. 1, c.n.n. [ins. 30].

In Florence, the enslaved/free status of children followed the status of the father (though even children taken captive at a young age were considered property, bought and sold). Since many children born to enslaved women were fathered by their owners or other freemen, such children were technically free. Lest we assume that such "freedom" serves as evidence of social good, scholars of Italian orphanages have suggested that as many as 30 percent of foundlings were born to enslaved women and perhaps forcibly given up for adoption.[81] Certainly, enslaved women were at an elevated risk of sexual assault, and enslaved men were also vulnerable to attack.[82]

An undated manuscript poem from the Medici archives, attributed to Ciro di Pers (1599–1663),[83] titled "To old Sig. Bali Alessandro Orso Cavaliere who has fallen in love with a Black slave when she comes to tend the fire in his house," conveys something of the place of enslaved women within the courtly domestic economy. In this poem, the feelings of the Black woman are casually ignored. Her presence and enslaved condition are taken as given,

---

[81] Kate Lowe, "Black Africans' Religious and Cultural Assimilation to, or Appropriation of, Catholicism in Italy, 1470–1520," *Renaissance and Reformation/Renaissance et Réforme* 31, no. 2, special issue on Sub-Saharan Africa and Renaissance and Reformation Europe: New Findings and New Perspectives (2008): 67–86, particularly 70–73. It is important to note that Lowe cites documents from the late fifteenth and sixteenth centuries, a period during which the orphanage records at the Ospedale degli Innocenti in Florence contained explicit documentation of the parentage of many foundlings. Even when infants were left anonymously, midwives on payroll at the Innocenti were called to testify who the parents were, based on who in the city was known to be pregnant or had recently given birth. Curious to know whether similar claims could be made about seventeenth-century foundlings, I consulted the archives of the Innocenti, without much luck. Florence was a larger city during the seventeenth century, and the large numbers of children left in the crib at the Innocenti (typically two or three children each night) were rarely associated with a specific family. While the details of the clothing of each child were recorded with obsessive attention to the quality and type of garment, along with any *contrasegno*—most commonly half a button or a specific type of jewelry, left so that the parents might reclaim the correct child at some future, more financially healthy date—next to nothing can be deduced about the families or context from which the children came. The vast majority of children died within days of their arrival at the orphanage and many more within the first year. Those who managed to survive the first few weeks were sent out to a wet nurse, typically living in the rural areas close to the city of Florence. Children who lived to the age of seven or eight were returned to the institution in order to begin their education and eventually learn a trade that would render them productive members of society. In I-FAoi 537, Balie e bambine (1599–1600) Q, the first volume associated with the seventeenth century, only two of the first one hundred listed children survived long enough to return to the Innocenti.

[82] Monga, *Galee toscane*, 18: "As for the sexual morality aboard the galleys, it was not surprising that a great number of young males, crowded together night and day in an extremely small space, could spawn episodes of homosexuality and sodomy, incidents which in the sixteenth century were punishable by death. In fact, to avoid these temptations among the troops that were to fight for Christianity in the campaign at sea of 1571, just before the papal galleys left the port of Civitavecchia, Pius V ordered Onorato Gaetani, the captain general of his infantry, to keep off the galley the young men who usually served the officers as pages: only mature (i.e. 'bearded') individuals were allowed aboard." See also, Tamar Herzig, "Slavery and Interethnic Sexual Violence: A Multiple Perpetrator Rape in Seventeenth-Century Livorno," *American Historical Review*, vol. 127, no. 1 (2022): 194–222.

[83] Notably, Ciro di Pers served as a knight of Malta. Of his several books of poetry, one (published posthumously in 1666) includes a poem about what it was like to serve on the galley.

and she serves primarily as a comic inversion of the ideal beloved. It is not enough that old Orso (lit. "Bear") has fallen in love (itself humorous, given his advanced age), but he has fallen for an enslaved woman who performs the lowest kind of manual labor, and she is Black. Di Pers constructs an elaborate poetic conceit about the color of the young Black woman's skin, the blackening effects of (literal) fire, the (metaphorical) fire of passion, and the purity (and thus "whiteness") of love. As such, the Blackness and servitude of the young woman are treated as merely incidental elements of the poetry, while their very mundanity explicates the normality of slavery within Italian courtly culture.

One place in which the historical memory of slavery within Italian courts has persisted is in scholarship on the genre painting of patron-prince (or princess) and Black page, in which the enslaved, racially marked Other serves a decorative function illustrating the financial and geopolitical power of the sitter.[84] In such contexts, the Black child is not just objectified but becomes a literal object (represented in paint) that is owned by the sitter and the owner of the painting. Faced with such images, it is difficult to find a vocabulary with which to discuss enslaved Black subjects that does otherwise than reinscribe their conscription into a colonialist project of white supremacy. It is important, however, to recognize the real historical people whose images have been preserved in these paintings and to acknowledge the extent to which slavery and bonded labor were integrated, essential elements of European culture. Over the last two decades, scholarship on European and Mediterranean enslavement during early modernity has increased dramatically, yet Salvatore Bono's apt designation of the phenomenon as a "repressed" memory persists.[85] Certainly, the presence of enslaved labor and enslaved musicians has been absent from large-scale music historical narratives.

Outside the galleys, the distinction between *serva* or *servo* (female or male servant) and *stiava* or *stiavo*[86] (female or male slave) referenced not only the

---

[84] Lowe has noted that the visual presence of Black individuals is relatively easy to trace in artwork, as opposed to archives. See Lowe, "Visible Lives," 426. See also David Bindman and Henry Louis Gates, eds., *The Image of the Black in Western Art*, 10 vols. (Cambridge, MA: Harvard University Press, 2010–2014). An increasing number of galleries and museums have begun to grapple with the legacy of slavery and Blackness in Western art; one example, with particular relevance to Medici patronage, is the 2020 interactive website developed by Justin Randolph Thompson in collaboration with the Uffizi Galleries in Florence (the website includes ten essays by scholars, including myself), "On Being Present: Recovering Blackness in the Uffizi Galleries," Uffizi Galleries, https://www.uffizi.it/en/online-exhibitions/on-being-present.

[85] Bono, "Slave Histories," 101.

[86] *Stiavo* is the Tuscan term, which appears in the Florentine documents more frequently than *schiavo* (the standardized Italian word).

status (free vs. enslaved) of the person thus described but also a difference in origin (local vs. foreign). The enslaved came from elsewhere, and their social position was rendered precarious by an absence of social connections and, in some cases, a limited linguistic fluency. In the sources I have consulted, enslaved people are quite regularly described as servants, and racially marked, obviously foreign servants are sometimes described as slaves; however, I have found no instances in which ethnically Italian servants are described as slaves.[87] This connotation of alterity as it relates to enslavement is important, particularly given the substantial presence of enslaved labor in Medici Florence. Such differences were cultural, religious, linguistic, and proto-nationalistic but also ethnic and racialized in important and historically specific ways.

Race

In May 1671, Sara—described as a *mora turca*, or "Black Muslim," originally from Tunisia and approximately thirty years old—petitioned for baptism in Florence along with her two children, Simonto (ca. sixteen years old) and Israele (ca. ten), both fathered by the late Abramo di Israele Hebreo (the Jew Abramo, son of Israele).[88] Sara described herself as a widow and called the deceased Abramo her husband: "My name is Sara—a Black muslim who was the wife—of the Jew Abramo son of Israele, now widowed."[89] Her children were described as simultaneously Black and Jewish, and they are not the only such individuals to appear in the archive. Notably, in other similar instances, marital status is less clear. Nearly ten years earlier, Benvenuta, *mora turca*, fled from the house of her Jewish owners, seeking baptism (and liberty) with her young son in tow:

> Benvenuta, *mora turca* from Angola, does not know the name of her father and mother, aged around 22 years, was taken by the Turks, and then purchased by Jews; [she has] a desire to come to the Holy Baptism [and] was helped by some Christians to escape from the house of the Jews her owners on the 6th of September, 1652, or thereabouts, along with her son,

---

[87] Lowe, talking about Black Africans who lived in Venice a full century earlier, notes that slaves are often called servants but that servants are never called slaves. See Lowe, "Visible Lives," 416.

[88] I-Fca, Pia Casa dei Catecumeni, f. 2, c.n.n. [ins. 65].

[89] I-Fca, Pia Casa dei Catecumeni, f. 2, c.n.n. [ins. 65]: "Mi haver nome Sara (^mora turca già moglie) di Abramo di Israele Ebreo vedova."

whom she had with one of her Jewish owners. She begs and supplicates your Most Illustrious Highness to concede her the grace of being admitted to Holy Baptism, along with her young son of around two years of age.[90]

Benvenuta (later baptized as Teresia) makes no mention of marriage or of voluntary sexual relations with Raffaello Ebreo, who is named as the father of her child, Mordacheo (later Giuseppe).[91] In yet another example, from 1674, the ten-year-old Samuello Ebreo Moro (Samuello, the Black Jew) fled the house of his father, Captain Chiaves, in Pisa and took refuge in the Pia Casa, requesting baptism.[92] In 1680, the fourteen-year-old Luna, daughter of Abram Costa, an Albanian Jew, was described as "Ebrea Mora" (Black Jewess).[93] As mentioned earlier, non-Christians were strictly forbidden from keeping Christian slaves, and so the conversions of Sara and of Benvenuta-Teresia and their children equated to manumission; such converts were highly reliant on Christian sponsors and patrons to ensure their stability within Christian society. From the scant documentation that has come to light, these women appear highly resourceful. Sara, in particular, seems poised to navigate a bearable living situation for at least a second time, having first married out of slavery (at the tender age of fourteen, if we take the approximate ages of mother and children seriously) and then converting to Christianity, presumably after the death of her Jewish husband rendered her situation in the Jewish community less tenable. Since both Simonto and Israele are described as having been born in Corfu, the family's ties to the Livornese Jewish community may have been particularly tenuous.[94]

The doubled adjectives of "Black" and "Jewish" deployed by church scribes to describe these children trace a descriptive biological inheritance that in modern terms is both racial and ethnic: Simonto, Israele, Mordacheo, and Samuello have inherited the black skin color of their mothers and the religious ethnicity of their fathers. This concept of (racial, ethnic) inheritance provides an element of

---

[90] "Benvenuta Mora Turca d'Angola in Morea senza sapere il nome di Suo padre e madre d'eta d'anni 22 in circa, fu presa da Turchi, e compra poi da Ebrei, con animo di venire al Santo Battesimo azzitata da alcuni Cristiani uscì di Casa degl'Ebrei suoi Padroni, a 6 di settembre 1652 o piu vero giorno con un suo figliolino havuto da uno de Padroni Giudei. Prega instantemente e supplica VS Illma a farli grazia di essere ammessa al Santo battesimo insieme con il suo piccolo figliolino d'eta circa anni 2." I-Fca, Pia Casa dei Catecumeni, f. 2, c.n.n. [ins. 11].

[91] Baptismal records can be found at I-Fd, Registri Battesimali, Femmine, reg. 271, fol. 309, and Registri Battesimali, Maschi, reg. 49, fol. 270, respectively. Both individuals were baptized on December 31, 1653.

[92] I-Fca, Pia Casa dei Catecumeni, f. 2, c.n.n. [ins. 87].

[93] I-Fca, Pia Casa dei Catecumeni, f. 2, c.n.n. [ins. 106].

[94] I-Fca, Pia Casa dei Catecumeni, f. 2, c.n.n. [ins. 65].

continuity between early modern racial formulations and the present, as well as the means to contextualize the differences between race in seventeenth-century Florence (or even Europe more broadly) and in the twenty-first-century Western world of academic writing. It also points up the specificity with which seventeenth-century Florentine sources use the term *moro* or *mora* to mean "Black." While in general "Moors [in early modern Europe] could be 'white,' 'brown,' 'black,' or anything in between," the Florentine sources I consulted were remarkably consistent.[95] Unless modified as *Moro bianco* ("white Moor," which seems to describe a small category of observant Muslims, visibly marked by clothing such as turbans), *moro* or *mora* can be understood to mean dark-skinned individuals, typically of African descent.

The literal Italian term for race—*razza*—was already in use. In *Il pazzo per forza*, a comic opera written in Florence and performed there at the Pergola theater during carnival in 1659, the character Anselmo uses the word *razza* in emblematic fashion when he reacts with surprise and sadness to the apparent madness of his only son:

ANSELMO	Oh figliuol mio diletto	Oh, son, my joy,
	Il senno hai perso, e pure	You have lost your sense, and
	Per una Donna un giovin della razza	Over a woman, no less; can a youth of a race [lineage],
	Sauia, come son'io si presto impazza?	as wise as I am, go so quickly insane?
	Filandro, uscite fuora.[96]	Filandro, snap out of it!

In *La serva nobile*, written and performed by the same troupe the following year, the word *razza* appears again:

FERNANDO	Io piglio donna	I take a bride
	Solo per aver razza,	Only for the sake of my race [lineage],
	E se ben questa di quella ragazza	And if this woman Is a little less beautiful [than the other],
	E un po manco bella,	
	Ch'importa? Al buio ogni gatta è morella.	What does it matter? At night all cats are black.
	Me ne contento.[97]	I am content.

---

[95] The quotation comes from Kate Lowe, "The Black Diaspora in Europe in the Fifteenth and Sixteenth Centuries, with a Special Reference to German-Speaking Areas," in *Germany and the Black Diaspora: Points of Contact, 1250–1914*, ed. Mischa Honeck, Martin Klimke, and Anne Kuhlmann (New York: Berghahn, 2013), 39.

[96] Giovanni Andrea Moniglia, *Il pazzo per forza, Dramma civile rusticale, Fatto rappresentare in Musica, Da gl'illustriss. Sig. Accademici Immobili Nel loro Teatro, Sotto la protezione del Sereniss e Reverendiss. Principe Cardinale Gio: Carlo di Toscana* (Florence: Il Bonardi, 1659), I, xxxii.

[97] Giovanni Andrea Moniglia, *La serva nobile*, in *Delle poesie dramatiche di Giovann'Andrea Moniglia, Accademic della Crusca, Parte terza* (Florence: Vincenzio Vangelisti, 1698), III, xxxv.

In modern English, this usage of *razza* is best translated (as Kate Lowe has argued elsewhere) as "lineage." In the examples above, we might say "of a sane lineage" or "I take a bride only to have descendants"; we might substitute "family" for "race." In early modern English, "race" was used in a similar way, in formulations such as "one comes from a race of kings" or "a race of thieves." I note that in each of these cases, race/lineage defines a set of qualities passed down through biological inheritance that are not limited to merely physical features—sanity, for example, or an aptitude for sovereignty or theft.

David Nirenberg has made a similar claim about early modern Spanish uses of the terms *raza*, *casta* ("caste"), and *linaje*, "already in the early fifteenth century . . . part of a complex of closely associated terms that linked both behavior and appearance to nature and reproduction."[98] With regard to *raza*, in particular, Nirenberg traces the use of the word in animal husbandry texts and its application to Jewish populations, "insisting" that *raza* was "already saturated with resonance to what contemporaries held to be 'common sense' knowledge about the reproductive systems of the natural world. . . . The natural science upon which such wisdom was based was not that of the nineteenth century, but it was nonetheless capable of generating conclusions startlingly similar to those of a later age."[99]

Lowe has called attention to the use of the Italian term *razza* in a discussion between Isabella d'Este and others on the topic of Blackness and enslaved African children, dated to 1491: Isabella was keen to procure a young Black girl—as young and "as Black as possible"—as part of a larger plan to breed up a supply of decorative Black court "buffoons."[100] She harbored similar aspirations to breed individuals with dwarfism, and the term *razza* appears there, too. In Isabella's usage, *razza* refers to an inherited set of traits (here Black skin but also, by implication, servitude) passed down from parent to child. The category thus carries a sense of inherited destiny: "blood will out."

It is, I believe, useful to think about lineage in this sense as a model for (early) modern conceptions of race and thus for a more capacious understanding of inherited difference and bodily residue. Lineage—or *razza*—circumscribed the clothes one wore, the educational and professional opportunities one had, the way one spoke, the person one married or was

---

[98] David Nirenberg, *Neighboring Faiths: Christianity, Islam, and Judaism in the Middle Ages and Today* (Chicago: University of Chicago Press, 2014), 180.
[99] Nirenberg, *Neighboring Faiths*, 181–182.
[100] Kate Lowe, "Isabella d'Este and the Acquisition of Black Africans at the Mantuan Court," in *Mantova e il Rinascimento italiano: Studi in onore di David S. Chambers*, ed. Philippa Jackson and Guido Rebecchini (Mantua: Editoriale Sometti, 2011), 70–71.

married to. Sumptuary law, learned social graces, and ossified class mobility functioned to extend the stereotypical personifications of such difference as if they were embodied, material truths. In short, *razza* sorted people, much the way that *race* has been understood to do within modernity. In this account, *razza* confounds both "race" and "class," though arguably, distinctions between these categories are blurry and difficult to parse even today. *Razza* designated one's place in life and was understood as legible both on the body's surface as physical traits (a visible likeness to one's parents, for example) and in the body's interior (in disposition or aptitude).

The force of such categories was (quite literally) dramatized in the standard *travestimento* of the Italian stage, where categorical differences of type were rendered visible and audible through costuming, gesture, voice, and vocabulary. In the commedia dell'arte and related literary genres, the denouement arrives through a series of recognitions and revelations: long-lost lovers, siblings, and children are identified; imposters are demoted; travestied nobles disguised as servants are elevated. Relationships that were doomed because of mismatched social status are returned to an even footing as everyone is returned to their rightful place.

Identification and distribution of these "rightful" places were visible and audible, biological and epigenetic, learned and disciplined. One prevalent critique of "race" as a heuristic for the study of early modernity pivots on a one-dimensional definition of race or racial discrimination as a function of skin color, rightly noting that discrimination in early modernity was more complex than mere color and highly influenced by religious, linguistic, and cultural designations. Yet *razza* makes clear that skin color was but one part of the complex materiality by which bodies—and thus people—were categorized.

In this sorting of phenotypes and costumes, skin color is neither negligible nor fully determining. Italian-language descriptions of missing persons—mostly Italian citizens who had been forced into foreign slavery—specify the skin color of those whom modern racial categories would classify as "white" with a variety of color-based adjectives, while the glorified "white skin" of poetic love lyrics reveals that differences of complexion were not equally valued.[101] Arthur Little, for example, has looked at the ways in which William

---

[101] Robert Davis, for example, in his work on "white" slavery in the Mediterranean, has the following to say about efforts to rescue Christian slaves held in North African cities: "Along with the names, each agent was ordered to collect all relevant details that might help identify the individual slaves: that is, 'their age, stature, skin [color], occupation, [and] every other clear indicator of [who

Shakespeare's noble characters mobilize the pale color of their cheeks to instigate a hierarchy that excludes those who labor in the fields.[102] Descriptions of foreign slaves in Italy also exploit a similar attention to the variation of skin color, even within fairly narrow ethnic parameters.[103]

Scholars of the African diaspora and early modernity have foregrounded skin color and its cultural meanings.[104] Yet the obvious relevance of skin color to the European treatment of Black Africans has complicated rather than clarified early modern race and racism on a larger scale. Joaneath Spicer has argued that "Attitudes to skin 'color' in the Renaissance encapsulate much of what today is grouped under 'race,'" yet she goes on:

> Although "race" and "racism" are used in scholarly discourse on ethnic discrimination in the Renaissance, the various European words used in the 1500s to suggest kinship relationships are not equivalent to our use of "race." They largely refer to either direct family descent from one person or "people" as "French people," involving cultural as much as visible genetic markers such as color.[105]

Race, however, is a category in which "cultural" markers need not be separated from "visible genetic markers." As the above discussion of *razza* makes clear, I advocate an alternative understanding of inheritance and race that foregrounds presumed aptitude among the complicated designations of difference and belonging as they were understood to cohere during early modernity. Recognizing this complexity is more useful than separating out a

they are], along with the time and the place where their capture took place'" (Davis's brackets). He quotes from I-Ras, Vat, Gonfolone, b. 8, f. 4, part 1; see Davis, *Christian Slaves*, 161.

[102] Arthur L. Little Jr., "Re-Historicizing Race, White Melancholia, and the Shakespearean Property," *Shakespeare Quarterly* 67, no. 1 (2016): 91–92.

[103] Discussing a significant archive of slave records from late-trecento Geneva, both Origo and Epstein emphasize the range of skin tones ascribed, even within fairly narrow ethnic parameters; the deed of sale, writes Origo, "described her origin, her price, and her appearance, her stature (small, rather small, medium, large), the color of her skin (black, *ulivigna* [olive], white, rosy, or even greenish), the shape of her face (round, long, square), the form of her eyes (sunken or with 'upturned eyelids') and any distinguishing scars or tattoos by which she was marked, as well as any illnesses from which she had suffered, especially small-pox, or any physical defect." Origo, "Domestic Enemy," 333. See also Stephen A. Epstein, *Speaking of Slavery: Color, Ethnicity, and Human Bondage in Italy* (Ithaca, NY: Cornell University Press, 2001), 108.

[104] A good review of current literature is provided in the introduction to Cassander L. Smith, Nicholas R. Jones, and Miles P. Grier, eds., *Early Modern Black Diaspora Studies: A Critical Anthology* (Cham, Switzerland: Palgrave Macmillan, 2018), 1–14.

[105] Joaneath Spicer, "European Perceptions of Blackness as Reflected in the Visual Arts," in *Revealing the African Presence in Renaissance Europe*, ed. Joaneath Spicer (Baltimore: Walters Art Museum, 2012), 36.

single embodied difference (skin color) from among the tangled nexus of religion, ethnicity, social class, (dis)ability, and gender. Crucially, this capacious understanding of *razza* and the heritable aptitude of social status—what Sylvia Wynter would call "an a-Christian premise of a by-nature difference" between races—makes room for embodiment, voice, and sound within the realm of the racially significant.[106] To deploy *razza* as analytic is to articulate how birth—lineage, family, social status, and inheritance—categorized people into predetermined categories or stock types.

* * *

As with the humanities more broadly, musicology has benefited from and contributed to a growing literature on race. In the wake of George Floyd's murder and the widespread Black Lives Matter protests of the Covid era, academics have paid renewed attention to disciplinary racism and the white-centric curricula of many fields. In musicology, this self-reflection has been particularly overdue, since—as I elaborate for my non-musicological readers—the history of music as it is predominantly taught in high schools and universities is the history of Western classical music, characterized by a pantheon of white male European composers and their masterworks. Not only has the ex-nominative whiteness of classical music sidelined racial questions, but the notational tradition of Western art music has facilitated a disciplinary investment in "the music itself," both as an aesthetic paradigm in which developmental musical textures are valorized over the kinds of complexity that arise in iterational or improvisational traditions and as a form of historiography in which scholars can write (and think) about music only where the particulars of the musical experience are notated or recorded in some form. Thus, much traditional music history has presumed that only Western art music has a history.

Further complicating the methodological pitfalls of historical work around race and "early music" (music from before 1750), much of the surviving (Western) music written for or about non-Western "Others" remains stubbornly consistent with European musical traditions. In the dominant musicological paradigm, an inability to build an argument on "the music itself" is perceived as weakness; to deal with the (poetic) text, with costumes or gestures, is to deal with surface rather than depth. Faced with this conundrum, many scholars encountering the question of race and early music have

---

[106] Wynter, "Unsettling," 296.

done one of two things. Either they retreat behind the notes, arguing that since the music itself is "Western," the situation is not one of *musical* exoticism and thus we musicologists need not deal with it at all. Alternatively, once problematic racial stereotypes are identified, the issue is put to one side, and the analysis (historical and/or musical) continues as before. Dymphna Callaghan might call this second set of circumstances an "inoculating critique," whereby a small dose of racial consciousness is inserted into the body of text, preventing the whole from succumbing to the disease.[107] In the rare cases where scholars have made claims for specifically musical exoticisms in early repertoires, they rely on stereotypical and oppositional assumptions of how non-European-ness should sound: namely, repetitive, non-developmental, noisy, or out of tune.[108] To search for the "Other" in music history has been to reify the supposedly neutral categories of aesthetic value as inherently European.

Such thinking presumes that the music of foreign others or music representing foreign others will be easily discernible as itself other: citations or imitations that stick out from a neutral, otherwise European texture. In contrast, in this book, I argue that markers of musical, cultural, and racial otherness were thoroughly embedded into and integral to the European tradition itself. In listening for the presence of foreign others within European musical sound, we can recognize an inherent slippage between here and elsewhere and discern through auscultation a vocal selfhood that participates in discourses that objectify people in the growing global economy of slaves and other material goods.

In certain musicological subfields, such as popular musics of the post-recording era and American art music, race has been a central analytic for a long time. Nina Sun Eidsheim's work (on race and timbre) and Matthew Morrison's (on Blacksound) have, for example, articulated a sophisticated analytic of the intersection of stereotype and musical style as they impact audible constructions of race.[109] Olivia Bloechl has been a trenchant advocate

---

[107] I learned of this very useful term from Bernadette Andrea, "Elizabeth I and Persian Exchanges," in *The Foreign Relations of Elizabeth I*, ed. Charles Beem (New York: Palgrave MacMillan, 2011), 182.
[108] Ralph P. Locke, *Music and the Exotic from the Renaissance to Mozart* (Cambridge: Cambridge University Press, 2015).
[109] Eidsheim, *Race of Sound*; Matthew D. Morrison, "The Sound(s) of Subjection: Constructing American Popular Music and Racial Identity through Blacksound," *Women & Performance: A Journal of Feminist Theory* 27, no. 1 (2017): 13–24; Matthew D. Morrison, "Race, Blacksound, and the (Re)Making of Musicological Discourse," *Journal of the American Musicological Society* 72, no. 3 (2019): 781–823.

of a postcolonial or global approach to music history, particularly in regard to the eighteenth century and the transatlantic world.[110] What once might have seemed like isolated essays in alternative historiography have begun to glom together into a rich yet coherent field, including work in historical ethnography, such as that of Katherine Butler Schofield and her collaborators;[111] in sound studies such as that of Richard Cullen Rath and Sarah Justina Eyerly;[112] in early American musics (both indigenous and settler musics), such as that of Glenda Goodman and Bloechl;[113] in Western art music and local practices in non-Western locations, such as that by Rogério Budasz, Ireri Chávez Bárcenas, Geoffrey Baker, Jesús Ramos-Kettrell, Cesar Favila, Makoto Harris Takao, Parkorn Wangpaiboonkit, Janie Cole, and many others, not least Kate van Orden's recent edited collection;[114] and the presence and representation of racialized musicians in Europe, including work by Budasz, Arne Spohr, Nathan Reeves, Berta Joncus, Eric Rice, Ralph Locke, Don Harrán, Ruth HaCohen, and Bloechl.[115] Such work has been my constant resource, and the scholars who have produced it have been valued interlocutors.

I imagine that few readers of this book will be simultaneously expert in seventeenth-century Italian musical-theatrical practice *and* in work on race, slavery, and early modernity. Most will, I anticipate, be scholars of

---

[110] Bloechl deals with this issue in many places, but see particularly Olivia Bloechl, "Race, Empire, and Early Music," in *Rethinking Difference in Music Scholarship*, ed. Olivia Bloechl, Melanie Lowe, and Jeffrey Kallberg (Cambridge: Cambridge University Press, 2015), 77–107.

[111] Francesca Orsini and Katherine Butler Schofield, eds., *Tellings and Texts: Music, Literature and Performance Cultures in North India* (Cambridge, UK: Open Book, 2015).

[112] Rath, *How Early America Sounded*; Eyerly, *Moravian Soundscapes*.

[113] Both are exemplified in the contributions to Emily Wilbourne and Suzanne G. Cusick, eds., *Acoustemologies in Contact: Sounding Subjects and Modes of Listening in Early Modernity* (Cambridge: Open Book, 2021).

[114] Rogério Budasz, *Opera in the Tropics: Music and Theater in Early Modern Brazil* (Oxford: Oxford University Press, 2019); Ireri Chávez Bárcenas, "Singing in the City of Angels: Race, Identity, and Devotion in Early Modern Puebla de los Ángeles" (PhD diss., Princeton University, 2018); Geoffrey Baker, *Imposing Harmony: Music and Society in Colonial Cuzco* (Durham, NC: Duke University Press, 2008); Jesús A. Ramos-Kittrell, *Playing in the Cathedral: Music Race, and Status in New Spain* (Oxford: Oxford University Press, 2016); Cesar Favila, "The Sound of Profession Ceremonies in Novohispanic Convents," *Journal of the Society for American Music* 13, no. 2 (2019): 143–170; Makoto Harris Takao, "'In Their Own Way': Contrafactal Practices in Japanese Christian Communities during the 16th Century," *Early Music* 47, no. 2 (2019): 183–198; Kate van Orden, ed., *Seachanges: Music in the Mediterranean and Atlantic Worlds, 1550–1800*, I Tatti Research Series 2 (Cambridge, MA: Harvard University Press, 2022).

[115] Rogério Budasz, "Black Guitar-Players and Early African-Iberian Music in Portugal and Brazil," *Early Music* 35, no. 1 (2007): 3–21; Arne Spohr, "'Mohr und Tropeter': Blackness and Social Status in Early Modern Germany," *Journal of the American Musicological Society* 72, no. 3 (2019): 616–663; Locke, *Music and the Exotic*; Don Harrán, "'Barucaba' as an Emblem for Jewishness in Early Italian Art Music," *Jewish Quarterly Review* 98, no. 3 (2008): 328–354; Ruth HaCohen, *The Music Libel against the Jews* (New Haven, CT: Yale University Press, 2011); Olivia Bloechl, *Native American Song at the Frontiers of Early Modern Music* (Cambridge: Cambridge University Press, 2008).

seventeenth-century Italy (possibly even of early baroque Italian music) but with little knowledge of Italian slavery or the widespread presence of racialized foreigners. Others will be scholars of race, slavery, and early modernity (possibly of music and sound) but with only a cursory familiarity with Medicean Florence in the seventeenth century. Yet others will be musicologists expert in vastly different places or periods, curious to rethink the sonic history of opera's emergence. Some will have no knowledge of music history whatsoever. I have tried to structure and word this book so that it can be useful to all such readers, as well as to others, unimagined at the point of writing.

In my turn to voice, to sound, and to the literal presence of marked "Others" within Medicean Florence, I hope to sidestep some of the more egregious presumptions of traditional musical historical thought. Rather than attempting to identify specific musical gestures as consistent with or foreign to European style, I consider questions of legibility and comprehension, comparing the vocal personas of variously situated characters. It matters when and where the voices of foreigners are comprehensible to other characters and audiences, it matters how their sounds and their music relate to norms of cultural expressivity and subjectivity, and it matters how present historical "Others" were within Italian culture at the time. Heard against the noisy, multiethnic, early modern Italian city, the voices amplified in this study complicate widely accepted musical historical narratives of cultural unity and autonomous stylistic development. As scholars, we need to denaturalize the expressive voice that cohered so effectively in the new music of Florence around 1600, for its musical and metaphorical success articulated a certain form of modern subjectivity and sound that persists into our present.

Voice, Slavery, and Race in Seventeenth-Century Florence is divided into two halves—labeled as "acts"—motivated by fundamentally different methodologies. Act I is both more archival and more theoretical; Act II is biographical, pursuing an extended case study of a specific enslaved Black singer, Giovannino Buonaccorsi. The two halves are mutually codependent, for without Act I, Buonaccorsi risks seeming like an exception to the status quo; it is the many other enslaved musicians discussed in Act I who prove his mundanity—even in the face of a clearly prodigious talent. Furthermore, without Buonaccorsi as a detailed example, the individuals cited in Act I risk reduction to a (largely) nameless, faceless crowd. The remarkably rich documentary trail that has survived with regard to Buonaccorsi helps flesh out the stories and the material presence that Act I describes.

In the first half of this book, I consider a variety of performances and people who were present in Florence during the first half of the seventeenth century. Each chapter (or "scene," as I have called them) in Act I considers the question of race, representation, and sound from a different angle: from elite courtly performances in front of foreign dignitaries to street songs performed during carnival, from scholarly efforts to transcribe foreign music or to recapture the enharmonic effects described in ancient Greek sources to the work songs performed by enslaved galley oarsmen in the Tuscan port city of Livorno. In each instance, I juxtapose evidence of contact and presence with extant traces of performed musical sound. In the process, I demonstrate the extent to which certain scholastic assumptions about authenticity and representation have worked to conceal the presence and significance of racialized difference within European musical sound and to provide contextual detail and analytic models for other scholars who work on similar questions. The fragmentary nature of the archival evidence has substantially shaped the presentation of my thoughts and findings. Rarely am I able to follow any individual for an extended period, while the sheer number of individuals and the rich detail of some of the evidence argue for broader implications even beyond the people and incidents I have found and discuss. Like Cassander L. Smith, I approach each individual as "a real, historical person whose actions were the material from which" history is recorded.[116] These people—unlike foreign characters in contemporary theater—were more than a metaphor or evidence about how (white) Italians constructed (white) history and appropriated the voices of racially marked "Others." I work to foreground the people who lived and worked within and through racial categories. I argue not only for the presence of foreign and enslaved individuals in sonic practices of early modern Florence but also for the ways in which certain genres became associated with enslaved and racially marked performers and then, in turn, how such genres were taken as evidence for the intrinsic characters and capacities—the *razza*—of such individuals and of the races from which they were drawn.

The chapters of the first half are deliberately short, each focused on a specific facet or manifestation of sound, voice, and racial difference, yet the impact of these chapters is best appreciated in their layering and interaction. Act I culminates in Scene 7, "Music Proper to Enslaved Singers," which

---

[116] Cassander L. Smith, "'Candy No Witch in Her Country': What One Enslaved Woman's Testimony during the Salem Witch Trials Can Tell Us about Early American Literature," in *Early Modern Black Diaspora Studies: A Critical Anthology*, ed. Cassander L. Smith, Nicholas Jones, and Miles P. Grier (Cham, Switzerland: Macmillan, 2018), 111.

falls structurally in place of the *imbroglio*. Here the various threads and arguments of the first half intersect, providing the strongest theoretical articulation of the major thesis of the book: that racialized bodies were aligned with the comic and thus with entertaining low-register music that signaled a seeming aptitude for enslavement. The voices ascribed and afforded to such individuals reflected and perpetuated the placement of racialized others within the European social hierarchy.

In the second half of the book, Act II, I turn to an extended case study of a single musician: Giovannino Buonaccorsi, an enslaved Black soprano (arguably castrato) singer and poet who was active at the Florentine court from at least 1651 until his death on August 15, 1674. A wealth of archival detail relating to Buonaccorsi is extant, including payment records, opera libretti, scores, descriptions, letters, costume designs, a portrait, and a poem attributed to him. He sang chamber music at the court and performed in a series of operas in mid-century Florence and at least one season on the public stage in Venice. Buonaccorsi is thus the rare seventeenth-century Black performer whose life in Italy can be documented with any accuracy. In many ways, Buonaccorsi is a singular figure, yet my time in the archives makes perfectly clear that Buonaccorsi was but one of numerous court retainers who were racially or ethnically marked and who labored as entertainers (singers, dancers, trumpet players, buffoons). His life and work resonate productively with the many other examples cited in the first half of the book, throwing into clear focus the presence and the voices of enslaved individuals.[117]

At the same time, Buonaccorsi's Blackness highlights the extent to which specific stereotypes cohered around individuals of African descent. Ottoman courts were known to utilize enslaved Black eunuchs and intact men in highly visible roles, and in the early seventeenth century, this knowledge shaped European models of Black slavery and performance in significant ways.[118]

---

[117] Two recent essays treat some of this material in a more fragmentary way. See Emily Wilbourne, "'... La Curiosità del Personaggio': 'Il Moro' on the Mid-Century Operatic Stage," in *Seachanges: Music in the Mediterranean and Atlantic Worlds, 1550–1880*, ed. Kate van Orden, I Tatti Research Series 2 (Cambridge, MA: Harvard University Press, 2022), 133–148; Emily Wilbourne, "Little Black Giovanni's Dream: Black Authorship and the 'Turks, Dwarves, and Bad Christians' of the Medici Court," in *Acoustemologies in Contact: Sounding Subjects and Modes of Listening in Early Modernity*, ed. Emily Wilbourne and Suzanne G. Cusick (Cambridge: Open Book, 2021), 135–165. I first learned about Buonaccorsi from Paul H. D. Kaplan, "Giovannino Moro: A Black African Servant, Musician, Actor and Poet at the Medici Court" (conference presentation at Staging Africans: Race and Representation in Early Modern European Theaters, Columbia University, New York, 2015).

[118] See, for example, Katherine Crawford, *Eunuchs and Castrati: Disability and Normativity in Early Modern Europe* (New York: Routledge, 2019), and also her current and forthcoming research, including "Race, Castration, and Confusion: An Epistemology of Silence" (conference presentation at Errant Voices: Performances Beyond Measure, University of Chicago, April 29–30, 2022).

The Mediterranean context of Florentine slavery resulted in a practice and development of unfreedom that was substantially different from those in operation in European sites of more globally oriented powers (such as Portugal, Spain, England, and the Netherlands); nevertheless, over the course of the seventeenth century, and certainly by the 1650s and 1660s, enslavement became more closely associated with Blackness, as part of a growing awareness of racial difference as a justification for the global slave trade.

In the conclusion of this book (the "Epilogo"), I do two things. First—with a nod to the late, great Eve Kosofsky Sedgwick—I solidify the arguments proposed throughout the book into a set of axioms that can articulate the ground of further scholarship into race and early modern music. Second—with an eye not just to future scholarship but also to the futures of the seventeenth-century sounds and ideologies articulated in the book—I turn to a close reading of *The Padlock* (1768) by Isaac Bickerstaffe and Charles Dibdin, a "comic opera" with spoken dialogue and sung interludes. The drama features a Black character, Mungo, played in the premiere season by the white composer Dibdin in blackface, who speaks (and sings) in a comic parody based on the patois of Black, Jamaican-born enslaved laborers. *The Padlock* is frequently cited in scholarship as a precursor or origin moment in the history of North American minstrelsy. In my reading of the drama, the character and costuming of Mungo, and the theatrical use of sound (including both dialect and music), I underscore the ways in which the comic theater of seventeenth-century Italy anticipates many elements that have been mistakenly labeled as novel representations of Blackness and racial difference. Like Robert Hornback, who has argued for the legacy of "Old Word" blackface practices in North American minstrelsy, I am "less interested . . . in making the conventional claim of having found *the* singular origin/invention of racism than in demonstrating instead that racism recycles/reinscribes a proto-racist archive of sources and ideas."[119] Pointing up the specific citations that *The Padlock* makes of Italian theatrical precedent clarifies the relevance of *Voice, Slavery, and Race in Seventeenth-Century Florence*, not only for scholars of the seventeenth-century but for all students of music history.

As a whole, this book argues for the power of sound. It is a call to listen attentively to historical acoustemologies and to what they narrate about bodies

---

[119] Hornback, *Racism and Early Blackface*, 28.

and their "natural" or appropriate noises. These are sounds that "sort and storify,"[120] voices that enunciate the organization of the social and political world. The new musics of the Italian seventeenth century provide a persuasive archive of such sounds and such voices, mapping their articulations in newly representational form.

---

[120] The quote comes from the introduction to Wilbourne and Cusick, *Acoustemologies in Contact*, 4.

ACT I

A maestro Francesco Ferri d.2 per dare ad uno beccaio, che haveva tolto una ferita da uno schiavo delle stalle.

To Master Francesco Ferri, two ducats, to give to a butcher who healed an injury of one of the slaves in the stables.
       I-Fas, Camera del Granduca, f. 2, August 1621, c. 20r

Scene 1
Songs to Entertain Foreign Royalty

At the Palazzo Pitti on February 11, 1614, the Medici court celebrated the end of *carnevale* with a performance of *Il passatempo*, a theatrical *favola* with text by Michelangelo Buonarroti *il giovane* and incidental music by Francesca Caccini and possibly others.[1] The evening's entertainment culminated—as such hybrid theatrical performances were wont to do—in semi-staged social dancing; in this instance, the pivot was negotiated by a sequence of scenes and songs entitled *Il balletto della cortesia*.[2] The *balletto* introduced a new scenario (separate from the play to which it was attached). Here I cite the poetic version of the *invenzione*, which was declaimed by the allegory of Gentilezza as part of the last scene of the play:[3]

---

[1] On Buonarroti, see Janie Cole, *Music, Spectacle and Cultural Brokerage in Early Modern Italy: Michelangelo Buonarroti il Giovane* (Florence: Olschki, 2011). Regarding the music, as listed by Suzanne G. Cusick, three pieces associated with this entertainment survive in the oeuvre of Caccini: "Chi desia saper che cosè Amor," the opening song for "Il passatempo in su la barca", is printed in Francesca Caccini, *Il primo libro delle musiche* (Florence: Zanobi Pignoni, 1618), 90; and "Egloga pastorale. Tirsi et Filli. 'Pascomi sospir,'" exists in manuscript, I-Ru, Ms. 279, fols. 61r–68r, attributed to "F.C." The third surviving piece comes from the final ballet and is discussed in more detail below. See Suzanne G. Cusick, *Francesca Caccini at the Medici Court: Music and the Circulation of Power* (Chicago: University of Chicago Press, 2009), 296–297. Cesare Tinghi attributes the music of the final ballet to Jacopo Peri and to another unnamed "maestro di cappella della chiesa de' Cavalieri di Pisa" (presumably Antonio Brunelli, who took up his appointment to the Cavalieri di S. Stefano in Pisa in 1612). See the transcription in Angelo Solerti, *Musica, ballo e drammatica alla corte medicea dal 1600 al 1637: Notizie tratte da un diario con appendice di testi inediti e rari, ristampa anastatica dell'edizione di Firenze, 1905* (Bologna: Forni Editori, 1969), 84. Cusick, however, cites a letter from Buonarroti to Christine de Lorraine that states that the music was entirely the work of Caccini (297). It was common at the Medici court for the musical composition of dramatic works to be divided among a number of different composers.

[2] The text of the *balletto* was published in a contemporary edition commemorating the performance. In that context, the "Invenzione del balletto" is given in prose: "Alcune Donzelle di Siria, che essendo in sú la riva del mare a coglier fiori, erano state sopprapprese da uno stuolo turchescho, e per iscampar da quello s'erano imbarcate sovra un picciol legnetto, approdano per fortuna a una spiaggia toscana. E vedute da alcuni Cavalieri da una torre, e udite chieder mercé, son raccolte da quelli, & informate del paese dove son giunte. Onde consolate, e riconfortate per letizia ballano, e cantano insieme co' Cavalieri, e sono inviate da loro alla toscana Regia, e inanimite a sperar pietà." See Michelangelo Buonarroti, *Il balletto della cortesia fatto in Firenze dalle SS.AA. di Toscana il di 11 di febbraio 1613 [more fiorentino] che fu introdotto da un'altro trattenimento rappresentato in'iscena* (Florence: Mariscotti, 1614), n.p. [3].

[3] Two autograph manuscript versions of the text to *Il passatempo* survive; here I quote from the version transcribed by Solerti. See Solerti, *Musica, ballo e drammatica*, 332.

Voice, Slavery, and Race in Seventeenth-Century Florence. Emily Wilbourne, Oxford University Press.
© Oxford University Press 2023. DOI: 10.1093/oso/9780197646915.003.0002

Di Siria alcune nobili donzelle	Several young noblewomen from Syria
Che del mar su la riva	That were on the coast by the sea
Intente a coglier fiori e far ghirlande	Intent on gathering flowers to make garlands
Furon sorprese dal nemico stuolo	Were surprised by the enemy troops
Del barbaro Ottomano,	Of the barbarous Ottomans,
E non avendo altro più certo scampo	And not having other more certain escape
S'eran commesse all'onde	They committed themselves to the waves
Sopra un picciol legnetto,	In a tiny little boat;
Col favor di fortuna	With the favor of fortune
Or pervenute alle tirrene spiagge,	They have now arrived on the Tirrenian [Tuscan] shore,
Son accolte, affidate e consolate	They are welcomed, entrusted to, and consoled
Da un drappel di Cavalier toscani.[4]	By a squad of Tuscan knights.

As we might expect, the Syrian refugee women of this scenario lament their rather dreadful ordeal, though the only section of the ballet for which music survives is "Io veggio i campi verdeggiar fecondi" ("I see the green, fertile, flourishing fields"), a celebratory text sung by one of the women expressing relief at her safe arrival and marveling at the beauty of the Italian countryside.[5] As intimated by the quote above, the exotic foreigners (who also happen to be female, beautiful, vulnerable, and noble) are quickly put at ease by the local menfolk, who welcome them to Tuscany with elaborate courtesy (the *cortesia* of the *balletto*'s title) and the promise of a safe haven from the "barbarous" (Eastern, male) Ottomans: "Thus consoled and comforted, [the Syrian women] dance with joy and sing, together with the noble knights."[6] The orientalist stereotypes of this scenario are entirely self-evident.

I have chosen to begin here, with an example of elite European theater in which the orientalist and exoticist elements of the plot are immediately obvious and those of the music difficult to discern. *Il balletto della cortesia* is a classic example of the kinds of musical theatrical performance where the analytic methodologies of traditional music scholarship have failed to do more than label such exoticisms, as if the label were sufficiently illuminating. The specific historical circumstances of this performance upend many assumptions about what these exoticisms were intended to convey, and they clarify the role of the voice with regard to identification.

If for modern auditors, the prospect of Syrian refugees washing up on European shores is all too vivid, the Tuscan port of Livorno seems an unlikely

---

[4] Michelangelo Buonarroti il giovane, *Il passatempo* (perf. 1614).
[5] See "Io veggio i campi verdeggiar fecondi," in Caccini, *Il primo libro*, 56–57.
[6] "Onde consolate, e riconfortate per letizia ballano, e cantano insieme co' Cavalieri." Buonarroti, *Il balletto*, n.p. [3].

point of arrival. Yet, as several scholars—including P. Paolo Carali, Francesca Casule, Maria Alberti, Kaled El Bibas, and Ted Gorton—have been at some pains to demonstrate, Syrian refugees had a specific political valence for Florentine audiences in the winter of 1613–1614.[7] Just a few months before, Fakhr ad-Dīn II, emir of significant territories in the Levant including modern-day Lebanon and parts of southern Syria, had docked in Livorno with three ships and an entourage of more than seventy followers, having fled from Sidon as an Ottoman army bore down upon the city. By February, the visitors had served their quarantine and transferred to Florence, where they stayed—as guests of the Grand Duke—for nearly two years. From Cesare Tinghi's court diary and his description of *Il passatempo* and *Il balletto della cortesia*, it becomes evident that Fakhr ad-Dīn himself (referred to here as "Caffardin," though more commonly named "Faccardino" in contemporary Italian sources)[8] was present at the performance:

> And on the 11th of February, day of Carnival, S.A. heard Mass at home; then, with the arrival of evening, wanting to give satisfaction to Her Most Serene Highness and to the entire court, he had ordered up, in the Sala della Commedia [the "room of plays" or the "performance room"][9] in the Palazzo

---

[7] P. Paolo Carali published many of the archival sources in a two-volume set as early as 1936 (one volume contains transcriptions of European-language texts and Italian translations of Arabic and Turkish sources; the other has Arabic versions of the Italian sources as well as transcriptions of the original Arabic and Turkish); that same year, Carali also published an Italian translation of the "Soggiorno di Fakhr ad-dīn II al-Ma'nī in Toscana, Sicilia e Napoli e la sua visita a Malta," written by Ahmad ibn Muhammad al Khalidi as-Safadi before his death in 1622. P. Paolo Carali, *Fakhr ad-Dīn II, Principe del Libano, e la corte di Toscana, 1605–1635*, Vol. 1 (Rome: Reale Accademia d'Italia, 1936); P. Paolo Carali, "Soggiorno di Fakhr ad-dīn II al-Ma'nī in Toscana, Sicilia e Napoli e la sua visita a Malta (1613–1618)," *Annali del Istituto Superiore Orientale di Napoli* 7, fasc. IV (1936): 14–60. More recently, Alberti has published a new version of the travel narrative. See Fakhr ad-Dīn II al-Ma'n, *Viaggio in Italia (1613–1618): La Toscana dei Medici e il Mezzogiorno spagnolo nella descrizione di un viaggiatore orientale*, ed. Maria Alberti (Milan: Jouvence, 2013). See also Maria Alberti, "Un emiro alla corte dei granduchi: Feste e spettacoli a Firenze in onore di Faccardino, Gran signore de' Drusi (1613–1615)," *Medioevo e Rinascimento* 11, no. 8 (1997): 281–300; Francesca Casule, "Un episodio esotico della scena fiorentina: La visita dell'emiro druso Fakhr ad-Din alla corte di Cosimo I de' Medici," *Levante* 28 (1986): 25–38; Kaled El Bibas, *L'emiro e il granduca: La vicenda dell'emiro Fakhr ad-Dīn II del Libano nel contesto delle relazioni fra la Toscana e l'Oriente* (Florence: Le Lettere, 2010); Ted J. Gorton, *Renaissance Emir: A Druze Warlord at the Court of the Medici* (London: Quartet Books, 2013). See also the contributions to Maurizio Arfaioli and Marta Caroscio, eds., *The Grand Ducal Medici and the Levant: Material Culture, Diplomacy, and Imagery in the Early Modern Mediterranean*, Medici Archive Project Series (Turnhout: Harvey Miller, 2015).

[8] Tinghi uses a variety of spellings to indicate the emir: Cafardi/Caffardi, Cafardin/Caffardin, Cafardini, Caffardino, Facardino, Facardin, Facardi. See the "Diario primo di Sua Altezza Serenissima," I-Fn, Capponi, 261/1, cc. 538rv, 541v, 542v, 543v, 544rv, 547v, 550v, 552v, 553r, 554v, 566r, 568r, 569r, 586r, 646r. I thank Francesca Fantappiè for these references.

[9] On the Sala delle Commedie, where many theatrical performances at the Medici court took place during the first two decades of the seventeenth century, see Francesca Fantappiè, "Sale per lo

Pitti, a most beautiful celebration and a most beautiful ballet: in which took part S.A., Her Most Serene Highness, her ladies, and the gentlemen of the court. And at the first hour of the night, S.A. dined above with Her Most Serene Highness and other princes: S.A. had many ladies invited and placed on the levels; Madama Ser*enissi*ma was there incognito with the Lady Princesses, and the Nunzio was there, the Resident of Venice, and other ambassadors; then, a little higher up on another bench was the Emir Caffardin incognito[10] and his wife along with several other women of his household.[11]

As Alberti has argued, historians have treated Fakhr ad-Dīn's visit as a symptom of the failed (and rather fanciful) ambitions of the Medici in the Middle East and have thus discounted its value, though to do so is to misunderstand the importance of this event for the Florentines at the time.[12]

The presence of Fakhr ad-Dīn and his entourage in Florence and at this particular performance provides a remarkable example of the co-presence of "Others" on Italian soil and as such militates against the presumed obliviousness typical of orientalist work, yet content-wise the storyline and setting of the *balletto* are difficult to distinguish from classic orientalist exemplars. Musically, the resolutely European aspects of the score seem to confirm assumptions that would abdicate racial representation: Caccini's *romanesca*, "Io veggio," is ostentatiously Florentine, and the long-breathed, exquisitely ornamented musical phrases are an oddly composed response (in both the emotional and musical senses of the word "composed") to a nominally traumatic set of circumstances (see Figure 1.1 and Musical Example 1.1).

Spettacolo a Pitti (1600–1650)," in *Vivere a Pitti: Una reggia dai Medici ai Savoia*, ed. Sergio Bertelli and Renato Pasta (Florence: Olschki, 2003), 135–180.

[10] Tinghi uses the term "incognito" not to mean that the emir and the grand duchess were disguised and completely unrecognizable but that they were not dressed for a state occasion or welcomed to the performance with the elaborate conventions that a state entourage would require. See, for example, the discussion of the Gonzagas' incognito days in Venice in 1623, particularly as juxtaposed with the official state visit that took place the same year. See John Whenham, "The Gonzagas Visit Venice," *Early Music 21*, no. 4 (1993): 528–531.

[11] "Et adì 11 di febraio, giorno di Carnovale, S. A. udì la messa in casa; poi, venuto la sera, volendo S. A. dare sadisfazione alla Ser.ma Arciducessa et a tutta la corte, aveva fatto ordinare su nella sala della Comedia nel palazzo de' Pitti una bellissima festa et un ballo bellissimo: dove intravenne S. A., la Ser.ma Arciducessa, le dame et camerieri di S. A. Et venuto l'ora una della notte S. A. cenò su di sopra con la Ser. ma et altri principi: aveva S. A. fatto invitare molte dame e messe su per e' gradi; vi era incognita Madama Ser.ma con le signore Principesse, et v'era il Nunzio, il Residente di Venezia et altri ambasciatori; poi più su in un altro palco incognito v'era l'Emir Caffardin et la mollie con altre sue donne." Solerti, *Musica, ballo e drammatica*, 81.

[12] Alberti, "Un emiro," 283–284.

Figure 1.1. Francesca Caccini, opening to "Io veggio i campi verdeggiar fecondi," from *Il primo libro delle musiche* (Florence: Zanobi Pignoni, 1618), p. 56.

Musical Example 1.1. Francesca Caccini, "Io veggio i campi verdeggiar fecondi," from *Il primo libro delle musiche* (Florence: Zanobi Pignoni, 1618).

SONGS TO ENTERTAIN FOREIGN ROYALTY 49

Musical Example 1.1. Continued

Musical Example 1.1. Continued

It is precisely these contradictions that make *Il balletto della cortesia* an ideal locus of analysis, though there are other court performances from the period that could have served equally well—*La stiava* (*The Slave Woman*, perf. 1607), for example, or *Il ballo delle donne turche* (*Dance of the Turkish Ladies*, perf. 1615). *Il balletto della cortesia* is emblematic of a genre, and as a whole the exoticisms of the genre have been undertheorized. Too often, the identificatory force of labels such as "exoticism" or "orientalism" can serve as an end in itself, such that the reasons for and the meanings of the terms and the situations they identify are assumed—as if the label had explained the historical circumstances in some way.[13] That is, to call a work such as *Il balletto della cortesia* "orientalist" does not get us very far. A cursory analysis of Caccini's "Io veggio" brings into sharp focus the relative paucity of disciplinary tools that can be brought to bear upon race and early modern music in comparison with the rich interpretive materials that have developed around

---

[13] I would like to thank Helen Hills and Hudson Vincent for some very engaging *pulmino* discussions on precisely this topic, which very much helped me to clarify my thinking on the issue.

stylistic difference, performance, power, and gender. In what follows, I consider the voice of Caccini's Syrian woman for what it communicates about the character and how she is represented as a communicating subject. My conclusions point to the historical specifics of the political interaction that the *balletto* celebrates and push toward a consideration of the special status of early modern class in relation to racial difference that will be taken up in subsequent chapters.

Io veggio i campi verdeggiar fecondi,	I see the green, fertile, flourishing fields,
E le rive fiorite, e i colli intorno,	And the flowering banks, and the hills all around
E gravidi di pomi arbori, e frondi,	And the arbors heavy with apples, and branches,
E d'infinite ville il lido adorno.	And the infinite towns with which the shore is adorned.
Sento i venti spirar dolci, e giocondi:	I feel the sweet and joyful sighing of the winds:
Serenissimo 'l Sol qui spiega il giorno.	The Sun reigns over the unfolding day.
Scendete omai, prendete alfin riposo,	Disembark now; finally take some rest,
Sperando a' vostri affanni il ciel pietoso.[14]	Entrusting your fears to the merciful heavens.

The hallmarks of a very early baroque style can be identified from a glance at the print. The piece is a monody for soprano with basso continuo accompaniment; the vocal ornaments preclude an ensemble performance and testify to the training and virtuosity of the intended singer. The rhythmic profile of the bassline distances this particular piece from recitative, though the time signature and solo texture indicate a flexibility of tempo, and the placement and nature of the ornaments (which interfere very little with the intelligibility of the words) associate the piece with Giulio Caccini's *nuove musiche*, the first volume of which was published in 1602.[15] The *romanesca* bassline, signaled in the published heading and audible to an attentive listener from the descending bass fourth of the very opening measure, repeats for the second half of the song (compare mm. 1 and 17). Here Caccini's setting preserves poetic features as musical structure: each line is the same length, and the two halves of the strophe break perfectly at the midpoint. Buonarroti has elegantly emphasized the connectedness of the unfolding clauses through the related sounds of each initial syllable: Es in the first half

---

[14] Michelangelo Buonarroti *il giovane*, text to "Io veggio i campi verdeggiar fecondi," as published in Caccini, *Il primo libro*, 56–57. The text also appears in Buonarroti, *Il balletto*, n.p. [4]. Note that Solerti's transcription from the Buonarroti manuscript has the second half of the verse as a single clause, punctuating the fifth line with a comma and the sixth with a colon; he also transcribes "vostri" as "nostri" in the last line of the verse.

[15] Giulio Caccini, *Le nuove musiche* (Florence: Marescotti, 1602).

of the canto and Ss in the second. In performance, and particularly through the use of female voice, this structural (though not melodic) repetition evokes the improvisatory ornamental practice of Vittoria Archilei and the virtuosic female vocality of the *concerto delle donne* tradition, a role that—in Florence—was filled by "le donne di Giulio Caccini" (the women of the Caccini family).[16] Thus, at a purely stylistic level, this piece makes a conscious display of courtly conceits and musical elements that were closely associated with Medici patronage.

None of these stylistic choices was aesthetically neutral. The coupling of opera and Giulio Caccini's "new music" to Medici patronage was part of a long tradition in which the arts (including music, painting, and theater) and academic experimentation were used to demonstrate and justify political power.[17] The sprawling lines of *Il passatempo*, a loose conglomeration of separate scenes held together by the central conceit of the court's desire "to entertain *Passatempo* ["Pastime"], who has entertained them many times," provided a kaleidoscopic vision of Medici competence, juxtaposing "a city scene, a pastoral scene, a scene with a boastful knight, a rustic scene, and in closing, a boat loaded with people" as a representation of discursive plenitude.[18] The danced finale—*Il balletto della cortesia*—permitted the show itself to culminate in the literal display of the Medici body; within scholarship, the noble gestures of courtly dance are almost reflexively assumed to represent political order and noble authority through kinesthetic analogy.[19] Furthermore, the dancing nobles were spectacularly costumed; the jewels and fabrics detailed in court records make explicit that such outfits track dynastic wealth.[20] Tinghi writes, for example, that in the *balletto*,

---

[16] See Nina Treadwell, "She Descended on a Cloud 'from the Highest Spheres': Florentine Monody 'alla Romanina,'" *Cambridge Opera Journal 16* (2004): 1–22; Nina Treadwell, *Music and Wonder at the Medici Court: The 1589 Interludes for "La Pellegrina"* (Bloomington: Indiana University Press, 2009). See also Hill, *Roman Monody*; Richard Wistreich, *Warrior, Courtier, Singer: Giulio Cesare Brancaccio and the Performance of Identity in the Late Renaissance* (Aldershot, UK: Ashgate, 2007); Susan McClary, "Soprano as Fetish: Professional Singers in Early Modern Italy," in *Desire and Pleasure in Seventeenth-Century Music* (Berkeley: University of California Press, 2012), 79–103; Cusick, *Francesca Caccini*.

[17] Alois Maria Nagler, *Theatre Festivals of the Medici, 1539–1637* (New Haven, CT: Yale University Press, 1964).

[18] "[P]er trattenere il *Passatempo* che tante volte ha trattenuto loro," and "[U]na scena civile, una scena pastorale, una scena di un cavaliere vantatore, et una scena rusticale, et in ultima una barca carica di persone." Tinghi, as transcribed by Solerti, *Musica, ballo e drammatica*, 82.

[19] Mark Franko, *Dance as Text: Ideologies of the Baroque Body* (Cambridge: Cambridge University Press, 1993).

[20] Valeria De Lucca, "Dressed to Impress: The Costumes for Antonio Cesti's *Orontea* in Rome (1661)," *Early Music 41*, no. 3 (2013): 461–473.

The Most Glorious Archduchess [Maria Maddalena of Austria] appeared, dressed in cloth of silver with a crimson overdress, with much gold and with a large veil, and at her neck and on her front she wore the rich and superb collar all made of diamonds that is called "Ferdinando's necklace," valued at a million pieces of gold, and with many other jewels in her hair and on her clothing.[21]

The ostentatious spectacle of such riches was intended to dazzle the watching crowds in direct and quite literal ways.

The fashion for virtuosic song (particularly as sung by women) aligned with a new division of musical labor within elite social circles. The equal-voiced madrigals typical of sixteenth-century prints were nominally part of a participatory amateur tradition in which the primary consumers of the music were the performers themselves.[22] As an interest in virtuosity grew, however, the music became significantly more difficult to sing, and a clear distinction emerged between an increasingly professionalized group of singers and the elite listeners who could afford to employ musicians of the necessary caliber.[23] This shift made the body of the performer something to be looked at and something to be owned. The performer was objectified.[24] As Melinda J. Gough has written about contemporary court ballet in France, "conspicuous consumption in Marie de Medici's courtly spectacles involved not only opulent, bejeweled costumes for dancers (as frequently noted in other contemporary reports) but also 'living, breathing luxury items' such as foreign women singers and dwarves."[25] (Notably, the "foreign singer" she references was almost certainly Francesca Caccini.)[26]

Although Tinghi lists the ladies who danced in the *balletto*—"The Most Glorious Archduchess, the Lady Countess San Secondo, the Lady Caterina

---

[21] "Era la ser.ma Arciducessa, vestita di tòcca d'argento con sopravesta scarnatina, con gran oro et con gran veliere et al collo et dinanzi aveva il ricco et superbo collare tutto di diamanti nominato il collare di Ferdinando, di valuta di un milione d'oro, et molte altre gioie in testa et per la vesta." Tinghi, as transcribed by Solerti, *Musica, ballo e drammatica*, 84.

[22] Laura Macy, "Speaking of Sex: Metaphor and Performance in the Italian Madrigal," *Journal of Musicology* 14, no. 1 (1996): 1–34.

[23] Hill, *Roman Monody*; Dell'Antonio, *Listening*.

[24] The place of musician, singer, or composer as servant is addressed in Tim Carter, "Non Occorre Nominare Tanti Musici: Private Patronage and Public Ceremony in Late Sixteenth-Century Florence," *I Tatti Studies in the Italian Renaissance* 4 (1991): 89–104.

[25] Melinda J. Gough, "Marie de Medici's 1605 *Ballet de la Reine*: New Evidence and Analysis," *Early Theatre* 15, no. 1 (2012): 116. The embedded quote is from Andrea, "Elizabeth I," 184.

[26] Melinda J. Gough, "Marie de Medci's 1605 *Ballet de la Reine* and the Virtuosic Female Voice," *Early Modern Women: An Interdisciplinary Journal* 7 (2012): 127–156.

Rosermini, the Lady Polita Agostini, the Lady Sofia Alemanna, [and] the Lady Strozzina"—he makes no mention of the name of the woman (or women) who sang.[27] Suzanne G. Cusick associates three further women with the performance of *Il passatempo* based on references in letters from the *cameriere* Domenico Motaguto to Buonarroti: "*la signora* Cecchina [Francesca Caccini], daughter of *signor* Giulio Romano; that woman who was the peasant in the comedy [*Il passatempo*], the wife of Mainardi; [and] the daughter of Pippo Sciamerone *pittore* [i.e., Angelica Furini, a student of Jacopo Peri]."[28] These women were apparently given gifts by Cosimo II to thank them for their participation. Caccini, of course, composed some music, so her participation may well have been entirely offstage, and the "wife of Mainardi" evidently performed in some capacity. However, these three women all came from the less-elevated ranks of the court and are good candidates to consider among the singers.[29] Several of the ladies of the women's court are known to have sung and even performed comedies "fra di loro" (among themselves), but there is no indication that noblewomen sang in such public circumstances.[30] Indeed, what little direct evidence we have from the period suggests that there was something socially suspect about the public performance of vocal virtuosity. It is more than likely that "Io veggio" was sung by a professional (quite possibly Caccini), which would align with the documentation of similar sung ballets.[31]

Quite possibly, the preservation of "Io veggio" is due in part to the self-contained formal structure of the song. Cusick has argued that Caccini's early success at the Medici court lay in her articulation of a complex model of female vocality, balancing virtuosity and decorum, *autorità* and *continenza*.

---

[27] Tinghi, as transcribed by Solerti, *Musica, ballo e drammatica*, 84.

[28] I-FcasaB, A.B. 50, no. 1255, February 26, 1614. See Cusick, *Francesca Caccini*, 297. The letter is transcribed in full as document 173 in Cole, *Music, Spectacle*, 548.

[29] The Mainardi were related to the Caccini, and at least one of them served as a lawyer for the Caccini family at various times.

[30] Cusick discusses the evidence for regular private performances in the women's court, often organized by Caccini and Buonarroti; see Cusick, *Francesca Caccini*, 62–66. The quote is taken from a letter from Caccini to Buonarroti on December 27, 1614, transcribed by Cusick, *Francesca Caccini*, 311–312.

[31] Famously, for example, in Claudio Monteverdi and Ottavio Rinuccini's *Ballo delle ingrate*, performed in Mantua in 1608. For the *descrizione*, see Federico Follino, "Compendio delle sontuose feste fatte l'anno MDCVIII: Nella città di Mantova, per le reali nozze del serenissimo prencipe D. Francesco Gonzaga, con la serenissima infanta Margherita di Savoia; facsimile," in *Cronache Mantovane (1597–1608)*, ed. Claudio Gallico (Florence: Olschki, 2004), 103–257. See also Bonnie Gordon, "Talking Back: The Female Voice in 'Il Ballo delle Ingrate,'" *Cambridge Opera Journal* 11, no. 1 (1999): 1–30.

Cusick has read Caccini's *Primo libro* of 1618 as "a self-reflexive course of study that winks simultaneously at problems of vocality and problems of womanhood."[32] The song "Io veggio" walks precisely this tightrope. In its long, sustained phrases, steady rhythms, and deftly placed melismas, the piece projects a restrained and highly educated model of female eloquence. The music embodies a cultivated and courtly nobility that justifies the "courtesy" of the listening Italian noblemen.

In this analysis, I have assumed that the music published by Caccini in 1618 resembles (if not replicates) that which was performed at court four years earlier. Not only would Caccini have had something to gain by thus recalling her participation in such an ostentatious courtly occasion, but the libretto positions this passage in such a way that an aria would have been entirely appropriate. The scene begins with eight lines of text in *endecasillabi* (poetic lines of eleven syllables), sung by a courtier who spies the arriving ship; this passage was almost certainly set as recitative (an effect magnified by the series of grammatical possibilities on which the passage elaborates).[33] The "Io veggio" text (cited in full above) is then sung by "one of the young ladies who has disembarked on the Tuscan shore."[34] Afterward, there is a sad chorus performed by the Syrian women as a group, a choral response by the assembled courtiers, and then a second solo text, this time structured as a lament:

O Siria, ò patrio nido,	Oh Syria, oh my country,
Onde siam miseramente or prive,	Of which we are now miserably deprived,
Odi 'l pianto, odi 'l grido,	Hear the lament, hear the cries
Di queste afflitte in sì lontano lido	Of these afflicted women on such a far shore
Peregrine donzelle, e fugitive.[35]	Wandering young ladies, and escapees.

The music to this second solo song does not survive, but the metrical choice of *versi sciolti* (mixed lines of seven and eleven syllables), the way in which several lines are broken down into fragments as the text restarts, and the repeated use of the open O vocable (O/ò/Onde/or/Odi/odi) suggest that the music would have fit the genre of theatrical lament, best known to scholars

---

[32] Cusick, *Francesca Caccini*, 114.
[33] The courtier sings: "Scorgesi press'a riva un picciol legno / Senza nocchier solcar l'onda marina. / Di Nettunno fuggendo il fiero sdegno / Forse al lido sen vien Teti Regina. / Forse che brama in terra un nuovo regno, / Figlia già della Terra, ma divina. / Forse, che Teti vien nemica a noi, / Che si spesso scorriam pe' regni suoi."
[34] "[U]na delle donzelle sbarcate in su la spiaggia toscana." Buonarroti, *Il balletto*, n.p. [4].
[35] "O Siria, ò patrio nido," from Buonarroti *Il balletto*, n.p.

through Claudio Monteverdi's widely studied "Lamento d'Arianna."[36] If we compare the poetry of "O Siria" to that of "Io veggio," then the balanced phrases of the earlier song come sharply into focus.

Buonarroti's *balletto* text thus gives space for a variety of musical genres (recitative, aria, chorus, lament), not dissimilar to the variety of dramatic genres that the poet juxtaposed in the evening's entertainment as a whole. If we assume that Caccini's music exploited such opportunities to the full, then we can recognize the astuteness with which she has excerpted "Io veggio" within her song collection, capitalizing not only on the structural self-sufficiency of the musical (and poetic) form but also allowing the courtly elegance of the selection to represent her participation as composer to the court, rather than something more literally theatrical, such as recitative lament, which might have carried unwelcome connotations of feminine indecency.[37] The composure and control that can be read from the long phrases and delicate ornaments of Caccini's setting presume that the lament of "O Siria" would (like the more famous and happily extant music of Arianna's lament) have the singer stumble over her words, interrupt herself, cry out, sob. The more generic lyrics of "Io veggio," which make no reference to a particular point of departure or of arrival, are also more amenable to anthologization than the specificity of the "O Siria" text.

Rather quickly, as the above discussion makes clear, we can build a gendered, politicized understanding of the function of the musical work in performance (and in publication): the densely woven semiminims of the printed vocal line testify to the sophisticated tastes and deep pockets of the house of Medici. The woman singer (and composer) and the complex material of her song are objects—like jewels and the arts themselves—that dazzle the audience, representing as spectacle the power of the sovereign.

All of this tells us nothing about the character's purported Syrian-ness, though Cusick—noting that the bassline as printed transposes the standard *romanesca* formula down a fourth—suggests that this displacement marks the character as out of place: a Syrian in Tuscany.[38] If transposition does mark the voice here as foreign (and in the absence of music from the rest of

---

[36] Monteverdi's text should be assumed to collate widely used lamenting gestures, not to invent them. See Wilbourne, *Seventeenth-Century Opera*, 51–91.

[37] Emily Wilbourne, "Musicological Indecency: Breastmilk, the Body, and the Interpellated Listener," *Echo: A Music-Centered Journal* 14, no. 1 (2016), http://www.echo.ucla.edu/volume-14-1-2016/article-breastmilk-exposed-bodies-politics-indecent/.

[38] Cusick, *Francesca Caccini*, 141. Cusick points out that only two published examples of transposed *romanescas* are known and that both appear in Caccini's *Primo libro*.

the *balletto*, it is difficult to know how obvious that shift might have been), it keeps intact the expressive rhetoric of the monodic texture. Indeed, the musical language of this unnamed female refugee turns out to be the highest and most sophisticated form of musical discourse—inherently noble and markedly Florentine. There is little reward in parsing the melody, harmony, rhythms, or cadences of this piece for some trace of an imagined Middle Eastern sound. Though instrumentation, timbre, or ornamental inflection may have characterized the performance as exotic in some way, the surviving sources suggest otherwise. According to prevailing rubrics of musicological interpretation, we need to assume that in this *balletto*, "Syrian" and "Florentine" were sonically indistinguishable. Furthermore, since it is literally the (foreign-born) archduchess and her ladies-in-waiting who eventually "dance with joy and sing, together with the noble knights," we can perceive a structural conflation of foreign nobilities that emphasizes class over race, language, or national difference. Indeed, this importance of class or lineage to musical representation and vocal expressivity will return as a crucial component of my argument.

What, however, are we to make of this scene? Literally (and quite simplistically), the allegory of *Il balletto della cortesia* can be understood as "Rebellious Middle Easteners fleeing Ottomans are welcome in Florence"—a meaning so straightforward that it barely counts as allegorical. The scene offstage is one of triumphant Florentine nationalism, with the special guests from Sidon emblematic of Florentine political heft and promising the tantalizing realization of large-scale military, geopolitical, and religious projects. The presence of such elevated foreign guests supersedes even the relatively frequent presence of (exotic) foreign ambassadors (Japanese ambassadors, for example, visited Florence with great pomp in 1584, and the Persian ambassador was present in 1609); Fakhr ad-Dīn was not a mere ambassador but himself foreign royalty.

While Fakhr ad-Dīn's arrival was unexpected, the event had an important prehistory that is worth rehearsing. The territory of modern-day Syria fell to the Ottomans in 1516 during the Ottoman-Mamluk war and was in principle controlled by the Ottoman Empire right through until World War I; the region attracted Florentine attention around 1606 when the then-governor of Aleppo, Ali Janbulad Pasha, revolted against Ottoman rule.[39] In October

---

[39] The previous governor, Janbulad's uncle, had been put to death by an Ottoman general after troops from Aleppo arrived late to a battle with the Safavid Empire, resulting in a large defeat for the Ottoman troops. Janbulad won his first battle and began to build alliances with other hereditary

1607, Janbulad negotiated a treaty with two of Ferdinando I de' Medici's agents, bartering Medici access to Syrian ports in return for Medici aid in the fight against the Ottomans—on the part of the Florentines, this was a component of a larger, more ambitious, and eventually failed plan in which an entire league of Christian nations (led by the Medici) was to participate in a crusade against the Ottomans, reclaiming the Holy Land for the Christians (and the Crown of Jerusalem for Ferdinando I and his heirs) and returning the Levant to the administration of local nobility.[40] Janbulad, unfortunately, was defeated even before the Grand Duke could sign the treaty and send it back;[41] however, the following year, the Medici signed a very similar treaty with Fakhr ad-Dīn, who had attracted the attention of European powers for his control over Galilee (and thus many of the important biblical sites) and for his nonconfrontational treatment of Levantine Christians.[42] One of Fakhr ad-Dīn's demands was that the Grand Duke of Florence "send a document of safe passage [*un salvo condotto*] in case [the emir] decided to travel to Italy and speak in person with His Highness for any reason or because of anything else that might occur, so that he [the emir] could arrive and return without any impediment to his person, his belongings, or his ships."[43] It was this *salvo condotto* that underwrote Fakhr ad-Dīn's eventual arrival in Livorno in 1613, though by this time, Ferdinando I had passed away, and his son, Cosimo II, had assumed the title.

The Arabic sources from the emir's visit include a description of the carnival celebrations with which we have been concerned, as narrated by an

---

families in the region—these included Fakhr ad-Dīn, who had assumed power in 1590 and had begun a sustained project of territorial expansion. Both Janbulad and Fakhr ad-Dīn were ecumenical in their search for allies, banking on the philosophy that the enemy of my enemy is my friend. During this same period, the Florentine fleet made a failed attempt to take the island of Cyprus, which the Ottomans had taken from the Venetians in 1570. These events are summarized by El Bibas, *L'emiro e il granduca*, 71–74; Franco Cardini, *Il turco a Vienna: Storia del grande assedio del 1683* (Rome: Laterza, 2011), 96–98. Their accounts rely heavily (and in El Bibas's case, sometimes plagiaristically) on the contextual introduction to Carali, *Fakhr ad-Dīn*, 84–93.

[40] Cusick makes the point that Christine of Lorraine could trace her ancestry back to the Crown of Jerusalem. See Suzanne G. Cusick, "'La Stiava Dolente in Suono di Canto': War, Slavery, and Difference in a Medici Court Entertainment," in *Acoustemologies in Contact: Sounding Subjects and Modes of Listening in Early Modernity*, ed. Emily Wilbourne and Suzanne G. Cusick (Cambridge: Open Book, 2021), 201–237.

[41] El Bibas, *L'emiro e il granduca*, 51.

[42] El Bibas, *L'emiro e il granduca*, 70.

[43] "Che l'A.V.S. gli mandi un salvo condotto per ogni occasione che si risolvessi trasferirsi in Italia ad abboccarsi con V.S.A. per qual si voglia negotio, ò altro che gli potessi occorrere, acciò sicuramente possi vener et ritornarsene senza impedimento alcuno nella sua persona, robba, ò Vascelli." Quoted from "IX. Accordo con Fakhr ad-Dīn," Angelo Bonaventura to Ferdinando I, I-Fas, Fondo Mediceo, f. 4275, fol. 167v, 1608, as transcribed in Carali, *Fakhr ad-Dīn*, 150.

anonymous observer to Khalidi as-Safadi.[44] Alongside details of festive masquerades, water bombs made from hollowed-out eggshells, tilts with a lance, boar fights, and a variety of horse, mule, and donkey races, we find details of a performance that—chronologically, at least—ought to have been *Il passatempo* and *Il balletto della cortesia*, though the descriptions of the scenery suggest that this account may provide a mash-up of several theatrical performances from the period:[45]

> That night they danced together, men with women, and they entertained themselves in a large room, the backdrop of which depicted a landscape that seemed far away, with the horizon reddened by the setting sun, where figures dressed as angels passed. On the floor, rolling wheels covered with blue fabric seemed, in their movements, waves of the sea. Boats passed, similarly mounted on wheels, as if they were sailing, from which disembarked fifteen young and very beautiful youths, who began to dance and to make speeches.
>
> The cities of Florence and Livorno were also represented with their rivers and ports, and even with their bridges, over which passed animals mounted on wheels. Livorno appeared with its forts, and its canal full of sea water. There were also many other games and extraordinary and marvelous representations.
>
> Men and women danced together, each with the lady of his social level: the wife of the Duke with the Duke, the other women with noblemen of their rank; because their women do not veil themselves before men, but socialize with them in meetings, dances, and in the street; in such a way,

---

[44] The details of this Florentine trip are so specific as to require the witness of someone who was present. Gorton (*Renaissance Emir*) suggests perhaps Suru (or Suror) Zecchiere, who, according to the Medici archives, "serve di secretario"; Carali (*Fakhr ad-Dīn*) believes that it was Fakhr ad-Dīn himself who dictated the history.

[45] Solerti transcribes Tinghi's description of the 1614 performance, which suggests that the women entered on foot rather than arriving in a boat: "Fu la scena un lago o più laghi continui vicino al mare, in sul qual lago nel parte anteriore si figurava una selva et un prato: il restante del lago era circondato di frondi, di rovine, di palafitte, di villaggi. . . . Torna la *Gentilezza* et avvisa il baletto esere ordinato dalle dame et da cavalieri, con l'invenzione che apparisce nel balletto stampato: che rappresentavano Cavalieri toscani et le Dame di Siria; escono per una grotta marina da un fianco della scena, scendendo alcuni gradi, et i cavalieri da una alta torre che era nell'altro fianco della scena, scendendo anch'essi certi gradi: et si fece il balletto da loro A.S." However, in his overall description of the entertainment, Tinghi notes "in ultima una barca carica di persone," indicating that water and boat effects were involved at some point. Solerti, *Musica, ballo e drammatica*, 82–83. The scenery was designed by Giulio Parigi, and the production is discussed by Blumenthal; however, his descriptions are based exclusively on Solerti's transcriptions of Tinghi. See Arthur R. Blumenthal, "Giulio Parigi's *Stage Designs*: Florence and the Early Baroque Spectacle" (PhD diss., New York University, 1984), 176–177.

that in the absence of the husband, the wife takes his place in the store, where she makes sales as he would.[46]

This observer was obviously struck by the stage machinery and scenery. He or she describes the perspectival backdrop, the recognizable architecture of Livorno and Florence, and the realistic movements of the wave machine, flying angels, moving animals, and arriving boats. No mention is made of the costumes; this is in notable contrast with Tinghi, who attentively— even aggressively—details the clothing and jewels worn by each group of noble dancers. When it comes to the dancing, the visitor emphasizes two things: first, that the women and men dance together (in pairs, organized by social status), and second, that the faces of the women are not veiled. This last point is so novel that it engenders a swerve away from the description of the performance, opening out into commentary on the role of women in Italian mercantile contexts. Evidently, whatever costuming our Syrian refugee characters wore, their visible faces and their interactions with men struck the watching foreigners as explicitly Italianate.

In this context, the elite, sophisticated, specifically Florentine musical utterance of "Io veggio" should be understood as part of a complex diplomatic welcome. The Medici saw themselves—and wished to present themselves— as powerful international figures, on a par with and equal to the visiting emir. The virtuosic, ornamented *romanesca* that Caccini put into the mouth of the arriving refugee signals the global aspirations of the Medici dukes with precision, extending Florentine musical rhetoric as representative of the Syrian visitors. What might—through the limited lens of exoticism—have seemed a tone-deaf or ignorant representation of the "Other" is revealed instead to be part of a larger, more heterogeneous project of mutual self-recognition and

---

[46] My translation from the Italian given by Carali: "La notte danzano insieme uomini e donne, e si divertono in una grande sala, al di cui fondo rappresentano un paesaggio che sembra lontano, con un orizzonte di crepuscolo rosso, ove passano figure a guisa d'angeli. Sul pavimento, delle ruote coperte di tessuto azzurro sembrano, muovendosi, onde del mare. Delle barche ugualmente montate su ruote vi passano, come se navigassero, da cui sbarcano una quindicina di giovani di tutta bellezza; i quali si mettono a danzare e a fare dei discorsi. / Rappresentano anche le città di Firenze e di Livorno con i loro fiumi e porti, nonchè con i loro ponti sopra dei quali passano degli animali montati su ruote. Livorno appare colle sue fortezze, con il suo canale pieno d'acqua del mare. Fanno ancora altri diversi giuochi e rappresentazioni straordinarie e meravigliose. / Danzano insieme uomini e donne, ciascuno colla dama di sua condizione; la moglie del Duca col Duca, le altre con i nobili del loro grado; giacchè le loro donne non si velano innanzi agli uomini, ma li frequentano nelle riunioni, balli e nelle strade; di modo che, in assenza del marito, la moglie tiene il suo posto nel negozio, ove sta a vendere come lui." Carali, "Soggiorno," 30–31. This passage is cited in (a different) English translation by Gorton, *Renaissance Emir*, 85.

international collaboration. Caccini's *romanesca* as Syrian song represents a claim to shared intelligibility and common cause.

My point here is not to rescue Caccini, Buonarroti, *Il balletto della cortesia*, or the Medici court from charges of exoticism or orientalism. Even less do I want to claim that this music—or the society within which it took shape—was antiracist or that racism didn't exist. Rather, I want to identify and unravel the ways in which anachronistic scholarly assumptions about race have concealed the workings of the early modern racial imaginary. As typically practiced, to listen for race is to search for something extraneous—as if there were a foreign sound that could be added to or quoted in the musical texture. It is to assume that race is not always already present.

"Io veggio i campi verdeggiar fecondi"—"I see the green, fertile, flourishing fields"—provides an opportunity to see the "Other" looking back at Europe, both in the first-person, subjective text articulated by the nameless refugee character (in which Buonarroti narrates Europe being seen as elite Florentines would wish it to be seen: green and welcoming) and in the surviving Arabic description of the dance. To bring this moment of reciprocal looking into focus, however, we need to listen to Caccini's music within the context of a highly specific set of historical circumstances. This specificity is crucial, for it leaves little that can be extrapolated out from this instance of musical exoticism to other pieces and performances. Orientalism here is not a destination but only an indication that something, some fine detail, might reward further investigation.

In context, the smooth, European surface of Caccini's "Io veggio" is less about presumed racial difference than about presumed class equivalence between the elite of different nations and a wishful cosmopolitanism that could read the art music of culturally Florentine court musicians as representative of the neutral international subject. Not necessarily white, or even Christian, this subject is patently civilized: educated, self-controlled, courteous, and cultured according to Christian European norms. The justness by which he or she claims sovereignty over geographic spaces and the inhabitants thereof is evidenced by their bodily comportment and underwritten by their noble lineage—by their *razza*. Sonically, genre sounds an ideal expressive register, for it is the inherent nobility of these women—as expressed in Caccini's vocal music—that engenders the hospitality of the Florentine welcome.[47] To inflect

---

[47] Cusick has made a similar point, noting that in *La stiava*, written by Buonarroti and Caccini and performed during carnival in 1607, it is the inherent nobility of the captured Persian princess's verbal

the voice away from this register is to descend immediately from the realm of serious art music to the level of the comic, and to change the representational affect from that of noble subject to that of lower-class comic character. Such voices—and their tight relationship to race and class—are the subject of the next chapter.

outburst—set by Caccini in the *stile recitativo*—that persuades her Tuscan captors to free her and accompany her home. See Cusick, "'La Stiava Dolente,'" 201–237.

A Bernardino Consalvi scudi centocinquantuno per dare a centocinquantuo stiavi riscattati dalle Galere del Serenissimo Gran Duca, disse la Serenissima Arciducessa.

To Bernardino Consalvi, one hundred and fifty-one *scudi* to be given to one hundred and fifty-one slaves ransomed from the Galleys of the Most Serene Grand Duke, as directed by the Most Serene Archduchess.

                        I-Fas, Camera del Granduca, f. 5, November 1623, c. 9v

Scene 2
Comic Songs Imitating Foreign Voices

The thick filiation of racial or ethnic difference and the voice is rendered particularly evident at moments in which dramatic characters are directed to speak Italian badly. In dialect theater, accent and vocabulary regularly mark a given interlocutor as an inhabitant of a specific region of the Italian peninsula or communicate their level of education or social class.[1] Foreignness, however, is invoked through linguistic errors and mispronunciations that spoof the common speech of a given immigrant population; crucially, in Italian drama, such voices are decidedly limited to the comic register, mutually imbricating race and class. Andrea Perrucci, writing in 1699, notes that "Foreign words [lit. *voci barbare*] are permitted [only] to the comic roles, and mangled by all tongues."[2]

An example illuminates the point. In Giovan Battista Andreini's commedia dell'arte play *La Sultana* (1622), the title character (played in the earliest performances by the operatic singer and actress Virginia Ramponi Andreini) is the wayward daughter of a Turkish sultan.[3] As the *prima donna innamorata*, the Sultana's foreignness is largely superficial. Her eventual union with the (Italian) *innamorato*, Lelio, is assumed, and she expresses herself in fluent Italian, speaking the elevated, courtly discourse shared by the other elite (Italian) characters. The plot hinges on the Sultana's search for her ex-lover, a (white) Italian, who was once enslaved in her father's palace in Constantinople. When the Sultana became pregnant to Lelio, she decided to

---

[1] Wilbourne, *Seventeenth-Century Opera*.
[2] "Le voci barbare sono concesse alle parti ridicole, storpiate da tutte le lingue, come nel fingere un Dottore, rompendo la testa a Prisciano [a Latin textbook author] quanto gli piace; Un Turco col contrafare il loro saluto da Salemelech, sabà, Iebunda, Iarafullà; de Tedeschi del Goth Morgen Mainer; de i Francesi col guì, gi meti vottre Scipaon; De gli Spagnuoli Reniego de Barrabas, befo fus manos; servidor sonor Alferez; De Fiorentini col oh oh ohi, tu mi rimiri io ti ripappo; Dei Genovesi con la meza lingua, e così di tutte le lingue, quali quanto piu stravolerà tanto più darà nel ridicolo." Andrea Perrucci, *Dell'arte rappresentativa premiditata ed all'improviso* (Naples: Michele Luigi Mutio, 1699), 344–345.
[3] Giovan Battista Andreini, *La Sultana* (Paris: Nicolas Della Vigna, 1622).

flee with him to Christendom; Lelio, however, took her money and ran. The Sultana followed, slowed by the birth and then a nursing child. Eventually reaching Naples (where Lelio is now living), she intends to find him and kill him. In order to approach without attracting suspicion, the Sultana disguises herself as a male slave (possibly in blackface) and fakes her resale, tricking Lelio into purchasing her.[4] This is where things get sonically interesting, as the Sultana also disguises her voice. As a slave, the Sultana manufactured the broken Italian, repetitive intonations, and punning mispronunciations that marked the voice of the Other as foreign, and as such, she enacts the Otherness of the enslaved through a relationship to class, servility, and vocal register.

In Act II, scene ii, the disguised Sultana encounters Lelio for the first time. She speaks in infinitives, uses verbal repetition and, presumably, a Turkish accent. The change in her voice is coupled with a change in her bodily comportment. "What the hell?" exclaims Lelio, "That you shove me so indecorously in the shoulder as you call my name? That's what they do in Turkey." The invasive physicality of "Turkish" interactions is confirmed when the Sultana threatens to punch Lelio in the face. On the most pragmatic level, linguistic drag of this nature makes good theater: the Sultana's "Turkish" voice is funnier than her typical eloquence, and an alternation between her two voices magnifies the opportunities for humor—for example, Lelio's harsh words, "I love no Turkish man, nor woman," pull from the Sultana an uncontrolled exclamation of woe in which she reverts to her "natural," idiomatically correct voice. The play text makes no visual distinction between lines meant as an aside and those intended for Lelio's ear, but a close reading and attention to the grammatical content of the Sultana's speech make the turning of her body and the different sounds of her discourse perfectly clear. In my transcription, I have differentiated between the two types of speech, placing the asides in italics.

---

[4] *La Sultana* (1622) is loosely based on the same scenario that underlies Giovan Battista Andreini, "Lo Schiavetto (1612)," in *Commedie dei comici dell'arte*, ed. Laura Falavolti (Turin: UTET, 1982), 57–213. Iconographic imagery from the earlier play implies that the lead actress, Virginia Ramponi Andreini, wore blackface when travestied as a male slave. It is possible that this costuming continued even as the play developed over the intervening decade.

SULTANA	O signor.	Ho, sir!
LELIO	Che diavolo hai, che tù m'urti nelle spalle così indiscretamente chiamandomi; s'usa così in turchia.	What the hell? That you shove me so indecorously in the shoulder as you call my name? That's what they do in Turkey.
SULTANA	Si signor, e quando nò responder alla prima, nò dar urton in le spalle: ma pugno in tel viso, intender ti. VS. mi.	Yes, sir, and when you do not respond to the first, I won't [just] shove your shoulder, but punch you in the face. Do you understand me, sir?
LELIO	Non solo t'hò inteso: ma quasi, quasi ancor sentito, tanto venivi risoluto con le pugna verso il viso.	Not only have I understood you: but nearly, nearly almost felt you, so threateningly did you bring that fist toward my face.
SULTANA	Turco star resoluto, resoluto, resoluto.	Turk be resolute, resolute, resolute.
LELIO	T'hò inteso, t'hò intesto, t'hò inteso. Caro fratello và à far i fatti tuoi.	I understand, I understand, I understand! Dear brother, go away and do your own thing.
SULTANA	Mi nò voler più partir da ti, tanto tò aria de ti piase a mi.	I do not want to leave you, so pleasing your style is to me.
LELIO	Ma la tua non piaser à mi; o che bello imbroglio.	But you are not pleasing to me; oh what a confused situation.
SULTANA	Mi saver che ti vorrà gran ben, ben à mi.	I know that you really, really love me.
LELIO	Il sai, male, perche nè turco, nè turca amai.	What you know is wrong, because I love no Turkish man, nor woman.
SULTANA	*Ah, traditore pur troppo il sò.* Guarda un poco tò signoria, che star questo, e, questo, e questo; *ah, ah, ti calarte.*	*Alas, traitor, unfortunately I know that!* Look here a moment, sir, that I have this, and this, and this; *ah ah, that draws you in to my lure.*[5]
LELIO	O quai belle cose.	Oh what beautiful things.
SULTANA	Ti guarda prest, che mi nasconder nasconder.	Look quickly, so I can hide them, hide them.
LELIO	Quest'è una Casacca alla barbaresca tutta tempestata di grosse perle, e di bellissimi diamanti. Quest'altro è un ricco gioiello da portar nel mezo al petto, ò com'è vago; e quest'è un cinto di grandissima valuta.	This is a coat in the Barbary style, all adorned with fat pearls and the most beautiful diamonds. This other thing is a rich jewel to be worn in the center of the chest, oh how beautiful it is; and this is a belt of the highest value.

---

[5] Among the several translations that John Florio gives of *calare* is "to stoope to a lure." This excellent Italian-English dictionary from 1611 is searchable online at http://www.pbm.com/~lindahl/florio/: John Florio, *Queen Anna's New World of Words, or Dictionarie of the Italian and English Tongues* (London: Melch and Bradwood, 1611).

SULTANA	Altre cose più belle mi haver; e tutte, donar à ti, tanto piaserme furbetto.	I have other, more beautiful, things, and I will give them all to you, since you please me so, little crafty boy.
LELIO	Mi tocca il viso, sotto il mento; questi turchi debbano esser molto carnali.[6]	He is touching my face, under my chin; these Turks must be very erotic [by nature].

At the core of this scene is the assumed incommensurateness of fluent, educated Italian emerging from the body of a foreign slave, even while the same linguistic discourse is presumed appropriate for a foreign princess, who remains fully available for incorporation into Italian society via marriage. For the Sultana, control of her voice provides autonomy over her legibility to others (even while she demonstrates little control over her emotions); as E. Natalie Rothman argues, "linguistic (in)competence became a marker of foreignness."[7] The Sultana's faked language is deliberately reductive and repetitive, with consequences for meter and declamation. Her "slave" voice sounds closer to the predictable rhymes and repetitious musical phrases of strophic song than to the long-breathed and flexible register of recitative. At "Turco star resoluto, resoluto, resoluto," we can imagine the hammered cadences of live performance (and the way in which Lelio spoofs her intonation with his threefold reply); her subsequent two statements both begin and end with "mi," insisting on her gesticulating presence and her impoverished verbal resources. The physical and verbal violence of the Sultana's disguise performs an aptitude for hard labor, which in turn justifies the harsh treatments used to encourage the enslaved to work.

Markedly comic, foreign voices of this type are part of a long tradition of verbal parody, prevalent both onstage and in semi-theatrical partsong repertoires. The stage voices of early modern Black characters have begun to attract scholarly attention (see, for example, the work of Nicholas Jones and Robert Hornback), while theatrical partsong is one of the few places where musicologists have engaged with racialized voice in any sustained fashion.[8] I touch on this literature—on sung *moresche*, along with other linguistically marked songs—as a means to foreground vocal sound and signification and to trouble the kinds of conclusions that can be drawn from such music and from

---

[6] Andreini, *La Sultana*, II, ii.
[7] Rothman, *Brokering Empire*, 18.
[8] Jones, *Staging Habla de Negros*; Hornback, *Racism and Early Blackface Comic Traditions*. See also Emily Wilbourne, "*Lo Schiavetto* (1612): Travestied Sound, Ethnic Performance, and the Eloquence of the Body," *Journal of the American Musicological Society* 63, no. 1 (2010): 1–44.

the sounding, living bodies that they represent. Juxtaposed with theatrical scenes in which a character transvests across racially marked boundaries and chooses to disguise their voice, a remarkably unified set of sonic stereotypes for the representation of racial and ethnic difference emerges within the comic register.

* * *

The best-known musical example of the parodic imitation of foreigners' Italian, repeatedly chosen for inclusion in musical historical anthologies, is Orlando di Lasso's "Matona, mia cara" (1581), in which a native German speaker is represented. Orthography transcribes linguistic holdovers from German: Ds are replaced with Ts, Vs with Fs; infinitives are used in place of conjugated verbs. The lusty "Lanze" (short for *lanzichenecco*, derived in turn from the German word *Lanzknecht*, signifying a mercenary soldier) sings under the window of his "Matona" (*Madonna*, or "My Lady"), accompanying himself on some kind of plucked string instrument, the ritornello of which is represented in the unaccompanied polyphonic song as onomatopoeic syllables (see Musical Example 2.1). German mercenaries were an integral part of the army of the Holy Roman Empire but were also very familiar to Italian audiences. In Florence, the "Guardia de' Lanzi" served as bodyguards to the Medici from 1541 until 1738; not only did the *cento lanzi* provide a way for Cosimo I and his descendants to claim a symbolic association with the Hapsburg emperor, but as foreigners, the *lanzi* were presumed less susceptible to manipulation by (local) enemies of the Medici.[9] Their allegiance was bought, paid for, and underwritten by their status as strangers in a strange land, with few local resources on which to rely other than the Grand Duke himself. The Lanze character in Lasso's song, however, is less concerned with political allegiances than with affairs of the heart and of the stomach:

Matona mia cara,	My dear lady,
mi follere canzon	me want a song
cantar sotto finestra,	To sing under window;
Lanze bon compagnon.[10]	Lanze is good companion!
Don don don diri diri don don don don	*Don don don diri diri don don don don*

---

[9] See, for example, the recent Uffizi exhibition, "Omaggio a Cosimo I—Cento Lanzi per il Principe," June 4–September 29, 2019, https://www.uffizi.it/eventi/omaggio-a-cosimo-i-i-cento-lanzi-del-principe.

[10] French endings add to the inept effect.

Musical Example 2.1. Orlando di Lasso, "Matona, mia cara," first published in *Libro de villanelle, moresche, et altre canzoni* (Paris, 1581), mm. 1–9.

Ti prego m'ascoltare	I beg you to listen to me,
che mi cantar de bon	because me sing good.
e mi ti foller bene	And I love you
come greco e capon.	as much as wine and chicken
Don don don diri diri don don don don	*Don don don diri diri don don don don*
Com'andar alle cazze,[11]	When I go hunting
cazzar con le falcon,	with a falcon
mi ti portar beccazze,[12]	Me bring you woodcocks,
grasse come rognon.	fat as a kidney.
Don don don diri diri don don don don	*Don don don diri diri don don don don*
Se mi non saper dire	Me not know how
tante belle rason	to say pretty things,
Petrarca mi non saper,	Me not know Petrarch,
ne fonte d'Helicon.[13]	nor the springs of Helicon.
Don don don diri diri don don don don	*Don don don diri diri don don don don*
Se ti mi foller bene	If you love me,
mi non esser poltron;	I won't be lazy!
mi ficcar tutta notte,	I will fuck all night,
urtar come monton.	thrusting like a ram!
Don don don diri diri don don don don	*Don don don diri diri don don don don*

While there are no literal German words in "Matona, mia cara," the text communicates the presumed familiarity of Lasso and/or his lyricist with actual Germans, in part because of academic musicology's familiarity with German pronunciation and in part because of the remarkable coherence of the cultural stereotype of the enthusiastic (if drunk and gluttonous) early modern "todesco" with the lederhosen-clad, sausage-toting, beer-drinking caricature who appears in many modern contexts. Archival sources suggest that the prospect of carousing German soldiers was a legitimate event: a report in the Medici archives, provided by the Bargello in Siena, recounts an evening of carousing in the city by German soldiers in January 1662, when "in a house belonging to a certain Catrina Corcigno, a large quantity of people played music and sang," and when the city guards turned up to keep the peace, the German soldiers fired shots.[14] (Lasso, of course, worked in Bavaria, where "courtiers were evidently amused by the parodies of their countrymen.")[15] An assumption of mutual recognition has limned scholarly work on parodies of

---

[11] The mispronunciation here of *caccia* (hunt) renders it as *cazzo*, meaning cock or penis.
[12] *Beccaccia* is rendered here to rhyme with *caccia/cazze*. The term *becco* could also mean cuckhold, to understandably humorous effect.
[13] In ancient Greece, the rivers with their origins on Mount Helicon were believed to provide (poetic) inspiration.
[14] I-Fas, Mediceo del Principato, f. 5487, c. 411rv: "in una casa di una tal detta Caterina Corcigno si sonava e cantava con gran quantità di persone."
[15] Donna G. Cardamone, "Todesca," *Oxford Music Online*, doi: 9781561592630.

European language speakers, while representations of less (academically) familiar linguistic populations have fueled different assumptions.

A case in point is the traditional musicological reception of the sung *moresche*—"a carnivalesque vocal genre popular in the sixteenth century whose texts parody the speech of Moors";[16] notably, several appear in the same Lasso volume of 1581. The parodic texts of the vocal *moresche* have long been identified as a key feature of the genre: "all [the Moorish characters] express themselves in a curious language, based on a somewhat distorted Neapolitan dialect, loaded with onomatopoeic sounds and words from an incomprehensible *gergo* of a pretended African origin."[17] The presence of this *gergo*—which can mean both jargon, in the less derogatory sense of an idiom used by a restricted group of speakers, and gibberish or nonsense—has served not only to cohere the genre of poetic texts associated with *moresche* but also as a measure of the genre's cruel humor, taken at the expense of the Black slaves and servants represented in the songs (presumably by "white" European composers to "white" European audiences): "They [the Moors] are represented as purely carnal creatures, and their scatological dialogue, a concoction of southern Italian dialects and pseudo-Moorish jargon, is filled with zoomorphizing images redolent of Carnival."[18]

Though described in the citations above as southern Italian (or specifically Neapolitan) dialect, the language of sung *moresche* is better understood in relation to Sabir, the lingua franca of Mediterranean ports, which evolved as a way to facilitate trade. Peppered with vocabulary derived from Turkish, Spanish, and Arabic and spoken with countless regional variations, Sabir was predominantly Italianate, though with irregular pronouns and largely unconjugated verbs. The language was regularly deployed as the theatrical speech of enslaved laborers and foreign servants throughout the seventeenth century, not only in Italian sources (we can, for example, recognize the reference to Sabir in the Sultana's "slave" dialect, cited above) but also in Portuguese and Spanish contexts, with a particular contiguity with Black

---

[16] The quote comes from the *New Grove* entry on the *moresca*. See Alan Brown and Donna G. Cardamone, "Moresca," Grove Music Online, Oxford Music Online, Oxford University Press, http://www.oxfordmusiconline.com.ezp-prod1.hul.harvard.edu/subscriber/article/grove/music/19125. Brown and Cardamone go on to specify that "Moors" were "then defined broadly as Muslims or narrowly as inhabitants of the Barbary Coast," which is not actually the "Moors" as most commonly represented in the *moresche* themselves.
[17] "[T]utte si esprimono in un curioso linguaggio, basato su un dialetto napoletano alquanto storpiato e intriso di onomatopee e di parole di un gergo incomprensibile, di pretesa origine africana." Elena Ferrari-Barassi, "La tradizione della moresca e uno sconosciuto ballo del cinqueseicento," *Rivista Italiana di Musicologia* 5 (1970): 38.
[18] Brown and Cardamone, "Moresca."

African characters.[19] Furthermore, as Gianfranco Salvatore observed in an important article from 2011, the "incomprehensible *gergo* of a pretended African origin" is not "pseudo-African speech"[20] in the slightest but instead belongs "to a precisely identifiable linguistic lineage: that of the Nile-Saharian languages"; along with "several idiomatic Arabic expressions," "the protagonists of the *moresca* . . . speak Kanuri."[21] With one stroke, Salvatore brings the *moresche* into line with a host of other parodic repertoires, both musical and theatrical. In a parallel theoretical move, Kate van Orden has identified comprehensible Turkish poetry (though transcribed with a French alphabet) in lyrics to a pair of "Turkish songs" published in Paris in 1604; earlier scholarship had presumed the words to be nonsense syllables.[22]

There is a simple object lesson that can be learned here. Linguists and musicologists have mined the *todesche* (German), *greghesche* (Greek), and *schiavonesche* (Slavic) repertoires for evidence of the use of foreign words in Italy; and theatrical and musical texts *all'ebraica* (Hebrew or Jewish) have proved a sometimes controversial but crucial archive for the study of Italo-Jewish dialects and the circulation of Hebrew.[23] The dialect texts of the *villanelle alla napolitana* have been presumed accurate (even as they range from the celebratory to the derogatory).[24] If we take the Kanuri words of the Italian *moresca* seriously, then the Black slaves and servants depicted in the

---

[19] Budasz, "Black Guitar-Players"; Jones, *Staging Habla de Negros*.

[20] "[L]a parlata pseudo-africana." Ferrari-Barassi, "La tradizione della moresca," 40.

[21] "Nelle nostre moresche compaiono (assieme ad alcune espressioni idiomatiche arabe) molti termini africani autentici. Essi appartenengono a un ceppo linguistico ben individuabile: quello delle lingue nilo-sahariane. I protagonisti della canzone moresca, oltre al loro napoletano stentato, parlano infatti il kanuri." Gianfranco Salvatore, "Parodie realistiche: Africanismi, fraternità e sentimenti identitari nelle canzoni moresche del cinquecento," *Kronos* 14 (2011): 103.

[22] Kate van Orden, "Hearing Franco-Ottoman Relations circa 1600: The *chansons turquesques* of Charles Tessier (1604)," in *Seachanges: Music in the Mediterranean and Atlantic Worlds, 1550–1800*, ed. Kate van Orden, I Tatti Research Series 2 (Cambridge, MA: Harvard University Press, 2022), 33–68.

[23] See, for example, Alfred Einstein, "The Greghesca and the Giustiniana of the Sixteenth Century," *Journal of Renaissance and Baroque Music* 1 (1946): 19–32; Manlio Cortelazzo, "Il linguaggio schiavonesco nel cinquecento veneziano," *Atti dell'Instituto Veneto di Scienze, Lettere ed Arti* 130 (1972): 113–160; Manlio Cortelazzo, "La figura e la lingua del 'todesco' nella letteratura veneziana rinascimentale," in *Scritti in onore di Giuliano Bonfante* (Brescia: Paideia, 1976), 173–182. On the use of Hebrew in Italian drama, see Erica Baricci, "La scena 'all'Ebraica' nel teatro del rinascimento," *Annali della Facoltà di Lettere e Filosofia dell'Università degli Studi di Milano* 63, no. 1 (2010): 135–163; Maria Luisa Mayer Modena, "A proposito di una scena 'all'ebraica' nello Schiavetto dell'Andreini," *Annali della Facoltà di Lettere e Filosofia dell'Università degli Studi di Milano* 43, no. 3 (1990): 73–81; Laura Falavolti, "Introduzione allo Schiavetto di Giovan Battista Andreini," in *Commedie dei comici dell'arte*, ed. Laura Falavolti (Turin: UTET, 1982), 7–36; Jaffe-Berg, *Commedia dell'Arte*.

[24] Donna G. Cardamone, *The Canzone Villanesca alla Napolitana: Social, Cultural, and Historical Contexts*, Variorium/Collected Studies (Aldershot, UK: Ashgate, 2008); Martha Farahat, "Villanescas of the Virtuosi: Lasso and the Commedia dell'Arte," *Performance Practice Review* 3 (1990): 121–137.

songs are reinscribed as Black Italians, or, in Salvatore's term, a "minoranza alloglotta," a minority linguistic community present within and among a native Italian-speaking majority: speaking subjects within Italian culture.[25] Salvatore's work and that of van Orden are thus a powerful argument for co-presence, inasmuch as it disturbs the sedimented (racialized) presumptions of musicology's Eurocentricity.

For Salvatore, the presence of Kanuri resuscitates the vocal *moresca* as ethnographic: "capable of celebrating, in the Neapolitan carnival or farcical contexts, the lively and often festive presence of Black Africans in Napoli."[26] Other scholars—perhaps most trenchantly those who work on *all'ebraica*—have been less likely to interpret familiarity as respect.[27] Furthermore, as many of the scholars working on such repertoires are quick to acknowledge, we cannot necessarily assume that a familiarity with foreign words (Kanuri, Hebrew, Arabic, German, or otherwise) indicates the close association of "white," "Italian" audiences with foreign bodies, as the audience may well have learned such words from the circulation of other similar songs.[28]

Here the mechanics of orthography and transcription can help distinguish among degrees of familiarity on the part of authors and audiences. When it comes to the vocal *moresca*, the corpus of surviving works is relatively limited, and yet the spelling of Kanuri words differs considerably; for example "a la lappia" versus "allalà pia," both of which Salvatore translates as the Kanuri phrase *álla lafia*, or "salute! salve!," "Good day! Good health!"[29] Even were all of the surviving *moresca* texts to have been written by the same poet, then we would have to assume that he or she was familiar enough with the sounds of Kanuri speech that the words in question were inscribed into Italian phonemes anew each time. That is, if the words themselves had been meaningless sounds for which the author was totally reliant on the report of another, we might expect their presentation in script to show that they had been literally copied. This is true whether we assume that there was a single author

---

[25] Gianfranco Salvatore, "Il teatro musicale delle lingue: Parodie di stranieri e minoranze nel Rinascimento italiano, dispensa per il corso di etnomusicologia 'Minoranze etniche nella musica rinascimentale,' a.a. 2011–2012," Università del Salento, 2011, n.p. [8].

[26] "[I]n grado di celebrare, nel Carnevale napoletano o in contesti farseschi, la vivace e spesso festosa presenza a Napoli dei neri africani." Salvatore, "Parodie realistiche," 125.

[27] Baricci, "La scena 'all'Ebraica.'"

[28] Natalie Operstein has noted a parallel between one of Lasso's *moresche* and an extant Spanish poem by Rodrigo de Reinosa. See Natalie Operstein, "Golden Age *Poesìa de Negros* and Orlando di Lasso's *Moresche*: A Possible Connection," *Romance Notes* 52, no. 1 (2012): 13–18.

[29] Salvatore, "Parodie realistiche," 122. He notes, "frasi o parole singole spesso si ripetono da un testo all'altro con grafie diverse: segno palese di una loro trasmissione esclusivamente orale, mai fissata in un unico testo di riferimento."

or multiple poets writing similar texts. The differences in spelling testify to the intervention of aural memory and thus to an assumption of meaning—even if the author didn't understand the Kanuri words incorporated into the texts, he or she recognized them as sounds.[30]

This association between words and sounds is a place where I want to linger, for it calls attention to the importance of sound to representation—an argument that I have been making for a long time, though the racialized dimensions of sound have not been sufficiently emphasized. In the early modern Italian theater, the use of differentiated vocal sounds figured the diversity of bodies and also their trajectories as a lived and audible history of migration from place to place. This is sound as an index of physical mobility, and importantly, the classic cityscape of the Italian theater was represented as essentially polyglot in nature. As the various voices and dialects of the stock commedia dell'arte characters relay information about each individual, their co-presence on stage represents the Italian city itself as inhabited and traversed by a heterogeneous, multiethnic population. Listening to the "minoranza alloglotta," we can hear not only various voices but also some of the meanings that coagulated around questions of diversity in the form of sound.

In Giovan Battista Andreini's *Lo Schiavetto* ("The Little Slave," first published in 1612), there is a much-discussed scene sequence that makes significant use of Hebrew words. I have written about the scene elsewhere: four Jewish merchants—Leon, Sensale, Caino, and Samuel/Scemoel—enter en route to present their wares at the palazzo. They are then joined by a Christian (though not particularly well-intentioned) character, Fulgenzio, who is disguised as a Jew.[31] On the point of joining the group, Fulgenzio realizes that while his costume—a "Jewish outfit and a yellow beret"—convincingly disguises his body, he risks revealing himself through sound: he cannot speak *ebraico* and so decides to pass himself off as mute.[32] Indeed, the

---

[30] In contrast, a very different approach can be seen in Giglio Artemio Giancarli's *La Cingana* (or *Zingara*, lit. "The Gypsy"), first published in 1540 but republished repeatedly through to at least 1610; the play is widely cited for its macaronic approach to language. Notably, the title character frequently speaks in Arabic, though she immediately translates each statement into Venetian dialect; for example, "*Anduch'mantil, enti, aber fazuleta?*" The Venetian is equivalent to "*Hai un fazzoletto?*" or "Do you have a handkerchief?" Giancarli, *La Cingana*, IV, 13. Quoted in Enzo Sardellaro, "Forme, struttura e lingua delle commedie di Giancarli: Studi sulla lingua della commedia veneta del cinquecento," *Studi Linguistici e Filologici Online* 6 (2008): 321. Sardellaro notes, "Come si può vedere, le parole arabe vengono subito tradotte in un veneziano storpiato, suscitando così l'ilarità del pubblico." While Giancarli's play thus demonstrates a remarkable fluency in Arabic on the part of the author, he ensures that his character's speech is comprehensible to others, while the audience itself is presumed not to speak or understand Arabic.

[31] Andreini, "Lo Schiavetto."

[32] The quote comes from the stage directions, "abito da ebreo con berretta gialla." Andreini, "Lo Schiavetto," 210.

use of *giudaico-italiano* in this scene is so extensive that scholars have turned to the script as a rare source for the preservation of spoken language,[33] and Claudia Burattelli has suggested that early Mantuan performances may have cast Jewish actors in the roles of the four Jewish merchants.[34] If this raises the specter of a profoundly alienating experience for the actors concerned, it also underlines the degree to which the deployment of semantically coherent Jewish words legitimizes the authenticity of these characters, even for modern commentators: whether or not Andreini's audience understood the actual import of each word, the use of *giudaico-italiano* marks the bodies under the costumes as legibly Jewish.

In a sonic economy of this nature, voice is a guarantee of truth, and muteness assumes a freighted role. Sensale, one of the "authentic" Jews—whose name means "middleman" or "broker" in Italian—claims to know how to speak "Mute" and translates the ensuing conversation for the benefit of his companions.[35] The name and actions of Sensale's character redouble his characterization: as middleman (a commercial role frequently filled by Jewish agents), Sensale literally creates lines of communication between parties unable or unwilling to communicate directly, and yet he makes apparent the potential for double-cross that middlemen are stereotypically assumed to exploit. Ultimately, Sensale is less interested in who Fulgenzio is under his yellow beret than in the benefit to be had in the role that he himself assumes as translator. Here is the scene:

---

[33] Both Laura Falavolti and Maria Luisa Mayer Modena have taken care to trace each dialect word back to its Hebrew or Yiddish cognate. Both point to a specifically northern Italian or central Italian vocabulary, with Falavolti suggesting Bergamo and Mayer Modena, in contrast, suggesting Pesaro—where, in fact, the play is nominally set. See Falavolti, "Introduzione," 32–33, notes on 109–118; Mayer Modena, "A proposito."

[34] Claudia Burattelli, *Spettacoli di corte a Mantova tra cinque e seicento* (Florence: Le Lettere, 1999), 164. The Jewish community in Mantua was required each year to provide a theatrical performance to the members of the Gonzaga court as part of their permit to live in the city. Thus, there was substantial interaction between the Jewish acting troupe and troupes of commedia dell'arte performers who were sponsored by the Gonzaga family. Jewish merchants in Mantua provided costumes, props, and lighting to professional actors; both groups participated in large celebrations, such as those of the Mantuan wedding festivities of 1608. Burattelli talks about the supply of costumes, etc.; see in particular 147–151.

[35] At this time, the role of the middleman was an economic and commercial reality for many Jews. In 1590, for example, Leone de' Sommi took advantage of his position at the Mantuan court to successfully petition Vincenzo Gonzaga on behalf of the Jewish middlemen. Christian businessmen were circulating a proposal to eliminate the services of the middlemen, a move that de' Sommi claimed would render a significant number of Jews unemployed and therefore penniless. Shlomo Simonsohn, *History of the Jews in the Duchy of Mantua* (Jerusalem: Kiryath Sepher, 1977), 267. On racially marked middlemen in Venice, see Rothman, *Brokering Empire*, 29–86.

FULGENZIO	Adesso è tempo ch'io mi cacci fra la turba; ma non sapendo parlare ebraico fingerò il mutolo. *Ba, ba ba, ba?*	It is now time that I threw myself into the crowd; but not knowing how to speak Hebrew I will pretend muteness. *Ba, ba ba, ba?*
LEON	Questo è muto e ne saluta, per quanto ne dimostra il gesto cortese; e di più convien che sia forestiero, non l'avendo qui giamai in Pesaro veduto.	This man is mute, and greets us, however he seems polite; and furthermore, not having ever seen him here in Pesaro, it seems that he is a foreigner.
SENSALE	Lasciate, ch'io l'intenderò, c'ho lingua muta, e in quel linguaggio parlo molto bene.	Leave it, I understand him. I know the mute tongue, and in that language I speak very well.
CAINO	Tu mi vuoi far ridere; che lingua muta?	You're kidding; what mute tongue?
SENSALE	Che lingua muta? O state a sentire. *Be, be, be, be?* Vedete voi, costui, co'l suo ba *ba ba ba*, n'ha detto buon dì a tutti e io, co'l mio *be, be, be, be*, gliho detto che tutti noi gli rendiamo il buon giorno.	What mute tongue? O listen! *Be, be, be, be?* You see, he, with his *ba ba ba ba*, said good day to everyone and I, with my *be, be, be, be*, said to him that we all render him good day.
SCEMOEL	Bene, per la Torrà, séguita, séguita, io stupisco di simil cosa.	Great, for the Torah's sake, continue, I am amazed!
LEON	E io.	Me too.
FULGENZIO	*Barau, babbù; gnaù, gnargnaù, gnaù gnaù?*	*Barau, babbù;* meow, meow meow, meow meow?
SENSALE	Oh? Vedete, questa è mo lingua gattesina, con la mutosina mescolata.	Oh? You see, this is cat language, mixed in with mute.
CAINO	E come gli risponderai? Eh, eh, eh.	And how will you respond to him? Ha, ha, ha.
SENSALE	Non ridete, perché la cosa va così.	Don't laugh, for things go like that.
LEON	Ma come risponderai?	But how will you respond?
SENSALE	O vi dirò: a questa lingua gattesina, risponderò con lingua sorzolina. Ma sapete voi quello che gattesinescamente, e mutescamente, ha detto? Vuoi che lo dica, muto? Bene, non intende questo linguaggio, e vedete che non s'è mosso, né ha risposto. Aspettate, che gle lo dirò. *Barabam, barabam, bi, be, ba?*	O I will tell you: to the cat language, I will respond with mouse language. But do you understand that which catlike and mutelike he has said? Do you want me to tell [them], mute? Good, he does not understand this language, and you see that he has not moved nor replied. Wait, I will say it to him. *Barabam, barabam, bi, be, ba?*
FULGENZIO	*Fi, fe, fo, fu.*	*Fi, fe, fo, fu.*

SENSALE	Dice di sì, che ve lo dica.	He says yes, I should tell you.
FULGENZIO	*Qua qui, quara, qui, qua, que qui?*	*Qua qui, quara, qui, qua, que qui?*
SENSALE	Di più, dice che vorrebbe vendere anch'egli, poiché se, per fare il mercante, ha perduto in man di Turchi la lingua, vuole anche, mercantando, perder la vita.	And further, he says that he, too, would like to sell things, since he lost his tongue at the hands of the Turks for having been a merchant, he would like to die a merchant.
CAINO	Tu mi fa stuppire, né so chi t'abbia insegnata questa lingua.	You amaze me, I don't know who taught you this language
SENSALE	Chi me l'ha insegnata? Un muto, che teneva scuola in questa lingua.	Who taught me? A mute, who ran a language school.
LEON	Or sù, muto, ci contentiamo che tu facci bene. Ma a che dimena il capo?	Let's go, mute, you have satisfied us that you are all right. But why is he moving his head?
SENSALE	Se vi dissi che non intende, se non il mio linguaggio? O questa è bella, io non so che mi dica, e costui m'intende. Lasciate fare a me. *Nebi, nebe, be, be?* Vedete, che china il capo? O cànchero, questa è bella! Non volendo io parlo muto. Or sù: *stipin, bipin, ripin?* Ho detto che stia cheto.	I told you that he doesn't understand anything except my language. O this is marvelous! I don't know what he is telling me, and he understands me. Leave it to me. *Nebi, nebe, be, be?* You see that he nods his head? This is quite something! Not wanting to, I speak mute. Let's go: *stipin, bipin, ripin?* I told him to stay quiet.
FULGENZIO	*Rispin, rispin.*	*Rispin, rispin.*
SENSALE	Sentite? Dice che tacerà. Or che dite, non sono un gran valent'uomo?	Did you hear that? He said that he will be quiet. Now what do you say, am I not a talented man?
CAINO	Tu n'hai fatto tutti stupire, e vogliosi di questa lingua mutesina, gattesina e sorzolina.[36]	You have amazed everyone and made them want to learn this mute, cat, and mouse language.

Two points leap out. First, that Fulgenzio is identified on sight as a foreigner (*forestiero*), an observation then borne out in sound; as the scene proceeds, he is apparently baffled by the Italian of his interlocutors, neither moving nor replying in response to their speech. Second, despite the comedy of muteness on which the scene ostensibly hinges, Fulgenzio is not mute at all but, on the contrary, noisily vocal. The carefully transcribed script of Fulgenzio and Sensale's discourse demonstrates a purported inability to make words rather than an inability to make sounds. These two axes—of the foreign and the unintelligible—intersect in Sensale's glib explanation, according to which

---

[36] Andreini, "Lo Schiavetto," II, ix.

78 ACT I, SCENE II

Fulgenzio's wordlessness is the result of a brutal encounter with the Turks. Metaphorically, the literal loss of the tongue (or *lingua*) is elided with the figurative loss of the Jewish tongue (or *lingua*), which should have guaranteed Fulgenzio's intelligibility amongst his coreligionists, no matter how foreign. Pragmatically, however, linguistic disability is normalized by mapping the violence of a slave economy over a global network of Jewish merchants.

The noises of Fulgenzio and Sensale's Mute speech fall into two basic categories. In the first, we have the repetition of single syllables: *ba ba ba, be be be*, and so on. These get more complex over the course of the scene, culminating in Fulgenzio's "Rispin, rispin." It is likely that the syllables chosen for the scene were intended to parody specific Jewish words; for example, the "Ba, ba, ba, ba" of Fulgenzio's initial foray into Mute—and recognized by Leon as a greeting—could reference "Barucaba," from the Hebrew *barukh ha-ba'*, a traditional greeting derived from the psalms.[37] The second category of sounds is made up of animal noises. The dehumanizing effect of animal sounds is immediately evident, as is their humorous (if cruel) potential. Furthermore, I would argue that the coincidence in this scene of "noisy" and "Jewish" is anything but. Some linguists have argued that the word "baruccaba" is a dialect Italian word that means hubbub, or noise, as derived from the Hebrew.[38] In a similar sense, the Mute sounds of this scene play on a nasty sonic stereotype that interpreted the sound of Judaism as incomprehensible babble, wrapping together the chanted rituals of religious observance and the Hebrew language into one nonsensical package. Accordingly, to the Christian auditor, Fulgenzio and Sensale's Mute conversation could have posited a hyperbolic claim to authenticity, since all Jewish speech could be figured as noisy nonsense, partway between sound and song.[39]

The audio profiling of Jews within Christian society was so prevalent that "Jewish" sounds provided ready material for programmatic musical representation within the comic partsong repertoire. A partsong representing Jews in Orazio Vecchi's *L'Amfiparnaso* is prefaced by a short, telling description: "In which Francatrippa goes to the Jews with a pawn, knocks loudly at the door, but only a Babel of voices and horrible tongues were heard."[40]

---

[37] Harrán, "'Barucaba' as an Emblem."
[38] *The Merriam-Webster New Book of Word Histories* (Springfield, MA: Merriam-Webster, 1991), 68.
[39] HaCohen, *The Music Libel*; Robert Bonfil, *Jewish Life in Renaissance Italy*, trans. Anthony Oldcorn (Berkeley: University of California Press, 1994), 233–241.
[40] "Va a gli Ebrei Francatrippa a porr'un pegno; / La porta forte scuote e una Babelle / S'ode di voci e orribili favelle." Text transcribed in Vecchi, *L'Amfiparnaso*, xxx. On Vecchi and his music, see Paul Schleuse, *Singing Games: The Music Books of Orazio Vecchi* (Bloomington: Indiana University Press, 2015).

The lyrics mix Hebrew words, biblical names, and Hebrew-esque sounds. Even once Vecchi's Jews begin to speak in Italian, their language is heavily inflected, with many words ending in an un-Italianate -t suffix. Their music, too, is immediately marked as "Jewish," as their first entry parodies the cantillation of Jewish religious practice (see Musical Example 2.2):[41]

FRANCATRIPPA	Tich, tach, toch	Knock, knock, knock,[42]
	Tich, tach, toch.	Knock, knock, knock.
	O hebreorum gentibus,	O, you Hebrew people,
	sù prest'avri, sù prest!	Hurry, open up, hurry up!
	Da hom da be cha tragh	I'm used to being received like a
	zo l'us.	gentleman.
HEBREO	Ahi, Baruchai,[43]	Ah, my blessed ones,
	Badanai,[44] Merdochai,[45]	In the name of the Lord,
	an Biluchan	Mordechai,
	ghet[46] milotranla Baruchabà.[47]	Blessed be he who comes in the name of the Lord.
FRANCATRIPPA	A no faro vergot maidè negot,	I won't be able to do business;
	ch'i fa la Sinagoga.	They're holding a synagogue.
	O che'l diavol v'affoga!	May the devil drown them!
	Tiche tach, tiche toch,	Knock, knock, knock,
	tiche tach, tiche toch.	Knock, knock, knock.

---

[41] The use of such sounds is far from unique. The repertoire of contemporary popular song that mocks Jewish characters has been called *musica ebraica*; see Anna Levenstein, "Songs for the First Hebrew Play *Tsahut Bedihuta Dekidushin* by Leone de' Sommi (1527–1592)" (DMA diss., Case Western University, 2006), 82–84. Another pertinent example, also from the madrigal comedy repertoire, is the "Sinagoga di Ebrei" from Adriano Banchieri's *Barca di Venezia per Padova: Venezia, 1605* (1998). This song, too, is prefaced by a description in which Jews are said to make a lot of noise: "Nel traghettar al Dolo (o dolce spasso) / fan sinagoga a instanzia d'un bresciano / Bethel e Samuel, con gran fracasso." In this second example, the use of purely nonsense syllables is even more exaggerated, and the same set of Hebrew words is deployed. A similar mock-cantillational style is utilized, in contrast with monophonic sections characterized by static harmony and simple voice exchange between the upper parts—both of these techniques are common to other examples of *musica ebraica* written by Banchieri, such as the Jewish song "Mascherata di Hebrei" in his *Canzonette a tre voci, novamente, sotto diversi capricci*, 20.

[42] Levenstein thinks that these sounds do not represent the knock at the door but rather "nonsense syllables in imitation of the glottal sounds and rhythm of Hebrew." See Levenstein, "Songs," 82.

[43] Baruchai = B'ruchai = "my blessed" (pl.). For this and other details concerning the Hebrew words in the text, I am indebted to Hila Tamir.

[44] Badanai = B'Adonai = "in God's name."

[45] Merdochai = Mordechai, a name from the Bible, more precisely the Megillah (or Book) of Ruth. The name Mordechai stands as metonymy for being Jewish, as throughout the Megillah, the character by that name is constantly referred to as "Mordechai the Jew." It bears noting that in this text, Mordechai has been transcribed as "Merdochai," presumably with the intention of invoking the Italian word for "shit": *merda*.

[46] The sound "ghet" is perhaps a transcription of the Hebrew word *khet*, which means "sin."

[47] Baruchabà = Barùch habbà = "Blessed by he that cometh [in the name of the Lord]," one of the Jewish forms of salutation, on which see Elio Piattelli's notes to Banchieri, *Barca di Venetia per Padova: Dilettevoli madrigali a 5 voci (1623)* (1969), iv.

HEBREO	Oth zorochot	Signs, afflictions,
	aslach muflach	Idols, Heathen.
	Iochut zorochot	Judah in distress,
	calamala Balachot.	[...]
FRANCATRIPPA	O ohi, o ohi, o messir Aron!	Ho there, ho there, O Messir Aaron!
HEBREO	C'ha pulset' à sto porton?	Who knocked at this door?
FRANCATRIPPA	So mi, so mi, messir Aron.	I did, I did, Messir Aaron.
HEBREO	Che cheusa volit?	What do you want?
	Che cheusa dicit?	What do you say?
FRANCATRIPPA	A vorraff' impegnà sto Bradamant.	I want to pawn this porter's strap.
HEBREO	O Samuel, Samuel, venit à bess,	O Samuel, Samuel
	venit à bess,	Come down, come down!
	Adanai, che l'è lo Goi	Lord, here is the Goy
	ch'è venut con lo moscogn	Come with a pawn
	che vuol lo parachem.	Who wants its countervalue.
	L'è Sabbà cha no podem.	It is the Sabbath, so we cannot.

While Vecchi's music was published as a collection of part songs, not as an explicitly theatrical work, the collection is structured as if it were a drama.[48] The cast list Vecchi provides in prefatory material to the madrigal collection describes the Jews as "Hebrei in Casa," or "Jews inside their house," and thus as imagined solely through their distinctive sound. Here, as in *Lo Schiavetto*, the sound of Judaism trumps the visible and vested trappings of the Jewish body, and the use of the voice marks the Jews as non-Italian or as foreign in important and insidious ways. In an era when sumptuary legislation pressed dress codes upon Jewish populations with increasing force, popular theatrical and musical cultures rendered such clothing merely the visual echo of an originary corporeal eloquence inseparable from the Jewish body.

L'Amfiparnaso notates ways in which the actors of *Lo Schiavetto* might have modified their voices, allowing the rhyming words of their "Mute" speech to imitate the meandering pitches that Christian audiences associated with the rites of Jewish religious ceremony, while the association of these two

---

[48] There is a small but significant literature on the madrigal comedy and the vexed question of whether dramatic performances were intended. See Laurie Dentenbeck, "Dramatised Madrigals and the *Commedia dell'Arte* Tradition," in *The Science of Buffoonery: Theory and History of the Commedia dell'Arte*, ed. Domenico Pietropaolo (Toronto: University of Toronto Press, 1989), 59–68; Warren Kirkendale, "Franceschina, Girometta, and Their Compaions in a Madrigal 'a Diversi Linguaggi' by Luca Marenzio and Orazio Vecchi," *Acta Musicologica* 44 (1972): 181–235; Martha Farahat, "On the Staging of Madrigal Comedies," *Early Music History* 10 (1991): 123–143; Wayne Allen Glass Jr., "The Renaissance Italian Madrigal Comedy: A Handbook for Performance" (PhD diss., University of Arizona, 2006); Schleuse, *Singing Games*.

Musical Example 2.2. Orazio Vecchi, "Tich, tach, toch," from *L'Amfiparnaso, comedia harmonica*, 5vv (first published 1597), mm. 13–16.

works does more than demonstrate a common vocabulary of aural Jewish stereotypes.[49] In combination, *L'Amfiparnaso* and *Lo Schiavetto* show that the syllables of Fulgenzio and Sensale's "Mute" conversation were integral semantic units, even in the absence of words.

In one sense, the noisy, linguistically marked Jew is but one among the cast of stereotyped commedia dell'arte characters, each of whom speaks in his or her own dialect and register (we could note, for example, that Francatrippa also speaks heavily modified Italian, and his attempts at Latin are deplorably inaccurate); in another, it reveals and reaffirms deep social anxieties concerning contagion and difference. As the elite, serious characters are elided seamlessly with the verbal signifiers of educated Italian, the Italian gentry are represented as a universal standard. At the same time, stubbornly unassimilated foreigners are relegated to society's lower echelons, the very familiarity of their vocal tics a testament to their substantial presence within the Italian soundscape. Each of the examples considered in this chapter coagulates around linguistic difference as a familiar theatrical trope but, more importantly, around the very sound of these characters as an integral—and far from arbitrary—element of characterization. Each example represents the sound of a foreign language as recognizable and familiar—as a "minoranza alloglotta," whether Jewish, Black African, Turkish, or German.

More importantly, in scenes of disguise, the voices of characters are treated as crucial evidence of their true selves—emerging from below the surface of the body and testifying to the materiality of that body as a quality inherent to it. This rendering of the flesh as sound provides a means by which a true inheritance can be heard and measured, fixing the place of a given character securely within societal categories. The Germans, Turks, Jews, and enslaved Africans whose voices were impersonated in this chapter were familiar sonic and physical presences in Italian cities. In the next chapter, I consider several theatrical depictions of a foreign Other that was decidedly less familiar to Florentine audiences, though not, as I show, entirely unheard: Native Americans, or *indiani*. Listening carefully to stage noises, and juxtaposing performances with the Florentine presence of literal "Indiani" and firsthand ethnographic witnesses, I push back against prevailing scholarly opinion that finds little trace of foreign sounds within the musical repertoire of European early modernity.

---

[49] During the 1590s, the characters named by Vecchi as the cast of *L'Amfiparnaso* regularly worked together as the Uniti or the Gelosi under the direction of Giovanni Pellesini and Isabella Andreini (Giovan Battista Andreini's mother); Giovan Battista was a regular member of the performing troupe; thus, the Vecchi may quite literally refer to performance practices of the Andreini, which would also have inflected stagings of *Lo Schiavetto*. See Wilbourne, "*Lo Schiavetto*," 16–17.

L'Indiano che al presente si trova in casa il S. Bartolomeo Corsini, fu donato in Londra, a me Ottavio Bernini da Filippo Barnardi Genovese, il quale disse che detto Indiano, era stato preso con altri tre Indiani da una sua nave, nella cuba, o Salmatra se bene, mi ricordo, e di piu disse, che detto Indiano non era batezato, e che dovessi farlo batezare come intesi poi che fece batezare li altri tre. Io non credo che detto Indiano sia di cuba, o Salmatea, ma che sia di quelle isole in quele parte, vicine, non ancora sogiogate dalli spagnoli, e che li spagnioli, li avessino presi come fanno giornalmente, per condurli poi alla margherita per pescare le perle e questo lo cognieturai, da quel poco discorso che alora da detto Indiano si pote cavare che e quanto informazione ne posso dare [in a new hand] e sono circa a anni cinque.

The Indian, who at present can be found in the house of Signore Bartolomeo Corsini, was given to me, Ottavio Bernini, in London, by Filippo Barnardi Genovese, who said that the aforementioned Indian was taken with three other Indians from one of their boats in Cuba or Salmatea, if I recall correctly. And furthermore [Barnardi] said that the aforementioned Indian hadn't been baptized and that I should have him baptized, which, as I later understood, he had done for the other three. I don't believe that the aforementioned Indian is from Cuba or from Salmatea, but instead that he is from an island in those parts, close by, but not yet subjugated by the Spanish, and that the Spanish had taken him, as they regularly do, in order to take him to fish for pearls at Margarita Island, and this I conjectured from what little conversation one could carve out from the aforementioned Indian at that time, and this is all the information that I can give, and it was about five years [ago].

Ottavio Bernini, November 1609, I-Fca, Pia Casa dei Catacumeni, f. 1, c.n.n. [ins. 28]

Scene 3
Music *all'Usanza Loro* (Performed in a Foreign Way)

In 1616, two Florentine entertainments staged so-called *indiani* in a noisy, spectacular fashion.[1] For carnival, the horse ballet *Guerra d'amore* was staged in Piazza Santa Croce, with a text by Andrea Salvadori; music by Jacopo Peri, Paolo Grazi, Gio: Battista Signorini, and Giovanni del Turco; choreography by Agnolo Ricci; and sets, costumes, and machines by Giulio Parigi.[2] The performing forces included two rival armies—one Asian, one African—with as many as 164 soldiers apiece. The "Indians" in this scenario were textually Asiatic: the cast includes "Indamoro, King of Narsingharh (*Narsinga*),"[3] played by the Grand Duke himself, as well as thirty-two "Brahmin priests, very famous in the East."[4] A host of textual and iconographical allusions make reference to Asian landmarks, such as the Ganges River. Yet Parigi's extant sketch of an Indian warrior (see Figure 3.1), repeated in Jacques Callot's prints of the festivities (see Figure 3.2), makes it clear that Florentines associated a specifically American set of visual influences with the term "Indian." On August 12, later the same year, a scenario attributed to Parigi provided the eye- and ear-catching framework to a *palio* (or foot race) held on the banks of the Arno.[5] The text, preserved in a broadsheet, describes a team of "Indians without heads," one of three groups accompanying the Sun, Fame, Summer, and the Hours in a procession that included both music and dance: "these Indians, who are born without heads, have their eyes, mouth, and nose in their chest, [. . .] armed with bows and arrows, and playing nackers and

---

[1] On French representations of Native Americans, see Bloechl, *Native American Song*; Bloechl, "Race, Empire, and Early Music."
[2] *Guerra d'amore, festa del Serenissimo Gran Duca di Toscana Cosimo secondo, fatta in Firenze il Carnevale del 1615* (Florence: Stamperia di Zanobi Pignoi, 1616), 52.
[3] *Guerra d'amore*, 29. Ironically enough, the Narsinga is a kind of curved metal trumpet, used throughout India.
[4] "Sacerdoti Bramanni tanto famosi nell'Oriente." *Guerra d'amore*, 8.
[5] An anonymous description of the *palio* was published; see *Descrizione del corso degli'indiani senza testa al palio* (Florence: Zanobi Pignoni, 1616). I consulted the copy at I-Fn, V.Mis, 123.17. Blumenthal claims that the descriptive "story" (his scare quotes) was invented by Parigi; see Blumenthal, "Giulio Parigi's Stage Designs," 357.

Figure 3.1. Giulio Parigi, costume design for "soldato indiano," *Guerra d'amore*, 1616. Pen and watercolor on paper, 280 × 176 mm. Biblioteca Marucelliana, Florence, B33. Used with permission of the Ministero della Cultura / Biblioteca Marucelliana, Florence. Further reproduction or duplication is expressly prohibited.

other instruments, according to the usage of their lands, make a delightful show of themselves."[6] Again, an explicit geographical origin for the "Indians" in this parade is far from clear, since they combine the headless aspect of

---

[6] "[Q]uelli Indiani, che nati senza testa, gl'occhi, la bocca, e'l naso nel petto dimostrano, [. . .] armati di archi, e faretre, e sonando naccare, & altri Instrumenti all'usanza de' paesi loro, fanno di se dilettosa mostra." *Descrizione del corso.*

Figure 3.2. Jacques Callot after Giulio Parigi. Printed in conjunction with the *Lettera al Sig. Alberico Cibo, Principe di Massa, Sopra il Giuoco fatto dal Gran Duca, Intitolato Guerra d'amore* (Pisa: Giovanni Fontani, 1616).

Pliny's Blemmyes with the bows and arrows of Native American populations, and they play instruments associated with the Middle East: the word used is *naccare*, which comes from the Persian word *nakar* or the Arabic *naqqāra*, meaning drum.[7] Both performances conflate the East and the West, the real and the imaginary, in their representation of the category *indiano*, yet I am less interested in critiquing such errors than in thinking about the ways in which they signify.[8] Visually, these Florentine Indians display an overwhelming dependence on iconography from the so-called New World. Indeed, as with Syria, America can be seen to have particular historical resonance for Florentine audiences of the early seventeenth century. Taking the specific Florentine circumstances seriously opens up a larger discussion

---

[7] "Antico strumento militare a percussione, costituito da due elementi, simili a timpani o tamburi, che si suonavano battendoli ritmicamente con due bacchette, per lo più stando a cavallo." http://www.treccani.it/vocabolario/nacchera/.

[8] See Elizabeth Horodowich and Alexander Nagel, "Amerasia: European Reflections of an Emergent World, 1492–ca.1700," *Journal of Early Modern History* 23 (2019): 257–295.

about racial difference and representation, and it points toward the meanings of representational sound beyond music, specifically staged noise.

Nearly eight years before the two 1616 performances, in the fall of 1608—the same year that Ferdinando I and Fakhr ad-Dīn signed their treaty—Cosimo de' Medici (heir to the Grand Duchy) married Maria Maddalena of Austria, daughter of the Austrian archduke Charles II and sister to Queen Margarete of Spain, wife of King Philip III. Among the entertainments was an intriguing representation of Florentine authority over the New World: the fourth *intermedio* to *Il giudizio di Paride*, performed on October 25, 1608, depicted Amerigo Vespucci in the moment of his arrival on "American" soil. The text of the *intermedio* (noted as the first historical subject of the Italian musical stage)[9] was written by Giovanbattista Strozzi *il giovane*, who had labored over an epic poem about the explorer some years previously,[10] and the topic itself was considered relevant not only because of the bride's connection to America (as Lia Markey points out, "ironically, or perhaps fittingly, Maria Maddalena's dowry was paid with gold from the 'fleets from the Indies'")[11] but also because less than two months previously, the Florentines had launched a (secret and technically illegal) expedition to scout the mouth of the Amazon in search of gold, Brazil wood, and land. The re-enactment foregrounds Florentine symbols on Vespucci's boat (lion, lilies) and body (an overcoat in the Florentine style):

> The scene became a placid and quiet sea, and the shore appeared, covered with trees of a kind unknown to us, and here and there among them were seen houses made of palms and reeds, some on the ground, others in the trees; the air full of parrots and similar varieties of birds, and on the ground, naked men, dressed as in the West Indies. On this ocean, a large sailboat appeared, with a lion on the prow and lilies over the masts, and among the sails, by these signs, one could recognize Amerigo Vespucci, Florentine, who sat armed on the poop deck, with an overcoat in the style of his country [i.e., Florence], and an astrolabe in hand.[12]

---

[9] Blumenthal, "Giulio Parigi's Stage Designs," 140.

[10] Lia Markey, *Imagining the Americas in Medici Florence* (University Park: Pennsylvania State University Press, 2016), 154.

[11] Markey, *Imagining the Americas*, 151. She quotes from an unsigned Spanish document in the Medici archives, dated July 17, 1609, partially transcribed by the Medici Archive Project, DocID 16566.

[12] "[L]a Scena si fece Mare placido, e quieto, e le sue rive apparvero vestite d'alberi incogniti a noi, e fra essi vedevansi qua, e la sparse case fatte di palme, e di canne, alcune in terra, altre sù gli

As the scene continued, the Florentine slant was further heightened, with choral singing provided by the (European) sailors and by a chorus of heavenly visitors, including "ten poets from various centuries and of various nationalities, each distinguished by his clothing and respective crown: Musaeus, Amphion, Linus, Orpheus, Homer, Pindaros, Virgil, Horace, Dante and Petrarch, and all together admiring the achievements of the Florentine captain, they began to sing."[13] Crucially, as a means to hear the voices of *indiani*, the *intermedio* fails. The "huomini nudi" described by Camillo Rinuccini in the quote above are absent from an extant sketch of the stage design by Parigi and from the widely circulated Remigio Cantagallina print derived from it (the Cantagallina print is reproduced as Figure 3.3).[14] Other visual sources from the 1608 wedding provide a possible indication of what these *indiani* might have looked like: the *gioco del ponte*, staged by Pisan nobles on October 28 on the Ponte Santa Trinita, involved one team costumed as warriors from around the world. Rinuccini writes that one squad of five noblemen were "dressed as Indians, with feathers."[15] The accompanying print, by Matthias Greuter (see Figure 3.4), shows the "Indians" alongside Germans, Greeks, Moors, and Turks but also Cyclops and lions; the visible feathers mark them as Native Americans rather than Southeast Asian soldiers.

The proto-ethnographic accuracies and silent inhabitants of the *intermedio* setting represent America as a paradise awaiting European discovery and exploitation—a phantasmic desire for the expedition that was then under way. By 1616, however, when the horse ballet and *palio* took place, the

---

alberi: l'aria piena di Pappagalli, e simil varietà d'uccelli, e per terra huomini nudi, come costuman nell'Indie Occidentali. In questo mare comparve a vela una nave grande, con un Leone in prua, e gigli sopra gli alberi, e nelle vele, da tal contrassegni, si riconobbe Amerigo Vespucci Fiorentino, che sedeva in poppa armato, con sopravvesta all'uso della patria, e l'Astrolabio in mano." Camillo Rinuccini, *Descrizione delle feste fatte nelle reali nozze de' Serenissimi Principi di Toscana D. Cosimo de' Medici e Maria Maddalena Archiduchessa d'Austria* (Florence: I Giunti, 1608), 40.

[13] "[D]ieci poeti di vari secoli, e di varie nazioni, Museo, Anfione, Lino, Orfeo, Omero, Pindar, Vergilio, Orazio, Dante, e il Petrarca, distinti ciascuno con gli abiti, e corone proprie, e tutti insieme ammirando l'opera del nocchier Fiorentino, cominciarono a cantare." Rinuccini, *Descrizione delle feste*, 41.

[14] Parigi's original design is visible at the website of the Victoria and Albert Museum, London, http://collections.vam.ac.uk/item/O1221883/set-design-parigi-giulio/. Parigi's image does not include the poets descending from the sky but in all other particulars is very similar to the Cantagallina print.

[15] "[V]estiti da Indiani, con penne." Rinuccini, *Descrizione delle feste*, 92. The squad consisted of Gio: Maria Ruccellai, Fabio Orlandini, Jacopo Nerli, and Cammillo Berzighelli, comanded by Orazio Moriani.

Figure 3.3. Remigio Cantagallina after Giulio Parigi, *The Ship of Amerigo Vespucci on the Shores of the Indies*, fourth *intermedio* from *Il giudizio di Paride* (perf. 1608). © Victoria and Albert Museum, London.

ambitious southern hemispheric plans hatched under Ferdinando I had been largely put aside, while knowledge acquired about the Indies persisted. As early as 1591, Ferdinando was actively collecting information on the region of Brazil and the prospect for trade there.[16] Throughout the early 1600s, a variety of plans were floated in an attempt to import sugar directly from the New World to Livorno (where a sugar refinery was to be built), and in 1608, even as the expedition was launched, Ferdinando made diplomatic inquiries at the court of Philip III about purchasing a portion of the Brazilian coast as a dominion for one of his younger sons.[17] When this came to no avail,

---

[16] Lucia Paoli, "Da Livorno a Nombre de Dios: Una dettagliata relazione inviata a Firenze e il progetto dei Medici per un possesso in Brasile," in *Percorsi di arte e letteratura tra la Toscana e le Americhe: Atti della giornata di studi Biblioteca Nazionale Centrale di Firenze, 3 Ottobre 2014*, ed. Nicoletta Lepri (Raleigh, NC: Aonia, 2016), loc. 2333–2930; Markey, *Imagining the Americas*, 147; Roberto Ridolfi, "Pensieri Medicei di colonizzare il Brazil," *Il Veltro* 6, no. 4 (1962): 705–720.

[17] Brian Brege, "Renaissance Florentines in the Tropics: Brazil, the Grand Duchy of Tuscany, and the Limits of Empire," in *The New World in Early Modern Italy, 1492–1750*, ed. Elizabeth Horodowich and Lia Markey (Cambridge: Cambridge University Press, 2017), 206–222.

Figure 3.4. Matthias Greuter, *Gioco del ponte*, from Camillo Rinuccini, *Descrizione delle feste fatte nelle reali nozze de' serenissimi prinipi di Toscana d. Cosimo de' Medici e Maria Maddalena, arciduchessa d'Austria*, 1608. The "Indian" soldiers are visible in the lower left quadrant of the main image. Gabinetto disegni e stampe, Galleria degli Uffizi, Florence. Photo Scala, Florence / Art Resource, NY. Used with permission.

he engaged in similar discussions with several Portuguese citizens regarding parts of what is now Sierra Leone.[18]

The Brazilian exploratory expedition financed by Ferdinando demonstrates the depth of his interest in the monetary and territorial benefits of colonial expansion and global trade, as well as his conception of the political position of Florence vis-à-vis other foreign powers.[19] The voyage was captained by Robert Thornton, an English sailor, based on detailed maps and instructions provided by the English cartographer and explorer Robert Dudley, illegitimate son of the earl of Leicester, who converted to Catholicism in the early years of the seventeenth century and moved to Florence in 1606, entering the service of the Grand Duke.[20] In 1594–1595,

---

[18] Paul Edward Hedley Hair and Jonathan D. Davies, "Sierra Leone and the Grand Duchy of Tuscany," *History in Africa* 20 (1993): 61–69.

[19] Several scholars have suggested that Ferdinando's training as a cardinal exposed him to a broader global politics and predisposed him to more ambitious endeavors; see, for example, Markey, *Imagining the Americas*, 141; Hair and Davies, "Sierra Leone," 61–62.

[20] Brege, "Renaissance Florentines," 219; Lia Markey, "Mapping Brazil in Medici Florence: Dudley's *Arcano del Mare* (1646–1647)," in *Far from the Truth: Distance and Credibility in the Early Modern*

Dudley himself had traveled to Trinidad, the mouth of the Orinoco, and Puerto Rico. He later published a report on the Thornton voyage in his *Arcano del mare*, printed in 1646 and 1661.[21] Further details about the expedition are provided by the ship's surgeon, William Davies, in his *True Relation of the Travailes and Most Miserable Captivitie*; he was guaranteed his freedom on the condition that he joined the exploratory journey.[22] According to Davies, Ferdinando furnished Thornton with a "good Ship called the *Santa Lucia* [*Bonaventura*], with a Frigot, and a Tartane, well victualled, and well manned, and chiefly bound to the River of *Amazones*, with other severall Rivers, the which the Duke would have inhabited, hoping for great store of gaine of Gold, but the Countries did affoord no such thing."[23]

Thornton and his party left Livorno on September 8, 1608,[24] arriving safely at the mouth of the Amazon, then following the coast west as far as the island of Trinidad.[25] They arrived back in Livorno on July 10, 1609, with a crew of forty-seven men[26] and six "indiani." Dudley writes:

> Furthermore, [Thornton] discovered the good port of Cayenne [*Chiana*], which is a well-defended and secure port, and which had not previously been well explored by Christians; and from here he took with him five or six Indians to present to Their Highnesses in Florence, which he did; they were of those Caribi who eat human flesh.[27] They then died in Florence, most of them of smallpox, which to them is more infectious than the plague itself, because in their countries they have no sign of such illness. Just one of them survived, and went on to serve the Most Serene Prince Cardinal de' Medici

World, ed. Michiel van Groesen and Johannes Müller (University Park: Pennsylvania State University Press, forthcoming). A number of English pirates were drawn to Italian service after the English-Spanish peace of 1604.

[21] Dudley's maps, engraved by Anton Francesco Lucini, are hugely important as the first maritime atlas of the entire world (including the first separately printed map of Australia) and as the first to use the Mercator projection. See Robert Dudley, *Arcano del mare*, 2nd ed. (Florence: Giuseppe Cocchini, 1661).
[22] Davies, *True Relation*. See also Neri, *Uno schiavo inglese*.
[23] Davies, *True Relation*, n.p.
[24] Paoli, "Da Livorno," 108.
[25] Dudley, *Arcano del mare*, Vol. 2, Libro VI, 33.
[26] Brege, "Renaissance Florentines," 221.
[27] The term "Caribe" has a long history, closely related to the representation of indigenous South Americans as consumers of human flesh; see, in particular, Surekha Davies, *Renaissance Ethnography and the Invention of the Human: New World, Maps and Monsters* (Cambridge: Cambridge University Press, 2016), 65–108.

at court for several years and learned to speak the Italian language comfortably well.[28]

The one Indian who survived was initially called Matteo, though he was later baptized with the name Giovanni.[29] His service in Florence reemphasizes the issue of co-presence, as does Davies's years in the slave *bagno* at Livorno and the presence of numerous English sailors and scientists at the court. Some further details of Matteo-Giovanni and his compatriots emerge in a document filed by Francesco Carletti in support of Matteo's petition for baptism. Carletti's account, written in 1611, complicates slightly the exact location of where Matteo-Giovanni boarded Thornton's ship, adds the details that the choice to do so was voluntary (this Carletti repeats for good measure), and resolves the question of whether five or six *indiani* were involved. Notably, Carletti is himself famous as the first private citizen to circumnavigate the globe. His account of his travels through the "indie orientali and indie occidentali" was originally delivered as an oral presentation in installments before the Grand Duke and circulated in contemporary manuscripts;[30] Carletti entered the service of Ferdinando in 1606:

> I, Francesco Carletti, maestro di Casa to His Highness, certify that, in the month of July 1609, I was commanded by His Highness to arrange

---

[28] "[Thornton] scoprì di più il buon porto di Chiana [Cayenne], che è porto Reale, e sicuro, il quale non fu mai bene scoperto da' Cristiani per i tempi passati; e di quivi egli menò seco cinque, ò sei Indiani per presentare alle loro Altezze in Firenze, si come fece; i quali erano di quei Caribi, che mangiano la carne humana: Questi morirono poi in Firenze, la maggior parte di vaioli, che a loro è più infettoso della peste istessa, perchè in detti paesi non hanno notizia di simil male: Uno solo di quelli campò, il quale servì poi in Corte per alcuni anni il Serenissimo Principe Cardinale de' Medici, & imparò a parlare comodamente bene la lingua Italiana." Dudley, *Arcano del mare*, Vol. 2, Libro VI, 33.

[29] The documents are at I-Fca, *Pia Casa dei Catecumini*, f. 1. I note that a Croatan indigenous American called "Manteo" befriended English explorers at Roanoke Island in 1584, suggesting that "Matteo" may be an Italianization of an original indigenous name. On Manteo's participation in a history of sound and colonial contact, see Patricia Akhimie, "Performance in the Periphery: Colonial Encounters and Entertainments," in *Acoustemologies in Contact: Sounding Subjects and Modes of Listening in Early Modernity*, ed. Emily Wilbourne and Suzanne G. Cusick (Cambridge: Open Book, 2021), 80–81.

[30] Carletti's account was published posthumously in 1701; the format reflects the oral origins of the material. Notably, he includes the Philippines as part of his discourse on the "West Indies" and only switches to the East Indies when he arrives in the free state of Japan. For more details, see Adele Dei, ed., *Ragionamenti del mio viaggio intorno al mondo di Francesco Carletti* (Milan: Mursia, 1987); Adele Dei, "Gli eden corrotti di Francesco Carletti," in *Percorsi di arte e letteratura tra la Toscana e le Americhe: Atti della giornata di studi Biblioteca Nazionale Centrale di Firenze, 3 Ottobre 2014*, ed. Nicoletta Lepri (Raleigh, NC: Aonia, 2016), loc. 1372–1615.

the way for five Indians who had come from the West Indies [*dal'Indie Occidentali*]; these [men] had been brought [to Tuscany] by the English Captain Thornton [*Tortone*] in the number of six, but one was sick in the hospital, where he died. And having spoken many times with the aforementioned Captain, who told me that he had brought them at their own volition from the banks of the Amazon River and from other places along the coast of the aforementioned Indies: places full of heathens, where he [Thornton] had gone the year before with a boat, and he said that there was not a single Christian there; furthermore he attested that they were a very simple, uncivilized people, as one can well believe from their having voluntarily come to this country without knowing where they were going. And having all arrived here, we see that among these Indians there was one, who was called Matteo by the aforementioned Captain, who, all his other companions having died, wants to become a Christian. Under orders from His Highness, he was regularly sent to San Giovannino, where he was instructed and indoctrinated by Fr. Claudio Seripenni, who gives his word that the aforementioned Indian is sufficiently instructed so as to be able to receive Holy Baptism, and this all being true, I have underwritten the present [text], on the 2nd day of January [1611].[31]

Despite Carletti's insistence that Matteo-Giovanni came to Italy of his own free will, the record of his baptism testifies that such nuances were not always evident to his Italian interlocutors:

Giovanni, Indian slave of the Grand Duke, about twenty-two years old. Baptized on the given day [February 28, 1611]. Godfather: the *Cavaliere*

---

[31] "Certifico Io Francesco Carletti m*a*stro di Casa di S.A.S. come sino nel mese di Luglio 1609 mi fu comandato dal S.A.S che io dovessi ordinare che fusse dato il via a cinque Indiani, che erano venuti dal'Indie Occidentali; quali haveva condoti Il Capitano Tortone [Thornton] Inghilese in n*u*mero di sei, che l'uno era allo spedale ammalato, dove morì. Et havendo io piu volte discorso con detto Capitano mi disse che gl'haveva menati di lor propria voluntà dal Rio delle Amazzone, et altri luogi di quella Costa delle dette Indie: Peasi tutti di Gentili, dove era andato l'anno innanzi con una Navetta, e disse che non vi era nessuno Cristiano anzi attestava che erano popoli semplicissimi, e barbari si come si può credere dal lor venire voluntariamente in questi Paesi senza sapere dove andavano; et Arrivarono qui tutti si vide, tra quali Indiani ven'era uno, che da d*e*tto Capitano fu nominato Matteo, Il quale essendo tutti gli altri suoi Compagni morti, si vuole far cristiano, e che con missione di S.A.S. si e sempre mandato a S. Giovannino dove e stato instruito e doctrinato dal Pre. Claudio seripenni, che fa fede, che d*e*tto Indiano sia sufficentemente ammaestrato da poter ricevere il santo battesimo e p*er* essere del sud*e*tto cosi la verita ho soscritta la presente q*ue*sto dì 2 Genn*ai*o 1610 [1611]." I-Fca, *Pia Casa dei Catecumini*, f. 1, c.n.n.

Fabbritio Coloreto, Godmother: Lady Nannina [daughter] of the Marchese del Monte at San Sovino.[32]

Whether enslaved or in voluntary service, Matteo-Giovanni's experience at the court would have been dramatically different from the hard labor endured by Davies in the *bagno* and on the galleys. A living, breathing, and Italian-speaking source on the Americas, Matteo-Giovanni provided forceful firsthand testimony, that we cannot now discount. Echoes of Matteo-Giovanni's voice can be heard in Dudley's writing:

> This Indian from Cayenne frequently recounted to the author [Dudley] and to others the fertility and wealth of the kingdom of Guinea, and how he had been to the famous city of Eldorado [*Monoa*], capital of the realm, where resided their king, whom they called Emperor, because he has many realms under his command; and [he recounted] that the city was rich in gold, and situated near a large lake; and that this city was eight days away from the port of Cayenne, given that the Indians walk very quickly by foot, and typically cover fifty miles a day and sometimes more. The aforementioned Indian also said that close to Cayenne (a hilly country) there was a quite rich silver mine, that they call Perota, and also of low gold, which they call Calcuri, with which they make certain images and half moons for ornament.[33]

The idea that Matteo-Giovanni could be heard "spesse volte" relating tales and details of his home country adds an ethnographic specificity to Florentine knowledge of the New World, even as the details of Eldorado imply that he quickly became adept at telling the Europeans precisely what they wanted to hear. Furthermore, the two maps Dudley provides of Matteo-Giovanni's home territory (nos. 13 and 14 of his America series; see Figures 3.5 and 3.6) are the only two to include ethnographically detailed

---

[32] "Giovanni, Indiano stiavo del gra' Duca, d'anni 22 in circa. Battezzato a dì detto. Compadre il cavaliere Fabbritio Coloreto, commadre La S.ra Nannina del Marchese del Monte a S. Sovino." I-Fd, *Registri Battesimali, Maschi*, reg. 28, fg. 60.

[33] "Quest'Indiano di Chiana raccontava spesse volte all'Autore, & ad altri la fertilità, e ricchezza del regno di Guiana, e com'egli era stato nella città famosa di Monoa [the mythical Eldorado] metropoli del Regno, dove risiede il Re da loro nominato Imperatore, perche ha parecchi regni sotto il suo Imperio; e che la Città era ricca d'oro, e situata vicino ad un gran lago; e che essa Città era da otto giornate lunghe lontana dal porto di Chiana, essendo che gl'Indiani caminano velocemente a piedi, e fanno comunemente da 50 miglia il giorno, qualche volta più. Diceva ancora il dett'Indiano, che vicino a Chiana (qual'è paese di colline) vi era una miniera d'argento assai ricca, che essi chimano Perota, come anco dell'oro basso, nominato da loro Calcuri, con il quale fanno certe immagini, e mezze lune per ornamento." Dudley, *Arcano del mare*, Vol. 2, Libro VI, 33.

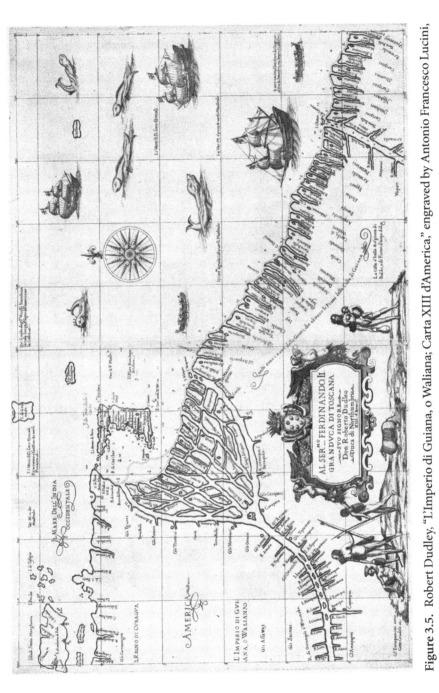

Figure 3.5. Robert Dudley, "L'Imperio di Guiana, o Waliana; Carta XIII d'America," engraved by Antonio Francesco Lucini, *Arcano del mare*, 2nd ed. (Florence, 1661).

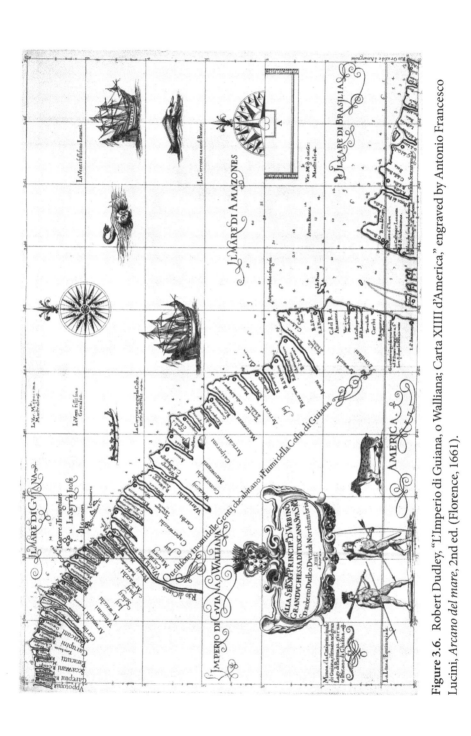

Figure 3.6. Robert Dudley, "L'Imperio di Guiana, o Walliana; Carta XIIII d'America," engraved by Antonio Francesco Lucini, *Arcano del mare*, 2nd ed. (Florence, 1661).

decorative drawings—in part, we can assume, because of their dedication to his Medici patrons but also perhaps because of his particular and personal experience in the region and his frequent discussions with Matteo-Giovanni. Along with the name of each river and inlet and soundings of the water depth off the coast, Dudley provides a precise accounting of the various tribes and nations who were resident in each segment of the coastline: "These are the names of the Peoples who live along the rivers of the coast of Guinea."[34] Dudley also provides a list of common indigenous words and their translations, to aid travelers who might wish to converse with native peoples.[35] In this list (part of which is reproduced in Table 3.1) and in the meticulously charted tribal names of the region, we can perhaps hear other echoes of Matteo-Giovanni's voice.[36]

Dudley's images bring us back to the question of performance, for his illustrations of Native Americans can be fruitfully compared with surviving images from the 1616 production of *Guerra d'amore* (see Figures 3.1 and 3.2). In both instances, the Indians carry long bows and quivers of arrows, one or two of which are held out for maximal visual effect. Both have bared chests and feather headdresses, though the costume for the *Guerra d'amore* covers the naked loins of the ethnographic image with a feathered skirt reminiscent of an ancient Grecian tunic and adds a helmet for good measure. Notably, the intricate body art visible in Dudley's drawing has not been replicated.

Unlike the silent *indiani* of the 1608 *intermedio*, those of the 1616 horse ballet are loud and warlike—they represent an army. Their noises tell us something important about their place in the Florentine imaginary and about the potential of sound to stage the body. In the *Guerra d'amore*, the arrival of each army was signaled by the "sound of Trumpets, of Drums, and of other Barbarous instruments."[37] Unsurprisingly, the musical material played by the trumpets, drums, and other barbarous instruments does not survive. Music for such instruments was rarely notated. The position of court

---

[34] "Questi sono i nomi delle Genti, che abitano li Fiumi della Costa di Guiana." The text appears on both maps.

[35] Dudley, *Arcano del mare*, Vol. 2, Libro VI, 33–34.

[36] Note that Dudley has similar lists for other places depicted in his atlas. I also note that at the beginning of this list (on page 33), he attests that he learned these words on his own trip to Guinea in 1595; however, on the following page, at the end of the list, he admits that he had forgotten the words and had taken these from written records provided by others: "Furono osservate molt'altre parole Indiane dell'Autore, delle quali se n'è perduto l'originale, e però è bisognato contentarsi delle parole sopradette, le quali ha ritrovato in altre scritture."

[37] "[S]uono di Trombe, di Tambur, e d'altri Barbari strumenti." *Guerra d'amore*, 29.

Table 3.1. Extract from the "Select words of the Indian language of Guinea, and of the island of Trinidad, observed by the author himself when he was in those parts during 1595." Robert Dudley, *Arcano del mare*, 2nd ed. (Florence, 1661), Vol. 1, 33–34. The Guinea words and their Italian translations appear in the original; English translation is author's own.

Guinea	Italian translation	English translation
Dabarah, *vuol dire*	I capelli della testa.	*Which means* The hairs of the head.
Caervvoda,	Una radice dolce.	A sweet root.
Guttemoc,	Un'huomo.	A man.
Dessie,	La fronte.	The forehead.
Tacosi, ò Tafereth,	Un'occhio.	An eye.
Delacoae,	La bocca.	The mouth.
Arehen,	I denti.	The teeth.
Daria,	Le gengive.	The gums.
[…]		
Sakel,	Io sto bene.	I am well.
Casparo,	Una spada.	A sword.
Tibetebe,	Conchiglie, o nicchi.	Shells (large or small).
Marahabo,	Un'arco.	A bow.
Semara,	Una freccia.	An arrow.
Huculle,	La corda dell'arco.	A bowstring.
Canua,	Le lor barchette.	Their boats (canoe).
[…]		
Caffique,	Un Re, o un regolo.	A king (cacique) or lord.
Marisce, e Maiz,	Grano Turchesco.	Turkish grain (corn, maize).

(or city) trumpeter was largely inherited, and the ensembles served a primarily civic function. Trumpeters and drummers are listed separately from "musicians" on court rolls from the period. Much of their music was learned by rote or improvised and, by early modern standards, may not have counted as "music" at all, being largely decorative, ceremonial, or militaristic. This does not mean, of course, that such instrumentalists were unable to produce music or sounds inspired by the military traditions of other places. Indeed, the frequency with which enslaved people (often enslaved Black people) were trained as trumpeters and/or drummers suggests that an invocation of racially marked music was part of the point; this is an issue to which I return in this book's Scene 6.

Sonic associations of foreignness arise even more strongly in the *palio* that took place that same year. The description of the *indiani*, quoted above, is worth repeating here: "these Indians, who are born without heads, have their eyes, mouth, and nose in their chest, [. . .] armed with bows and arrows, and playing nackers and other instruments, according to the usage of their lands, make a delightful show of themselves."[38] The other groups of performers included "a host of peasants and shepherdesses [. . .] playing flutes, whistles, and similar rustic instruments" and "a long line of corpulent men with smiling faces, some of whom displayed precious foodstuffs, and others held in their hands various kitchen implements, in imitation of musical instruments, and the most noble played and sang making a ridiculous and noisy harmony [*una ridicolosa, e strepitosa armonia*]."[39] The corpulent men are described as coming from "Cuccagna," an imaginary land of plenty, part of Italian folklore since the late medieval period; the rustic peasants were presumably Tuscan. In addition, the Sun himself, seated on his float, held a golden cetra and sang the praises of the Tuscan realms,[40] and printed verses imply that Fame also sang.

It is important that each of these groups played music that was different in instrumentation, style, and affect. We can also underscore that the Indians played their instruments "according to the usage of their lands": *all'usanza de' paesi loro*. This music is not notated and does not survive, but the description differentiates between the way music is typically played in Florence and the way it is played (by these musicians, in this performance, in imitation of the way it is played) elsewhere.

Makato Harris Takao has noticed two similar phrases in Jesuit descriptions of Japanese hymn singing from the 1500s: *á sua maniera* ("in their own way") and *á sua costume* (which he translates as "in accordance 'with their traditions'"), arguing that these words index a qualitative difference in how the musical sounds of Japanese Christians differed from those of European missionaries.[41] The same phrase—*all'usanza de' paesi loro*—or variants

---

[38] "[Q]uelli Indiani, che nati senza testa, gl'occhi, la bocca, e'l naso nel petto dimostrano, [. . .] armati di archi, e faretre, e sonando naccare, & altri Instrumenti all'usanza de' paesi loro, fanno di se dilettosa mostra." *Descrizione del corso.*

[39] "[U]na schiera di Contadini, e villanelle, [. . .] & altri vanno sonando flauti, sordine, & simili rusticali Instrumenti," and "una lunga schiera di huomini corpulenti, e di faccia allegra parte de' quali fanno mostra di preziosissime vivande, & altri sostengono in mano varij instrumenti di Cucina, che imitando gl'instrumenti musicali, & i piu nobili sonando, e cantando formano una ridicolosa, e strepitosa armonia." *Descrizione del corso.*

[40] "[S]ostenendo in mano la Cetra d'oro, su la quale è udito cantare le glorie de' Toscani Regi," *Descrizione del corso.*

[41] Takao, "'In Their Own Way,'" quotations from 187.

thereof appear repeatedly in travel writing, for example, in Pietro della Valle's *Viaggi, descritti da lui medesimo in lettere famigliari*, which was (nominally) written at precisely the same period as the Florentine performances discussed above, though it didn't appear in print for several years.[42] Della Valle writes, for example, in a description of Persia:

> In the presence of the king and of all the bystanders, the young women did several dances according to their usage [*all'usanza loro*], to the sound of the *cerchio*, or as they say *dairà*, which they carry with them, similar to that of young Roman girls in the month of May, but larger and more sonorous, with which they combine also the sound of the *cetri*. I am not sure whether they are of wood of ebony or bones of ivory or of other similarly hard materials, long enough, here called *ciaharparà*, which means "four pieces," of which they hold two of them in each hand, and banging them together in time to the music, they make an indescribable musical noise [*un non so che di ronzo musicale*].[43]

This "ronzo musicale" is both like and not like practices in Rome, specifically the celebratory musical practices understood to welcome the spring and typically performed by girls from the rural or peasant classes. In della Valle's description and in Parigi's scenario, we hear musical noises—della Valle writes of "un non so che di ronzo musicale," Parigi of "una ridicolosa, e strepitosa armonia"—used in ways that delineate different categories of people. In the *Corso degl'indiani senza testa*, three different groups of individuals played three different types of instruments: the *indiani* with "nackers and other instruments, according to the usage of their lands," the peasants "playing flutes, whistles, and similar rustic instruments," and the corpulent men of Cuccagna with "various kitchen implements, in imitation of musical instruments"—here we can imagine lutes or guitars disguised as ladles or saucepans, as well as percussive instruments of many types. This

---

[42] Pietro della Valle, *Viaggi di Pietro della Valle, detto il Pellegrino, descritti da lui medesimo in lettere familiari all'erudito suo amico Mario Schipano, divisi in tre parti, cioè la Turchia, la Persia e l'India* [Gioseffo Longhi, 1672] (Rome: Vitale Mascardi, 1845).

[43] "[L]e dame giovani alla presenza del re e di tutte le circostanti, fecero alcuni balli all'usanza loro al suono del cerchio, o come essi dicono *dairà* che portavano con loro, simile a quello delle fanciulle romane il mese di maggio, ma più grande e più sonoro, col quale concertano anche il suono di certi, non so se legni d'ebano, ovvero ossi di avorio o di simile altra materia soda, lunghetti alquanto, chiamati qui *ciaharparà*, che vuol dir quattro pezzi, de' quali tenendosene due per mano, e sbattendoli insieme a tempo di suono, fanno un non so che di ronzo musicale." Della Valle, *Viaggi*, La Persia, lett. VI.

unruly soundscape *narrates*, in precisely the way that operatic music is presumed to do, testifying to the recognizable coherence of sonic categories and—through timbre, meter, and sound itself—testifying to the geopolitical origins of the characters concerned. Class and function emerge as key components of representational sonicity.

Unlike the solo Syrian refugee of Francesca Caccini's "Io veggio," the characters from the *palio* are primarily entertaining. They represent no internal subjectivity with which the (noble) listener is expected to identify but rather a chaotic, noisy world of difference within which the subject himself or herself enjoys the "delightful show." The music of these performances steps away from the subtle inflections of the *nuova musica* in favor of strophic verses, improvised accompaniments, and boisterous percussion. These choices reflect their location—the two 1616 works were performed outside and thus were available for consumption by larger numbers of people and a much larger cross section of Florentine society; the *Guerra d'amore* was reputedly witnessed by an "immense multitude of people,"[44] and later that evening the participants paraded through the streets in order to entertain the entire city[45]—but they also reflect a hierarchy of sonic representation that will emerge as central to the argument of this book, whereby popular musical performances are repeatedly conflated with foreign bodies displayed as entertainment.

Notably, many of the foreigners invoked as co-presences in this chapter were enslaved or described as enslaved, including both Matteo-Giovanni (the Indian) and Davies (the Englishman who was freed from the *bagno* in Livorno on the condition that he serve on the Brazilian expedition). Their lives highlight the long-established practice of the Mediterranean slave trade, enabled in Tuscany by the development of the port of Livorno, as well as a more exotic trade in singular individuals who turned up at court. To this number, besides Matteo-Giovanni, we can add Antonio Corea, reputedly the first Korean to travel within Italy, who arrived in Florence in 1606 in the service of Francesco Carletti;[46] it is also worth mentioning that the first step

---

[44] "[I]mensa moltitudine di popolo." *Guerra d'amore*, 6.

[45] *Guerra d'amore*, 50–51.

[46] "Da queste Provincie [di Corea], ma particolarmente da quelle più marittime, ne conducevano per ischiavi numero grande d'Uomini, e di Donne d'ogni età; fra le quali vi erano assai belle fanciulle, e tutti indifferentemente eran venduti a vilissimo prezzo; ed io ne comprai in fino a cinque per poco più di dodici scudi e fattili battezzare gli menai meco, e nella Città di Goa li lasciai liberi, e solo uno di essi condussi con me in questa Città di Firenze, che oggi si ritrova in Roma, chiamato Antonio Corea." See Francesco Carletti, *Ragionamenti di Francesco Carletti Fiorentino sopra le cose da lui vedute ne' suoi viaggi, si delle'Indie Occientali, e Orientali come d'altri paesi* (Florence: Giuseppe Manai, 1701), 39–40.

of Carletti's long journey was a trip to Cape Verde to load a cargo of enslaved Black Africans bound for the "New World."[47] The material presence at court of Matteo-Giovanni and Antonio Corea, in conversation with the world traveler Carletti and the cartographer-explorer Dudley, testifies to a deep understanding of cultural and geographic difference that could and did operate in tandem with less precise invocations of foreign sound.

It has become a truism of music history that early modern Europeans had no interest in replicating, imitating, or invoking the sounds of non-European music. Ralph P. Locke, introducing his work on musical exoticism from 1500 to 1800, notes that the "awareness of non-Western musics will be treated only briefly in the present book because published descriptions and transcriptions of, say, Chinese music had little or no echo in Western musical works that evoked the respective land or people."[48] Owen Wright, discussing early modern *turqueries*, emphasizes that, "however realistic the costumes may have been, there is nothing authentically Turkish in the music."[49] Wendy Heller, summarizing the literature, concludes, "It would be some time before the sounds of Asia or the Americas were absorbed by composers."[50] Yet the stage directions and descriptions of this chapter suggest otherwise: the term *all'usanza loro* testifies to a clear invocation of stylistic difference. In the following chapter, I examine evidence that the Medici court was regularly exposed to foreign musical and military sounds associated with their Mediterranean foes and allies. This exposure would have provided a ready resource for representational noise that was both foreign and familiar.

---

[47] Dei, "Gli eden corrotti," loc. 1372.

[48] Locke, *Music and the Exotic*, 8.

[49] Owen Wright, "Turning a Deaf Ear," in *The Renaissance and the Ottoman World*, ed. Anna Contadini and Claire Norton (Farnham: Ashgate, 2013), 147–148. He summarizes the general consensus that later repertoires (including the *alla turca* march, which came to prominence in Viennese instrumental music of the late eighteenth century) incorporate "partial and distant impressions [. . .] of the *mehter* [or Janissary] sound" (165).

[50] Wendy Heller, *Music in the Baroque: Western Music in Context* (New York: W. W. Norton, 2014), 53.

[*E*] *piu volte venduta fui condotta a Livorno da Pier Lodovico Gambonni, e morto d*etto [Gambonni] *fui con gli altri effetti venduta.*

I was sold many times and then taken to Livorno by Pier Lodovico Gambonni, and when he died I was sold along with his other effects.
Covia di Mustafa Bas (later baptized as Anna Maria Teresia),
February 1658, I-Fca, Pia Casa dei Catacumeni,
f. 2, c.n.n. [ins. 20]

Scene 4
"Turkish Music" in Italy

In the first chapter of my previous book, *Seventeenth-Century Opera and the Sound of the Commedia dell'Arte*, I discussed a scene that could have served equally well as the beginning of this one. Giovan Battista Andreini's play *La Sultana* (published in 1622) contains an extended sequence at the beginning of the fourth act in which Turkish soldiers and then enslaved Black African court retainers arrive in the city of Naples and parade across the stage, interacting with an ethnically Italian character, Parsenio. In *Seventeenth-Century Opera*, I argued that the sounds of this scene were used to convey crucial information about characters and context, including not only Parsenio's use of dialect and the Turkish words and bad Italian of the Turkish soldiers (Mustafà and Ferahat) but also the drums and trumpets that herald their arrival. Indeed, the military instruments are deployed in such a way that their noise intrudes upon and interrupts the production of conventional (Western) music during the *intermedio*, prefiguring and rendering audible the intrusion of foreign characters into the Italian setting:

Qui mentre si farà la musica, o di strumenti, o di voci per separazione frà l'Atto Terzo, e Quarto s'udiranno suonar trombe, e tamburi: ma brevemente, nè però la musica, o vero i suoni cesseranno, fatto così due volte finirà la melodìa, & uscirà Parsenio. [1]	Here, while the music is playing to separate Act Three from Act Four, which could be either instrumental or vocal, one should hear trumpets and drums sound—but just briefly—however, neither the music nor the noises should cease. Once this has happened twice, the melody should finish and Parsenio should enter the stage.

In Andreini's stage direction, the juxtaposition of music and noises—*musica* and *suoni*—reiterates a point I touched on earlier: the functional sounds of trumpets and drums occupied a liminal space with regard to the category of "music." To hear them as identifiably foreign sounds, however, takes us a step further, leaning heavily on the shared instrumentation of war—particularly naval warfare and piracy on the Mediterranean. In this chapter, I trace a fascinating seam of archival sources documenting the presence of enslaved, ethnically marked musicians performing on the

---

[1] Andreini, *La Sultana*, IV, i.

galleys in Livorno, both for their enslaved and convict fellows and for the Florentine elite. These sources resonate with Maria Alberti's work on the 1589 *naufragia* and with Nathan Reeves's work on the use of music on the Neapolitan galleys; Reeves has documented the "ubiquitous" presence of drums and trumpets and has traced several of the enslaved and convict instrumentalists whose labor most often produced the military signals exchanged by the galleys with other craft, forts, and ports and the drumbeat that served as the "means of entrainment," "that which kept *galleotti* rowing to a singular rhythm."[2] To understand the "instruments of the maritime war" (the *strumenti da guerra marattima*; the term comes from Francesco Settimanni's diary of 1589) as integral to the complex infrastructure of Mediterranean slavery and political power is to articulate the signification of musical noise (particularly "trumpets, drums, pipes, nackers," and "artillery pieces") as a soundtrack for cultural contact and alterity, on- and offstage.[3]

In April 1624, the Medici court visited Livorno, and Grand Duke Ferdinando II—as was typical—took the opportunity to inspect the galleys. In addition to tips for the marine guards, the enslaved laborers of the caravan, and the *biscotteria*,[4] the accounts record an intriguing payment to "Carzio, master of the Turkish music, and his companions, of whom there are twenty-seven in total."[5] Twenty-seven is a large ensemble by any standard, and such inflated numbers are infrequent. For purposes of comparison, the court trumpets during this period averaged six players and the *tamburi* more typically four. In February 1627, however, on a similar visit to Livorno, "the Turkish drummers and trumpeters" were paid a "half scudo each," for a total of nine scudi; there were thus eighteen players.[6] On that same visit, "certain instrumentalists who played wind instruments" were tipped a (single) scudo

---

[2] Nathan Reeves, "The Oar, the Trumpet, the Drum: Music and Galley Servitude in Spanish Naples," 2018.

[3] "[T]rombe, tamburi, pive, nacchere, ed altri strumenti da guerra marittima, con sparare molti pezzi d'artiglieria." From Francesco Settimanni, "Diario," I-Fas, Ms. 130, c. 147, as cited in Alberti, "Battaglie navali," 21.

[4] The *biscotteria*, staffed by enslaved labor, produced enormous quantities of hard ship's biscuit which served as the primary foodstuff for those at sea on the galleys and those in the *bagno*. For more details, see Lucia Frattarelli Fischer, "Il bagno delle galere in 'Terra cristiana,'" *Nuovi Studi Livornesi* 8 (2000): 69–94.

[5] "A Carzio m'ro della musica turchesca, e suoi compagni che sono in tutto ventisette, et a otto guardie di Marinari mezzo scudo per ciascuno disse il Signor Cavaliere Gio: Cosimo 17.3.10.-." I-Fas, Camera del Granduca, f. 5, 28v.

[6] "Alli Tamburini e trombetti Tucheschi per mancia mezzo scudo per ciascuno 9.-." I-Fas, Camera del Granduca, f. 7, 17v.

to be shared among them.[7] The following month, "the Turks who sang and carried the wood so that the Galley would be well supplied" were tipped one scudo (to share), and "the nineteen Turkish musicians who played when the Galley was launched" netted a total of nine scudi, three lire, and ten soldi (once again, a half scudo each).[8]

This is a particularly dense flurry of activity, though citations of "la musica turchesca," "i Turchi della Tuba, e Trombetti" or "la musica delle Galere" from 1636, 1637, 1640, 1654, and 1665 strongly imply that the presence of such ensembles was ongoing, even when not mentioned in the granducal accounts.[9] Indeed, almost every year musicians (*trombe, tamburi*, occasionally *sonatori*) are recognized in Livorno, though without racial or ethnic modifiers that would confirm the participation of enslaved or foreign musicians. On one occasion, in January 1630, the instrumentalists (*sonatori*) of an English ship were tipped twenty-four lire.[10]

While we should assume that granducal visitations involved a greater degree of pomp and spectacle than was habitual in the absence of elite guests, these sources suggest that the Livorno *bagno* had a standing ensemble involving a considerable number of participants. We can infer that music of some kind was regularly used to accompany the hard labor of galley life: loading ships, carting heavy materials, rowing at oar. This music could be sung or played and was regularly performed by "Turkish" musicians or in a "Turkish" style. The rather indeterminate meanings of this term notwithstanding, here it seems to indicate musical sounds that are recognizably non-European, either Middle Eastern or North African. These musicians likely sounded "Ottoman" to early modern Italians, who saw the Ottomans as their primary adversaries in the region.

The instrumental makeup of the large ensemble is never listed, though at various times the sources mention *tamburi, trombetti, istrumenti di fiato*, and in one instance a *tuba*. Contemporary images of enslaved musicians in Livorno provide a suggestive complement to these scant descriptions. The *Figure con istrumenti musicali e boscherecci* was published by the Florentine

---

[7] "A Certi suonatori, che sonarono istrumenti di fiato uno scudo." I-Fas, Camera del Granduca, f. 7, 17r.

[8] "Alli Turchi che cantavano, e portavano il legnio che la Galera era fornita uno scudo disse S.r Gio: Cosimo," and "A Diciannove Musici Turcheschi che sonorno quando li varo' la Galera 9.3.10.-." I-Fas, Camera del Granduca, f. 7, 19r and 19v (respectively).

[9] I-Fas, Camera del Granduca, f. 17 (1635–1636), c. 35r; f. 18 (1636–1637), c. 38r; f. 21 (1639–1640), c. 32r; f. 25 (1653–1654), c. 18v; f. 34 (1664–1665), c. 92r.

[10] "Ai sonatori d'un vascello Inglese ventiquattro lire, 3.3.-.-." I-Fas, Camera del Granduca f. 11, c. 24v.

Figure 4.1. Giovanni Battista Bracelli, from *Figure con istrumenti musicali e boscherecci* (published ca. 1630). This image shows "Turkish" musicians enslaved in the *bagno* in Livorno playing a kettledrum and a pair of cymbals (in Turkish, *zil*, pl. *ziller*). Rare Book and Special Collections Division of the Library of Congress, Washington, D.C. Used with permission.

artist Giovanni Battista Bracelli around 1630; his one previous publication, the *Bizarrie di varie figure* (1624), was dedicated to Don Pietro de' Medici, then governor of Livorno. The *Figure* includes three etchings of exoticized instrumentalists, who almost certainly represent inhabitants of the Livorno *bagno* (see Figures 4.1, 4.2 and 4.3).[11] Bracelli studied in Florence under the more famous Jacopo da Empoli, whose school—according to the late-seventeenth-century art historian Filippo Baldinucci—was full of "young men enthusiastically drawing from nature."[12] From 1619 until 1623, Bracelli resided in Livorno, where he assisted Jacopo with decorations for the

---

[11] I thank Lucia Frattarelli Fischer for introducing me to these images.
[12] As cited in Sue Welsh Reed, *Giovanni Battista Braccelli: Bizzarie di Varie Figure (Livorno, 1624)* (Evansville, IN: Octavo, 2000), 2.

Figure 4.2. Giovanni Battista Bracelli, from *Figure con istrumenti musicali e boscherecci* (published ca. 1630). This image shows "Turkish" musicians enslaved in the *bagno* in Livorno playing a plucked lute, known generically in Turkish as a *saz*, and a bowed spike fiddle or *kemane* (in Arabic, *rabab*), each of which has two visible pegs for tuning the strings. Rare Book and Special Collections Division of the Library of Congress, Washington, D.C. Used with permission.

cathedral and would have had many opportunities to observe and sketch the inhabitants of the granducal *bagno*.[13]

The musicians in Bracelli's images wear the rough uniforms distributed to the *bagno*'s inhabitants, open at the collar and belted around the middle with cloth. Where visible, their hair is shaved into the *ciuffo* that was imposed during enslavement; others wear the *berettino*: "the granducal slaves were shaved, with the exception of a hank of hair in the center of their heads; they wore shirts, linen trousers, small caps of red wool and rough jackets."[14]

---

[13] Reed, *Giovan Battista Braccelli*, 2.
[14] "[G]li schiavi del granduca, rapati con l'eccezione di un ciuffetto nel centro della testa, vestivano camicie, calzoni lini, berrettini di lana rossi e giubba di panno di Empoli." Frattarelli Fischer, "Il bagno," 71.

"TURKISH MUSIC" IN ITALY   109

Figure 4.3. Giovanni Battista Bracelli, from *Figure con istrumenti musicali e boscherecci* (published ca. 1630). This image shows "Turkish" musicians enslaved in the *bagno* in Livorno playing the nackers or *naccare* (small kettledrums played in pairs; in Turkish, *nekkare*) and a reed instrument, presumably the Turkish *zurna*, though possibly the (European) shawm which was similar in construction. Rare Book and Special Collections Division of the Library of Congress, Washington, D.C. Used with permission.

In Figure 4.2, the men wear leg irons. The instruments are depicted with a degree of detail that suggests an attempt at ethnographic accuracy; consider, for example, the two differently and distinctively shaped drumsticks used by the kettledrummer in Figure 4.1, which records a traditional Middle Eastern and Asian performance practice still in use today. These images show "Turkish" slaves playing a kettledrum and a pair of cymbals (in Turkish, *zil*, pl. *ziller*); a plucked lute, known generically in Turkish as a *saz*, as well as a bowed spike fiddle or *kemane* (in Arabic, *rabab*), each of which has two visible pegs for tuning the strings; and finally, the nackers or *naccare* (small kettledrums played in pairs; in Turkish, *nekkare*), mentioned earlier in relation to the *indiani* of 1616, as well as a reed instrument, presumably the Turkish *zurna*, though possibly the (European) shawm, which was similar in construction.[15]

The instrumentalists in Bracelli's prints are not necessarily the same musicians who played on or in tandem with the hard labor of the galleys; however, they testify to a sonic, musical presence in the city. Indeed, enslaved workers and *forzati* were a common sight on the streets of Livorno. A description of the city published by the English traveler John Evelyn in 1644 is noisily evocative: "Here, especially in this *piazza*, is such a concourse of slaves, Turks, Moors, and other nations, that the number and confusion is prodigious; some buying, others selling, others drinking, others playing, some working, others sleeping, fighting, *singing* [my emphasis], weeping, all nearly naked, and miserably chained."[16] Particularly during the winter months, when the Livorno galleys and the enslaved laborers and convicts who powered their movement were confined to the city, many of the enslaved circulated widely within the town, their leg irons, haircuts, uniforms, and racialized features considered sufficient to prevent escape. Indeed, as Lucia Frattarelli Fischer makes evident, "to put on the cassock of the slave did not signify isolation from urban society, in fact, contact with the city [of Livorno] appears to have been continuous and constant."[17] During daylight hours, enslaved laborers and convicts who were not otherwise occupied were permitted to roam the city and to engage in small businesses, trades, or errands in return for money. As previously cited, Stephanie Nadalo writes that "slaves in Livorno were employed as barbers and vendors of water, wine, tobacco, and used clothing within and near the *bagno*."[18] In rare cases, enterprising individuals earned enough to purchase their freedom; even small quantities of money could ease life in the *bagno* through the purchase of extra food or other creature comforts.

Reeves, in his discussion of music and the Neapolitan galleys, cites several descriptions of enslaved musicians, including one account by Jean-Jacques Bouchard, a Frenchman who visited Naples during Holy Week in 1632 and described a church where "a band of *cornetti* and shawms played by galley slaves, who perform whenever a nobleman or lady of quality enters or leaves

---

[15] I thank Jonathan Shannon for his expertise about these instruments.
[16] Evelyn's diary was published in 1901 and is now available online through Project Gutenberg. William Bray, ed., *The Diary of John Evelyn, Edited from the Original MSS by William Bray* (Washington, DC: M. Walter Dunne, 1901), 88–89.
[17] "[I]ndossare la casacca dello schiavo non significava poi l'isolamento dalla società urbana, anzi il contatto con la città appare continuo e costante." Frattarelli Fischer, "Il bagno," 83.
[18] Nadalo, "Negotiating Slavery," 296.

[the church] and also at the elevation of the Host," which was "pleasing to hear."[19] Similar—musical—activities may well have taken place in Livorno as a means of earning coin or as part of quotidian life (recall the "singing" listed in Evelyn's catalogue of noises). The "musica turchesca" of the Livorno galleys demonstrates the many opportunities that Italian citizens would have had to hear the music of "Others," not only elite Florentines and other less-elevated members of the court who would have visited the galleys in the train of the Grand Duke's official viewings but merchants, visitors to Livorno, and military personnel of various ranks and social levels who were regularly stationed on the galleys or at the fort. "European" military drummers and trumpeters would have had ample opportunity to absorb "Turkish" musical sounds, in close quarters and over many months of any given campaign.

With Livorno's *musica turchesca* ringing in our ears, I want to revisit the "sound of Trumpets, of Drums, and of other Barbarous instruments" that announced the arrival of the foreign armies with such *strepitoso* flair in the 1616 horse ballet *Guerra d'amore* (discussed in the previous chapter),[20] and the "sounds" of "trumpets and drums" called out in Andreini's stage directions above. Where brass and percussion and the other instruments of the "guerra marittima" perform dramatic functions, particularly in relationship to exotic or othered characters, we need to assume that the sounds produced could invoke the sounds of foreign others—even if these sounds were also largely familiar. Indeed, in several instances, it is clear that the Medici drew upon the sonic drama of their "Turkish" musicians in explicitly performative contexts.

Consider the staged naval battle that famously entertained audiences in Florence during the wedding festivities for Ferdinando I de' Medici and Christine of Lorraine in 1589. One of the more spectacular enactments of a perennial crowd favorite (an epic battle between Islam and Christianity), this particular performance is preserved in several detailed descriptions (as well as frequently reproduced images; see, for example, Figure 4.4). The courtyard of the Pitti Palace was flooded for the occasion, and awed spectators watched the show from the internal balconies. Alberti has traced specific galley slaves and convicts who were brought from Livorno in order to row the boats:

---

[19] Jean-Jacques Bouchard, *Journal*, Vol. II, 184, cited in Reeves, "The Oar," 12.
[20] *Guerra d'amore*, 29.

Figure 4.4. Orazio Scarabelli after Bernardo Buontalenti (Bernardo delle Girandole), *Naumachia in the Court of Palazzo Pitti*, from an album with plates documenting the festivities of the 1589 wedding of Ferdinando I de' Medici and Christine of Lorraine. Purchased by the Harris Brisbane Dick Fund, 1931. Metropolitan Museum of Art, New York. 31.72.5(11). Used with permission.

The soldiers and rowers of the Palazzo Pitti naval battle thus came from the most diverse coastal and inland locations of the Mediteranean, there included the territories of the Ottoman Empire, just as normally happened in each of the crews in every fleet. . . . In this case the ethnic promiscuity conferred greater spontaneity and realism on the performance, since, in the middle of the combat "one heard those who were injured shout in Turkish [Turchesco], as they fell into the water."[21]

Alberti cites from the contemporary diary of Giuseppe Pavoni. In the words of another diarist, Francesco Settimanni, in order to attend the naval performance, the audience members—who had been dining inside the Pitti Palace, at some distance from the windows—were called back from their dinner by "trumpets, drums, pipes, nackers, and other instruments of the marine war, with the sound of many pieces of artillery, and at that noise, the Princes abandoned their meal."[22]

The hyperrealism of this scene is embedded in sounds (the Turchesco language, the instruments of the maritime war, and gunfire) and in the visible, physical, and aural presence of enslaved bodies. To presume that the musical noises of this melee were exclusively "European" seems wantonly deaf to contemporary circumstances.

Further documents from 1608 reveal a similar use of enslaved foreigners for dramatic "realness," this time with specific reference to musicalized sound. Two newly discovered letters, shared with me by Francesca Fantappiè, relate to the transportation from Livorno to Florence of thirty-two trumpeters, enslaved and *forzati* (convicts), to serve in the "battaglia" that was staged for the dynastic wedding celebrations of Prince Cosimo (later Cosimo II). On October 22, Ugolino Baritoli wrote to Francesco Paulsanti, secretary to the Grand Duke:

> I am sending 32 trumpeters, there not being any others in the *bagno* at this point, to serve on the same occasion, I am also sending 38 slaves [awaiting]

---

[21] "I combattenti e i rematori della battaglia navale di palazzo Pitti provenivano quindi dalle più diverse località costiere e insulari del mediterraneo, compresi i territori dell'Impero ottomano, proprio come normalmente avveniva in tutti gli equipaggi di tutte le flotte. . . . In questo caso la promiscuità etnica contribuiva a conferire maggiore vivacità e realismo allo spettacolo, dal momento che, nel mezzo del combattimento 'si sentiva gridare in Turchesco quelli che erano feriti, e quelli cascavano in acqua.'" Alberti, "Battaglie navali," 23–24. The Pavoni citation comes from p. 41 of the original.

[22] "[T]rombe, tamburi, pive, nacchere, ed altri strumenti da guerra marittima, con sparare molti pezzi d'artiglieria, al qual rumore i Principi abbandonarono la colazione." From Francesco Settimanni, "Diario," I-Fas, c. 147, Manoscritti, 130, as cited in Alberti, "Battaglie navali," 21.

ransom, there not being any greater number that could be sent at the present time. The Captain of this endeavor will be <u>Consalvo Aurino Reale</u>, a very diligent man, <u>to whom have been assigned 48 sailors</u> who will serve as guard and accompaniment and if necessary, they too can be of service in the battle.[23]

Paolo Vinta noted receipt of the letter, specifying that Cosimo Latini was to be responsible for "the enslaved and convict trumpeters [*trombetti schiavi et forzati*] and of the 38 slaves sent to serve on the Galley," for whom Florentine lodging had to be found, somewhere secure.[24] A second letter, from October 27, notes that the "stiavi forzati trombetti" were put in the prison (Le Stinche) because of the "better security and capacity of the place" when compared with the fort.[25]

These letters make explicit that the trumpeters in the Livorno *bagno* and on the galleys were drawn from enslaved and convict populations and, that in 1608, thirty-two of them were considered competent enough to perform in front of the gathered dignitaries and elite guests of a Medici wedding. Once again, these performers demonstrate the access that Italian audiences would have had to such sounds. As literal examples of performance, these sounds are caught up with the racialized and ethnically marked bodies of the "Other" in ways that illuminate more traditionally theatrical representations.

In closing, I want to return to Andreini's *La Sultana* and specifically to the musical performance of the Black slaves from the latter half of the scene mentioned earlier. The Moors (enslaved Black retainers of the Turkish sultan, who is himself disguised as a Persian ambassador) are described as playing the *cennamela* (pipes or bagpipes) and two drums held up on camelback. The specificity of the number (two) makes this a clear reference to nackers. By the final refrain, cymbals have been added. The instruments that these singing

---

[23] "Si <u>mandano 32 Trombetti</u> non se ne sendo più nel bagnio al preposito per servirsi in simili occasione, si mandano <u>anchora 38 schiavi di ricatto</u>, non ve ne sendo maggiori quantità da poter mandare al presente. Capo di questa Condotta sarà <u>Consalvo Aurino Reale</u> homo molto diligente al quale <u>li s'è conseg*n*ato 48 marinari</u> li quali serviranno per Guardia et accompag*n*amento et se occorrerà potranno ancho servire a qualcosa nella battaglia." Underscores in the original. I-Fas, Guardaroba medicea, f. 245, c. 100r.

[24] "Cosimo Latini riceva et dia ricapito a questi trombetti schiavi et forzati et alli schiavi no. 38 mandati per servitio della Galleria quali deveno restare a Firenze et gli sorregga di alloggiamento et di spese o alla Fortezza o Zecca Vecchia et in somma in luogo dove possino stare sicuri." I-Fas, Guardaroba medicea, f. 245, c. 100r.

[25] "Mandai alle Stinche per più sicurtà e meglio capacità di luogho li no. 32 stiavi forzati trombetti, e li stiavi turchi li ò messi tra gli altri." I-Fas, Guardaroba medicea, f. 245, c. 101r.

slaves carry and play directly cite the *musica turchesca* instrumentation of the Livornese sources, including those engraved in Bracelli's images.

PARSENIO	[...] che diavolo è quello, che quì viene? Per mia fè sono duo camelli, e sopra vi sono duo mori e duo altri neri li conducono, ò uno d'essi vuol sonare una cennamela, l'altro duo timpani cola sopra stando, ò quanti fanciulli seguitano.	[...] what the hell is this thing which now comes? By my faith, it is two camels, and riding them are two Moors and two other Black men leading them. Oh, one of them wants to play the pipes, the other has two drums up there [on the camel] with him. Oh, see how many children are following them!
	Qui s'udiranno i nominati, & i putti gridar tal volta, viva i mori, viva i mori; poi usciranno.	*At this point everyone mentioned will be heard and the children should shout several times, "Long live the Moors! Long live the Moors!" then leave.*
MORO I	Napoli bello tutto pien di fiori Vengon di Persia per vederti i Mori.	[*sings*] Beautiful Naples, full of flowers The Moors have come from Persia to see you.
	Qui faranno le riprese con cennamelle, e timpani.	*Here they play the refrain on pipes and drums.*
MORO II	Benche Mori noi siamo del Persiano, In Napoli parliamo ancor toscano.	Although we are Moors from the Persian Gulf, In Naples we still speak Tuscan [Italian].
	Qui fanno le riprese simili alle prime.	*Here they play the refrain, similar to the first time.*
MORO I	Questi Camelli ogn'hora cavalchiamo Che de l'Ambasciador i Cuochi siamo.	We always ride these camels For we are the Ambassador's cooks.
	Qui fanno le solite riprese.	*Here they do the usual refrain.*
MORO II	E quì le masserie d'argento, e d'oro De la Cucina custodisce il Moro.	And here is the silver and gold crockery Of the kitchen, which the Moor protects.
	Qui fanno l'istesse riprese, e di più li duo mori, che conducono i camelli havranno un cimbalo per uno da suonare.[26]	*Here they do the same refrain, and furthermore, the two Moors leading the camels have a cymbal each to play.*

Even in the absence of musical notation, the structure of the song is clear: four strophes are parsed out between two alternating soloists, each separated by a ritornello. Given that each of the eight lines of song has a standard eleven syllables, the music for each verse may well have been improvised over stock chord progressions. We can note that no bass instrument is mentioned; the verses

---

[26] Andreini, *La Sultana*, IV, I.

may have been sung unaccompanied or over a drone (from the *cennamela*). The singers—who joke about their command of the Italian language—could have imitated ornaments or vocal timbres associated with Turkish song.

As with the mock naval battle discussed above, to assume that this music was performed "straight"—with "little or no echo" of Turkish music—requires a willfully obtuse reading of the sources. The musical noises of each of these performances (including the *musica turchesca*, the thirty-two *trombetti schiavi forzati*, and the singing slaves of Andreini's *La Sultana*) disrupt an ingrained set of assumptions about musical notation and cultural difference that has shaped histories of instrumental musics. It is worth reiterating the standard narrative of orchestral *alla turca*—that is, the use in Western art music of timbres and musical figures drawn from janissary music in order to represent Ottoman aggression or the "East": the phenomenon of notated *alla turca* is largely limited to the eighteenth century and is repeatedly treated as a precursor to the full-blown (musical) exoticisms of nineteenth-century opera. The eighteenth-century fashion for operatic and instrumental music *alla turca* consolidates the narrative of its purported newness and thus its absence from earlier periods and repertoires. The *New Grove* entry on janissary music begins: "The Turkish ensemble of wind and percussion instruments known in the Ottoman Empire as *mehter*, introduced into Europe in the 17th century and later imitated there using Western instruments." Mary Hunter elaborates:

> Although travelers' descriptions of Turkish music begin long before 1700, they continue in profusion during the eighteenth century, and the many musical treatises of the time also routinely mention Turkish musical devices or practices. Janissary (i.e. Turkish military) bands were among the principal agents of cultural exchange; they played quite frequently in Europe from the early eighteenth century on and were found in a number of European courts after the Polish and Russian monarchs had ordered them in the 1720s. European imitations of these bands were commonplace by the second half of the century, and the *alla turca* style or topos, as it is normally understood, is based principally on janissary music.[27]

Yet the Livornese *musica turchesca* was an integral part of the port city's soundscape, long before the "early eighteenth century," and the sounds of

---

[27] Mary Hunter, "The *Alla Turca* Style in the Late Eighteenth Century: Race and Gender in the Symphony and the Seraglio," in *The Exotic in Western Music*, ed. Jonathan Bellman (Boston: Northeastern University Press, 1998), 43.

the cymbals, *cennamela*, and nackers in Andreini's *La Sultana* are enough to categorize this music as *alla turca*, though the play's publication predates the purported emergence of the phenomenon by more than a century. It is my contention that Italian musicians (and audiences) were conversant with a range of ways in which performance could be inflected in order to sound foreign—including an explicit range of *alla turca* gestures *avant la lettre*. The familiarity of the *musica turchesca* suggests as well that other ornamental, melodic, timbral, rhythmic, or accompanimental elements could have been added to notated repertoires or improvised as necessary in order to signify sonic difference. Such inflections are highly unlikely to show up in notation. Rather, evidence for such sounds is more likely to emerge when we consider un-notated repertoires, such as military musics, performed sound effects and atmospheric musical sound (including trumpets and drums), civic and courtly brass, wind, and percussion ensembles, and popular, formally repetitious musics, such as strophic verse settings and dance music, where the repetitions themselves facilitate the use of differentiated ornaments.

In this equation, the question of ethnographic accuracy or "authenticity" is not completely irrelevant. With regard to *La Sultana*, excerpted above, it is worth repeating that the playwright's father—Francesco Andreini—reputedly spent eight years of an early military career enslaved to the Turks before returning to Italy and giving up his sword for the stage. Giovan Battista trained under Francesco, although there is no guarantee that long familiarity with Ottoman culture translated into "authentic" representation. The first-degree relationship to slavery, the Turks, and the "East," however, is an important reminder of the co-presence of the Other within Europe. For many early modern Italian residents, knowledge of the Ottoman East was close to hand and often personal.

The common critique of musical exoticisms as a failure of authenticity—that the conventions of exotic musical difference "were arrived at less by direct borrowing than by developing (or distorting or even suppressing) pre-existing elements"[28] of the Western musical language—implies that a more accurate portrayal would be somehow more valuable. But if, as Matthew Head notes, "music's signs for the Other are most often constituted by materials already existing within European music,"[29] it might be more useful to consider this as indicative of an Other that was always already present, always already

---

[28] Wright, "Turning a Deaf Ear," 148.
[29] Matthew Head, "Musicology on Safari: Orientalism and the Spectre of Postcolonial Theory," *Music Analysis* 22, nos. 1–2 (2003): 224.

European. I am reminded of Judith Butler's argument that the concepts of "sex" and "gender" cannot be separated, because there is no idyllic, pre-linguistic, pre-cultural space in which sex exists a priori and unmarked.[30] Similarly, there is no monolithic European music (or even a "Europe") that exists prior to contact with the Other. Early modern Italy was inhabited by Syrian refugees, Turks, Jews, Black Africans, and their descendants. The immigration and assimilation problems they faced then were different from the ones active now, but the Italy of the seventeenth century was far from the unified (white) monoculture that regularly appears in the political imagination. Listening for the racialized sounds of early modern performance helps to dismantle that same phantasmically white, innocent, and pure "Europe" as it has populated musicological fantasies of the past.

In this chapter, I have demonstrated the fluency with which the racialized, ethnic, and political meanings of "foreign" sounds could be re-cited in performance. If anything, a lack of notation suggests a coherent idea of what such music should sound like, so self-evident that musicians could be relied upon to produce the appropriate noises with the minimum amount of instruction. To say so is to apply the logic of historically informed performance and "authentic" performance practice to the performance of non-Western repertoires of sound.[31] The *musica turchesca* of the Livorno *bagno* disrupts histories of listening that remain overly reliant on notated music and on rigid teleologies that presume a continual development of increased knowledge, integration, and cultural contact that through a logical extrapolation is projected backward to configure the past as always less accurate than the times that came afterward. In the un-notated stage musics of trumpet, winds, and percussion, we can recognize a range of sounds that were potentially "Other," familiar and yet terrifying, quotidian and yet significant.

In the next chapter, I discuss a related phenomenon. Rather than ensembles of (enslaved) foreign-born musicians playing identifiably foreign-sounding music for Italian auditors, or the imitation of such sounds in musical-theatrical performances, I turn to the presence of racially marked, foreign-born, and/or enslaved musicians within court ensembles (presumably playing music that was aurally identified with European conventions); that such musicians were frequently associated with the military instruments of trumpet and drum indicates a slippery if persistent codependence.

---

[30] Judith Butler, *Gender Trouble: Feminism and the Subversion of Identity* (New York: Routledge, 1990).

[31] Stanley Boorman, "The Musical Text," in *Rethinking Music*, ed. Nicholas Cook and Mark Everist (Oxford: Oxford University Press, 1999), 403–423.

A un povero vecchio che haveva la moglie, e figluolo stiavi sei giuli -.4.-.

For a poor old man whose wife and son are enslaved, six giuli [equivalent to 4 lire].

        I-Fas, Camera del Granduca, f. 6, June 1625, c. 31r

Scene 5
Trumpets and Drums Played by Enslaved Musicians

In this chapter, I directly take up an association between musical performers and (visibly) foreign bodies that has been regularly attested in more general work on Black Africans and enslaved retainers in early modern Europe.[1] Kate Lowe, for example, has argued that many enslaved Africans in Italy worked at trades and occupations in which they had already been trained prior to their enslavement, with specific reference to the large number of Black court musicians.[2] Joaneath Spicer makes a similar point, suggesting that "Black salaried court entertainers were often musicians, usually their occupation before manumission."[3] The use of the term "musician" in this context refers almost exclusively to trumpeters and drummers. Writing about Black court musicians in Germany, Arne Spohr has argued that "The history of black people in early modern Germany is inseparable from that of the princely court and its music."[4] Working with a database of "380 black court servants present at German courts between the late sixteenth century and ca. 1800," Spohr has identified "ten court trumpeters, twenty-one kettledrummers, and nearly one hundred military pipers and drummers ('Tambours') at the courts of German-speaking states."[5] He argues that this statistically extraordinary correlation—more than one-third—reflects an aural dimension of what has been understood as a (primarily visual) iconography, whereby the dark skin of Black court servants represents "their patrons' far-reaching trade connections . . . and thus their economic power."[6]

---

[1] The topic of Black musicians warrants an entire subheading in the Italian section of Bindman and Gates, *Image of the Black*; See Paul Kaplan's essay on Italy in Vol. 3, Part 1, specifically 122–126.
[2] Kate Lowe, "The Stereotyping of Black Africans in Renaissance Europe," in *Black Africans in Renaissance Europe*, ed. T. F. Earle and K. J. P. Lowe (Cambridge: Cambridge University Press, 2005), 19, 32–41.
[3] Joaneath Spicer, ed. *Revealing the African Presence in Renaissance Europe* (Baltimore: Walters Art Museum, 2012), 87.
[4] Spohr, "'Mohr und Tropeter,'" 614.
[5] Spohr, "'Mohr und Trompeter,'" 614.
[6] Spohr, "'Mohr und Trompeter,'" 622.

Tightly linked to civic power, military exercises, and the galleys of the Mediterranean littoral, the noises made by brass and percussion served to announce and to signal, to communicate information and coordinate movements. Such sounds could be familiar or strange, reassuring or threatening, local or foreign. Largely un-notated, these repertoires were passed down by an apprenticeship system, learned by rote, or improvised according to formulas. Only in the seventeenth century were the first trumpet treatises written. In 1614, the Veronese trumpeter Cesare Bendinelli, who spent most of his professional life at courts in Vienna and Munich, dedicated his manuscript text *Tutta l'arte della trombetta* ("The Complete Art of Playing the Trumpet") to the Accademia Filarmonica of his native town.[7] In 1638, the Florence-based, Spoleto-born trumpet virtuoso Girolamo Fantini (known in Medici court documents as Girolamo Trombetto) published his *Modo per imparare a sonare la tromba tanto in guerra quanto musicalmente* ("Method to Learn to Play the Trumpet, Both in Battle and Musically").[8] For military and civic purposes, the Medici court and the city of Florence each kept ensembles of *trombe* (trumpets) and *tamburi* (drums); the aforementioned Fantini directed the court ensemble from 1630 or 1631 until his death after 1675. Trumpeters and drummers show up in the accounts of the Camera del Granduca with some frequency. Not least, these instrumentalists were regularly tipped at Christmas, at Ferragosto, and on the Grand Duke's birthday. Similar ensembles in Pisa and Livorno were recognized during state visits to those cities.

I concentrate on a series of archival sources from the 1630s that document the training of several ethnically marked (almost certainly enslaved) musicians who were incorporated into ensembles at the court; two were trained on trumpet by Fantini. Building on the previous chapter, in which I excavated both the familiarity of Florentine audiences with foreign musical sounds and the fluency with which military instruments could invoke or re-cite *alla turca* associations, here I consider the ways in which racialized

---

[7] Mario Bertoluzzi, "Bendinelli's *Entire Art of the Trumpet* of 1614: A Modern Edition" (DMA diss., University of Northern Colorado, 2002).

[8] Girolamo Fantini, *Modo per imparare a sonare di tromba (1638)*, ed. Ignio Conforzi (Bologna: Ut Orpehus Edizioni, 1998). See also Robert Douglas, "The First Trumpet Method: Girolamo Fantini's *Modo per Imparare a Sonare la Tromba* (1638)," *Journal of Band Research* 7, no. 2 (1971): 18–22; Igino Conforzi, "Girolamo Fantini 'monarca della tromba': Nuove acquisizioni biografiche," *Recercare* 2 (1990): 225–239; Igino Conforzi, "Girolamo Fantini, 'Monarch of the Trumpet': New Light on His Works," trans. Alexandra Amati-Camperi, *Historic Brass Society Journal* 6 (1994): 32–60; Peter Downey, "Fantini and Mersenne: Some Additions to Recent Controversies," *Historica Brass Society Journal* 6 (1994): 355–362.

bodies maintained a significant rapport with particular musical sounds. The various payments made by the Grand Duke to the musicians of the *musica turchesca* indicate an awareness of foreign sound that the Florentines may have explicitly worked to replicate within their own musical ensembles. The authoritative acoustic power of military signaling instruments invokes the pomp and implicit violence that the elaborately bedecked court slave reflects (visually) on his (or her) person.[9] It is to the "grain" of this association that I now turn.

In August 1633, Girolamo Fantini *detto* Trombetto was given five scudi to purchase "a trumpet [*tromba*] for the Morino who is learning to play."[10] The lessons must have gone reasonably well, for in September, the "Moro who plays the trumpet" received three testoni in order to purchase a belt, and a few days later, he was rewarded with a scudo. In July 1634, "the *Moro trombetto*" was paid a zecchino (equivalent to a scudo and three lire) for having "played in the chamber of His Highness [the Grand Duke]."[11] In August that same year, he received another zecchino on the Grand Duke's recommendation.[12] Also that August, "Brancone, Tromba, and Moro" were tipped one and a half scudi for having "all three sung together in harmony."[13] Here "Tromba" or "Moro" might reference the Black trumpeter; there were, however, several Black retainers within the Grand Duke's court at the time, and we cannot assume this individual to be the trumpeter under consideration based on a racial moniker alone.

From 1635 until at least 1640, the Grand Duke paid to train two *turchi* into specifically musical pursuits, supporting their studies with an allowance of five scudi a month (the rate is comparable with other student allowances):[14]

---

[9] Monica L. Miller, *Slaves to Fashion: Black Dandyism and the Styling of Black Diasporic Identity* (Durham, NC: Duke University Press, 2009); Jörg Jochen Berns, "Instrumental Sound and Ruling Spaces of Resonance in the Early Modern Period: On the Acoustic Setting of the Princely *Potestas* Claims within a Ceremonial Frame," trans. Benjamin Carter, in *Instruments in Art and Science: On the Architectonics of Cultural Boundaries in the 17th Century*, ed. Helmar Schramm, Ludger Schwarte, and Jan Lazardzig (Berlin: De Gruyter, 2008), 479–503.

[10] "A Girolamo Trombetto *per* una Tromba *per* il Morino che impara a sonare cinque scudi." I-Fas, Camera del Granduca, f. 14, 54r.

[11] "Al moro che sona la Tromba tre testoni *per* comprare un Brachiere"; "Al moro che sona la Tromba uno scudo disse SA"; "Al moro trombetto un *zecchino* sonò in camera di SA 1.3.-.-." I-Fas, Camera del Granduca, f. 14, 6r, 6v, 48v.

[12] "Al moro trombetto un *zecchino* disse SA." I-Fas, Camera del Granduca, f. 15, 6v.

[13] "A Brancone, Tromba e Moro che *tutti* tre cantorno in concerto 1.3.10.-." I-Fas, Camera del Granduca, f. 15, 51v.

[14] Rosoan and Solefar are on salary in I-Fas, Camera del Granduca, f. 17, 18, 19, 20, 21. I note that Conforzi considers Fantini's salary of ten scudi a month rather generous; however, he does not comment on whether the salary includes compensation for students; see Conforzi, "Girolamo Fantini 'monarca,'" 235.

Solefar Turco (occasionally written Turcho) was trained to "play the Trombetta," and "Rosoan Turco" was taught to dance and to fence; in one instance, Rosoan is described as studying dance "along with other skills [*virtù*]."[15] In November 1635, a *chitarra* ("guitar") was purchased on Rosoan's account, so evidently his musical education went somewhat beyond choreographic steps.[16] The association of swordplay and dance should not surprise: both draw on a shared repertoire of fancy footwork, physical dexterity, and rhythmic control.[17] Both disciplines also foreground a spectacularity of the body in performance—a physicality that is to be gazed at and admired by the audience. Though Rosoan played neither trumpet nor drum, his training in fencing links him (and his visible "Turkishness") tightly to the military. While Solefar's allowance was paid (without exception) directly to Fantini, Rosoan's went to a variety of different people (on one occasion only, he took possession of the money himself), although most frequently it was paid to his presumed teacher, Jacopo (or Jacopino) dell'Armaiolo (lit. "of the Armory"). Jacopo was both a fencer and a choreographer, and his *soprannome* confirms Rosoan's location among the weapons of war.[18]

Unfortunately, the Camera del Granduca accounts from 1640 to 1650 are missing, so it is not clear how long the education of Solefar and Rosoan continued beyond the five years for which documentation survives. Five years, however, is already a considerable apprenticeship, suggesting that the two *turchi* may have been relatively young when they arrived.[19] Solefar and Rosoan can perhaps be identified as "the two young Turks [*li due Turchetti*]" transported from Livorno to Florence in September 1635, precisely as their

---

[15] See I-Fas, Camera del Granduca, f. 21, 21r; these accounts cover the year 1639–1640. Özden Mercan has suggested (personal communication) that perhaps the presence of Sultan Yahya in Florence in 1634 had something to do with the cultivation of Solefar and Rosoan; however, Yahya was in Florence only very briefly in early 1634 (during February), and his pretensions to the throne were not taken very seriously at this time—unlike, for example, in 1609.

[16] I-Fas, Camera del Granduca, f. 17, c. 14v.

[17] On the relationship of dance and swordsmanship, see Kate van Orden, *Music, Discipline, and Arms in Early Modern France* (Chicago: University of Chicago Press, 2004).

[18] In 1621, Jacopo dell'Armaiolo was listed as fencing teacher to the Medici court pages. See Maria Pia Paoli, "Di madre in figlio: Per una storia dell'educazione alla corte dei Medici," *Annali di Storia di Firenze* 3 (2008): 139n16. In 1647, Jacopino dell'Armaiolo choreographed the dances for the first-known opera staged in Siena, presumably *La Datira*, under the patronage of Prince Mattias. See Coleen Reardon, *A Sociable Moment: Opera and Festive Culture in Baroque Siena* (Oxford: Oxford University Press, 2016), 13.

[19] The two Black African trumpeters discussed by Spohr each served a two-year apprenticeship, apparently the standard in Germany; see Spohr, "'Mohr und Trompeter.'"

names appear on the rolls of the Camera del Granduca.[20] Notably, within five months of Solefar's inscription into the court roll, both he and his teacher were rewarded by the Grand Duke, indicating that the student's progress was rapid (at least initially): "to Solefar Trombetto, two scudi, and to his teacher Girolamo, four scudi."[21] We do not know whether Solefar had studied the trumpet or knew how to play before September 1635, though presumably his aptitude, at least, was ascertained in advance.

The sources do suggest that Solefar's visible "Turkishness" was prized (above and beyond his *soprannome* "Turco"): in May 1636, Solefar Turco was paid a giulio (thirteen soldi and four denari) "to have his head shaved."[22] In other instances, court dwarves or Moors are paid to have their hair cut, but the verbs used in such instances are "farsi levare i cappelli" or "fare la barba," not "rapare" or shave, which instead is the verb consistently used to describe the shaved pates and distinctive *ciuffetto* of the enslaved denizens of the Livorno *bagno*. Solefar's hair confirms a racialization of his body, maintained through dress and grooming. He thus participates—like the "Moro trombetto" discussed above—in the audiovisual association of racialized bodies and the trumpet sound. The deliberate and continued association of enslaved court retainers with foreign, even exotic, dress was typical (in the second half of this book, I discuss several instances with regard to Black African individuals). Similarly, records from the *guardaroba* from 1601 describe pieces of white bombazine being given to "Maomet [Mohammad] and Abaman, Turkish slaves of His Most Serene Highness, so that they can make turbans for themselves."[23]

Jörg Jochen Berns has argued that early modern sovereignty relied on aurality as a means to manifest and sustain power: "inherent in such sound signs was a tendency towards expansion that *does not* stop at territorial boundaries but transgresses them."[24] To control sound is to fill up even the immaterial spaces between objects under one's dominion; it demonstrates power over a faculty (that of listening) largely understood

---

[20] While the *ruolo* itself survives for the previous year, the *spese straordinarie* do not. Thus, Solefar and Rosoan may have been paid from the Camera for some months previous to their official inscription on the payroll.

[21] "A Solefar Trombetto due scudi, et a Girolamo suo maestro quattro scudi tutto sei scudi." I-Fas, Camera del Granduca, f. 17, 23v.

[22] "A Solefar Turco p*er* farsi rapare un Giulio, -.-.13.4." I-Fas, Camera del Granduca, f. 17, 42r.

[23] "Sciugatoi d'ogni sorte di contro . . . alla turchesca bianchi di bambagino mandati a Maomet e Abraman turco stiavi di SAS per farsene turbanti." I-Fas, Guardaroba medicea, Libro di vestiri della Guardaroba, f. 235 (inv. 881), c. 44d. I thank Francesca Fantappiè for this reference.

[24] Berns, "Instrumental Sound," 500; emphasis in original.

as involuntary. In this system, Berns traces the presence of controlled sounds of various types, including the fake bird calls and obediently gurgling waters of the carefully groomed princely estate. Outside of the palace and during ceremonial events, trumpets and drums were instrumental (in both senses of the word) to European sovereignty: "the prince builds around himself an acoustic cocoon. This is largely produced by trumpets and drums."[25]

The ceremonial and civic functions of brass and percussion sound, in five-part chordal splendor, were a constant invocation of military power and the sovereign claim to force. Playing "militarily"—as it is called by Marin Mersenne (aptly, in a description of Fantini's celebrated virtuosity)—always already invokes a potential battle and thus an "Other" who is to be defeated, subdued, or brought into line.[26] To produce these sounds from the body of the racially and visibly marked "Other" is thus to proclaim (and the choice of verb here is deliberate) that the battle has already been won. The "Other" has already been subdued; indeed, his docile (though potentially ferocious) body has already bent to the task of enforcing the law of the sovereign, as heard in the ceremonial trumpet sound. Thus, the race of the performer is anything but incidental. The persistent, sticky association of racialized bodies and military music inscribes a violence into and onto the body and the subjectivity of the body which gives voice—sounds the trumpet—to the direct will of the sovereign. The racialization of the Turkish or Moorish trumpeter as a subject who emits sound is not merely visible but also audible. The racially marked trumpeter performs (quite literally) his enslavement—in the implicit violence of battle and his subjection to foreign power.

Such sound signals re-cite or transpose the Blackness and racialized appearance of court servants as they appear in early modern portraiture and in art history. Importantly, however, the sources cited above regarding both Solefar and the "Moro trombetto" indicate that their education under Fantini transgressed the military repertoire of civic and courtly ceremonial to include the newer "musical" repertoire for which Fantini was renowned. Consider that, on at least one occasion, the "Moro trombetto" played in the Grand Duke's chambers, an architectural specificity that suggests he was learning the more intimate and technically challenging repertoire foregrounded in

---

[25] Berns, "Instrumental Sound," 493. A more metaphorical analysis of the power of trumpets can be found in the first chapter of Sarah Finley, *Hearing Voices: Aurality and New Spanish Sound Culture in Sor Juana Inés de la Cruz* (Lincoln: University of Nebraska Press, 2019), 13–57.
[26] Downey, "Fantini and Mersenne."

Fantini's *Modo per imparare*. The payment to both Solefar and his teacher (from January 1636) suggests that he, too, was playing something worth listening to in a musical sense.

The dual adjectives of Fantini's book's title—explicitly labeled as a method for playing both in battle ("militarily") and musically—reflect the virtuoso's fame as an actual musician, at the forefront of a new practice of playing the trumpet in "concert with other instruments."[27] Fantini's textbook, written between 1634 and 1638, addresses both styles of playing, although the military style is given relatively short shrift, with the greater part of the book concentrated on chamber music for solo trumpet and basso continuo, along with several pieces for paired trumpet or for trumpet choir.

A comparison of the military signals and the musical pieces is illustrative. In "La Marciata,"[28] shown as Musical Example 5.1, all of the notes fall within the third octave of the trumpet's compass, where the notes facilitate an arpeggiation of the C chord, save a brief excursion in the penultimate phrase. The syllables underlaid beneath the notes are simultaneously a mnemonic aid for memorization and a means of articulation for tone and rhythm. "In the battle toccatas," explains Fantini, "there are words that say *da ton della*, *atta non tano*, and *attanallo*, which mean 'saddle up' [*buttasella*, lit. "throw yourself into the saddle"],[29] 'to ride' [*cavalcare*], and 'to horse' [*a cavallo*], and *tin ta* means 'everyone' [*tutti*]; they are pronounced in this manner because, with the trumpet they are better preferred, and are rendered easier to articulate with the tongue, which is the true way to play."[30] The seemingly nonsense text of the "Marciata" thus takes on a very specific meaning: "everybody ride, to ride, to ride; everybody, everybody ride, to ride, to ride." The aggregating structure of the call builds on the initial rhythmic (and minimally melodic) cell, repeating it with ornamental differences and rhythmic extensions, building into the higher register and culminating in a brief moment of virtuosic passagework in the penultimate phrase before cascading downward to a reprise of the opening motif.

---

[27] Fantini, *Modo*, xvi.

[28] Florio defines *Marchiare* not only in terms of military or unified movement but also in terms of its aural component: "to march in order by sound of drum."

[29] Florio defines the *Butta in sella* as "a charge that trumpeters sound as a warning to take horse."

[30] "Nelle toccate di Guerra vi sono parole che dicono *da ton della*, *atta non tano*, e *attanallo*, voglion dire buttasella, a cavalcare, e a cavallo, et il *tin ta* vuol dire tutti; si son dettate in questa maniera, perché con la Tromba si proferiscono meglio, e si rendono più facili a punteggiarle con la lingua, quale è il vero modo di sonare." Fantini, *Modo*, xvi.

Musical Example 5.1. Girolamo Fantini, "La Marciata," from *Modo per imparare a sonare la tromba tanto in guerra quanto musicalmente* (published 1638).

In performance, the notated melody could be readily converted into an ensemble piece for five-part trumpet choir. Mario Bertoluzzi, paraphrasing Bendinelli, provides a clear explanation:

> Each of the five players enters one at a time, from lowest to highest. The first to begin is the *Grosso* player, who plays the rhythm of the entire piece on the tonic note. The next to enter was the *Vulgano* player, who, like the *Grosso*, plays the rhythm of the entire piece, but at the fifth, or *Vulgano* pitch level. The third player to enter is the *Altebasso*, who copies the rhythm and melodic shape of the *Principale*, though one harmonic lower. The fourth player to enter is the *Principale*, the only person in the ensemble to play the Sonata as written. The fifth and last to enter is the *Clarino* player, who improvised in the uppermost register of the trumpet spanning the eighth through the twelfth partials.[31]

Bertoluzzi uses the standard terms for the register of the instrument: *grosso*, *vulgano*, and so on. Fantini's particular skill lay in the "clarino" register, or the fourth octave of the trumpet, where the diminishing intervals of the harmonic series permit a close approximation of the Western major scale (see Figure 5.1, taken from Fantini's textbook, in which the notes of the harmonic series are mapped against the register names). It can be noted that while Bendinelli largely keeps his clarino writing within the lower fifth, Fantini exploits the whole octave.

With few exceptions (principally the toccatas and the military signals), each of the pieces in Fantini's collection is named in honor of a member of the Medici court—for example, the "Ricercata detta la Torrigiani," the "Baletto detto l'Albizi," the "Brando detto il Rucellai," even an "Esercizio di passaggi detto il Maffei."[32] The "First sonata for trumpet paired with the organ, named after Colloreto" is shown as Musical Example 5.2. To a certain degree, I chose this example at random, though I limited myself to those with basso continuo. The name, however, leaped out at me, since in July 1638—the same year in which Fantini's volume was published—the Grand Duke tipped a scudo "to the Morino of Sig. Marchese Colloredo who played the drum."[33] The same sheet of accounts rewards the court "drummers

---

[31] Bertoluzzi, "Bendinelli's *Entire Art*," 322–333.
[32] Fantini, *Modo*.
[33] "Al Morino del Signore Marchese Colloredo che sonò il tamburo uno 1.-.-.-." I-Fas, Camera del Granduca, f. 19, 50r. Conforzi notes that the name "Colloreto" is spelled "Colloredo" in "documenti fiorentini dell'epoca." See his editorial apparatus to Fantini, *Modo*, xiii.

Figure 5.1. Girolamo Fantini, illustration of the harmonic series, from *Modo per imparare a sonare la tromba tanto in guerra quanto musicalmente* (published 1638).

and trumpets who played for the birthday celebrations of His Highness."[34] This "Morino" can perhaps be identified as the young "Ametto fanciullo schiavo" (lit. Ametto, "young male-child slave"), who served the Colloreto family and was baptized with the name Antonio in 1635 at around the age of ten.[35] Colloreto can thus be understood to participate in precisely the same recruitment of racially marked military musicians that is central to this chapter and his Black drummer recognized as a virtuosic performer in his own right (worthy to be singled out by the Grand Duke for financial reward).[36] While there is no indication that Solefar, the Grand Duke's Black trumpeter, or Colloreto's Black drummer performed this specific piece—or,

---

[34] They received ten scudi among them, presumably four drummers and six trumpeters, as was then typical. I-Fas, Camera del Granduca, f. 19, 50r.

[35] See I-Fca, Pia Casa dei Catecumini, f. 1, c.n.n. [ins. 108]; I-Fd, Registri Battesimali, Maschi, reg. 40, fg. 139.

[36] Two years later, in July 1639, the "Moro del Signor Marchese Collaredo" was tipped a scudo on the recommendation of Giorgio Todesco. Given the ethnic *soprannome* given to Giorgio, he was quite possibly a member of the *cento lanzi del Principe*, indicating that this may have been a military event, plausibly involving drums. It may also indicate that a second "Moro" was a member of the Colloreto household. See I-Fas, Camera del Granduca, f. 21, 52r.

Musical Example 5.2. Girolamo Fantini, "First sonata for trumpet paired with the organ, named after Colloreto," from *Modo per imparare a sonare la tromba tanto in guerra quanto musicalmente* (published 1638).

indeed, that anything other than opportunism on Fantini's part connects Colloreto to this specific tune (ninety-nine different members of the court are recognized with such dedications in Fantini's oeuvre)—the marquis's connection with the rehearsal of Black aurality is a useful corollary to the present discussion.[37]

Comparing the Colloreto sonata with the "Marciata" discussed above, the relatively melic focus of the second piece is clear. Though the chosen pitches remain reliant on the harmonic series, this piece is primarily located in the fourth octave of the instrument—the clarino register—where stepwise motion, turns, and trills become possible. In addition, a melodic preponderance of F♯s turns need into virtue, capitalizing on the precariously tonal eleventh harmonic to permit modulation away from C major. Only once (in m. 9) do the organ and the trumpet interact in any significant way, with the bass and trumpet indulging in a brief moment of melodic imitation. The primary function of the bass is chordal support on C or G—as Fantini warns in his note to his readers, "many bass lines are not in [rhythmic] diminutions [*non si sono diminuiti*], because it is necessary to support such an instrument [the trumpet] with a great deal of harmony."[38]

All but two of Fantini's sonatas in this later section of the book begin in common time, then switch to triple time (however briefly), before moving back to common meter; the Colloreto sonata is no exception.[39] The entire last three systems are part of an elaborate cadential gesture, with repeating musical cells "echoed" back with contrasting dynamics. The echo and its use of stepped dynamics is a quintessentially baroque musical gesture; its prominent use in this early trumpet collection invokes the more traditional function of the instrument, both in the external space of the echo itself (where the trumpet was more traditionally heard) and in the repetition of brief musical motifs (which in their repeatable brevity recall the military calls of the traditional trumpet repertoire).

---

[37] The Marchese Colloredo or Colloreto was the same Cavaliere Fabbritio Coloreto who stood as godfather to Matteo-Giovanni, the converted "indiano," in 1611. He was elevated to the rank of *marchese* only in 1615. He can also be associated with the ownership of at least two other enslaved converts who are recorded in the Pia Casa documents: Acamed Turco from Cairo, who applied for baptism in 1627 at approximately twenty-seven years old, and Maometto from Tunisia, who was baptized with the name Giovan Battista in 1629 at approximately twenty-five. See I-Fca, Pia Casa dei Catecumini, f. 1, c.n.n. [ins. 83 and 88]; I-Fd, Registri Battesimali, Maschi, reg. 37, fg. 130.

[38] "[M]olti bassi non si sono diminuiti, perché è necessario per reggere tale strumento d'assai armonia." Fantini, *Modo*, xvi.

[39] The earlier sonatas published in the same book do not follow this same practice. While also written for trumpet and basso continuo, they do not explicitly call for the organ.

Thinking about the Grand Duke's Black trumpeter or Solefar playing this kind of music in the Grand Duke's private chambers evokes an intimacy, a musicality, and the explicitly pleasurable consumption of enslaved labor. I want to note the necessary musicality—including musical literacy—that such repertoires demand and the implied subjectivity of a musical voice that can ironically invoke the practice of playing "militarily" while playing "musically," as, for example, in the echo effects of the Colloreto sonata. Furthermore, I want to directly consider these players in conjunction with the musicians and the *musica turchesca* discussed in the previous chapter: the documented and deliberately cultivated presence of *turchi* and *mori* within the ranks of court ensembles begs the question of whether non-European musics were part of their sonic remit. The answer—frustratingly—is that I do not know. I have not been able to ascertain the ages of any of the racially marked musicians discussed in this chapter; thus, it is difficult to infer what level of instrumental training or musical exposure they might have had prior to their arrival at court. Other scholars have encountered similar lacunae in the historical record. Lowe's suggestion that many Black court musicians may have been musicians in their earlier lives is speculative and largely based on the close association of musicianship with talent and on the parallel situation of Black Venetian gondoliers, a number of whom had prior experience on boats.[40] The two Black trumpeters discussed by Spohr—Christian Real and Christian Gottlieb—both received apprenticeships in Europe, and no indication is given that they had had musical training before their enslavement or their arrival in German-speaking lands.[41]

Ultimately, it may not matter whether Solefar and his colleagues played "authentic" non-Western music. As I intimated in the previous chapter, brass and percussion ensembles were well able to imitate a range of janissary sounds, and Fantini may himself have taught his pupils how to play a *musica* inflected *alla turchesca*. On this point, it seems opportune to mention that the one trumpet method that proceeded Fantini's *Modo*, Bendinelli's *Tutta l'arte della trombetta*, which was presented in manuscript to the Accademia Filarmonica in Verona in 1614, contains three pieces labeled "sarissinetta." The etymology of the term is contested; however, Thurson Dart has argued that it relates to "sarazinades" or "music of the Saracens," further stating

[40] Lowe, "Visible Lives."
[41] Spohr, "'Mohr und Trompeter.'"

that the genre is characterized by "dramatic leaps" of a downward sixth.[42] Bendinelli's collection also includes two sonatas "in the style of a Hungarian dance [ball'ongaro]." Of these dances, Bertoluzzi notes that "Since the natural trumpet was not a chromatic instrument, Bendinelli was not able to use Hungarian melodic elements such as special or altered scales. He was instead left with rhythm as the vehicle for expressing Hungarian elements."[43]

Bendinelli's text confirms that foreign musical styles were available for instrumental impersonation. And regardless of whether Solefar and others played music that was literally or "authentically" non-Western, the racialization of their bodies and the freighted reception thereof may have sufficed. The large numbers of Black and otherwise racialized musicians who were incorporated into court ensembles and their persistent association with the military instruments of trumpet and drum were far from casual. In subsequent chapters, I linger longer on the specifically musical and entertaining aspects of enslaved labor, though first I take a short detour through musical notation and ethnographic transcriptions.

---

[42] Bertoluzzi, "Bendinelli's *Entire Art*," 346.
[43] Bertoluzzi, "Bendinelli's *Entire Art*," 342.

All'orefice per *un Orecchino con una perla* per *il Morino, -.5.-.-.*

For the jeweler, for a pearl earring for the little Black boy, [five lire], -.5.-.-.
>I-Fas, Camera del Granduca, f. 11, November 1629, c. 18r

Scene 6
Scholarly Transcriptions of Foreign Musical Sounds

While I have argued that the appropriation of foreign musical sounds was available and familiar within un-notated popular and military traditions, there are also two seventeenth-century Italian musical cultures in which scholars labored to transcribe and recreate eastern Mediterranean sounds, both of which deserve a fleeting mention.

In the first instance, a widely recognized culture of scholarship on the musical practice and theory of ancient Greece was instrumental in academic circles in Florence and Rome, contributing to the development of early opera. Such studies were strongly promulgated by the Florentine-born scholar Girolamo Mei, whose letters and writings were read and debated in the musical circles around Giovanni de' Bardi in the late sixteenth century, and hugely influential on the writings and experiments of Vincenzo Galilei, Giovanni Battista Doni, and Pietro della Valle.[1] Inspired by ancient Greek tuning systems and the complicated concepts of mode and genera, Doni had a number of enharmonic instruments constructed in order to hear, play, and compose music that exploited microtonal sounds, rarely heard in Western art music until very much later; the most famous of these instruments, the "lyra Barberina" (named after his Barberini patrons), was capable of playing in all of the ancient modes and the transpositions that his theoretical works adumbrated.[2] Doni's enthusiasm (and that of his patrons) culminated in a series of musical compositions and performances from the years around 1640 by composers including Girolamo Frescobaldi, Domenico Mazzocchi, Luigi Rossi, and the widely

---

[1] Palisca, "Florentine Camerata"; Patrizio Barbieri, "Gli stumenti poliarmonici di G. B. Doni e il ripristino dell'antica musica greca (c. 1630–1650)," *Analecta Musicologica* 30 (1998): 79–114. Forthcoming scholarship by Pier Mattia Tommasino revisits Doni's work.

[2] Claude Palisca, "G. B. Doni, Musicological Activist and His *Lyra Barberina*," in *Modern Musical Scholarship*, ed. Edward Olleson (Stocksfield, UK: Oriel Press, 1980), 180–205; Claude Palisca, ed., *G. B. Doni's Lyra Barberina: Commentary and Iconographical Study, Facsimile Edition with Critical Notes* (Bologna: Antiquae Musicae Italicae Studiosi, 1981).

traveled Florentine Pietro della Valle, whose travel accounts I have already had occasion to cite. Della Valle spent time in Turkey, Persia, and India between 1614 and 1626, and his letters describing his travels were published repeatedly from mid-century.[3] Della Valle composed an oratorio on the book of Esther (1640; the music is unfortunately lost), as well as an extant oratorio for the feast of purification (1641). Della Valle's music drew explicitly on contemporary Middle Eastern practice for inspiration, assuming that Eastern repertoires retained ancient musical elements.[4] Writing from Shiraz in the second decade of the seventeenth century, he explains in one letter:

> He sent for a musician with a flute, from whom, in my presence, he had diverse things played, following the teachings of Avicenna, ordering him how and when he had to vary them. But because it was played on a single flute, without the voice, and for the scant knowledge that I have, even now, of the technical terms in the Persian language, I could not understand well what was happening; I do think that it could have been the variety of tones that the ancients had, now little understood by us moderns.[5]

Though the "musica erudita" that was composed in imitation of ancient Greek music was heard only in very limited circles and arguably had little influence on wider dramatic or musical trends, sonic experimentation with pitched material beyond and between the (semi)tones of the Western chromatic scale was an essential part of the musical-scientific plane. Such thinking was part of the experimental context that generated interest in music drama and early opera and in proto-museums and Kunstkammer

---

[3] Raffaella Salvante, *Il "Pellegrino" in Oriente: La Turchia di Pietro della Valle (1614–1617)* (Florence: Edizioni Polistampa, 1997).

[4] Amanda Wunder has argued that many early modern travelers saw the Middle East as a modern-day repository of antiquities. See Amanda Wunder, "Western Travelers, Eastern Antiquities, and the Image of the Turk in Early Modern Europe," *Journal of Early Modern History* 7 (2003): 89–119.

[5] "[F]ece venire un musico con un flauto, dal quale, in presenza mia, fece suonar diverse cose, secondo la dottrina di Avicenna, ordinandogli esso, quando ed in che modo le aveva da variare. Ma io, per suonarsi con un solo flauto senza voce, e per la poca intelligenza che ho sin ora, in lingua persiana, dei termini di quell'arte, non potei comprender bene che cose fossero: penso ben che potessero esser le varietà dei tuoni che avevano gli antichi, ora da noi moderni non ben conosciute." Della Valle, *Viaggi*, 389. The passage begins on the previous page with this introduction: "ed un giorno, convitatomi in casa sua, [Scerèf Gihon] ragionando a proposito delle opere che ha scritte Avicenna di musica, per quanto dicono, assai sottilmente e con molta leggiadria, secondo i modi degli antichi, e qui vanno per le mani de' dotti, e sono oltre modo stimate."

centered on sound, such as that of Kirscher in Rome. We also need to remember that at this time European tuning systems were flexible. The challenges of keyboard temperament were widely acknowledged; awareness of the "wolf" fifth engendered a range of tuning solutions, and as my earlier discussion of tuning and the harmonic series in relationship to the "musical" trumpet makes clear, the affordances of various instrumental bodies were part and parcel of early modern composition and performance.

In della Valle's letter, cited above, we can see the early traces of a persistent idea that the music of non-Western cultures preserves the earlier developmental stages of Western music history itself. Eric Ames has argued that early ethnomusicologists, particularly Erich Moritz von Hornbostel, saw the phonograph as a means to listen back in time and "to plot temporal change along an evolutionary axis, charting the morphological and historical transformations of music across the sweep of time and space."[6] Even without the hungry horn of the phonograph to inscribe noises and sounds outside standard Western practice, early modern musicians operated in full awareness of the limitations of the staff's grid as record, and contemporary scholarly discourse explicitly acknowledged the difficulties of musical transcription and translation.[7]

In 1688, Giovanni Battista Donà (also known as Donado) published *Della letteratura de' Turchi* after a stint in Constantinople as the Venetian ambassador to the Sublime Porte. Donà went so far as to learn Turkish himself and included translations of several Turkish songs and transcriptions of their music in his publication (the poetic translations are credited to Gio: Rinaldo Carlì, public dragoman, and the transcriptions are also implied to be the work of a collaborator).[8] Donà's volume has been lauded by literary historians as one of the first close engagements with Ottoman literature on the part of a European outsider, while the musical transcriptions he

---

[6] Eric Ames, "The Sound of Evolution," *modernism/modernity* 10, no. 2 (2003): 297–325, quote from 298. In large part, Ames's text is a response to Alexander Rehding, "The Quest for the Origins of Music in Germany circa 1900," *Journal of the American Musicological Society* 53, no. 2 (2000): 345–385.

[7] For a postcolonial critique of early modern transcriptions, see Glenda Goodman, "Sounds Heard, Meanings Deferred: Music Transcription as Imperial Technology," *Eighteenth-Century Studies* 52, no. 1 (2018): 39–45.

[8] "Vedrà, & udirà dunque Lei le seguenti, che hò procurato raccogliere, e far ponere sù la Carta, perche possano essere tasteggiate, & intese." Giovanni Battista Donà, *Della letteratura de' Turchi: Osservationi fatte da Gio. Battista Donado senator veneto, fu bailo in Constantinopoli* (Venice: Andrea Poletti, 1688), 133.

Figure 6.1. First page (of eight) transcribing Turkish music, from Giovanni Battista Donà, *Della letteratura de' Turchi* (Venice, 1688), appendix. Used with permission of the Ministero della Cultura / Biblioteca Nazionale Centrale, Florence. Further reproduction or duplication is expressly prohibited.

published have occasioned more ambivalence.[9] Donà hews to Western notational conventions—even down to the replication of a bass staff which is then left deliberately blank. He explains: "in the music, the bass is not shown. This happens in order to leave the Turkish songs as they are, and as they are practiced by the Turks, since in their music they have no bass."[10] (See Figure 6.1 and Musical Example 6.1.)

The replication of this empty staff is compelling. After all, it would have been simple enough (and, one would assume, cheaper) to omit the extra staff entirely and to present the melodic transcription in a fashion closer to that of the partbook. To do so, however, would imply—by the conventions of (Western) musical publication—that there were other parts available

---

[9] Ennio Concina, ed., *Venezia e Istanbul: Incontri, confronti e scambi* (Udine: Forum, 2006), 236.
[10] "[N]ella Musica non si vede il Basso, questo accade, per lasciar le Canzioni Turchesche nell'aria appunto che stanno; & la praticano i Turchi, poiché loro nella Musica non hanno il Basso." Donà, *Della letteratura de' Turchi*, 140.

Musical Example 6.1. Transcription of Turkish music as reproduced in Giovanni Battista Donà, *Della letteratura de' Turchi* (Venice, 1688), appendix.

Musical Example 6.1. Continued

elsewhere. Printed on a double staff, the transcription is an insistent claim to representational totality. At the same time, with that empty staff, Donà (or his accomplice transcriber) makes clear that the mode of transcription is an uneven match with the material he has at hand. He himself says, "I wanted to have you see and hear some of their songs, in their idiom and with the melodies that they compose, and I even had them translated for you into our [notation]; but I do not know if they will come out as well as I would like, since given the difficulty of translating them, I am very doubtful that they will."[11]

Donà's transcriptions are regularly paired (and unfavorably compared) with those published slightly more than a century later by the Jesuit scholar Giambattista Toderini in 1789.[12] Toderini's *Letteratura turchesca*, compiled after his own stint in the Ottoman Empire, includes a different transcription of some Ottoman music—this time instrumental—which evidences a clear methodological difference in transcription practice (see Figure 6.2).[13] Toderini makes a notational distinction between European and Turkish musics, using extra symbols in an attempt to convey the distance between the original sounds and any European attempt to recreate their effects. Furthermore, he includes a diagram of the instrument on which the music is typically played, which presumes from the start that European equivalents will differ.

The comparison between these two authors originated with Toderini himself, who reports "having arranged to have [Donà's transcription] played by a native in front of an audience of Turks, who were unable to recognize it and who were even amused because of the 'tonal' result produced by the piece in European notation."[14] In Toderini's account, Donà is naive, culturally oblivious, and musically tone-deaf to the differences between Western notation and authentically Turkish pitch, while Toderini embraces a proto-ethnomusicological mindset that strives for objectivity and invests in the

---

[11] "Ho parimente voluto far vedere, & udire a lei alcune delle Canzoni loro, nell'idioma, e su l'arie, che loro compongono, e le ho pure fatte tradur nel nostro; ma non so se riusciranno bene come vorrei, poiche per le difficultà (già addotte) di trasportarle, ne dubito molto." Donà, *Della letteratura de' Turchi*, 130.

[12] Giambattista Toderini, *Letteratura turchesca* (Venice: Giacomo Storti, 1787).

[13] I note that when a digital version of the book was produced by the Biblioteca Nationale di Firenze, the technician did not bother to unfold and photograph the musical examples at the end. They are photographed in their folded form and are thus unavailable to the viewer.

[14] "[H]a provveduto a farla intonare da un nativo di fronte a un uditorio di turchi, i quali non hanno saputo riconoscerla e si sono anzi divertiti a causa del risultato 'tonale' prodotto dal pezzo in notazione europea." See also Ivano Cavallini, "La musica turca nelle testimonianze dei viaggiatori e nelle trattatistica del sei-settecento," *Rivista Italiana Musicologia* 21 (1986): 155–156.

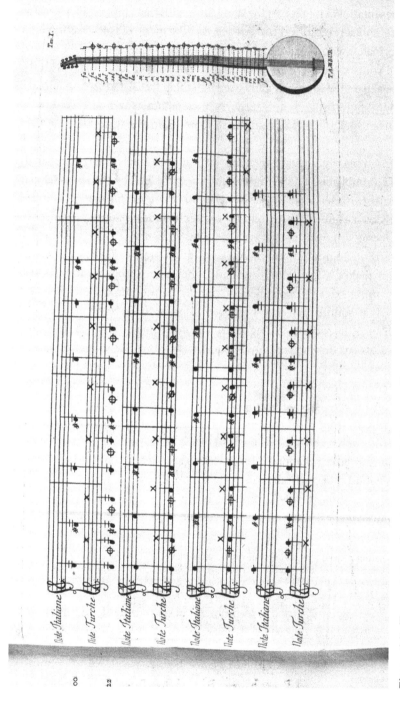

Figure 6.2. Transcription of a microtonal scale (lower staff) compared with the Western chromatic scale, from Giambattista Toderini, *Letteratura turchesca* (Venice: Giacomo Storti, 1789). Image courtesy of the Newberry Library, Call Number Y 37.88.

authority of his native informants.¹⁵ Still, we needn't be too quick to laugh along, for Toderini has failed to recognize the comfortable conventions of Donà's print. Donà himself talks of learning to hear differences between genres, and multiple travelers' accounts from the sixteenth and seventeenth centuries make clear that the sounds of Middle Eastern musics were widely understood to differ substantially from European idioms.¹⁶ Della Valle, for example, emphasizes the sonic differences:

> In the evening we had music performed at the house, by a few female Muslim singers and dancers, because, among the Gentiles there is no one who practices such art. These women, with their Indian instruments— that is: little drums [*tamburini*], little bells [*campanelli*] tied to their arms, and other [instruments], all very noisy [*di strepito grande*]—gave us a performance, playing, singing, and dancing while we dined: but to me, their music was more irritating than pleasing, because it was too raucous [*strepitoso*].¹⁷

A somewhat later account, provided by an anonymous French traveler in Turkey and published in 1680, "invokes the delights of music during the nocturnal encampments, and in particular the hilarity of the reciprocal imitations, conducted to the sound of the *tanbūr*, of French, Arab, and Turkish melodies."¹⁸ In its acknowledgment of musical parody, this idyllic scene of cross-cultural exchange illustrates the interpretive force of performance and the wide spectrum within which any given performance could be inflected with racialized sounds. Donà's musical script presumes a gap between notated text and performance which the historical performance practice movement has effectively normalized in our consumption

---

[15] In the late nineteenth and early twentieth centuries, emergent sound-recording technologies were seized upon by Western scholars of non-Western musics as a way to sidestep the problems of transcription—both the limits of a notational form designed for the semitonal division of the octave and for specific metrical patterns and the cultural deafness of the heavily conditioned ears of the Western transcriber. Erika Brady, *A Spiral Way: How the Phonograph Changed Ethnography* (Jackson: University Press of Mississippi, 1999).

[16] Donà, *Della letteratura de' Turchi*, 131–132.

[17] "La sera di notte avemmo in casa musica, di alcune cantatrici e ballatrici maomettane, perchè fra' gentili non vi è chi faccia tal arte, le quali coi loro strumenti indiani, che son tamburini, campanelli legati alle braccia ed altri, tutti di strepito grande, ci diedero trattenimento, suonando, cantando e ballando, mentre cenavamo: ma a me la loro musica, per esser troppo strepitosa, dà piuttosto fastidio che gusto." Della Valle, *Viaggi*, 537.

[18] "Grelot rievoca le delizie della musica durante gli accampamenti notturni, e in particolare l'ilarità delle reciproche imitazioni, condotte al suono del *tanbūr* su arie francesi, arabe e turche." See Cavallini, "La musica turca," 149.

of notated Western repertoires; we shouldn't be so surprised to see it at work in the notation of non-Western musics, too. To cite Stanley Boorman, "notations are imprecise; they conceal many well-understood elements; and they are influenced by the style of their presentation and the occasions for their use."[19]

---

[19] Boorman, "Musical Text," 410.

A Pietrino nano ballò meglio del ~~Nano~~ Moro un Testone -.2.-.

For Little Peter the dwarf who danced better than ~~the Dwarf~~ the Moor, a *Testone* [equivalent to 2 lire]
                I-Fas, Camera del Granduca, f. 11, March 1630, c. 35v

Scene 7
Music Proper to Enslaved Singers

In early June 1610, members of the Florentine court filed a petition for baptism in the name of Giovanni, a "Morino," then approximately eleven years old. The documents held in the Pia Casa attest repeatedly that the "aforementioned little Black boy affirms his desire to be baptized,"[1] and even Giovanni's choice of name was linked to his longed-for conversion:

> I, Michele Zotti, tailor, attest that I have instructed a little Black boy belonging to Madama [Christine of Lorraine], whose name is Giovanni, so called because he intends that he will be thus called after the baptism.[2] I have taught him the Our Father, the Hail Mary, and the Credo; even though he does not know them well, being rather thick [*assai duro*], I promise to teach him so often that he will know these and other things necessary to a Christian, and this much I promise to do, and this being the truth, it is written in my own hand.[3]

---

[1] "[D]etto Morino afferma haver desideri d'esser battezato." I-Fca, Pia Casa dei Catecumini, f. 1, c.n.n. [ins. 32].

[2] I note that Zotti also educated at least one other enslaved convert during this time, a certain Ali di Reenet or Ali di Maometti, from Algeria, age around twenty-two, who was owned by Cardinal Francesco Antonio Soldari; Ali was baptized with the name Francesco on April 17, 1611. See I-Fca, Pia Casa dei Catecumini, f. 1, c.n.n.; I-Fd, Registri Battesimali, Maschi, reg. 28, fg. 45. Interestingly, twenty years earlier, when the grand duchess wanted "her *Moretto Abissino*, of around 14 years of age," instructed and catechized with an eye to his eventual conversion to Christianity, she assigned the task to the priest Giuliano Guglielmi, who testified not only that he instructed the boy directly but that he assigned him to "accompany the lessons of the children of the late Signor Agostino Sacchettini, who were being educated under the discipline of Maestro Vettorio Pennini." "[I]l suo Moretto Abissino d'età 14 in circa"; "Io fin ora l'ho esercitato in simili operationi, e p*er* mio aiuto l'ho accompagnato con i figlioli del gia S. Agostino Sacchettini educati sotto la diceplina del M. Vettorio Pennini." I-Fca, Pia Casa dei Catecumeni, f. 1, c.n.n. [ins. 91], August 28, 1630. Translated literally, *Moretto Abissino* means "little Black Ethiopian," though the term should be understood to represent Black skin in general, not a specific point of geographical origin. The boy was renamed Giovambattista when he was baptized; see I-Fd, Registri Battesimali, Maschi, reg. 38, fg. 55.

[3] "Fassi fede per me Michele Zotti Sarto come è la verità che io ho istruito, un morino di Madama il nome del quale e Giovanni così chiamato per avere intentione che così si chiami al battesimo. L'io insegnato il Pater Noster, l'Ave Maria et il credo, se bene non li sa bene, per essere assai duro, prometto insegnarli tanto che sappia questo et altre cose necessarie, al cristiano e tanto prometto fare e per essere la verità scrissi di propria mano." I-Fca, Pia Casa dei Catecumini, f. 1, c.n.n. [ins. 32].

Giovanni's case was complicated by the question of whether or not the applicant had been previously baptized. It is in this context that some scant details of his pre-Florentine life emerge, as narrated by an English Catholic, Tommaso (or Thomas) Jong (an archaic spelling of Young, also spelled Yong); the archived letter is written in Italian:[4]

> Messer Lorenzo, I received your dear [letter], and about the little Black boy I can tell you nothing except what I have heard related by others. I had him purchased from an English Heretic sea captain in Livorno: and he said that he got [the boy] in Spain, where the boy had been in a Convent of Friars for many months. And this has the ring of truth since (as you know) when he first came he did nothing but sing Litanies and other airs [*arie*] that one sings in church, and he also preached.[5] And all of this, he would not have been able to learn (having such a hard head [*il Capo tanto duro*]) if not for daily exposure and long practice in the aforementioned Convent. Now it is worth considering (assuming all this to be true) that the Fathers where he was would not have kept this young boy such a long time without baptizing him or without having some indication that he had been baptized. However, I do not know this for certain and if one were to baptize him conditionally, I think it would be all right. I defer to those who better understand such cases, and thus I finish my letter, I salute you, and ask you to remember me with great affection to Messer Michele [presumably Zotti]. May Our Lord God keep you in his Holy Graces.[6]

According to Jong's account, Giovanni arrived in Livorno from Spain on a Protestant English ship. All that is known of Giovanni before this point is

---

[4] Thomas Jong is presumably the Englishman of the same name who delivered letters from Florence to Ottaviano di Lotti (then the Medici ambassador in London) in 1610; see the Medici Archive Project, Person ID 13220.

[5] It is not clear what is meant by preaching (*predicava*); perhaps Giovanni imitated the preacher giving a sermon, or perhaps Jong intended to say that the boy prayed (*pregava*).

[6] "Mes. Lorenzo hebbi la cara vostra, & circa al Morino non vi posso dir cosa alcuna senon per relatione d'altri. Io lo feci comprare da un Eretico Inglese Capitano di Nave, in Livorno: & disse costui haverlo havuto nella Spagna dove il ragazzo era stato parecchi mesi in un Convento di Frati, & questo ha del verosimile poichè (come voi sapete) quando venne prima non faceva altro che cantare Letanie, e altre arie che si cantano nelle chiese, e anche predicava. & tutto questo non poteva lui imparare (havendo il Capo tanto duro) senon per una consuetudine grande, e pratica longa fatto nel primo detto Convento. Hora egli è da pensare (essendo tutto questo vero) che quei Padri dove egli era non havrebbono tenuto questo figliuolo tanto tempo senza battezzarlo, o senza haverne qualche inditio che fusse battezzato. Pero Io non ne so certezza, & quando si havessi a battezzarlo conditionalmente credo saria bene. Io mi rimetto a chi bene intende questi casi, & cosi fo fine, vi saluto, e pregovi di risalutare Maestro Michele da mia parte con molto affettione. Nostro Signore vi conservi nella sua Santa gratia. Di Villa A di 5 di Maggio 1610." I-Fca, Pia Casa dei Catecumini, f. 1, c.n.n. [ins. 32].

hearsay, though the veracity of the story can be measured against the young Black body that stands in Florence and clamors for baptism. Giovanni's long stay in the Spanish monastery is confirmed not only by his musical fluency but also by his "Capo tanto duro"—which, in combination with the music he had absorbed and regurgitated continually, testified to a considerable stay within the monastery walls. The "hardness" of Giovanni's head is likewise noted by his catechism tutor, the tailor Zotti, who acknowledges Giovanni as "rather thick," as well as one of the several priests involved in the deliberations: "Because the aforementioned little Black boy is so young and quite thick [*duretto d'ingegno*] he is not as well educated as he would be were he older and smarter, I judge, however, that he may be baptized."[7] For modern readers, the purported *durezza* of this young child is overshadowed by his traumatic biographical trajectory; language delays and learning disabilities are common in displaced populations. At an age of only eleven, Giovanni has already been long separated from his family (if he ever knew them), spent considerable time in an institutional setting, traversed the Mediterranean, and experienced both the bustling port of Livorno and the city and court of Medici Florence. At the very least, we can presume his exposure to Spanish, Latin, English, and Italian. Rather than an innate stupidity, we might read his *durezza* as a consequence of trauma.

Yet despite his hard, hard head, Giovanni learned to sing. Indeed, when Giovanni first arrived in Florence, he did little else except sing litanies and other airs that were sung in churches. This melic predilection, Jong tells us, was widely known and evidently memorable.

Giovanni's early performances must have transmitted a sense of the miraculous: the "Letanie, e altre arie" of Christendom emerging from a young and visibly foreign body.[8] Such singing—learned by rote (in Jong's words, "daily exposure and long practice") and disconnected from a presumption of semantic comprehension (given Giovanni's hard head)—stands in polar opposition to the kinds of vocal performance more commonly associated with the court of Florence in the years around 1600. Yet to think about Giovanni's arrival in terms of musical sound and performance makes clear that his selection for court service was influenced by his song. If Giovanni's

---

[7] "Il Morino soprascritto per essere assai piccolo, e duretto d'ingegno non c'è ammaestrato come sarebbe se fusse grande e ingegnoso, tuttavia giudicherei che si potutta battezzare." I-Fca, Pia Casa dei Catecumini, f. 1, c.n.n. [ins. 32].

[8] While I do not (yet) know when Giovanni arrived at the court, his age in 1610 (around eleven) and his ability to sing at the time of his arrival suggest that it must have occurred at some point between 1603 and 1610.

song can be presumed to have entertained his audience at court—the ducal family, courtiers, visitors, clerks, and tailors—on the slave ship, the young boy's singing singled him out as a prime candidate for courtly service precisely because song performs the decorative labor of the Black page. His singing voice thus articulates what Matthew Head calls "[t]he relationship between the troping of music as Other and orientalism's constructions of Otherness."[9]

The presence of Black children as luxury slaves in Italian courts is well documented, best known from the long lineage of (double) portraits depicting patron and (Black) page; thus, most of the scholarship on the phenomenon has arisen from within art history. Paul Kaplan has argued that Titian's *Ritratto di Laura Dianti* (painted around 1520–1525) was the first exemplar of the genre,[10] though Isabella d'Este's well-documented attempts to secure a steady stream of young children—"as Black as possible," she wrote in a previously discussed letter from 1491—make it clear that the practice of keeping young Black retainers predated Titian's decision to memorialize it, just as several mid-seventeenth-century examples among Justus Sustermans's Florentine portraits and those of his school evidence the continued relevance of the genre painting and thus the Black courtly presence more than a century later.

The children depicted in the double-portrait tradition are difficult to discuss without reinscribing the process of objectification that would render their complexion a self-evident expression of servitude. But Giovanni's singing, by pointing away from the visual surface of race, draws attention to the sonic and to the expressive potential of voice, even while the materiality of his voice-as-musical-object solidifies his value as an object of exchange. Giovanni, then, is the commodity who sings—while to say so is to signify on Fred Moten's powerful assertion that the slave, contradicting Karl Marx, is the commodity that speaks.[11] Recognizing Giovanni in such terms allows us to notice a similar, previously unmarked vocality in others who have been understood as primarily visual pendants to white sovereignty. Isabella d'Este, still in 1491, wrote, "we couldn't be more pleased with our Black girl even if she were blacker, because from being at first a little disdainful she has now

---

[9] Head, "Musicology on Safari," 216.

[10] Paul H. D. Kaplan, "Titian's 'Laura Dianti' and the Origins of the Motif of the Black Page in Portraiture (1 and 2)," *Antichità Viva* 21, no. 1 (1982): 11–18, no. 2 (1982): 10–18.

[11] Fred Moten, *In the Break: The Aesthetics of the Black Radical Tradition* (Minneapolis: University of Minnesota Press, 2003), 1–24.

become pleasing in *words and acts* [my emphasis], and we think she'll make the best buffoon in the world."[12]

The word "buffoon" (in the original Italian, *buffone*) makes clear that this young girl was in training as a professional entertainer and not merely learning a more deferential demeanor. This is a crucial component of Black courtly experience that has gone underrecognized.[13] In the Medici archives, the connection between Black bodies and buffoonery is repeatedly cited. For example, in February 1627, when the court was in Livorno, "certain Turks who played the buffoon (*fecero il Buffone*) for the carriage of His Highness" were rewarded with a scudo,[14] and later that month, "that *moro* who plays the buffoon" was given two testoni.[15] In March, the "two *mori* who play the buffoon" were given three giuli.[16] Similarly, in 1630, "the *moro* who plays the buffoon in Livorno" was tipped six giuli (equivalent to four lire).[17]

Furthermore, when the Medici accounts cite the actions of court Moors in any detail, the activities for which they are rewarded are distinctly buffoonish. On one occasion, for example, in October 1630, an unnamed woman and "the Moor" were set to box each other.[18] In January 1631, the "Morino" was given a scudo for extinguishing a candle with his mouth,[19] and that March, Jacopo Capoletto was paid for "two beasts, which served for the Moor and the Buffoon to go about in costume [*andare in maschera*]."[20] In November 1632, "the Moro" was given two testoni (equivalent to 4 lire), which he swallowed.[21]

---

[12] "Nui achora non poteressimo esser più satisfacte de la nostra [moretta], se la fusse più negra, perchè essendo stata nel pricipio un poco desdegnosetta è poi venuta tanto piacevole de parole et atti, che existimiamo se farrà la megliora buffona del mundo." Cited in Alessandro Luzio and Rodolfo Renier, "Buffoni, schiavi e nani alla corte dei Gonzaga ai tempi d'Isabella d'Este," *Nuova Anthologia* 19 (1891): 67–68.

[13] Kaplan, writing about a link between court jesters and African court servants in relationship to the young child in the Titian portrait of Laura Dianti, has suggested that "the entertainment this and other African children generally afforded was probably less aggressive and performative in character than that of a traditional jester." Kaplan's essay is in Vol. 3, Part 1, of Bindman and Gates, *Image of the Black*, 109.

[14] "A Certi Turchi che fecero il Buff*one* alla Carrozza di SA uno scudo." I-Fas, Camera del Granduca, f. 7, 18r.

[15] "Al S.M. Gonzaga quattro test*oni* due dati a quel moro che fa il Buffone e due *per* ricuperare il Giobbone di M. Gian quando era sopra la Galera 1.1.-.-." I-Fas, Camera del Granduca, f. 7, 18r.

[16] "A due Mori Turchi che fecero il Buff*one* un test*one per ciascuno* -.4.-.-." I-Fas, Camera del Granduca, f. 7, 19r.

[17] "Al Moro che fa il Buffone in Livorno sei giuli -.4.-.-." I-Fas, Camera del Granduca, f. 11, 38v.

[18] "A quella Donna che fece alle pugnia col Moro al paretaio -.3.10.-." I-Fas, Camera del Granduca, f. 12, 10r.

[19] "Al Morino uno scudo spense la Candela in Bocca 1.-.-.-." I-Fas, Camera del Granduca, f. 12, 25r.

[20] "A Jacopo Capoletto *per* le due Bestie, che servirono a' andare in maschera il Moro, e il Buffone sei giuli -.4.-.-." I-Fas, Camera del Granduca, f. 12, 33v.

[21] "Al Moro due testoni che gli ingoiò -.4.-.-." I-Fas, Camera del Granduca, f. 14, 16v.

I could cite many other examples. Cumulatively, they demonstrate that the register of the comic was actively associated with racially marked bodies, whose performative antics were rewarded by the sovereign with direct cash payments, while—for Italian audiences—such actions testified to the aptitude of such performers for enslavement, drawing on deeply embedded assumptions about performance, display, and consumption. In Italian courts, enslaved Black and foreign children and racially marked enslaved adults rubbed up against and shared space with other jester figures, including madmen, dwarves, and mutes—a human menagerie, whose visible differences shored up the able-bodied, white, male, European norm.[22]

Within this context, I am interested in voice and the extent to which the genealogy of Black song articulated by the figure of the Black buffoon—what Matthew Morrison might call "Blacksound"[23]—forecloses on agential voice: Giovanni's song confirms his aptitude for court slavery not because he sings the flexible, expressive music of recitative but precisely because he doesn't.[24] Indeed, Giovanni sings in what Saidiya Hartman, writing about nineteenth-century chattel slavery in North America, has called "the appropriately simple tones of the enslaved."[25] Hartman argues that the enduring association of Black bodies and a natural, ingrained musicality was taken as evidence for the unaffected simplicity of the Black mind and thus an aptitude for enslavement.

Thinking back across the earlier examples from this book, we can note that Giovanni's voice, that of the *indiani senza testa*, the rural peasants of the *palio*, and Caccini's Syrian refugee fit into and cohere within the economy of musically expressive sound that solidifies in early operatic practice. To think about all of this music in terms of expressivity is instructive, for Giovanni and his (Black) colleagues are ascribed a strictly delimited emotional range, constrained—we could call it typecast—by their Black bodies and servile status. If song and performance help identify why some enslaved children were understood as suitable for courtly service and—with Solefar,

---

[22] Critical disability studies have articulated a very sophisticated understanding of the social norm. Rosemary Garland Thompson proposes the term "normate" to describe "the figure outlined by the array of deviant others whose marked bodies shore up the normate's boundaries." Rosemarie Garland Thompson, *Extraordinary Bodies* (New York: Columbia University Press, 1997), 8.

[23] Morrison, "Sound(s) of Subjection."

[24] Saidiya Hartman articulates a pertinent critique of scholars who search for and celebrate agential behavior on the part of enslaved people. See Saidiya V. Hartman, *Scenes of Subjection: Terror, Slavery, and Self-Making in Nineteenth-Century America* (Oxford: Oxford University Press, 1997), 8.

[25] Hartman, *Scenes of Subjection*, 53.

Rosoan, the "Moro Trombetto," and the unnamed little girl described by Isabella d'Este—demonstrate how they were trained or educated in order to fulfill their courtly labors, then the repeated re-citation of this trope, the Black singer/musician, marks the ways in which the association of racial difference and musical facility was naturalized in the European sonic imaginary. In what the Black court buffoon is permitted to sing, we can hear the parceling out of full humanity only to certain characters and the association of a natural, musical predisposition with the marked bodies of (foreign) slaves. In contrast, the refugee who sings the sophisticated musical rhetoric of courtly song sounds their readiness to be welcomed and celebrated as (foreign) equal.

This representational schema reflects the intersection of expressive voice (that is, the sound of the character's voice as a reflection of their nature) with an understanding of categorical and fundamental distinctions among different types of people—we can recall here the "peasants and farm girls" of the 1616 *carnevale* parade, along with their "flutes, whistles, and other similarly rustic instruments": different categories of people made different types of sounds.[26] In early opera, expressive voice entailed a strict hierarchy with regard to song and character type. The main, serious, characters—almost all of whom were represented as noble—sang recitative with occasional arioso passages. Gods and allegories performed florid, ornamented, or melismatic music. Comic and low-class characters (including servants and the enslaved) got to sing real songs. While in later operatic repertoires, recitative came to be heard as the (brief) connective tissue between arias (which in turn became the genre's emotional and dramatic kernel), in early opera, recitative was disproportionately valued, both for its affinity to speech and for the opportunities it offered for more sophisticated poetry. The qualities that modern listeners tend to identify as musical—a predictable metric pulse, balanced phrases, solidly tonal areas, and formal repetitions—served a predominantly decorative function and were placed in the mouths of peripheral characters. Exceptions were governed by the rules of theatrical verisimilitude—specific activities that could be understood to require formally patterned or heightened utterance, such as diegetic musical performance (for entertainment or as serenade), prayer, lament, or magical incantation.[27] The hierarchy of character

---

[26] The quote comes from *Descrizione del corso*. See also the discussion of instruments and their relative registers in Berns, "Instrumental Sound," particularly 496–497.
[27] *Il corago, o vero alcune osservazioni per metter bene in scena le composizioni drammatiche*, ed. Paolo Fabbri and Angelo Pompilio, Studi e Testi per la Storia della Musica 4 (Florence: Olschki, 1983),

types and musical form incorporated a long tradition of categorizing poetic genres along a spectrum from simplicity to complexity, from easy to difficult, from natural to learned, from musical to the poetic. Writing one hundred years before the invention of opera, the poet and critic Vincenzo Colli *detto* Il Calmeta divided vernacular poetry into various categories governed by an inverse relationship between the quality of the text and the sophistication of the meter on the one hand and the use of musical accompaniment on the other:

> There will be those who, delighting in the act of song, desire to delight their woman with song—maximally ornamented—and to insert amorous words into such music. These people, not wanting to proceed any further with the institution [of poetry], should for the verses occupy themselves with *barzellette, frottole* and other pedestrian styles, . . . which, when accompanied by music, are not only adorned, but covered, in such a way that they cannot be discerned.[28]

By linking poor poetry, florid or robust musical declamation, and the company of women, Calmeta states quite baldly an association that feminist musicologists of the early 1990s went to some length to point out: the "music itself" is feminized and thus devalued by cultural tropes of sensuality, superficiality, and simplicity. More complicated poetry, however, can appeal to a higher quality of listener—assuming that the music is suitably deferential:

> [T]hey are to be esteemed with the highest judgment those who, when singing, put all of their effort into expressing the words well, when they are of substance, and who make the music accompany [the words] in the same

---

64. See also Nino Pirrotta, "Early Opera and Aria," in *Music and Theatre from Poliziano to Monteverdi* (Cambridge: Cambridge University Press, 1982), 237–280, particularly 63ff; Ellen Rosand, *Opera in Seventeenth-Century Venice: The Creation of a Genre* (Berkeley: University of California Press, 1991), 246.

[28] "Saranno alcuni altri i quali, dilettandosi d'arte di canto, disiderano col cantar, massimamente diminuito, gratificar la sua donna, e in quella musica parole amorose inserire. Costoro, non volendo più avanti di tale instituto procedere, circa le stanze, barzelette, frottole e altri pedestri stili deveno essercitarsi . . . le quali, quando con la musica s'accompagnano, sono non solo adombrate, ma coperte per modo che non si possono discernere." Vincenzo Calmeta, *Prose e lettere edite e inedite (con due appendici di altri inediti)*, ed. Cecil Grayson (Bologna: Commissione per i Testi di Lingua, 1959), 21. See also Brian Richardson, "Sixteenth-Century Italian Petrarchists and Musical Settings of Their Verse," in *Voices and Texts in Early Modern Italian Society*, ed. Stefano Dall'Aglio, Brian Richardson, and Massimo Rospocher (Abingdon, UK: Routledge, 2017), 124–125.

way that *patrons are escorted by servants* [my emphasis], in order to appear more honorably, not making the affects and the sentences servants of the music, but the music servant of the sentences and affects.[29]

Prima le parole o prima la musica—the debate is perennial and the terms long familiar, not least from music history surveys, from Giovanni Artusi's famous spat with Claudio Monteverdi, and from the reflexively defensive prefaces of early libretti, in which author after author hurries to excuse the poor quality of the poetry as a deliberate strategy intended to maximize the musical efficacy of the text.[30] My point is that with such a hierarchy in operation, musicality itself can be understood as a marker of servility or cultural devaluation—gendered, classed, or raced difference.

To take what Head calls "Western music's Otherness"[31] seriously is to recognize and analyze the representational logic by which the enslaved and singing Black Africans of *La Sultana*, who performed *alla turca* from atop their camels, were consolidated as "Other"—as Black slaves—in part through their affinity for song. It is to note that young Giovanni's song was a crucial component in Thomas Jong's decision to gift him to the grand duchess. Or that the "Moro Trombetto's" race was instrumental in his selection and training. To put things another way: what happens if we think through Monteverdi's pithy—and epoch-defining—adage that music should be servant to the text: "far che l'orazione sia padrona del armonia e non serva," that is, in a nonliteral translation, "ensure that the text has control over the music and is not subservient to it."[32] In what way does (the) music (itself) constitute the conditions of servitude? And what can music tell us about the voice (or subjectivity) of the servile class, whether servant or enslaved?

---

[29] "[S]ono da essere essi stimati di sommo giudicio coloro che cantando mettono tutto lo sforzo in esprimer ben le parole, quando sono di sustanza, e fanno che la musica le accompagna con quel modo che sono i padroni da' servidori accompagnati, per poter più onorevolmente comparire, facendo non gli affetti e le sentenze della musica, ma la musica delle sentenze e degli affetti esser ministra." Calmeta, *Prose e lettere*, 22.

[30] See Suzanne G. Cusick, "Gendering Modern Music: Thoughts on the Monteverdi-Artusi Controversy," *Journal of the American Musicological Society* 46 (1993): 1–25; Carter, *Composing Opera*.

[31] Head, "Musicology on Safari," 216.

[32] The difficulties in translating this phrase are particularly pronounced when the feminine noun "padrona" (so chosen to match the arbitrarily feminine term "orazione") is translated as "mistress," with the heavily gendered, sexual connotations that the word "mistress" currently conveys. I note that Massimo Ossi has argued that Giulio Cesare misrepresents Claudio's intentions, and that the seconda prattica is more correctly about the music becoming more liberated from pure text representation. See Ossi, *Divining the Oracle*.

Such associations are difficult to bring into focus, particularly within musicological studies where music is, by definition, valued and where historical sources are selected, in large part, for their demonstrable musical content. Even while modern repertoires based on repetitions, simple chord progressions, and widely recognized formulas remain devalued (consider pop music), we need to work to recognize the extent to which popular musics and genres themselves signified on the early modern stage.[33]

In *La Sultana*, when the title character fakes her sale into slavery (and tricks Lelio into purchasing her), she illustrates her worth as a slave by breaking into song.[34] The stage directions indicate that the Sultana is to be dressed as a slave and carry a Spanish guitar; the Nudrice (her nurse, who pretends to be her current owner) is to be dressed "alla levantina" (in a Middle Eastern style); and Momolo (the innkeeper, who stages the sale) should have a "trumpet (*tromba*) and a banner decorated with half-moons."[35] The scene begins with sound:

Qui suonerà la tromba, e mentre terrà continuamente suonato usciranno tutti i nominati per diverse parti del Theatro, & alhor che saranno tutti in scena, si fermerà; avvertendo che taccia suanando alcuna breve intermissione, per non assordar il Theatro, e gli spettatori. [36]	Here [Momolo] *will play the trumpet, and while he plays continually, all the named characters will come out from different parts of the theater, and when they are all on the stage, he will stop [playing]; Note that he should stop playing for a few brief intermissions, in order that the Theater and the spectators are not deafened.*

As the sale itself gets under way, the (onstage) spectators demand to see the slave's talent in order to justify the asking price, and here vocality comes to the fore. In the first instance, the Sultana and Nudrice speak together in (relatively accurate) Turkish, demonstrating the slave's command of tongues, yet since the audience cannot understand what they are saying, something more useful is requested. At this point, the Sultana sings (presumably

---

[33] We also need to work to recognize the ways in which our analytic language devalues such repertoires. See Emily Wilbourne, "Affect and the Recording Devices of Seventeenth-Century Italy," in *Sound and Affect: Voice, Music, World*, ed. Stephen Decatur Smith, Judith Lochhead, and Eduardo Mendieta (Chicago: University of Chicago Press, 2021), 325–341.

[34] *La Sultana* is not the only contemporary play in which such scenes occur. One example, mentioned to me by Patricia Akhimie, is *A Very Woman*, by John Fletcher and Philip Massinger, first performed in England in 1634 and published in 1655. In III, i, several enslaved characters on the auction block are instructed to sing.

[35] "Nudrice vestita alla levantina Momolo con tromba, e stendaro con entrovi delle meze Lune, haverà la Sultana addosso un mazzo di carte Francesi, un sonaglio, della farina, havrà una chitarra alla spagnola." Andreini, *La Sultana*, 56–57.

[36] Andreini, "Lo Schiavetto," transition from scene vi to scene vii.

accompanying herself on the "chitarra alla spagnola" called out in the stage directions). Later in the scene, the text seems to mock the dehumanizing context of the slave sale, when the potential buyers demand to see the slave walk (to ensure he/she is not lame) and examine his/her teeth. The nurse responds, "As if you are buying a horse!"[37]—echoing, unconsciously or not, one of the fundamental critiques of the slave trade.[38]

PARSENIO	Hor sù alle virtù, e poi al prezzo.	Get on with [showing] the skills, and then tell us the price.
NUDRICE	Aahali.	Hello.
SULTANA	Ne isterse Sultanum.	What do you want, my Lord [lit. "Sultan"]?
NUDRICE	Ben, seni satar.	I want to sell you!
SULTANA	Ne, isterse hala.	Why do you want that?
NUDRICE	Alla hatala vl'e ister.	Allah, in error, wants it.[39]
FEGATELLO	Se voi, altri non parlate in altro linguaggio, che in questo scommunicato, non sarete intesi.	If you cannot speak in some language other than this excommunicated one, you will not be understood.
NUDRICE	Ti parlar ben, ti scomenza un poco à mostrar virtù.	[*To Sultana:*] You speak fine, get on with it and show your skills.
MOMOLO	E monstrela tuta vè, perche ti hà una virtùe che fà voia.	[*To Sultana:*] And show them everything, because you have a virtue that will make them want you.
	Quì canterà à suo capriccio un aria alla spagnola, e sapendone alcuna alla schiavona, o vero alla turchesca pur non starebbe male: e mentre canterà potranno diversi, dire; buono; ò canta ben; val ogni danaro &c. finito il canto, seguirà Momolo suonando: avvertendo, che il primo tocco di tromba, hor lo suonerà nell'orecchio dell'uno, hor dell'altro comperatore.[40]	*Here she should sing a Spanish aria of her choosing, and if she knows a slave song [possibly Slavic song],*[41] *or even a Turkish one, that would not be bad, either; and while she sings, various [bystanders] will say, "Good," "She sings well," "Worth every penny," etc. When the song is finished, Momolo will follow playing [the trumpet]; take note, that with the first blare of the trumpet, first he will play it in the ear of one buyer, then of another.*

---

[37] "Nudrice. E che ti compri caval." Andreini, *La Sultana*, 63.

[38] William Davies echoes this complaint at least twice in his 1614 book about his enslavement, Davies, *True Relation*.

[39] I thank Jonathan Shannon for his translation from the Turkish. For a translation of this section of dialogue into Italian, see Luca D'Onghia, "Aspetti della lingua comica di Giovan Battista Andreini," *La Lingua Italiana: Storia, Strutture, Testi* 7 (2011): 70n1.

[40] It is possible that "aria alla schiavona" is meant to describe a Slavic aria; the original repurposing of the term "schiava" to mean slave came from the large numbers of Slavic women in domestic slavery.

[41] Andreini, *La Sultana*, II, vii.

This is a crucial moment for the musicological inquiry into race: an Italian actress, impersonating a Turkish sultana, disguised as a male slave (quite possibly in blackface), singing in Spanish—though a Turkish or slave (possibly Slavic) song would also be appropriate. By most measures, this scene is one of exotic representation. We can note the casual assumption—on the part of the author—that both "slave songs" and "Turkish" songs are in circulation, available (and legible) to potential performers and audience members; here we can recall the *minoranza alloglotta*, discussed earlier, and Kate van Orden's work on Turkish songs in French chanson collections of the early seventeenth century. The use of Spanish guitar suggests a lighter, strophic repertoire; the strummed technique and *alfabeto* notation of the instrument was better suited to the more popular register, and, as I have argued elsewhere drawing on Rogério Budasz's work, Italian performances may have evoked associations with enslaved Black street musicians.[42] While the turn toward Spanish-language song might be seen to collapse all diversity into a homogeneous soup of undifferentiated "Otherness," it pays to remember that in 1622 (when this play was published), Naples (where the play is set) was occupied by the Spanish; Spanish song was thus, indeed, a marker of "Otherness" but one with a very specific contextual application, connoting a precise relationship to political power. We can be certain that this power relationship was evident to the play's author, since in the final scenes, when the Sultana's father makes his long-anticipated arrival onstage, he is accompanied by a group of Spanish courtiers. For an enslaved human on the Neapolitan auction block, an ability to sing in Spanish would be a valuable skill, though it is important not to let the specificity of such details detract from the larger observation that I want to make here: the value of this slave is located in the efficacy and entertainment of his/her musical labor.

As a demonstration of what this particular singer-actress could do, song lies at the dense nexus of professionalism, femininity, racialization, and objectification that I am attempting to bring into focus. The recourse made by the Sultana-as-slave to jargon (as discussed in this book's second scene), foreign language, and song draws upon the tight association between slavery and "Otherness" but also upon the functional or servile status of musical entertainment. This is a singer or musician who is called upon to perform

---

[42] Budasz, "Black Guitar-Players"; Wilbourne, "*Lo Schiavetto*."

at the will of a patron (or owner)—a playback device or music-producing object.[43]

Frequently, for the enslaved, musical labor was a step up from other types of physical labor and in many cases a way to increase one's value in the eyes of a slaveholder or the market. Yet as the literate traditions of Western vocal music moved inexorably away from an amateur, participatory culture toward professionalized, commoditized practices in which voices and performances could be bought and sold, the musically literate enslaved performers discussed here and in earlier chapters make a forceful argument that musical performance itself could represent the Other. While "Western music's Otherness" does not render all musical performance as a sign of slavery or foreign difference, its representational coherence in the mouths of slave characters calls for heightened scholarly attention to the ways in which the presence of music itself signified—in addition to more traditional, hermeneutic readings of text or word painting.

"Far che l'orazione sia padrone dell'armonia e non serva." The very familiarity of Monteverdi's injunction has naturalized the servile status of music: there were certain kinds of music understood as proper to the register of the comic, of servants, and of the enslaved. Indeed, in *La stiava* (performed for the Medici court in Pisa for carnival of 1607), it is the verbal outburst of the title character, set by Francesca Caccini as a *stile recitativo* lament, that convinces her auditors that she is of royal descent and no candidate for enslavement.[44] The same could be said of the female Syrians in *Il balletto della cortesia*. The music of the Black buffoon, on the other hand, is "songlike"—which by early modern European standards was securely collocated to the entertaining, the popular, and the "lowbrow." Whether we think of this categorial distinction as primarily one of class—and in the study of early modern voice, the association of the music itself with markedly devalued characters has long been acknowledged as a function of class[45]—Giovanni's voice (and the voices of others like him) makes a forceful claim that *razza* is a more useful term than "class" (or even "race" alone). Giovanni's song interpolates racial difference into the known hierarchy of character types, as his body and its echoes illustrate the sonic and musical labor that was deemed verisimilar for young Black court slaves such as himself.

---

[43] This instrumentalization of the singer's body resonates with Giulio Cesare Brancaccio's reluctance and Alfonso d'Este's delight that the *concerto delle donne* should repeat the music as written, precisely the same each time. See Wistreich, *Warrior, Courtier, Singer*.
[44] Cusick, "'La Stiava Dolente.'"
[45] Wistreich, *Warrior, Courtier, Singer*.

Crucially, the epistemology of expressive voice conflates the aesthetic labor of Giovanni's performance with his subjectivity. The purported inheritability of *razza* ties these voices and their inherent musical categories to structural possibilities that conditioned the lives of the individuals concerned. The enslaved singers of the Italian court and stage produced a soundtrack that justified their enslavement, registering their purportedly contented participation in the institutions of slave labor and of racialization. The role of music in this equation is not neutral. Though produced through a stylized performance, music purports to express genuine emotion. If, in Monica Miller's words, the "luxury black symbolizes the extreme wealth of his owner in the denial of his laboring power and potential. He is, perhaps, the perfect example of conspicuous consumption,"[46] then the investment (of time and money) in musical training allows the (white, elite) listener to presume the contentment of the enslaved, as the enslaved themselves labored to entertain.

Patricia Akhimie has noted the "inherent instability" of the term "entertainment" in early modernity:

> The primary denotative meaning is provision: monarchs, lords, and masters make provision for those under their protection, whether material or financial, providing money, goods, food, land, or shelter for servants, soldiers, and livestock. To entertain is to retain service and repay that service with worldly care. Yet to entertain is also to provide amusement, courtesy, and welcome; and in this case entertainment is often offered by the recipients of patronage or largesse to those monarchs, lords, and masters, as a token of love and loyalty. Entertainment describes the offer of hospitality, especially banquets, or the offer of pretty speeches, music or dance.[47]

In this sense, the entertaining, servile status of racially marked enslaved musicians coheres, as the very act of singing and dancing for the

---

[46] Miller, *Slaves to Fashion*, 49.

[47] Akhimie, "Performance," 68. I note that John O'Brien makes a similar claim for the importance of "entertainment" in eighteenth-century British contexts: "'entertainment' designated a specific class of performances . . . by implication, such performances were understood to be intended for diversion rather than for moral uplift, to be less serious than the plays that constituted the mainpiece repertory. . . . In the eighteenth century, entertainment was a keyword with several core meanings and numerous associations, the proliferation of which testifies to its significance to a culture that used the term to designate crucial relationships that were both hierarchical (between literature and mere entertainment, for example) and lateral (between the observer and the spectacle)." See John O'Brien, *Harlequin Britain: Pantomime and Entertainment, 1690–1760* (Baltimore: Johns Hopkins University Press, 2004), xiv–xv.

entertainment of the sovereign is understood as a proclamation of contentment with and even thanks for the servile status of enslavement. In the courtly and operatic context of seventeenth-century Florence, the fungibility of the enslaved Black character with the comic servant relies precisely on this paradox of the voice: purporting to express a limited and simplistic subjectivity while merely reflecting the entrained vocality of singers and performers under duress.

In closing, it is worth noting that Giovanni's petition for baptism was approved. On June 6, 1610, three enslaved members of the Medici court were baptized in the baptistry of San Giovanni, Florence. Both our Giovanni and another male slave, Muslì of Andrinopoli (now Edirne in Turkey), were given the Christian name Giovanbattista, and a female slave, Fatilena or Fatilemia Turca, was renamed Lisabetta.[48] Notably, both Muslì-Giovanbattista (who was approximately thirty-five to forty years of age) and Fatilena-Lisabetta (around age thirty) were already married to other members of the enslaved community, and both gave the earlier conversion of their respective spouses as factors in their own decision to convert.[49] Opening up from Giovanni, then, his baptismal trail points toward the large Florentine community of enslaved "Others," in various degrees of integration into Florentine society.

In the second half of this book, I turn to a singular figure, Giovannino Buonaccorsi, an enslaved Black soprano active at the Medici court from 1651 until his death in 1674. A remarkable number of surviving documents flesh out Buonaccorsi's musical and theatrical activities in the years between 1657 and 1664. In the larger context of unfree labor and musical performance, Buonaccorsi is a compelling case study of Black Italian musical experience, demonstrating how early modern *razza* preconditions modern racist ideologies.

---

[48] For Muslì-Giovanbattista, see I-Fd, Registri Battesimali, Maschi, reg. 27, fg. 196; for Fatilena-Lisabetta, see I-Fd, Registri Battesimali, Femmine, reg. 249, fg. 177.

[49] See I-Fca, Pia Casa dei Catecumini, f. 1, c.n.n. [ins. 27, 30].

Giovanni detto Gio: Moro si fuggi di casa il di 15 di Giugno 1628 d'Anni 15 incirca.

Giovanni, called Gio: Moro [lit., "the Moor" or "Black"], ran away from the house [the orphanage of the Innocenti] on June 15, 1628, aged approximately 15 years.

I-FAoi 1655, Esito delli Allevati delli Innocenti,
1628, alphabetical, G

Intermezzo Primo

Thinking from Enslaved Lives

In the fall of 2019, during the first blissful months of my sabbatical (and before the global Covid-19 pandemic confined me to my house and redirected my intellectual energies away from this book and toward fourth-grade fractions and preschool literacy), I took an opportunity to write a program note about Barbara Strozzi (1619–1677) in what was the quatercentenary of the singer-composer's birth.[1] I expected my time with Strozzi to be a brief and pleasurable digression from the book project, but instead, I found that I couldn't do otherwise but see the sources on Strozzi through the lens of voice, slavery, and race. Strozzi's unique position in music history has raised questions about why and how she happened into the musical and compositional activities that single her out. Considering her life and oeuvre in relationship to race and slavery raises some new answers to such questions and shows how the issue of enslavement resonates far beyond the Florentine court and into the echelons of the most celebrated seventeenth-century musicians.

For feminist musicologists, scholars of seventeenth-century Italian music, and teachers of the Western music survey, Strozzi is a familiar figure.[2] A woman composer—itself a relatively rare category—Strozzi was also a performer, she worked independently of both court and church and was a canny adapter to print culture, making her one of the period's most published composers (male or female) of secular vocal music.[3] Seven volumes of

---

[1] In musicological terms, of course, the title of this "intermezzo" is a nod to the classic essay by Suzanne G. Cusick, "'Thinking from Women's Lives': Francesca Caccini after 1627," *Musical Quarterly* 77, no. 3 (1993): 484–507.
The concert, "The Secret Lover: Strozzi @ 400," was performed by Tenet Vocal Artists on October 26, 2019, at the House of the Redeemer, New York.
[2] Ellen Rosand, "Barbara Strozzi, *Virtuosissima Cantatrice*: The Composer's Voice," *Journal of the American Musicological Society* 31 (1978): 241–281; Beth Glixon, "New Light on the Life and Career of Barbara Strozzi," *Musical Quarterly* 81, no. 2 (1997): 311–335; Beth Glixon, "More on the Life and Death of Barbara Strozzi," *Musical Quarterly* 83, no. 1 (1999): 134–141.
[3] Strozzi is regularly cited as the most prolific composer of published vocal music in this period; however, Barbara Swanson points out that Maurizio Cazzati (1616–1678) was more prolific, noting, too, that Cazzati owned a printing press and was responsible for most of his own publications. See Barbara Swanson, "Barbara Strozzi, *Appresso ai molli argenti* (1659)," in *Analytical Essays on Music*

Strozzi's music survive (an eighth is lost); a handful of other pieces appear in anthologies or manuscript. Except for one volume of sacred songs, all of Strozzi's music is secular, typically dealing with romantic love.[4] Genres range from lighter strophic forms (*ariette, canzonette*) to complex, multisection cantatas.

Strozzi's life and her musical output swirl with a permissive female sexuality that has added to the composer's modern appeal. The illegitimate daughter of a domestic worker, later adopted by the poet, librettist, academician, and libertine Giulio Strozzi (himself the illegitimate son of an illegitimate son), in whose house she lived from a young age, Strozzi went on to become the unmarried mother of four children, at least three of whom have suggestive links to the (married) patrician Giovanni Paolo Vidman, who was presumably their father.[5] Scholars have assumed Strozzi's participation in sex work; her identification as a courtesan is supported by the bared flesh of the *Female Musician with Viola da Gamba* by Bernardo Strozzi (no known relation), widely believed to be a portrait of the composer (see Intermezzo Primo Figure 1, reproduced after page 240).[6]

While musical performance, particularly song, was a standard component of the education of courtesans, composition was not. Strozzi's unusual relationship with her patron and adoptive father provided rare, perhaps unique, musical opportunities for a woman of her era. Strozzi studied musical composition with the celebrated operatic composer Francesco Cavalli and possibly also with Nicolò Fontei. In the mid-1630s, when Barbara was still a teenager, Giulio began to sponsor regular meetings of the Accademia degli Unisoni at his house. She became a regular fixture at these meetings, performing and improvising for the exclusively male membership and acting as a master (or mistress) of ceremonies. Particularly in Venice, where honorable women were strictly constrained in their interactions with men, Strozzi's

---

by *Women Composers*, ed. Laurel Parsons and Brenda Ravenscroft (Oxford: Oxford University Press, 2018), 74n2.

[4] A notable exception is "Il lamento (sul Rodano severo)," which responds to a contemporary political execution.
[5] Glixon, "More on the Life," 136–140.
[6] David Rosand and Ellen Rosand, "Barbara di Santa Sofia and Il Prete Genovese: On the Identity of a Portrait by Bernardo Strozzi," *Art Bulletin* 63 (1981): 249–258. See also Franca Trinchieri Camiz, "'La bella cantatrice': I ritratti di Leonora Barone e Barbara Strozzi a confronto," in *Musica, scienza e idee nella Serenissima durante il seicento: Atti del convegno internazionale di studi, Venezia, Palazzo Giustinian Lolin, 12–15 dicembre 1993*, ed. Francesco Passadore and Franco Rossi (Venice: Fondazione Ugo e Olga Levi, 1996), 285–294.

participation in elite intellectual circles carried an erotic charge associated with sexual availability. Her performances put her body on display, and the highly erotic content of many of her songs can only have magnified the effect. Furthermore, unlike her male contemporaries, who rarely, if ever, published chamber cantatas (which were closely identified with intimate performance, elite audiences, and erotic texts), Strozzi made her oeuvre available for purchase in improvisatory settings that implied her own performance practice.[7] Given her gender, the transactional nature of this calculus is clear.

Ellen Rosand has argued that Strozzi's adoption by Giulio implies his (natural) paternity, which may well be true.[8] This is a highly reasonable claim, and there is some evidence that contemporaries leaped to similar conclusions; for example, a letter from 1678, cited by Beth Glixon, states, "I learned that the aforementioned Signore [Giulio Strozzi] had a daughter with one of his servants."[9] Strozzi's mother, Isabella, worked in Giulio's house, and it was she who was first named as his heir. Isabella was still alive at the time of Giulio's death in 1652; however, Barbara was to inherit all of Giulio's effects ("including furniture, property, and especially his writings").[10] Yet even for an acknowledged libertine, Giulio's efforts to sponsor Barbara into public life were unorthodox: more typical for natural daughters was marriage to a friend (thus guaranteeing access to the "correct" social class) or entry into a convent.

Contemporary scholarship on Strozzi sidesteps the irregularity of Giulio's behavior—part and parcel of an understandable feminist desire for more female composers. Scholars have been more likely to ask why other fathers did not provide their musical daughters with composition lessons and a private performance arena and less likely to question Giulio's role in pimping out his adopted daughter (Vidman was a friend of Giulio's and a member of the Accademia degli Unisoni; the same letter cited by Glixon and mentioned above, which ascribes parentage to Giulio, describes Vidman as having "raped [*stuprata*]" Barbara, though the term possibly indicates his legal inability to marry her rather than non-consensual sex).[11]

---

[7] In publishing improvisatory work, Strozzi is aligned with contemporary instrumental composers, such as Girolamo Frescobaldi. On the chamber cantata and its implications, see Ellen T. Harris, *Handel as Orpheus: Voice and Desire in the Chamber Cantatas* (Cambridge, MA: Harvard University Press, 2004).

[8] Rosand, "Barbara Strozzi."

[9] Glixon cites a letter from an unidentified informant, dating from 1678 (shortly after Strozzi's death): "Ho saputo che detto signore [Giulio Strozzi] hebbe d'una sua serva una figlia." See Glixon, "More on the Life," 141n8.

[10] Glixon, "New Light," 329n29.

[11] Glixon, "More on the Life," 141n8.

Why weren't more women provided the professional opportunities afforded to Strozzi? That is a question far beyond the scope of this book; however, when I revisited the documentary records that reference Strozzi's mother, I saw them in a new light, with consequences for how I thought about the composer and about her musical and family life.

Strozzi's mother makes her first documentary appearance in the record of Strozzi's baptism. Rosand summarizes the document:

> Her baptismal record, in the archives of the parish church of Santa Sofia, now housed in the church of San Felice in Venice (*Battezzati* no. 3, 1606–23), is dated 6 August 1619. The document lists her mother as Isabella Griega and her father as "incerto" [lit. "unknown"].[12]

Griega, we can note, is the Spanish word for "Greek." Both Barbara and Isabella reappear in Giulio's will from 1628, where Isabella has the surname Garzoni and the nickname "the little Greek woman":

> Of the furniture, writings, contracts, and money that shall be found in Venice at the time of my death ... I want and intend that they shall be left to Madonna Isabella Garzoni *detta la Greghetta* [lit. "called the little Greek woman"], and this not because of any dishonorable interest, but only for the faithful and long service that, together with her daughter [then aged eight and a half], she has given to me over many years, not having had from me either wage or salary, so that this legacy shall be rather a payment owed for services rendered than a voluntary act [done] without reason, and for this reason she should be preferred above all others, and if she is missing, all this should go to Madonna Barbara Valle her daughter.[13]

In a later will, from 1650, Giulio described Barbara as "Barbara from Santa Sofia, my chosen daughter [*figliuola elettiva*], commonly however called La

---

[12] Rosand, "Barbara Strozzi," 241n3.

[13] "Dei mobili, scritti, contratti, e danari, che si troveranno al tempo della mia morte in Venetia ... voglio, e intendo che sia mia legataria Madonna Isabella Garzoni detta la Greghetta, e questo senza alcun cativo interesse, ma solo per la fedele, e lunga servitù, che insieme con la figliola mi ha prestata in molti anni, non havendo da me alcuna mercede ne salario, onde questo legato le sarà più tosto un dovuto pagamento del servitio prestatomi, che un lascito volontario, e gratuito, che per questo capo doverà esser preferita ad ogni altro, e mancando lei, vadi tutto questo in madonna Barbara Valle sua figliola." I-Vas, Notarile, Testamenti chiusi, Atti Erizzo, b. 1182.4, April 27, 1628; transcribed by Rosand, "Barbara Strozzi," 242n4.

Strozzi."[14] What interests me here is the intersection of racialized terms used to describe Isabella (Griega, la Greghetta) and her long period of unpaid labor. Certainly, in modern terms, to work "many years" without "wage or salary" amounts to slavery, and indeed, in Venice, as throughout the Italian peninsula, domestic slavery of foreign women—including Greek Orthodox women—was common. When she is viewed as the child of an ethnically marked unpaid domestic worker, certain aspects of Strozzi's life appear less radical, not least her early and evidently extensive education in music, since life as a *cortegiana onesta* or a professional singer would have been a distinct step up the social scale.

E. Natalie Rothman's work on Venetian immigrants, including religious converts and enslaved domestic workers, details several incidents in which enslaved workers were manumitted or financially rewarded for long and faithful service in their owners' wills as well as instances in which the children of converts were adopted by childless Venetian citizens in the market for an heir.[15] In this broader context, Giulio need not have been Barbara's natural father to have felt a sense of ownership over her and her education, and the professionalization of her education, publication, and life as a working woman seems far less strange. For Giulio to have sponsored into prostitution the talented daughter of his enslaved domestic servant is more plausible than his having done the same for his biological daughter. A generation later, three of Strozzi's own four illegitimate children went into monasteries (including both of her daughters), and the fourth (with little evident success) attempted to purchase a position in the office of the Doge.[16] Within her lifetime, it seems Strozzi achieved for her children the respectability that (perhaps luckily, from a musical historical perspective) was denied to her.

While this is not a book about Strozzi or, indeed, about Venice, the resonance of her unusual biography with the widespread practice of Italian

---

[14] "Barbara di Santa Sofia mia figliuola elettiva, e però chiamata comunemente la Strozzi." I-Vas, Notarile, Testamenti, Notaio Claudio Paulini, b. 799, no. 269, January 1, 1650; transcribed by Rosand, "Barbara Strozzi," 242n5.

[15] Regarding the adoption of converted and/or previously enslaved children, Rothman writes, "In most cases, it was the culmination of long periods of cohabitation between adoptive parent(s) and child, often under a different header, such as domestic service." Rothman, *Brokering Empire*, 154.

[16] For details about the attempts of Giulio Pietro (presumed son of Vidman, born ca. 1641) to purchase an office, see Glixon, "More on the Life," 136. Strozzi's two daughters, Isabella (born ca. 1642) and Laura (born ca. 1644), entered the monastery of Santo Sepolcro in 1656; Isabella died only six months later at the age of fifteen, before she could take her vows; Laura took the name Lodovica. Both are presumed to be children of Vidman. See Glixon, "More on the Life," 137–138. Strozzi's other son, Massimo, became a monk at Santo Steffano in Belluno in 1662; he was still alive in 1680. See Glixon, "New Light," 320–321.

slavery underscores the relationship of musical labor to the enslaved and the failure of musicological scholarship to account for slavery in the extant historical models. Strozzi's voice—quintessentially Italianate and freighted with a female sexuality that modern performers, listeners, and scholars have read as liberated—testifies to how quickly the children of immigrants were incorporated into Italian society and the contested, embodied locus of personal agency and musical performance as labor.

ACT II

Al Morino e a Brancone che cantarono avanti a SA due [scudi].

For the little Moor and for Brancone, who sang before His Highness, two [scudi].
I-Fas, Camera del Granduca, f. 17, May 1635, c. 41v

Scene 8
Introducing Giovannino Buonaccorsi

Giovannino Buonaccorsi was an enslaved Black singer in the retinue of Cardinal Prince Giovan Carlo de' Medici (1611–1663), a younger brother of Grand Duke Ferdinando II. Archive documents imply that Buonaccorsi lived at the Medici court from at least 1651 until his death on August 15, 1674. In contrast with the many other enslaved and racialized performers discussed in the first half of this book, details of Buonaccorsi's life and performances are preserved in a wide range of sources: account books, administrative documents, letters, costume designs, set drawings, libretti, scores, descriptions of performances, a portrait, and, in one remarkable instance, a poem. Described as a "chamber singer" (*musico da camera*) in 1663, he is known to have performed in a series of mid-century Florentine operas and in at least one season on the public opera stage in Venice. Buonaccorsi's life and work foreground the relevance of race to an analysis of European music history in three important ways. First, his very presence at the court and his participation as a singer in the elite genre of opera make it clear that race and racial difference were an important part of Florentine life. Second, the operatic roles Buonaccorsi played and the performance opportunities that were available to him demonstrate the structural importance of stereotypes— including racial stereotypes—to the development of musical and dramatic forms. Third, the extant details of Buonaccorsi's life stand in for the missing information about the larger community of racialized performers. Indeed, in Buonaccorsi's own work, this community emerges as a central component of Florentine court life. The emergent expressive and metaphorical meanings of "voice"—which coalesced in opera—intersected with characters (onstage and in real life) to distribute insidious stereotypes about the innate humanity of raced, classed, gendered, and differently abled bodies; these formulations are legible in Buonaccorsi's Blackness and persist into the present moment.

As is frequently the case for performers and other little-studied individuals of the period, the surviving material on Buonaccorsi is confusing and at times contradictory; such circumstances are only exacerbated when the individual concerned is largely identified by a racial moniker—here Moro, or "the Moor," which, as has been seen, was both a descriptive noun and a name used for many of the individuals I have discussed. Modern scholarship has struggled to account for Black characters and for Black lives in early modern Europe; however, placing this particular Black singer front and center promises to give the discussion a rare historical specificity, producing avenues with which to think about race and representation in terms that reach beyond "exoticism" or "orientalism" and troubling the presumed whiteness of European music history and music making.

Buonaccorsi features as one of two sitters in the double portrait *Ritratto di suonatore di liuto con cantore moro* (*Portrait of a lute player with a Black singer*), painted by Baldassarre Franceschini *detto il* Volterrano and thought to date from late 1662, reproduced as Figure 8.1, after page 240. Art historians have long identified the two men as "Giovannino Moro" (lit. "little Black Giovanni") and "Pan bollito" (lit. "boiled bread"), based on two seventeenth-century descriptions of the painting.[1] The earliest description dates from 1663, in a list of Cardinal Giovan Carlo's effects compiled shortly after his death on January 22:

> A painting on canvas, without a frame, oblong, 2½ *braccia* wide and 1¾ *braccia* tall, that is a portrait of Pan Bollito who plays the lute, and the Moro with a sheet of music in hand, with a violin and books, [done] in the hand of Baldassarre.[2]

The unframed nature of the painting suggests that it was a recent acquisition. Almost twenty years later, the art critic and historian Filippo Baldinucci published a description of the same work alongside other paintings produced by Volterrano for the cardinal during the last few years of Giovan Carlo's life:

---

[1] Fabrizio Guidi, "Pitture fiorentine del seicento ritrovate," *Paragone* 25, no. 297 (1974): 58–62; Gerhard Ewald, "Appunti sulla Galleria Gerini e sugli affreschi di Anton Domenico Gabbiani," in *Kunst des Barock in der Toskana: Studien zur Kunst unter den letzten Medici*, ed. Florence Kunsthistorisches Institut (Munich: Bruckmann, 1976), 344–358; Riccardo Spinelli, "Ritratto di suonatore di liuto con cantore moro (Panbollito e Giovannino moro)," in *Volterrano: Baldassarre Franceschini (1611–1690)*, ed. Maria Cecilia Fabbri, Alessandro Grassi, and Riccardo Spinelli (Florence: Ente Cassa di Risparmio di Firenze, 2013), 244–245; Kaplan, "Giovannino Moro."

[2] "Un quadro in tela senza adornamento bislungo di braccia 2½ largo, et alto braccia 1¾ entrovi il Ritratto di Pan Bollito che suona il Liuto, et il Moro con una Carta di musica in Mano, con il Violino et libri di mano di Baldassarre." I-Fas, Miscellanea medicea, n. 31, ins. 10, c. 133v. The list locates the painting as being in the Medici Villa of Castello, in a room with a view of a meadow and a fountain.

then [Volterrano] represented for [the cardinal] a young footman [*staffiere*] of his court, with Giovannino his Moor, who was a pretty good musician [*musico*], in the act of singing.³

In his (as yet unpublished) work on this painting, Paul Kaplan was able to connect the figure of Cardinal Giovan Carlo's Giovannino Moro to a Black singer-performer variously mentioned in musicology and theater studies, pulling together references that had been separated by discipline and complicated by the various names by which Buonaccorsi was known. Nomenclature has immediate consequences for the ease with which Buonaccorsi can be traced in both secondary and primary sources, and the confusion quickly bleeds into the loaded question of whether this singer was a servant or a slave. In many sources (primary and secondary), he is merely "il Moro"; this is true for much of the musicological literature, including Robert and Norma Weaver's *A Chronology of Music in the Florentine Theater 1590–1750* and James Leve's introductory essay to Jacopo Melani's *Il potestà di Colognole*.⁴ Françoise Decroisette, however, a theater historian who has worked on the La Pergola theater and on the singers of Cardinal Giovan Carlo, has called him Giovanni Buonaccorsi throughout her writings,⁵ an identification echoed by Sara Mamone in several publications in 2003, though Mamone spelled his name "Bonaccorsi"⁶ (without the u). The use of "Bonaccorsi" persists in Sergio Monaldini's excellent work on Carlo Righenzi (another singer in the

---

³ "[D]ipoi gli rappresentò in un quadro un giovanetto staffiere di sua Corte, con Giovannino suo moro, che fu assai buon musico, in atto di cantare." The quote continues: "Trovasi oggi questo quadro in mano di Girolamo Gerini Senatore Fiorentino." The mention of the picture comes as part of a section beginning on the previous page describing works done by Volterrano for Cardinal Giovan Carlo de' Medici around 1662. Filippo Baldinucci, "Decenn. V. della Part. I. del sec. V. dal 1640. al 1650," in *Notizie de' professori del disegno da Cimabue in qua* (Florence, 1682), 400.
⁴ Robert Lamar Weaver and Norma Wright Weaver, *A Chronology of Music in the Florentine Theater 1590–1750*, Detroit Studies in Music Bibliography (Detroit: Information Coordinators, 1978); Jacopo Melani, *Il potestà di Colognole*, ed. James Leve (Middleton, WI: A-R Editions, 2005).
⁵ See Françoise Decroisette, "Un exemple d'administration des theatres au XVIIème siecle: Le theatre de la Pergola a Florence (1652–1662)," in *Arts du spectacle et histoire des idées: Recueil offert en hommage à Jean Jacquot* (Tours: Publications de la Société des Amis du Centre d'Études Supériures de la Renaissance, 1984), 81n17; Françoise Decroisette, "I virtuosi del Cardinale, da Firenze all'Europa," in *Lo "spettacolo maraviglioso": Il Teatro della Pergola: l'Opera a Firenze*, ed. Marcello de Angelis et al., Ufficio Centrale per i Beni Archivistici (Florence: Pagliai Polistampa, 2000), 85; Giovanni Andrea Moniglia, *Il vecchio balordo*, ed. Françoise Decroisette, Biblioteca Pregoldoniana (Venice: Lineadacqua, 2014), 149.
⁶ See Sara Mamone, ed., *Serenissimi fratelli principi impresari: Notizie di spettacolo nei carteggi medicei: Carteggi di Giovan Carlo de' Medici e di Desiderio Montemagni suo segretario (1628–1664)* (Florence: Le Lettere, 2003), XXXVI, XXXVII; Sara Mamone, "Most Serene Brothers-Princes-Impresarios: Theater in Florence under the Management and Protection of Mattias, Giovan Carlo, and Leopoldo de' Medici," *Journal of Seventeenth-Century Music* 9 (2003): 4–8.

Table 8.1. Extract from "Ruolo dei provvisionati del Serenissimo Principe Cardinale Giovan Carlo di Toscana, provvisioni il mese," I-Fas, Mediceo del Principato, f. 5358, cc. 756r–758r, as transcribed in Sara Mamone, ed., *Serenissimi fratelli principi impresari: Notizie di spettacolo nei carteggi medicei: Carteggi di Giovan Carlo de' Medici e di Desiderio Montemagni suo segretario (1628–1664)* (Florence: Le Lettere, 2003), as document 1, p. 6.

Principio del servizio [Date service began]	Nome [Name]	Cariche [Responsibility]	Provvisione [Provision]
14 settembre 1651	Gio Bonaccorsi	musico di camera	scudi 4

cardinal's household).[7] Even this seeming agreement provides no clarity, however, since Monaldini cites Mamone, Mamone cites Decroisette as the source of the identification, and Decroisette cites a list of *salariati* employed by Giovan Carlo that Mamone herself published; the transcription shows the name "Gio Bonaccorsi" but no indication that he was or was called "il Moro" (see Mamone's transcription, reproduced as Table 8.1). Indeed, by 2013, Mamone had identified the designation "il Moro" with a different singer, Giovanni Michele de Bar.[8] The salary cited in Mamone's transcription—4 scudi per month—is roughly comparable with those of the other singers on Giovan Carlo's roll, where singers' salaries range from 2 to 16 scudi per month, leading several scholars to categorize Buonaccorsi/Bonaccorsi as a paid servant and not a slave, assuming Decroisette was correct in her association of the name with the cardinal's Moor. Kaplan, citing small payments to "il Moro" from the Camera del Granduca's *spese straordinarie* from 1656 and 1657, has also questioned the individual's enslaved status.[9]

Importantly, however, the published transcription of Giovan Carlo's *provvisionati* is inaccurate on a number of counts, and when corrected, the information it contains clarifies several points. My transcription is shown in Table 8.2; I have also transcribed entries pertaining to the cardinal's other singers and several other relevant court members (the full list runs to 143 individuals over four and a half dense pages).

---

[7] Sergio Monaldini, "Leandro: Carlo Righenzi musico e comico," *Musicalia* 8 (2011): 75–111.

[8] See the index to Sara Mamone, ed., *Mattias de' Medici serenissimo mecenate dei virtuosi: Notizie di spettacolo nei carteggi medicei: Carteggio di Mattias de' Medici (1629–1667)* (Florence: Le Lettere, 2013). I note that this seems like a simple error on her part; she makes no justification for the change.

[9] Kaplan, "Giovannino Moro." He cites I-Fas, Camera del Granduca f. 28b (1656–1657), 17r, 43v.

Table 8.2. Extract from "Ruolo dei provisionati del Serenissimo Principe Cardinale Gio: Carlo di Toscana," I-Fas, Mediceo del Principato, f. 5358, c. 756r–758r; my transcription.

				Provvisione il mese [Provision each month]	
	Principio del servizio [Date service began]	Nomi de' servitori [Name of service provider]	Cariche [Responsibility]	Dal Tesoriore [From the Treasury]	Dalla Camera [From the Chamber]
c. 256r	March 15, 1656	Dottore Gio: Andrea Moneglia	Medico [doctor]	10.-.-	
c. 256v	June 1, 1638	Domenico Anglesi	Aiutante di Camera [personal manservant]	10.-.-	
	September 14, 1651	Pier Gio: Albizzi [P. Bollito]	Staffiere [footman]	6.1.10.-	
c. 257v	February 1, 1651	Antonio Rivani	Musico di camera* [chamber singer]	16.-.-	
	September 14, 1651	Gio: Buonaccorsi Moro	Musico di camera	Vitto e vestito [food and clothing]	-.4.-
	May 1, 1653	Francesco Leonardi	Musico [Soprano]	6.-.-	
	May 20, 1656	Carlo Righenzi	Musico [Tenore]	10.6.-	
	October 31, 1659	Lorenzo Bertoni	Sonatore di tiorba [theorbo player]		-.3.-
		Anton: Maria Bertoni	Sonatore di violino [violin player]		4.-.-

(*continued*)

Table 8.2. Continued

			Provvisione il mese [Provision each month]	
Principio del servizio [Date service began]	Nomi de' servitori [Name of service provider]	Cariche [Responsibility]	Dal Tesoriore [From the Treasury]	Dalla Camera [From the Chamber]
September 1, 1660	Vincenzo Oliviviani	Mus*ico* ^Soprano^	5.-.-	
October 1, 1661	Gregorio Kiglier	Sona*tore* di flauti [flute player]	2.-.-	
December 1, 1662	Bartolomeo Melani	Mus*ico* ^Contralto^	3.-.-	
June 1, 1646	Do*nna* Lucia Coppa	Musica		10.-.-
December 31, 1656	Angela Solij fanciulla	Musica	2.-.-	
July 4, 1657	Do*nna* Lisabetta Falbetti Nacci	Musica		3.-.-
December 8, 1657	Francesca Chiarelli Fanci*ulla*	Musica	8.-.-	
November 1, 1658	Do*nna* Leonora Falbetti Ballerini	Musica	6.-.-	
March 20, 1661	Luisa Massai fanciulla	Musica		3.-.-
[November 5, 1652]	Stefano Nano	[Dwarf]		6.-.-
c. 758r	Gio: Antonio Gaeta Mutolo	[Mute]	Vitto e vestito [food and clothing]	

* Each of the singers is listed here as *musico* or *musica* (lit. "musician"), while the instrumentalists are listed as *sonatore* (lit. "player"). In several cases, the voice range of the singer has been added in later, with a different ink and smaller hand (these annotations appear in my transcription in superscript). While in many contemporary documents *musico* is used as a euphemism for castrato, the use here of the term to describe the tenor singer Carlo Righenzi indicates that a broader meaning is intended. Still, many of these male singers are described as having high voices, and most can be identified as castrati from other documents.

From this corrected list, we can clearly identify "Gio: Buonaccorsi" (with a u) as "il Moro" and note that he was indeed enslaved. Instead of a salary of 4 scudi a month (as claimed by Mamone), he received his food and clothing along with a small allowance of 4 lire a month—far too little to be anything more than pocket money—drawn from a separate source of funding.[10] This lack of salary explains why Buonaccorsi's name is missing from other contemporary lists of the cardinal's household, which typically catalogue the *salariati* or "salaried" employees (such as the list from 1661 that appears in the same *filza*).[11] The *ruolo* at cc. 756r–758r, however, from which the corrected transcription is drawn, includes all of the *provvisionati*, or "provisioned." The only other person on this list of 143 *provvisionati* who is "provisioned" with food and clothes rather than a monetary disbursement is Gio: Antonio Gaeta *mutolo*, or "mute," who—much like the enslaved—had little or no autonomy over his life.

In this list, the singers and instrumentalists are ranked in order of their arrival at court. Giovan Carlo kept six male singers and six female singers, as well as three instrumentalists (a theorbo player, a violinist, and a flutist), all men. Antonio Rivani, a well-regarded castrato singer, had been with Giovan Carlo the longest and was the best compensated; however, the rate of payment does not map directly onto length of service. Most of the male singers were castrati; the only singer explicitly identified as having a non-altered or natural voice is the comic tenor and commedia dell'arte performer Carlo Righenzi, who received one of the largest salaries among the performers, second only to Rivani and more than equal to the salary paid to the footmen on staff.[12]

I have included only one footman, or *staffiere*, in my transcription, though there are twelve in the original document, all of whom received the same salary, of 6 scudi, 1 lire, and 10 soldi per month. Beside the name of Pier Giovanni Albizzi, the text "P. Bollito" (an abbreviation of "Pan Bollito") has been added in a smaller hand. The nickname refers to a cheap and rustic soup commonly eaten by Tuscan peasants; Giovanni Andrea Moniglia provides the following definition: "Bread cooked in water, properly mush, bread

---

[10] In the conversion equivalency at the time, 1 scudo = 7 lire; 1 lire = 20 soldi; 1 soldo = 12 denari. My thanks to Francesca Fantappiè for the time she spent helping me make sense of the Medicean account books.

[11] I-Fas, Mediceo del Principato, f. 5358, cc. 751r–753v. Notably, this list, dated 1661, contains only those who were paid from the treasury and omits payments that came from the Camera del Granduca.

[12] On Righenzi's career, see Monaldini, "Leandro."

mush."[13] We can thus identify Albizzi as the lutenist who appears alongside Buonaccorsi in Volterrano's double portrait. I note that according to the list of *provvisionati*, Albizzi and Buonaccorsi began their service at the court on exactly the same day. Their presence together in the portrait and their shared start date raise the intriguing possibility that they arrived together or shared a history even before 1651, though it should also be noted that of the twelve footmen listed, five began on September 14, 1651, and four others shared an initial date of August 1, 1642. It is equally likely that Giovan Carlo expanded his staff at certain points in his career and that Buonaccorsi and Albizzi were coincidentally entered onto the *ruolo* at the same time.[14]

It is not clear how Buonaccorsi entered the cardinal's service. Unfortunately, while some of the cardinal's accounts do survive, the more detailed register of his Camera and petitions to enter his service have been found only for the period leading up to August 1651, breaking off precisely at the time that might have provided more detail on Buonaccorsi or Albizzi. On October 12, 1650—more than a year before Buonaccorsi officially entered his service—Cardinal Giovan Carlo de' Medici paid 4 lire to the "Morino del Buonaccorsi";[15] this may be a reference to our singer, or it may refer to another young Black man who was owned by the Buonaccorsi family. Similarly, in September 1653, the Grand Duke paid the "Morino del Buonaccorsi" a total of 6 lire.[16] Given that the accounts after 1651 regularly mention the "Morino" or "Moro del Card. Giovan Carlo" (presumably a reference to our singer), it seems that this later granducal payment refers to a different Black African. The naming conventions for converted Christians make it difficult to be certain either way. While several scholars have assumed that Buonaccorsi's given name (cited in documents as "Giovannino" or with the abbreviation "Gio:") was a reference to the cardinal's name (Giovan Carlo), the other baptized Giovannis discussed in this book evidence the high prevalence of that name among converts. Furthermore, had Giovan Carlo de' Medici sponsored

---

[13] Giovanni Andrea Moniglia defines the term *pan bollito* in the list of definitions provided as an appendix to his 1660 opera, Giovanni Andrea Moniglia, "La serva nobile," in *Delle poesie dramatiche di Giovann'Andrea Moniglia, Accademic della Crusca, Parte terza* (Florence: Vincenzio Vangelisti, 1698), 284.

[14] Mamone transcribes a reference to "Moro" from January 1651 that may or may not describe Buonaccorsi: "il Moro" is described as helping out a German "giocolatore," presumably a tumbler or acrobat: "Pippo et il Moro furono gl'aiuti che fecero bella scena." I-Fas, Mediceo del Principato, f. 5393, Cardinale Leopoldo a Mattias (1624–1657), c. 418r; transcribed as lett. 659 in Mamone, *Mattias de' Medici*, 312.

[15] I-Fas, Depositeria generale, parte antica, f. 1604, c. 116r.

[16] I-Fas, Camera del Granduca, f. 25, c. 9r.

Buonaccorsi for baptism, his surname—following convention—would have been Medici, not Buonaccorsi.[17] The Buonaccorsi were an established and wealthy Florentine family. Giulio Buonaccorsi was on the board of the Pia Casa dei Catacumeni from at least 1643 until 1673; a Giovanni Buonaccorsi was made bishop in 1645.[18] Either of these men would have been a highly eligible candidate to sponsor a converting slave. A conversion would suggest that Buonaccorsi himself was brought to Italy as a slave, rather than being born there to enslaved persons or to descendants of the enslaved.

It should also be noted that in July 1651, the Camera del Granduca made a single payment of 28 scudi and 4 lire to a Roman slave trader.[19] The timing of this payment—the only direct payment to a slave trader in the accounts I examined—is certainly noteworthy; however, the sum involved is relatively modest compared with the standard purchase price for healthy slaves at the time, particularly one with such noteworthy musical skills. I thus do not think it particularly likely that this slaver sold Buonaccorsi to the court. The traffic among skilled court slaves was more typically part of the gift economy, demonstrating the generosity (and thus nobility) of the gift giver.

I want to return to the list of Giovan Carlo's *provvisionati* from which Table 8.2 is transcribed. Though the list is undated and has been attributed to 1661 and 1656, my consultation of the documents makes clear that it was produced (like the list of paintings cited earlier) in the aftermath of the cardinal's death. First, the latest "start date" given in the first column is December 1662, and so it cannot have been written before then. More important, however, the document is closely related to and cross-referenced by a second document, written in the same hand and titled "Roll of the Courtiers of the Most Serene Cardinal Gio: Carlo, who, after the death of his most illustrious highness, need to be reassigned."[20] This related document exists in several copies (the most detailed is reproduced as Table 8.3) and separates a number of the cardinal's dependents into one of five categories (reading from left to

---

[17] To give just one example, see Ferdinando Medici, described as "Ferdinando Medici Battezzato" in the Libro di Salariati from 1664 to 1665; I-Fas, Depositeria generale, parte antica, f. 397, c. 63s. In 1667, the same individual received a sum of 10 doble (equivalent to 28 scudi, 4 lire) for serving as "interpreter for the Armenians": "A Ferdinando Medici interprete degli Armeni." I-Fas, Camera del Granduca, f. 39, c. 11r.

[18] There is a book of regulations for the Pia Casa dei Catacumeni that lists Giulio Buonaccorsi's name in several places. See I-Fas, Mediceo del Principato, f. 5363. See also the entry on Giovanni Buonaccorsi in the Medici Archive Project, Person ID 17256.

[19] I-Fas, Camera del Granduca, f. 22, c. 37v.

[20] "Ruolo dei Cortigiani del Ser*enissi*mo Car*dinal*e Gio: Carlo, à quali doppo la morte di S.A.Ill*ustrissi*ma doveva dargli impiego," I-Fas, Mediceo del Principato, f. 5358, cc. 728r–729r.

Table 8.3. "Ruolo dei Cortigiani del Serenissimo Cardinale Gio: Carlo, à quali doppo la morte di S.A.Illuminissimi doveva dargli impiego," I-Fas, Mediceo del Principato, f. 5358, cc. 728r–729r.

	Offizi		Carità		Buoni		Carità di donne		Licenzare
1630	Franc:o Conti è vecchio, non può più servire alla Cam:ra, Sarà impiegato p un'Anno, chè buono p un'uffizio o in Guardaroba.	1647	Bargiacchi, non buono, ma p la servitù della Nonna, padre e sua, e p carità, e p non esser buono ad altro	1655	Monsù Riccardo, ottimo Barb:e e buon'huomo	S.8.-		1655	Desiderio Lacchè è stato un'Anno, non corre. Luccattini ha del suo, e può operare. Macinghi Spostacolo. Bernieri Garzon' di Bottig:a.
1636	Citerni, ha qualcosa del suo Véditore di Dog:na, o Cassiere.	1631	Bechino Portiere. Carità non buono	1642	Aless:o Lungo Staffiere	S.10.-	Dom:co Betta Portiere Vecchio o La Ser:ma, o Pri'pino, o P.pessa	1629	Garzon' di Cucina stato un Anno. Ministro di fonderia.
1638	Anglesi, sapere la Provisione che ha, e non volendolo alcun pigliare, dargli tanto che non parta.	1634	Gio: Aggravi Portiere con motiss. mi fig.li senza niente	1651	Buttero	S.10.-	Cesere Buono, l'istessa	1632	M:ro di Stalla, sentesi haver del suo. S.10.- Lettighere accomodato. S.20.- Serv.re della Valigia. Valigiaio, Mestiero. Morosini. Manescalco Mestiero.
1637	Bambagino. S.A. lo piglia p la Caccia.	1636	Gio: M.a Mozzo. Carità non buono	1651	Panbollito	S.6.1.10			Boccardio, ha del suo.
1638	Benvenuto staffiere.	1642	Elmi sotto Maestro di Casa Povero storpiato	1658	Lorenzino Lacchè	S.6.1.10			I Min'ri dello scrittorio saranno impiegati p un'Anno nell'Eredità. In tanto può venire occasione d'impiego essendo buoni.
1642	Barbetta. Forse la Ser.ma per haverlo messo vorrà sia accomod.a.	1629	Gio: Piero Bottigliere. Carità	1630	Rasperino	S.10.-			
1642	Rocchio Tiratore.	1645	Vannini Cantiniere	1655	Il Credenziere	S.10.-			
1642	Scarpettini.	1651	Simone Cantiniere	1655	Garzone	S.6.-			
1643	Menichella.	1650	Petrini Cuoco Aiuto	1651	Poppino	S.6.1.10			

1651	Tozzi.	1645	Marco P.o Cocchiere	S. 7.-	1650	Nottolone, forse il S:r Pr̄cp.e	S.6.1.10
	Burattino.	1651	Baccaloro, Storpiato, Povero	S 6.-	1658	Bernini, forse il S:r Pr̄cp.e	S.6.1.10
							S.79.3.10
1642	Picchietto Bracchiere.	1634	Stefano Stroziere cieco	S 5.-			
1651	Vinc.o Dini Bracchiere.	1634	Guarda Vecchio	S 5.-			
1652	Marchionne Cacciatore		Moro	S 8.-			
1657	Niccolo del'Buono Stroppiere.		Mutolo	S 8.-			
1657	Benvenuto Bracchiere.		Tartufo	S 8.-			
	Quattro si possono accomodare p Stradieri in due, o tre mesi di tempo, et il resto propongo p soldati di Livorno, o Fortezze, con due scui il mese d'augumento, che p dieci facienzo, S. 20	1629	Ipolito già Cocchiere. S.A. li ha dato intenzione in riguardo del fig.lo Bassetti, e può contentarsi di	S. 8.- S.137			

right): hired directly into a new position by the Grand Duke, given a charitable donation, given a pension, eligible for charity to be distributed via the women of the family, and fired. Reading the two lists together, we can see that "Panbollito" was allocated a monthly pension at the same rate he was paid during his patron's life.[21] Buonaccorsi however, who, as we recall, received no salary, also fails to receive a pension. After Giovan Carlo died, "il Moro," the mute Gio: Antonio Gaeta, and the dwarf, called here by his nickname "Tartufo," meaning "Truffle," but identified elsewhere as Stefano Nano ("the Dwarf"), were each paid a one-time charitable handout of 8 scudi, which for Buonaccorsi amounted to a little more than his total annual income.[22] This treatment is in contrast not only with that of Albizzi but also with that of the other chamber singers, male and female, none of whom appears on the list. Notably, several of the cardinal's singers appear in a list of *salariati* employed by the Grand Duke in 1664–1665.[23]

We can understand the bundling together of "Il Moro," "Il Muto," and "Tartufo" (Moor, Mute, and Dwarf) as a moment of productive opacity, a term I borrow from Édouard Glissant.[24] Evidently, these three individuals occupied a similar category for the court functionaries in charge of these accounts. Moor, Mute, and Dwarf—each is physically marked, each is at some remove from the category of the fully human. Tartufo, however, it should be noted, did receive a salary, at the rate of 6 scudi per month.

The economic and categorical disparities that these documents manifest in their treatment of Buonaccorsi and the lute-playing footman Albizzi provide a useful counterpoint to Volterrano's portrait of the two men, for one of the most striking aspects of the painting is the visual equivalence of the two sitters. In contrast to the traditional model of courtly portraiture, in which a Black child or retainer is depicted in a subservient position to a central white patron, the two sitters in Volterrano's canvas are united in deference to the patron-viewer, their attention and their music making directed to a

---

[21] I note that despite this assignation of funds, the footmen Scarpettini, Tozzi, Benvenuto, Menichelli, and Roccio go on to receive payments (at this rate) from the Camera del Granduca—"tutti staffieri della Beata Memoria del Card. Gio:Carlo"—although Pan Bollito does not. See, for example, I-Fas, Camera del Granduca, f. 33, c. 13v.

[22] In March 1663, Tartufo was placed on the rolls of the Camera del Granduca with a salary of 2 scudi per month; however, in August of that year, he left for Parma, and the payments ceased. See I-Fas, Camera del Granduca, f. 32b, c. 25.

[23] Anton Maria Bertoni, Vincenzo Oliviviani, Gregorio Kiglier, Lucia Coppa, and Lisabette Falbetti Nacci (all singers) are listed in I-Fas, Depositeria generale, parte antica, f. 397, as are Domenico Anglesi and Ferdinando Tacci.

[24] Édouard Glissant, *Poetics of Relation*, trans. Betsy Wing (Ann Arbor: University of Michigan Press, 1997).

specific goal. Both men make eye contact with the viewer, initially identifiable as the cardinal patron and/or his selected guests. Albizzi fingers a chord with his left hand, his right poised in anticipation; he seems to wait for a signal. Buonaccorsi has his lips slightly parted. This is a common iconography of song or singing, though here it looks as if he is breathing in or holding a breath, poised like Albizzi and ready to begin.[25] There are bound music books visible on the table, yet the performers are reading from loose sheets; thus, the listener/viewer is about to hear something fresh and new, likely something written expressly for the patron's enjoyment. Presumably—given the small-scale instrumentation, the intimate physical setting, and the newness of the composition—the work is a chamber cantata. As Ellen Harris has argued, the chamber cantata had specific currency as a marker of intimacy and exclusive access to highly restricted social spaces.[26] Here the literacy of the two musicians underscores their importance as playback devices (even as it testifies to their level of education): before recording technologies, only the wealthiest Europeans could listen to music on demand. Recall Jörg Jochen Berns's arguement that precisely this ability to control the aural environment—over which a listener typically has little control—is an intrinsic element of early modern sovereignty.[27] Thus, in this image, musical sound (specifically the rarefied, rarely circulated sound of a chamber cantata) unites both musicians as subject to the sovereign viewer. Our ears pricked in anticipation, the soundscape of this painting impinges on our notice, imbuing Buonaccorsi with action and with voice—in ways that blur the boundaries between the two categories.

Importantly for my analysis, the work is a portrait, depicting recognizable individuals (Buonaccorsi and Albizzi) in a customary occupation (chamber music performance) in a recognizable location (Palazzo Pitti, with a section of the Boboli Gardens and the famous artichoke fountain visible through the open window). There is a studied casualness to the composition, as if Volterrano has captured a candid glimpse of an ordinary and intimate afternoon of musical performance. Formally, however, the painter has constructed a striking contrast between the pale-skinned white lutenist, depicted in somber dark clothing and seated in shadow, and the Black-skinned singer who sits with the light behind him, wearing a brightly striped

---

[25] Riccardo Spinelli suggests that Buonaccorsi might be quickly looking over his part, singing softly to himself, while Albizzi looks to the viewer (originally, of course, Cardinal Giovan Carlo) for a sign to begin; see Spinelli, "Ritratto," 245.
[26] Harris, *Handel as Orpheus*.
[27] Berns, "Instrumental Sound."

non-Western tunic. This play of light and dark, outside and inside, exotic and European, splits the painting precisely down the middle, belying the sense it exudes of a natural occurrence, happily captured by the painter-as-observer. Yet even as Buonaccorsi and Albizzi are markedly contrasted, their unity and coordination are emphasized by subtle visual cues such as the parallel angle of Albizzi's left hand and the back of Buonaccorsi's right and the similarly open collars of their two very different outfits. Nothing is included in Volterrano's frame by mistake or happenstance, not the music, not the outfits, and certainly not the enslaved Black singer.

Within this frame, the clothing of the two men calls attention to itself, with both depicted in costly, even luxurious outfits. Black fabric was particularly expensive, and the textured velvet and voluminous folds of Albizzi's jacket and undershirt make it clear that whoever paid for the outfit spared no expense. While the satiny fabric of Buonaccorsi's tunic also makes a claim to volume (and thus expense), the brightly striped pattern and the Middle Eastern style have a dramatically different effect. Indeed, it is productive to consider Buonaccorsi's outfit as a costume, though he likely wore this outfit or something very similar as his everyday wear.[28] The splendor of Buonaccorsi's outfit iterates a long tradition of what Monica Miller calls "black spectacularity," where the "garish but expensive outfits" of Black children and young men kept as luxury items represent an iconography of international wealth.[29]

Early modern servants and retainers wore livery supplied by their employers, and the enslaved typically wore clothing that marked them us foreign. Accounts from 1666, for example, document an outfit made for the *morino*, or "Black boy," belonging to Ferdinando II, presumably Ali Moro, who would have been around ten at the time.[30] This individual received an "outfit in the Moorish style [*alla moresca*] made of green cloth, silk slippers, and stockings made in one piece and a long cassock down to the knee, all decorated with green trim."[31] The outfit cost more than 88 lire, twenty-two times the monthly allowance that was distributed to Buonaccorsi, and

---

[28] On racially marked outfits and their use in Italian courts (particularly in Florence), see Elizabeth Currie, "Clothing and Cross-Cultural Perspectives at the Medici Court, 1550–1650" (conference presentation at The Medici and the Perception of Sub-Saharan Africa, Medici Archive Project, Florence, June 2–3, 2022).

[29] Miller, *Slaves to Fashion*, 39, 49.

[30] For Ali's age, see his baptismal details at I-Fd, Registri Battesimali, Maschi, reg. 58, fol. 22. Ali took the baptismal name Cosimo Maria Medici.

[31] I-Fas, Camera del Granduca, f. 35, 77r.

reminds us of the "vitto e vestito" Buonaccorsi received rather than a salary. With regard to Buonaccorsi's everyday costume (as depicted by Volterrano), it is notable that Kaplan has traced an iconography of stripes in the outfits of Italian court slaves and that the Black page in the 1658 Florentine performance of Moniglia and Francesco Cavalli's opera *L'Hipermestra* was described as wearing "incarnata" livery, that is, striped red and white.[32] A costume sketch by Stefano della Bella represents one of the six (non-singing) pages who accompanied the title character—clearly depicting a Black African individual (see Figure 8.2, reproduced after page 240).[33] The high collar, ballooning sleeves, and striped fabric are highly reminiscent of Buonaccorsi's outfit as depicted by Volterrano. While the role of this page may have been double cast with Alindo (the Moorish valet played by Buonaccorsi in the same production), the face of the young boy is not recognizable as Buonaccorsi's face, and the sketch presumably represents another of the Medici's Black retainers.

The (literal) costume that Buonaccorsi wore as Alindo was described by Orazio Ricasoli Rucellai in the published *descrizione* of *L'Hipermestra*: "he was dressed in black taffeta in semblance of nude skin, with a rich vest of light blue Turquoise [Turkish] satin, all trimmed with silver and beautifully studded with scarlet coral."[34] Similarly, Buonaccorsi's costuming in a 1661 performance of *Ercole in Tebe* was described at some length by Alessandro Segni in a published appendix to Moniglia's libretto:

Iolao, the Black servant of the Athenian monarch appeared on the shore. He wore a vest of blue satin in the African style, adorned with splendid

---

[32] See Kaplan, "Titian's 'Laura Dianti.'"; Kaplan, "Giovannino Moro." Buonaccorsi's costuming in performances is also discussed in the introduction to Francesco Cavalli, *Scipione affricano*, ed. Jennifer Williams Brown (forthcoming).

[33] The entire set of costume designs associated with this series of operas is described at length by Phyllis Dearborn Massar, "Costume Drawings by Stefano della Bella for the Florentine Theater," *Master Drawings* 8, no. 3 (1970): 243–266. Massar makes some strange assumptions about the parts of various performances that were sung or spoken and has some inaccuracies with regard to the dating of *L'Hipermestra* and the death of the cardinal but includes nice reproductions of the relevant images. Descriptions of many of these images, illustrated with a set of much smaller reproductions, are included in Marcello de Angelis et al., eds., *Lo "spettacolo maraviglioso": Il Teatro della Pergola: l'opera a Firenze* (Florence: Pagliai Polistampa, 2000).

[34] Original Italian: "nella medesima Scena quivi Alindo Moro valletto d'Arbante, il quale era di taffettà nero in sembianza di nudo vestito, con una ricca giubba di raso turchino celeste, tutta guarnita d'argento, e di purpurei coralli vagamente tempestata." The description of the scene continues: "feronsi accoglienza scambievole, ed Alindo di concerto col suo Signore con bella circuizion di parole accennò a Vafrino il nuovo amor d'Ipermestra, ed andossene." Orazio Ricasoli Rucellai, as reproduced in Giovanni Andrea Moniglia, *Delle poesie dramatiche di Giovann'Andrea Moniglia, Accademico della Crusca, Parte prima* (Florence: Vincenzio Vangelisti, 1689), 55–56.

embroidery; the dark color of his Black legs was covered by elegant boots of white silver, and the many jewels adorning him all over denoted the grandness of his master.[35]

Notable in both of these descriptions is an exoticization of Buonaccorsi's skin and costume alike, from the "black taffeta in semblance of nude skin" and "the dark color of his Black legs" to the "Turquoise" satin of his coral-studded vest and his jacket "in the African style." These descriptions make explicit the function of Buonaccorsi's offstage costume of bright red stripes. Buonaccorsi's racialized appearance reflected back—like the jewels of his costume in performance as Iolao—onto the greatness of his master.

Taken as a whole, Volterrano's painting communicates the fabulous wealth of the Medici court, including the decorative nature of the painting itself, the leisurely enjoyment of new music, the expensive clothing of the court functionaries, and even the architectural and botanical vistas glimpsed in the background. The poses of the waiting musicians flatter the patron directly, implicating him as the reason for and the controlling force over their imminent performance, flaunting his sovereignty over the bodies, products, and sounds depicted in the painting—true not only of the two visible musicians but also of the painter whose labor resulted in the image and the composer who produced the newly composed song indicated by the loose sheets.

Still, I find something compelling about this image of Buonaccorsi that goes beyond the objectification of his race and of his performance as luxury commodity, conspicuously and artfully displayed. In part, as I have already indicated, his visual equivalence with Albizzi unsettles the generic dyad of Black slave/white master; however—less objectively—I find something striking about the confidence with which Buonaccorsi sits in his chair. European representations of confident, relaxed Black men are rare even today, such that the very pastness of this image pushes back against

---

[35] Original Italian: "mentre la nave dilungandosi si toglieva dalla veduta degli spettatori, Iolao moro servo del monarca Ateniese comparve sul lido. Egli vestia all'Affricana una giubba di raso mavì, adornata con ricamo splendente; copriva l'oscuro colore della sua nera gamba gentile calzare di candido argento, e le molte gioie, che d'ogn'intorno il fregiavano, la grandezza dinotavano del suo Signore." The description of the scene continues: "Questi nel viaggio, che ci fe verso Dite, seco il condusse fin quivi, ove aspettandone il ritorno, egli pur'anco dimorava, dolendosi con giocose rime, che la sterilità, e solitudine di quel brutto paese, gli togliesse il valersi della sua zingaresca industria; Sifone [the hunchback, stuttering servant character, played as usual by Carlo Righenzi] il riconobbe, e dopo varj discorsi, pieni di detti faceti, e di proverbi mordaci, risolvero d'accordo, abbandonando quella diserta spiaggia, di tornarsene alle fertili campagne di Tebe; e come dissero, sì fecero." Alessandro Segni, as reproduced in Giovanni Andrea Moniglia, *Ercole in Tebe* (Florence: Stamperia all'Insegna della Stella, 1661), 134.

narratives of Black otherness within Europe and against the presumedly cumulative arc of moral history as it tends toward justice. Volterrano's portrait, to cite Saidiya Hartman, provides a rare "glimpse of the vulnerability of [Buonaccorsi's] face" and charges us to answer to "what looking at such a face might demand."[36] To understand all of the Black and ethnically marked individuals at the court on their own terms is an admirable if difficult task, though one in which Buonaccorsi's voice provides some purchase, for—literally and metaphorically—the voice emerges from under the visual surface of race and testifies to the presence of an acting body. Buonaccorsi's complicated status as part of the court pushes us to think carefully about how the court itself is defined and how we think about who and what counts as European.

Perhaps illuminating in an attempt to rethink who counts or how people counted—with particular relevance to Buonaccorsi—is a document held in the archives of the Accademia degli Immobili (the academy in charge of La Pergola theater and the operatic productions held therein), transcribed here as Table 8.4; this document provides an intriguing witness to Buonaccorsi's status in relation to the other court singers and to the nobility for whom they (collectively) performed. It dates from 1662 and relates to the scheduled performances of *Amore vuole ingegno*, intended for carnival of 1663 though canceled after Cardinal Giovan Carlo died. The list distributes financial responsibility for costuming the singers among pairs of academy members. Many of these singers are familiar from the *ruolo* of Cardinal Giovan Carlo, who served as protector to the Immobili—indeed, as Decroisette has made clear, the theater and its active run of operas between 1657 and 1663 should be understood as a semiprivate affair, largely sponsored by Giovan Carlo and operating in a gray area between court theater and public spectacle.[37]

In this opera, Buonaccorsi was to sing the role of Moro Birbone (lit. "Moorish Rascal" or "Black Rascal"), and two noblemen—Signore Bernardo Pecori and Signore Domenico Caccini (no relation of the famous musicians)—assumed responsibility for his outfit. Described elsewhere, Buonaccorsi's intended costume was "like an Italian soldier, in tatters."[38] Along with three others, he was to carry "a staff, a flask, pouches, and

---

[36] Saidiya V. Hartman, "Venus in Two Acts," *Small Axe* 12, no. 2 (2008): 2.
[37] Decroisette, "Un example," particularly 75.
[38] "Moro Birbone, Gio: Buonaccorsi, Va vestito da soldato Italiano: stracciato." I-FImmobili, f. 1.17, c. 6v.

Table 8.4. Archivio dell'Accademia degli Immobili, I-FImmobili, f. 1.17, c. 7r. The left column is a list of academy members, arranged in pairs and then matched up on the right with names of performers in the opera *Amor vuole ingegno* (intended perf. 1663). The paired academicians were to be responsible for the costuming of their assigned performer. Diplomatic transcription. Words transcribed in italics have been added in a different hand; the same later hand was also responsible for the crossouts.

Sig:r March.e Salviati S:r March.e Corsi	}	Sig.ra Lucia *Rivani*
S:r Filippo Franceschi S:r Pier Gio: Federighi	}	Sig.ra Leonora *Ballerini*
S:r Carlo Taddei S:r Lionardo Mastellini	}	Sig.ra Luisa *Massaj*
S:r March.e Gerini S:r Vieri Guardagni	}	S:r Ant.o Rivani
S:r Jacopo Ricciardi S:r Lionardo Grazzini	}	S:r Dom:co Bellucci
S:r March.e dal Monte S:r March.e Corsini	}	S:r Paolo Rivani
S:r March.e del Bufalo S:r Cav.r Suarez	}	~~S:r~~ Carlo Righenzi *da Tartaglia*
S:r Grifoni S:r Mattia M.a Bartolomei	}	S:r Vincenz~~ino~~o *Olivicciani*
Mons:r Bentivogli S:r March.e Niccolini	}	~~S:r~~ ^*S.r* Gio: Michele *de Bar*
S:r Bernardo Pecori S:r Dom:co Caccini	}	~~S:r~~ Gio: Buonaccorsi Moro *non ci va Sig.re*
S:r Balì Gianfigliazzi S:r Cosimo Pasquali	}	Il ^*Carlo* Righenzi da Todesco
S:r Baron Alamanni S:r Piero Strozzi	}	Gio: Grossi da Spagnolo
S:r Co: Visconti S:r Baron Luigi M.a del Nero	}	Lorenz*ino* da Franzese

bundles."[39] While no illustration of this costume survives, the description is highly reminiscent of an extant Stefano della Bella sketch of Buonaccorsi's costume for the role of Moro Monello (lit. "Moorish Rascal" or "Black Rascal")[40] in the 1657 production of *Il potestà di Colognole*, a costume that

---

[39] "Tutti con Bordone, Fiasca, Tasche, e Fagotti." I-FImmobili, f. 1.17, c. 6v.
[40] In a definition the librettist Moniglia provided for the term "Monello," the link between these two rascally terms is made clear: "Monello. Furbo, baro, birbante." Moniglia, "La serva nobile," 290.

was described in Immobili documents as an "outfit of a rascal, good quality, but tattered."[41] This earlier sketch is reproduced as Figure 8.3, after page 240. In this image, Buonaccorsi's outfit shows courtly touches, particularly the stylish way in which the sleeves meet the vest and the shape of his breeches, yet the ensemble is—as described—rendered in rags. Buonaccorsi carries a staff, and several visible pouches and bundles are strung around his torso.

What interests me in Table 8.4 are the titles given to the singers, several of whom are addressed as "Signora" or "Signore." Someone has then crossed out some of these titles, in particular for Righenzi, the comic tenor and actor, and for Buonaccorsi (the title for Signore Gio: Michele de Bar has been crossed out mistakenly and then added back in); family names and character details have been added. In Buonaccorsi's case, the scribe did not merely cross out "Signore" but was moved to protest in writing, "non ci va Signore," or "Signore does not apply here!"[42] We cannot assume that racial difference is the prime motivation for Buonaccorsi's demotion or for the anger inherent in the scrawled protestation. Note that Righenzi, too, was demoted, although in other places, he merits the Signore title—see, for example, the printed cast list of *Il potestà di Colognole*, reproduced here as Figure 8.4, where Buonaccorsi is described as "the Moor who belongs to His Most Reverend Highness," that is, to Cardinal Prince Giovan Carlo de' Medici.[43]

Both Buonaccorsi and Righenzi played comic roles and frequently appeared together in comic scenes. Righenzi's character was typically a stuttering, hunchbacked servant, a stock conflation of physical disability with verbal disability that reappears throughout commedia dell'arte and operatic history. While I am not suggesting that Righenzi himself was necessarily disabled in any way, his performances as such inhabit a category of person (disabled) that was regularly conflated with racialized others in the courtly imaginary—recall the treatment of "Moor," "Mute," and "Tartufo" (dwarf) in the accounts I discussed earlier. It is this space of the marked other that both Buonaccorsi and Righenzi seem to inhabit, their comic stage personas difficult to disaggregate from their lived experience as men with no claim to the title "Signore."

[41] "Monello, Moro di S.A.S., Abito da Monello buono sotto e soppra ^ma Straccione." I-FImmobili, f. 1.7, ins. 4, c. 1v.

[42] I-FImmobili, f. 1.17, [c. 7r].

[43] In the document partially transcribed as Table 8.2, none of the male singers is provided with a title, though three of the women merit the honorific "Donna" (lit. "Lady"); the other women are described as "fantesca" ("young girl").

190 ACT II, SCENE VIII

Figure 8.4. Published cast list from Giovanni Andrea Moniglia, *Il potestà di Colognole, Dramma civile rusticale: A gl'illustrissimi signori academici Immobili* (Florence: il Bonardi, 1657), n.p. [82].

It is also worth noting that while Buonaccorsi appears only infrequently in the Immobili archives, his presence accrues a particularized weight over time: in 1657, he is referred to as the "Moor of His Highness";[44] in 1661, as "Gio:, the Moor of His Most Reverend Highness";[45] and only in 1662 is he "Gio: Buonaccorsi Moro."[46] The increased specificity of the Immobili accounts suggests a gradual incorporation of Buonaccorsi into Florentine society, such that his name eventually takes precedence over the generic designation "Moor." Still, he never entirely disassociated himself from the category of "Moor" or "Turk."

---

[44] "[I]l Moro di SAS." See I-FImmobili, f. 1.7, ins. 1, p. 13, and ins. 4, c. 1v. Note that this would translate as "the Moor belonging to the Grand Duke"; the printed libretto, however, identifies the actor-singer as "il Moro di S. A. Reverendiss.," which gives ownership to the cardinal. See Giovanni Andrea Moniglia, *Il potestà di Colognole, Dramma civile rusticale: A gl'illustrissimi signori academici Immobili* (Florence: Il Bonardi, 1657), c.n.n. [81v].

[45] "Gio: Moro di S.A.R.ma." See I-FImmobili, f. 1.14, 19v–20r.

[46] I-FImmobili, f. 1.17, c. 6v and 7r.

On August 15, 1674, the death of "Gio: Buonaccorsi Turco Battezzato"— "Giovanni Buonaccorsi, baptized Muslim [lit. 'Turk']"—was recorded in the Florentine death registry.[47] A few further details are included in the parish records:

> Gio: del Buonaccorsi, Black, baptized Muslim [lit. *moro, turco battezzato*], who was in service to the Sig. Cardinal Leopoldo Medici, he lived at la Lupica, died with all the sacraments, and was buried in our church [San Felice in Piazza] with 10 [officiants] counting priests and clerics, on this day, 15th of August 1674.[48]

Though the details are sparse, the death record confirms that "Buonaccorsi" is a baptismal name, not a family name (or, at least, that the religious authorities interpreted it as such). At the time of his death, he was still in courtly service (specifically to Cardinal Prince Leopoldo de' Medici, the youngest brother of Ferdinando II). I am inclined to believe Buonaccorsi may also have labored in the household of Prince Mattias de' Medici between the death of Cardinal Giovan Carlo (in 1663) and the death of Mattias (in 1667), since several letters to Mattias from this period mention Buonaccorsi and his movements (these letters are discussed in the final chapter of this book). San Felice in Piazza is a parish church just blocks from Palazzo Pitti. Canto "alla Lupica" was, by some accounts, located close behind the church, just off the via di Sitorno; neither street is in existence today; however, via di Sitorno can be seen on early modern maps of the city.[49] At the time of his death, Buonaccorsi lived close in the shadows of the Medici residence where, in Volterrano's portrait, he still sings.

---

[47] I-Fas, Arte di Medici e Speziali, Registro dei morti della città di Firenze, n. 260, c. 141r.

[48] "Gio: del Buonaccorsi moro, turco batte*zz*ato stava in servitù del Sig. Cardinale Leopoldo Medici, habitava da la Lupica, morto con tutti sac*rem*enti e fù sepolto in chiesa no*st*ra con 10 fra P*re*ti e ch*ier*ici q.to di 15 di Agosto 1674." I-Fca, S. Felice in Piazza, Morti dal 1627 al 1686, RPU 0025.13, c. 236v.

[49] A poetic description of the city of Florence published in the early eighteenth century includes a reference to the Canto alla Lupica; see canzone 2 and particularly the key given to understand the poetic allusions. Antonio Domenico Giovanetti, *Descrizione allegorica della città di Firenze divisa in più canzoni* (Florence: Francesco Moücke, 1733), 18–21. Given the later date of the poem (published in 1733, more than fifty years after Buonaccorsi's death), it is possible that the canto was named after a particular woman or residence, though presumably the reference here is directly to the location. Canto alla Lupica does not come up in the searchable census data from 1561 or 1632. Via di Sitorno does; see, for example, the searchable interactive map at https://decima-map.net.

Al Morino della Gondola lire sei per *portare gli Orioli al Pignone et scaricare a Pisa (come la nota) -.6.-.*

For the little Moor of the Gondola, six lire, for transporting the orioles to Pignone and unloading in Pisa (as per the note), -.6.-.
    I-Fas, Camera del Granduca, f. 33, December 1663, c. 42r

Scene 9
Buonaccorsi Sings on the Florentine Stage

Between 1657 and 1663, Cardinal Giovan Carlo de' Medici and the Accademia degli Immobili sponsored a series of operas at the Pergola theater in Florence; these operas are listed in Table 9.1a. While the theater, completed in 1656, was deliberately constructed at some distance from Palazzo Pitti and from the bustling city center in order to minimize external noise, the institution was not so easily separated from courtly politics or influence.[1] The theater operated in a semiprofessional fashion, with a core troupe of professional singers and a resident playwright (Giovanni Andrea Moniglia), composer (Jacopo Melani), and engineer (Ferdinando Tacca). Most of these individuals—singers included—were supported by regular payments by Cardinal Giovan Carlo, and those few who were not paid directly by the cardinal were on payroll to other members of the Medici family. Furthermore, as Françoise Decroisette has noted, the Accademia degli Immobili consisted almost entirely of noblemen who were members of the cardinal's court.[2]

As a singer in the cardinal's employ, Buonaccorsi was a key part of the Pergola ensemble, and most of the operas performed in the theater included a role written specifically for him. Notably, the Black roles of the Florentine operatic stage are closely delimited. With the single exception of a female Egyptian "gypsy" (a racialized, gendered, and ethnically marked role), the *mori* of these mid-century libretti are all servants or slaves—effectively replicating onstage the role that Buonaccorsi played in "real life." In general, Moniglia's libretti develop a local vein of civic comedy, tightly linked to characterological and narrative conventions of the commedia dell'arte and to the early comic operas of 1640s Rome.[3] Several characters reappear

---

[1] According to Decroisette, the decision to build the theater was taken in 1652. See Decroisette, "Un exemple." A contemporary description of the theater architecture and decoration is included in the *Presa d'Argo* published with the libretto for Giovanni Andrea Moniglia, *L'Hipermestra, festa teatrale, rappresentata dal Sereniss. Principe Cardinale Gio. Carlo di Toscana, per celebrare il giorno natalizio del Real Principe di Spagna* (Florence: Stamperia di S.A.S., 1658).

[2] Decroisette, "Un exemple."

[3] Wilbourne, *Seventeenth-Century Opera*. See also Maria Anne Purciello, "And Dionysus Laughed: Opera, Comedy and Carnival in Seventeenth-Century Venice and Rome" (PhD diss., Princeton University, 2005); Susan Gail Lewis, "*Chi Soffre Speri* and the Influence of the Commedia dell'Arte on the Development of Roman Opera" (MMus thesis, University of Arizona, 1995); William C. Holmes, "Comedy—Opera—Comic Opera," *Analecta Musicologica* 5 (1968): 92–103.

Table 9.1a. Operas staged at La Pergola theater, Florence, under the aegis of Cardinal Giovan Carlo de' Medici and the Accademia degli Immobili, 1657–1663.

Year	Title	Librettist	Composer	Black character or role
1657, rev. 1661	*Il potestà di Colognole*	Gio: Andrea Moniglia	Jacopo Melani	Moro Monello
1658	*Il pazzo per forza*	Gio: Andrea Moniglia	Jacopo Melani (music lost)	Moretta, Zingara
1658	*L'Hipermestra*	Gio: Andrea Moniglia	Francesco Cavalli	Alindo
1659	*Il vecchio balordo*	Gio: Andrea Moniglia	Jacopo Melani (music lost)	Caralì, moro, schiavetto
1660	*La serva nobile*	Gio: Andrea Moniglia	Jacopo Melani (music lost)	
1661	*Ercole in Tebe*	Gio: Andrea Moniglia	Jacopo Melani	Iolao, moro servitore di Teseo
1663	*Amore vuole ingegno*	Gio: Andrea Moniglia	Jacopo Melani (music lost)	Moro

in multiple operas; others fall into characterological types or stock roles.[4] A number of these operas went on to Venetian adaptations,[5] and singers from the Medici court circle were sought after for Venetian seasons.[6] Buonaccorsi's participation in the Pergola performances, the roles he played, and his position within a functional, professionalized troupe of performers provide a unique opportunity to think about race, the voice, and dramatic convention in seventeenth-century opera. Over time—as Buonaccorsi matured and honed his craft—the roles he played expanded in size, though his stock character remained within tight characterological limits.

For four of the Pergola operas, cast lists printed with the libretti or surviving in the archives mention the person of "il Moro" directly. For *Il potestà di Colognole* (1657, reprised 1661), which inaugurated the Pergola theater, documents in the Immobili archives name the performer of the character Moro Monello as the "Moro di S.A.S." (that is, belonging to the Grand

---

[4] The character of Anselmo, for example, played by the singer Michele Grasseschi, appeared in *Il potestà di Colognole*, *Il pazzo per forza*, and *La serva nobile*.

[5] Decroisette, "Un exemple."

[6] Mamone, "Most Serene Brothers."

Duke); the printed libretto, however, includes a cast list specifying that the role was played by "il Moro di S.A. Reverendiss."[7] (that is, belonging to the cardinal prince). A costume sketch for the role, briefly discussed in the previous chapter and reproduced as Figure 8.3, shows the outfit designed for the performance; notably, della Bella's figure is depicted with explicitly Black skin. In *Il pazzo per forza* (1658), the printed libretto attributes the role of Moretta *zingara* (lit. "Little Black gypsy girl") to "il Moro di S.A. Reverendiss."[8] For *Ercole in Tebe* (1661), the Immobili archives include a cast list identifying Iolao, "the Moorish servant to Teseo," as "Gio: Moro di S.A. Rev.ma."[9] And, for *Amor vuole ingegno*, which was written and rehearsed for *carnevale* in 1663 but then canceled after the cardinal died on January 23, archive documents (some of which were discussed in the previous chapter) assign the character of Moro Birbone to the performer "Gio: Buonaccorsi Moro."[10] All four of these libretti are by Moniglia, and the music, which survives for both *Il potestà di Colognole* and *Ercole in Tebe*, was composed by Melani.[11] One further Moniglia-Melani collaboration, *Il vecchio balordo* (performed in 1658), features the character "Caralì, moro, schiavetto di Clarice" ("Caralì, a young Black slave belonging to Clarice").[12] *La serva nobile* (1660) is the only

---

[7] I-FImmobili, f. 1.7, ins. 1, p. 13, and ins. 4, c. 1v. For the libretto, see Moniglia, *Il potestà di Colognole*. No sources document the performers of the reprised performances of 1661; however, the work was staged at very short notice as part of an exchange with visiting musicians in the retinue of Archduke Ferdinando of Austria (the guests performed Antonio Cesti's *La Dori*), and presumably the original performers participated.

[8] See Moniglia, *Il pazzo per forza*, 124.

[9] I-FImmobili, f. 1.14, 19v–20r. Weaver and Weaver cite a list transcribed by Ademollo that incorrectly cites "Iolar—Moro di S.A.S." See Weaver and Weaver, *A Chronology*, 131.

[10] The text of *Amor vuole ingegno* was published as Giovanni Andrea Moniglia, "La vedova, ovvero Amore vuole ingegno," in *Delle poesie dramatiche di Giovann'Andrea Moniglia, Accademic della Crusca, Parte terza* (Florence: Vincenzio Vangelisti, 1698), 299–403. For Buonaccorsi's participation, see I-FImmobili, f. 1.17, cc. 6v, 7r. The scholarly account of casting in this opera includes a number of confusing claims. Weaver and Weaver transcribe a list of performers compiled by the early historian of theater Palmieri Pandolfini, which he claimed to have transcribed from the Immobili archives: "Lucia Rivani, Leonora Falbetti Ballerini, Lucia Massai, Antonio Rivani, Domenico Bellucci, Paolo Rivani, Gio. Michele de Bar, Vincenzio Bonaccorsi, Carlo Righensi, Giovanni Grossi, Lorenzo Pettore, La Pollarolina, il ragazzo Cerroni." See Weaver and Weaver, *A Chronology*. There is an error here, eliding Vincenzio Oliviciani and Gio: Buonaccorsi. This error was silently corrected by Decroisette. See particularly the table of singers and roles she provides in Decroisette, 85.

[11] Both scores are widely available: *Il potestà di Colognole* was published in modern edition as part of the Yale University Collegium Musicum series. See Melani, *Il potestà di Colognole*. *Ercole in Tebe* is published in facsimile as part of the Garland series, with an introductory essay by Howard Mayer Brown. See Jacopo Melani, *Ercole in Tebe* (New York: Garland, 1978).

[12] In some sources, this opera is referred to by the title *Il vecchio burlato*. The original libretto survives in manuscript, two copies of which are extant in Florence (I-Fn, Ms. Magliab., D. VII.252, and I-Fl, Ms. Antinori 244). Weaver and Weaver list the characters, mis-transcribing Caralì as Corali. The music is assumed to have been written by Melani but doesn't survive. A modern edition of the libretto has been published. See Moniglia, *Il vecchio balordo*.

opera in this string of carnival offerings written by Moniglia that does not include a specifically Black character.[13]

Two other Black roles have been noted on the Florentine operatic stage during this period. Orazio Ricasoli Rucellai's detailed description of the premiere of *L'Hipermestra* (composed by the celebrated Venetian composer Francesco Cavalli to a libretto by Moniglia in 1654, with intent to inaugurate the Pergola theater, though the performance was delayed until 1658) describes the servant character Alindo as "the Moorish valet to Arbante" (the *descrizione* also details the character's clothing, as was previously discussed).[14] Given Moniglia's authorship of the libretto, the role of Alindo may have been intended for Buonaccorsi from the outset—as Jennifer Williams Brown has noted, his parting words in Act II, scene xviii, are "Vafrin[o], ti sono schiavo" ("Vafrino, I am your slave").[15] That a role in the opera would have been carved out for Buonaccorsi is altogether unsurprising given his participation in the Pergola troupe and—as I wish to emphasize—given the strong association of Blackness with servitude and the large number of servant roles in comedic Italian theater. There is also a specifically Black character in the anonymous opera, *Scipione in Cartagine*, which was performed in 1657 at the competing theater, Il Cocomero, under the sponsorship of the Accademia dei Sorgenti (see Table 9.1b).[16] The extant libretto (the music is lost) includes a dedication to Cardinal Giovan Carlo de' Medici, and the Black character, Caralì, is described as "a Moor, enslaved on the Roman galleys."[17]

In sum, there are seven libretti (six by Moniglia, one anonymous) and three scores (two by Melani, one by Cavalli) documenting Black characters on the

---

[13] The music for *La serva nobile* was composed by Domenico Anglesi (or so Moniglia claims in the published libretto). The Immobili archives make no mention of Buonaccorsi or "il Moro" in relation to this work. The singers and their relative roles are listed in Decroisette, "I virtuosi," 85. She lists ten performers, though there are twelve speaking roles.

[14] Moniglia, *Delle poesie, Parte prima*, 55–56.

[15] See the introductory material to Cavalli, *Scipione affricano*.

[16] On the Sorgenti and performances at Il Cocomero, see John Walter Hill, "Le relazioni di Antonio Cesti con la corte e i teatri di Firenze," *Rivista Italiana di Musicologia* 11 (1976): 27–47.

[17] "Caralì, moro schiavo su le navi Rom*a*ne." The dedication to this libretto is signed by Giovanni Battista Rontini; however, the libretto itself is anonymous. Some scholars (beginning with Allacci) have assumed that the lyrics and music were likely to have been produced by the Moniglia-Melani pair who did so many of the Immobili works during this period (Rontini also signed another of Moniglia's early libretti). Weaver and Weaver emphasize, however, that the libretto does not appear in Moniglia's collected works (which were published in three volumes under the title *Delle poesie dramatiche*, beginning in Florence in 1689). James Leve (in the introduction to his edition of *Il potestà di Colognole*) cites an anonymous biography of Moniglia that does list the libretto of *Scipione in Cartagine* among his works; I-Fl, Ms. Antinori 184, fols. 17r–18v. See Melani, *Il potestà di Colognole*, xvii, n. 16.

Table 9.1b. Opera staged at Il Cocomero theater by the Accademia Sorgenti and dedicated to Cardinal Giovan Carlo de' Medici.

Year	Title	Librettist	Composer	Black character or role
1657	Scipione in Cartagine	Anon.	Anon. (music lost)	Caralì Moro schiavo su le navi Romane

mid-century Florentine operatic stage.[18] Typically, the Black character appears in only one or two scenes, often in dialogue with a stuttering hunchback servant, played in performances by the cardinal's comic tenor Carlo Righenzi. Comparing scenes across multiple works, it is fascinating how closely these excerpts adhere to the system of stock characters that (public) opera inherited from the commedia dell'arte—even in this semiprivate and lavishly funded context where we might imagine greater liberties were accorded.[19] The stuttering servant, played by Righenzi, and "il Moro" shared scenes in *Il potestà di Colognole, Il vecchio balordo, Ercole in Tebe,* and *Amore vuole ingegno*; evidently, the two singers—or the librettist, Moniglia, who wrote all four libretti—had a shtick. In three separate cases, the text exploits the Moro's dark complexion as a surprise for Righenzi's character, leading to his mis-recognition as supernatural or inhuman. The three passages that follow are extracts, not the full scenes, but they show a shared reliance on whiteness as a visual norm.

Gio: Andrea Moniglia, *Il potestà di Colognole* (perf. 1657), II, xi

DESSO, MORO	Oste, oste, oste, Porta un lume.	Innkeeper, innkeeper, innkeeper! Bring a light!
MORO	Per certo Facciam a non c'intendere.	Clearly We are making it so we don't understand each other,
	Per il vero comprendere, Rispondi, chi è l'oste, tu o io?	So that it is perfectly clear, Respond! Who is the innkeeper, you or me?
DESSO	I-, i-, i-, io …	I-, I-, I-, I …

---

[18] I also deem it highly likely that Buonaccorsi performed as the personification of Africa in Moniglia and Anglesi's balletto a cavallo *Il mondo festeggiante* at the Palazzo Pitti for the Medici wedding of 1661; the music is unfortunately lost. The libretto is included in Moniglia, *Delle poesie dramatiche, Parte prima*, 261ff. The singers who represent the four corners of the earth (Europe, Asia, America, and Africa) are described as beautiful women—with exposed breasts—though the Medici regularly used male singers to represent female personifications (of the planets, for example, in the Medici wedding festivities of 1589).

[19] Wilbourne, *Seventeenth-Century Opera*.

MORO	Se dunque L'oste tu sei, perché Domandi il lume a me?	Well then, If you are the innkeeper, Why are you asking me for a light?
DESSO	...Io non son oste.	...I am not the innkeeper.
MORO	E nemmen io.	Well, me neither.
DESSO	Ma vedo una lanterna. Lascia ch'io ti discerna.	OK, I see a lantern. Let me take a look at you.
	(*Piglia la lanterna lasciata da Anselmo.*)	(*He takes the lantern left by Anselmo.*)
MORO	Guarda pur quanto vuoi. Ma tu chi sei?	Look all you want. But who are you?
DESSO	Il diavolo.	The devil!
MORO	Il diavolo, sicuro.	The devil, for sure!
DESSO	O-, o-, o-, o-...	O-, o-, o-, o-...
MORO	Per la mia vita rendere, Gambe mie, voi sappiatemi difendere.	In order to save my life, Legs, you'd better know how to defend me!

Gio: Andrea Moniglia, *Ercole in Tebe* (perf. 1661), III, vi

SIFONE	Per tro-, trovare Alceste vò cercando per tutto oh, che paese bru-, bru-, bru-	To f-, find Alceste I am searching everywhere Oh, this place is ug-, ug-, ug-
IOLAO (MORO)	In queste parti e come Per qual strana occasione arrivasti Sifone? Che fai, non mi conosci? Guardami, chi son io	In these parts, and how? And for what strange reason Did you arrive, Sifone? What are you doing? Don't you recognize me? Look at me! Who am I?
SIFONE	bru-, bru-, bru- bru-, bru-, bru-, brutto. Ohimè, un Demonio, ohimè	ug-, ug-, ug- ug-, ug-, ug-, ugly. Alas, a demon, alas!
IOLAO (MORO)	Di che paventi? Iolao son' io.	What are you so scared of? It is me, Iolao!
SIFONE	È quando sei venuto nella patria di Pluto?	And when did you arrive in the land of Pluto?

Gio: Andrea Moniglia, *Amore vuole ingengo* (rehearsed for carnival 1663), II, xxxi

FRASIA	Desso, Desso?	Desso, Desso?
DESSO	Signora?	My lady?
FRASIA	Tira in là quella botte	Pull that barrel over there.
ISABELLA	Il Ciel m'aiuti	Heaven help me!
DESSO	Pe, pe, pesa che spiomba	It's very he- he- heavy.
FLAVIO	Muovila piano	Move it carefully

LIGURINO	Vuol seguir del male	Something bad will happen
MARCHIONNE	Ch'v'è egli dentro?	What is inside?
DESSO	Ca, ca, caviale	Ca- ca- [shit] caviar,
	Ta, tant'è nero; Uimè	It is s- s- so black; Oh no!
	Il De, Demonio!	The de-, devil!
MORO	Scapperò di quà	I need to get out of here!
	Desso nel muover la Botte vede entrovi il Moro, s'impaurisce, la Botte si roverscia, e n'escono fuori tutte le cose ripostevi, e spaventati il Moro, e Desso fuggono.	*While moving the barrel, Desso sees the Moro inside, he takes fright, the barrel tips over, and all the stuff that had been put in there falls out. Frightened, Moro and Desso run away.*

The identification of Blackness with demons or devils has a long history within Christian iconography.[20] Its citation in these operas reflects the ways in which an increased familiarity with sub-Saharan Africans gave such metaphorical associations an explicitly racial dimension. Della Bella's costume sketches for *L'Hipermestra* include a fury—one of twelve, danced by noblemen at the end of Act I—who emerged from the underworld (see Figure 9.1, reproduced after page 240).[21] The facial features and the coloring depicted in this sketch are explicitly sub-Saharan; the published description emphasized how repulsive the figures were to seem: "the furies appeared naked, with drooping, bruised breasts, and with splotches of putrid blood and rust on all their limbs: they had terrifying whirls of toads, [and] of eels attached in strange ways to their nasty, poisoned heads, and, above their rough hair, their fierce temples were bound with vipers, asps, serpents and snakes."[22] There are some similarities, too, with the chorus of "infernal monsters" who appeared in *Ercole in Tebe* (see Figure 9.2); though the print is harder to read, the braided, snakelike hair of these dancers and the skirts of their outfits resonate with the *furie* of *L'Hipermestra* and with the "grotesque" faces that decorate the set. In this context, Righenzi's repeated misrecognition of Buonaccorsi as a demon naturalizes an association of racial Blackness with an underworld of unredeemed sin and eternal torment.

[20] For a discussion of black devils in relationship to blackface performing traditions and early modern racisms, see Hornback, *Racism*.

[21] The description of the festivities, published as an appendix to the 1658 libretto, lists the names of the noblemen who danced the parts. See "Descrizione della presa d'Argo e degli amori di Linceo con Hipermestra; Festa teatrale," published with Moniglia, *L'Hipermestra*, Appendix, 17–18.

[22] "[L]e Furie ignude apparivano con cascanti, e livide poppe, e con macchie di putrido sangue, e di ruggine per tutte le membra: havevano spaventosi girelli di rospi, d'anguille di lor teste attossicate, confusamente composti, e sopra i ruvidi crini di vipere, di aspidi, e di serpentelli, e ceraste le fiere tempie erano avvinte." Moniglia, *L'Hipermestra*, Appendix, 17.

Figure 9.2. Set design for Act III, scene vi, of *Ercole in Tebe*. Libretto by Gio: Andrea Moniglia, music by Jacopo Melani. Etched plate by Valerio Spada after a design by Ferdinando Tacca. Printed between pages 56 and 57 of the ceremonial libretto (Florence: Stamperia all'Insegna della Stella, 1661).

Yet while Blackness and its presumed (visual) abnormality function as comic punchlines in each of the three extracts cited above, vocally and linguistically, the Black character is far more adept than the stuttering hunchback. These Moors speak excellent Italian, and in contrast with the destructive, dehumanizing sounds of stuttered speech, they articulate the action and respond in logical fashion to surrounding events.[23] In the extract from *Il podestà*, for example, Desso thinks Moro a devil because of his Black skin, but Moro thinks Desso a devil because grammatically speaking, he claims to be one: Q. "But who are you?" A. "The devil!" Had the hunchback character known that the Moor was Black from his voice or speech alone, there would have been no surprise at seeing his face.

The neutral, "Italianate" voice used by Buonaccorsi's character is prevalent but not entirely consistent across all of the roles under discussion here. In reference to the character of Caralì in Moniglia's *Il vecchio balordo*, Decroisette writes, "this figure of the Moor is typical in the dramas of Moniglia, who gives him an exotic, macaronic language, dominated by a final *ù*, by the substitution of *b* for *p*, by the use of infinitive verbs, and by the omission of grammatical articles."[24] The three excerpts just discussed make it clear that this "exotic" Black voice—though consistent with the *gergo* (jargon) or Sabir regularly used for theatrical representations of Black or enslaved characters—is not necessarily typical for Moniglia. He deploys it only in the travesty role of the Gypsy Moretta (*Il pazzo per forza*, 1658) and for Caralì (*Il vecchio balordo*, 1659). Coincidentally, in the anonymous libretto for *Scipione in Cartagine*, performed at Il Cocomero in 1657, the Black slave character—also called Caralì—does speak *gergo*. These three particular Black characters are noticeably less elevated—less educated, more comic—and specifically singled out as recent immigrants. The linguistic deformations of this slaves' *gergo* are remarkably consistent with linguistic tics familiar from Sabir and *moresche* stretching back into the previous century, which, as Gianfranco Salvatore has shown, incorporate the speech patterns of enslaved communities.[25] Across this audible axis of dialect and signification, we can recognize a contemporary distinction whereby the roles of "galley slave" and "court servant" are

---

[23] On the topic of musical stutters, see Wilbourne, "Demo's Stutter." For a discussion of the animalistic noises of mute characters in relation to noble Black characters, see Wilbourne, "*Lo Schiavetto*."

[24] "[Q]uesta figura di moro è abituale nei drammi di Moniglia, che gli dà un linguaggio esotico maccaronico, dominato dalla ù finale, dalla sostituzione di -p- in -b-, dall'uso degli infinitivi verbali, e dalla soppressione degli articoli." See the editorial apparatus to Moniglia, *Il vecchio balordo*, 149.

[25] Salvatore, "Parodie realistiche."

markedly different, even when both individuals might well be Black, Muslim, and literally enslaved.

I include here an extract from the anonymous libretto for *Scipione in Cartagine*, in which the slaves' jargon given to the Moor is particularly dense. In the scene directly preceding this one, Caralì learned that Scipione had liberated all the slaves; this scene is Caralì's song of celebration. Given the heavily marked Italian, the deliberate grammatical errors, and the use of both foreign and dialect words, I have provided two translations: one into comprehensible, if still ungrammatical, Italian (and, where relevant, Arabic), then a second that translates the text into English, with no attempt to reproduce the orthographic or grammatical errors of the original *gergo*.[26]

Anon., *Scipione in Cartagine* (perf. 1657), I, xv

CARALÌ	O Quanto star contentu	O, quanto sto contento	Oh, how happy I am,
	Baes miu andar,	Paese mio andar,	To return to my country
	Marmorata trovar;	Innamorata trovar;	To find my beloved;
	Legressa grandu Diù,	Largesa[27] del grande Dio,	Generosity of the great God,
	O fatma core miù.	O, Fatima, core mio.	O, Fatima, my love.
1	Camarata nesciumù,	Dalla camerata esciamo,	Leave the cabin,
	Non biscottu mansgiar,	Non biscotto mangiar,	We will not eat ship's biscuit,
	Non corbasciù tuccar;	Non curbascio toccar,	Nor be touched by the whip,
	Tenimu libertà;	Teniamo libertà;	We hold our liberty;
	Scibiona gentilisco	Scipione gentile	Noble Scipione
	Fasito carità;	Ci ha fatto carità;	Has done us this good deed;
	Salamalech Ikallà, Ikallà.	*As-salāmu 'alaykum, in sha Allah!*	*Peace be upon you, God willing!*
2	Ber chistu ligramente	Per questo allegramente,	For this happily,
	Frofalla, & Ebrahin,	Frofalla, & Ebrahim,	Frofalla, and Ebrahin,
	Corcùt, Dragùt, Selin,	Corcùt, Dragùt, Selim,	Corcùt, Dragùt, Selin,
	Soliman, Mustafà,	Soliman, Mustafà,	Soliman, Mustafà,
	Ballar, e ghimberì.	Ballare, e cimbali	Dance and [with] cymbals,
	Sonar, Alì, Cassa,	Sonar; Alì, Cassa.	Play, Alì, Cassa.
	Salamalech Ikallà, Ikallà.	*As-salāmu 'alaykum, in sha Allah!*	*Peace be upon you, God willing!*

---

[26] I would like to extend my thanks to Riccardo Strobino and Giuliano Mori for their help translating this particularly complex text.

[27] It is possible that "Legressa" is intended to signify "allegrezza," in which case the English translation would read "Happiness."

Though the score of *Scipione in Cartagine* does not survive, the poetic meter of this scene suggests an introductory recitative followed by two verses of aria. Direct reference is made to the lives of the enslaved on the galleys—no longer will they have to eat ship's biscuit!—while the names of Caralì's fellows are recognizably ethnic, even Ottoman. The refrain cites the traditional Arabic greeting: "Assalāmu 'alaykum," or "Peace be upon you," possibly with the word "Allah" or "in sha Allah" ("God willing") tacked on the end. The "Italian" text reflects precisely the final *ù* as described by Decroisette, as well as the transposed *p/b* (see, for example, Scipione's name, which is rendered as "Scibiona"). The same *gergo* is used by the Caralì character in *Il vecchio balordo*. In the scene cited next, he appears in conversation with a stuttering servant, Piero (played by Righenzi), who in this particular instance is not shocked by the slave's Black skin, having assumed his Blackness from the beginning of the interaction.

Giovanni Andrea Moniglia, *Il vecchio balordo* (perf. 1659), II, xiv

PIERO	Schia, schia, schia, schia, schiavetto Caralì, mo, mo, morino vien qui.	Sl, sl, sl, sl- little slave Caralì, Mo, mo, little Moor, come here.
CARALÌ	Salamalecch', dù star Badruna.	Peace be upon you, where is my master?
PIERO	Or ora ve, ve, verrà.	Na, now He co, co, comes.
CARALÌ	Ber ti star sciamatù. Dicir pipa tabaccu avir?	I was called by you. Tell me, He wants pipe tobacco?
PIERO	Vi, vi, vi, vino vuol essere.	W-, w-, w-, wine It has to be.
CARALÌ	Biager vinù, si donar libertà, e non bibir, io campar non putir.	I like wine, If I had freedom and could not drink I could not bear it.
PIERO	Ti, ti diletta questo paese?	You, you like This country?
CARALÌ	Multo golentieri son schiavù; ma sciamar Anselma signura.	I like very much I am a slave; but I call Anselmo master.
PIERO	Come spesso ti da, danno? di?	How often Does he gi-, gi-, give it to you?
CARALÌ	Non bastuna ber mi. Non bastuna ber mi.	He never beats me. He never beats me.
PIERO	Ecco che viene.	Here he comes!

There is a stark contrast between the low register of Caralì's dialogue, as seen here, and the vocal polish demonstrated by the characters of Iolao and Moro Monello in the other operas under discussion. This contrast is indicative of the varieties of Black experience—court retainer versus galley slave—and one interpretation would see this characterological variety (so unusual by seventeenth-century standards of performance and repertory) as documenting the breadth and flexibility of Buonaccorsi's performance abilities. Something I found in the archives, however, undermines this presumption.

I have looked at some length (as yet unsuccessfully) for the baptismal records of "Gio: Buonaccorsi Turco Battezzato," although I have found a considerable number of records for other Medici-owned slaves. One in particular stood out. Here is a section of one of the Pia Casa interviews, dated July 21, 1657:

My name is Caralì; I do not know the name of my father, and I was born in Barbary, in Zeila [a coastal city in present-day Somalia], of the race [*razza*] of Granadians, [I claim] to be 16 years old, to live in Florence, and being on the sea, the boat where I found myself was captured by Captain Flaminio, who brought me to Livorno and gave me to Prince Mattias.[28]

On August 1, "Caralì, Moor from Barbary of the race [*razza*] of Granadians, approximately 16 years old," was sponsored for baptism by the Most Serene Prince Mattias of Tuscany, although it was Andrea Pellegrini, his *cappellano*, who stood up for the prince at the ceremony. Caralì took the baptismal name "Mattia Medici."[29] During this period, Prince Mattias owned at least three *mori*, including the siblings Ali (baptized as Ferdinando in 1657, born ca. 1641) and Tuffega (baptized as Maria Adelaide in 1657, born ca. 1648).[30] A Florentine painting from the same period (shown as Figure 9.3, reproduced after page 240), attributed to the school of Sustermans, depicts Prince Mattias with a young Black man, presumably Ali-Ferdinando or Caralì-Mattia. Here the Black African retainer is represented in the traditional configuration—as pendant to the

---

[28] "Io mi chiamo Caralì, non so il nome di mio padre, e sono nato in Barberia a Zeila di razza di Granatini, esser d'anni 16. abitare in Firenze et essendo in mare fu preso il legno dove mi ritrovavo dal Cap. Flaminio, il quale mi condusse a Livorno e mi dono al S.r Principe Mattia." I-Fca, Pia Casa dei Catecumini, f. 2, ins. 18, c.n.n. [3]. It is not clear whether the scribe recorded errors that Caralì himself made (the unconjugated verbs are suggestive on this front) or whether the infinitive verbs indicate a notational shorthand in which "he declares himself" has been omitted.

[29] I-Fd, Registri Battesimali, Maschi, reg. 51, fg. 236, August 1, 1657.

[30] On Ali and Tuffega, respectively, see I-Fca, Pia Casa dei Catecumini, f. 2, [ins. 17 and 19], c.n.n. (for conversion records); I-Fd, Registri Battesimali, Maschi, reg. 51, fg. 191, and Femmine, reg. 273, fg. 220 (for baptismal records).

white master. The enslaved sitter wears stripes, with a heavy gold chain around his neck, and is shown passing a helmet (a "morione") to the prince, in what was a well-worn if grotesque pun. Given Caralì's assumption of the baptismal name Mattia, it is credible that he was chosen as the sitter in the Sustermans-school portrait, since the doubling of Mattia/Mattias and *moro/morione* reinforces the grotesque humor that juxtaposes the two men.

It seems likely to me that the thickly accented Caralì roles were taken by and/or written for Caralì (an ex-galley slave), rather than Buonaccorsi. Characterologically, having two different performers makes sense, as the roles fall into two distinct types. In neither case is there extant documentation of the singer who performed the role of "Caralì" (though scholars have assumed it to be Buonaccorsi). Furthermore, among the hundreds of slaves and immigrants referenced in seventeenth-century Florentine accounts, I came across the name of Caralì only twice; it is highly coincidental that one of these men should be present at the court at precisely this time.[31] I also note that in August 1665, the "mori" (plural) of Prince Mattias were tipped 2 scudi and 6 lire "for having played music [*sonato*] with Batistone" (a dwarf in the service of Prince Mattias).[32] Unfortunately, neither the score of *Scipione in Cartagine* nor that of *Il vecchio balordo* survives; comparison of the vocal ranges and the melodic profile might help rule out or confirm Buonaccorsi's suitability or participation. By 1657, when *Scipione in Cartagine* was performed, the historical Caralì had been in Florence for four years; he was baptized the summer of that same year.[33] Captured at sea at the tender age of twelve, Caralì was deemed young enough (and presumably handsome enough) to be taken to court and given to a prince. Caralì himself may have spoken the slave jargon represented in these libretti or may have known—through intimate experience—how to effectively perform it.

---

[31] The other Florentine Caralì applied to the Pia Casa for baptism in November 1683. He gave his name as "Caralì di Mele Align" and his place of origin as Moira in Borno; he is described as "moro" and states that he has been in Florence for several years, see I-Fca, Pia Casa dei Catecumini, f. 2, c.n.n. [ins. 112]. Roman records mention three Muslim converts named Caralì during the length of the seventeenth century, two of whom were described as Black; two other Roman converts give Caralì as their father's name. See Rudt De Collenberg Wipertus, "Le baptême des musulmans esclaves à Rome aux XVIIe et XVIIIe siècles. I. Le XVIIe siècle," *Mélanges de l'École Française de Rome. Italie et Méditerranée* 101, no. 1 (1989): 9–181.

[32] "Ai mori dell Prin*cipe* Mattias per haver sonato con Batistone, 2.6.-.-." I-Fas, Camera del Granduca, f. 35, c. 11r.

[33] I-Fca, Pia Casa dei Catecumini, f. 2, ins. 18, c.n.n. [1].

I—like Decroissette, Kaplan, and surely all modern scholars who had thought about these operas—had assumed there to be but one Black operatic singer in the court at this time. But if Caralì made a cameo in the two roles that bear his name, then we are dealing with (at least) two opera-singing enslaved Black men.[34] And given the sheer number of enslaved court retainers and their contiguity with comic song, we shouldn't be particularly surprised. Caralì (aka Mattia Medici battezzato) reminds us that the "cortigiani di basso servizio" (lit. "the courtiers at the lowest service level")—the buffoons, jesters, Moors, and dwarves of early modern courts—were regularly engaged in performance and in music making that has largely been lost.[35] What is unique about Buonaccorsi and Caralì is not that they made music—for many Black Europeans clearly made music—but that they performed in the high-cultural form of opera, which has allowed some level of documentation to survive. In the next chapter, I turn to a poem (arguably sung), that exemplifies the kinds of performances in which such *cortigiani* engaged within the quotidian spaces of the court. Buonaccorsi's poem records an improvisatory or ephemeral practice that has been largely lost and, as the lyrics make clear, testifies to the very real courtly presence of the "Other"—too familiar to their more evidently European interlocutors (the princes, patrons, nobles, clerics, and artisans with whom Western history has largely been concerned) to be truly strangers or truly strange, even while it was their physical, racial, and religious differences that brought them into the court.

---

[34] Archival documents describing an opera production in Siena in 1690 mention another singer nicknamed "Moretto," quite possibly also racially Black. See Reardon, *A Sociable Moment*, 180.
[35] Ignatius Hugford, *Vita di Anton Domenico Gabbiani* (Florence: n.p., 1762), 10.

A Ludovico staffiere per fare una Giubba al Moro Indiano lire trenta, 4.2.-.-.

For Ludovico the footman to make a doublet for the Black Indian, thirty lire, -.6.-.-.
                    I-Fas, Camera del Granduca, f. 36, December 1666, c. 35r

Scene 10
Buonaccorsi as Court Jester

The poem "Il sogno di Giovannino Moro" survives in a single, undated manuscript copy in the Medicean archives in Florence; the first page (of three) of the manuscript is reproduced here as Figure 10.1.[1] Throughout my discussion of the "Sogno," I attribute authorship to Giovannino Buonaccorsi, who was often identified in contemporary sources by the name "Giovannino Moro" (lit. "Little Black Giovanni") and thus can be associated with the work by the title alone. Both Alessandro Grassi and Paul Kaplan—the only scholars to have previously discussed the poem (in both instances, in relation to the Volterrano portrait of the singer)—also attribute authorship to Buonaccorsi (though they refer to him as Giovannino).[2] They do so with a rather pleasurable naivete, assigning authorship to the most obvious contender—as if he were not Black or not enslaved, as if he were an autonomous subject fully capable of artistic endeavor. They neatly sidestep the qualifications and disavowals that typically shield such assertions from the charge of overreaching, for indeed, to identify Buonaccorsi as author is, in Kaplan's words, to consider him "one of the earliest known Italian writers of color."[3]

As I hope by now to have made clear, Buonaccorsi was but one of a considerable number of Black African and Middle Eastern Muslim and newly Christianized court retainers who arrived in Florence under conditions of enslavement, and his very presence in Italy testifies to an endemic practice of Italian slavery with which scholars are only recently beginning to grapple. Within academia, the work of documenting the historical presence of Black Africans, enslaved people, and other racialized minorities within early modern Europe (as Kaplan long has done) has itself been seen as a radical

---

[1] I'd like to thank Paul Kaplan for having introduced me to this poem and for sharing with me his working translation of the text (which differs quite substantially from my own translation). The poem can be found in I-Fas, Mediceo del Principato, f. 6424, c.n.n.

[2] The poem is referenced (though not transcribed) by Alessandro Grassi in his catalogue entry on the Volterrano painting *Ritratto di suonatore di liuto con cantore moro*. See Maria Cecilia Fabbri, Alessandro Grassi, and Riccardo Spinelli, eds., *Volterrano: Baldassarre Franceschini (1611–1690)* (Florence: Ente Cassa di Risparmio di Firenze, 2013), 245.

[3] Kaplan, "Giovannino Moro," [1].

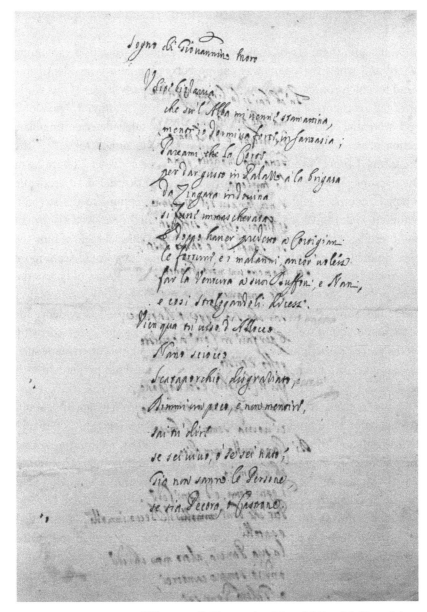

Figure 10.1. First page of "Il sogno di Giovannino Moro," I-Fas, Mediceo del Principato, f. 6424, c.n.n. Used with permission of the Ministero della Cultura / Archivio di Stato, Florence. Further reproduction or duplication is expressly prohibited.

and often destabilizing project. To make a further claim for Black authorship is bold.

To be sure, there is no smoking gun, no explicit dedication explaining where and when the poem was composed, no signature, no identifiable hand to which comparisons could be made. In the early stages of this work, I hedged my claims of authorship with words such as "presumed," "possibly," and "potential" and located my conclusions in the safely deferred linguistic fiction of the subjunctive: "if Buonaccorsi *were* the author, *then* . . ." The more time I spent with the text, however, the more convinced I became of Buonaccorsi's authorship. The purportedly neutral skepticism of academic practice requires a higher burden of proof for exceptions to the straight, white, cis-male model, insisting on the foreignness of the enslaved Black man and presuming his incapacity. According to the traditional logic of musicological practice, the authorial attribution to Buonaccorsi would seem more convincing if I could point to mistakes in the text: mistakes would *prove* the foreignness of the author and might illustrate a reliance on spoken dialect or foreign words. But grammatical errors can only be used as evidence for Black authorship if we presume an incapacity to write and speak correctly on the part of Black humans. Contemporary Italian authors often made such assumptions or traded in their familiarity, but we need not perpetuate such readings.

In my translation of "Il sogno di Giovannino Moro" (which appears in full below), I have rendered the title as "Little Black Giovanni's Dream." This is only one of several possible translations. First, I should note that the use of *di* to express possession leaves it ultimately unclear whether it is the dream or the poem that belongs to Giovannino; the title could be translated either as "The Dream *of* Giovannino Moro" or "The Dream" *by* Giovannino Moro. My use of the possessive apostrophe is intended to incorporate both possibilities. Second, it could be argued that since "Giovannino Moro" was a name by which Buonaccorsi was known, it ought to be retained unchanged. Importantly, however, both the -*ino* suffix and the word *moro* had literal indexical meanings implicit in their use— whether or not their use as a nickname normalized the interpolative work they did in the mouths, ears, and minds of Buonaccorsi and his contemporary interlocutors. I have chosen, therefore, to translate the (nick)name itself quite literally, in order to restore something of the shock inherent in the words: to be called (and to answer to) the name "Little Black Giovanni" meant *something*, and though we cannot know exactly what, reminding ourselves of the content and context of Buonaccorsi's nomenclature is important.[4]

In the opening lines of the "Sogno," the narrator-performer Giovannino speaks in the first person (I use the name "Giovannino" when referring to the speaking subject of the poem and "Buonaccorsi" when I refer to the historical individual). Describing a dream (the "Sogno" of the title), Giovannino invokes and then impersonates a "Zingara indovina" (a "gypsy" fortune teller)[5] who mocks a motley crew of Turks, dwarves, and buffoons—labeled in the poem as "mal'Cristiani" (the bad Christians) of the court, most of whom I have identified with contemporary historical figures. The "Sogno di Giovannino Moro" thus documents the way in which the literal bodily differences—of (racially marked) enslaved retainers, freaks, and fools— were enjoyed by the court and provides a rare opportunity to exemplify the ephemeral entertainments provided by the "cortigiani di basso servizio." The poem resonates with other extant buffoonish texts, such as Margherita Costa's *Li buffoni* (Florence, 1641), a *comedia ridicola* set at the Medici court and populated by similar strata of courtly inhabitants; indeed, at least one historical person appears in both Buonaccorsi's poem and Costa's play.[6] As I argue here, the "Sogno di Giovannino Moro" epitomizes the impromptu courtly entertainments produced by buffoons, jesters, dwarves, and enslaved court functionaries—a type of performance known to have occurred at court with some regularity but which was infrequently documented or recorded.

The surviving text is bound into the unpaginated volume I-Fas, Mediceo del Principato, f. 6424, where an unhelpful if well-intentioned archivist saw fit to extract and collate poetic material from disparate archival sources, thus separating the poems from any accompanying letters or documentation that might date or contextualize them.[7] This particular

---

[4] In a similar spirit, Cassander Smith writes, "We cannot fully recover the nuances of how and why [Candy] matters, but that does not mean we should approach mediation as an impasse; this critical approach has for too long rendered mute and invisible the literary significance of historically marginalized racial, ethnic, and gendered groups in the earliest textual archives of the Americas." See Smith, "'Candy No Witch," 123.

[5] I use the term "gypsy" here and in other chapters to describe a common stereotype and dramatic character, not to reference people of Romani heritage who, historically, have been described using the term.

[6] An excellent translation of the Costa has recently been published. See Margherita Costa, *The Buffoons, A Ridiculous Comedy: A Bilingual Edition*, trans. Sara Díaz and Jessica Goethals, ed. Sara Díaz and Jessica Goethals (Toronto: Iter Press, 2018). A facsimile of the 1641 print is also available online.

[7] The series "Poesie e Pasquinate" runs from 6420–6427. See *Archivio Mediceo del Principato: Inventario sommario* (Pubblicazioni degli Archivi di Stato 1, Rome: s.n.: 1951, 240ff.

volume (one of eight such *filze* held in the archive) includes an important early version of Ottavio Rinuccini's *La Dafne*, recently brought to light by Francesca Fantappiè.[8] It also includes a number of texts for singing associated with the circle of Cardinal Giovan Carlo de' Medici and at least one other racially charged text: the poem by Ciro di Pers discussed in the Introduction.

The hand that copied the "Sogno" is clear, neat, and practiced. A single error (omitting two words) was made on the second page and corrected seemingly immediately. This is a clean copy, not a draft. The text consists of seven strophes, the first and last of which are composed in *versi sciolti* (unrhymed or blank verse in freely alternating line lengths of seven and eleven syllables), providing both a structural and narrative frame to the poem. These two bookend strophes are spoken in the poetic voice of Giovannino Moro himself; the first explains the dream that he had, and the last recounts the moment in which he woke up. The five central strophes, in contrast, are enunciated in the voice of the "gypsy" who appears in his dream; they are highly rhythmic, with a tightly controlled rhyme scheme: AaBCcBDD. Here capitalization refers to metric form, with lowercase letters indicating shorter *quaternario* lines (of four syllables each) and capital letters indicating *ottonari* (eight syllables each). The first four of the central five strophes treat individual members of the court, addressing each figure in turn using the second-person singular ("tu"), while the fifth discusses the group as a whole. The form, as I discuss later, implies a musical performance.

Il sogno di Giovannino Moro	Little Black Giovanni's Dream
[1r]	
Udite bizzarria	Listen to this strange thing
che su'l'Alba mi venne stamattina,	which came to me this morning at dawn
mentr'io dormiva forte, in fantasia;	while I was deep asleep, in a dream;
Pareami, che la Corte	It seemed to me that—
per dar gusto in Palazzo à la brigata[9]	to give delight to the Palace crew—
da Zingara indovina	the Court was disguised
si fusse immascherata.	as a Gypsy fortune teller.
E doppo haver predetto a Cortigiani	And after she had predicted the fortunes
le fortune, e i malanni, ancor' volesse	and the misfortunes of the Courtiers,
far la Ventura a suoi Buffoni, e Nani,	she wanted to read the destiny of the buffoons and dwarves,
e cosi strologandoli dicesse.	and so, astrologizing, she said:

---

[8] Francesca Fantappiè, "Una primizia rinucciniana: La *Dafne* prima della 'miglior forma,'" *Il Saggiatore Musicale* 24, no. 2 (2018): 189–228.
[9] Florio defines *brigata* as "a company, a crew, a knot or rout of good fellowes."

Vien qua tu' viso d'Allocco[10]	[Scatapocchio]
Nano sciocco	Come here, you wide-eyed fool,
Scataporchio disgraziato;	Silly dwarf,
Dimmi un poco, e non mentire,	Disgraceful Scatapocchio [little prick];
sai tu' diresse	Tell me a little something, and don't lie,
sei vivo, ò se sei nato;	Do you know how to say
Gia non sanno le Persone,	whether you're alive or if you're newborn;
se sia Pecora, ò Castrone.	People can't even tell
	whether you're a ewe or a gelding.
Tu' ch'hai sì la lingua aguzza,	[Gabriello Martinez]
mà che puzza	You, who have such a sharp tongue,
da vicino, e da lontano.	but who stinks,
Getta via monello getta	from up close and from far away.
la muletta	Throw it away, tramp, throw away
e non far' più del'Malsano	that little cane [*muleta*],
soffierai, soffi, e soffiasti;	and stop being dishonest,
sei spagnolo, e tanto basti.	you will spy, you do spy, you have spied,
	you're Spanish, and that's enough.
[1v]	[Maometto Turco]
Sei Mametto un moro bianco,	You're Mohammad, a white Moor,
che non anco	who knows neither
sai che sia legge, ò Ragione;	law or reason,
E per fare in Corte acquisto,	And in order to make a career at Court,
goffo, e tristo	clumsy, and evil,
fai il Coniglio, e sei volpone;	you pretend to be a rabbit, when you are a crafty fox;
ma per quanto io ti conosco,	but given what I know of you,
ci vorria seme di bosco.	you'd do better to sow your seeds in the bush.
Di Canà[11] nulla non dico	[Canà or Becco (lit. "Beak"). Possibly Caralì?]
ch'è nemico	Of Canà I have nothing to say,
d'ogni setta, e d'ogni fede.	because he is the enemy
Pur'che bene immolli il Becco[12]	of every sect and of every faith,
immolli,	As long as his Beak is kept wet,
e satolli	and his stomach
la sua Pancia, altro non chiede	is sated, he asks for nothing else;
ond'io sempre canterei,	therefore I would always sing,
ò Galera dove sei.	"Oh, galley where are you?"

[10] Literally, the word "Allocco" means a tawny owl, though the wide eye feathers and the resultingly shocked or stunned expression of the bird have meant that in Italian, the word has taken on a metaphorical meaning: the Treccani: "2. fig. persona sciocca, balorda, . . . intonito." Díaz and Goethals translate the word as "pimp" in their translation of Costa's *Li buffoni*, though that meaning does not seem relevant here. See Costa, *Buffoons*, 333n28.

[11] Kaplan keeps "Canà" and adds "scoundrel" in square brackets, presumably based on the Crusca's definition of Canaglia: "gente vile, e abbietta" (1st ed., 1612, 147). Boggione and Casalegno note that Canà is a Piedmont word for a canal or drain (and thus an occasional euphemism for female genitalia).

[12] This could also be a name or nickname, and the reference to keeping the beak wet could be both a sexual euphemism and a reference to the consumption of alcohol; in some sources, "becco" is used as a euphemism for cuckold.

[2r]
Son di Corte i Turchi, e Nani	They are of the Court: the Turks and dwarves,
mal'Cristiani	the bad Christians,
e sottile hanno l'udito	and they have a well-developed sense of hearing,[13]
Poi ch'infatti à tutti piace,	In fact, they all like—
con lor'pace,	Peace be with them—
il soffiar' nel' Panbollito	to spy on Panbollito [lit. "to blow on their bread soup"]
han Vescica che non tiene	they have bladders that do not hold,
raspan male, e cantan' bene.	they scratch badly, and sing well.
Qui mi parve, ch'allora	Here it seemed to me, that at that point
venisse a me Costei	she [the fortune teller] came toward me,
per legger del morin'sul'libro ancora.	to read more about the little Moor in her book,
quando da gli occhi miei,	when from my eyes,
mentre manco il pensai,	without me realizing it,
fuggi la Corte, il sogno, e mi destai.	the Court, and my dream, fled; and I woke up.

The poem begins with an invocation, calling the attention of onlookers and setting the scene with a gradual layering of information that then permits the direct address and individualized punchlines of the central verses. Though Giovannino himself takes on the role of the gypsy, he cleverly displaces the responsibility for the insults he dishes out: he himself is not telling their fortunes, the court is, in disguise, and anyway, it was just a dream. The barbed humor of the central verses is remarkably individualized, rendering discernible physical and behavioral traits of the personalities in question.

In the first instance, Giovannino mocks the dwarf Scatapocchio (lit. "Little Prick," familiar to scholars as one of the characters in Costa's *Li buffoni* and identified by Teresa Megale as a *nano* in the service of Prince Leopoldo de' Medici from at least 1640;[14] I have seen his name in the granducal accounts as late as 1656.[15] Costa explained for those of her readers unfamiliar with the Medici buffoons that Scatapocchio was a "nanetto piccolissimo" (a particularly small dwarf), and his diminutive stature was emphasized in her play where he served as a "bravo" (henchman) to another dwarf.[16] In the "Sogno," the joke about whether or not Scatapocchio is a newborn implies a similar reference to his size, and the *battuta* about whether he is to be understood as

---

[13] Lit. "They have a subtle sense of hearing."
[14] Teresa Megale, "La commedia decifrata: Metamorfosi e rispecchianti in *Li buffoni* di Margherita Costa," *Il Castello di Elsinore* 2 (1988): 70.
[15] I-Fas, Camera del Granduca, f. 28b, c. 22r.
[16] The quote "nanetto piccolissimo" comes from the advice "A' lettori." Costa, *Buffoons*, 76.

a female sheep or a *castrone* (a gelded male sheep) suggests that Scatapocchio had a noticeably high-pitched voice, a common side effect of primordial dwarfism.

The Spanish dwarf referenced in the following verse is almost certainly Gabriello Martinez, "famed in his own time for his ability to 'soffiare' [lit. to blow], that is to be a spy,"[17] and who regularly appears in the account books of Grand Duke Ferdinando II.[18] The poem accuses Martinez of being smelly (an insult regularly directed at Spaniards by other Europeans)[19] and also of using a crutch when it wasn't necessary. The word that Giovannino uses for cane is *muletta*, an Italicization of *muleta*, a Spanish term for a short wooden stick with a red cloth tied to one end, used in the closing stages of a bullfight. He thus cleverly implicates the spectacularized death of a powerful animal and a thoroughly Spanish pastime in his roasting of Martinez.

The subject of the third verse, Mametto (Mohammad), appears in the account books of the Camera del Granduca as Maometto Turco several times during 1653.[20] He is referred to in the poem as a "moro bianco" (a white Moor), a term I have found with some regularity in contemporary Florentine sources and which seems to have indicated Ottoman Muslims, frequently dressed in recognizably foreign style, including turbans or the shaved pates familiar from the granducal slaves in Livorno.[21] This particular verse of the poem gave me the greatest difficulty to parse, though each word taken individually is easily translated. The poet makes a euphemistic pun based on woodland animals and the natural environment. The reference, I believe, is to sodomitical behavior—which Giovannino accuses Mametto of exchanging

---

[17] "[L]o spagnolo Gabriello Martinez, uno dei nani di Ferdinando II, celebre ai suoi tempi per l'abilità nel 'soffiare' ovvero nel far da spia." Anna Bisceglia, in her description of the painting *Ritratto del nano Gabriello Martinez*, anonymous, ca. 1640. Cited from Anna Bisceglia, Matteo Ceriana, and Simona Mammana, eds., *Buffoni, villani e giocatori alla corte dei Medici* (Livorno: Sillabe, 2016), 80.

[18] In September 1667, Gabriello nano and Giovannino moro are both mentioned in the accounts in relatively quick succession. See I-Fas, Camera del Granduca, f. 39b c. 4r.

[19] Clara Rico Osés, *L'Espagne vue de France à travers les ballets de cour du XVIIe siècle* (Geneva: Éditions Papillon, 2012).

[20] I have seen mention of "Maometto" and "Maometto Turco" in the account books of the Grand Duke in several instances during 1653. See I-Fas, Camera del Granduca, f. 24, c. 47rv (July 1653), and f. 25, 4r, 12v, 14v (September–December 1653).

[21] For example, on February 15, 1641, Vincenzio Ferrari, the *maestro di stalla* (stable master) of the Grand Duke, wrote a letter describing three enslaved stable workers, in which both Smirro and Gemer, originally from Tunisia, were described with the term "moro bianco." See I-Fca, Pia Casa dei Catecumini, f. 1, c.n.n. [ins. 120]. The two men had arrived in the Medici stables from Livorno in 1636 as part of a consignment of eight enslaved workers. Smirro was baptized with the name "Carlo Medici." See I-Fd, Registri Battesimali, Maschi, reg. 43, fg. 32.

for financial and social reward;²² Ottoman Turks were widely held to be sodomites by early modern European commentators.²³

I have not identified the addressee of the fourth verse, "Canà," possibly nicknamed "Becco" (lit. "Beak," though the capitalization may just emphasize a euphemistic reference to male genitalia). The poem describes him as without faith—not only a non-Christian but an enemy of all sects—and as a bottomless pit of gluttony. The poet suggests that Canà—like many of the Medici court slaves and like the many hundreds of Medici slaves held in Livorno—was once on the galleys. From a musicological perspective, the reference in the "Sogno" to the galleys through song is particularly fascinating. Here song itself is presented as a medium through which a colleague or companion can be subtly teased, and a past existence—in which presumably much less food was available—can be brought back to mind; the text suggests that "O Galera dove sei" ("Oh, galley, where are you?") was a popular song that would have been recognizable to contemporary audience members. In this verse, Buonaccorsi calls attention to the difference between life on the galleys and at court: the harsh conditions, physical labor, and deprivations of the galley were far removed from the rich fabrics and abundant food of court servitude. Canà, who asks for nothing as long as his stomach is sated, is highly redolent of Caralì (the character, not the individual), who in *Scipione in Cartagine* sang in celebration: "Non biscottu mansgiar, / Non corbasciù tuccar."²⁴ (It is possible that Canà should or does read Carà and that this passage in the poem was directed at Caralì.)²⁵

---

²² *Bosco* is offered as a euphemism for "vagina" in the *Dizionario storico del lessico erotico italiano* by Valter Boggione and Giovanni Casalegno). According to Salvatore Battaglia's *Grande dizionario della lingua italiana*, *bosco* can also mean "intrico, confusione (di cose fitte fitte e intricate)," in which case the punchline could translate as "the beginnings of some trick or plot are needed." I thank Francesca Fantappiè for her recommendation of the Battaglia text, Jessica Goethals for the Boggione and Casalegno, Diana Presciutti for being willing to talk about this one phrase for a very long time, and all the members of the Alterities seminar, May 2018, for helping me figure out various possible significations of this phrase.

²³ See Walter G. Andrews and Mehmet Kalpaklī, *The Age of Beloveds: Love and the Beloved in Early-Modern Ottoman and European Culture and Society* (Durham, NC: Duke University Press, 2005); Mustafa Avci, "Köçek: A Genealogy of Cross-Dressed Male Belly Dancers (Dancing Boys) from Ottoman Empire to Contemporary Turkey" (PhD diss., New York University, 2015). See also the discussion of Ottomans, sodomy, and musical performance at the Florentine court in Cusick, "'La Stiava Dolente."

²⁴ Anon., *Scipione in Cartagine, dramma musicale; Fatto rappresentare da gli Accademici Sorgenti, nel loro Teatro, sotto la protezione del Sereniss. e Reverendiss. Princ. Card. Gio: Carlo di Toscana* (Florence: Gio: Anton Bonardi, 1657), I, xv.

²⁵ If so, the poem presumably dates from before 1657, when Caralì converted to Christianity and was baptized with the name Mattia Medici.

The text of the "Sogno" also mentions "Panbollito," deploying the nickname of Pier Gio: Albizzi, the *staffiere* depicted alongside Buonaccorsi in Volterrano's double portrait of the two musicians (see Figure 8.1). The *mal'Cristiani* of the poem are described as spying on Panbollito—literally, "blowing in their boiled bread soup." Thus, Panbollito may be a stand-in for the higher levels of court life more generally, capitalizing on the double meaning of Albizzi's *soprannome*. If we include Buonaccorsi, the text of the poem makes reference to six specific members of the court—Giovannino, Scatapocchio, Martinez, Mametto, Canà (Caralì?), and Panbollito. When Giovannino mocks his companions, he does so in a highly individualized fashion. That is, rather than using broader, more generic insults—bombast, sexual euphemisms, or scatological humor—each verse calls out specific features of the person in question, relying on recognition as an integral part of each joke. Cruel and brief as they are, Buonaccorsi's verses stand as portraits of his companions.

Interestingly, and importantly, the person of Giovannino Moro himself is never mocked, and this, to my mind, is the strongest argument for Buonaccorsi's authorship of the poem. Not only are no jokes made at his expense, but Giovannino is not introduced or described as part of the exordium. Were this written by someone else, we might expect Giovannino's character to be more fully fleshed out: my name is Giovannino, I come from afar, my skin is black as night, and so on. Such phrases are habitual in the opening verses of masking songs and carnivalesque texts. Indeed, not only is such material conspicuously absent from the poem's introduction, but Giovannino wakes up precisely at the moment in which the gypsy is moving toward him, about to read his fortune. The poet thus makes Giovannino's escape from mockery the structural pivot of the poem, retaining and emphasizing his position as narrator-author, a verse-making subject, not subject of the verse.

The various characters portrayed by Buonaccorsi stand in ribald intimacy. Giovannino makes fun of his peers with an impunity that implies a relative degree of friendship—we can assume that (superficially, at least) the insults delivered by the poem were taken as good fun; there is no implication that Giovannino risked physical retribution. At the same time, the antagonistic structure of the poem invokes the competitiveness of the more visible layers of court culture, with the *buffoni* and *nani* engaged in competition for the resources and favors of those in power, much as the noble courtiers competed for precedence within each court and the various courts themselves (and or their ruling families) acted within the political arena of the Italian peninsular and European public life through military, artistic, and matrimonial displays of influence and power. The clever sidestep of the poem's final verse (in which the "Zingara indovina" evaporates precisely at the moment in which she approaches Giovannino and is expected to point out his flaws) permits Buonaccorsi a moment of literary and performative triumph over his rivals. The "Sogno di Giovannino Moro" stands as a moment of articulate Black excellence in which Buonaccorsi speaks back, his voice, wit, and performative force echoing still, hundreds of years after the fact.

* * *

The pointed humor of the "Sogno" and Buonaccorsi's role as humorist bear comparison with a scene written for Buonaccorsi by Moniglia and Melani in the lavish 1661 opera *Ercole in Tebe*. Figure 10.2 shows the set design, with Iolao and his interlocutor Sifone visible at the bottom right (Iolao is closer to the river, pointing).[26] Previously, I discussed the opening interaction of this scene—in which Iolao (played by Buonaccorsi) and Sifone (a stuttering hunchback played by Righenzi) encounter each other on the banks of the Styx, and Sifone mistakes Iolao for a demon. I will also discuss Iolao's entrance aria, "E a chi non scapperebbe la patienza," from Act III, scene v, in a later chapter. Here, however, I want to focus on the duet sung by the two comic servants (see Musical Example 10.1). Iolao (Buonaccorsi) sets up the duet with the unexpected announcement that despite his eagerness to leave the underworld, he is not sorry to have visited. Indeed, he has learned a valuable lesson: that appearances can be deceiving and, specifically, that many individuals who pass themselves off as morally unimpeachable are hiding their more scurrilous thoughts and activities and will therefore be sent to hell when they die. The duet proper illustrates this claim with examples; I have translated the introductory patter of the two comics as well as their duet, while the musical transcription begins at "Tra ta- tanti infelci," twenty-one lines later.

---

[26] Sergio Monaldini identifies the figure of Sifone/Righenzi through reference to other costume sketches of the stuttering hunchback character that feature the puffy short pants, visible stripes, and a long scarf. See Monaldini, "Leandro," particularly 81, 93–94.

Figure 10.2. Set design for Act III of *Ercole in Tebe*, libretto by Giovanni Andrea Moniglia, music by Jacopo Melani. Etched plate by Valerio Spada after a design by Ferdinando Tacca. Printed between pages 44 and 45 of the ceremonial libretto (Florence: Stamperia all'Insegna della Stella, 1661).

Musical Example 10.1. "Or fidisi chi vuole," duet; Iolao (Giovannino Buonaccorsi) and Sifone (Carlo Righenzi). *Ercole in Tebe* (perf. 1661); libretto by Gio: Andrea Moniglia, music by Jacopo Melani, Act III, scene vii.

Musical Example 10.1. Continued

Musical Example 10.1. Continued

Musical Example 10.1. Continued

IOLAO	Son contento,	I am happy [to leave],
	Ma d'esser qui venuto non mi pento	But I do not regret coming here.
SIFONE	Pe- pe- perchè?	Wh-, wh-, why not?
IOLAO	Conobbi,	I learned,
	Che nella nostra Corte	That in our Court,
	Più non s'alloggia verità sincera.	True sincerity no longer resides!
SIFONE	In qual ma- ma- maniera?	In what w-, w-, way?
IOLAO	Per esser condannate	Whether to be condemned
	Ai sempiterni horrori	To eternal horrors
	O per goder dentro i beati Elisi,	Or to enjoy the blessed Elysium,
	Sappi, o fido compagno,	Know, oh faithful companion,
	Che vengon l'alme tutte a questa riva.	That all souls come to this river.
SIFONE	Pa- pa- partiam,	Le-, le-, let's get out of here.
	che qui non c'è guadagno,	Here there is nothing to be earned.
	Co i morti non stà ben la gente viva.	The dead do not go well with the living.
IOLAO	Non temere: io pur vidi	Don't be afraid. I have even seen
	Giunger su i neri lidi,	Arrive on the black shore
	E tombolar nel baratro infernale	And fall into the infernal abyss,
	Tal'un che per bontà del mondo insano	Such a one of whom, for the generosity of the mad world,
	Di Giove si credea fratel carnale.	One would believe them the brother of Jove.
SIFONE	Tra ta- tanti infelici	Among so, so many poor souls,
	Hai, notizia d'alcun?	Do you have news of anyone [in particular]?
IOLAO	Son[27] nostri amici,	These are our friends!
	Non conoscevi in Tebe	Didn't you know, in Thebes,
	Quel dotto Satrapon, ch'era in concetto	That learned Satrap,[28] who conceived the idea
	Di rintracciare ogni virtù smarrita?	To search out every lost virtue?
SIFONE	Quel con la fa- fa- faccia scolorita,	Him with the discolored fa- fa- face,
	Con larga barba, e venerando aspetto?	With the large beard and venerable aspect?
IOLAO	Questo sì, sì, poc'anzi,	Him, yes, yes, just now
	Scese nel fondo, e non a passi corti.	He descended into the depths, and not slowly.
a 2	Or fidisi chi vuol di colli torti.	Now, trust he who will in bent necks!

---

[27] In the printed libretto, this word is "Fur," or "they *were* our friends."

[28] A Satrap was an ancient Persian official; in European languages (English and Italian included), the term had a strong sense of someone who abused or exaggerated their authority. Florio defines the term: "Satrapo, a Governor, a president, a Captaine or chiefe Ruler of a Province or Country under another, a Chieftaine, a Chiefe-ruler or Peer of a Realme, but rather now taken in bad than in good part." Note that he also provides definitions for Satraperia, Satrapia, and Satrapico; thus, the term was presumably used relatively frequently. Since this opera is set in ancient times, the use here may be intended as historicizing detail; given the "discolored skin" and "large beard" associated with this particular figure in the following lines of poetry, Moniglia may have seized on the term "Satrap" precisely for its racializing connotations.

IOLAO	So che ben ti sovviene	I know that you well recall,
	Di quella gran matrona,	That great matron,
	Che cinta il crin di maestoso velo	Who wrapped her hair in a magnificent veil,
	Gli occhi sempre tenea rivolti al cielo.	Her eyes always turned toward heaven.
SIFONE	Che parlava si poco, e si modesta?	She who spoke so little and so modestly?
IOLAO	Attendi, appunto questa	Precisely her. Pay attention:
	Molto non è che venne	It is not that long since she passed by
	Tra le schiere malvagie, e maladette.	Among the wicked, and cursed ranks.
a 2	Or fidisi chi vuole di bocche strette.	Now, trust he who will in closed mouths!
IOLAO	Ti ricordi di quello,	Do you remember that man,
	Ch'impastato parea di carità,	Who seemed swollen with charity,
	Di zelo, e di pietà?	With zeal and with pity?
SIFONE	Che pa- pa- pa- parlando	He who when sp- sp- sp- speaking,
	Facea spallucce, riverenze, e inchini?	Pleaded with humility, made reverences, and bowed?
IOLAO	Questo dentro i confini	Him! Inside the confines
	Di casa calda tormentato stassi.	Of the warm house he is in torment.
a 2	Or[29] fidisi chi vuol di baciabassi!	Now, trust he who will in obsequies[32]!
	Se dunque così è,	If indeed it is so,
	Voglio, amico, alla fè,	My friend, I swear I want to
	Con ragione imparar su questo loco	Learn a logical lesson from this place:
	A creder niente,[30] & a fidarmi poco.[31]	Believe in nothing, and trust less!

Moniglia's libretto is more allusive than Buonaccorsi's poem—no one in Iolao's scene with Sifone is identified by name, and no one is described in enough detail for scholars to easily identify them at this distance—still, Iolao's specific insistence that "these are our friends" makes it clear that figures from the Medici court were to be found hidden behind the descriptions that follow. As with Buonaccorsi's "Sogno," the Moorish court servant in this opera plays the role of court jester, producing a humor that skewers the denizens of the court in rhyme and in song and articulating a knowing circle of those who can identify the joke's targets (the "in" crowd), excluding those who can't.

This scene has all the hallmarks of an operatic set piece, drawing on the specific skills of known performers (including Reghenzi's stage stutter) and incorporating specific textual references to events and personalities, aimed at a

---

[29] In the libretto, this appears as "O"; the score has it as "Hor," which makes more sense given the text of the previous two refrains.

[30] In the libretto, this appears as "A viver bene."

[31] Moniglia, *Ercole in Tebe*, III, vii.

[32] The Treccani translates *baciabasso* as "Inchino profondo accompagnato dal bacio della mano o del lembo della veste in segno di riverenza. Con senso spregiativo, atto di umiliazione, di esagerato ossequio, specialmente col fine di ottenere qualcosa."

particular audience at a particular time. In revivals, scenes such as this were (and still are) liable to be replaced, cut, or substantially rewritten. For historians, they are thus doubly useful, as they record the particularity of a given performer's affect. In *Ercole in Tebe*, Buonaccorsi makes a cameo appearance as entertaining court servant. He mocks members of his audience, and he does so in song. In Melani's setting, the verses are set as simple patter over largely static or cadential chords, allowing the words to be clearly understood, while the three refrains are increasingly complex variants rather than direct musical repeats.

The very musicality of "Or fidisi chi vuole" illuminates certain structural elements of the "Sogno." Textually (in terms of what the words of the poem say) and structurally (how the poem is put together), the "Sogno" implies a live performance. We can imagine the interpellative force of the second-person-indicative text, with the body of the performer (of Buonaccorsi) turning with the start of each new strophe, in order to mock his companions one after another. I would suggest that Buonaccorsi's poem was almost certainly sung, and again, the Iolao-Sifone duet is a productive point of comparison. By mid-century, *versi sciolti* (such as those used by Buonaccorsi in the first and last strophes) were tightly linked to recitative, while full strophes of *versi pari* (lines of verse in even meters, as used in the central five strophes) were rarely seen outside of musical performance. *Versi pari* could be easily paired with a repeating musical unit, with each verse of text sung to the same music or a lightly altered variant thereof. The framework of the poem, its introduction and recitative conclusion, calls for the dramatism of registral change and performative flair.

The musical implications of the "Sogno" text are strengthened still further when we consider the long association between buffoonery and musical performance. In Costa's *Li buffoni*, for example, when Marmotta (the princess of Fessa) and Tedeschino (a buffoon) discuss the requirements of buffoonery (part of a longer joke about courtiers and the court), music is the first item on the princess's list:

MARMOTTA	A tal sorte di gente	For that class of people [buffoons]
	Convien saper cantare,	it's best to know how to sing,
	Sonare, motteggiare,	to play music, to banter,
	Aver frasi galanti,	to have smooth sayings,
	Botte ridicolose,	ridiculous retorts,
	Bei motti all'improvviso,	smart offhand quips,
	Saper tacere a tempo,	to know when to keep silent,
	Non parlar fuor di tempo.[33]	to not speak out of turn.

---

[33] Costa, *Li buffoni*, I, x.

In the "Sogno," Buonaccorsi mirrors precisely this mix of singing, banter, quips, and ridiculous retorts. Furthermore, much like Costa, he represents the individuals referenced in his text as an essential substrata of courtly life ("Son di Corte," he writes) and as a group with a particular affinity for (musical) sound. While Costa, in the quote above, describes the community of *buffoni*, *nani*, and *schiavi* as knowing "how to sing" but also "when to keep silent / to not speak out of turn," the *Turchi*, *Nani*, and *mal'Cristiani* of Buonaccorsi's text "have a well-developed sense of hearing"; "they scratch badly, and sing well." In both accounts, sound is central: the protagonists speak and sing, and they listen carefully and attentively in ways that show them as aurally literate participants in the complex protocols of courtly behavior.

Alongside Costa's (theatrical) portrait of buffoonish humor and competitive collaboration, Buonaccorsi's poem can be productively juxtaposed with Anton Domenico Gabbiani's visual *Ritratto di quattro servitori della corte medicea* (*Portrait of Four Servants of the Medici Court*), dated to slightly later in the century and reproduced as Figure 10.3, after page 240. Gabbiani's first biographer and erstwhile student, Ignatius Hugford, described the *Ritratto* along with a second Gabbiani work that hung with it in the Medici Villa di Castello, just outside Florence: "various portraits of several youths of barbarous nations who lived at the court of Grand Duke Cosimo III, that is Moors, Tartars, Cossacks, etc., various Courtiers of the lowest level of service; among them is a dwarf who holds a plate in his hand with a few leaves of fresh spinach, in order to indicate his particular inclination for passing on the business of other people, in which skill, he [the dwarf] stands out above all others."[34] Hugford's description is rich, not only identifying the *Ritratto* securely but codifying the documentary quality that the painting would have had for contemporary viewers. Several parallels with Buonaccorsi's poem are immediately evident, both in the racial and physiognomic diversity of the grouping and in the association of such figures with eavesdropping practices and with impromptu entertainment, illustrated by Gabbiani through framing and the directed gazes of the sitters.

---

[34] Hugford, *Vita*, 10. I note that the Villa di Castello was the same villa in which Volteranno's double portrait of Buonaccorsi and Albizzi was located at the time of Cardinal Giovan Carlo's death.

"Nella Villa di Castello si conservano due altri simili Quadri rappresentanti varj Ritratti di alcuni giovani di barbare nazioni, che stavano alla corte del Gran Duca Cosimo III., cioè Mori, Tartari, Cosacchi, ecc. vari Cortigiani di basso servizio, e tra gli altri vedesi un Nano, che tiene nelle mani un piatto con alcune foglie fresche di Spinaci, per così denotare l'inclinazione particolare di quello in riferire gli altrui fatti, nel che fare spiccava sopra d'ogni altro."

The three central (and more dramatically "Othered") figures of Gabbiani's portrait are gathered in a relatively orderly, well-choreographed fashion, with the two dwarves engaged over the prominently placed plate of spinach. On the right, the stone column and red silk curtain reference standard conventions of formal portraiture, while on the left, a rather dissolute and unkempt older white man—identified by Marco Chiarini as "Corporal Buccia"[35]—crowds his way into the frame like a seventeenth-century photobomb. The pained, almost apprehensive expression on the young Black man's face suggests that the late arrival is unwanted and even unexpected; the impression of discomfort is magnified by Buccia's pointing hand, which rests suggestively on the Black man's hip. Presumably, this gesture and Buccia's looming appearance referenced some gossipy event or *lazzo* (slapstick routine or joke) that would have been familiar to contemporary viewers. The evident discomfort of the young Black man calls to mind the transactions that Buonaccorsi attributes to Mametto, exchanging homosexual acts in return for acquisitions at court (ll. 31–35), as well as the tribulations of the Black maidservant who found herself the target of an old nobleman's lust in Ciro di Pers's poem (see the Introduction). Despite the luxurious trappings of court slavery—Gabbiani's Black African sitter wears an extraordinarily beautiful silk cassock, belted in the Ottoman style and decorated with a long row of buttons; a double strand of coral beads is visible at his neck—enslaved bodies were appropriated for the physical pleasures of slaveholders at every turn.[36]

In addition to providing a name for Corporal Buccia, contemporary documents identify the young man holding the plate of spinach as "Christofanino Gobbo" (lit. "Little Christopher the Hunchback") and the other individual with dwarfism as "the little hunchback who came from Livorno."[37] The young Black man is, unsurprisingly, identified solely as "il Moro." A plausible sitter, based on his relative youth, is Mehmet, "Turco & etiope" (lit. "Turkish & Ethiopian," though more accurately "Muslim & African"), who was baptized with the name Giuseppe Maria Medici in

---

[35] Marco Chiarini, "Quadro raffigurante famigli della Corte di Cosimo III de' Medici," in *Curiosità di una reggia: Vicende della guardaroba di Palazzo Pitti*, ed. Kirsten Aschengreen Piacenti and Sandra Pinto (Florence: Centro Di, 1979), 59.

[36] The "Moorish" outfit depicted here is reminiscent of the green cassock with many buttons fabricated for Ali Moro in 1666, as discussed in this book's eighth chapter.

[37] "[I]l Gobbino . . . che venne di Livorno." Chiarini gives credit for having found the document to Silvia Meloni Trkulija but does not transcribe the entire document or provide a citation. Chiarini, "Quadro raffigurante," 59.

1685.³⁸ Mehmet described himself as from Mussa, Borno, in modern-day Nigeria; he would have been around fourteen when Gabbiani's painting was made. Documents in the Pia Casa note that Mehmet was living in the house of one of the Grand Duke's footmen, and since the Grand Duke himself is cited as godfather at his eventual baptism, Mehmet-Giuseppe Maria can be assumed a resident at the court, much as Hugford describes, among the "several youths of barbarous nations."

Gabbiani's *Four Servants* are not so different from the two dwarves, the ex-galley slave, and the *moro bianco* whom Buonaccorsi roasts in the "Sogno."³⁹ The tight coupling evidenced between racial, religious, and physical differences in Buonaccorsi's poem and elsewhere, including the Gabbiano painting, marks the contiguity of these categories to a degree that scholars have yet to fully account for—neither for what this contiguity illustrates about race and physical deformity as "wondrous" (in a Daston/Parks sense of the word) exceptions to the white, able-bodied norm nor the ways in which the court servitude of dwarves, buffoons, and fools approached slavery.⁴⁰ An expanding literature on court dwarves has noted that they were effectively owned by the court and that their opportunities for upward social mobility were simultaneously enabled and limited by their marked physical differences.⁴¹ The intimacy and access of the court dwarf role meant that they (like many itinerant performers) could be effective spies (like Martinez and Christofanino) and trusted confidants (a notable example is the letters exchanged by the young Prince Giovan Carlo de' Medici and the court dwarf Battistone, published by Teresa Megale).⁴²

---

³⁸ I-Fd, Registri Battesimali, Maschi, reg. 65, fg. 214; see also I-Fca, Pia Casa dei Catecumini, f. 2, c.n.n [ins. 119].

³⁹ Aside from the Volterrano portrait of Buonaccorsi and Albizzi, Cardinal Giovan Carlo owned at least one other painting of a moor (unfortunately now lost), described in inventories from 1647 and 1663, of "a Moor and the dwarf Petricco, half figure, both eating ricotta." See I-Fas, Miscellanea Medicea, n. 31, ins. 10, c. 9v: "Numero 1 quadro, entrovi un moro e Petricco nano, mezza figura, che mangiano una ricotta, ornamento fondo nero, rabescato e profilato d'oro." The painting is unlikely to represent Buonaccorsi, as it was also described in 1647. See I-Fas, Possessioni, 4279, transcribed and published by the Fondazione Memofonte onlus, http://www.memofonte.it/home/files/pdf/CASINO_VIA_DELLA_SCALA_1647.pdf.

⁴⁰ Lorraine Daston and Katharine Park, eds., *Wonders and the Order of Nature, 1150–1750* (New York: Zone Books, 1998). It is worth reiterating that the cardinal's "mute," Gio: Antonio Gaeta, was—like Buonaccorsi—paid only in "vitto e vestito."

⁴¹ Thomas V. Cohen, "Furto di nano" (2018). See also Eleonora Ferraro, "Ventura e sventura dei nani nelle corti del Seicento," *Rivista Internazionale di Filosofia Online* 12, no. 23 (2017): 201–214; Giuseppe Crimi and Cristiano Spila, eds., *Nanerie del Rinascimento: "La Nanea" di Michelangelo Serafini e altri versi di corte e d'accademia* (Rome: Vecchiarelli, 2006); Luzio and Renier, "Buffoni, schiavi e nani."

⁴² These letters are included as part of the editorial introduction to Benardino Ricci's buffoonish text. See Teresa Megale, "Bernardino Ricci e il mestiere di buffone tra cinque e seicento," in *Il*

Each of the identifiable people in the "Sogno," including the author, was present at the Medici court in 1653, several for a number of years on either side of that date. In Buonaccorsi's able hands, each of the characters described assumes an agential role, from the details of Martinez's crutch to the dubious sexual behavior ascribed to Mohammad. The "Sogno" illuminates the kinds of performances produced within the court and the kinds of relationships that Western hegemony imposed on the "Turchi, e Nani, mal'Cristiani" who lived and labored in courtly spaces. Like these individuals, who had to make their way through a hostile and highly political environment, we historians need to develop a "subtle sense of hearing" (to borrow Buonaccorsi's elegant turn of phrase, "e sottile hanno l'udito") in order to understand their place and the rules of comportment they were obliged to follow.

Tedeschino overo Difesa dell'Arte del Cavalier del Piacere (Florence: Le Lettere, 1995), 7–75. See also Touba Ghadessi, *Portraits of Human Monsters in the Renaissance: Dwarves, Hirsutes, and Castrati as Idealized Anatomical Anomalies* (Monsters, Prodigies, and Demons: Medieval and Early Modern Constructions of Alterity, Kalamazoo, MI: Medieval Institute Publications, Western Michigan University, 2018).

Allo schiavo del Mendes Ebreo che fa i sorbetti uno scudo.

To the slave of Mendez the Jew who makes the sorbets, one scudo.
        I-Fas, Camera del Granduca, f. 37, March 1667, c. 20r

Scene 11
Buonaccorsi as a Black Gypsy

It is noteworthy that Giovannino Buonaccorsi's "Il sogno di Giovannino Moro" is written in precise, idiomatic Italian and not the slave *gergo* favored by (white) Italian authors and poets to represent the speech of both *mori* (which Buonaccorsi was) and *zingari* (which the poem impersonates). This linguistic level, too, encourages an association with Buonaccorsi, who frequently sang Black roles written in proper Italian. Recall that, of the Black parts featured on the Florentine stage at mid-century, only three used *gergo*, and, as I have argued, only one of these three—the Black gypsy[1] "Moretta," in Gio: Andrea Moniglia's *Il pazzo per forza* of 1659—can be linked directly to Buonaccorsi (the other two roles, I suggest, were played by Caralì). The published libretto of *Il pazzo per forza* identifies the performer who sang the role of "Moretta" as "il Moro di S.A. Reverendiss."; it is thus unlikely to have been anyone other than Buonaccorsi, since the cardinal prince was not known to have an association with any other Black singers.[2]

It is revealing to contrast Buonaccorsi's operatic performance as "Moretta" with the gypsy impersonated in the "Sogno." Notably, the libretto of *Il pazzo per forza* includes a range of different *zingari*. There is a chorus of gypsies, sung (according to the cast list) by Michele Mosi, Francesco Leonardi, Antonio Ruggieri, Niccola Coresi, and Gio: Michele de Bar; and a gypsy dance was performed by various noblemen of the academy to conclude Act II.[3] There was also a fake gypsy, "Muretta," impersonated by the page character Ligurino, played by the castrato Antonio Rivani disguised using Moretta's clothes. The largest of these roles is that played by Rivani as Ligurino/Muretta. (The archival document reproduced here earlier as

---

[1] I use the term "gypsy" here and in other chapters to describe a common stereotype and dramatic character, not to reference people of Romani heritage who, historically, have been described using the term.

[2] Moniglia, *Il pazzo per forza*, 124.

[3] The same singers also performed as the chorus of madmen (*pazzi*). Moniglia, *Il pazzo per forza*, 124. The dancers' names are provided in archival documents, which make clear that male dancers performed both the male and female dancing roles. See I-FImmobili, f. 1.8.

Table 8.2 identifies Rivani as the longest-serving and most highly paid of the cardinal's singers.) Ligurino is given many opportunities to show off his cleverness and cunning, fulfilling the stock commedia role of the *primo zanni*, a wily servant who ensures the convoluted story's happy ending.[4] Part of the joke is that Ligurino successfully pulls off his gypsy disguise by assuming not just the clothes but also the name and the language of the real gypsy. He assures his dubious master:

LIGURINO	Quando presi la veste	When I took the clothes
	Di Zingara, pur anco 'l nome presi	Of the Gypsy, I also took the name
	Di Moretta da lei, ch'a me la diede,	Of Moretta from she who gave them to me.
	Per Moretta mi spaccio a chi mi vede;	I pass myself off as Moretta to all who see me;
	L'abito è in tutto eguale al suo, se vengo	My outfit is equal to hers in all ways, if I am
	Scoperto, getto via	Discovered, I will throw away
	(Badi vo signoria)	(Be careful, master)
	Linguaggio, panni, e nome.[5]	Language, clothes, and name.

By "language," Ligurino means slave *gergo* or Sabir, that by-now-familiar mash-up of Neapolitan dialect words, un-conjugated verbs, and often a substitution of *b* for *p*. Ligurino's disguised voice would itself have been funny for contemporary audiences, but the elevation of sound also makes a joke about visual (racial) difference, since Muretta (Rivani) was white and Moretta (Buonaccorsi) was Black. This color change would have made it immediately obvious to the audience whether Moretta or Muretta was onstage at any given time and magnified the foolishness of the onstage characters who were tricked. Indeed, Ligurino is quite explicit about this difference, telling Trottolo that (s)he has the power to change the color of her skin:

LIGURINO	Mi gran virtù tinir,	The biggest talent that I have is the
	Chillu, ch'è biancu nigru,	ability to turn what is white, black,
	Chillu, ch'è nigru biancu far vinir.[6]	and what is black, white.

When Trottolo later encounters Moretta, he assumes that the real and the false gypsies are one and the same person, placing his faith not in skin color but in the continuity of voice (language) and in clothing:

---

[4] Wilbourne, *Seventeenth-Century Opera*.
[5] Moniglia, *Il pazzo per forza*, II, xii.
[6] Moniglia, *Il pazzo per forza*, II, xvi.

TROTTOLO	Quanto è furba costei:	How sneaky she is!
	Ma io ben più di lei	But I—far better than she—
	Son di calca: Moretta,	Am a trickster: Moretta,
	Alle vesti, al parlar ti riconosco;	By your clothes and way of speaking I recognize you!
	E ben ch'adesso nera, e dinazi bianca,	And even if now you are black, and before were white,
	Questo a fe non ti franca,	This does not absolve you, I swear,
	Variare i colori	You told me that you know how
	Saper tu mi dicesti,	To vary your colors
	Come appunto facesti,	Just like you have done now
	per mascherar l'inganno.[7]	To mask the trick.

The Black Moretta appears only a few times, most notably at the ends of the first and second acts, emphasizing her relationship to comedy rather than narrative. Her presence serves to set up the two end-of-act dances and thus the *intermedii*. In Act I, scene 37, Moretta enters to find Sgaruglia, Bellichino, and a troupe of *battilani* (wool workers) drinking. She sings a short da capo aria and then offers to read their palms. Sgaruglia and Bellichino make it quite clear that they are not so easily tricked, at which point the Moretta offers each of them a piece of advice. She whispers in their ears, "If you don't watch out, your companion will steal your purse," picking their pockets as she does so (in the process, she knocks out a letter which drops to the floor, a mishap that ultimately proves crucial to the plot). Moretta takes her leave, and only later do both men realize that they have been robbed and—misled by her earlier advice—blame each other. They thus fight (dance) along with the *battilani*, which serves to conclude the act.

Moretta, Sgaruglia, Bellichino, Truppe di Battilani   *Moretta, Sgaruglia, Bellichino, troop of wool workers*

MORETTA	Ligrizza, ligrizza,	Happiness, happiness,
	Si nun avir billizza	Even if I have no beauty,
	Nun vulirmi dispirar:	I don't want to despair.
	Ballar,	To dance,
	Cantar,	To sing,
	Miu curi,	My heart,
	Miu amori,	My love,
	Muritta cusì	Thus, Moretta,
	Star tutta pir ti:	Is all yours.
	Per visu liggiadru	For a pretty face,
	I Mundo star ladru;	The world becomes a thief.
	Chi bella vidir,	Whoever sees a beautiful woman
	Bramusu vulir	Wants, with desire,
	Cun munita d'amur cumprar vaghizza.	To buy that beauty with the money of love.
	Liggrizza, ligrizza &c.	Happiness, happiness etc.

---

[7] Moniglia, *Il pazzo per forza*, II, xxviii[b] (note that the scene is misnumbered in the printed libretto).

SGARUGLIA	Zinganina, degnate.	Little gypsy, look at my hand.
MORETTA	Manu vustra	[In] your hand,
	Guardar, buna vintura	I see, good fortune
	Pir vui tinir sicura.[8]	Comes for you, for sure.

Unfortunately, the music composed by Jacopo Melani for this opera has not survived. Visually and metrically, the text of Moretta's opening aria is striking, for the lines get longer as the song progresses. This *zingara* offers to read palms but is rebuffed; she picks pockets without being caught; she speaks *gergo*. Later in the opera, Moretta is the unexpected (but delighted) recipient of money that "Muretta" had hoped to collect, and in the final scene of Act II, Moretta delivers the money to her gypsy companions. The scene is a "field with gypsy wagons," where a chorus of *zingari* sing "Di stelle o crudità," a melancholy lullaby, which alternates between various groups of voices (one, two, and four singers) as well as the chorus as a whole (five singers).[9] All of these singers sing in *gergo*. When Moretta arrives, she tells them not to lament, because now she has lots of money; they celebrate with song and dance.[10]

We can recognize familiar elements of the modern gypsy stereotype: foreign wanderers, poor trickster fortune tellers, pickpockets, and thieves, who live in wagons and camp in fields. During this time, people identified as Romani occasionally appear in the Medici accounts. On March 16, 1662, for example, the Granducal Camera distributed 40 lire to "certi Zingari" (certain Rom); and in May 1627, two *zingari* and a stable boy were rewarded for having worked with the camels.[11] Despite this historical presence, the *zingara* in both Buonaccorsi's poem and Moniglia's libretto is most important as a figure available for impersonation: the fake gypsy is more important to either plot than any "real" gypsies. The mask of the gypsy doubles down on the clever tricks in which Ligurino/"Muretta" delights, and it is Ligurino's craftiness that the opera ultimately celebrates. Indeed, it is this same deliberate distancing through disguise and yet flagging of trickery on which the "Sogno" relies, even as Buonaccorsi's two characters, Moretta and the

---

[8] Moniglia, *Il pazzo per forza*, I, xxxvii.
[9] "Prato con trabacche di Zingari." Moniglia, *Il pazzo per forza*, 88. Florio defines *trabacche* as "Pavillions, Tents, that are remooved too and fro, and suddainely set up. Also boothes or bowres. Also shelters or skaffolds made of boordes."
[10] Moniglia, *Il pazzo per forza*, II, xxxv and xxxvi.
[11] For these two references, see, respectively, I-Fas, Camera del Granduca, f. 31, c. 116r, and I-Fas, Camera del Granduca, f. 7, c. 23r. The longer citation reads: "A due Zingari, e a un Garzone di stalla sette giuli per ciascuno che fecero travagliare li Cammelli in tutto due scudi."

"Zingara indovina," represent two strongly contrasted versions of the gypsy character: in Buonaccorsi's poem, Giovannino dreams of the court disguised as a gypsy whom he then goes on to impersonate—a mask within a mask within a mask.

Fascinatingly, while Moretta falls victim to the foreignness of the gypsy stereotype—an element explicitly marked by the linguistic distortions of the *gergo* sound—Giovannino flaunts his ability to assume the gypsy disguise while remaining thoroughly Italianate. The "Sogno" is remarkable in the extent to which it frames the speaker as a canny viewer of, articulate commentator on, and consummate participant in Italian court life. In this context, Buonaccorsi's excellent Italian and the subtle distinctions he makes between the subjunctive space of his dream (*venisse, dicesse*) and the *passato remoto* of his morning activities (*mi venne, mi destai*) suggest a long engagement with the Italian language, placing his arrival at court (in Florence or elsewhere) at a very young age—and making his poem the consequence or afterlife of the young Black children whose presence persists in Italian court portraiture.

A due mori che uno ballò e l'altro sonò 1.-.

To two Moors, one who danced and the other who played music, 1 scudo.

                        I-Fas, Camera del Granduca, f. 34, March 1665, c. 92r

Scene 12
Buonaccorsi as a Soprano

Thanks to Giovannino Buonaccorsi's participation in the elite genre of opera, a limited access to sound and vocality is retained through the notational technologies of musical reproduction. Four scores survive for operas in which Buonaccorsi is known to have sung, and each of his known roles is scored for soprano. Thus, either Buonaccorsi sang in falsetto (the voice type commonly known in modern English as countertenor) or he was a castrato (that is, castrated young enough to retain his high-pitched, prepubescent voice into adulthood).[1] Historically, the second option is far more likely. During the seventeenth century, musically motivated castration was common throughout the Italian peninsula; castrato voices dominated in Italian courts and churches, and the castrato voice was the normalized male lead in professional opera and elite chamber music. There are no documents that would confirm or deny Buonaccorsi's status as castrated or intact male; however, castrato singers were often (though not exclusively) known by diminutive names such as "Giovannino," and the term *musico*—which was given as Buonaccorsi's job title in 1663 and in Baldinucci's description of his portrait—was often (though, again, not exclusively) used as a euphemism for castrato. Of the five other male singers in Cardinal Giovan Carlo's retinue, none sang bass or baritone, and only Carlo Righenzi sang tenor; the other four had high male voices: Antonio Rivani soprano, Francesco Leonardi soprano, Vincenzo Olivicciani soprano, and Bartolomeo Melani contralto.[2] Of these, three are described in historical documents as castrati (Rivani, Olivicciani, and Melani), and at least two were known by diminutive names ("Tonino" Rivani and "Vincenzino" Olivicciani).[3] By early modern aesthetic standards,

---

[1] Since we do not know when Buonaccorsi was born, there is a third possibility that his voice had yet to break. While he looks relatively young in Volterrano's portrait of him (ca. 1662), his body does not seem sufficiently childlike to support such a claim.

[2] The list of the cardinal's singers also includes six female singers, three *donne*, three *fanciulle*: Donna Lucia Coppa, Angela Socii fanciulla, Donna Lisabetta Falbetti Nacci, Francesca Chiarelli fanciulla, Donna Leonora Falbetti Ballerini, and Luisa Massai fanciulla, all of whom can be assumed to have had high voices. See I-Fas, Mediceo del Principato, f. 5358, c. 757v.

[3] Rivani's diminutive name appears in the accounts of Cardinal Giovan Carlo. See, for example, I-Fas, Depositeria generale, parte antica, f. 1604, c. 116r. See also Reardon, *A Sociable Moment*, 12. The entry on Rivani in the Archivio Multimediale Attori Italiani also gives the nickname "Ciccolino"

the castrato voice was considered explicitly "natural"—despite the surgical intervention required to produce the voice—as the singer retained his (natural) boyish voice into adulthood rather than artificially manufacturing a small, false voice (lit. "falsetto") in the adult throat.[4]

If Buonaccorsi were not Black, if he were not enslaved, the question of whether he was castrated or not would be largely academic. After all, at the time, most serious male singers were. Yet here Buonaccorsi's hypervisible difference interrupts the naturalized circuits of identification. I mean this quite literally. In early presentations of my work on Buonaccorsi, some listeners questioned how I could prove he was castrated, offering resistance to the idea because of his Blackness and thus the presumed belatedness of his arrival on Italian soil. Other listeners insisted that as a Moor, he would have reached Italy already castrated, since castration was common in the (barbarous) Ottoman Empire. Both responses are steeped in racialized stereotypes. I argue here that the castrato voice—which confounds modern taxonomies of gender difference—also provides a way to think about Buonaccorsi's racial difference. Simultaneously, his race helps us to think more carefully about castration as a socio-musical practice, since Buonaccorsi's Black body forces attention to the ways in which the violence of slavery and the violence of castration cohere in their instrumentalization of the human body. While music, particularly vocal music, invokes beauty, expressivity, and emotional sincerity, the forced physical labor of Buonaccorsi's body makes evident what Saidiya Hartman calls the "apparently unsettling juxtaposition of the festive and the obscene." His vocal performances "outline a problematic of enjoyment in which pleasure is inseparable from subjection, will indistinguishable from submission, and bodily integrity bound to violence."[5]

As I have already intimated, Buonaccorsi's roles fell into a standard type, iterating his performance techniques over a series of performances. The same can be said about the music composed for him to sing, as is evident from a comparison of the two extant scores by the resident compositional team at the Pergola theater, Giovanni Andrea Moniglia and Jacopo Melani. Melani,

---

(with variable spellings). Olivicciani is identified as "Vincenzino" in various scholarly sources. See, for example, Beth Glixon and Jonathan Glixon, *Inventing the Business of Opera: The Impresario and His World in Seventeenth-Century Venice* (Oxford: Oxford University Press, 2008), 183–184; Warren Kirkendale, *The Court Musicians in Florence during the Principate of the Medici: With a Reconstruction of the Artistic Establishment* (Florence: Olschki, 1993), 409–411.

[4] Freitas, *Portrait*.
[5] Hartman, *Scenes of Subjection*, 33.

who was on the payroll of Prince Mattias de' Medici, served as singing teacher to at least one of Giovan Carlo's young singers and can be assumed to have had a good grasp of the capacities of the Florentine performers.[6] In each of Melani's surviving scores for La Pergola, Buonaccorsi's music is written for soprano (cleffed as C1 and C2, respectively), ranging from B♮ just below middle C, to the D a tenth higher.[7] The music that survives for the role of Alindo, in Cavalli's *L'Hipermestra*, which was also composed specifically for a Florentine performance, is also notated in C1, though the page sings only a few lines. While the opening line of Alindo's music is set as much as a third higher, the rest of the part is firmly notated within the same range.[8]

Both Monello (Buonaccorsi's role in *Il potestà di Colognole*, 1657) and Iolao (his role in *Ercole in Tebe*, 1661) get a short aria in common time for their first entrance, followed by a ritornello; Iolao has a brief B section in triple time and then repeats the opening two lines to conclude. In the later opera, Buonaccorsi's role also includes the extended comic scene and duet with Righenzi (as Sifone) that was previously discussed (see this book's tenth chapter and Musical Example 10.1).

A comparison of Buonaccorsi's entrance arias is productive. In *Il potestà*, Act III, scene iii, Buonaccorsi sang "Più durar io non la posso" ("I can't take it any longer"); in *Ercole*, Act III, scene v, he sang "E a chi non scapperebbe la pazienza?" ("And who wouldn't lose their patience?"). The two titles express a similar sentiment, and they appear at similar points in the drama. Poetically, the text of each aria follows the same structure, with an opening line reiterated to close out the stanza, simultaneously rhyming with the penultimate line (closing *chiusette* were common in the improvised vernacular theater of the commedia dell'arte and in contemporary opera libretti). The

---

[6] For Melani's presence on Mattias's rolls, see Mamone, *Mattias de' Medici*, lett. 1103–1104. Alessandro and Jacinto Melani were also on Mattias's rolls during the late 1650s. See I-Fas, Mediceo del Principato, f. 5417, cc. 942–943. Bartolomeo Melani is listed as a singer in Giovan Carlo's household in I-Fas, Mediceo del Principato, f. 5358. For the reference to Jacopo as a singing teacher, see Mamone, *Serenissimi* fratelli, lett. 803.

[7] I have not seen the original score of *Il potestà*, only the Leve edition of 2005, but I thank Jennifer Williams Brown for information regarding the cleffing. The other Melani score has been published in facsimile. See Melani, *Ercole in Tebe*. Moro Monello sings from middle C to D (a ninth higher); Iolao sings from B♮ to the same D.

[8] Francesco Cavalli, *L'Hipermestra* (Biblioteca Nazionale Marciana, Venice; Codex Contarini 3621654), II, 18, c. 78r-79v. My enormous thanks to Judy Tsou for copying this music for me from the microfilm at the University of Washington at an early stage in my research. Alindo's part ranges from middle C to at least the F (possibly the G) above the staff; the top notes appear only in the first line of music; after that, the range stays below D (a ninth above middle C), with a possible E in the last phrase. Brown has noted that the Venice score is Cavalli's own preproduction original, composed several years before the actual performance and almost certainly modified at some point.

Figure P.1 Artemisia Gentileschi, *Esther before Ahasuerus*, ca. 1630. Oil on canvas, 208.3 × 272.7 cm. Metropolitan Museum of Art, Gift of Elinor Dorrance Ingersoll, 1969, 69.281.

Figure P.2. Paolo Caliari *detto* Veronese, *L'évanouissement d'Esther*, ca. 1570. Oil on canvas, 198 × 306 cm. Musée du Louvre, 05-514759, inv. 138. Photo © RMN-Gran Palais (musée du Louvre) / Gérard Blot / Art Resource, NY. Used with permission.

Figure P.3. Detail of Artemisia Gentileschi, *Esther before Ahasuerus*, ca. 1630. Oil on canvas, 208.3 × 272.7 cm. Metropolitan Museum of Art. Gift of Elinor Dorrance Ingersoll, 1969, 69.281.

Figure P.4. Domenico Fetti, *Bacco e Arianna a Nasso*, 1611–1613? Oil on canvas. Private collection. Formerly with the The Matthiesen Gallery, London. Used with permission.

Figure P.5. Interior of the Berenson Library, Villa I Tatti, Florence. Photo by author.

Figure I.2. Ignazio Fabroni, *Album di ricordi di viaggi e di navigazioni sulle galere toscne dall'anno 1664 all'anno 1687*. Fondo Rossi Cassigoli, Biblioteca Nazionale Centrale di Firenze, Ms. 199, imm. 129, detail. Used with permission of the Ministero della Cultura / Biblioteca Nazionale Centrale, Florence. Further reproduction or duplication is expressly prohibited.

Figure I.3. Ignazio Fabroni, *Album di ricordi di viaggi e di navigazioni sulle galere toscne dall'anno 1664 all'anno 1687*. Fondo Rossi Cassigoli, Biblioteca Nazionale Centrale di Firenze, Ms. 199, imm. 27, detail. Used with permission of the Ministero della Cultura / Biblioteca Nazionale Centrale, Florence. Further reproduction or duplication is expressly prohibited.

Intermezzo primo Figure 1. Bernardo Strozzi, *Female Musician with Viola da Gamba*, ca. 1630–1640. Widely assumed to be a portrait of Barbara Strozzi (no relation). Oil on canvas, 126 × 99 cm. Gemäldegalerie Alte Meister, Dresden. Gal.-Nr. 658. Bpk Bildagentur / Art Resource, NY. Used with permission.

Figure 8.1. Baldassarre Franceschini (1611–1690) *detto* Il Volterrano, *Ritratto di suonatore di liuto con cantore moro* (*Panbollito e Giovannino moro*), 1662. Oil on canvas, 95 × 144 cm. Private collection. Photo by DEA / G. NIMATALLAH / De Agostini via Getty Images.

Figure 8.2. Stefano della Bella, costume sketch for Hipermestra, from *L'Hipermestra* (perf. 1658). Black chalk, with watercolor and some pen and brown ink. London, British Museum, 1887,0502.34. Image © The Trustees of the British Museum. All rights reserved.

Figure 8.3. Stefano della Bella, costume sketch for Monello, from *Il podestà di Colognole* (perf. 1657 and 1661). Pen and brown ink, with brown wash, over black chalk. London, British Museum, 1887,0502.5. Image © The Trustees of the British Museum. All rights reserved.

Figure 9.1. Stefano della Bella, costume sketch for Furies, presumably from the ballet that accompanied *L'Hipermestra* (perf. 1658). Pen and brown ink, with watercolor, over graphite. London, British Museum, 1887,0502.59. Image © The Trustees of the British Museum. All rights reserved.

Figure 9.3. School of Giusto Sustermans (1597–1681), *Ritratto di Prencipe Mattias de' Medici*, ca. 1660. Oil on canvas, 128.3 × 104.2 cm. National Gallery of Art, Washington, DC. 1950.10.1. Gift of Ursula H. Baird and Sally H. Dieke in memory of their grandmother, Constance Cary Harrison. Reproduced under open access courtesy of the National Gallery of Art, Washington, DC. The young Black man depicted holding Mattias's helmet is likely the enslaved African Caralì, who was baptized in 1657 with the name "Mattia Medici."

Figure 10.3. Anton Domenico Gabbiani (1652–1726), *Ritratto di quattro servitori della corte medicea*, ca. 1684. Oil on canvas, 205 × 140 cm. Florence, Gallerie degli Uffizi, Galleria Palatina e Appartamenti Reali, depositi, inv. 1890 no. 3827. Used with permission of the Ministero della Cultura / Uffizi gallery, Florence. Further reproduction or duplication is expressly prohibited.

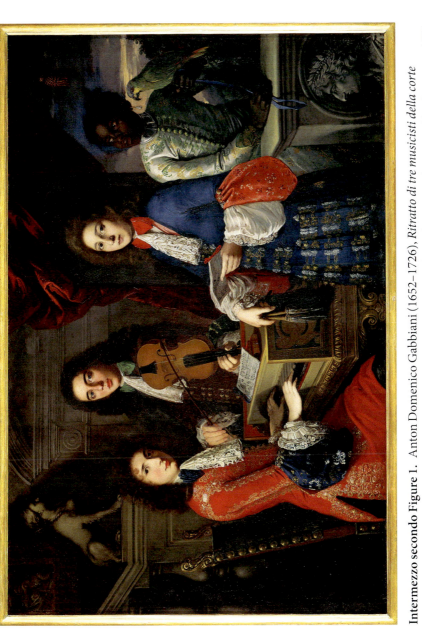

Intermezzo secondo Figure 1. Anton Domenico Gabbiani (1652–1726), *Ritratto di tre musicisti della corte medicea*, ca. 1687. Oil on canvas, 141 × 208 cm. Florence, Galleria dell'Accademia. Erich Lessing/Art Resource, NY. Used with permission.

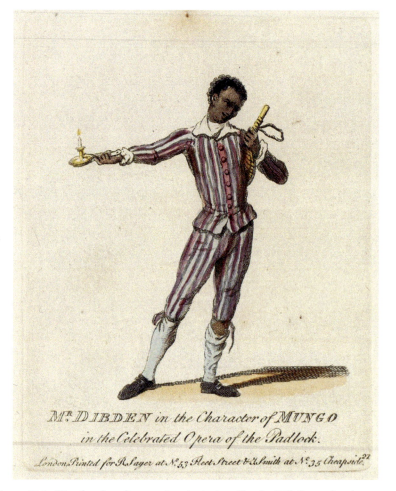

Figure E.1. Hand-colored engraving depicting Charles Dibdin as the character of Mungo in a production of *The Padlock*, ca. 1769. © Victoria & Albert Museum. S.443-1997. Used with permission.

internal verses rhyme in pairs, either alternately or *baciate*: abbccaa in the first instance, abcbcddaa in the second. If the first (and then, when repeated, last) lines summarize the affect of each outburst, the central lines detail the specific complaints of the character and their unlucky lot in life.

Gio: Andrea Moniglia, *Il potesta di Colognole* (perf. 1657), III, iii

MORO	Più durar io non la posso.	I can't take it any longer.
	Donde l'è	From where it is:
	Per ficcarsi intorno a me	To get close to me,
	La disgrazia veloce ogn'or galoppa,	Disgrace gallops quickly without stopping,
	Ma poi diventa zoppa	But then becomes lame
	Nel partirmisi da dosso.	When it comes to getting off my back.
	Più durar io non la posso.	I can't take it any longer.

Gio: Andrea Moniglia, *Ercole in Tebe* (perf. 1661), III, v

IOLAO	E a chi non scapperebbe la pazienza?	And who wouldn't lose their patience?
	La paura mi tormenta	Fear torments me
	E la fame m'assassina;	And hunger assassinates me.
	La caritade in questi luoghi è spenta,	In such places, charity is exhausted
	E non c'è modo à viver di rapina.	And there is nothing to steal.
	Per qual grave peccato	For what grave sin
	Sono, ohime, condennato	Have I, alas, been condemned
	A tanta rigorosa penitenza?	To such a harsh punishment?
	E a chi non scapperebbe la pazienza?	And who wouldn't lose their patience?

Musically, there are also similarities. Both pieces make use of a shared B♭ ("Più durar" is effectively in F, "E a chi" opens in d minor), and in both instances, the composer reuses the same music when setting repeated words. In "Più durar" (Musical Example 12.1), the setting indulges in some humorous (if unsubtle) word painting. Each full line of poetry engenders a new musical idea. A quarter-note walking pace is established in the opening line, stepping up in the bass all the way through an ascending octave, then up a step, down a fifth, until it hits the cadence. In the next full line, as Buonaccorsi sings of Disgrace galloping toward him, the pace of the bass line doubles, and then, when Disgrace limps away, Melani slows the bass back down while the vocal line initiates a sequence of suspensions that hop up and down, a step then a third, a step then a third, limping toward closure. In this short piece (the entire aria is over in only twenty-four measures), the closing ritornello draws on the vocal material used for the galloping Disgrace, displaced by one beat, and romping to a finish.

242   ACT II, SCENE XII

Musical Example 12.1. "Più durar io non la posso," as sung by Moro Monello (Giovannino Buonaccorsi). *Il potestà di Colognole* (perf. 1657), Act III, scene iii. Libretto by Gio: Andrea Moniglia, music by Jacopo Melani.

Musical Example 12.1. Continued

In "E a chi non scapperebbe la pazienza" (Musical Example 12.2), the setting (and the poetry) are slightly more complex—representing, I believe, the development of Buonaccorsi's skills and his growing participation in the ensemble. Again, the poetic form dictates the musical structure. The opening A section is highly redolent of the music for "Più durar." The bass line here moves quickly, emphasizing the tonic and dominant chords of the d minor key. This section is jaunty, giving a rollicking, humorous energy to Iolao's energetic complaints. The bass line cycles through a series of different stock formulae. From m. 9, for example, the bass moves up a step and down a third repeatedly until the end of the phrase; in the following phrase, from m. 14, the bass descends stepwise through an octave plus a fifth, and so on. Iolao reaches an energetic climax as he repeats the punchline ("E non c'è modo à viver di rapina") on an ascending sequence, followed by an orchestral ritornello; as in "Più durar," the ritornello is scored for two violins. When the affect and rhyme scheme change at "Per qual grave peccato," Melani seizes the opportunity for a contrasting B section in triple time. This would almost certainly have been sung more slowly, allowing Buonaccorsi to spoof the moment of introspection before returning to the opening complaint, repeating the first two lines of the A section to conclude.

Musical Example 12.2. "E a chi non scapperebbe la patienza?," as sung by Iolao (Giovannino Buonaccorsi). *Ercole in Tebe* (perf. 1661), Act III, scene v. Libretto by Gio: Andrea Moniglia, music by Jacopo Melani.

Musical Example 12.2. Continued

Musical Example 12.2. Continued

In each of these solo scenes, both of which represent the first arrival of the character in the drama, Buonaccorsi's immediate launch into song (into aria rather than recitative) marks him as a lower-status character; the rhythms and repeating melodic cells emphasize his expressive register. Interestingly, with "E a chi," the poetic form is *versi sciolti* throughout, so the scene could have been set as recitative; however, Moniglia has repeated the last line, and Melani has used more insistent repetitions—sometimes of whole lines, sometimes of single words—to break down the elevated poetic affect into something much simpler and more popular in style. When we look at the lyrics, the impression of simplicity and rustic naturalness is deepened. Iolao complains of bodily distress—terror and hunger—far removed from the political and romantic crises that trouble the serious characters. The punchline of the song confirms the character's lowbrow essence: there is not even anything here worth stealing.

Unfortunately, music does not survive for the 1663 Moniglia-Melani collaboration *Amore vuole ingengo*. The last opera in the series created by the duo for the Pergola, *Amore vuole ingengo* contains an expanded role for Buonaccorsi (a circumstance I discuss in the following chapter). Neither does music survive for Buonaccorsi's turn as the Black gypsy girl Moretta in *Il pazzo per forza* (1658), though presumably, his soprano voice contributed to his personification of a female character and to the substitution of "Muretta" for Moretta, played by the well-reputed castrato singer Antonio Rivani; it would have been particularly interesting to know whether the music written for Rivani as Muretta was—stylistically, melodically, or rhythmically—any different from his music as the comic servant Ligurino.

The potential expansion of Buonaccorsi's musicking is evident in his juxtaposition with and contiguity to the stuttering tenor character played by Righenzi (as Desso in *Il potestà* and Sifone in *Ercole*), whose work is explicitly and unquestionably comedic. Much of what I have written about the similarly stuttering hunchbacked character Desso in Giacinto Andrea Cicognini and Francesco Cavalli's *Giasone* is applicable to Righenzi's performances.[9] In *Il potestà*, Act I, scene xv, for example, Bruscolo (played by Simone Martelli) and Desso (Righenzi) engage in a *lazzo* of musicalized stuttering that, as with Desso and Oreste (in *Giasone*, II, ix), turn the rhythmicized syllables of attempted (yet stuttered) speech into music: "ta- ta-" in Moniglia-Melani's opera is mocked as trumpet music; "mi sol-" and later "la be-" in *Giasone* are mocked as popular song. The stuttering hunchbacked servant was a staple of the Italian theater; the humorous affect of the role relied on the specific materiality of the tenor voice and on the sonic-linguistic distortions of the stutter effect.[10] It is no coincidence that the character is regularly portrayed as "gobbo," a misshapen voice tightly conflated with the misshapen body.

In contrast, Buonaccorsi's soprano voice (like the explicitly Italianate orthography of his dialogue) has a fungibility with other soprano voices that, while aggressively aligned with comic or witty material in his stage roles, implies a possible expansion into other vocal sounds. We do not know, for example, what music Buonaccorsi is about to sing in Volterrano's double portrait (Figure 8.1), though his calm demeanor and relaxed body language, combined with the musical signifiers of lute and loose paper, suggest an elevated musical register such as the chamber cantata. There is little indication

---

[9] Wilbourne, "Demo's Stutter."
[10] *Il Giasone* was written for Venice and first performed in 1649; we do not know the names of the original cast.

in the Volterrano of the propulsive energy of "Più durar" or the physical gestures suggested by the walking, galloping, limping effects of the text and music. In contrast, the body in motion indicated in Stefano della Bella's costume sketch for the "Più durar" role (Figure 8.3) gives a better sense of how Buonaccorsi would have embodied the Moro Monello character.

Within the context of mid-seventeenth-century Italy, Buonaccorsi's adult soprano voice suggests his identification as a singer at a very young age. That is, for someone (the Medici, the Buonaccorsi family, a singing teacher—possibly Melani—or even Buonaccorsi himself) to have considered castration, the prepubescent Buonaccorsi must have shown substantial promise as a singer. He thus must have received musical instruction prior to that point. Buonaccorsi-as-castrato makes Western music itself integral to his being in the world. For any (male) singer, a castrato voice opened a larger range of dramatic roles and an expanded access to elevated musical repertoires, including chamber cantatas and sacred music. Castration was an investment—on the part of whoever organized and paid for the operation—in a melophilic future. To transpose Esther Terry's assertion about dance into the register of song: "We must not only be able to image sub-Saharan Africans as present within Early Modern Europe, but also as active contributors to Early Modern [music] within and outside of their homelands."[11]

Thus, Buonaccorsi's Black body helps to throw certain assumptions about music-oriented castration into clear focus. For much music scholarship of the twentieth century, castration was figured as proof of the barbarity of the past and indicative of the artificial, effeminate, overgrown baroque of the pre-Enlightenment Italian style. In the rare instances when seventeenth- or early-eighteenth-century vocal repertoire was performed, castrato parts were regularly transposed downward such that solidly masculine tenor voices could provide satisfyingly heteronormative and timbrally reassuring renditions. Things began to change, however, in the 1990s with the parallel emergence of the "new musicology" and "historically informed" ("authentic") performance practice. (Male) countertenors and (female) mezzo-sopranos began to sing castrato roles in far greater numbers, and musicologists, newly emboldened to talk about the relationships between music, gender, and sexuality, found the castrato—with his explicitly genital relationship to musical

---

[11] Esther J. Terry, "Choreographies of Trans-Atlantic Primitivity: Sub-Saharan Isolation in Black Dance Historiography," in *Early Modern Black Diaspora Studies: A Critical Anthology*, ed. Cassander L. Smith, Nicholas R. Jones, and Miles P. Grier (Cham, Switzerland: Palgrave Macmillan, 2018), 73.

sound—a privileged figure through which to elaborate theories of sound and sexuality.[12] Much of this early work, exemplified by scholars such as Joke Dame and Michel Poizat, saw castration through a post-Freudian or psychoanalytic account of castration anxiety, reading the soprano voices of castrati as a direct displacement of a lost phallus into vocal sound.[13]

A further disciplinary shift happened with what we might call the "third wave" of castrato scholarship, catalyzed by the work of scholars such as Roger Freitas and Giuseppe Gerbino, who were interested in understanding the castrato in historical context. Both authors normalized the castrato within early modern Italian society. Freitas argued for the ways in which castration preserved a boyish adolescence in line with early modern aesthetic priorities, clarifying—in crucial ways—how castrati could be understood as desirable and how their high-pitched voices could represent lovers, heroes, and warriors on the operatic stage.[14] Gerbino painted a picture of the vast numbers of sixteenth- and early-seventeenth-century castrati.[15] Martha Feldman's excellent work on the castrato, particularly as he was received into the eighteenth century, and Bonnie Gordon's forthcoming work on the seventeenth century are indicative of recent scholarship.[16] Recent work by Hedy Law and Katherine Crawford and my own castrato article puts the historical figure of the castrato into dialogue with trans* scholarship and disability theory.[17]

If the normalization of castration within early modernity has helped neutralize the violence of the practice for modern scholars, Buonaccorsi's body brings the brutality, the "cruel and unusual" tenor of castration crashing back into play. Buonaccorsi breaks open the category of the castrato, revealing the

[12] For a more detailed analysis of this historical trajectory, see Emily Wilbourne, "The Queer History of the Castrato," in *The Oxford Handbook of Music and Queerness*, ed. Fred Everett Maus and Sheila Whiteley (Oxford Handbooks Online, 2018), https://doi.org/10.1093/oxfordhb/9780199793 525.013.14.

[13] Some early modern listeners made a similar interpretive leap. Giovanni Angelini Bontempi, for example, in his *Historia Musica* of 1695 (rept. 1976), saw the voice of castrato singer Baldassare Ferri in terms of an "exchange of potencies . . . the procreative power of semen replaced by the magical power of song"; the quote comes from Martha Feldman, "Castrato Acts," in *The Oxford Handbook of Opera*, ed. Helen Greenwald (Oxford: Oxford University Press, 2014), 403.

[14] Freitas, *Portrait*. See also Freitas, "Eroticism."

[15] Giuseppe Gerbino, "The Quest for the Soprano Voice: Castrati in Sixteenth-Century Italy," *Studi Musicali* 32, no. 2 (2004): 303–357.

[16] Feldman, "Castrato Acts"; Martha Feldman, *The Castrato: Reflections on Natures and Kinds* (Berkeley: University of California Press, 2015); Bonnie Gordon, "The Castrato Meets the Cyborg," *Opera Quarterly* 27 (2011): 94–122.

[17] Hedy Law, "A Cannon-Shaped Man with an Amphibian Voice: Castrato and Disability in Eighteenth-Century France," in *The Oxford Handbook of Music and Disability Studies*, ed. Blake Howe et al. (Oxford Handbooks Online, 2018), https://doi.org/10.1093/oxfordhb/9780199331444.013.11; Crawford, *Eunuchs and Castrati*; Wilbourne, "Queer History."

exnominative power of whiteness in castrato scholarship, as his Blackness and enslavement aggravate the question of agency and consent.[18] "Certainly," as Hartman writes, "the notion of the autonomous self endowed with free will is inadequate and, more important, inappropriate to thinking through the issue of slave agency."[19] If scholars of North American chattel slavery have made good use of sovereignty to emphasize the power of white citizens over the Black slave, then Buonaccorsi's position at the court of a literal sovereign (the Medici Grand Duke) creates differently distributed lines of political power. His juxtaposition with (white) castrati, including Rivani and Bartolomeo Melani (the fourth of seven brothers to be castrated), confronts us with "the difficulty of installing an absolute distinction between slavery and freedom."[20] At the same time, Buonaccorsi's demonstrable affinity with the "Turchi, e Nani, / mal'Cristiani" of the court indicates his categorical distance from Rivani, Melani, and other (white), non-enslaved singers. We do well to recall the list of singers, academicians, and costumes (transcribed here earlier as Table 8.4), where "Signore" has been crossed out from in front of Buonaccorsi's name, and an outraged secretary has scrawled "Non ci va Signore" in the margin.

The smug presentism that limns much writing on the castrato (diagnosed by Gordon as a "squeamishness about castrati" coupled to a "privileged sense of civil rights") masks the extent to which the "abolition" of castration has merely transposed (not eradicated) the intersection of entertainment, virtuosity, and bodily violence in contemporary modern society.[21] A pertinent example is the young female gymnast, whose rigorous pursuit of excellence can interrupt and deform the "natural" sexual development of the body; another is the mostly Black boys whose bodies and brains are damaged in the production of professional North American football. The prurient interest of modern commentators in the sexual functioning of the castrato's altered genitalia (even while—as I have argued elsewhere—"only the conflation of penile penetrative sex with sexual activity more generally allows the metonym

---

[18] The term "exnomination" was coined by Barthes to refer to the bourgeoisie; it is particularly useful when transposed to include whiteness and racial marking. Robin DiAngelo, "White Fragility," *International Journal of Critical Pedagogy* 3, no. 3 (2011): 54–70.

[19] Hartman, *Scenes of Subjection*, 53. In a similar vein, Alexander Weheliye writes that "resistance and agency assume full, self-present, and coherent subjects working against something or someone." See Alexander G. Weheliye, *Habeas Viscus: Racializing Assemblages, Biopolitics, and Black Feminist Theories of the Human* (Durham, NC: Duke University Press, 2014), 2.

[20] Hartman, *Scenes of Subjection*, 139.

[21] Gordon, "Castrato Meets," 111.

to hold")[22] sounds a disturbing resonance with the "white witness of the spectacle of [Black] suffering."[23]

By the 1660s, the castrato voice was the natural choice for musico-dramatic representation of sovereignty, and yet the castrato voice itself (as a measure of physical objectification and readiness to serve as entertainment) was achieved through a *loss* of agency—directly contradicting deep-seated assumptions about the voice, its production within the body, and its testimonial force as resonant breathy messenger from within the flesh.[24] When Frederick Douglass wrote, for example, "I have sometimes thought that the mere hearing of these songs would do more to impress some minds with the horrible character of slavery, than the reading of whole volumes of philosophy on the subject could do,"[25] he articulated a dense nexus of voice, bodily history, and opaque communicative power that resonates centuries before he wrote and still today. As Alexander Weheliye puts it, "[h]ere, the black singing voice signals both a radical alterity by pointing to the aspects of slavery that cannot be represented visually and stands as a marker for knowability, since it assumes that the black voice can encode the horrors of slavery aurally."[26] In this context, Buonaccorsi can provide a useful case study for critical race theory, too, for when we turn to his surviving music, it lacks the expressivity or the aural excess that the analyst might read as a vibrational stand-in for subjectivity or acts of resistance (often glossed as evidence for personal agency).[27] In "Più durar io non la posso" and "E a chi non scapperebbe la pazienza," Buonaccorsi represents his character's frustrations (at hunger, mistreatment, and disgrace) in a comic register that invites his audience to laugh at him. His expressed desires (for food and for something worth stealing) solidify his status both as servile and as requiring supervision. Buonaccorsi is an important ancestor in the lineage of what Matthew D. Morrison calls "Blacksound,"[28] naturalizing a physical association between Black bodies and natural-yet-servile musicality.[29] At the same time, Buonaccorsi's success

---

[22] Wilbourne, "Queer History," n28.
[23] Hartman, *Scenes of Subjection*, 19.
[24] Jessica Gabriel Peritz's forthcoming book, *The Lyric Myth of Voice: Civilizing Song in Enlightenment Italy*, promises to address this issue in more depth.
[25] Frederick Douglass, *Narrative of the Life of Frederick Douglass, an American Slave* (New York: Penguin Books, 1986), 50–51.
[26] Weheliye, *Habeas Viscus*, 102.
[27] For an example, see Hartman, *Scenes of Subjection*, 8.
[28] Morrison, "Sound(s) of Subjection"; Morrison, "Race."
[29] My argument here resonates with Robert Hornback's claims about the enduring power of blackface representation on the early modern English stage, though he is talking about white performers in blackface rather than about a Black singer. See Hornback, *Racism*.

as a castrato is predicated on his thorough internalization of Italian musical sounds and his entry into Western musical pedagogy early enough for the castration to have taken place. The soprano voice of Buonaccorsi is something that modern scholarship needs to take seriously: his (Black) body labored in the production of this music, and the ease with which his body was absorbed into the material production of operatic music and the facility with which his enslaved Black body slipped down unmarked into the footnotes of music history is a methodological warning. Historiographically, we need to find a language that can account for Buonaccorsi's centrality and thus for the central importance of racial difference to the monument of European opera.

Alli schiavi che tengono ripulita la Fortezza uno scudo 1.-.-.-.

To the slaves who keep the Fortezza clean, one scudo, 1.-.-.-.
                        I-Fas, Camera del Granduca, f. 37, April 1667, c. 38v

Scene 13
Buonaccorsi Sings on the Venetian Stage

On October 14, 1662, the opera impresario Vettor Grimani Calergi wrote to Prince Mattias de' Medici, requesting the Moor who belonged to Cardinal Prince Giovan Carlo as a singer for an upcoming season in Venice:

> About the Moor, I supplicate the good grace of Your Highness to help me have him, since as much as I esteem his talent, even more I am banking on the novelty [*curiosità*] of his character; given that here in Venice it will be new, and never before seen, that which perhaps is considered ordinary there [in Florence]; and if the good grace of the Prince Cardinal were to favor me in this, I would send him a similar voice, or perhaps a better one.[1]

Above and beyond the Moor's talents as a singer, Grimani professed interest in his novelty: perhaps merely "ordinary" in Florence, "il Moro" would be "new, and never before seen" on the Venetian stage. Indeed, Grimani promised to send a singer of equal or better talent to replace the Moor, emphasizing that the draw was something other than or supplementary to Buonaccorsi's vocal skill. While this letter seems not to have borne immediate fruit, just over a year later, Grimani mentioned the Moor again, insisting that he "set out" for Venice.[2] That Buonaccorsi did eventually arrive and perform in the 1664 Venetian season is documented in a third letter addressed to Prince Mattias, this last written by the famous castrato

---

[1] "Del Moro, io supplico la benignità di Vostra Altezza farmelo avere, poiché sì come stimo la sua virtù altretanto fo capitale della curiosità del personaggio; già che qui a Venezia sarà nuovo, e non più veduto; che costì forse sarà stimato ordinario; e quando la benignità del Principe Cardinale mi volesse far grazia, io le manderei voce simile, e forse migliore." Vettor Grimani Calergi to Prince Mattias de' Medici, October 14, 1662, I-Fas, Mediceo del Principato, f. 5487, Registro di riscontri di pagamenti; lettere di segretari e auditori (1632–1663), cc. 666rv. Transcribed in Sara Mamone, ed. *Mattias de' Medici*, lett. 1590, 796.

[2] "Già è tempo, ch'il Moro s'incammini a questa volta, che perciò potrà Vostra Altezza restar servita ordinarle, che se ne venga." Grimani to Mattias, November 9, 1663, I-Fas, Mediceo del Principato, f. 5477, Diversi, con minute di risposta (1662–1663), c. 175r. Transcribed in Mamone, *Mattias de' Medici*, lett. 1625, 814.

singer-turned-diplomat Atto Melani, who was in Venice and reporting back to the Medici on the local reception of their singers.[3]

Grimani's enthusiasm and his assessment of Buonaccorsi's novelty demand further attention. Importantly, Buonaccorsi's "new, and never before seen" appeal cannot merely have been that he played a Black servant or a slave character: the *personaggi* of any number of Venetian operas include Black characters who are enslaved or in service (two pertinent examples are discussed below). More probably, though much harder to document, Grimani's interest may have been piqued by the authenticity of Buonaccorsi's racial presentation. Grimani's desire for Buonaccorsi in particular (to the point where he was willing to send a better singer to take his place) and his emphasis on Buonaccorsi's ordinariness in Florence (perhaps a reference to other Black Florentine singers, such as Caralì) underscore the peculiar situation of Black entertainers within the court system—simultaneously exceptional and quotidian—as well as the centrality of Buonaccorsi's performances at La Pergola and within the cardinal's court in Florence (that a replacement is required demonstrates Buonaccorsi's importance).

In this chapter, I consider the surviving evidence of Buonaccorsi's performances in the period directly preceding and following Cardinal Giovan Carlo's death, on January 23, 1663. The cumulative weight of Grimani's initial letter and the Volteranno double portrait—both dated to late 1662—suggest that the young singer was achieving some notoriety as he matured. This supposition is supported by Buonaccorsi's increased presence in the Immobili archives (where his full name is used for the first time that same year in documents related to the production of *Amore vuole ingegno*) and by his seemingly expanded dramatic role in the later operas. The Moro Birbone character in *Amore vuole ingegno* is highly consistent with Buonaccorsi's earlier roles (particularly the Moro Monello from *Il potestà di Colognole*); however, in the earlier works, Buonaccorsi appeared exclusively in scenes that were extraneous to the various plot arcs, serving as comic interpellation. In *Amore vuole ingegno*, the Moro provides such comic moments but is also integrated into essential plot developments. His importance is such that he is named as present in the final ensemble scene for the first time, and his overall number of lines increases substantially (see Table 13.1,

---

[3] Atto Melani to Mattias de' Medici, February 16, 1664, I-Fas, Mediceo del Principato, f. 5478, Diversi, con minute di risposta (1662–1664), cc. 427r–428r. Transcribed in Mamone, *Mattias de' Medici*, lett. 1636, 818–819.

Table 13.1. Scenes and lines sung by Buonaccorsi in the La Pergola operas.

Year	Title	Black character or role	No. of scenes	No. of lines
writ. 1654, perf. 1658	*L'Hipermestra*	Alindo	1	20
1657, rev. 1661	*Il potestà di Colognole*	Moro Monello	4	46
1658	*Il pazzo per forza*	Moretta, Zingara	3	46
1661	*Ercole in Tebe*	Iolao, moro servitore di Teseo	2	56
1663*	*Amore vuole ingegno*	Moro	12	153

* Note that the scheduled performances of this opera were cancelled after the death of Cardinal Giovan Carlo. The libretto which survives was published much later, under the alternate title *La vedova*, and may reflect changes that were made to the original text. {Moniglia, 1698 #534@299-403}

which tabulates Buonaccorsi's lines in the Florentine operas, organized chronologically).

Unfortunately, neither score nor contemporary libretto survives for *Amore vuole ingengo*, though the text was published in 1698 as part of Gio: Andrea Moniglia's collected works under the alternative title *La vedova*. According to prefatory material by Moniglia, by the late stage at which the opera season of 1663 was canceled after Giovan Carlo's unexpected death, the work "had already been set to music by the famous Sig. Jacopo Melani, and the parts had already been distributed to the performers."[4] Some years later, in 1680, a performance reputedly took place in gardens near the Porto di Prato owned by Marchese Bartolommeo Corsini. Corsini had been an active member of the Immobili and was involved in the original plans for the 1663 production; he is listed, for example, in the document transcribed here earlier as Table 8.4, where he was assigned joint responsibility for Paolo Rivani's costume. By 1680, several of the original participants had passed away—not least the composer (who died in 1676) and Buonaccorsi (who died in 1674). No information is known about the eventual performers beyond Moniglia's generic (if enthusiastic) claim that they were "a selection of musical performers as rare and perfect as any others, such that never was such heard in the most renowned of theaters."[5] Nor does Moniglia indicate that the text or music was altered in any fashion,

---

[4] "[G]ià era stato messo in musica del famoso Sig. Jacopo Melani, e n'erano di già state distribuite le parti a i recitanti." Moniglia, "La vedova," 301.

[5] "[U]na scelta di musici rappresentanti così rara, e perfetta, che non invidiò alcuna altra, che mai si fusse udita sopra i più rinominati Teatri." Moniglia, "La vedova," 302.

though presumably some changes were made to suit the new location and new singers.[6] Tangentially, we can note that the Corsini family can be associated with at least three enslaved retainers. Prince Giovan Carlo de' Medici tipped the "Morino" of "Sig*nore* Marchese [Bartolommeo] Corsini" at least twice, in 1650 and 1651,[7] while the Pia Casa documents from 1663 record the presence of an eleven-year-old girl, Raima di Asmat Lubini, in the house of "Sig*nore* Andrea Corsini," and in 1671, another young girl, Lattifa Turca, approximately thirteen years of age, was resident in the house of Signora Lucrezia Corsini.[8]

Despite the distance that separates the libretto's eventual publication from the original intended premiere, the role of the Moro Birbone provides an intriguing backdrop to the question of Buonaccorsi's "novelty." A comparison of the roles as listed in 1663 (see the *Immobili* document transcribed here earlier as Table 8.4) with those in the libretto (see Figure 13.1) suggests substantial continuity. In both, a quartet of foreign *birboni* is led by the Moro. In one scene (as discussed in this book's ninth chapter), the Moro's Black skin shocks the stuttering servant Desso (written for Carlo Righenzi), who flees screaming about having seen a devil. As in Iolao's duet with Sifone (*Ercole in Tebe*) or "Il sogno di Giovannino Moro," the Moro Birbone stage manages the humorous presentation of other characters, most obviously during Act II, scene ix, where he and the other vagabond *birboni* make their appearance and shake down the wealthy Marchionne for food, wine, and money. Notably, each of the other three *birboni* speaks in a distinctly marked "foreign voice," while the Moro not only speaks proper Italian but also serves as translator or middleman, emphasizing the vocal continuity of this role with Buonaccorsi's character (in contrast with the *gergo* used for Caralì and the gypsy):

	Marchionne, Moro, Tedesco, Franzese, Spagnuolo	Marchionne, Moor, German, Frenchman, Spaniard
MORO	Fate la carità.	Alms for the poor.
MARCH.	Andate al fatto vostro Via mostaccio d'onchiostro[9]	Mind your own business, Get your inky snout out of here.

---

[6] Some scant evidence in the 1698 print implies that the division of scenes may have been reorganized: the glossary of dialect terms and local expressions that Moniglia provides at the end of the libretto groups words and phrases from Act II, scenes ix and x together under the heading "scene ix." See Moniglia, "La vedova," 392.

[7] I-Fas, Depositeria generale, parte antica, f. 1604, c. 112r, August 1650: "Al Morino del Sig*nore* Marchese Corsini 1.-.-.-"; c. 120r: "Al Morino del Sig*nore* Marchese Corsini che porse i Torli a donare 1.-.-.-."

[8] I-Fca, Pia Casa dei Catecumeni, f. 2, c.n.n. [ins. 32 and 65].

[9] Moniglia provides an appendix to the drama which translates typical Tuscan phrases for other audiences. He glosses *Mostaccio d'onchiostro* as "Viso d'inchiostro, viso nero," lit. "Face of ink, black face."

258 ACT II, SCENE XIII

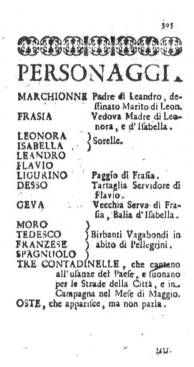

Figure 13.1. Published cast list from *Amore vuole ingegno*, which appears in Giovanni Andrea Moniglia, "La vedova," *Delle poesie dramatiche di Giovann'Andrea Moniglia, Accademico della Crusca, Parte terza* (Florence: Vincenzio Vangelisti, 1698), 303.

MORO	Se brunetto Il viso avrò, Dentro al petto Bianca fede asconderò.	My face May be dark, [But] inside my chest I hide a white faith.
MARCH.	Forse sì, e forse no.	Perhaps, perhaps not.
MORO	Sete tanto crudeli?	Are you so cruel?
MARCH.	Tu abba alla Luna.[10]	You're barking at the moon.
MORO	Sono un'Uomo da ben senza fortuna.	I am a good man, out of luck.
FRAN.	De chel male che le sor me pursuive Ne du tè pà de mà fidelitè Me si giapran ch'un'otre vu cattive Votre prison serà ma libertè.[11]	No matter what ills fortune attacks me with, Do not doubt my faithfulness. But if I learn that someone else has captured you, Your prison will be my liberty.

[10] Glossed by the playwright as "Tu chiedi in vano," lit. "You ask in vain."
[11] In correct French: "De quel mal que le sort me poursuive, / Ne doutez pas de ma fidelité; / Mais si j'apprens qu'un autre vois captive, / Votre prison sera ma liberté." My thanks to Anne Stone and Emery Snyder for their help.

MARCH.	Ch'arziguogolo[12] è questo?	What fool is this?
MORO	Un mio compagno.	One of my companions.
FRAN.	Monsieur s'il vù plèF et muà la sciaritè.	Monsieur, please, Give me some charity.
MARCH.	Dond'è egli?	Where is he from?
MORO	Franzese.	[He is] French.
MARCH.	Se gli arriva in Firenze, Lo fan maestro delle liverenze.[13]	If he were to go to Florence, They would make him the courtesy master.
SPA.	Vaia el mal per donde và, Y el bien per donde quisiere, Que io yrè per donde fuere, Que el buon tiempo bien me dà.[14]	Evil goes where it wishes, And Goodness wherever it may wish to go, I will go wherever I wish, And may good fortune bring me good things.
MARCH.	O vè quanta brigata![15] Moro, chi è egli?	O, look how many there are in this crew! Moro, who is this one?
MORO	Un nostro camerata.	One of our society.
SPA.	Che'l Zielo fea alabado, La caridad a este noble soldado.[16]	May the Heavens be praised, Charity for this noble soldier.
MARCH.	Donde viene?	Where is he from?
MORO	Di Spagna, a quel ch'ei dice	From Spain, from what he says.
MARCH.	Questo s'aggiusta con una radice.	That can be straightened out with a root.
TED.	Bin ich sin armer Cavallier Das becchennì selfsten Hier Dù aller scenste dammen Hab ich kein Ghelt, und auch kein guet So bin, ich doch von Thijstchen bluet Von itterliche stammen.[17]	I am but a poor soldier, I myself confess that here, [To the] most beautiful of ladies; Though I have no money, and also no estate, Even so I am of German blood, From a noble lineage.

[12] Florio provides a truly wonderful definition for *Arzigogolo*: "a lifter, a heaver, a leaver, a sherer, an underprop. Also a foolish silly gull." *Arzigogolare* is "to rave or be franticke"; Moniglia, for his part, provides the gloss "Invenzione sottile, e fantastica," or a "subtle and fantastical invention."

[13] Moniglia glosses *liverenze* as "Riverenze." The latter term is defined in the 1612 Crusca: "Reverenza diciamo a qualunque segno d'onore, che si fa altrui, inchinando 'l capo, o piegando le ginocchia, o movendo qualche altra parte del corpo."

[14] In correct Spanish, this passage would read, "Vaya el mal por donde vaya, / Y el bien por donde quisiere, / Que yo iré por donde fuere, / Que el buen tiempo bien me da." My thanks to Ana Beatriz Mujica Lafuente.

[15] Moniglia: "O vedi quanta gente adunata insieme."

[16] Corrected (with thanks to Ana Beatriz Mujica Lafuente), this passage would read: "Que el cielo sea alabado, / La caridad a este noble soldado."

[17] In corrected German, this passage would read, "Bin ich ein armer Cavallier, / Das bekenne ich selfsten hier, / Du aller schönste Damen; / Hab ich kein Geld, und auch kein Gut / So bin ich doch von deutschen Blut / Von [r]itterliche[r] Stammen." My thanks to Janette Tilley and Emery Snyder.

MARCH.	Moro, che mi minchioni? Guarda quanta genìa![18]	Moro, why are you tricking me? Look what a monstrous variety [of people]!
	Oggi quest'Osteria Doventa l'arsenal de' ribaldoni.[19]	Today this inn Has become an arsenal of knaves!
TED.	A vune Tarsce poserine Mocch le limossine.	Give alms to a poor German.
MARCH.	Ecco un'altro arfafatto.[20]	Here's another lowlife!
MORO	È Tedesco bizzarro, e bell'umore.	He's German, crazy but cheerful.
MARCH.	Lo conosco all'odore, Puzza di baccalà.	I recognize him from the smell, He stinks of salted cod.
MORO	Fate la carità.	Alms for the poor!
SPA.	Caridad.	Charity!
TED.	Limossine.	Charity!
MARCH.	Uimè, uimè!	Help, help!
FRAN.	Fet muà la sciaritè.	Give me your charity.
MARCH.	E che vorreste voi?	And what do you want?
SPA.	Un pochitto de pan.	Just a little bread.
MORO, SPA., TED., FRAN.	*a 4* Pan, pan, pan, pan.	*a 4* Bread, bread, bread, bread.
MARCH.	Che invenzionaccia è questa? Mi stordiscon la testa. Dagli del pane.	What terrible composition is this? You're making me dizzy. Give them some bread.
SPA.	Un pochitto de vin.	Just a little wine.
MORO, SPA., TED., FRAN.	*a 4* Vin, vin, vin, vin.	*a 4* Wine, wine, wine, wine.
MARCH.	Diavol'empigli; Reca Del vin, Corpo di bacco Gli spalancano il sacco, Guarda che fiasche! Tengono un barile; No, no, mutiamo stile; Olà meder Dagli un tozzo di pane, e un po da bere.	May the Devil take them! Fetch Some wine, dammit, They are opening their sack, Look at those flasks! They have a barrel. No, no, let's change plans. Here! Give them a heel of bread and a little to drink.
MORO, SPA., TED., FRAN.	*a 4* Pan, vin, pan, vin, pan, vin.	*a 4* Bread, wine, bread, wine, bread, wine.

---

[18] Moniglia: "*Genìa*, Generazione vile, ed abietta."
[19] Florio's definition of *Ribaldaglia* is wonderful: "the basest or vilest kind of people, the common rascalitie." Moniglia glosses this phrase: "*L'Arsenal de' ribaldoni*. L'Arsenale degl'isciagurati, degli scellerati."
[20] Moniglia: "*Arfafatto*. Uomo vile, e di poco pregio."

MARCH.	O discrizione!	Oh, too much!
	Abbassate il bordone.	Lower your sticks! Be quiet!
	Dagli quanto domandano; Vo a risco	Give them what they want; I run the risk
	Di riuscirne con cattiva cera,²¹	Of getting out of this the worse for wear,
	Ed in questa maniera,	And in this way,
	S' i' fo un'altra limosina, fallisco.	If they ask for another donation, I will go bankrupt.
	Volet'altro?	Do you want anything else?
SPA.	Dinero.	Money!
TED.	Ghelt.	Money!
FRAN.	Arsgian.²²	Money!
MARCH.	Abbassate il bordone.	Lower your sticks! Be quiet!
SPA.	Dinero.	Money!
TED.	Ghelt.	Money!
FRAN.	Arsgian.	Money!
MARCH.	Ecco la borsa!	Here is my purse!
MORO, SPA., TED., FRAN.	*a 4* Pan, vin, pan, vin, pan, vin.	*a 4* Bread, wine, bread, wine, bread, wine.
SPA.	Dinero.	Money!
TED.	Ghelt.	Gold!
FRAN.	Arsgian.	Silver!
MORO, SPA., TED., FRAN.	*a 4* Pan, vin, pan, vin, pan, vin.	*a 4* Bread, wine, bread, wine, bread, wine.
MARCH.	Pur se ne sono andati; Che gente al Mondo sta!	Now they have gone! What people there are in this world!
MORO	Fate la carità.	Alms for the poor!
MARCH.	Vattene via di qua.²³	Get out of here!

Through Marchionne's various exclamations, this scene frames the four *birboni* as evidence of the monstrous variety of foreign peoples. Each of the three European "Others" apostrophizes on generic expositional material, with little—if any—connection to the drama. The German, for example, speaks as if wooing a beautiful woman, though no woman is present; Marchionne's response implies that the outburst was directed at him. The versification is not consistent across these three passages, suggesting that

---

[21] Moniglia: "*Riuscirne con cattiva cera*. Riuscirne male, escirne con poco onore."

[22] *Arsgian* is a Milanese dialect word for silver but here presumably represents the French word *Argent*.

[23] Moniglia, "La vedova," II, ix.

different music (possibly preexisting songs or music spoofing national styles) would have characterized the performance of each role. Given the vocal and sonic play of the other three *birboni* roles, it would have been very simple to write the Moro's part in *gergo*. Without a differentiated vocality, Buonaccorsi's flesh stands in as a marker of authentic diversity, even as his eloquence and Italian fluency telegraph his particular skills.

At one point, the text makes a clever musical pun, playing on the double meaning of "bastone," used to simultaneously signify both the pilgrim staffs carried by the *birboni* (here raised threateningly toward Marchionne) and a repetitive musical ground (evidently describing the four-part harmony of the "bread, wine, bread, wine" chorus, also described with the term "invenzionaccia," lit. "horrible composition").[24]

In a later scene, the Moro Birbone decides (for little apparent reason) to hide inside a barrel. This sets up his surprising (and, to Desso, terrifying) reappearance and allows him to eavesdrop on the complicated love lives of the *innamorati* and their elderly relatives (who also aspire to romance). Thus informed, the Moro collaborates with the wily servant, Ligurino—the character is familiar from his romp as "Muretta" in *Il pazzo per forza*, though in 1663, Ligurino was intended for performance by the younger Vincenzino Olivicciani rather than by Antonio Rivani, who had matured into the lover's part of Leandro.[25] Together, the Moro and Ligurino concoct an unlikely *lazzo* involving Desso, disguised (against his better judgment) as a dragon tamer, and a large, fire-belching lizard, who first devours and later regurgitates the four young *innamorati*—once Marchionne has coughed up a gold ransom large enough to justify their re-emergence. As the trick unfolds, Ligurino laments, convincing Marchionne that his son (Leandro) and his purported fiancée (Leonora) have been eaten, while the Moro swoops in with the promised solution. Here the text makes one of many allusions to the character's dark skin, as the Moro gives his (untruthful) word: "Affe da Uomo nero" (lit. "I give my word as a Black man"). (The racism of this quip—intended for performance by a man of Black African descent—is palpable.) Desso, who is humiliated and coerced into his role as dragon tamer, sings an aria in which he attributes the blame for his own actions to hunger rather than bad

---

[24] Moniglia glosses *Bordone* as "Bastone, che usano i Pellegrini in viaggio per appoggiarsi." Florio, in contrast, includeds several meanings in his definition: "*Bordone*. a prop or underlaier of timber. Also the burdon of a song, or a tenor and keeping of time in musicke. Also the second base string of any instrument. Also a humming noise or sound. Also a shepheards hooke, but chiefly a pilgrims or palmers staffe."

[25] Decroisette, "I virtuosi," 85.

choices. In the recitative, he inveighs against the Moro Birbone, calling him a "monello" ("rascal," using the name for Buonaccorsi's same character in the earlier opera *Il potestà di Colognole*) and attributing the Moro's participation to greed and deceit:

DESSO	Que, que, questo Morino	Thi-, thi-, this little Moor
	È un mo, monello fino;	Is a fine ra-, rascal;
	Con promesse, e guadagno	With promises, and money
	Vuo, vuo, vuol ch'io l'aiuti	He wa-, wa-, wants me to help him
	Trappolare il compagno;	Trick my companion;
	Io, che son Uom da bene,	Me! who am a good man,
	So che no si conviene;	I know that this is not OK;
	Ma se divento infame,	But if I become villainous,
	La colpa non è mia, ma della fame.[26]	The fault is not mine, but that of hunger.

The sight and sound of the stuttering hunchback and the Black African tricking and teasing each other for the amusement of courtly spectators cannot but have recalled quotidian scenes of buffoonery among the "cortigiani di basso servizio," exemplified by "Il sogno di Giovannino Moro" and echoed in the "monstrous variety" of foreign beings that the four *birboni* stage. The familiarity of these characters and their interactions can be seen to illustrate Buonaccorsi's ordinariness in Florence, not only in operatic performances but in a wide range of comedic contexts.

* * *

The scant surviving evidence for Buonaccorsi's Venetian performances suggests that (as Grimani predicted) the ordinariness and familiarity that existed in Florence between performer and audience were lost, though perhaps without the crowd-pleasing novelty on which Grimani was banking.

Black characters, and even Black servants or enslaved characters, were familiar denizens of the Venetian stage, though no evidence has yet emerged that other Black African performers had sung in Venetian opera prior to Buonaccorsi's debut. An emblematic Black character is Vaffrino, from Giovan Francesco Busenello and Francesco Cavalli's *La Statira principessa di Persia*, which was staged at the Grimani theater of Santi Giovanni e Paolo in 1656 under Giovanni Grimani (cousin to Vettor Grimani Calergi). In the cast list, Vaffrino is described as the "servant [*servo*] to Nicano."[27] Vaffrino

---

[26] Moniglia, "La vedova," III, xiii.
[27] Giovanni Francesco Busenello, *La Statira principessa di Persia: Drama per musica* (Venice: Appresso Andrea Giuliani, 1655), n.p. [19].

speaks in proper Italian (not *gergo*) and repeatedly refers to his dark complexion; indeed, the final lines of this quote use the same Black man/white faith analogy as deployed by the Moro Birbone:

VAFFRINO	Non t'inganni, Signore,	Do not be fooled, Signore,
	Sotto queste caligini del volto,	Under the smoke of this face,
	De purissimo zelo arde il mio core;	My heart burns with the most pure zeal;
	Dentro a negra miniera è ascosto l'oro,	Inside the black mine is hidden gold,
	Sta bianca fe, sotto sembiante moro.[28]	A [pure] white faith resides under my black countenance.

Though Vaffrino is never explicitly called a slave, his master Nicano offers him his freedom in exchange for delivering a love letter, speaking to entrenched assumptions of bonded labor and Black skin.[29] Such assumptions remain operative in complicated ways. Consider, for example, a letter written by the castrato singer Giovanni Antonio Cavagna to the Venetian librettist Giovanni Faustini in 1666. This letter has been cited in scholarly literature as a crucial piece of evidence in ongoing discussions about the ability of singers to negotiate the finer details of their roles, but it also testifies—with evident displeasure on Cavagna's part—to a practice of blackface costuming. "Two things alone worry me," he wrote, "the first is the need to sing in a black Moor's mask [*con la Maschera da Moro*], a thing that I no longer do, and which I did not realize [was necessary] until after I read the third act."[30] (For what it is worth, Cavagna's other concern was the potential embarrassment of singing between two "angels," beside whom he feared his own talents might fade into insignificance.) Ellen Rosand has suggested that the role in question might be that of Megaristo, Alciade's servant in Faustini and Pietro Andrea Ziani's *Alciade*.[31] Other

---

[28] Busenello, *La Statira*, I, viii.

[29] Rather creepily, Nicano's opening lines of the scene are: "Vaffrin, fin da fanciullo, / Nelle mie case ti guidò fortuna, T'ho sempre amato, hor voglio, / Darti dell'amor mio sicuro pegno." See Busenello, *La Statira*, I, viii.

[30] "Due cose sole mi spaventano, l'una, di dover cantar con la Maschera da Moro, cosa non più usata da me, et non mai compresa che doppo haver letto il terzo atto; l'altra dover cantar in mezo di due angioli, la Sig.^{ra} Antonia et la Sig.^{ra} Giulia; la canzonetta che mi manda per agionta mi scusi chi l'à fatta, è per un contralto et non per Soprano, et molto diferente dalla maniera del Sig.^{r} Ziani, onde mi contenterò cantare il duetto et che la Sig.^{ra} Giulia canti la sua canzone sola." Cavagna's letter is transcribed by Ellen Rosand, *Opera*, as doc. 16 in Appendix 3A.

[31] Rosand writes: "The role in question was probably that of Megaristo, Alciade's servant." See Rosand, *Opera*, 239 and n61. *Alciade* was initially scheduled for the 1666 season, but the production was postponed until the following year.

letters discussing the production, however, make it clear that Cavagna was to play the title role.[32]

The *argomento*, published with the libretto in 1667 when the production was ultimately staged, makes it clear that both Megaristo (a servant described as Libyan) and Alciade (the Sicilian king) donned blackface before the action of the opera began: "The African [Megaristo] had learned the secret from an old Gaetuli[33] woman, and had experimented in dyeing himself Black with a tisane made from several herbs; so both of them [Megaristo and Alciade], in a mean shepherd's hut, transformed themselves into the color of Ethiopians."[34] Though several of the other characters comment on Alciade's dark complexion, he himself does not; were Cavagna learning only his own lines, it would have been relatively straightforward for him to have presumed his character's whiteness right up to the moment of explicit unmasking, which takes place in Act III, scenes ii and iv.[35] Alciade is given a whole scene offstage in order to complete his transformation from "Moro" back to "King." Though the *argomento* describes the characters as having dyed their skin ("tingersi Moro"), it is more likely that a thin cloth mask was used.[36] We can also note that even the "African" character of Megaristo is here understood as fundamentally white.

Returning to Cavagna's letter, it is unclear whether his objection to the "Maschera da Moro" was at the prospect of singing in a mask (in general) or singing as a Moor (specifically), while it is clear that he once did so, perhaps regularly.[37] As we might expect, in *Alciade*, the purportedly Black skin

---

[32] See, for example, Ziani to Faustini, November 28, 1665, I-Vas, Scuola grande di San Marco, b. 188, c. 354: "V.S. osserverà ne la scena 12 del 2.o Atto la Cantata in forma di lamento d'Alciade, Più per me non vi è contento, che è la mia favorita per il S. Cavagnino, che stimo portera il Vanto di tutto il resto, pur che sia cantata adasio e le Viole discrete, e qui place tanto à S.M. che ne ho fatto copia e aggionte parole per non perderla."

[33] Gaetuli was the Romanized name of an ancient Berber tribe inhabiting Getulia, located in the large desert region south of the Atlas Mountains, bordering the Sahara.

[34] "Haveva l'Africano appreso da una vecchia di Getulia secreto sicuro, & esprimentato di tingersi Moro con la decottione d'alcune Erbe; onde ambo trasformatisi nella capanuccia d'un povero pescatore in Etiopi di colore." Giovanni Faustini, *L'Alciade* (Venice: Francesco Nicolini & Steffano Curti, 1667), 12.

[35] In Act III, scene ii, Alciade declares, "Vado sì, vado, o bella, / Queste tenebre false a dispogliarmi" Faustini, *L'Alciade*, 67. He disappears for all of scene iii, and when he reappears in scene iv, he proclaims, "Ecco il pazzo, ecco il moro, / Candido, e saggio" (70).

[36] The use of a cloth mask is discussed in the accompanying text to Jacopo Cicognini, *La finta mora* (Florence: I Giunti, 1626). See also Miller, *Slaves to Fashion*.

[37] Coincidentally, Cavagna is known to have performed in *La Statira*, though it is highly unlikely that he played the role of Vaffrino, which is scored for tenor. See Cavagna to Faustini, October 17, 1665, transcribed in Rosand, *Opera*, lett. 6: "[P]er altro poi io intendo di cantar sopra li instrumenti della orchestra accordati al giusto tono di Roma, e non più come ho fatto nella Statira, nel Teseo et altri, e questo per esser di maggior vantaggio alla mia voce, e lo dico io hora acciò niuno si

displayed by the main character for much of the performance is sufficient to disguise his identity—this is true of the *travestimento* of countless operatic and dramatic characters throughout Italian stage history, who become immediately unrecognizable, even to their closest family members, as soon as they don a disguise. Alciade repeatedly proclaims his true identity throughout, yet nobody—with the exception of his beloved, Charisde—believes him. Alciade is dismissed as crazy and Charisde as foolish and impressionable. As "Etiope di colore," Alciade's claim to sovereignty is laughable; his true nature is revealed, however, along with his "candido" complexion. Historiographically, we can diagnose a distressingly persistent economy of racial valence at work in the easy scholarly assumption that Cavagna-in-blackface must have sung the role of the African servant, Megaristo, rather than the Sicilian king. The whole incident—from Cavagna's outraged protestations onward—is a useful reminder of the wide variety of black(face) and Black roles that were depicted on the Italian stage and of the deep cultural implications of Black skin. Taken together, the characters of Vaffrino, Megaristo, and Alciade make it clear that the novelty Grimani ascribes to Buonaccorsi's performances—"never before seen" on the Venetian stage—was not merely the Black character but possibly Buonaccorsi's naturally black face.

* * *

Of the two operas staged by the Grimani at Santi Giovanni e Paolo in 1664, the first was *La Rosilena* by Aurelio Aureli and Giovanni Battista Volpe *detto* Rovettino; the dedication of the libretto was signed January 4, 1664.[38] The music is unfortunately lost; however, the libretto includes a character seemingly made for Buonaccorsi: "Ergisto Moro servo d'Ariadeno" (Ariadeno is an Assyrian prince). Ergisto functions primarily as the bearer of information, repeatedly informing his master about events that have just happened or are just about to happen. Brief flashes of Buonaccorsi's more comedic persona emerge only in the third act. In Act III, scene xiii, for example, the elderly nursemaid Fidalba attempts to persuade Ergisto to save her from the

---

lamenti di ciò." Cavagna played the role of Teseo in *L'incostanza trionfante overo il Theseo* (libretto by Francesco Piccoli and others, music by Pietro Andrea Ziani; perf. at S. Cassiano in the 1657–1658 season under the direction of Marco Faustini). The full performing cast is listed in the published libretto, transcribed by Beth Glixon and Jonathan Glixon, *Inventing the Business*, 329. It is also unlikely that Cavagna played the heartthrob lead in some operas and the servant (canny or otherwise) in others.

[38] Aurelio Aureli, *La Rosilena, drama per musica* (Venice: Francesco Nicolini in Spadaria, 1664).

approaching enemy army; Ergisto recommends that she save herself, adding a quip about her advanced age:

| FIDALBA | Deh soccorrimi Ergisto! | Argh! Help me, Ergisto! |
| ERGISTO | Hò che pensar a me: fuggi i tuoi danni
Se non t'aggrava il piede
Il gran peso degl'anni.[39] | I have to think about myself: flee your own troubles,
If the heavy weight of your years
Does not slow your feet. |

A few scenes later, Ergisto manages to distract Clito, his captor and would-be executioner, with talk of hidden gold; he then seizes the opportunity to flee, leaving Clito cursing:

CLITO	Vien qui demone Assiro; A fe, che questa volta Se ben tutt'ombra sei Fuggir tu non potrai da gli'occhi miei	Come here, Assyrian demon! I swear, that this time Even if you are all shadows, You will not escape from under my eyes!
ERGISTO	Pieta d'un infelice.	Take pity on an unhappy soul.
CLITO	Che pieta? Sol rigore Amministro col brando: Ti ricordi all'hor quando Volevi saettar il mio Signor?	What pity? Only severity Will I administer with my sword: Do you remember when You wanted to shoot my Lord with arrows?
ERGISTO	Del mio Prence a i comandi Fui costretto ubbidire.	I was constrained to obey The commands of my Prince.
CLITO	Se qui fosse ancor lui Teco unito vorrei farlo morire.	If he were still here, I would kill him, along with you.
ERGISTO	Dunque uccider mi vuoi.	Then you want to kill me!
CLITO	Vò che discendi Su la Stigia pallude Con la tua nera fronte A spaventar nel legno suo Caronte.	I want you to descend, To the swampy Stygian shore, To frighten Charon in his boat, With your black face.
ERGISTO	Crudele io morirò; ma almen concedi Che di molt'oro ascoso Possa dispor.	Cruel one! Then I will die; but at least permit Me to dispose of My piles of hidden gold.
CLITO	Dov'è quest'oro?	Where is this gold?
ERGISTO	Vedi, Quel diroccato volto? Colà molte monete Da me avanzate in guerra Hò nascose sotterra.	Do you see, That rocky mountain face? Up there, many coins, Ransacked by me in battle, I have hidden underground. [aside]
CLITO	O ch'Etiope mal nato! Io le godrò!	Oh, wicked Ethiopian! I will enjoy them!

---

[39] Aureli, *La Rosilena*, III, xiii.

		[*aside*]
ERGISTO	Se ti posso scernir fuggir io vò.	If I can trick you, I will flee!
CLITO	Seguimi; piano; orsù.	Follow me, slowly, up we go.
	Vieni: ma no, stà qui.	Come, but no, stay here.
ERGISTO	T'inganni a fe, se credi havermi più.	You deceive yourself if you believe that you have me still!
		[*Ergisto escapes.*]
CLITO	All'acquisto d'un tesoro	The acquisition of a treasure
	Desto in me strani pensieri;	Awakens strange thoughts,
	Vò goder tutti i piaceri	I will enjoy all the joys
	Che si comprano con l'oro.	That one can buy with gold.
	Ma non trovo, che sassi;	But I don't find anything except rocks;
	Ergisto, Ergisto, ohime, certo è fuggito!	Ergisto, Ergisto, alas, he has escaped for sure!
	O maledetto moro che m'hà schernito.[40]	O cursed black, who has made a fool of me.

The racialization of Clito's insulting speech toward Ergisto is depressingly familiar; Ergisto (Buonaccorsi) is a cursed, unlucky, Ethiopian demon, and the sight of his face would terrify even Charon, long habituated to the task of ferrying the dead. Insidiously, Clito elides Ergisto's skin color with subterfuge and deceit from the outset, justifying a heightened surveillance on Clito's part to prevent Ergisto's escape. Indeed, confronted with the enemy, Ergisto quite literally fears for his own skin:

ERGISTO	E son cosi adirati	And they are so enraged
	Contro di noi, che se prigione io resto[41]	Against us, that if I become a prisoner,
	Mi scortican sicuro,	They will surely flay me
	E della pelle mia fanno un tamburo.[42]	And make a drum from my skin.

Stereotype and comedic caricature aside, there is a genuine malevolence underlining much of the language in these scenes. Even the fear that Ergisto expresses about his potential treatment at the hands of the Armenian troops objectifies his own body as a site of sanctioned violence, and the barbarity he imagines reflects unsubtly back onto his own person as the generative locus of violent threat.

---

[40] Aureli, *La Rosilena*, III, xviii.

[41] The line doesn't make grammatical sense and could perhaps have been meant to say either "che se prigioner io resto" (which would change the meter), or "che se'n prigione io resto."

[42] Aureli, *La Rosilena*, III, xiii.

While the fifty-five lines given to Ergisto are structured as if for recitative, without a surviving score it is impossible to know how they were set or how often the character resorted to arioso effect.[43] Certainly, as published, there is no evidence that Buonaccorsi sang a comic aria of the type familiar from his performances at La Pergola.

As a whole, *La Rosilena* was not particularly well received, despite the presence of the star soprano Giulia Masotti.[44] In the second opera that Grimani produced that season, Buonaccorsi's role is even more tenuous. Confirming Buonaccorsi's presence in Venice and in the performances, Atto Melani reported that "the Moor has not had much chance to bring honor upon himself, because he has had a very small role [*pochissima parte*] in this second opera."[45] Melani's faintly damning assessment is particularly disappointing given the work in question: *Scipione affricano*, with a libretto by Nicolò Minato and music by Cavalli; the dedication to the libretto was signed February 9, 1664.[46] The explicit confluence of an opera set entirely on African soil with this rare Italian singer of African descent would seem (at least for modern scholarship) a unique opportunity to confront the tangled nexus of race and representation—if it wasn't for Buonaccorsi's reported "pochissima parte" and the lack of honor that his performances accrued.

Jennifer Williams Brown, editor of a forthcoming scholarly edition of *Scipione affricano*, has suggested that Buonaccorsi could have played the small role of the Sibyl—noting that the comic servant Lesbo runs away at the sight of the otherworldly creature.[47] Lesbo's horrified response chimes with

---

[43] Jennifer Williams Brown cites fifty-two lines of recitative and notes that the character sings no arias or ensembles; personal communication. My own count is fifty-five lines of text, though one is incorrectly attributed in the libretto to Zaffira (Act III, scene xiii).

[44] De Lucca cites a letter from Colonna to Faustini from October 20, 1666: "Mi fo lecito però di dire che spendendo tutto in musici si dovrebbe cercare a fare un'opera che nelle parole, e nella musica accompagnasse l'eccellenza de' recitanti, et in questo fa parlare con raggione la Sig.ra Giulia; mentre lei fu molto più stimata e accetta nella Dori opera vecchia, che nella Rosilena opera nuova, e forse la sua parte inviatagli in Roma sarrà stata riconosciuta per mediocre." Colonna, Lorenzo Onofrio. 1666. I-Vas, SGSM, b. 188, f. 345. See Valeria De Lucca, "Patronage," in *The Oxford Handbook of Opera*, ed. Helen Greenwald (Oxford: Oxford University Press, 2014), 658.

[45] "Il Moro non ha avuto troppo campo di farsi onore, perché ha avuto pochissima parte in questa seconda opera." Atto Melani to Mattias de' Medici, February 16, 1664, I-Fas, Mediceo del Principato, f. 5478, Diversi, con minute di risposta (1662–1664), cc. 427r–428r. Transcribed in Mamone, *Mattias de' Medici*, lett. 1636, 818–819.

[46] Details of both productions are listed in Appendix 1 of Glixon and Glixon, *Inventing the Business*, 333. The Glixons note that the dedication of *La Rosilena* is dated January 4, 1664, that of *Scipione affricano* February 9 (thus, *La Rosilena* is the "first" opera, and *Scipione affricano* is the "second"). It is possible that Melani was referring (by mistake or by a schedule change) to *La Rosilena*; however, while fifty-five lines is hardly an enormous part, neither is it "pocchissima."

[47] Personal communication. Brown also discounts the role of Lesbo (soprano) for Buonaccorsi based on the number of lines the character sings: "Atto implies that [Buonaccorsi's] role in *Scipione*

the various scenes in Moniglia's libretti in which Buonaccorsi's skin shocks an unsuspecting viewer; however, the music written for the Siblyl (particularly the second scene in which she appears) is scored a full third higher than Buonaccorsi's regular tessitura (see Musical Examples 13.1 and 13.2).[48] Brown believes that the Sibyl would have been double cast with the messenger (possibly both the "Messo del Prencipe di Luceio, e di Polinio" and the "Paggio d'Ericlea") and an onstage musician, each of whom sings only a line or two.[49] Such doublings were common in the public theater, particularly with a work such as *Scipione affricano*, which has a large number of very

Musical Example 13.1. "De Latini eccelsi eroi," as sung by Sibyl (possibly Giovannino Buonaccorsi). *Scipione affricano* (perf. Venice 1664), Act I, scene xix. Libretto by Nicolò Minato, music by Francesco Cavalli.

was smaller than in *La Rosilena*, where he had fifty-two lines of recitative and no arias or ensembles. For this reason, it is unlikely that Il Moro sang either Lesbo or Ceffea, whose parts are much more substantial than that of Ergisto in *La Rosilena*."

[48] The repetitive rhythmic unit of the Sibyl's predictions recalls other scenes of magic and incantation, for example, "Dell'antro magico," sung by Medea in Francesco Cavalli's *Il Giasone*.
[49] Personal communication, January 18, 2018. See also Cavalli, *Scipione affricano*. The 1664 libretto lists two separate characters, "Un Messo del Prencipe di Luceio, e di Polinio" and "Un Paggio d'Ericlea" (given in that order), who both appear in the score as "Messo," where they are scored for

Musical Example 13.2. "Odi, Campion Latino" and "Poco grate," as sung by Sibyl (possibly Giovannino Buonaccorsi). *Scipione affricano* (perf. Venice 1664), Act II, scene xix. Libretto by Nicolò Minato, music by Francesco Cavalli.

minor roles. To modern sensibilities, the obvious casting for a Black singer in *Scipione affricano* would be as one of the African characters (imagine Buonaccorsi, for just a moment, in the celebrated castrato role of Siface, king of the Massessuli),[50] yet Grimani and his peers obviously thought otherwise.

C1, which would sit well for Buonaccorsi's voice. Certainly, the first messenger, in Act I, scene xi (as numbered in the libretto; note that in the Vm score, this scene is numbered as I, xii), seems to come from the princely brothers. "Messo," who sings in II, xvi, is described by Ceffea as "un forastiero" (according to the score) or "un straniero" (according to the libretto) and claims to have been sent by the father of Luceio and Polinio; it thus seems unlikely that he would have been played by the same character as the Messo who introduced them in the previous act. The "Messo" in III, xii (described as Paggio in the libretto), in contrast, seems to act on behalf of Ericlea. They could therefore represent three separate people but played by the same singer. The musicians of the opening scenes sing the praises of Scipione in his role as conqueror of Carthage, a depressingly likely role for a Black singer.

[50] Coincidentally, the singer who sang Siface in the 1671 Roman revival of the opera—becoming so famous for the role that he assumed "Siface" as his stage name—was Giovanni Francesco Grossi, who reputedly sang the role of Nettuno in *Ercole in Tebe* in Florence in 1661, at which point he was only eight or nine years old ("Grossi" is named in the list of singers transcribed by Ademollo). A "castratino" who sang in *Ercole* attracted the attention of the queen of France, who requested that he be sent—along with Antonio Rivani and Leonora Ballerini—to the French court to sing; Cardinal

As the (Black) page, as a (Black) musician, as a (Black) Sibyl, Buonaccorsi's performance once again confirms the representational associations of Black skin and servitude and of Black skin and devilishness.[51] Ironically, Buonaccorsi's presumed role as the Black pageboy points up not only a European obliviousness to Africa but also the thoroughly normalized presence of Afro-Europeans within Italian society, such that Blackness and servitude were so typical of contemporary culture that even in representations of Africa, the Black presence enslaved to white masters is unremarkable.

Buonaccorsi's potential double casting in *Scipione affricano* draws attention to a further complication implied by his racial identity, above and beyond typical considerations of voice type, tessitura, and dramatic range. Theatrical texts of the period regularly describe the use of costume to make characters seem visibly similar,[52] but for Buonaccorsi, his skin acted as if it were already a costume—while to say so is to foreshadow by more than three centuries Leontyne Price's famous comment, "When I sang Aida, my skin was my costume."[53] The exonominative whiteness of the Venetian stage renders racialization itself as something to be slipped on and off at will. All of the main characters are white, while Buonaccorsi's marked skin makes him unable to easily play multiple roles within the same work.[54] Unlike the effectively private stagings that took place at La Pergola, the commercial enterprise of the Venetian theater was intended to turn a profit, and as such, there was little point in employing a singer for a single scene or comic effect.[55]

Giovan Carlo refused, citing the castratino's weak state and his need to remain longer with his singing teacher, Jacopo Melani. See Mamone, *Serenissimi fratelli*, lett. 803 and 13.

[51] The relatively substantial roles of the princely brothers Luceio and Polinio are both scored as sopranos, while the characters are described as "Celtiberi" and were thus "Spanish." When first reading through the score, I spent some time considering Polinio as a possible role for Buonaccorsi. While Lucieo is the hereditary prince and Polinio is sworn to serve him, the two switch identities, and several characters comment on how much more noble the "servant" Lucieo appears than his "prince" Polinio. Buonaccorsi's Black skin could easily have turned this into a running gag; however, to do so would have cast him as a relative of the sovereign. This also would negate the "pocchissima parte" that we know him to have played.

[52] For directions on how to clothe actors so that they pass as twins, see the introduction to Giovan Battista Andreini, *Li due Lelii simili* (Paris: Nicolas Della Vigna, 1622).

[53] Price has made this comment in a variety of places, including in her book for children: Leontyne Price, Leo Dillon, and Diane Dillon, *Aida* (New York: Voyager Books, 1991).

[54] A similar point was made in reviews of Ira Aldridge in the mid-nineteenth century. See Urvashi Chakravarty, "What Is the History of Actors of Color Performing in Shakespeare in the UK?," in *The Cambridge Companion to Shakespeare and Race*, ed. Ayanna Thompson (Cambridge: Cambridge University Press, 2021), 194.

[55] Documents from the archives of the Academia degli Immobili show the large-scale, celebratory operatic performances in which Buonaccorsi took part costing as much as 105,500 lire (*Hipermestra*) and 122,500 lire (*Ercole in Tebe*), paid in large part by Cardinal Giovan Carlo or the Medici court.

Onstage in Florence, Buonaccorsi played a version of his offstage role—not just a Black buffoon but a particular Black comic, familiar and recognizable as a member of the court and as an inhabitant of the city. In Venice, however, he is rendered more generic; his ability to poke fun at other (white) Italians emerges as more disturbing and less funny. Despite a legion of enslaved Black characters, an actual (enslaved) Black singer is harder to cast. Furthermore, Buonaccorsi's free movement across the operatic stage was limited by his race to an extent that was magnified and perpetuated by the infrastructure of the Italian theater. The system of stock characters that seventeenth-century opera inherited from the commedia dell'arte constrained the categories through which his performances could be understood, reproducing his conduct as servile in ways that both reflected and reinforced cultural norms. Singers were associated with specific roles through vocal sound, costumes, gesture, and musical genre. And under this system, Buonaccorsi could only ever play the slave, the demon, or the messenger, never the African king.

As yet, no evidence has surfaced regarding Buonaccorsi's performances between the documented season he spent in Venice during carnival of 1664 and his death a decade later in August 1674. (He does, however, make occasional appearances in the granducal accounts.)[56] While it seems unlikely that Buonaccorsi would have entirely ceased to perform, it also seems as if, absent the presence of the opera-loving Cardinal Giovan Carlo de' Medici, the opportunities for such performances diminished significantly.

Despite Atto Melani's less than celebratory assessment of Buonaccorsi's debut Venetian season, it is worth considering a continued role for Buonaccorsi in the Grimani theater and elsewhere. The following year, in 1665, Grimani staged Aureli and Andrea Mattioli's *Perseo*, which includes a whole slew of Ethiopian and Mauritanian characters (several of whom are servants), as well as a remake of *Ciro* (libretto by Giulio Cesare Sorrentino,

---

See Hill, "Le relazioni," 34. He in turn cites U. Morini, *La R. Accademia degli Immobili* (1926). Performances staged during those same years by the less wealthy Sorgenti academy, which sold tickets in an attempt to cover costs, reportedly clocked in at 532 lire (for a spoken play with musical *intermedii*, in 1658) and 5,239 lire (for Cavalli's *L'Erismena*, in 1661). See Hill, "Le relazioni," 32–33.

[56] For example, in September 1667, "A Giovannino moro una dobla, 2.6.-.-," I-Fas, Camera del Granduca, f. 39, c. 4r; also in July 1669, "A Giovannino Moro scudi due," I-Fas, Camera del Granduca, f. 40, c. 32r. A reprise of *Scipione* in Pisa in 1672 (presumably Cavalli's work) may have included Buonaccorsi in his original role; the performance and some of the singers are mentioned in I-Fas, Camera del Granduca, f. 42, cc. 62r–66r. *La Cleopatra* was performed during the same celebrations. The libretto, which was published anonymously, survives in a single copy in the Braidense in Milan; the text, minus the prologue, is that of Giacomo Dall'Angelo's 1662 libretto, which was performed in Venice that season with music by Daniele Castrovillari.

with music by Francesco Provenzale and Cavalli, substantially updated by Mattioli). *Ciro* includes the character "Fatama Mora, slave to [Cleopilda,] dressed as a gypsy," which would have been an ideal role for Buonaccorsi, who had previously played the gypsy Moretta in *Il pazzo per forza*.[57] Fatama's role is cleffed for C3; however, the tessitura sits squarely in the octave above middle C and is consistent with the music Buonaccorsi is known to have sung.

Indeed, the similarities between the gypsies in the two libretti are striking. In *Ciro*, as in *Il pazzo*, we find two gypsies, one white and one Black, though this time, both characters are in disguise. There is an interesting slippage between Fatama as Black and Fatama as gypsy, magnified by her servitude to an Egyptian princess (tradition had long held that European gypsies originated in Egypt).[58] Fatama Mora speaks (sings) the same *gergo* as Moretta;[59] like her, she is repeatedly linked to the act of fortune telling or palm reading; and like Moretta, Fatama closes out one of the acts. At the end of Act I, Fatama steals a key from Delfido (a stuttering hunchback), and when he puts his hands on her in an attempt to get it back, she cries rape. A chorus of Ethiopian Moors comes running to Fatama's rescue—they call her their "Paesana" or "countrywoman"—and after Delfido flees, they dance and sing; this scene is reproduced here as Musical Example 13.3.[60] (As I mentioned in my discussion of Buonaccorsi's performance as Moretta, the association with the danced finale emphasizes the character's relationship to comedy and to entertainment rather than character development.)

Unlike *Il pazzo per forza*, which was written with specific Florentine singers in mind, the libretto for *Ciro* relied on an earlier Neapolitan opera, first modified for Venetian performance in 1654 and then changed even

---

[57] The production schedule of 1665 is listed by Glixon and Glixon, *Inventing the Business*, 333. For the list of "intervenienti" (characters, not performers), see Aurelio Aureli, *Perseo, dramma per musica* (Venice: Francesco Nicolini, 1665). The character lists of both the 1665 and 1654 editions mistakenly name Fatama as "Fatama Mora, Schiava d'Elmera, vestita di Zingara," but the libretto makes clear her relationship to Cleopilda, not Elmera, and indeed, Cleopilda is also "in habito di Zingara." See Giulio Cesare Sorrentino, *Ciro, drama per musica: Nel teatro a SS Gio: e Paolo l'anno 1665* (Venice: Per il Giuliani, 1665).

[58] The association between Egypt and European gypsies is traced in Leonardo Piasere, "L'invenzione di una diaspora: I nubiani d'Europa," in *Alle radici dell'Europa: Mori, giudei e zingari nei paesi del Mediterraneo occidentale*, Vol. 1: *Secoli XV–XVII*, ed. Felice Gambin (Florence: Seid, 2008), 185–199. See also Hornback, *Racism*, 185–186.

[59] Indeed, Fatama has such a slim grasp on Italian that she misunderstands Euretto: he declares that he who loves is foolish, finishing with the word "*innamora*"; she repeatedly hears her own name (Mora, Black woman) in the final syllables *-mora* and wants to know why he calls for her. See Sorrentino, *Ciro*, Act II, scene v, 47–48.

[60] See Sorrentino, *Ciro*, Act I, scene xvii, 40–41. The second-act ballet also involves Delfido, who is accused of smuggling goods into the city under his hunched back; he is then stoned by a chorus of pages with slingshots; see Act II, scene xvii, 63.

Musical Example 13.3. Fatama Mora, Delfido, and a chorus of Ethiopian Moors. *Il Ciro* (rev. Venice 1665), Act I, scene xvii. Libretto by Giulio Cesare Sorrentino and others, music by Francesco Provenzale, Francesco Cavalli, and Andrea Mattioli.

Musical Example 13.3. Continued

Musical Example 13.3. Continued

Musical Example 13.3. Continued

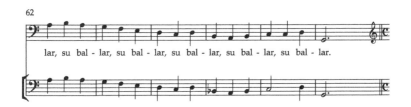

further for 1665. It is an intriguing possibility that Buonaccorsi's presence in the performing ensemble may have influenced the revival of this particular work.

DELFIDO	La tela è ben ordita; tra se, se, Elmera tra le selve attenderà.	The web [of deceit] is woven well! Elmera will be waiting by herself among the trees.
FATAMA	Camerata dicir?	Are you a courtier?
DELFIDO	Ahime! ahime!	Help, help!
FATAMA	Fa fuggir femine ti? Su dicir verità; che star di Curt?	Do women make you flee? Come on, tell the truth; are you of the court?
DELFIDO	Camerier di Ciro: Quest'aurea chiave è de le Regie stanze.	I am a chamberman to Ciro: This golden key is that of the Royal chamber.
FATAMA	Veder.	Let me see.
DELFIDO	Vedila sì.	See!
FATAMA	Voler per mi.	I want it for myself.
DELFIDO	Temeraria tù sei, Rendila, ò proverai li sdegni miei.	You are foolhardy! Give it back, or you will feel my wrath!
FATAMA	O gente soccorrer! Voler chiste sforzar.	Oh, people, to the rescue! This one wants to force me.
CHORO	Fermar, ò là fermar.	Stop! Hey there, stop!
DELFIDO	Non m'uccidete ahime, pietà, clemenza!	Don't kill me! Help! Take pity!
CHORO	A Paesana ti far violenza?	You try to violate our countrywoman?
DEFIDO	Ella mi vuol robbar.	She wants to rob me.
CHORO, FATIMA	Uccidir, nù parlar.	Let's kill him. No talking.
DELFIDO	Deh lasciatemi andar.	Ah! Let me go.
CHORO, FATIMA	Uccidir, nù parlar.	Let's kill him. No talking.
DELFIDO	Con fuga spedita Si sa, salvi la vita. Vado di qua? Si, si; no, no, di là, Che fò? dove m'ascondo? O potessi volar fuori del Mondo!	With a fast escape— It is said—life can be saved. Should I go this way? Yes, yes: no, no, that way, What do I do? Where should I hide? Oh, if only I could fly out of this world!
FATIMA	Compagni veder, E Gobbo lasciar Chi chiave mi haver.	Companions, look— And let the Hunchback go— What key I have.
CHORO	Bella star, bella star. Se piacir Ti sentir Su ballar, su ballar.	Stay, beautiful lady, stay, If pleasure, You feel, And dance, and dance.

FATIMA	Temer mi, che chiave Andar, come venire. Ballar compagni, e Fatama fuggir.	I am afraid that this key Will leave me the way it came. Dance, companions, while Fatama flees.
	Il Choro delli Ethipoi forma un ballo.[61]	*The Chorus of Ethiopians does a dance.*

The dramatic premise of *Ciro* is that the son of the king and that of a humble shepherd were switched at birth. The truth is eventually discovered due to the innate nobility of the presumed shepherd and the innate uncouthness of the peasant-presumed-kingly-heir, who does not know how to behave, despite his upbringing in the royal household. *Ciro* thus highlights the manifestation of birth and lineage through aptitude and social graces, an issue of central importance in seventeenth-century Italian drama. This concept of lineage—of *razza*—shores up both sovereignty and slavery. To imagine Buonaccorsi at work in this opera, his body travestied as an enslaved Black gypsy, his voice articulating a thick *gergo*, is to recognize the role that seventeenth-century opera and European culture at large have delineated for Black-skinned peoples. The association of Blackness with comic servility sustains a conflation of character type and the moral or intellectual character of an entire race of people. Black humans are typecast as the enslaved, the inheritability of Black skin written large as the legacy—the *razza*—that passes down the privileges and deprivations of social status from generation to generation, no matter their upbringing or their geographical location.

Such stereotypes persist throughout operatic history. In 1955, for example, when Marian Anderson desegregated the Metropolitan Opera in New York City, she did so in the role of Ulrica, the Black gypsy sorceress in Giuseppe Verdi's *Un ballo in maschera*. The libretto explicitly calls out her race, with another character describing her as being "of the vile race of negros"—thus, the Black gypsy fortune teller stereotype was alive and well in Verdi's time (the opera dates from 1859) and also in the minds of the Met administration and audience members a century later.[62] Rudolf Bing, then general manager of the Met, noted in his autobiography: "I planned to engage black artists at the earliest opportunity, which provoked another storm. (In fact, I had already asked Max Rudolf to sound out Marian Anderson on

---

[61] Sorrentino, *Ciro*, I, xvii.
[62] "S'appella / Ulrica—dell'abbietto / Sangue de' negri." *Un ballo in maschera*, Act I, scene iv. Text by Antonio Somma, 1859.

the possibility of singing Azucena in *Il Trovatore* for us, but nothing came of it)."[63] Azucena is also a gypsy, and thus coincidence slides over into predisposition. Again and again—1658, 1859, 1955—the operatic gypsy is Black, and the Black singer, no matter their concertizing reputation, is typecast as a gypsy, whose connections to the mystical, not-quite-human realm are distinctly racialized.

---

[63] Rudolf Bing, *5,000 Nights at the Opera* (London: Hamilton, 1972), 156; I thank Matthew Timmermans for the reference.

Pagati a P. Gio. Bat.a Amori Priori di S. Paolo . . . per suo rimborso di tanti spesi in revestire le due minori figliole della Maria schiava di Roverscino Rosso fine, e per otto Camicie, et Otto Grembiuli di panno nostrale, servito per la Madre, et tre sue figlie, e fatture de Vestiti e Camicie sudette 28.5.2.-.

Paid to Father Giovan Battista Amori, Prior at St. Paul's, . . .to reimburse him for several expenses incurred outfitting the two younger daughters of Maria the slave in fine red fabric, and for eight shirts, and eight aprons of local fabric, to be used by the mother and three of her daughters, and for the cost of making the clothes and the aforementioned shirts, 28.5.2.-.

        I-Fas, Camera del Granduca, f. 42, December 1671, c. 45r

Intermezzo Secondo

Thinking from Giovannino Buonaccorsi's Life

Anton Domenico Gabbiani's *Three Musicians of the Medici Court* (see Intermezzo secondo Figure 1, reproduced after page 240) has an evident relationship to his *Four Servants* painting (shown earlier as Figure 10.3). Both paintings form part of a series depicting court functionaries, conceived with documentary intentions, and, more important, both include a Black youth dressed in a pale green silk cassock. The fabric of the cassock is the same in both paintings, with delicate floral curlicues in green and yellow, and while the features of the two individuals are clearly differentiated, their resemblance is emphasized by their posture. These two Black children share the turn of the head, the direction of the gaze (all the better to display the whites of their eyes), the right hand held across the body, and the low stone walls against which they lean. There are subtle differences: the younger child in the *Three Musicians* has more elaborate frogging down the front of his or her cassock and larger green buttons. Their hair is longer, with no widow's peak; this person wears a silver slave collar and a distinctive pearl drop earring. (The earring is reminiscent of the one worn by Pietro Moro in Justus Sustermans's painting *Madonna "Domenica delle Cascine," la Cecca di Pratolino e Pietro Moro*; documentation also survives for a pearl earring purchased for a "Morino" in 1629.)[1] While the three *virtuosi* have been named and discussed by art historians and musicologists—the harpsichordist has been identified as Antonio Pagliardi, the violinist as Marino Bitti, and the singer as the castrato Francesco de Castris *detto* Cecchino—the Black child remains nameless.[2] Yet

---

[1] "All'orefice per un Orecchino con una perla per il Morino, -.5.-.-.," I-Fas, Camera del Granduca, f. 11, c. 18r.

[2] Marco Chiarini, "Anton Domenico Gabbiani e i Medici," in *Kunst des Barock in der Toskana: Studien zur Kunst unter den letzten Medici*, ed. Florence Kunsthistorisches Institut (Munich: Bruckman, 1976), 333–335. Maddalena De Luca has disputed the identification of the harpsichordist as Pagliardi; she argues that in the mid-1680s, he would have been too old to be identified with the sitter of the portrait. See Annamaria Giusti and Cristina Acidini Luchinat, eds., *Masters of Florence: Glory and Genius at the Court of the Medici*, exhibition catalogue (Memphis: Wonders, 2004), 288.

in this image, where the Black child's presence falls below the radar of the painting's title, his or her inclusion is far from casual and is integrally tied to the task of representing musical sound.

Specifically, the child holds a parrot, representing a natural, musicalized, and explicitly foreign noise, against which the learned and artificial music of the white European sitters is juxtaposed. The elaborately coiffed hair, fussy cravats, and literate musical repertoire of the three European *virtuosi* are figured as civilized precisely through the inclusion of the child. The natural/civilized divide is heightened by the split backdrop of the image. Like Giovannino Buonaccorsi, in Volteranno's double portrait with Albizzi (see Figure 8.1), Gabbiani's Black child appears against an outdoor vista, while the white musicians are located in the cool interior space of the villa.

In Florence, the imitative vocality of the parrot was well known. References to the birds, their travel, and their delivery appear frequently in the granducal accounts.[3] At least during the late 1620s and early 1630s, musical performances of the court parrots were closely associated with the practice of singing "Maggio" (lit. the month of "May"), a rustic inauguration of the spring celebrated in Tuscany with traditional songs, red scarves, colored ribbons, and hats covered in flowers. *Contadine* ("peasant girls") were regularly brought before the Medici to sing at such times. Nearly every year between 1628 and 1635 (and again in 1640), the Grand Duke's *mezzo da camera* Paolo da Merlupo was tipped for singing Maggio with a parrot—the comicity of this event is underscored by the indication that in 1633, he sang instead with a cat.[4] Other Maggio events included (in 1629) a *moresca* danced by the *contadini* and (in 1630) singing by the dwarf Petrino, performances (including singing, games, and the procession of a decorated carriage) by one hundred inhabitants of the castle, as well as singing by "certain impoverished young girls."[5] Tangentially, we can note that Merlupo

---

[3] For example, in August 1633, a boatman was tipped for the transportation of parrots and other things: "Al navicellaio che condusse li Pappagalli e altre Robe *per* Mancia, 2.-.-.-.," I-Fas, Camera del Granduca, f. 14, c. 53v. And in May 1639, a Venetian gondolier was tipped the equivalent of 2 lire for the transportation of a parrot: "Al Veneziano Gondoliere tre giuli di portatura del Pappogallo, -.2.-.-.," I-Fas, Camera del Granduca, f. 20, c. 39r. Such citations appear with some regularity.

[4] "A Merlupo che cantò Maggio col pappagallo una doppia 2.4.10.-," I-Fas, Camera del Granduca, f. 10, c. 39r. "A Merlupo che cantò Maggio col pappagallo un zecchino 1.3.-.-.," I-Fas, Camera del Granduca, f. 11, c. 41r. "A Merlupo che cantò Maggio con la Gatta due scudi," I-Fas, Camera del Granduca, f. 14, c. 49r. "A Merlupo che cantò Maggio con il Pappagallo un zecchino," I-Fas, Camera del Granduca, f. 15, c. 39r. "A Merlupo che cantò Maggio con il Pappagallo due 2.-.-.-.," I-Fas, Camera del Granduca, f. 17, c. 41r. "A Merlupo che cantò Maggio due scudi disse SA," I-Fas, Camera del Granduca, f. 21, c. 35r.

[5] I-Fas, Camera del Granduca, f. 10 and f. 11.

was also responsible for the upkeep and housing of at least one Black court retainer: in October 1632, he was paid an allowance to cover food for the "Moro Spagnolo" (lit. "Spanish Moor" or "Black Spaniard") and then, in November, for the "Morino," presumably (given the chronological continuity) the same individual.[6]

The conflation of seasonal (almost pagan) celebrations, rustic (unpolished) music making, the lower classes, and the imitative natural noises of the exotic birds cohere—almost seamlessly—with the ways in which Black musical sounds were understood within the late-seventeenth-century Medici court. This nameless Black child stands alongside Buonaccorsi, Caralì, Mehmet-Giuseppe Maria Medici, and the countless other Black entertainers who lived in Florence. His or her signification here is dependent on a long tradition of court performance in which enslaved Black entertainers were trained to fulfill specifically limited roles, while their successful performances were understood to indicate the natural aptitude of their *razza* for servitude and for musical performance and to justify their continued exploitation.

Even the white sitters in this portrait can be linked to the circumstances of Black servitude: the white castrato singer Francesco de Castris is best remembered today for his intimate relationship with Crown Prince Ferdinando de' Medici. However, as noted by theorbist Niccolò Susier, de Castris also kept a "Moretto" as lackey, who in 1701 fathered the celebrated opera singer Vittoria Tesi *detta* La Moretta.[7] Baptismal records give Tesi's father's name as Alessandro di Antonio Tesi;[8] certainly, the Black child shown in this painting (ca. 1687) may well have been old enough to father a daughter fourteen years later.[9] De Castris was not the only castrato to flaunt a Black servant or enslaved retainer. Both Francesco Bernardi *detto* Senesino (1686–1758) and Carlo Broschi *detto* Farinelli (1705–1782)

---

[6] "A Merlupo cinque scudi *per* il Vitto del Moro spagnolo finito il mese alli 16. del presente [Ottobre]"; "A Merlupo tre scudi *per* il vitto del Morino a buonconto," I-Fas, Camera del Granduca, f. 14, c. 11v and 15r.

[7] As this book goes to print, I am continuing to work on the figure of Vittoria Tesi (1701–1775), whose dates put her outside the limits of this volume. Susier's voluminous handwritten diary is held at the I-Fn, Biblioteca Moreniana, Acquisti Diversi, 54.1; facsimile scans can be viewed at http://www 405.regione.toscana.it/ImageViewer/servlet/ImageViewer?idr=TECA00000266335&keyworks= niccolo%20susier. The entry regarding Tesi and her father is dated April 14, 1753.

[8] I-Fd, Registri Battesimali, Femmine, reg. 295, fg. 130.

[9] It is also possible that Alessandro Tesi *detto* Il Morino was himself a singer (given the occupation of his owner and of his daughter). Reardon references an opera singer in Siena in 1690 who was nicknamed Il Moretto. See Reardon, *A Sociable Moment*, 180.

purchased or employed Black boys, and even Tesi—herself descended from a Black African father—employed a Black maidservant, Maria Labita, whom she raised from childhood.[10] For star singers attempting to distance themselves from the category of servility, the purchase of Black children was a reliable technique, casting the singer-owner (by contrast) in the role of white sovereign.

Like Giovanni Antonio Cavagna (cited in the previous chapter), who did not realize he was to wear a "Maschera da Moro" until after he read the third act of *Alciade*, musicologists are only belatedly coming to recognize the importance of race to the development of seventeenth-century musical tropes— and the importance of seventeenth-century musical tropes to Western configurations of race. To understand the deeply constitutive associations between voice, slavery, and race, we need not only to acknowledge the substantial number of foreign people who were present in Italy under conditions of enslavement but also to listen to them and to auscultate the ways in which their voices sounded and signified: "Voice's source," in Nina Sun Eidsheim's powerful formulation, "is not the singer; it is the listener."[11] The rare documentary plenitude that characterizes certain periods of Buonaccorsi's life provides a stethoscope with which to amplify the echoes of other voices. Even as Vettor Grimani Calergi declares that Buonaccorsi will be "new, and never before seen" on the Venetian operatic stage, he points up the singer's very ordinariness in Florence. In a similar vein, the many *mori*, *turchi*, and *stiavi* listed in this text and its accompanying Appendix militate against Buonaccorsi's exceptionalism. Gabbiani's choice of a young Black child as the visual embodiment of musical sound relies upon and documents the central importance of enslaved, racially marked court performers to the Western conception of music. The historical facticity of this child's life—and that of all the performers, buffoons, musicians, dancers, fencers, and court retainers

---

[10] On Senesino and the sad fate of the young Black boy who died in his service in 1725, see Ilias Chrissochoidis, "Senesino's Black Boy (1725)," *Handel Institue Newsletter* 21, no. 1 (2010): 7–8. Records from the Venetian Pia Casa from 1734 note that the "turco moro" Vaiton, originally from the Congo and purchased by Farinelli in Livorno, was admitted for baptism and renamed Carlo (after Farinelli) Grimani (after his godfather, Michele Grimani). These documents are cited and discussed in Pietro Ioly Zorattini, *I nomi degli altri: Conversioni a Venezia e nel Friuli Veneto in età moderna* (Florence: Olschki, 2008), 236–237. Ioly Zorattini notes that later that year, Vaiton-Carlo was sent to Naples in the service of the celebrated castrato's mother. For details of Tesi's last will and testament and some biographical data about Maria Labita, see Michael Lorenz's fascinating blog post at http://michaelorenz.blogspot.com/2016/03/the-will-of-vittoria-tesi-tramontini.html.

[11] Eidsheim, *The Race of Sound*, 9.

discussed in this book—insists that we pay closer attention to historical sources and rethink our assumptions about who lived and worked in the artistic genres that persist. Absent even from the title of the Gabbiani painting, this child and the one re-emerging from the Artemisia Gentileschi painting with which this book began demand to know how they have remained unseen and unheard for so long.

*Pagati a Cosimo Battezzato già Turco nominato Almansor d*ucati *due di Coman*d*amento di SAS p*er *havere havuto uno figliolo, 2.-.*

Paid to Cosimo Battezzato, previously a Turk named Almansor, two ducats, as commanded by His Most Serene Highness, for having had a son, 2.-.
    I-Fas, Camera del Granduca, f. 42, December 1671, c. 43v

Epilogo (Axiomatic)

In the archives of seventeenth-century Florence, I have searched for two things. First, I have sought the presence of racially marked individuals (whether visitors, voluntary or involuntary immigrants, or those born in the city) and the ways in which the identities of these people were understood through or figured in sound, particularly vocal sound. Second, I have looked at musical and theatrical representations of racialized characters. I contend that these two poles of existence worked together. The historical "real" of once living people and the sonic and gestural verisimilitude of stage and song cohered through the naturalized expressivity of vocal sound as testimony to the fundamental truths of body, character, and the capacious early modern concept of *razza* as inherited aptitude or social status. The operatic voice fleshes out—in sound—the desires, the proclivities, and the potential of each singing subject; similarly, the familiar tales and characters of the Italian theatrical imaginary narrativized the quotidian experience of audiences and artisans, rendering the foreign familiar. In this way, the entrained affective repertoire required of court buffoons cast them in the role of the comic servant character. The voices afforded to racially marked entertainers naturalized their confinement on the lowest step of a pre-Enlightenment social hierarchy that was predicated on birthright, and in the rhythmic, tuneful strains of their expressive vocabulary, seventeenth-century European listeners heard a rustic sensibility aligned with hard labor and unsophisticated bodily pleasures. The very musicality of these figures—on- and offstage—spoke to their social place, signaling a fundamental suitability of the singing subject for servitude and justifying their (continued) enslavement. In the formulation associated with Monteverdi, "Far che l'orazione sia padrona dell'armonia e non serva."

From the various examples detailed in this book, we can extrapolate a number of axioms to guide future research and teaching about voice, slavery, and race in seventeenth-century Europe.

Axiom 1: People (and Information) Traveled

The various archive sources consulted in the course of researching this book make it clear that the courts and cities of Europe were home to many individuals with ties to geographically distant places. Nobles and merchants traveled for work or pleasure, and a constant stream of visitors, travelers, diplomats, and unfree laborers circulated along trade routes, roads, and rivers. The list of names and citations provided in the Appendix insists that slavery was not merely a North American problem and that the inhabitants of Europe were neither ethnically nor racially unified. In addition to the *turchi*, *mori*, and *schiavi* compiled in the Appendix, we need to consider the priests, pilgrims, and other visitors. Spanish, English, and Greek travelers are regularly mentioned in the sources, as are Italians who have themselves been enslaved (typically in Ottoman territory) and are returning home or traveling as a way to sell their story and earn a living.

Premodern societies were more static and less mobile than the jet-setting present (though under Covid, that calculus was perhaps temporarily changed); however, that does not mean that people stayed put or did not have a sense of what was going on beyond the outskirts of their village. Certainly, the classes and individuals who were making and consuming the musical and artistic products that were preserved and that we continue to study today were—in general—exposed to a large amount of very up-to-date information about the world, both through the circulation of information in written and verbal forms and through their interactions with people from foreign places or who had themselves traveled to foreign places.

One consequence of such mobile bodies and the information they trailed with them is that the artistic and cultural products that have survived into the present regularly reflect knowledge of and interaction with people and ideas from geographically distant places. What to modern auditors has seemed an orientalist fantasy of the Other or the ascription of nonsense comic or animalistic sounds to nonnative-speaking populations can often be understood as representations of known or familiar cultural differences. To recognize such reflections, however, it is necessary to understand what contemporary geopolitical information was available and the specific context within which such representations were created and consumed. The historical specificity of given performances is a weak theory, which cannot translate or decode racial representation on a large scale. We need more studies of this kind to flesh out the common assumptions of early modern audiences in various locales.

Axiom 2: Racialized and Ethnic Differences Shaped Musical Forms and Sounds

In early chapters of this book, I demonstrated that non-Western sounds were occasionally—perhaps even frequently—incorporated into non-notated repertoires, including military and theatrical musics, and some evidence indicates that enslaved musicians performed their own musics in ways that were actively consumed by European audiences. I also showed that different genres of music could indicate characterological differences that included racialized and ethnic elements. References to racial or ethnic difference were not necessarily represented by citations of musical materials that can be unequivocally understood as non-Western, foreign, or incorrect according to the musical logics of early modern music theory. The truism that Western art music is characterized by notation has created a feedback loop—Western notation transmits Western music—that can foreclose other interpretations. The dense sites of interaction characteristic of European cities, ports, and courts, however, made more sounds familiar to Western ears (and available to Western notation) than has been presumed by such facile correlations. We cannot assume that racially marked or foreign musical sound will stand out against the familiar textures of Western art music or that such sounds will be immediately audible as such to the modern musical ear.

Axiom 3: Class Interacted with Race in Complex Ways

Members of the European elite were accustomed to socializing across geographic and linguistic borders in highly stratified fashion, deploying complex diplomatic protocols of procedure and courtesy. The rules of international diplomacy secured military treaties, trade agreements, and marriage contracts through a presumption of mutually legible subjectivity, sovereignty, and the binding power of the written word (properly witnessed, signed, and sealed). The shared horizon of elite humanity can be seen in the interactions of the Medici court with Emir Fakhr ad-Dīn and his entourage, discussed in this book's first chapter. Such frameworks also marked the early European incursions into Africa and the Americas, with ships' captains, explorers, and agents of the would-be colonial powers seeking local sovereigns for diplomatic discussion.[1]

By beginning with Fakhr ad-Dīn and finishing with Giovannino Buonaccorsi, this book implies a trajectory from presumed class equivalence across linguistic, geographic, and even religious boundaries, to a situation in which racialized difference itself functioned as a categorical hierarchy of human types in which Blackness signified as servile. Though my work here does not itself contain enough examples to sustain this claim, the implication resonates within broader histories of race in the West.

The aggressive colonial aspirations of early modern Europe resulted in the forcible occupation of large swaths of land and required a mental gymnastics in which the sovereign subjects of foreign territories were disenfranchised. Nurtured by wealth extracted from colonial territories and the labor of enslaved workers, the European middle class clamored for access to educational opportunities and cultural products that had heretofore been restricted to elite consumption. The upward social mobility of considerable portions of the European population, coupled with the vast number of Africans who were sold as chattel and shipped across the Atlantic, served to reconfigure phenotype as a categorical marker of difference. If the French, the Spanish, or even the Venetians had once seemed foreign by Florentine standards, shared epistemologies of European identity came into sharp focus when juxtaposed with the "uncivilized" expanse of the New World or the "barbarous" space of the African interior. Political sovereignty was expanded to the category of whiteness writ large and denied to Black and indigenous individuals.

To understand this shift, the term *razza* is particularly useful, for through the category of "lineage," *razza* demonstrates the extent to which "class" (as it is now understood) was once fundamentally biological, rigid in ways that have since been obfuscated by the modern promise of fluid capital, social mobility, and universal education. In the modern, capitalist West, we can all aspire to the role of employer—to be the boss (or even the "girl boss")—even while entire (racially marked) categories of humans are restricted, en masse, to the lower strata of the service economy. In early modernity, the categories

---

[1] Herman L. Bennett, *African Kings and Black Slaves: Sovereignty and Dispossession in the Early Modern Atlantic*, The Early Modern Americas (Philadelphia: University of Pennsylvania Press, 2019).

of "serva" and "padrona" were heritable; the terms described fundamentally different types or lineages of people. And, as Italian dramatic norms reiterated again and again, true identity was inherent in and passed through the body; the conventions of *travestimento*, *imbroglio*, and late-in-show revelation reinstated the social order at the end of each evening's entertainment. Parents and lovers reunited despite years apart (often in captivity), *padrona* and *serva* returned to their proper (inherited) place. "Race"—in its modern and pseudoscientific formulations—retains the connotations of lineage and biology that the more expansive category of *razza* once extended to other markers of human difference. *Razza* shows that race was not invented in the service of colonialism or mass racial slavery but that—flushed with the success of the colonialist enterprise and the vast economic engines of transatlantic slavery—early modern whiteness was imbued with a fluidity that allowed it to supersede some of the limitations of *razza* as they had previously been impressed upon white subjects, extending the possibility of sovereignty to all educated, white, male citizens and in a limited fashion to other white people.

There are musical consequences to this categorical system that our own, theoretically more mobile society has served to conceal. Hearing the category of *razza* in sonic terms implicates both race and class in early modern music making through the notion that the voice reliably and transparently expresses the body and character.

Axiom 4: To Have a Voice Was Not Necessarily to Have Agency

In modern, democratic terms, to have a voice is to participate in society or politics, to speak up or claim agency. Yet the voices discussed in this book make it clear that not all voices were (or are) agential, even as such voices could be heard, actively listened to, and consumed by elite audiences. The exploitation of enslaved performers (and professional singers) as entertainment forces the performance of contented subjugation, objectifying the bodies of performers as playback devices and their sounds as an acclamation of willing participation. Listening critically to such voices, exemplified by the Black castrato, underscores the potential violence of musical labor and the insidious valence of voice as an expressive, autonomous channel for self-expression. Enslaved voices point up the contradictions at the heart of words such as "agency," "subjectivity," and "entertainment." Etymologically, an agent is one who is authorized to speak or act on behalf of a more powerful entity. Similarly, subjectivity can be understood to represent the sense of oneself as a human being within the context of laws and social rules to which one is involuntarily subject. For the enslaved, who were not free to voice their inner thoughts or desires but instead could serve only as the voice of those in power over them (like the Moro trombetto, discussed in this book's fifth chapter) or as entertainment for their social superiors, voice can only be misread as agency through a presumption of contentment or as an expression of a servile nature. To have a voice, particularly a trained singing voice, was not necessarily reflective of agential speech or song.

Axiom 5: The Racialized Voices That Coalesced in the Seventeenth Century Have Had Long, Durable Afterlives

During the seventeenth century, sonic epistemologies of the racialized subject consolidated around the figure of the Black servant or enslaved retainer in ways that conditioned and preempted blackface minstrelsy and sonic racial stereotypes of the nineteenth and twentieth centuries. Histories of blackface performance and "Blacksound" have gestured at earlier theatrical models of black masking, particularly at the black masks that were traditionally worn by the commedia dell'arte character of Arlecchino, who became Harlequin on the British pantomime stage.[2] Still, this body of scholarship has yet to account for the extent to which seventeenth-century acoustemologies of voice, race, and slavery provided a vocabulary and a sonic script for legible (and limited) representations of Black subjectivity, though the work of Robert Hornback has made a forceful argument for the importance of early modern theatrical examples.[3] The extent to which racialized sound is embedded into Western art music through the conventions of operatic style and genre distinctions has not been fully recognized. Even a cursory examination of minstrelsy's acknowledged early precursors demonstrates the importance of seventeenth-century sonic and characterological legacies to the later

---

[2] Henry Louis Gates, *Figures in Black: Words, Signs, and the "Racial" Self* (Oxford: Oxford University Press, 1987), 51–58; O'Brien, *Harlequin Britain*, 117–137; Felicity Nussbaum, "'Mungo Here, Mungo There': Charles Dibdin and Racial Performance," in *Charles Dibdin and Late Georgian Culture*, ed. Oskar Cox Jensen, David Kennerley, and Ian Newman (Oxford: Oxford University Press, 2018), 26–27.

[3] Hornback, *Racism*.

formations of stereotypical theatrical Blackness and the visual, sonic, and gestural afterlives of the practices examined throughout this book. In what follows, I turn to a late-eighteenth-century precursor of blackface minstrelsy in order to foreground the specific ways in which seventeenth-century operatic practices of Black representation—familiar now from throughout this book—were incorporated, rehearsed, and recycled into the later repertoire.

The Padlock (Perf. 1768)

Several moments in blackface minstrelsy history are recognized as particularly formative. Crucially, the 1830s can be identified as a decade of active consolidation and articulation: largely Irish and working-class white communities in North America bricolaged popular and traditional songs to gross visual and characterological stereotypes of Blackness, including Zip Coon and Jim Crow.[4] These figures have a characteristic repertoire of sonic and gestural material that circulated through local theatrical routes, sheet music publications, and the sound-ways of repeated entertainment in public and in private. From earlier still, the blackface servant character of Mungo, from *The Padlock*, a "comic opera" first performed in London in 1768, has attracted considerable scholarly attention as a historical "first." *The Padlock* has spoken dialogue and sung interludes, text by Isaac Bickerstaffe, music by Charles Dibdin, and a long performance history on both sides of the Atlantic. The work was presented 142 times over eight seasons at Drury Lane by the original London cast,[5] and in eighteenth-century North America, there were, according to Marianne Cooley, fourteen known productions in New York City (where the work was staged within nine months of the London premiere), thirty-two productions in Philadelphia, and performances in Savannah, Charleston, Richmond, Washington (Kentucky), Baltimore, Newport, and Boston.[6] The work was also performed in eighteenth-century Jamaica, where it was staged at least ten times between 1777 and 1813.[7] The show was a huge success, and so was the Mungo character, who was memorialized in printed

---

[4] Morrison, "Sound(s) of Subjection." See also Ayanna Thompson, *Blackface*, Object Lessons (New York: Bloomsbury, 2021).

[5] Robert Fahrner, "David Garrick Presents *The Padlock*: An 18th-Century 'Hit,'" *Theatre Survey* 13 (1972): 52.

[6] Marianne Cooley, "An Early Representation of African-American English," in *Language Variety in the South Revisited*, ed. Robin Sabino and Cynthia Bernstein (Tuscaloosa: University of Alabama Press, 1997), 51.

[7] Nussbaum, "'Mungo Here,'" 24n7.

imagery, souvenirs such as tea caddies and decorative handkerchiefs, masquerade costumes, and frequent references in conversation and the press.[8] Gretchen Gerzina notes that on the heels of the play's success, "Mungo" became a British slang term for both "servile" and "uppity" Blacks; the term is still cited as such in the Oxford English Dictionary.[9] The definitive nature of Mungo as a representation of Black comicity can be seen in Ira Aldridge's performances of *The Padlock* in a double-header with Shakespeare's *Othello* when he toured England in 1833, billed as the first Black actor to walk the London stage.[10] Other sources suggest that a Black actor may have played the role in a Dublin production as early as 1770.[11]

The resounding success and wide dissemination of *The Padlock* and the Mungo character consolidate the importance of show and role in the history of blackface minstrelsy. Contemporary reviews lauded the role as "well drawn" and "almost wholly new to the stage,"[12] and the sense of Mungo as a "radically new representation of black servitude"[13] has persisted in criticism and commentary.[14] The perceived novelty of Mungo has been theorized on three fronts (each of which I discuss in more detail below): his use of Black dialect; his glitzy, boldly striped costume; and his "cheeky" character, "alternating servility and humorous impertinence."[15] Each of these elements has clear precursors in the seventeenth-century Italian context, particularly in the Black servant and enslaved representations that were prevalent in the court and operatic contexts. Their re-citation and re-performance in the figure of Mungo is not necessarily an indication of what Mungo's composer and first performer, Dibdin, might have called direct "assistance" but rather of the epistemological force of racialized voices as they cohered around characteristic types. Here, too, the concept of *razza* (or "lineage") is crucial, for we can simultaneously point to the characterological lineage of the Mungo role

---

[8] Julie A. Carlson, "New Lows in Eighteenth-Century Theater: The Rise of Mungo," *European Romantic Review* 18, no. 2 (2007): 142. See also W. J. Lawrence, "An Old English Music Handkerchief," *Musical Quarterly* 3, no. 4 (1917): 503–508.

[9] Gretchen Gerzina, *Black London: Life before Emancipation* (London: John Murray, 1995), 10.

[10] Joyce Green MacDonald, "Acting Black: *Othello*, *Othello* Burlesques, and the Performance of Blackness," in *Ira Aldridge: The African Roscius*, ed. Bernth Lindfors (Rochester, NY: University of Rochester Press, 2010), 135–156.

[11] Chakravarty, "What Is the History," 197.

[12] The citations are taken from the *Critical Review* (November 1768), as cited in Fahrner, "David Garrick Presents," 58.

[13] Miller, *Slaves to Fashion*, 31.

[14] The purported "newness" of US blackface minstrelsy has come under pressure. See Hornback, *Racism*.

[15] The quotes come, respectively, from Carlson, "New Lows," 139; Hans Nathan, "Negro Impersonation in Eighteenth-Century England," *Notes* 2, no. 4 (1945): 253.

and the importance of this role in emergent categories of racialized thought. Analyzing Mungo in light of his Italian forebears demonstrates the extent to which the racialized voices of seventeenth-century Black individuals and Black characters have been lost to history, even as scholars have noted the reliance of *The Padlock*'s composer, Dibdin, on Italian musical forms and that of the playwright, Bickerstaffe, on that "longstanding European theatrical tradition, the comic servant."[16] For modern scholars, "the comic servant" has been "a device designed to speak more to a class relationship than it did to race-based slavery";[17] however, with the racially marked voices of Buonaccorsi and Caralì ringing in our ears, we can think of Mungo's lineage differently. The *razza* of servility and the seventeenth century's crucial articulation of voice, slavery, and race to popular comic song help to contextualize the ways in which sound signified and continues to signify though race, subjectivity, and agency.

Voice

Bickerstaffe and Dibdin's Mungo "spoke an identifiable version of West Indian speech—a first for the London stage"[18]—at least, we might add, in terms of the transcription of such speech into the play text and song lyrics. From the outset, Mungo's words were endowed with a putative authenticity grounded in earwitness testimony. The role was initially intended for the white actor John Moody, who had spent several years during the 1740s in the Jamaican colonial town of Kingston. Kathleen Wilson notes that Moody had previously garnered praise in his stint as a drunken Black servant in James Townley's *High Life below Stairs* of 1759, "a performance which bore the marks of Moody's facility with Jamaican patois."[19] According to Dibdin's autobiography, "The part [of Mungo] would never have been written as it is but for Moody's suggestions, who Had been in the West-Indies, and knew, of course, the dialect."[20] Dibdin also asserts that he deliberately wrote the music

---

[16] Melinda Lawson, "Imagining Slavery: Representations of the Peculiar Institution on the Northern Stage, 1776–1860," *Journal of the Civil War Era* 1, no. 1 (2011): 30.

[17] Lawson, "Imagining Slavery," 30.

[18] Miller, *Slaves to Fashion*, 28–29.

[19] Kathleen Wilson, "Introduction: Three Theses on Performance and History," *Eighteenth-Century studies* 48, no. 4 (2015): 382.

[20] Dibdin published his autobiography in 1803; here I cite from Wilson, "Introduction," 382. She comments dryly that it is worth "[l]eaving aside for now the notion of a 'negro dialect,' apparently culled from the twenty or so West African language groups spoken by the enslaved in Jamaica." It is

such that it would be too difficult for Moody to sing, allowing the composer himself to take on the role, which he reportedly did with public "reluctance and secret indignation": "I knew what I could do with it, and I knew I ought to have had it from the beginning."[21]

It should be noted that in subsequent years, Dibdin composed a number of songs in similarly idiomatic representations of Black speech. These include "Kickaraboo," reproduced and analyzed in some detail by Hans Nathan in 1945.[22] Several of Dibdin's "Black" dialect songs were reproduced in songbooks that circulated in North America and made appearances in later minstrel shows. For his part, Dibdin featured such songs in one-man performances that he gave seated at a keyboard, imitating a range of different ethnicities and English stock characters through linguistic and narrative means. Dibdin's "Table Entertainments" (as he called them) were thus entirely reliant on sound and speech patterns for their dramatic impact.[23] These songs demonstrate how clearly voice was indicative of character through the sound and quality of language and register and how crucial Mungo's Black voice was to his reception as a new and authentic representation of Black subjectivity. Much like *gergo*, Sabir, or the *minoranza alloglotta* used to represent the speech of enslaved laborers and recent immigrants on the seventeenth-century Italian stage, Bickerstaffe's patois and that of Dibdin's later songs involve mispronunciations and ungrammatical formulations to comic effect.

The plot of *The Padlock* was derived from a short story by Cervantes, first published in Spanish as "El celoso estremeño" in 1613 and widely circulated in English translations as "The Jealous Husband," numerous versions of which were published during the eighteenth century.[24] Cervantes's tale is

---

also worth noting that the performer who created the role in New York (Lewis Hallam the Younger) had also spent time in Jamaica. Cooley notes of Hallam: "His success, like Moody's role as an adviser, was attributed to his study of the dialect and manners of African-Americans in Jamaica, where the Company had stayed from 1754 to 1758 and where he had married a West Indian." Cooley, "An Early Representation," 52.

[21] Cited from Wilson, "Introduction," 382; Fahrner, "David Garrick Presents," 63.
[22] See Nathan, "Negro Impersonation," particularly 245–250. I note that Nathan assumes "kickaraboo" to be a nonsense word, "whose approximate modern equivalent seems to be 'Kicking the bucket,'" (248); however, its use in accounts of the Middle Passage suggest that it was a word or phrase of African origin meaning "We are dying." See the use of the term by ship's surgeon Thomas Trotter in an account from 1790, cited and discussed in Danielle Skeehan, "Black Atlantic Acoustemologies and the Maritime Archive," in *Acoustemologies in Contact: Sounding Subjects and Modes of Listening in Early Modernity*, ed. Emily Wilbourne and Suzanne G. Cusick (Cambridge: Open Book, 2021), 121.
[23] Nathan, "Negro Impersonation."
[24] All the citations below come from Miguel de Cervantes Saavedra, "The Jealous Husband," in *Instructive Novels: Viz. The Story of Two Damsels, The Lady Cornelia Bentivoglio, The Generous Lover,*

ripe for operatic adaptation, since music—and its seductive, persuasive power—figures as central plot device. The cast is full of familiar stock figures of the Italian and Spanish theatrical imaginary: a miserly old man, his nubile though naive wife, a chaperone who mourns the passing of her younger years and the amorous opportunities she once had, a handsome young lover who has fallen for the young bride, and a host of servants and enslaved retainers—most important, for our purposes, a music-loving Black eunuch, Luys, whose task is to guard the door (and thus protect the chastity of the young wife); in the comic opera version of the story, Luys becomes Mungo.

Few words of direct speech are reported in the Cervantes story, and those few are glossed in standard grammar even when the surrounding text describes their inaccuracy. Critics have thus emphasized that the Black dialect affected or imitated by Bickerstaffe and Dibdin's Mungo is a new addition. Yet two other enslaved Black characters from the original story do speak in marked fashion (I quote here, and throughout the discussion, from an eighteenth-century translation that was in wide circulation): "two blackamoor she-slaves, who knew no other language but their own, save a little broken Spanish."[25] One of these women is given a name—Guiomar—and, as I argue below, provides the inspiration for several other aspects of Mungo's character that modern critics have mistakenly considered new. It seems very likely that Cervantes had the *habla de negros* in mind as he wrote his story; the prevalence of the Black voice in seventeenth-century Spanish literary and theatrical representations has been highlighted in the work of Nicholas R. Jones.[26] Mungo's speech thus conflates the "new immigrant" voice of Guiomar and her companion with that of Luys rather than inventing it wholesale, while modernizing (and authorizing) the particular mispronunciations of Mungo's role through reference to British colonial outposts in the West Indies rather than the quotidian "Portugueze" or Brazilian inflections that are attributed to Guiomar by Cervantes (which, in turn, reflect the Spanish playwright's daily encounters with an enslaved Black community in his own time).[27]

The Force of Blood, The Spanish Lady, The Jealous Husband, trans. Thomas Shelton (Glasgow: Robert Urie, 1750), 285–342.

[25] Cervantes, "Jealous Husband," 292.
[26] See Jones, *Staging Habla de Negros*.
[27] Cervantes, "Jealous Husband," 329.

One significant change to the voice of Cervantes's Luys as he was reimagined by Bickerstaffe and Dibdin is that of vocal register or pitch. Luys is explicitly described as a eunuch, and the lover comments to him, "that organ of thy voice tells me, that it is a treble, and thou shouldst therefore sing wondrous clear and well."[28] The Black castrato voice is—as I discussed in relationship to Buonaccorsi's soprano in my twelfth chapter—made for music in a very literal sense.[29] Through voice, Luys is emasculated, simultaneously authorizing his presence within the largely female space of the house and underscoring a love or inclination for music that is violently (and, according to Cervantes) naturally manifest in his (Black, castrated) body. Mungo, in contrast, sings with the voice of an unaltered male. Indeed, his place within the house as a possible threat to the young bride's chastity is never addressed in *The Padlock*, leading Monica Miller to note that in the later version of the story, the Black man is emasculated by default.[30]

Dibdin's music for Mungo is (as with all the male parts) notated in treble clef; yet, the accompanimental texture throughout the opera and, specifically, the placement of Mungo's voice below that of the lover, Leander, in the *quartetto* chorus, "Let's be merry," indicates a baritone range (see Musical Example E.1).

Importantly, by the eighteenth century, the musical-stylistic associations of class hierarchy had shifted in comparison with the earlier dramatic repertoires that were discussed in the main part of this book. Up through the middle of the seventeenth century, serious, noble, elite-class characters were represented by recitative or arioso music, with complex, through-composed forms. Metrical music with predictable tonal and rhythmic structures was closely aligned with lower-class, comic characters. This I have labeled the "songlike" music of the (Black) buffoon, discussing the extent to which the production of such song provides a soundtrack associated with entertainment and simple unaffected joy, effectively justifying the perceived suitability of such subjects for enslavement and servitude from the perspective of the (white, elite or middle-class) listener. The increased popularity of opera, however, and the ensuing normality of sung drama led to an increased

---

[28] Cervantes, "Jealous Husband," 300.
[29] On the castrato as a man-made device, see Gordon, "Castrato Meets."
[30] "Mungo's master opens the opera by singing, 'My doors shall be lock'd / My windows be block'd, / No male in my house, / Not so much as a mouse, / Then horns, horns, [of a cuckold], I defy you' (act I, sc. i), insisting that no man will gain entrance into his house, while also implying that no man (besides himself) already lives there. In *The Padlock*, Mungo is not a man, not a mouse, apparently not a threat to the chastity of the beautiful woman confined within." See Miller, *Slaves to Fashion*, 33.

Musical Example E.1. "Let's be merry," opening measures of the *quartetto* from *The Padlock* (perf. London, 1768). Text by Isaac Bickerstaffe, music by Charles Dibdin.

musicalization of operatic music along with a decrease in the quantity of recitative and a simultaneous increase in its formulaic construction. In later operas, a greater range of characters got to be musical, though the ways in which they expressed themselves and their audible characteristics continued to be differentiated through sonic means. These differences manifest at the level of linguistic and stylistic register, with elaborate similes and metaphors decorating the convoluted and highly poetic language written for elite, serious characters, which were then reflected in melodic writing with long, technically challenging vocal lines and dense ornamentation. The virtuosity of opera seria castrati roles such as those composed for celebrated performers like Farinelli or Senesino are indicative of this serious yet exceedingly musical style. The castrati who performed in England during the eighteenth century were exclusively imported from Italy; they commanded lucrative contracts and appeared in elite repertoires such as opera and oratorio. To cast

Mungo as such would have marked him as foreign and emasculated, though also as exceedingly cultured. Indeed, it is the lovers' roles in Dibdin's music that claim some allegiance with the Italianate vocality of the castrato through ornamentation and elaborate melodic lines.

In Cervantes's story, it is explicitly through music and Luys's love thereof that the ardent young *innamorato* weasels his way into the tightly locked house. He begins from the street outside, playing and singing "some pleasant witty ballads of Moors and Moorish women":[31]

> And Luys the Negro laying his ears as close as he could between the two doors, was so mightily taken with this music, that he would have opened the door with a very good will, and did endeavour it, but all in vain, that he might to his greater contentment more fully hear it; such, and so great is the inclination which your Negroes naturally have unto music.[32]

Here Cervantes states that this inclination to music is naturally Black and characteristic of Black listeners in general, yet as the story unfolds, all listeners (regardless of race, gender, and social class) fall under the singer's spell. Even in this first serenade scene, described above, "as many as past along that street made a stand to hear,"[33] and eventually the chaperone, the young bride, "four white female slaves" ("burned . . . with a hot iron in their cheeks and forehead" by the old man, "setting his mark upon them"),[34] as well as the two Black "she-slaves"—"All the servants of the house, great and small, black and white"—succumb to the lover's song.[35] In the English adaptation, Mungo, too, loves music—as evinced by his set piece, "Let me when my heart a sinking / hear the sweet Guittar a clinking," discussed further below—but the telescoped timeline of the comic opera means that both Mungo and the chaperone hear the *innamorato*'s serenade at the same time and are thus seduced together.

That the music for *The Padlock* is "Italianate" has been widely accepted by scholars, though the specific qualities of this designation are rarely explored. In the dedicatory letter from the music's original publication, Dibdin asserts:

---

[31] Cervantes, "Jealous Husband," 299.
[32] Cervantes, "Jealous Husband," 299.
[33] Cervantes, "Jealous Husband," 299.
[34] Cervantes, "Jealous Husband," 292.
[35] Cervantes, "Jealous Husband," 299.

I am indeed told there are some who affect not only to doubt my having set the Musick of the Padlock, but even to name the Composer, some Italian Master (God knows who) that I stole it from, but if any such Composer Exists, my Enemies would do well to produce his Works, for I Declare, I am not Conscious of having received any Assistance, in what I here do my self the Honour to present to you, but from the Author of the Opera, and my obligations to his Taste and Judgement I am very ready to Acknowledge.[36]

This simultaneous disavowal and advertisement of the purported Italianicity of the music has been sufficient for most critics, though we would do well to consider the matter further. What signified for English audiences of the later eighteenth century as Italian musical style was the operatic works of George F. Handel, though by 1768, the German-born, Italian-trained, naturalized English composer had been dead for nearly a decade. Handel's long run of opera seria productions, featuring Italian singers, loomed large in audience memory.

Dibdin's music is strongly tonal, often elaborating a single chord for entire phrases. Small melodic units are repeated, often identically, and in instrumental instantiations with alternating forte and piano dynamics. Phrases are predictable and balanced, in multiples of two or four measures.[37] This is true for comic and more serious characters alike, as can be seen in a comparison of Mungo's song "Let me when my heart a-sinking" with the young bride-to-be Leonora's apostrophe to freedom "Was I a Shepherd's Maid to keep" (see Musical Examples E.2 and E.3). Both begin with an arpeggio of the tonic chord over an orchestral tremolo. The vocal ornaments of Leonora's part get gradually more complicated, and here we can hear an echo of castrato virtuosity as associated with a serious operatic sound. Notably, it is the young lovers' parts that include such ornaments—almost exclusively as melismatic runs—while the comic characters sing largely syllabic passages. Never does Mungo sing more than two notes to a single syllable. This difference maps complexity and high art (operatic) associations onto the lovers and simplicity, popular, or low art associations onto the enslaved Black servant.

---

[36] From Dibdin's dedication to David Garrick's wife, in Charles Dibdin, *The Padlock: A Comic Opera as It Is Performed at the Theatre-Royal in Drury-Lane* (London: J. Johnston, 1769), n.p.

[37] Nussbaum notes, "Some listeners found the rapid repetition of the two- or four-bar phrases annoying but credited it with making the music easy to memorize and imitate." See Nussbaum, "'Mungo Here,'" 32–33.

Musical Example E.2. "Let me when my heart a-sinking," mm. 1–60, as sung by Mungo (Charles Dibdin), from *The Padlock* (perf. London, 1768). Text by Isaac Bickerstaffe, music by Charles Dibdin.

Musical Example E.2. Continued

Musical Example E.2. Continued

Musical Example E.3. "Was I a shepherd's maid to keep," as sung by Leonora (Mrs. Arne), from *The Padlock* (perf. London, 1768). Text by Isaac Bickerstaffe, music by Charles Dibdin.

308 EPILOGO

Musical Example E.3. Continued

Musical Example E.3. Continued

Musical Example E.3. Continued

Musical Example E.3. Continued

Both Leonora and Mungo want to change their situations, yet Leonora's imagined freedom soars and flies (melodically as well as textually) in ways that rely on solidified notions of the musically beautiful and on conventions of sentimental song, while Mungo's desire for liberty is tightly linked to freedom from disagreeable tasks. Under the influence of music, he is distracted to the point where he "soon am cur'd of tinking" (soon is cured of thinking). His voice leaps back and forth in a comic imitation of his master, swinging from his garters; Mungo is unable to conceive of freedom in abstract or ideological terms, and his voice is incapable of the lyrical effusions that would express such ideas.

The difference between these pieces and their affective power is in literary register and melodic quality, even while both rely on the same chordal and structural devices. Crucially, the poetry and music provided for Leonora are expressive and lyrical in ways that the material for Mungo is not. This can be seen at the level of the music itself. Leonora's part provides the musical interest (see, for example, the melodic figuration in mm. 28 and 30, then echoed by the orchestra in m. 35). In contrast, the "music" of Mungo's song fills the pauses between his vocalizations rather than being manifest through his own song (see, for example, the pizzicato "guitar" of mm. 19–22 or the tooting flute of mm. 37–38). These sounds are not part of the music that he creates or that he expresses as indicative of his internal state but instead represent music that distracts him, subjecting him to sound even as it acts on his body in ways that he is incapable of controlling. As such, he entertains his audience, representing a simple, unrefined character for their amusement.

Costume

The second aspect of the Mungo role that has been recognized as new is his "ostentatious silk costume," by some measures, "even more outrageous than his confrontational, unusual accent."[38] Dibdin's outfit, presumably chosen by the impresario David Garrick, is memorialized in at least three commemorative prints, the most famous of which is reproduced as Figure E.1, after page 240.[39] Scholars have disagreed about the valence of Mungo's stripes, with some presuming them a direct citation of clothing practices in Caribbean slavery contexts[40] and others suggesting that the stripes recall an entirely European iconography representing "handicap or liability," in effect, erasing the character's African heritage.[41] The costume itself may well have been recycled from earlier productions in which it was associated with villainous though noble characters.[42]

In the context of this book, it is difficult not to read the red and white stripes of Mungo's outfit as a direct reference to Buonaccorsi's similarly

---

[38] Miller, *Slaves to Fashion*, 29.
[39] "The character [of Mungo] was depicted in three different prints dating between 1769 and 1773: the first, *Mr. Dibdin in the Character of Mungo*, was produced by the prolific engraver and London printseller Butler Clowes; the second, printed by Carington Bowles, was a slight variation on the first; and the third formed part of a collection of small engravings entitled *Dramatic Characters* that were available to buy individually from Robert Sayer's print shop on Fleet Street in the 1770s." Prathiba Kanakamedala, "Staging Atlantic Slavery," in *The Oxford Handbook of the Georgian Theatre, 1737–1832*, ed. Julia Swindells and David Francis Taylor (Oxford: Oxford University Press, 2014), 676.
[40] Nussbaum, "'Mungo Here,'" 30.
[41] Kanakamedala, "Staging Atlantic Slavery," 676–677.
[42] On Garrick's costuming conventions, see Raymond J. Pentzell, "Garrick's Costuming," *Theatre Survey* 10 (1969): 18–42, particularly 30; Fahrner, "David Garrick Presents," 52–70.

spectacular and identically patterned outfit as rendered in the double portrait by Volterrano. As Miller has noted, "The costume works on Mungo because ... black slaves resident in England ... were often used and regarded as luxury items and ornaments rather than as laborers."[43] If the shared red stripes of these two images reflect a degree of coincidence, they both draw upon a language of conspicuous consumption. Miller writes that "what made these slaves conspicuous was, in large part, the irony-laden dichotomy of their status as debased beings in uniforms of sumptuous dress."[44]

The British "vogue" for "luxury blacks" ran from approximately 1650 to 1800,[45] emerging (much like British colonial expansion) somewhat belatedly in comparison with the European continent. Certainly, in Italy, we can trace the fashion back as far as Isabella d'Este in the late fifteenth century and iconographical exemplars to the paintings of Titian in the early sixteenth. Dibdin's Mungo costume similarly recycled extant signifiers; in doing so, however, Garrick and Dibdin did not create something new but instead sutured Mungo's apparel to the striped liveries worn by legions of Black boys in northern Italian courts. Given the considerable quantity of portraiture that documents the practice and remains extant even today, it seems unlikely that Garrick and Dibdin would have been entirely insensible of the connotations.[46]

Character

The third "new" aspect of Mungo's performance as identified by critics is his "sassy," "cheeky" personality, which differs from Luys's more naive affect and has allowed some scholars to read Mungo as part of an abolitionist discourse.[47] As I intimated earlier, this change can be traced to the "negress Guiomar" from Cervantes's original story. For example, Guiomar alone is skeptical of the lover's assurances of good behavior:

> Hereupon, said Guiomar the negress, who could speak a little broken Spanish; for my part, swear or swear not, be he what he will, let him come

---

[43] Miller, *Slaves to Fashion*, 39.
[44] Miller, *Slaves to Fashion*, 49.
[45] The word "vogue" and the date range come from Peter Freyer, as cited by Miller, *Slaves to Fashion*, 48. "Luxury blacks," however, is Miller's term.
[46] See Kaplan, "Titian's 'Laura Dianti'"; Kaplan, "Giovannino Moro."
[47] The quotes come from Miller, *Slaves to Fashion*, 41; Carlson, "New Lows," 139. For a discussion of Mungo in relationship to abolition, see Lawson, "Imagining Slavery," 25–55.

in; for though he swear never so much, when he is once in, he will forget all his oaths.[48]

Later in the story, left behind as "centinel" lest the drugged elderly husband wake to find the lover within the house, Guiomar comments pointedly on her own racialized status: "The black must stay, whilst the white must play."[49] Later still, her mocking impersonations of the house chaperone garner laughter from the other enslaved women:

> But that which moved most laughter in those that heard them, were the words which Guiomar the negress uttered; who, for that she was a Portugueze, spake no good Spanish, yet very unhappily, and in a strange kind of witty manner did play upon [the chaperone], taxing her loose and wanton carriage.[50]

We should note that Guiomar's humor imbricates the savvy, disgruntled attitude that marks her performance (and that of Mungo) with broken or fragmented speech patterns representative of the foreign presence in Europe. She, like the various Black and enslaved characters whose voices have been discussed elsewhere in this book, is a familiar presence for her readers, indicative of the considerable number of enslaved individuals who were living in Europe and part of the culture that produced and consumed such stories and their theatrical representations. Lining Mungo up alongside these comic Black theatrical forebears helps to contextualize his arrival on the English-speaking stage, and his dissemination through North America underscores the ways in which later impersonations of blackface and Black voices drew upon and presumed the coherence of sound, subjectivity, and musical/characterological identity.

As a pendant to this book, the radical newness of Mungo's characterization is rendered immediately dubious. Mungo's "Blacksound" reiterates the conjunction of servitude and popular song that is—by now—familiar from seventeenth-century operatic sources. My intent here is not to claim an unbroken line of direct influence between Buonaccorsi's Iolao, Cavalli's Vaffrino, and Bickerstaffe and Dibdin's Mungo—as if the librettist and composer took "assistance" from an earlier score. Rather, I note that the similarities and consistency in the specific musical-theatrical vocality of the enslaved Black

---

[48] Cervantes, "Jealous Husband," 320.
[49] Cervantes, "Jealous Husband," 322.
[50] Cervantes, "Jealous Husband," 329.

character reflect an epistemology of racialized voice that is tightly coupled to buffoonery, to popular musical sounds, to entertainment, and to *razza*—as a defining and heritable set of traits associated with character type and classed categories of the human.

***

If the similarities between Mungo and his Italian forebears help to illustrate the relevance of the material covered in this book to historians and scholars of later time periods, so do the differences help scholars of the seventeenth century grasp what was novel about racialized voices of the Seicento. Most important, in the later (eighteenth-century) work, musicality itself is not a marker for enslavement, though the popular or "low" style of Mungo's music persists, sharply differentiating his modes of expression from those of the "high" style of the lover characters. Not only does this low/high dichotomy re-emerge in the 1830s as an essential structural element of the North American minstrelsy circuit, but it also persists today in the moralizing associations of classical or Western art music as a civilizing force. The appreciation of complex, cerebral, and transcendentally beautiful music is taught at the college level as a means of cultural uplift, disciplining students into a decorous relationship to musical sound that—ideally—will transport them out and away from their everyday, bodily experience. Popular musics, in contrast, are understood to act directly on the body, moving one to dance and to distraction, as a lowest common denominator of physical and musical pleasure. The presumed moral force of high art music can be traced back far further than the origins of opera (cf. Plato); however, in the pursuit of voice, it is the representational musical turn of the seventeenth century's "new musics" that has made this project possible. The voices of operatic characters represent their interior states and the drama of their interactions to a degree that has been effectively neutralized in modern reception. These voices—scripted into musical sound—were so persuasive and so imitated as to affect other, non-operatic musical genres, in effect creating an acoustemology of self and subjectivity articulated through vocal sound that modern auditors need to work to decouple.

The foreign, Black, indigenous, and otherwise marked voices amplified in this book demonstrate precisely how circumscribed such voices were in agential and expressive terms—with long-lasting consequences for the bodies who labored to produce such voices. In this account, musical sound and vocal conventions are far from neutral. To listen for race in the echoes of music history requires what Giovannino Buonaccorsi called a "subtle sense of hearing." "*Udite!*" he warns us: "Listen up!"

APPENDIX

Archival References to Enslaved, Moorish, and "Turkish" ("Non-Christian") Individuals

This Appendix provides a list of archival references to *schiavi* (enslaved people, including enslaved Europeans), *mori* (Blacks), and *turchi* (lit. "Turks" but commonly Muslim) that I found in the documents I consulted during the research for this project—plus a few other foreigners who seemed to deserve special mention. Note that some of the uses of the term "moro" cited here may have been intended as nicknames or family names for white individuals rather than racialized descriptions; not all of the individuals listed here are explicitly identified as enslaved, though some are. Many uses of "moro" or "mora" are accompanied by the word "di"—a possessive pronoun used to show that the individual "belongs" to someone else. The list is sorted into different categories, based on the presence of identifiable names: alphabetically by given name (where possible), and by date where names are not used. I have separately grouped references to anonymous people "owned" (explicitly or by implication) directly by the Medici family. Please note that the spelling of many names including place names is highly approximate; these references were culled from handwritten documents, and with regard to ethnically unfamiliar names, Italian scribes were themselves quite inconsistent. As a consequence, if you are tracking an individual, you will need to look for various spellings, to check both the given and baptismal names, as well as any common nicknames, and to consider entries where an explicit name has not been given. The Appendix is divided into three tables: (1) Individuals Identified by Name (note that this list includes many individuals owned by the Medici family); (2) Anonymous Individuals Who Can Be Strongly Linked to the Medici Family; and (3) Anonymous Individuals and Groups of People.

Individuals Identified by Name

Reference (as given in document)	Baptismal name (if known)	Other descriptors in document	Year	Citation	Owner (if known)
Abissino Moretto	Giovanni Battista	Etiopio, abissino, moretto, approx. 14y.	1630	I-Fca, Pia Casa, 1	Maria Maddalena of Austria
Abissino Moretto	Giovanni Battista	8/29/1630.	1630	I-Fd, Battesimi m, reg. 38, fg. 55	
Achamed Turco		Stiavo, turco, from Cairo, approx. 47y.	1627	I-Fca, Pia Casa, 1	Marchese Coloreto
Achemet di Machmet		Stiavo, turco, from Trapani in Barbary. Worked in the stables for the Grand Duke.	1612	I-Fca, Pia Casa, 1	SAS
Achmet d'Asan d'Alep	Cosimo	Turco, stiavo, from Cairo, moro bianco. Worked in the stables for the Grand Duke.	1611	I-Fca, Pia Casa, 1	SAS
Achmet d'Asan d'Alep	Cosimo	12/11/1611.	1611	I-Fd, Battesimi m, reg. 28, fg. 149	
Adrame		Stiavo, moro, turco, approx. 10y, from Briscia. Purchased in Livorno.	1612	I-Fca, Pia Casa, 1	Paolo Montauti
Aeob		Tartaro, approx. 5y. Described as living in the same house as Curilat di Camvechi, who lives with the Auditore Barducci and is in service to SAS.	1698	I-Fca, Pia Casa, 3	SAS
Agbassi di Sitian		Tartaro, approx. 14y. Described as an "oratore."	1686	I-Fca, Pia Casa, 2	SAS

Name		Year	Description	Archive	Folio
Agnelo Pandolfini gondoliere		1667	For the rent, paid to him and Agnelo Miniati.	I-Fas, Camera del Granduca, f. 38b	1r
Agniolo	[Agniolo Pandolfini?]	1666	Money to cover the rent on the house that stores the gondola.	I-Fas, Camera del Granduca, f. 35b	107r
Agniolo della Gondola	[Agniolo Pandolfini?]	1665		I-Fas, Camera del Granduca, f. 34b	103v
Agniolo Pandolfini		1664	Possibly *il morino della gondola*, since this document lists Agniolo Miniati, *capo pescha*, and Agniolo Pandolfini as having received money to cover the rent of a house that serves to store the fishing equipment and "robe della gondola."	I-Fas, Camera del Granduca, f. 33b	123r
Agniolo Pandolfini		1665	"[P]er la pigione della Casa dove tenghono le Rete come la sua Ricevuta."	I-Fas, Camera del Granduca, f. 34b	117r
Agniolo Pandolfini		1665		I-Fas, Camera del Granduca, f. 34b	124r
Agniolo Pandolfini		1666	Receipt for money to cover rent.	I-Fas, Camera del Granduca, f. 35b	113r
Agniolo Pandolfini	Agniolo Pandolfini	1667	"[L]ire sei disse haver spese in haver fatto condurre alle Gondole gli occhiali e li fatti scaricare a Pisa e a Livorno."	I-Fas, Camera del Granduca, f. 37b	39v
Agniolo Pandolfini		1670	Money to cover the rent on the house that stores the gondola.	I-Fas, Camera del Granduca, f. 41c	74r
Agniolo Pandolfini		1672	Paid for the rent of the house where the gondola is stored, along with the other Agniolo.	I-Fas, Camera del Granduca, f. 42	84l
Agniolo Pandolfini		1673	Rent allowance for the house where the gondola is stored.	I-Fas, Camera del Granduca, f. 42	199r

Reference (as given in document)	Baptismal name (if known)	Other descriptors in document	Year	Citation	Owner (if known)
Agniolo Pandolfinj Gondoliere		Salaried for the year.	1664	I-Fas, Depositeria Generale, parte Antica, f. 397	
Agnolo and Filippo Pandolfini		On a list of the hunters and other personel involved in the hunt at Pisa.	1667	I-Fas, Camera del Granduca, f. 37b	
Agnolo Pandolfini Gondoliere		Rent for a house to store the gondola.	1668	I-Fas, Camera del Granduca, f. 39b	
Aice di Marco Lichechi	Maria Giovanna Felice	Turca, approx. 26y, from Candia.	1666	I-Fca, Pia Casa, 2	Magalotti
Aice di Marco Lichechi	Maria Giovanna Felice	Age in baptismal records given as approx. 18y; 12/8/1666.	1666	I-Fd, Battesimi f, reg. 278, fg. 94	
Aice di Mecmette		Turca, schiava, approx. 25y. Baptized at home while ill, 2/19/1665.	1666	I-Fca, Pia Casa, 2	Sinibaldo Gaddi
Aice di Sachin		Turca, from Dalmatia, approx. 22y, schiava. Domenico de' Melani is presumably the castrato singer mentioned by Freitas: "Domenico Melani (no relation to Atto), who after years of service abroad, returned, ennobled, to his native Florence as a wealthy philanthropist" (Freitas, 5).	1686	I-Fca, Pia Casa, 2	Domenico de' Melani
Aicia		Turca, stiava, "di raze turca," from Vidin, approx. 15y.	1690	I-Fca, Pia Casa, 3	SAS
Aifas di Salech	Giorgio Pazzi	Tucho, stiavo, approx. 30y, from Salonich. Has been enslaved for 8 or 9 years.	1660	I-Fca, Pia Casa, 2	Michele Grifoni

Name	Godparent	Date	Description	Year	Reference	Other
Aifas di Salech	Giorgio Pazzi	10/9/1660		1660	I-Fd, Battesimi m, reg. 53, fg. 53	
Ais di Marco Leie			Turca, stiava, from Dalmatia.	1663	I-Fca, Pia Casa, 2	Vincenzio Allegri
Aise (or Aice) d'Addella e Fattume	Vittoria		Turca, "di color nero," 8y, from Bona. Presumably not the child of Fattume/Caterina, given their respective ages.	1608	I-Fca, Pia Casa, 1	Silvio Piccolomini
Aise (or Aice) d'Addella e Fattume	Vittoria	9/24/1608		1608	I-Fd, Battesimi f, reg. 249, fg. 103	
Aissa di Onoi Umpsa			Turca, approx. 33y, maritata. Fled from Jewish owners in Livorno and wishes to convert. Described as the wife of Barca Moro, possibly the Barca/Flavio Francesco who was baptized six years previously or Barca/Cosimo Francesco Maria.	1672	I-Fca, Pia Casa, 2	
Aissa, wife of Brachia Gianicchi			Turca, approx. 30y. Has two children.	1672	I-Fca, Pia Casa, 2	Cavacci
Aita (or Aica) di Regepe	Maria Angela		Stiava, turca, approx. 9y.	1648	I-Fca, Pia Casa, 1	Lorenzo Strozzi
Aita (or Aica) di Regepe	Maria Angela	8/14/1649.		1649	I-Fd, Battesimi f, reg. 269, fg. 232	

Reference (as given in document)	Baptismal name (if known)	Other descriptors in document	Year	Citation	Owner (if known)
Aivas di Memet		Turco, approx. 16y. The owner, Burij, is a "staffiere" to SAS.	1692	I-Fca, Pia Casa, 3	Giuseppe Burij
Al Coggia	[Ferdinando Medici Battezato]		1666	I-Fas, Camera del Granduca, 34v f. 36b	
Albercader		Stiavo, turco, from Bona. Purchased in Livorno.	1618	I-Fca, Pia Casa, 1	Don Antonio de' Medici
Albraim		Turco, from Transylvania, approx. 34y. Fascinating life story. Had been a slave for many years, polylingual, worked in Flanders and Prague, then became a soldier.	1627	I-Fca, Pia Casa, 1	
Alcima di Amatti Bascia		Turca, approx. 17y.	1665	I-Fca, Pia Casa, 2	Vincenzo del Sera
Alcina di Ecmat Acmammac		Turca, schiava, approx. 18y.	1666	I-Fca, Pia Casa, 2	Vincenzo del Sera
Ali			1637	I-Fas, Camera del Granduca, 9v f. 19b	
Ali		Turco, stiavo, from Candia, approx. 15y.	1655	I-Fca, Pia Casa, 2	Prince Mattias de' Medici
Ali	Ferdinando	Moro, turco, stiavo, from Borno, approx. 16y. Brother of Tuffega/Maria Adelaide.	1657	I-Fca, Pia Casa, 2	Prince Mattias de' Medici
Ali	Ferdinando	7/1/1657.	1657	I-Fd, Battesimi m, reg. 51, fg. 191	

Name	Godparent	Description	Year	Archive ref		Sponsor
Ali		Turco, approx. 13y.	1665	I-Fca, Pia Casa, 2		Alessandro Guadagni
Ali	[Cosimo Maria?]		1666	I-Fas, Camera del Granduca, f. 35b	137v	
Ali	Cosima Maria	Moro, Ali Moro, Ali Negro, from Smyrna, approx. 14y.	1670	I-Fca, Pia Casa, 2		SAS
Ali	Cosima Maria	8/5/1670.	1670	I-Fd, Battesimi m, reg. 58, fg. 22		
Ali		Turco, schiavo, approx. 16y. Was taken into slavery at a very young age.	1692	I-Fca, Pia Casa, 3		Francesco Malegonnelli
Ali (or Eli)	Antonio Medici	Stiavo, from Cairo.	1612	I-Fca, Pia Casa, 1		SAS
Ali Agha	Antonio Medici	Turco, moro, etiope, from Scio, approx. 19y.	1696	I-Fca, Pia Casa, 3		SAS
Ali Agha		7/1/1696.	1696	I-Fd, Battesimi m, reg. 71, fg. 9		
Ali ben'Asen		Turco, stiavo, from Tripoli in Barbary.	1616	I-Fca, Pia Casa, 1		SAS
Ali d'Assman		Turco, from Tunisia, approx. 15y.	1684	I-Fca, Pia Casa, 2		
Ali del Qu Veli	Giovanni Battista	Stiavo, from Constantinople, mother also enslaved, approx. 12y.	1606	I-Fca, Pia Casa, 1		SAS
Ali del Qu Veli	Giovanni Battista	7/161606.	1606	I-Fd, Battesimi m, reg. 25, fg. 184		
Ali del'Quondam Amet Riva	Carlo Francesco	Turco, from Dalmatia, approx. 15y.	1671	I-Fca, Pia Casa, 2		Carlo Francesco Ceva
Ali del'Quondam Amet Riva	Carlo Francesco	8/15/1671.	1671	I-Fd, Battesimi m, reg. 58, fol. 133		
Ali di Ale	Leopoldo Maria Groppi	Turco, negro, schiavo, approx. 20y, from Moira.	1659	I-Fca, Pia Casa, 2		Paolo del Bufalo
Ali di Ale	Leopoldo Maria Groppi	4/14/1659.	1659	I-Fd, Battesimi m, reg. 52, fg. 181		

Reference (as given in document)	Baptismal name (if known)	Other descriptors in document	Year	Citation	Owner (if known)
Ali di Basc	Giovan Carlo	From Zin in Scaderia, approx. 37. Explicitly described as a freeman, not a slave. Worked as a soldier.	1644	I-Fca, Pia Casa, 1	
Ali di Basc	Giovan Carlo	1/26/1645.	1645	I-Fd, Battesimi m, reg. 45, fg. 97	
Ali di Brahmin	Pietro	Turco, stiavo, moro bianco, from Bona. Worked in the stables for the Grand Duke.	1611	I-Fca, Pia Casa, 1	SAS
Ali di Brahmin	Pietro	12/11/1611.	1611	I-Fd, Battesimi m, reg. 28, fg. 231	
Ali di Cassan		Turco, from Tunisia, approx. 38y.	1696	I-Fca, Pia Casa, 3	
Ali di Etternadar	Pietropaolo	Turco, stiavo, moro bianco, approx. 25y, from Alexandria. Worked in the stables for the Grand Duke.	1611	I-Fca, Pia Casa, 1	SAS
Ali di Etternadar	Pietropaolo	9/11/1611.	1611	I-Fd, Battesimi m, reg. 28, fg. 229	
Ali di Lecaino	Carlo Girolamo	Turco, approx. 12y.	1664	I-Fca, Pia Casa, 2	Alessandro Gallo
Ali di Lecaino	Carlo Girolamo	9/7/1664.	1664	I-Fd, Battesimi m, reg. 55, fg. 30	
Ali di Lima		Turco, approx. 4y. Son of Lima and possibly of her late husband, Amet/Francesco, who died in Genoa.	1697	I-Fca, Pia Casa, 3	
Ali di Machamust Nogiscit	Francesco Maria	Turco, stiavo, from Dalmatia, approx. 13y.	1663	I-Fca, Pia Casa, 2	Cosimo Pasquali

Name		Date	Reference	Other
Ali di Machamust Nogiscit	Francesco Maria	3/25/1664.	I-Fd, Battesimi m, reg. 55, fg. 44	
Ali di Mamuet	Pietro	Turco, approx. 75y. A copy of the ex-slave's manumission papers are included in his file; this was the only time I saw such a document. I note that Ali/Pietro was of a very advanced age when he was given his freedom.	1641	I-Fca, Pia Casa, 1	Pietro de' Medici
Ali di Meomet	Cosimo	Turco, stiavo, approx. 12y, from Aleppo.	1611	I-Fca, Pia Casa, 1	
Ali di Meomet	Cosimo	5/22/1611.	1611	I-Fd, Battesimi m, reg. 28, fg. 27	
Ali di Reenet	Francesco	Turco, moro, stiavo, approx. 22y. Was instructed by the same Michele Zotti, tailor, who instructed Giovanni/ Giovanni.	1611	I-Fca, Pia Casa, 1	Cardinal Antonio Soldari
Ali di Reenet	Francesco	4/17/1611.	1611	I-Fd, Battesimi m, reg. 28, fg. 45	
Ali di Solimano	Giuseppe	Turco, stiavo, from Candia, approx. 8y.	1663	I-Fca, Pia Casa, 2	Senatore Tempi
Ali di Solimano	Giuseppe	9/8/1663.	1663	I-Fd, Battesimi m, reg. 54, fg. 153	
Ali di Tarri	Paolo	Moro biancho, stiavo, approx. 28y, from Alexandria.	1611	I-Fca, Pia Casa, 1	SAS
Ali di Tarri	Paolo	12/11/1611.	1611	I-Fd, Battesimi m, reg. 28, fg. 231	
Ali Morino	[Cosimo Maria?]		1666	I-Fas, Camera del Granduca, f. 35b	133r
Ali Morino			1667	I-Fas, Camera del Granduca, f. 38b	34r

Reference (as given in document)	Baptismal name (if known)	Other descriptors in document	Year	Citation	Owner (if known)
Ali morino			1667	I-Fas, Camera del Granduca, f. 39b, 4r	
Ali Morino			1668	I-Fas, Camera del Granduca, f. 39b, 164v	
Ali Morino	[Cosimo Maria?]		1669	I-Fas, Camera del Granduca, f. 40c, 32r	
Ali Moro	[Cosimo Maria?]		1666	I-Fas, Camera del Granduca, f. 36b, 15r	
Ali Moro			1667	I-Fas, Camera del Granduca, f. 38b, 53r	
Ali moro		"[P]er la fiera di S. Simone."	1669	I-Fas, Camera del Granduca, f. 41c, 19v	
Ali Moro gia schiavo al Sr. Marchese Paolo del Bufalo		Talks about a collection that will be taken up to defray the cost of the baptismal celebration.	1658	I-Fas, Mediceo del Principato, f. 5363, 421r	Paolo del Bufalo
Ali schiavo di Carlo di Lorenzo		Giovanni Talducci is given 4 scudi to transport Ali from Florence to Livorno.	1621	I-Fas, Camera del Granduca, f. 2b, 22v	Carlo di Lorenzo SAS
Ali Turco	Agostino	Stiavo, turco, approx. 8y, from Bona.	1609	I-Fca, Pia Casa, 1	
Ali Turco	Agostino	11/1/1610.	1610	I-Fd, Battesimi m, reg. 27, fg. 125	
Ali Turco			1637	I-Fas, Camera del Granduca, f. 19b, 9r	
Ali Turco			1653	I-Fas, Camera del Granduca, f. 25b, 14v	
Ali Turco Levantino	Raffaello	Levantino, approx. 40y, stiavo.	1630	I-Fca, Pia Casa, 1	Benedetto del Maestro

Name		Date/Note	Year	Source	Folio	Extra
Ali Turco Levantino	Raffaello	3/30/1630.	1630	I-Fd, Battesimi m, reg. 37, fg. 164		
Ali Turco Moemot	Stefano	Turco, stiavo, approx. 18y, from Constantinople. Was training as a horseman.	1610	I-Fca, Pia Casa, 1		SAS
Ali Turco Moemot	Stefano	12/26/1610.	1610	I-Fd, Battesimi m, reg. 28, fg. 107		
Allife (or Aliffe) di Sati	Caterina Leonora	Stiava, turca, approx. 15y, from Smyrna.	1606	I-Fca, Pia Casa, 1		SAS
Allife (or Aliffe) di Sati	Caterina Leonora	7/16/1606.	1606	I-Fd, Battesimi f, reg. 247, fg. 138		
Almancor turco		"A Vincentio Spettiale per vitto di Almancor turco per tutto 7 mesi, cioe dal principio di maggio per tutto novembre di cinque scudi il mese."	1669	I-Fas, Camera del Granduca, f. 41c	13v	
Almancor turco			1669	I-Fas, Camera del Granduca, f. 41c	33r	
Almansor			1671	I-Fas, Camera del Granduca, f. 42	12r	
Almansor turco		"[C]he lavora il Ciocolatto."	1668	I-Fas, Camera del Granduca, f. 39b	28r	
Almansor turco			1668	I-Fas, Camera del Granduca, f. 40c	5v	
Almansor turco			1669	I-Fas, Camera del Granduca, f. 40c	15v	
Almansor turco			1669	I-Fas, Camera del Granduca, f. 40c	17r	
Almansor turco		"A Vincentino speziale per vitto di Almansor turcho di mesi sei cioe dal primo novembre fino a tutto Aprile a scudi cinque il mese."	1669	I-Fas, Camera del Granduca, f. 40c	18v	

Reference (as given in document)	Baptismal name (if known)	Other descriptors in document	Year	Citation	Owner (if known)
Almansor turcho			1669	I-Fas, Camera del Granduca, f. 40c, 21r	
Almansor turcho			1669	I-Fas, Camera del Granduca, f. 40c, 25v	
Almansor turcho			1669	I-Fas, Camera del Granduca, f. 40c, 27v	
Almansor turcho			1669	I-Fas, Camera del Granduca, f. 40c, 32v	
Almansor turcho		5 scudi per month for his upkeep, paid to Vincenzio.	1670	I-Fas, Camera del Granduca, f. 41c, 74v	
Almansore turcho			1668	I-Fas, Camera del Granduca, f. 39b, 33r	
Almanzor Turco Cioccolatero			1668	I-Fas, Camera del Granduca, f. 39b, 23v	
Almarchor turcho			1670	I-Fas, Camera del Granduca, f. 41c, 54v	
Almonsor turcho		"[C]he fabrica il ciocolatte."	1669	I-Fas, Camera del Granduca, f. 41c, 13r	
Aman di Uber	Giovan Carlo	Stiavo, turco, from the Black Sea, approx. 40y. Gifted to Alamanni by Prince Giovan Carlo de' Medici.	1645	I-Fca, Pia Casa, 1	Raffaello Alamanni
Aman di Uber	Giovan Carlo	9/13/1645.	1645	I-Fd, Battesimi m, reg. 45, fg. 250	
Amber di Solimano	Jacopo	Turco, moro, from Cairo, approx. 16y.	1607	I-Fca, Pia Casa, 1	SAS
Amber di Solimano	Jacopo	7/29/1607.	1607	I-Fd, Battesimi m, reg. 26, fg. 72	

Amere Nero		Turco, nero, stiavo, approx. 7y.	1670	I-Fca, Pia Casa, 2	Donna Costanzia
Amet		Turco, approx. 8y.	1628	I-Fca, Pia Casa, 1	Alberto Marzichi
Amet	Pier Francesco	Stiavo, turco, approx. 14y, from Zebenich. Was taken into slavery "piccolino" (at a very young age).	1649	I-Fca, Pia Casa, 1	
Amet	Pier Francesco	"Amet da Zebenicco Turco schiavone battezzato Adulto," 9/26/1649.	1649	I-Fd, Battesimi m, reg. 47, fg. 268	
Amet Turco	Ricovero	Stiavo, turco, from the Black Sea.	1633	I-Fca, Pia Casa, 1	Buonaccorso Uguaccioni
Amet Turco	Ricovero	9/28/1633.	1633	I-Fd, Battesimi m, reg. 39, fg. 240	
Amet Turco		Moro bianco, stiavo.	1635	I-Fca, Pia Casa, 1	Ruperto Capponi
Ametto d'Amore	Carlo Giovanni	Turco, approx. 58y, from Algeria.	1664	I-Fca, Pia Casa, 2	Giovanni Ricasoli
Ametto d'Amore	Carlo Giovanni	8/31/1664.	1664	I-Fd, Battesimi m, reg. 55, fg. 30	
Ametto d'Argeri		Fanciullo, schiavo, turco, approx. 10y.	1635	I-Fca, Pia Casa, 1	Marchese Fabrizio Coloreto
Ametto da Trapani		Stiavo, turco, from Barbary. Was purchased in Livorno from Captain Franschetto in 1634 for 70 scudi.	1635	I-Fca, Pia Casa, 1	Paolo del Bufalo
Ametto di Ansa	Zanobi	Turco, from Constantinople, approx. 53y. Taken by the galleys in 1607.	1615	I-Fca, Pia Casa, 1	SAS
Ametto di Ansa	Zanobi	3/23/1616.	1616	I-Fd, Battesimi m, reg. 30, fg. 181	
Ametto di Fiore		Stiavo, turco, approx. 12y, from Alessandria. Taken captive at the age of 8y.	1635	I-Fca, Pia Casa, 1	Gabriello Riccardi

Reference (as given in document)	Baptismal name (if known)	Other descriptors in document	Year	Citation	Owner (if known)
Ametto Mita Crecci	Francesco Maria	Turco, approx. 15y.	1664	I-Fca, Pia Casa, 2	Jacinto Ganucci
Ametto Mita Crecci	Francesco Maria	9/7/1664.	1664	I-Fd, Battesimi m, reg. 55, fg. 50	
Ametto Turco Schiavo		"[F]attura d'un Zimarrone alla Turchesca fatto a punto Inghilese," etc.	1668	I-Fas, Camera del Granduca, 177r f. 39b	
Amolo di Memet Addalo		Etiopo, stiavo, from Borno in Ethiopia, approx. 22y. Currently lives in the rooms of the Cardinal, presumably Francesco Maria de' Medici.	1704	I-Fca, Pia Casa, 3	Cardinal de' Medici
Amore di Jesuff		Turco, approx. 21y, from Algeria.	1672	I-Fca, Pia Casa, 2	Camillo Giudi
Amumach di Maumet da Corone	Giorgio Antonio	3/8/1665.	1665	I-Fd, Battesimi m, reg. 55, fg. 93	
Amurat(to)	Benedetto	Turco, stiavo, from Brescem in Hungary, approx. 20y.	1605	I-Fca, Pia Casa, 1	Paolo Ricasoli
Amurat(to)	Benedetto	3/5/1606.	1606	I-Fd, Battesimi m, reg. 25, fg. 133	
Amut di Casme	Agostino	Turco, stiavo, approx. 10y, from Bona.	1608	I-Fca, Pia Casa, 1	Silvio Piccolomini
Amut di Casme Anasar	Agostino Paolo	9/24/1608. Moro, turco, approx. 30y. Not explicitly described as a slave. Has been in Florence for 3 months.	1608 1649	I-Fd, Battesimi m, reg. 27, fg. 1 I-Fca, Pia Casa, 1	

Anasar	Paolo	1/25/1650.	1650	I-Fd, Battesimi m, reg. 47, fg. 271	
Anassar	Giovan Gualberto	Turco, moro, approx. 13y, stiavo, from Borno. Has been in Florence for 3 years.	1647	I-Fca, Pia Casa, 1	SAS
Anassar	Giovan Gualberto	7/12/1648.	1648	I-Fd, Battesimi m, reg. 47, fg. 78	
Anastasio di Morea fatto Cristiano			1626	I-Fas, Camera del Granduca, f. 7b 8r	
Andrea Bernadelli ebreo		"[P]er averlo fatto cavare delle stinche."	1668	I-Fas, Camera del Granduca, f. 40c 13r	
Andrea de Silvera (un Indiano Chiamato)		"[P]er tornare al paese."	1667	I-Fas, Camera del Granduca, f. 38b 2v	
Andrea di Silvez di Gao muratto		"[C]he desse piu relazioni delli Indie."	1667	I-Fas, Camera del Granduca, f. 37b 2v	
Angiolo Pandolfini		Rent for a house to store the gondola.	1668	I-Fas, Camera del Granduca, f. 39b 31r	
Anna Agata		Turca, from Russia, approx. 23y.	1670	I-Fca, Pia Casa, 2	Doctor Fortebraccio
Anna moglie gia di Mezzomoro staffiere			1634	I-Fas, Camera del Granduca, f. 15b 31r	
Ansano di Jussup		Turco, approx. 15y.	1672	I-Fca, Pia Casa, 2	Ferdinando Ridolfi
Ansano Turco di Apedi		Stiavo, turco, "storpiato dal braccio sinistro."	1618	I-Fca, Pia Casa, 1	SAS
Ansano Zuchi	Tommo	6/13/1668.	1668	I-Fd, Battesimi m, reg. 57, fg. 118	
Aracab Negro (aka Ali)		Moro, turco, negro, approx. 16y. Was born in Seville to an enslaved mother and sold away from her at the age of 4y.	1651	I-Fca, Pia Casa, 2	Michel Diaz Ebreo

Reference (as given in document)	Baptismal name (if known)	Other descriptors in document	Year	Citation	Owner (if known)
Aramada		Turco, stiavo, approx. 11y. Was enslaved at the age of 3y and remembers nothing of his parents.	1675	I-Fca, Pia Casa, 2	Lorenzo di Bernardo Cimini
Archimia di Mammut		Turca, comprata, from Bosnia, approx. 20y.	1686	I-Fca, Pia Casa, 2	Caterina Fioravana nei Bocchirierei
Aretto di Ussain	Giovanni Battista	Turco, stiavo, approx. 26–30y, from Constantinople. Was previously a galley slave.	1607	I-Fca, Pia Casa, 1	Alessandro Risalite
Aretto di Ussain	Giovanni Battista	9/7/1607.	1607	I-Fd, Battesimi m, reg. 26, fg. 161	
Arsano		Turco, persiano, fanciullo, approx. 14y.	1675	I-Fca, Pia Casa, 2	
Artigia di Mustafa Memicogicci		Turca, gia schiava, approx. 55y. Was previously enslaved to Giovanni Bogos, a merchant in Livorno.	1677	I-Fca, Pia Casa, 2	
Asan d'Aiuath Turco	Francesco	Stiavo, from Constantinople, over 80y. Was baptized in the hospital.	1635	I-Fca, Pia Casa, 1	SAS
Asano d'Osmano		Fanciulletto, from the Levante, stiavo. Purchased in Naples.	1632	I-Fca, Pia Casa, 1	Bernardino Attavanti
Asano di Ramadan		Turco, stiavo. Was captured approx. 16 years previously.	1617	I-Fca, Pia Casa, 1	SAS
Asano Rocchiovich		Turco, schiavo, from Moscow.	1668	I-Fca, Pia Casa, 2	Antonio Generotti
Assain		Stiavo, approx. 3y. Was taken by the galleys while travelling with his parents.	1638	I-Fca, Pia Casa, 1	Antonio Simoni

Assan	Giuseppe Maria	Turco, schiavo, from Volo, approx. 10y. Has been with his current owner for 2 years.	1660	I-Fca, Pia Casa, 2	Bartolomeo Corsini
Assan	Giuseppe Maria		1660	I-Fd, Battesimi m, reg. 53, fg. 42	
Assan d'Ebraim Suppachi		Turco, approx 9y. Presumably the son of the Ebraim di Memco Suppachi who also converted the same year but was owned by the Corsini.	1664	I-Fca, Pia Casa, 2	Pier Francesco Marcometi
Assano Atticer Attigia d'Amet Spaia		Turco, from Negroponte, approx. 16y. Stiava, turca, approx. 45y, from Scro. Turca, schiava, approx. 35y. Wife of Arsano Tobice of the city of Livorno.	1692 1609 1687	I-Fca, Pia Casa, 3 I-Fca, Pia Casa, 1 I-Fca, Pia Casa, 2	Piero Angeli SAS Serenissima. Granduchessa Davide Ebreo Levantino SAS
Auzza di Macometto Bamnen (or Ramnen) di Lanan		Stiava, mora, nigra, approx. 25y.	1609	I-Fca, Pia Casa, 1	
		Idolatro, moro, from Guinea in Africa, approx. 12y, etiope. Living in the house of Giovanni Maria de' Medici. Was enslaved in Livorno for a year before he was brought to Florence.	1701	I-Fca, Pia Casa, 3	
Barbara		Turca, approx. 10y, schiava, believed to be from Negroponte. Describes being enslaved in various Venetian households from a young age; she notes that none of her Venetian owners gave her an education or instruction in Christianity.	1694	I-Fca, Pia Casa, 3	Cosimo Pecori
Barca		Schiavo. Lenzini was director of the galleys.	1612	I-Fca, Pia Casa, 1	Girolamo Lenzini

Reference (as given in document)	Baptismal name (if known)	Other descriptors in document	Year	Citation	Owner (if known)
Barca	Flavio Francesco Ghighi	Turco, moro, schiavo, approx. 16y.	1666	I-Fca, Pia Casa, 2	Prince Mattias de' Medici
Barca	Flavio Francesco Ghighi	5/16/1666.	1666	I-Fd, Battesimi m, reg. 56, fg. 45	
Barca di Ali Bornau		Etiopo, stiavo, from Borno in Ethiopia. Currently lives in the rooms of the Cardinal, presumably Francesco Maria de' Medici.	1704	I-Fca, Pia Casa, 3	Cardinal de' Medici
Barca di Nasser		Turco, moro, approx. 20y.	1687	I-Fca, Pia Casa, 2	SAS
Barca Moro	Cosimo Francesco Maria Medici	"[F]igliolo di Macamà di Bornia di anni 19."	1662	I-Fd, Battesimi m, reg. 54, fg. 17	SAS
Barcha di Macama		Moro, from Borno, also described as from Tripoli, approx. 19y. Was enslaved (possibly still enslaved), currently living in the house of Giampaolo Prato.	1662	I-Fca, Pia Casa, 2	
Bartangi turcho			1668	I-Fas, Camera del Granduca, 7r f. 40c	
Bellallo di Ali Nero Indiano	Cosimo	Indiano, stiavo, nero.	1611	I-Fca, Pia Casa, 1	SAS
Bellallo di Ali Nero Indiano	Cosimo	9/11/1611.	1611	I-Fd, Battesimi m, reg. 28, fg. 146	
Benvenuta	Teresia	Mora, turca, approx. 22y, from Angola. Mother of Mordacheo/Giuseppe.	1653	I-Fca, Pia Casa, 2	Raffaello Ebreo

Name	Baptismal name	Date	Notes	Year	Source	Folio	Sponsor
Benvenuta	Teresia	12/31/1653.		1653	I-Fd, Battesimi f, reg. 271, fg. 309		
Berricato schiavo				1652	I-Fas, Camera del Granduca, f. 24b	19r	SAS
Bila (or Beliel) Moro	Marco Rottoli	Stiavo, moro, stanchiere. Baptized in the hospital 7/18/1606.		1606	I-Fca, Pia Casa, 1		
Bileada di Maumet Movech		Turca, approx. 37y.		1664	I-Fca, Pia Casa, 2		Niccolo Santa Paolina Sergardi
Bizirre di Smain		Turco, approx. 24y. Currently imprisoned on suspicion of having stolen from the family who purchased him in Livorno (the Sergardi).		1671	I-Fca, Pia Casa, 2		
Burghassi di Ciaballa	Giovanni Battista	Stiavo, from Bona, approx. 12y.		1609	I-Fca, Pia Casa, 1		SAS
Burghassi di Ciaballa	Giovanni Battista	11/1/1610.		1610	I-Fd, Battesimi m, reg. 27, fg. 181		
Caddira di Usain	Maria Maddalena	Turca, approx. 28y; from Dalmatia. Baptized while ill.		1665	I-Fca, Pia Casa, 2		Alessandro Fiorini Pietro Gattolini
Caggie Mebiliti		Turco, from Famagosta, approx. 45y.		1688	I-Fca, Pia Casa, 2		
Camera di Ali	Maria Cornelia	Presumably, based on the date, this is the same individual as Camera di Osman; the age given also matches, 9/7/1664.		1664	I-Fd, Battesimi f, reg. 277, fg. 101		
Camera di Osman		Turca, approx. 40y.		1664	I-Fca, Pia Casa, 2		Alessandro Gallo Zanobi Bucherelli
Canum (or Alice)		Stiava, from Greece, 10y in 1611.		1613	I-Fca, Pia Casa, 1		
Capauzzo Turco				1627	I-Fas, Camera del Granduca, f. 7b	15v	

Reference (as given in document)	Baptismal name (if known)	Other descriptors in document	Year	Citation	Owner (if known)
Capuzzo Turco		Rewarded for having presented a lion and a tiger.	1626	I-Fas, Camera del Granduca, f. 6b 24r	
Caral'; Moro			1654	I-Fas, Camera del Granduca, f. 25b 37r	Mattias de' Medici
Carali	Mattia	Moro, stiavo, Granatino, from Barbary (Zelia), approx. 16y.	1657	I-Fca, Pia Casa, 2	Prince Mattias de' Medici
Carali	Mattia	8/1/1657.	1657	I-Fd, Battesimi m, reg. 51, fg. 236	
Carali di Mele Align Carali moro		Turco, moro, from Borno, approx. 20y.	1683 1654	I-Fca, Pia Casa, 2 I-Fas, Camera del Granduca, f. 25b 37r	
Cariccia di usaino Carlo battezzato sta alle stalle		Turca, from Dalmatia, approx. 19y.	1689 1666	I-Fca, Pia Casa, 3 I-Fas, Camera del Granduca, f. 36b 19r	
Carlo detto Maometi dal gran Cairo	Giovan Carlo	Records that Giovan Carlo (approx. 25y) has been officially baptized and thus can now collect a salary.	1630	I-Fas, Mediceo del Principato, f. 5178 21r	Prince Giovan Carlo de' Medici
Carzio		Maestro della musica turchesca. He and his 26 companions are tipped, as are 8 guards from the marina.	1624	I-Fas, Camera del Granduca, f. 5b 28v	
Casella	Caterina	Stiava, turca, father's name was Ali; from Barbary, had traveled to Constantinople; approx. 16y.	1606	I-Fca, Pia Casa, 1	SAS
Casella	Caterina	7/16/1606.	1606	I-Fd, Battesimi f, reg. 247, fg. 138	

Cechere di Alesemesch	Caterina	Turca, stiava, from Notolia via Malta, approx. 25y.	1606	I-Fca, Pia Casa, 1	Raphaello de' Pazzi
Cechere di Alesemesch	Caterina	6/27/1606.	1606	I-Fd, Battesimi f, reg. 247, fg. 138	
Cesmina Emacheri	Caterina Angela	6/3/1668, approximately 14 y.	1668	I-Fd, Battesimi f, reg. 279, fg. 23	
Cherma	Alessia	Schiava, serva, from Natolia. Her daughter also served Capponi and had been baptized 3 years previously.	1618	I-Fca, Pia Casa, 1	Piero Capponi
Cherma	Alessia	10/21/1618.	1618	I-Fd, Battesimi f, reg. 254, fg. 53	
Chiarima di Brachin Duramiscevich		Turca, schiava, approx. 38y. Sister of Mametto di Brachin Durmiscevich.	1674	I-Fca, Pia Casa, 2	Fabio Cantucci
Chienan		Stiavo, from Russia, approx. 13y.	1654	I-Fca, Pia Casa, 2	Prince Leopoldo de' Medici
Chierichinio figlio di Mezzomoro			1623	I-Fcas, Camera del Granduca, f. 5b	2v
Chinan		Along with Maometto and Pier. Giovanni.	1653	I-Fas, Camera del Granduca, f. 24b	47v
Chinan		Along with Mutolo and Moro.	1654	I-Fas, Camera del Granduca, f. 25b	34v
Chinan		Along with il Moro.	1655	I-Fas, Camera del Granduca, f. 26b	45r
Chinan del S. Principe Leopoldo		Christmas.	1655	I-Fas, Camera del Granduca, f. 27b	26r
Chinan Turco			1653	I-Fas, Camera del Granduca, f. 24b	47v

Reference (as given in document)	Baptismal name (if known)	Other descriptors in document	Year	Citation		Owner (if known)
Chinan Turco			1653	I-Fas, Camera del Granduca, f. 25b	15r	
Cicco Moro			1644	I-Fas, Depositeria generale f. 1604	5v	Prince Giovan Carlo de' Medici
Cicco Moro			1644	I-Fas, Depositeria generale f. 1604	6v	Prince Giovan Carlo de' Medici
Cicco Moro			1644	I-Fas, Depositeria generale f. 1604	8v	Card. Gio:Carlo de' Medici
Cicco Moro			1644	I-Fas, Depositeria generale f. 1604	9r	Card. Gio:Carlo de' Medici
Cicco Moro			1644	I-Fas, Depositeria generale f. 1604	10v	Card. Gio:Carlo de' Medici
Cicco Moro			1644	I-Fas, Depositeria generale f. 1604	11r	Card. Gio:Carlo de' Medici
Ciuch Ali di Alimemer		Turco, from the Black Sea, approx. 75y.	1676	I-Fca, Pia Casa, 2		
Coccia (or Coggia)	Ferdinando Medici	Turco, stiavo, approx. 45y, from Marocco. Works as a translator for the Medici.	1666	I-Fca, Pia Casa, 2		SAS

Coggia		1667	I-Fas, Camera del Granduca, f. 37b	19v
Coggia		1667	I-Fas, Camera del Granduca, f. 38b	31v
Coggia batezzato	[Ferdinando Medici Battezato]	1666	I-Fas, Camera del Granduca, f. 36b	19r
Cosimino Turco Battezzato		1633	I-Fas, Camera del Granduca, f. 14b	26v
Cosimiro Paggio Nero pollacco		1634	I-Fas, Camera del Granduca, f. 15b	35v
Cosimo Battezzato che sta in spezieria	Cosimo/Almansor	1672	I-Fas, Camera del Granduca, f. 42	106r
Cosimo Battezzato di Spezeria	Cosimo/Almansor	1674	I-Fas, Camera del Granduca, f. 43	24r
Cosimo Battezzato gia detto Almansor		1671	I-Fas, Camera del Granduca, f. 42	15l
Cosimo Battezzato gia Turco chiamato Almansor		1672	I-Fas, Camera del Granduca, f. 42	78l
Cosimo Battezzato gia Turco detto Almansor		1671	I-Fas, Camera del Granduca, f. 42	50l
Cosimo Battezzato gia Turco detto Almansor		1672	I-Fas, Camera del Granduca, f. 42	157r

Descriptions (middle column, in row order):

- Money is given to the Sr. Prov.re Cappelli for cinnamon, gloves, and the upkeep of Cosimino Turco Battezzato.
- Payment for clothing; the 3 Flemish chefs and a Flemish stablehand are also provided with outfits.
- Tipped for the Grand Duke's birthday.
- Money paid to Mattio Fontebuoni for materials used by Cosimo/Almansor and by Mustafà Moro.
- Paid to cover six months of the rent on his house.
- Tipped for Christmas.
- Tipped for Christmas.

Reference (as given in document)	Baptismal name (if known)	Other descriptors in document	Year	Citation		Owner (if known)
Cosimo Battezzato gia Turco nominato Almansor		"Pagati a Cosimo Battezzato gia Turco nominato Almasor per due moneta di Comandimento di SAS per havere uno figliolo."	1671	I-Fas, Camera del Granduca, f. 42	44l	
Cosimo Battezzato Moro		Tipped for Christmas.	1672	I-Fas, Camera del Granduca, f. 42	157r	
Cosimo Battezzato Moro di Camera		Tipped for Christmas.	1671	I-Fas, Camera del Granduca, f. 42	50l	
Cosimo Battezzato prima Turcho chiamato Almansor		Rent allowance for the semester.	1673	I-Fas, Camera del Granduca, f. 42	198l	
Cosimo Battezzato, gia Tucho che si chiamava Almansor			1671	I-Fas, Camera del Granduca, f. 42	28r	
Cosimo Battezzato, gia Tucho che si chiamava Almansor		"[P]er il semestro decorso per tutto Ottobre prossimo passato, a conto di pigione di Casa."	1672	I-Fas, Camera del Granduca, f. 42	143l	
Cosimo Maures Ebanista		Salaried for the year.	1664	I-Fas, Depositeria Generale, parte Antica, f. 397	33	
Cosimo Moro	[Cosimo Maria?]	Along with Batistone and Fegatello.	1666	I-Fas, Camera del Granduca, f. 36b	34r	
Cosimo Moro		"Pagati a Girolam Miliotti portiere scudi cinque moneta per il vitto di Cosimo Moro che tiene in Casa."	1671	I-Fas, Camera del Granduca, f. 42	39l	
Cosimo Moro			1673	I-Fas, Camera del Granduca, f. 42	163r	

Name	Owner/Baptism	Description	Year	Archive reference	Notes
Cosimo Turco Battezzato			1634	I-Fas, Camera del Granduca, f. 15b	32v
Covia di Mustafa Bas	Anna Maria Teresia	Stiava, from Dalmatia, approx. 21y.	1658	I-Fca, Pia Casa, 2	Bartolo Castelli
Covia di Mustafa Bas	Anna Maria Teresia	3/25/1658.	1658	I-Fd, Battesimi f, reg. 274, fg. 1	
Cuper stato schiavo	Michele Cuper		1670	I-Fas, Camera del Granduca, f. 41c	44r
Cuper stato schiavo	Michele Cuper		1670	I-Fas, Camera del Granduca, f. 41c	54v
Curilat di Camvechi		Tartaro, approx. 7y. Living in the house of the Auditore Barducci and in service to SAS; living in the same house as Aeob, possibly a brother.	1698	I-Fca, Pia Casa, 3	SAS
Curso (or Curto) Ali		Turco, stiavo, from Constantinople. Purchased from the galleys.	1616	I-Fca, Pia Casa, 1	Biagio Capizecchi
Curt (known as Niccolo)		Claims to be a Greek Christian who was enslaved in Ottoman territories and has now fled in search of freedom.	1621	I-Fca, Pia Casa, 1	
Curt di Urem		Turco, approx. 16y.	1666	I-Fca, Pia Casa, 2	Andrea Corsini Doctor Gregorio Redi
Curtus di Memia Mattitaiace		Turco, stiavo, approx. 70y.	1671	I-Fca, Pia Casa, 2	
D d'Ghevarra stato schiavo			1665	I-Fas, Camera del Granduca, f. 34b	169r
Demera (lady "donna" of Curem Cadrovich)		Turca, approx. 40y.	1670	I-Fca, Pia Casa, 2	Antonio Mari

Reference (as given in document)	Baptismal name (if known)	Other descriptors in document	Year	Citation	Owner (if known)
Dimitrio greco			1623	I-Fas Camera del Granduca, f.5b	12r
Donna Maria Maddalina di Nazione Turca		Given permission to take a room in the Orbatello cloisters, which were reserved for impoverished women.	1678	I-Faoi, 10452, Orbatello	c. 797
Donna Maria Sammiabelli Ebrea fatta Cristiana		Given permission to take a room in the Orbatello cloisters, which were reserved for impoverished women.	1668	I-Faoi, 10452, Orbatello	c. 653
Doria di Mustafa	Maria Vittoria	Turca. Was enslaved (possibly still enslaved), currently living in the house of Marco Lambeati.	1662	I-Fca, Pia Casa, 2	
Doria di Mustafa	Maria Vittoria	5/31/1662.	1662	I-Fd, Battesimi f, reg. 276, fg. 51	
Dramadà d'Asan	Giovan Carlo	Stiavo, tuco, from Tripoli, approx. 24y.	1652	I-Fca, Pia Casa, 2	Carlo Geraldini
Dramadà d'Asan	Giovan Carlo	9/12/1652.	1652	I-Fd, Battesimi m, reg. 49, fg. 95	
Durach di Zuco Rolcovich	Giuseppe Maria	Turco, from Dalmatia, approx. 18y. Taken captive 4 years previously.	1667	I-Fca, Pia Casa, 2	Vincenzio Allegri
Durach di Zuco Rolcovich	Giuseppe Maria	4/4/1667.	1667	I-Fd, Battesimi m, reg. 56, fg. 193	
E'nene Turca	Caterina	Turca, stiava, daughter of Macheber Ruca/Maddalena, approx. 26 months old.	1607	I-Fca, Pia Casa, 1	Christine of Lorraine
E'nene Turca	Caterina	9/24/1607.	1607	I-Fd, Battesimi f, reg. 248, fg. 129	

Name	Owner	Description	Date	Source	Notes
Ebraim		Turco, approx. 14y.	1665	I-Fca, Pia Casa, 2	Barone del Nero Pietro Corsini
Ebraim di Memco Suppachi	Pietro Francesco	Turco, approx. 30y. Presumably the father of Assan d'Ebraim Suppachi who converted the same year but was owned by the Marcometi.	1664	I-Fca, Pia Casa, 2	
Ebraim di Memco Suppachi	Pietro Francesco	9/7/1664.	1664	I-Fd, Battesimi m, reg. 55, fg. 123	
Ebraimo di Joan		Turco, from Hungary, approx. 13y. The owner, Mangiacani, is a "staffiere" to the Cardinale de' Medici (presumably Francesco Maria)].	1693	I-Fca, Pia Casa, 3	Rocco Mangiacani
Ebrain		Turco, stiavo, from Belgrade.	1604	I-Fca, Pia Casa, 1	Gio: Bandini Cardinal de' Medici
Ehemet		Turco, from Belgrade, approx. 9y. Presumably the cardinal is Francesco Maria de' Medici.	1688	I-Fca, Pia Casa, 2	
Emina di Accemet	Maria Francesca	Turca, schiava, approx. 14y.	1668	I-Fca, Pia Casa, 2	Antonio Pitti
Emina di Accemet	Maria Francesca	5/12/1668.	1668	I-Fd, Battesimi f, reg. 279, fg. 75	
Emina di Assan	Maria Maddalena	Turca, stiava, approx. 15y.	1663	I-Fca, Pia Casa, 2	Margherita della Fonte
Emina di Assan	Maria Maddalena	9/8/1663.	1663	I-Fd, Battesimi f, reg. 276, fg. 180	
Emma		Turca, from Bosnia, approx. 7y.	1686	I-Fca, Pia Casa, 2	Ottavio Galilei and Lucretia Grifoni Concorsi
Emne		Turca, approx. 12y. Described as "al servizio," so it isn't explicitly clear whether she is a servant or enslaved.	1686	I-Fca, Pia Casa, 2	

Reference (as given in document)	Baptismal name (if known)	Other descriptors in document	Year	Citation	Owner (if known)
Enmina di Amet Frabosci		Turca, schiava, approx. 20y.	1668	I-Fca, Pia Casa, 2	Lorenzo Gherardini
Ernine (or Emine)		Turca, schiava, approx. 20y. Letter is written in the first person, seemingly by Ernine/Emine herself.	1695	I-Fca, Pia Casa, 3	Anna Angeli nei Mori Ubaldini
Fatima		Turca, stiava, approx. 16y, believed to be from Bosnia.	1694	I-Fca, Pia Casa, 3	Francesco Gaino Bichi
Fatima di Acmet		Turca, approx. 10y. Was enslaved (possibly still enslaved), currently living in the house of Cosimo Pasquali.	1662	I-Fca, Pia Casa, 2	
Fatima di Acmet	Maria Caterina 9/8/1663.		1663	I-Fd, Battesimi f, reg. 276, fg. 180	
Fatlemia Turca	Lisabetta	Stiava, from Schiavonia, approx. 30y. Wife of Sulfiare/Simone who had previously converted to Christianity.	1610	I-Fca, Pia Casa, 1	SAS
Fatlemia Turca	Lisabetta	6/6/1610.	1610	I-Fd, Battesimi f, reg. 249, fg. 177	
Fattama		Stiava, turca. Was captured with her daughter, who was baptized in Pisa at age 3y and given the name Caterina.	1633	I-Fca, Pia Casa, 1	Angelmaria Stufa
Fattama Turca		Stiava, from Bona. Purchased three years previously in Livorno.	1614	I-Fca, Pia Casa, 1	Don Antonio de' Medici
Fattima		Turca, schiava, approx. 10y.	1666	I-Fca, Pia Casa, 2	Maddalena Galli
Fattima		Alla Mora fattima.	1657	I-Fas, Camera del Granduca 33r f. 28b	

Name	Baptismal name	Notes	Year	Source	Sponsor
Fattima d'Abram	Angela Vettoria	Possibly Fattima Mulam, who is also 21. Baptized 5/30/1668.	1668	I-Fd, Battesimi f, reg. 279, fg. 4	
Fattima d'Echemet		Turca, schiava, approx. 17y.	1666	I-Fca, Pia Casa, 2	Giovanni Uguccioni
Fattima di Aecmet Opplamich	Maria Teresa	5/31/1662.	1662	I-Fd, Battesimi f, reg. 276, fg. 51	
Fattima di Amet Dilichich		Turca, schiava, approx. 64y.	1674	I-Fca, Pia Casa, 2	Marco Rabbuiati
Fattima di Bariam	Maria Maddalena	Turca, from Constantinople, approx. 30y. Was baptized at home on 12/11/1670; was previously enslaved and owned by Jews.	1671	I-Fca, Pia Casa, 2	Lorenzo Marzoppini
Fattima di Isacco		Turca, stiava, from Smirne, approx. 20y. Has been enslaved since childhood, is married to Sola, a Turk, from Tripoli who is enslaved in the bagno in Livorno.	1677	I-Fca, Pia Casa, 2	Verrazzano
Fattima di Leomeo		Turca, schiava, vedova, approx. 30y. Widow of Mamut.	1674	I-Fca, Pia Casa, 2	Luisa Corsini
Fattima di Memmia Calimichi	Maria Angiola	Turca. Was enslaved (possibly still enslaved), currently living in the house of Vincenzio Salvi.	1662	I-Fca, Pia Casa, 2	
Fattima di Memmia Calimichi	Maria Angiola	5/31/1662.	1662	I-Fd, Battesimi f, reg. 276, fg. 51	
Fattima di Solemo di Isacolee		Turca, schiava, approx. 28y.	1674	I-Fca, Pia Casa, 2	Luisa Corsini
Fattima Mora	Maria Vittoria Medici	Mora, turca.	1652	I-Fca, Pia Casa, 2	SAS
Fattima Mora	Maria Vittoria Medici	3/26/1652.	1652	I-Fd, Battesimi f, reg. 271, fg. 112	SAS

Reference (as given in document)	Baptismal name (if known)	Other descriptors in document	Year	Citation	Owner (if known)
Fattima Muchimeri	Maria Maddalena	Presumably Moschiva Fattima, baptized 5/19/1668.	1668	I-Fd, Battesimi f, reg. 279, fg. 76	
Fattima Mulam		Turca, schiava, approx. 21y.	1668	I-Fca, Pia Casa, 2	Conte Caprara Bernardo Birri
Fattima Russcim		Turca, schiava, approx. 13y.	1668	I-Fca, Pia Casa, 2	
Fattima turca	Maria Maddalena	Possibly Fattima Russcim, given her age (14y), 4/15/1668.	1668	I-Fd, Battesimi f, reg. 279, fg. 72	
Fattuma		Turca, schiava, from Bagnaluga, approx. 18y.	1699	I-Fca, Pia Casa, 3	Niccolo Quarateri Silvio Piccolomini
Fatume (or Fattume) di Metasen	Caterina	Turca, stiava, approx. 12y, from Bona.	1608	I-Fca, Pia Casa, 1	
Fatume (or Fattume) di Metasen	Caterina	9/24/1608.	1608	I-Fd, Battesimi f, reg. 249, fg. 13	
Ferdinando	[Ferdinando Medici Battezzato]	"[I]nterprete degli Armeni."	1668	I-Fas, Camera del Granduca, f. 39b 35r	
Ferdinando Batezzato			1666	I-Fas, Camera del Granduca, f. 35b 123v	
Ferdinando Batezzato			1666	I-Fas, Camera del Granduca, f. 36b 2r	
Ferdinando Batezzato			1666	I-Fas, Camera del Granduca, f. 36b 33r	
Ferdinando Batezzato			1667	I-Fas, Camera del Granduca, f. 39b 43r	
Ferdinando Batezzato			1667	I-Fas, Camera del Granduca, f. 39b 67r	

Ferdinando Batezzato alias Coggia		1666	I-Fas, Camera del Granduca, f. 36b	20r
Ferdinando Batezzato, che si chiamava Chioggia	Tipped for Christmas.	1671	I-Fas, Camera del Granduca, f. 42	51l
Ferdinando Batezzato, che si chiamava Chioggia	Tipped for Christmas.	1672	I-Fas, Camera del Granduca, f. 42	158r
Ferdinando battezzato	Maestro Frediano is reimbursed for shirts and other items he provided for Ferdinando battezzato.	1631	I-Fas, Camera del Granduca, f. 12b	52r
Ferdinando battezzato		1632	I-Fas, Camera del Granduca, f. 14b	7r
Ferdinando battezzato	"Al Battesimo del figluolo di Ferdinando Battezzato che sta al Condotto"; 10 scudi on the baptism of his son.	1634	I-Fas, Camera del Granduca, f. 15b	52v
Ferdinando Battezzato detto Coggia		1667	I-Fas, Camera del Granduca, f. 36b	69v
Ferdinando Battezzato detto Coggia		1667	I-Fas, Camera del Granduca, f. 37b	18v
Ferdinando Battezzato detto Coggia		1667	I-Fas, Camera del Granduca, f. 37b	38r
Ferdinando Battezzato detto Coggia		1667	I-Fas, Camera del Granduca, f. 37b	40r

Reference (as given in document)	Baptismal name (if known)	Other descriptors in document	Year	Citation	Owner (if known)
Ferdinando Battezzato detto Coggia			1667	I-Fas, Camera del Granduca, f. 38b	1v
Ferdinando Battezzato detto Coggia			1667	I-Fas, Camera del Granduca, f. 38b	15r
Ferdinando Battezzato detto Coggia			1667	I-Fas, Camera del Granduca, f. 38b	16r
Ferdinando Battezzato detto Coggia			1667	I-Fas, Camera del Granduca, f. 39b	7r
Ferdinando Battezzato detto Coggia			1668	I-Fas, Camera del Granduca, f. 39b	17v
Ferdinando Battezzato detto Coggia			1668	I-Fas, Camera del Granduca, f. 39b	19r
Ferdinando Battezzato detto Coggia			1668	I-Fas, Camera del Granduca, f. 39b	29r
Ferdinando detto Coggia			1667	I-Fas, Camera del Granduca, f. 37b	1v
Ferdinando Inteprete	[Ferdinando Medici Battezato]	Served as interpreter for the two turchi del Capitano della torra.	1668	I-Fas, Camera del Granduca, f. 40c	6v

Name	Alt	Description	Year	Archive	Folio	Patron
Ferdinando Medici	[Ferdinando Medici Battezato]	"[I]nterprete degli Armeni."	1667	I-Fas, Camera del Granduca, f. 39b	11r	
Ferdinando Medici Battezzato		Salaried for the year.	1664	I-Fas, Depositeria Generale, parte Antica, f. 397	63	
Ferdinando Medici detto Chioggia		"Pagati a Girolamo Miliotti e per detto a Ferdinando Medici detto Chioggia scudi cinque moneta per il Vitto del Morino."	1672	I-Fas, Camera del Granduca, f. 42	611	
Ferdinando Moro		"Pagati a Arrigo Vinter . . . tanti se li fanno dare per il vitto di numero 6 fra nani, e mori legl'appiè nomi per il mese di ottobre passato . . . Batistone, Andrea frattello di Batistone, Pier Gio, Ferdinando Moro, Filippino, Mattio Moro."	1657	I-Fas, Mediceo del Principato f. 5487	107v	Prince Mattias de' Medici
Filippo Moro			1643	I-Fas, Mediceo del Principato f. 5279b	ins. 6, c. 90	Prince Giovan Carlo de' Medici
Filippo Moro schiavo			1642	I-Fas, Mediceo del Principato f. 5279b	ins. 3, c. 16	Prince Giovan Carlo de' Medici
Filippo Pandolfini detto il Morino			1667	I-Fas, Camera del Granduca, f. 37b	19v	
Filippo Spagnolo Moro	Filippo	Paolosanti is paid for his upkeep.	1633	I-Fas, Camera del Granduca, f. 14b	55r	
Filippo Spagnolo Moro		Is given 5 ducati a month for his food.	1633	I-Fas, Camera del Granduca, f. 15a	20r	
Filippo Spagnolo Moro		5 scudi each month for his food.	1634	I-Fas, Camera del Granduca, f. 16a	19r	

Reference (as given in document)	Baptismal name (if known)	Other descriptors in document	Year	Citation		Owner (if known)
Filippo Spagnolo Moro		5 scudi each month for his food; listed as training in the "mestiero dell'Arc're."	1635	I-Fas, Camera del Granduca, f. 17a	27r	
Filippo Spagnolo Moro		"[C]he impara il Mestiero dell Arc*hierere*"; 5 scudi a month to cover his food; however, payments go only through the end of March 1637. Payments are often given directly to Maestro Giuseppe Archiere.	1636	I-Fas, Camera del Granduca, f. 18a	24r	
Filiziana	Maria Antonia	Mora, turca, fanciulla, approx. 20y, from Lisbon.	1671	I-Fca, Pia Casa, 2		Marco Abriuti
Fortunato Moro		"Alla Balia di Fortunato Moro due scudi per settembre." The wet nurse of Fortunato Moro is paid for the month of September.	1635	I-Fas, Camera del Granduca, f. 17b	9v	
Fortunato Moro		Another payment to the wet nurse.	1635	I-Fas, Camera del Granduca, f. 17b		
Fortunato Moro		Another payment to the wet nurse.	1635	I-Fas, Camera del Granduca, f. 17b	18v	
Fortunato Moro		Another payment to the wet nurse.	1636	I-Fas, Camera del Granduca, f. 17b	24v	
Fortunato Moro		Another payment to the wet nurse.	1636	I-Fas, Camera del Granduca, f. 17b	39r	
Fortunato Moro		Another payment to the wet nurse.	1636	I-Fas, Camera del Granduca, f. 17b	39r	
Fortunato Moro		Another payment to the wet nurse.	1636	I-Fas, Camera del Granduca, f. 17b	51r	

Name	Description	Year	Source	Folio	Other
Francesco	Turco moro, approx. 11y in 1594.	1603	I-Fca, Pia Casa, 1		Gucci
Francesco detto il Moretto	Given a license to leave the orphanage of the Innocenti, having reached maturity.	1617	I-Faoi, 1654, Exito di fanciulli (1617–)	F	
Francesco Moro del S. Cardinale		1637	I-Fas, Camera del Granduca,	5v	
Francesco Paulsanti Indiano furiere		1636	I-Fas, Camera del Granduca, f. 17b	37r	
Ga Moro	[Gave a gift of food.]	1650	I-Fas, Camera del Granduca, f. 22b	4v	
Ga Moro	[Gave a gift of food.]	1651	I-Fas, Camera del Granduca, f. 22b	40r	
Ga Moro	[Gave a gift of food.]	1651	I-Fas, Camera del Granduca, f. 22b	44r	
Ga Moro	[Gave a gift of food.]	1651	I-Fas, Camera del Granduca, f. 23b	4r	
Ga' Moro	Delivered melons.	1651	I-Fas, Camera del Granduca, f. 22b	40r	
Ga' Moro	Delivered melons.	1651	I-Fas, Camera del Granduca, f. 22b	44r	
Ga' Moro	Delivered melons.	1651	I-Fas, Camera del Granduca, f. 23b	4r	
Ganza di Ermetto	Turca, schiava, approx. 20y.	1666	I-Fca, Pia Casa, 2		Andrea Benvenuti
Gavone Ebreo	"A Vincentino spetiale, per Caccai comprato da Gavone Ebreo, come per nota."	1669	I-Fas, Camera del Granduca, f. 40c	21r	
Gelsima di Canza Criccheli	Turca. Was enslaved (possibly still enslaved), currently living in the house of Isabela Verazzini; has two children who are not named in the documents (see turco).	1662	I-Fca, Pia Casa, 2		

Reference (as given in document)	Baptismal name (if known)	Other descriptors in document	Year	Citation	Owner (if known)
Gelsima di Machemet		Turca, schiava, approx. 31y.	1666	I-Fca, Pia Casa, 2	Francesco Maria Capponi
Gelsima di Mostafa Arsia		Turca, approx. 17y.	1669	I-Fca, Pia Casa, 2	Benedetto Dragomanni SAS
Giafer Turco di Lader		Turco, stiavo, from Boreali.	1618	I-Fca, Pia Casa, 1	
Gio: Buonaccorsi Moro	Giovanni Buonaccorsi	Mus:o di Cam:a, paid vitto, e vestito, 4 lire. List of the prince's household members.	1663	I-Fas, Mediceo del Principato f. 5358	Prince Giovan Carlo de' Medici
Gio: d'Angola	Giovanni Battista	Stiavo, moro, turco, from Angola, approx. 18y. Described as a lackey of the prince.	1639	I-Fca, Pia Casa, 1	Prince Mattias de' Medici
Gio: d'Angola	Giovanni Battista	2/7/1640.	1640	I-Fd, Battesimi m, reg. 42, fg. 256	
Gio: detto ga Moro		[Gave a gift of food.]	1650	I-Fas, Camera del Granduca, f. 22b	4r
Gio: Moro		Delivering food.	1626	I-Fas, Camera del Granduca, f. 6b	33v
Gio: Moro			1628	I-Fas, Camera del Granduca, f. 8b	25v
Gio: Antonio Gaeta Mutolo	Gio: Antonio Gaeta		1664	I-Fas Camera del Granduca, f. 33b	135r
Gio: Antonio Gaeta Mutolo		Salaried for the year.	1664	I-Fas, Depositeria Generale, parte Antica, f. 397	80

Name		Note	Year	Source	Folio
Gio: Battista Chigi, moro		Lacche.	1660	I-Fas, Camera del Granduca, f. 30b	49r
Gio: Battista Faciullacci gia Ebreo fatto Cristiano			1672	I-Fas, Camera del Granduca, f. 42	103r
Gio: Battista Moro	[Chigi]	Lacche.	1660	I-Fas, Camera del Granduca, f. 30b	30r
Gio: Battista Moro	[Chigi]	Lacche.	1661	I-Fas, Camera del Granduca, f. 30b	79r
Gio: Battista Moro	[Chigi]	Lacche.	1661	I-Fas, Camera del Granduca, f. 30b	171r
Gio: Battista Moro	[Chigi]	Lacche.	1661	I-Fas, Camera del Granduca, f. 30b	184r
Gio: Battista Moro	[Chigi]	Lacche.	1662	I-Fas, Camera del Granduca, f. 31b	67r
Gio: Buonaccorsi	Giovanni Buonaccorsi	"Moro Birbone, va vestito da soldato Italiano: stracciato."	1662	I-Fimmobili, 1.17	6v
Gio: Buonaccorsi Moro	Giovanni Buonaccorsi	"Non ci va Signore" (see transcription published in main text of book).	1662	I-Fimmobili, 1.17	7r
Gio: de' Buonaccorsi Moro	Giovanni Buonaccorsi	"Gio: del Buonaccorsi moro, turco battezato stava in servitù del Sig. Cardinale Leopoldo Medici, habitava da la Lupica, morto con tutti sacrimenti e fu sepolto in chiesa nostra con 10 fra Prete e chierici questo di 15 di Agosto 1674."	1674	I-Fca, S. Felice in Piazza, Morti dal 1627 al 1686, RPU 0025.13	236v
Gio: de' Buonaccorsi Moro	Giovanni Buonaccorsi	"Gio: del Buonaccorsi moro, turco battezato stava in servitù del Sig. Cardinale Leopoldo Medici, habitava da la Lupica, morto con tutti sacrimenti e fu sepolto in chiesa nostra con 10 fra Prete e chierici questo di 15 di Agosto 1674."	1674	I-Fca, S. Felice in Piazza, Morti dal 1664 al 1745, RPU 0025.14	c.n.n.

Reference (as given in document)	Baptismal name (if known)	Other descriptors in document	Year	Citation	Owner (if known)
Gio: di Damasco			1636	I-Fas, Camera del Granduca, f. 18b 10v	
Gio: di Damasco			1637	I-Fas, Camera del Granduca, f. 18b 61v	
Gio: di Damasco			1637	I-Fas, Camera del Granduca, f. 18b 62v	
Gio: gia' Moro		Delivered melons.	1650	I-Fas, Camera del Granduca, f. 22b 4r	
Gio: Moro		Delivered melons.	1637	I-Fas, Camera del Granduca, f. 18b 59v	
Gio: Moro		Delivered melons.	1638	I-Fas, Camera del Granduca, f. 19b 53r	
Gio: Moro		Delivered melons.	1638	I-Fas, Camera del Granduca, f. 19b 54v	
Gio: Moro		Delivered melons.	1638	I-Fas, Camera del Granduca, f. 20b 4r	
Gio: Moro			1639	I-Fas, Camera del Granduca, f. 20b 52v	
Gio: Moro		Delivered melons.	1639	I-Fas, Camera del Granduca, f. 21b 8v	
Gio: Moro			1640	I-Fas, Camera del Granduca, f. 21b 55r	

Name	Description	Year	Source	Folio	Notes
Gio: Moro ser.e di S.A. Rev. [Gio Carlo de' Medici]				19v, 20r	
	Giovanni Buonaccorsi				
	"Iolao Moro ser.e di Teseo e Suo Abito / Calza radice di Taffetta nero con manica dell'istesso / Gubetta di raso mavi ricamata d'arg:to e coralli / Girello con busto di raso bianco ricamato d'oro, e Turchina / manica di Camicia al Imperiale / p in piedi scarpe alla Greca / al fianco scimitarra nobile con gioie e Corallo / In mano guanti / In testa berrettone mavi ricamato con pagio al Ingherina / con penne bianche e nere."	1661	I-FImmobili, 1.14		
Gioia	Turca mora, approx. 20y. Described as of Portuguese origin, though she claims to have been born in Livorno, presumably into slavery.	1678	I-Fca, Pia Casa, 2		
Giovambattista Morino	Christmas tips.	1630	I-Fas, Camera del Granduca, f. 12b	21r	
Giovambattista Morino	Tipped for Christmas.	1632	I-Fas, Camera del Granduca, f. 14b	23v	
Giovambattista Morino	Christmas.	1633	I-Fas, Camera del Granduca, f. 15b	21v	
Giovan Battista	Turco, stiavo, from Portugal, approx. 15y.	1677	I-Fca, Pia Casa, 2		
Giovan Battista da Messina	Che era sopra le Galere ricattato.	1628	I-Fas, Camera del Granduca, f. 10b	8r	
Giovan Moro	Delivered melons.	1639	I-Fas, Camera del Granduca, f. 20b	51v	
Giovanni	Turco, moro, approx. 11y. Instructed by Michele Zotti, tailor.	1610	I-Fca, Pia Casa, 1		
	Giovanni Battista				Armenian merchant in Livorno
					Christine of Lorraine

Reference (as given in document)	Baptismal name (if known)	Other descriptors in document	Year	Citation	Owner (if known)
Giovanni	Giovanni Battista	6/6/1610.	1610	I-Fd, Battesimi m, reg. 27, fg. 196	
Giovanni	Giovanni	"[S]tiavo del Cav. Lorenzo Corboli d'eta di anni 14 in circa, non si sa ne' patria ne nome di parenti, battezzato detto di sotto condittione non sapendosi se prima era battezzato." 10/14/1643.	1643	I-Fd, Battesimi m, reg. 44, fg. 232	
Giovanni (Morino Giovanni)		Possibly the Morino Giovanni owned by the grand duchess who converted in 1630.	1629	I-Fas, Camera del Granduca, f. 11b	18r
Giovanni (Morino Giovanni)			1629	I-Fas Camera del Granduca, f.11b	18v
Giovanni detto Gio Moro		"[S]i fuggi di casa il di 15 di Giugno 1628 d'Anni 15 incirca".	1628	I-Faoi, 1655, Esito delli Allevati delli Innocenti (1628)	G
Giovanni di Damasco			1637	I-Fas, Camera del Granduca, f. 18b	42r
Giovanni di Damasco			1637	I-Fas, Camera del Granduca, f. 19b	7r
Giovanni Indiano	Jacopo	Servo, stiavo, from Cuba, approx. 18–20y. Described as the servant of Nero Corsini and the slave of Bartolomeo Corsini in two different documents.	1609	I-Fca, Pia Casa, 1	Bartolomeo Corsini
Giovanni Indiano	Jacopo	11/5/1609.	1609	I-Fd, Battesimi m, reg. 27, fg. 200	

Name	Description	Date	Source	Folio	SAS
Giovanni Mezzo Moro	List of household members of the Grand Duke, undated, but given the membership, presumably from around 1630. Includes Giovanni Mezzo Moro (and Pietro Moro) as "staffieri del Granduca."	c. 1630	I-Fas, Mediceo del Principato f. 5385	90v	
Giovanni Moro	Delivered melons.	1631	I-Fas, Camera del Granduca, f. 12b	48v	
Giovanni Moro	Delivered melons.	1633	I-Fas, Camera del Granduca, f. 14b	52v	
Giovanni Moro	Delivered melons.	1640	I-Fas, Camera del Granduca, f. 21b	52v	
Giovannino moro	[Buonaccorsi?]	1667	I-Fas, Camera del Granduca, f. 39b	4r	
Giovannino moro	[Buonaccorsi?]	1669	I-Fas, Camera del Granduca, f. 40c	32r	
Giovannino Moro	Giovanni Buonaccorsi	Copy of poem "Il sogno di Giovannino Moro."	I-Fas, Mediceo del Principato, f. 6424	c.n.n.	Prince Giovan Carlo de' Medici
Giulia di Brachino Jacrambassa	Turca, from Croatia, approx. 28y.	1688	I-Fca, Pia Casa, 2		Niccolo Ronconi
Hakmet di Alia Bosu Kovi	Turco, schiavo, approx. 11y.	1686	I-Fca, Pia Casa, 2		Ferdinando Suarez
Hali	Stiavo, turco.	1621	I-Fca, Pia Casa, 1		Christine of Lorraine
Hamer Ben'Nassedin	Turco, stiavo, from Alessandria.	1616	I-Fca, Pia Casa, 1		Benedetta Guerrieri
Hanzada di Sacman	Turca, bambina, approx. 7y.	1669	I-Fca, Pia Casa, 2		Boccherini

Reference (as given in document)	Baptismal name (if known)	Other descriptors in document	Year	Citation	Owner (if known)
Has		Approx. 12y.	1608	I-Fca, Pia Casa, 1	SAS, then gifted to Nannina del Nero
Haser di Selem	Niccolo	Turco, stiavo, moro bianco. Worked in the stables for the Grand Duke.	1611	I-Fca, Pia Casa, 1	SAS
Haser di Selem	Niccolo	12/11/1611.	1611	I-Fd, Battesimi m, reg. 28, fg. 221	
Hassardino di Maccometto Hierme		Turco, stiavo, from Alessandria. Was captured approx. 9 years previously.	1617	I-Fca, Pia Casa, 1	SAS
		Stiava, turca, approx. 8y. Previously owned by Christine of Lorraine and then gifted to Filippo Uguccione's brother.	1614	I-Fca, Pia Casa, 1	Filippo Uguccione
Humicana di Mostafa Colcebacia		Turca, from Mostara, approx. 18y. Baptized while ill. The name Vincenzon Salvadore is given as her owner but then crossed out and replaced with Lorenzini.	1670	I-Fca, Pia Casa, 2	Antonio Francesco Lorenzini
Iach	Cosimo Fortunato Medici	Turco, moro, schiavo, approx. 14y.	1666	I-Fca, Pia Casa, 2	Prince Mattias de' Medici
Iach	Cosimo Fortunato Medici	5/16/1666.	1666	I-Fd, Battesimi m, reg. 56, fg. 30	
Iaia di Ali		Stiavo, from Tripoli. Worked in the stables; has been enslaved for 10 years.	1635	I-Fca, Pia Casa, 1	SAS

Name	Description	Year	Archive Reference	Owner
il Morino di Credenza		1644	I-Fas, Depositeria generale, f. 1604	Francesco II de' Medici
Ina di Cersein	Turca, schiava, approx. 9y. Has been enslaved for 3 years according to the document, though no owner is mentioned, and she is currently living in the Pia Casa dei Catecumeni.	1666	I-Fca, Pia Casa, 2	
Ismaelino di Mustafa	Piermaria Stiavo, turco, from Saline in Capri.	1627	I-Fca, Pia Casa, 1	
Ismaelino di Mustafa	Piermaria 5/3/1627.	1627	I-Fd, Battesimi m, reg. 36, fg. 64	Pietro Medici
Israele, son of Sara and Abramo	Antonio Moro, hebreo, approx. 10y, from Corfu.	1671	I-Fca, Pia Casa, 2	
Issa	Turca, stiava, from Smyrna, approx. 20y.	1684	I-Fca, Pia Casa, 2	Artemesia della Corgnia Medici SAS
Isuff d'Abudala	Stiavo, from Anatolia. Worked in the stables; has been enslaved for 28 years.	1635	I-Fca, Pia Casa, 1	
Jacob Ferrandei Ebreo Cioccalattiere		1668	I-Fas, Camera del Granduca, f. 39b	20r
Jacopo detto morino	"[S]i licentio' dal nostro spedale sotto di 18 Giugno 1630."	1630	I-Faoi, 1655, Esito delli Allevati delli Innocenti (1628)	J
Jacut	Francesco Schiavo, moro, from Sudan, approx. 20y.	1612	I-Fca, Pia Casa, 1	Conte Tassoni
Jacut	Francesco 2/26/1613.	1613	I-Fd, Battesimi m, reg. 29, fg. 51	
Jacut (or Jacutto)	Moro, stiavo, turco.	1638	I-Fca, Pia Casa, 1	Giovan Battista Baccelli

Reference (as given in document)	Baptismal name (if known)	Other descriptors in document	Year	Citation	Owner (if known)
Josepho (aka Giuseppe) di Mustafa		Turco, stiavo, from Bossina, approx. 24y.	1696	I-Fca, Pia Casa, 3	Zanobi Giorgi
Jusa di Constantonopoli	Giovanni Antoni	11/9/1665.	1665	I-Fd, Battesimi m, reg. 55, fg. 218	
Jusef di Cassan Pessivocich		Turco, schiavo, from Dalmatia, approx. 16y.	1692	I-Fca, Pia Casa, 3	Cosimo Maria del Sera
Jusein		Turco, from Cipri.	1630	I-Fca, Pia Casa, 1	
Jusse		Turco, approx. 17y, from Bossina.	1695	I-Fca, Pia Casa, 3	
Jussino		Turco, approx. 6y. Son of Meliam di Pace.	1676	I-Fca, Pia Casa, 2	
Jussuf di Bechir	Cosimo	Stiavo, approx. 45y, from Algeria, blind in one eye. Has been enslaved for 17 years. File includes a letter from a previous owner.	1609	I-Fca, Pia Casa, 1	Girolamo Tati
Jussuf di Bechir	Cosimo	11/19/1609.	1609	I-Fd, Battesimi m, reg. 27, fg. 127	
Jusuf		Turco, approx. 10y.	1665	I-Fca, Pia Casa, 2	Senatore Boromei
la Mora Fattima			1657	I-Fas, Camera del Granduca, 33r f. 28b	
la Mora Fattima			1668	I-Fas, Camera del Granduca, 36r f. 39b	
Latore Turco detto Suf	Giuseppe	Turco. Described as staying with Agnolo Firenzuola.	1630	I-Fca, Pia Casa, 1	

Name		Date	Description	Reference	Sponsor
Latore Turco detto Suf	Giuseppe	7/15/1630.		I-Fd, Battesimi m, reg. 38, fg. 54	
Lattifa	Maria Maddalena	1671	Turca, Lattifa Turca, approx. 13y.	I-Fca, Pia Casa, 2	Lucrezia Corsini
Lattifa	Maria Maddalena	1671	5/3/1671.	I-Fd, Battesimi f, reg. 280, fg. 167	
Lelia (or Zelia) di Memet Mustapine	Maria Margherita	1664	Turca, approx. 36y, from Dalmatia.	I-Fca, Pia Casa, 2	Girolamo Bardi
Lelia (or Zelia) di Memet Mustapine	Maria Margherita	1664	9/7/1664.	I-Fd, Battesimi f, reg. 277, fg. 101	
Lighiam moro		1619	Stiavo, moro, from Guinea, approx. 18y.	I-Fca, Pia Casa, 1	Antonio Simone
Lima		1697	Turca, from Algeria, approx. 50y. Describes herself as the widow of Amet, later baptized as Francesco, who died in Genova. Mother of Ali di Lima.	I-Fca, Pia Casa, 3	
Luna di Abram Costa		1680	Ebrea mora, approx. 14y.	I-Fca, Pia Casa, 2	
Luna di Amette	Maria Maddalena	1668	Turca, schiava, approx. 30y.	I-Fca, Pia Casa, 2	Dottor Moniglia
Luna Modiari Mora	Maria Maddalena	1668	5/19/1668; described as "mora."	I-Fd, Battesimi f, reg. 279, fg. 76	
Macheber Ruca	Maria Maddalena	1607	Turca, stiava, from Constantinople, approx. 40y.	I-Fca, Pia Casa, 1	Christine of Lorraine
Macheber Ruca	Maddalena	1607	9/24/1607.	I-Fd, Battesimi f, reg. 248, fg. 183	
Machmet d'Achmet		1612	Stiavo, approx. 17y.	I-Fca, Pia Casa, 1	Don Ottaviano de' Medici

Reference (as given in document)	Baptismal name (if known)	Other descriptors in document	Year	Citation	Owner (if known)
Maddalena	Maddalena	Turca; baptized 3/27/1606.	1606	I-Fd, Battesimi f, reg. 247, fg. 200	Benedetto Macchiavelli
Maddi Negro	Giovanni Battista Nardi	Turco, moro, stiavo, approx. 22y. Was enslaved from a very young age even in Borno.	1659	I-Fca, Pia Casa, 2	Pietro Paolo Nardi
Maddi Negro	Giovanni Battista Nardi	2/10/1659.	1659	I-Fd, Battesimi m, reg. 52, fg. 61	
Madi		Stiavo, moro, approx. 27y. Was sold into slavery in Constantinople at the age of 8.	1647	I-Fca, Pia Casa, 1	Lionardo and Tommaso Generotti
Maemet		Stiavo, turco, from Constantinople, approx. 22y.	1621	I-Fca, Pia Casa, 1	Ugolino Grifoni
Maemet		From Tunisia.	1623	I-Fca, Pia Casa, 1	
Maemet (known as Giorgio) Ipostoli		Claims to be a Greek Christian who was enslaved in Ottoman territories and has now fled in search of freedom.	1621	I-Fca, Pia Casa, 1	
Maemett di Ramadan	Paolo	Turco, stiavo, from Laiazzo, approx. 14y. Was purchased for 90 ducats.	1611	I-Fca, Pia Casa, 1	Grazia Grifoni
Maemett di Ramadan	Paolo	5/29/1611.	1611	I-Fd, Battesimi m, reg. 28, fg. 100	
Mahamed di Ben'Hamar		Turco, stiavo, from Alessandria	1616	I-Fca, Pia Casa, 1	Christine of Lorraine
Mambucca di Ali Barbier		Turco, from Tunisia, approx. 30y.	1706	I-Fca, Pia Casa, 3	
Mamet	Carlo	Stiavo, from Cairo, approx. 25y.	1630	I-Fca, Pia Casa, 1	Prince Giovan Carlo de' Medici

Mamet	Carlo	7/8/1630.	1630	I-Fd, Battesimi m, reg. 38, fg. 21	
Mamet		Turco, approx. 12y. The owner, Mavelli, is a "staffiere" to SAS; Mamet is described as the brother of Milos.	1692	I-Fca, Pia Casa, 3	Daniando Mavelli
Mametto di Brachin Durmiscevich		Turco, schiavo, approx. 13y. Brother of Chiarima di Brachin Duramiscevich.	1674	I-Fca, Pia Casa, 2	Fabio Cantucci
Mametto di Giuli		Turco, from Algeria.	1624	I-Fca, Pia Casa, 1	
Manetta Moro		Fece la lucia.	1629	I-Fas, Camera del Granduca, f. 11b	18v
Maomet d'Ali	Antonio	Turco, from Prenesa, stiavo, approx. 8y; baptized 6/24/1606.	1606	I-Fd, Battesimi m, reg. 25, fg. 125	
Maometto	Giovanni Battista	Turco, stiavo, from Tunisia, approx. 25y.	1629	I-Fca, Pia Casa, 1	
Maometto	Giovanni Battista Andrea	3/25/1630.	1630	I-Fd, Battesimi m, reg. 37, fg. 130	
Maometto		Stiavo. Baptized in the hospital.	1632	I-Fca, Pia Casa, 1	
Maometto		Along with Moro.	1653	I-Fas, Camera del Granduca, f. 24b	47r
Maometto		Along with Chinan and Pier. Giovanni.	1653	I-Fas, Camera del Granduca, f. 24b	47r
Maometto Turco			1653	I-Fas, Camera del Granduca, f. 25b	1r
Maometto Turco			1653	I-Fas, Camera del Granduca, f. 25b	12v
Maometto Turco			1653	I-Fas, Camera del Granduca, f. 25b	14v	Bartolomeo della Staffa
Maometto Turco					Antonio Grimani Marchese Fabrizio Coloreto

Reference (as given in document)	Baptismal name (if known)	Other descriptors in document	Year	Citation	Owner (if known)
Mara		Turca, from Dalmatia, approx. 15y.	1687	I-Fca, Pia Casa, 2	Antonio Norzi in Careggi
Marco		Negro, schiavo.	1614	I-Fca, Pia Casa, 1	Comitiz de Vazlies
Margiano		Stiavo, moro, turco, from the Levant.	1639	I-Fca, Pia Casa, 1	Raffaello Alamanni
Maria Maddelena Convoni Turca Battezzata		Given permission to take a room in the Orbatello cloisters, which were reserved for impoverished women.	1683	I-Faoi, 10452, Orbatello c. 824	
Maria schiava		"Pagati a P. Gio: Batista Amori Priori di S. Paolo … per suo rimborso di tanti spesi in revestire le due minori figliole della Maria schiava di Roverschino Rosso fine, e per otto Camicie, et Otto Grembuili di panno nostrale, servito per la Madre et tre sue figle, e fatture de Vestiti e Camicie sudette."	1671	I-Fas, Camera del Granduca, 45r f. 42	
Marragone delle Galere		"[C]he va alla Madonna dell'Loreto."	1637	I-Fas, Camera del Granduca, 6r f. 19b	
Marzocco stiavo			1624	I-Fas, Camera del Granduca, 28r f. 5b	
Matteo di Gio Battista Delli di Pisa		Supplication to Prince Mattias de' Medici to have his 5-year sentence on the galleys reduced.	1662	I-Fas, Mediceo del Principato, 347r, 348r f. 5487	

				SAS
Matteo Indiano	Giovanni	Indiano, stiavo, from the "indie occidentali." 2/28/1611.	1610	I-Fca, Pia Casa, 1
Matteo Indiano	Giovanni		1611	I-Fd, Battesimi m, reg. 28, fg. 60
Mattia Medici			1672	I-Fas, Camera del Granduca, f. 42 130r
Mattia Medici			1673	I-Fas, Camera del Granduca, f. 42 191r
Mattia Medici			1673	I-Fas, Camera del Granduca, f. 42 202l
Mattia Medici			1673	I-Fas, Camera del Granduca, f. 42 212l
Mattio Battezzato			1672	I-Fas, Camera del Granduca, f. 42 101l
Mattio Battezzato			1672	I-Fas, Camera del Granduca, f. 42 160l
Mattio Battezzato … che serviva il Generale delle galere			1672	I-Fas, Camera del Granduca, f. 42 80l
Mattio Battezzato … che serviva il Generale delle galere			1672	I-Fas, Camera del Granduca, f. 42 87l
Mattio Battezzato che serviva il Generale delle galere			1672	I-Fas, Camera del Granduca, f. 42 92r

Reference (as given in document)	Baptismal name (if known)	Other descriptors in document	Year	Citation	Owner (if known)
Mattio Battezzato che serviva il Generale delle galere			1672	I-Fas, Camera del Granduca, f. 42	96l
Mattio Battezzato che serviva il Sig. Ammiraglio Ricasoli			1672	I-Fas, Camera del Granduca, f. 42	73l
Mattio figlio di Giorgio moro			1653	I-Fas, Camera del Granduca, f. 24b	52v
Mattio Medici			1672	I-Fas, Camera del Granduca, f. 42	147l
Mattio Medici			1673	I-Fas, Camera del Granduca, f. 42	165l
Mattio Medici			1673	I-Fas, Camera del Granduca, f. 42	171r
Mattio Medici			1673	I-Fas, Camera del Granduca, f. 42	220r
Mattio Medici Battezzato		"[P]er sua provisione di tutto il sopradetto mese, a ragione di 40 pezze da 8 reali l'anno, e questa e' la prima pagha."	1672	I-Fas, Camera del Granduca, f. 42	106r
Mattio Medici gia Turcho del S. Sergardi Genereale delle Galere			1672	I-Fas, Camera del Granduca, f. 42	126l

Name			Description	Year	Source	Owner
Mattio Moro			"Pagati a Arrigo Vinter... tanti se li fanno dare per il vitto di numero 6 fra nani, e mori legl'appiè nomi per il mese di ottobre passato.... Batistone, Andrea fratello di Batistone, Pier Gio, Ferdinando Moro, Filippino, Mattio Moro."	1657	I-Fas, Mediceo del Principato, f. 5487	Prince Mattias de' Medici
Maumet Chiaus Maumetto			Turco, from Greece, stiavo. Turco, approx. 50y, from Constantinople.	1617 1681	I-Fca, Pia Casa, 1 I-Fca, Pia Casa, 2	SAS Giuseppe Rossano
Mechmet di Mussa	Giuseppe Maria		Turco etiope, stiavo, approx. 14y, from Borno.	1685	I-Fca, Pia Casa, 2	SAS
Mechmet di Mussa	Giuseppe Maria		7/22/1685.	1685	I-Fd, Battesimi m, reg. 65, fg. 214	
Mecometo di Homer			Turco, approx. 20y.	1696	I-Fca, Pia Casa, 3	
Mecrema di Memmia Sarevichi			Turca. Was enslaved (possibly still enslaved), currently living in the house of Count Bentivoglio. Wife of Joseph Calamichi.	1662	I-Fca, Pia Casa, 2	
Meemest Aecheinen Colisisci	Giuseppe Maria	Piero	5/7/1668.	1668	I-Fd, Battesimi m, reg. 57, fg. 54	
Meliam di Pace			Turca, from Smyrna, approx. 22y. Mother of Jussino.	1676	I-Fca, Pia Casa, 2	
Mellucia			Turca, approx. 12y.	1608	I-Fca, Pia Casa, 1	SAS, then gifted to Nannina del Nero

Reference (as given in document)	Baptismal name (if known)	Other descriptors in document	Year	Citation	Owner (if known)
Meme di Canza	Filippo Maria	Turco, stiavo, from Croatia, approx. 15y.	1663	I-Fca, Pia Casa, 2	Bernardo Arighetti
Meme di Canza	Filippo Maria	9/8/1663.	1663	I-Fd, Battesimi m, reg. 54, fg. 131	
Memet		Turco, approx. 17y, from Bossina. Was purchased from Bernardo Guainai.	1692	I-Fca, Pia Casa, 3	Rev. Giuseppe Guainai
Meometto d'Ebraim	Francesco	Stiavo, turco, from the Archipelago, approx. 27y. Interesting account of having been enslaved in Alessandria on an Ottoman boat and smuggling himself to Europe in order to convert to Christianity.	1642	I-Fca, Pia Casa, 1	
Meometto d'Ebraim	Francesco	9/14/1642.	1642	I-Fd, Battesimi m, reg. 44, fg. 47	
Merceo schiavo del Cap. Cardi			1653	I-Fas, Camera del Granduca, 44v f. 24b	
Merema di Sulan		Turca, from Dalmatia, approx. 20y.	1687	I-Fca, Pia Casa, 2	Gio: Filippo Michelozzi Boni
Merema di Teamen	Maria Angiola	Turca, approx. 19y.	1664	I-Fca, Pia Casa, 2	Francesco Caccini
Merema di Teamen	Maria Angiola	9/7/1664.	1664	I-Fd, Battesimi f, reg. 277, fg. 101	

Name	Baptismal name	Description	Year	Archive	Folio	Notes
Mero di Ahmet		Turco, approx. 14y, schiavo. Describes himself as having been stolen and then sold.	1669	I-Fca, Pia Casa, 2		Pietro Cavvo Armeno
Mesenet di Mostafa	Cosimo	Stiavo, turco, approx. 20y. Had been enslaved for 1 year.	1606	I-Fca, Pia Casa, 1		SAS
Mesenet di Mostafa	Cosimo	7/16/1606.	1606	I-Fd, Battesimi m, reg. 25, fg. 141		
Mesenet di Mostafa	Cosimo					
Micco di Jure	Alberto Maria	Turco, stiavo, approx. 14y.	1663	I-Fca, Pia Casa, 2		Cavaliere del Rosso
Micco di Jure	Alberto Maria	9/8/1663.	1663	I-Fd, Battesimi m, reg. 54, fg. 94		
Michele Cuper			1671	I-Fas, Camera del Granduca, f. 42	41l	
Michele Cuper		"[A]ccio giocassero."	1672	I-Fas, Camera del Granduca, f. 42	147l	
Michele Cuper		"[A]ccio giocassero."	1672	I-Fas, Camera del Granduca, f. 42	147r	
Michele Cuper		"[A]ccio giocassero."	1672	I-Fas, Camera del Granduca, f. 42	148l	
Michele Cuper			1673	I-Fas, Camera del Granduca, f. 42	162l	
Mina di Abramo		Mora, schiava, approx. 30y.	1666	I-Fca, Pia Casa, 2		Pietro and Felice Catani
Mina di Badchino Gregatovich	Maria Antonia	Turca, approx. 12y.	1664	I-Fca, Pia Casa, 2		Benedetto Dragomanni
Mina di Badchino Gregatovich	Maria Antonia	9/7/1664.	1664	I-Fd, Battesimi f, reg. 277, fg. 101		

Reference (as given in document)	Baptismal name (if known)	Other descriptors in document	Year	Citation	Owner (if known)
Mine	Cristina	Turca, stiava, approx. 12y.	1608	I-Fca, Pia Casa, 1	Christine of Lorraine, or Girolamo di Angolo Guicciardini
Mine	Cristina	4/7/1608.	1608	I-Fd, Battesimi m, reg. 248, fg. 137	
Minia	Maria Anna	From Cecina, approx. 13y.	1663	I-Fca, Pia Casa, 2	Carlo Corbinelli
Minia	Maria Anna	9/8/1663	1663	I-Fd, Battesimi f, reg. 276, fg. 180	
Minia (or Maria) di Stefano	Maria Caterina	Turca. Was enslaved (possibly still enslaved), currently living in the house of the Geani.	1662	I-Fca, Pia Casa, 2	
Minia (or Maria) di Stefano	Maria Caterina	5/31/1662.	1662	I-Fd, Battesimi f, reg. 276, fg. 51	
Mocareme di Usain Sabacicacie		Turco, from Dalmatia, approx. 18y.	1691	I-Fca, Pia Casa, 3	
Mochiba		Turca, from Bosnia, approx. 28y. Has a husband (named Mostafa) and a son, both of whom she believes are still alive somewhere. Was taken 3 years ago and sold in Livorno.	1671	I-Fca, Pia Casa, 2	Vettorio Nelli
Mochiva		Schiava, approx. 19y.	1668	I-Fca, Pia Casa, 2	Marchese del Bufolo

Name		Description	Date	Source	Owner
Moglietto Moro della Galeazza Nuova Momi			1634	I-Fas Camera del Granduca, f.15b	
		Stiavo, from Negroponte, approx. 14y.	1613	I-Fca, Pia Casa, 1	Zanobi Bucherelli SAS
Monsor di Achmetem Casme Morassi		Turco, schiavo, from Algeria, approx. 38y.	1670	I-Fca, Pia Casa, 2	
		Schiavo, creduto turco, approx. 15y. Has been with his current owner for approx. 8 years.	1659	I-Fca, Pia Casa, 2	Gio: Maria Petracchi
Morato Corono		From the Levant, schiavo.	1664	I-Fca, Pia Casa, 2	Antonio Serristori
Mordacheo di Raffaello Ebreo	Giuseppe	Moro, ebreo, approx. 2y. Son of Benvenuta/Teresa.	1653	I-Fca, Pia Casa, 2	
Mordacheo di Raffaello Ebreo	Giuseppe	12/31/1653.	1653	I-Fd, Battesimi m, reg. 49, fg. 270	
Morello Cerusico		"[P]er la Compagna di Pisa."	1669	I-Fas, Camera del Granduca, f. 40c	27r
Morello Cerusico		"[D]ella Compagnia di Pisa."	1670	I-Fas, Camera del Granduca, f. 41c	61v
Moretta Schiava	Maria Angiola	Stiava, approx. 13y.	1606	I-Fca, Pia Casa, 1	Maddalena Salvetti, wife of Zanobi Acciaiuoli
Moretta Schiava	Maria Angiola	9/27/1606.	1606	I-Fd, Battesimi f, reg. 248, fg. 75	
Morino schiavo		Morino, schiavo.	1647	I-Fca, Pia Casa, 1	Pompeo del Monte

Reference (as given in document)	Baptismal name (if known)	Other descriptors in document	Year	Citation	Owner (if known)
Moro	Giovanni Buonaccorsi	3 copies of the same list, shows the re-distribution of the prince's staff after his death.	1663	I-Fas, Mediceo del Principato, f. 5358	Prince Giovan Carlo de' Medici 701–702, 706–707, 728–729
Moschiva Fattima		Turca, schiava, approx. 26y.	1668	I-Fca, Pia Casa, 2	Gio Carlo Ridolfi
Moselinium Mehemetum		Turco.	1624	I-Fca, Pia Casa, 1	Alessandro de' Medici
Mossoli		Stiavo, turco, from Constantinople.	1623	I-Fca, Pia Casa, 1	Ottaviano de' Piccardini
Mostafa	Ferdinando	Stiavo, turco, from Constantinople.	1606	I-Fca, Pia Casa, 1	SAS
Mostafa	Ferdinando	7/16/1606.	1606	I-Fd, Battesimi m, reg. 25, fg. 162	
Mostafa	Carlo	Moro, stiavo, turco.	1611	I-Fca, Pia Casa, 1	SAS
Mostafa	Carlo	12/8/1611.	1611	I-Fd, Battesimi m, reg. 28, fg. 149	
Mostafa	Gio: Antonio	Previously baptized at home 7/9/1663, rebaptized in church 9/8/1663	1663	I-Fd, Battesimi m, reg. 54, fg. 153	
Mostafa di Ali	Domenico Antonio	Moro, turco, approx. 12y, from Candia.	1663	I-Fca, Pia Casa, 2	Niccolo Santa Paolina
Mostafa di Ali	Domenico Antonio	9/8/1663.	1663	I-Fd, Battesimi m, reg. 54, fg. 120	
Mostafa di Cairo	Francesco Maria	Turco, stiavo, moro, approx. 12y. Worked in the stables for the Grand Duke.	1611	I-Fca, Pia Casa, 1	SAS
Mostafa di Cairo	Francesco Maria	9/11/1611.	1611	I-Fd, Battesimi m, reg. 28, fg. 162	

Mostafà di Tolombotto	Cosima Maria	Turcho, moro, from Persia, approx. 15y.	1671	I-Fca, Pia Casa, 2	SAS
Mostafà di Tolombotto	Cosima Maria	9/8/1671.	1671	I-Fd, Battesimi m, reg. 58, fol. 133	
Mucametto Amech Solivich		Turco, schiavo, approx. 17y.	1668	I-Fca, Pia Casa, 2	Ferdinando Capponi
Mucchia Musuet de Stola	Maria Maddalena	5/27/1668.	1668	I-Fd, Battesimi f, reg. 279, fg. 77	
Muccio di Racchezemo	Vincenzo	Stiavo, approx. 18y, from Presensa. Knows how to write in Turkish.	1606	I-Fca, Pia Casa, 1	SAS
Muccio di Racchezemo	Vincenzo	7/16/1606.	1606	I-Fd, Battesimi m, reg. 25, fg. 231	
Muchiba di Idrighe		Turca, approx. 15y.	1672	I-Fca, Pia Casa, 2	Tommaso Geppi
Muchibe (wife of Osman Oroccevich)		Turca, approx. 34y, schiava. Wife of Osman Oroccevich.	1670	I-Fca, Pia Casa, 2	Pietro Capocci
Muchina		Turca, stiava. Though owned by SAS, she is currently living in the house of Artemesia della Corgnia Medici.	1685	I-Fca, Pia Casa, 2	SAS
Mus di Osman		Turco, from Belgrade, servo, approx. 16y.	1693	I-Fca, Pia Casa, 3	Gaetano Risaliti
Musli di Hascif	Giovanni Battista	Stiavo, turco, approx. 35y.	1609	I-Fca, Pia Casa, 1	SAS
Musli di Hascif	Giovanni Battista	6/6/1610.	1610	I-Fd, Battesimi m, reg. 27, fg. 196	
Musso d'Osman		Turco, from Schiavonia, approx. 12y.	1665	I-Fca, Pia Casa, 2	Carlo Ughi Prince
Mussolino di Ali	Giovanni Battista	Stiavo, turco, from Constantinople, approx. 50y.	1646	I-Fca, Pia Casa, 1	Lorenzo de' Medici

Reference (as given in document)	Baptismal name (if known)	Other descriptors in document	Year	Citation	Owner (if known)
Mussolino di Ali	Giovanni Battista	5/19/1646.	1646	I-Fd, Battesimi m, reg. 46, fg. 77	
Mustafa	Leonardo	Stiavo, from Vesprino in Hungary. Had been baptized 8 years previously while desperately ill but wanted to repeat the ceremony in the church.	1608	I-Fca, Pia Casa, 1	Jacopo Dati
Mustafa	Leonardo	4/5/1608.	1608	I-Fd, Battesimi m, reg. 26, fg. 188	
Mustafa	Carlo Maria	Turco, schiavo, approx. 5y, from Tunisia.	1668	I-Fca, Pia Casa, 2	Marchese Cerini
Mustafa	Carlo Maria	6/22 1668.	1668	I-Fd, Battesimi m, reg. 57, fg. 26	
Mustafa		Described as having been captured at a very young age.	1686	I-Fca, Pia Casa, 2	
Mustafa (of Joseph)		Turco, from Serbia. Salvagio is a "furiere" for SAS.	1685	I-Fca, Pia Casa, 2	Luigi Salvagio
Mustafa d'Osman		Turco, from Begrade, approx. 20y.	1698	I-Fca, Pia Casa, 3	Antonio Temperini
Mustafa di Amat Moro	Ferdinando	Stiavo, turco, moro, from Rodos, approx. 20y.	1646	I-Fca, Pia Casa, 1	SAS
Mustafa di Amat Moro	Ferdinando	9/23/1646.	1646	I-Fd, Battesimi m, reg. 46, fg. 61	
Mustafa di Assano		Turco, stiavo, approx. 18 or 20y.	1672	I-Fca, Pia Casa, 2	Ronconi

Name	Owner	Description	Year	Archive		Other
Mustafa di Chassan	Anton Francesco Maria Peruzzi	Stiavo, turco, from Smyrna, approx. 45y. Has been enslaved for 27 years. His file includes a letter of support from another convert, Giovanni Battista, who serves Prince Lorenzo de' Medici (presumably Mussolino/Giovanni Battista).	1647	I-Fca, Pia Casa, 1		Jacopo Peruzzi
Mustafa di Chassan (or Assan)	Anton Francesco Maria Peruzzi	10/4/1647	1647	I-Fd, Battesimi m, reg. 46, fg. 175		
Mustafa di Maemet Solac	Giovan Paolo	Turco, stiavo, from Constantinople, approx. 52y. Has worked as a soldier, has been enslaved for 18 years. Baptismal date given as 10/10/1631.	1631	I-Fca, Pia Casa, 1		The heirs of Paolo Rucellai
Mustafa di Mista Mustafà Moro		Turco, stiavo, approx. 9y. Money paid to Mattio Fontebuoni for materials used by Cosimo/Almansor and by Mustafà Moro.	1690 1671	I-Fca, Pia Casa, 3 I-Fas, Camera del Granduca, f. 42	151	Lenzoni
Mustafat di Niccolo		From Constantinople. Claims to be a Greek Christian who was enslaved in Ottoman territories and has now fled in search of freedom.	1621	I-Fca, Pia Casa, 1		
Mustaffa Turcho		Stiavo, from Rodi, approx. 14y.	1613	I-Fca, Pia Casa, 1		Ubertino Ricasoli
Nebbia di Alia Orobaschichi		Turca, maumettana, approx. 30y.	1665	I-Fca, Pia Casa, 2		Carlo Ughi
Nebbia di Mico		Turca, from Dalmatia, approx. 35y. Described as the wife of Sciachi (possibly Sciaba, given the timing).	1689	I-Fca, Pia Casa, 3		

Reference (as given in document)	Baptismal name (if known)	Other descriptors in document	Year	Citation	Owner (if known)
Nebbia di Sacri		Turca, schiava from Dalmatia, approx. 16y.	1686	I-Fca, Pia Casa, 2	Barbara Ronconi nei Neri
Nebi (or Anabi)		Stiavo, approx. 44y.	1622	I-Fca, Pia Casa, 1	Cosimo del Sera
Olmeda Ebreo		"[C]he fabrica il Ciocolatte."	1669	I-Fas, Camera del Granduca, 18v f. 40c	
Orsumanno (or Osman) di Mustafa	Gio: Batista	Turco, approx. 8y. Was enslaved (possibly still enslaved), currently living in the house of Ottomanna Biaghi.	1662	I-Fca, Pia Casa, 2	
Osman d'Ansan Popprichi		Turcho, approx. 10y. Was enslaved (possibly still enslaved), currently living in the house of Francesco Carnischi.	1662	I-Fca, Pia Casa, 2	
Osman di Mustafa	Gio: Batista	3/30/1662.	1662	I-Fd, Battesimi m, reg. 54, fg. 36	
Osmano di Cassano	Antonio Maria	Turco, from Croatia, approx. 20y.	1668	I-Fca, Pia Casa, 2	Piero da Verrazzano
Osmano di Cassano	Antonio Maria	5/15/1668.	1668	I-Fd, Battesimi m, reg. 57, fg. 3	
Ottula di Jezuf		Turco, stiavo, approx. 14y.	1675	I-Fca, Pia Casa, 2	
Pandolfini della barca			1666	I-Fas, Camera del Granduca, 69r f. 35b	SAS
Pandolfini detto il Morino	[Agniolo Pandolfini?]		1663	I-Fas, Camera del Granduca, 72r f. 33b	
Paolo Carlovich		From Croatia, gia soldato a Livorno.	1623	I-Fas, Camera del Granduca, 10r f. 5b	

Name	Description	Date	Archive reference	Folio	Patron
Pattima (or Pattituma)	Chiara	Turca, stiava, approx. 32y, from Bona. Was catechized by the house priest and by another convert, "Paolo Turco fatto Christiano."	1608	I-Fca, Pia Casa, 1		Giulio Estense Tassoni
Pattima (or Pattituma)	Chiara	9/14/1608.	1608	I-Fd, Battesimi f, reg. 249, fg. 12		
Per' figluolo di Juan turco	Andrea	"[D]i anni 10 in circa."	1662	I-Fd, Battesimi m, reg. 54, fg. 3		Corsini
Piale (known as Andrea) di Andrea		Claims to be a Greek Christian who was enslaved in Ottoman territories and has now fled in search of freedom.	1621	I-Fca, Pia Casa, 1		
Piale Greco		Stiavo, turco, approx. 26y.	1602	I-Fca, Pia Casa, 1		
Pier Maria Pertinari Ebreo battezzato			1667	I-Fas, Camera del Granduca, f. 38b	15r	
Piero Albanese		Gia soldato a Livorno.	1623	I-Fas, Camera del Granduca, f. 5b	10r	
Pietro		Approx. 85y.	1641	I-Fas, Mediceo del Principato, f. 5363	421v	Pietro de' Medici
Pietro Moro		Money spent for his outfit, including 12 new shirts.	1624	I-Fas, Camera del Granduca, f. 5b	29r	
Pietro Moro		Tipped for Christmas.	1625	I-Fas, Camera del Granduca, f. 6b	16r	
Pietro Moro		Rewarded for having shot down two birds.	1626	I-Fas, Camera del Granduca, f. 6b	23v	
Pietro Moro			1626	I-Fas, Camera del Granduca, f. 6b	24v	
Pietro Moro			1626	I-Fas, Camera del Granduca, f. 7b	12v	

Reference (as given in document)	Baptismal name (if known)	Other descriptors in document	Year	Citation		Owner (if known)
Pietro Moro			1627	I-Fas, Camera del Granduca, f. 8b	7r	
Pietro Moro			1627	I-Fas, Camera del Granduca, f. 8b	13r	
Pietro Moro			1628	I-Fas, Camera del Granduca, f. 10b	18r	
Pietro Moro		Christmas.	1629	I-Fas, Camera del Granduca, f. 11b	20v	
Pietro Moro		Christmas tips.	1630	I-Fas, Camera del Granduca, f. 12b	21r	
Pietro Moro		"[D]ue scudi d'elemisina per il Ragazzo amalato."	1636	I-Fas, Camera del Granduca, f. 17b	51r	
Pietro Moro		List of household members of the Grand Duke, undated, but given the membership, presumably from around 1630. Includes Pietro Moro (and Giovanni Mezzo Moro) as "staffieri del Granduca."	c. 1630	I-Fas, Mediceo del Principato, f. 5385	90v	SAS
Pietro moro del Sr. Cardinale			1628	I-Fas, Camera del Granduca, f. 9c	25v	
Pietro Moro lacche			1631	I-Fas, Camera del Granduca, f. 12b	35r	
Pietro Moro lacche		Rewarded for a trip to Pratolino.	1634	I-Fas, Camera del Granduca, f. 15b	47r	
Piloto il Moro		There is no comma in this list between these two names, implying they are a single person, but it may well refer to Piloto and to il Moro.	1630	I-Fas, Camera del Granduca, f. 12b	2r	

Name	Baptismal name	Description	Year	Archive	Folio	Sponsor
Pistacchio		Turco, muto, approx. 28y. His owner works as a "speziale" for SAS; described as a deaf mute. In Pisa.	1681	I-Fca, Pia Casa, 2		Vincenzo Sandrini
Pizzicata Schiavo			1661	I-Fas, Camera del Granduca,	134r	
Porre (or Piero) d'Ivvan	Andrea	Turco, approx. 10y. Was enslaved (possibly still enslaved), currently living in the house of Bernardo Percori.	1662	I-Fca, Pia Casa, 2	f. 30b	
Pugniatta Moro			1634	I-Fas, Camera del Granduca, f. 15b	24r	
Racchema di Druach Laicie		Turca, approx. 11y.	1664	I-Fca, Pia Casa, 2		Francesco Maria Bontalenti Senatore Panciatici
Raffia		Greca, approx. 13y. Was enslaved to Turks at the age of 3y and then later captured by Christians.	1686	I-Fca, Pia Casa, 2		
Raima di Asmat Lubini	Maria Maddalena	Approx. 11y.	1663	I-Fca, Pia Casa, 2		Andrea Corsini
Raima di Asmat Lubini	Maria Maddalena	9/8/1663.	1663	I-Fd, Battesimi f, reg. 276, fg. 180		
Raima di Mussein	Maria Verginia	Turca, approx. 25y. Was enslaved (possibly still enslaved), currently living in the house of Pier Francesco Bartolini. Mother of Salia di Raima and wife of Macometto Calimichi.	1662	I-Fca, Pia Casa, 2		
Raima di Mussein	Maria Verginia	5/31/1662.	1662	I-Fd, Battesimi f, reg. 276, fg. 51		
Ramada di Smida		Turco, stiavo, from Tunisia, approx. 54y.	1680	I-Fca, Pia Casa, 2		Luca degli Albizzi

Reference (as given in document)	Baptismal name (if known)	Other descriptors in document	Year	Citation	Owner (if known)
Reggep di Omer Peralic		Turco, schiavo, from Dalmatia, approx. 21y.	1665	I-Fca, Pia Casa, 2	Ferrante Capponi
Reggeppe Assanmoisinovichie		Turco, approx. 12y.	1686	I-Fca, Pia Casa, 2	Filippo Senghieri
Rigeppe d'Aggi	Francesco	Turco, moro, from Bona, approx. 35y. The Pia Casa documents include an official description detailing his physical appearance including moles and scars. His skin is described as "negro olivastro", or a dark/black brownish green like an olive.	1607	I-Fca, Pia Casa, 1	Silvio Piccolomini
Rigeppe d'Aggi	Francesco	3/9/1608.	1608	I-Fd, Battesimi m, reg. 26, fg. 155	
Risuani di Eusene Selenti		Turco, stiavo, from Cairo, approx. 22y.	1631	I-Fca, Pia Casa, 1	Niccolo Giugno
Romandan Mehcante		Servitore, turco, from Rodis in Greece. Was taken into slavery 10 years previously. These documents describe him using the term servant.	1638	I-Fca, Pia Casa, 1	Duca di Guisa
Rosa di Ismael		Stiava, turca, from Paias, approx. 27y. Captured by the galleys 9 years previously.	1646	I-Fca, Pia Casa, 1	Giacob Ebreo
Rosoan		"A Jacopino dell'Armaiolo per una Chittara per Rosoan."	1635	I-Fas, Camera del Granduca, 14v f. 17b	
Rosoan Turco		"[C]he impara a Ballare e schermire." 5 scudi each month for his food.	1635	I-Fas, Camera del Granduca, 30r f. 17a	

Rosoan Turco			"[C]he impara a Ballare e schermire." 5 scudi a month to cover his food.	1636	I-Fas, Camera del Granduca, f. 18a	27r
Rosoan Turco			"[C]he impara a Ballare, e schermire." 5 scudi a month to cover his food.	1637	I-Fas, Camera del Granduca, f. 19a	25r
Rosoan Turco			"[C]he impara a Ballare e schermire."	1638	I-Fas, Camera del Granduca, f. 20a	24r
Rosoan Turco			"[C]he impara a Ballare e altre Virtu." 5 scudi per month.	1639	I-Fas, Camera del Granduca, f. 21a	21r
Saba di Arsonovicchio	Giovanni Filippo Maria		Turco, approx. 11y.	1664	I-Fca, Pia Casa, 2		Mattias Bartolommei
Saba di Arsonovicchio	Giovanni Filippo Maria		9/7/1664.	1664	I-Fd, Battesimi m, reg. 55, fg. 75	
Saccia d'Ali Orlovich			Turca, from Bosnia, approx. 23y.	1687	I-Fca, Pia Casa, 2		Francesco Rigolgi
Saccina			Turca, approx. 15y. Has been enslaved for 7 years; mentions that her mother is also living in Florence and has been baptized into Christianity.	1668	I-Fca, Pia Casa, 2		Filippo Nerli
Saccina di Vileada Maumet	Maria Angiola		Turca, approx. 11y.	1664	I-Fca, Pia Casa, 2		Filippo Nerli
Saccina di Vileada Maumet	Maria Angiola		9/7/1664.	1664	I-Fd, Battesimi f, reg. 277, fg. 101	
Sadet'Albini detto Gregorio			Turco, from Circassis, approx. 12y.	1684	I-Fca, Pia Casa, 2		Armenians
Saigma di Meemet Assano			Turco, moro, approx. 20y.	1688	I-Fca, Pia Casa, 2		Alessandro and Francesco Ambrogi

Reference (as given in document)	Baptismal name (if known)	Other descriptors in document	Year	Citation	Owner (if known)
Saino di Comer		Turco, from Macedonia, approx. 13y.	1686	I-Fca, Pia Casa, 2	Bernardo Maria Baldi
Salceh di Assano	Simone	Turcho, approx. 10y.	1664	I-Fca, Pia Casa, 2	Simone Taganucci
Salceh di Assano	Simone	9/7/1664.	1664	I-Fd, Battesimi m, reg. 55, fg. 131	Simone Taganucci
Salcia di Ebraim		Turca, approx. 11y.	1665	I-Fca, Pia Casa, 2	Beatrice Tarlati
Salcina di Seidin		Turca, schiava, approx. 13y.	1666	I-Fca, Pia Casa, 2	Maddalena Lapini
Salcina Velchiere d'Alimicio	Maria Maddalena	Turca, schiava, approx. 22y. Describes being enslaved and having transited through Livorno, but no owner's name is given.	1668	I-Fca, Pia Casa, 2	
Salcina Velchiere d'Alimicio	Maria Maddalena	7/20/1668.	1668	I-Fd, Battesimi f, reg. 279, fg. 83	
Salemme	Margherita	Turca. Baptized at the hospital 6/21/1606.	1606	I-Fca, Pia Casa, 1	SAS
Salemme di Acometto		Turco, stiavo, from Alessandria. Was captured approx. 9 years previously.	1617	I-Fca, Pia Casa, 1	SAS
Salemme di Solimano		Stiavo, from Algeria. Worked in the stables; has been enslaved for 23 years.	1635	I-Fca, Pia Casa, 1	SAS
Saletta Micucca Mora	Maria Maddalena	Turca, schiava, approx. 2y. Baptized at home 12/17/1668.	1668	I-Fca, Pia Casa, 2	Lucrezia Strozzi
Saletta Micucca Mora	Maria Maddalena	6/8/1668.	1668	I-Fd, Battesimi f, reg. 279, fg. 78	

Sali di Brachino		Turco, approx. 11y.	1686	I-Fca, Pia Casa, 2	Zanobi Giorgi SAS
Sali di Cassan		Turco, approx. 24y.	1687	I-Fca, Pia Casa, 2	
Salia		Turca, approx. 14y. Fled from Jewish owners and wishes to convert.	1672	I-Fca, Pia Casa, 2	
Salia di Ali		Turca, schiava, approx. 15y.	1666	I-Fca, Pia Casa, 2	Teodoro Levantino
Salia di Homer	Maria Teresa	Turca. Was enslaved (possibly still enslaved), currently living in the house of Ferrante Capponi.	1662	I-Fca, Pia Casa, 2	
Salia di Homer	Maria Teresa	5/31/1662.	1662	I-Fd, Battesimi f, reg. 276, fg. 51	
Salia di Juso Miochi		Turca, from Dalmatia, approx. 9y.	1685	I-Fca, Pia Casa, 2	Laura Ubaldini Franchi Niccolo Mardelli
Salia di Mustafà	Maria Teresa	Schiava, approx. 48y.	1668	I-Fca, Pia Casa, 2	
Salia di Mustafà	Maria Teresa	6/21/1668.	1668	I-Fd, Battesimi f, reg. 279, fg. 79	
Salia di Raima	Maria Felice	Turca, approx. 7y. Was enslaved (possibly still enslaved), currently living in the house of Maria Cimeni; daughter of Raima di Mussein.	1662	I-Fca, Pia Casa, 2	
Salia di Raima	Maria Felice	5/31/1662.	1662	I-Fd, Battesimi f, reg. 276, fg. 51	
Salia di Uscein	Maria Felice	Turca, approx. 18y.	1664	I-Fca, Pia Casa, 2	Carlo Ballerini
Salia di Uscein	Maria Felice	9/7/1664.	1664	I-Fd, Battesimi f, reg. 277, fg. 101	

Reference (as given in document)	Baptismal name (if known)	Other descriptors in document	Year	Citation	Owner (if known)
Salica di Jusuph Galiot	Maria Catherina	Turca. Was baptized at home while ill.	1687	I-Fca, Pia Casa, 2	
Salica di Zucchanzich Ocanzilz		Turca, from Bosnia, approx. 15y.	1686	I-Fca, Pia Casa, 2	Marchese Riccardi
Salich di Saline Samimabasea	Filippo Maria	Turco, approx. 14y.	1664	I-Fca, Pia Casa, 2	Vincenzo del Sera
Salich di Saline Samimabasea	Filippo Maria	9/7/1664.	1664	I-Fd, Battesimi m, reg. 55, fg. 50	
Salima d'Amet Vrmovich	Margherita	Turca, approx. 33y.	1664	I-Fca, Pia Casa, 2	Piero da Verrazzano
Salima d'Amet Vrmovich	Margherita	9/7/1664.	1664	I-Fd, Battesimi f, reg. 277, fg. 101	
Salma di Arstanovicchio	Giuseppe Luigi Maria	Turco, approx. 13y.	1664	I-Fca, Pia Casa, 2	Mattias Bartolommei
Salma di Arstanovicchio	Giuseppe Luigi Maria	9/7/1664.	1664	I-Fd, Battesimi m, reg. 55, fg. 74	
Salma di Camboza		Approx. 13y, from Dalmatia.	1663	I-Fca, Pia Casa, 2	Mattias Bartolommei
Samuello di Captain Chiaves		Ebreo moro, approx. 10y.	1674	I-Fca, Pia Casa, 2	
Sara di Abramo di Israele		Mora, turca, vedova, approx. 30y, from Tunisia. Now working as a servant (serva) to Lorenzo Lorenzini; mother to Simonto and Israele/Antonio.	1671	I-Fca, Pia Casa, 2	

Name		Description	Year	Source	Notes
Sara di Brida		Turca, approx. 13y. Described as currently living in the Pia Casa dei Mendicanti in order to learn a trade.	1690	I-Fca, Pia Casa, 3	
Schian d'Oxman		Turco, schiavo, approx. 35y.	1692	I-Fca, Pia Casa, 3	Lorenzo Gualtieri Gaddi Francesco Ghiberti Cardinal de' Medici Maracelli
Sciaba di Soglio		Turco, stiavo.	1689	I-Fca, Pia Casa, 3	
Sciater di Gines	Margherita	Stiava, turca	1634	I-Fca, Pia Casa, 1	
Selim		Turco, from Bosnia, approx. 12y, schiavo.	1693	I-Fca, Pia Casa, 3	
Selima		Turca, approx. 4y, from Dalmatia.	1665	I-Fca, Pia Casa, 2	
Selima di Be		Turca, mora, from the Morea, approx. 24y.	1687	I-Fca, Pia Casa, 2	
Simonte, son of Sara and Abramo		Moro, hebreo, approx. 16y, from Corfu. Living in the house of Antoinio Armaleoni.	1671	I-Fca, Pia Casa, 2	
Smirro Turco	Carlo	Stiavo, turco, moro bianco, from Tunis. Worked in the stables.	1641	I-Fca, Pia Casa, 1	SAS
Smirro Turco	Carlo	3/3/1641.	1641	I-Fd, Battesimi m, reg. 43, fg. 32	
Soin di Basche		Turco, stiavo, approx. 30y. Works in the stables.	1679	I-Fca, Pia Casa, 2	SAS
Solefar Trombetto		"A Solefar Trombetto due scudi, et a Girolamo suo maestro quattro scudi"	1636	I-Fas, Camera del Granduca, f. 17b	23v
Solefar Turcho		"[C]he impara a sonare la Trombetta." 5 scudi each month for his food.	1635	I-Fas, Camera del Granduca, f. 17a	29v
Solefar Turco		"A Solefar Turco per farsi rapare."	1636	I-Fas, Camera del Granduca, f. 17b	42r

Reference (as given in document)	Baptismal name (if known)	Other descriptors in document	Year	Citation	Owner (if known)
Solefar Turco		"[C]he impara a sonare la Tromba." 5 scudi a month to cover his food.	1636	I-Fas, Camera del Granduca, f. 18a 26v	
Solefar Turco		"[C]he impara a sonar la Tromba." 5 scudi a month to cover his food.	1637	I-Fas, Camera del Granduca, f. 19a 24v	
Solefar Turco		"[C]he impara a sonar la Tromba."	1638	I-Fas, Camera del Granduca, f. 20a 23v	
Solefar Turco		"[C]he impara a sonare la tromba." 5 scudi per month.	1639	I-Fas, Camera del Granduca, f. 21a 20v	
Solimano		Turco, moro, approx. 23y, from Bornio.	1608	I-Fca, Pia Casa, 1	SAS or Christine of Lorraine
Speranza di Bernardo		Turca, mora, from Cape Verde, approx. 15y. Fled from Jewish owners in Livorno and wishes to convert.	1677	I-Fca, Pia Casa, 2	
Stella di Abram Barù		Turca, originally from Smyrna but lived in Amsterdam, approx. 48y. Was taken into slavery at a young age.	1677	I-Fca, Pia Casa, 2	
Stella Mus	Maria Maddalena	Turca, schiava, from the Levant, approx. 22y.	1668	I-Fca, Pia Casa, 2	Anton Francesco Ticcia
Stella Mus Mora	Maria Maddalena	6/30/1668.	1668	I-Fd, Battesimi f, reg. 279, fg. 80	
Sunibol (or Srimbol) di Merbret	Francesco	Stiavo, from Moglo di Cappa in Barbary.	1606	I-Fca, Pia Casa, 1	SAS
Sunibol (or Srimbol) di Merbret	Francesco	7/16/1606.	1606	I-Fd, Battesimi m, reg. 25, fg. 162	

Name		Date	Archive	Owner
Surcia Scavoli stiavo		1636	I-Fas, Camera del Granduca, f. 17b, 35r	
Tessa	Approx. 7y. She and her sister, Sofia, were taken from a boat near Malta.	1610	I-Fca, Pia Casa, 1	Lorenzo Usimbardi Signora Caccini
Timisillo di Mehemecht Prealinich	Turco, stiavo, approx. 28y.	1673	I-Fca, Pia Casa, 2	
Tommaso che viene dell'Indie	"[S]tato altre volte."	1672	I-Fas, Camera del Granduca, f. 42	123l
Tommaso Costa Moro Indiano	"[I]n occasione che egli se ne ritorna al Paese."	1673	I-Fas, Camera del Granduca, f. 42	192r
Tommaso Moro che è stato in India		1673	I-Fas, Camera del Granduca, f. 42	160r
Tommaso Moro Indiano		1673	I-Fas, Camera del Granduca, f. 42	171r
Tommaso Moro Indiano		1673	I-Fas, Camera del Granduca, f. 42	188r
Trasuma di Anza di Livibuschi	Maria Angiola 5/31/1662.	1662	I-Fd, Battesimi f, reg. 276, fg. 51	
Truffo	Turco, from Algeria, approx. 8y.	1686	I-Fca, Pia Casa, 2	Senatore Panciatici Prince Mattias de' Medici
Tuffega	Maria Adelaide Mora, fanciulla, approx. 9y., from Borno. Sister of Ali/Ferdinando.	1657	I-Fca, Pia Casa, 2	
Tuffega	Maria Adelaide 7/29/1657.	1657	I-Fd, Battesimi f, reg. 273, fg. 220	
Uisir di Chiarali	Turco moro, ethiope, from close to Constantinople.	1680	I-Fca, Pia Casa, 2	

Reference (as given in document)	Baptismal name (if known)	Other descriptors in document	Year	Citation	Owner (if known)
Umana di Ali Andai Bei		Fanciulla turca, stiava.	1611	I-Fca, Pia Casa, 1	Christine of Lorraine, then gifted to Filippo Salviati Raffaello Giusti
Vaida di Cechie	Francesca	Schiava, approx. 60y.	1668	I-Fca, Pia Casa, 2	
Vaida di Cechie	Francesca	11/29/1668.	1668	I-Fd, Battesimi f, reg. 279, fg. 49	
Veli di Mustafa		Turco, approx. 23y.	1687	I-Fca, Pia Casa, 2	
Viladea di Maumet	Maria Domenica	Presumably Bileada di Maumet. 9/7/1664.	1664	I-Fd, Battesimi f, reg. 277, fg. 101	
Vincenzo Moro			1624	I-Fas, Camera del Granduca, f. 5b	36v
Vincenzo Turchino del S. Conte di Novellara		Delivered cheese.	1671	I-Fas, Camera del Granduca, f. 42	401
Zachida di Baiaziti		Schiava, turca, approx. 46y.	1668	I-Fca, Pia Casa, 2	Gio: Paolo Prato
Zaffira	Margherita Medici	Turca, stiava, approx. 30y., from Croatia.	1658	I-Fca, Pia Casa, 2	Ottavia Altoviti Medici
Zaffira d'Orace		Turca, stiava, approx. 10y.	1661	I-Fca, Pia Casa, 2	Princess de' Medici
Zaffira Santa	Margherita Medici	1/1/1659.	1659	I-Fd, Battesimi f, reg. 274, fg. 211	

Zaida di Sein	Maria Niccola	Turca, schiava, approx. 26y.	1668	I-Fca, Pia Casa, 2	Argentina Ridolfi
Zaida di Sein	Maria Niccola	7/31/1668.	1668	I-Fd, Battesimi f, reg. 279, fg. 84	
Zaime	Maria	Stiava, turca. Baptized at the hospital 6/21/1606.	1606	I-Fca, Pia Casa, 1	SAS
Zanobi battezzato		Zanobi is given 4 lire to buy shoes. This occurs nearly every month during the year.	1621	I-Fas, Camera del Granduca, f. 2b	10v, passim
Zanobi battezzato		Money for his shoes.	1622	I-Fas, Camera del Granduca, f. 3b	10r, passim
Zanobi battezzato		Paid for his shoes; also in one instance paid for having made or brought toothpicks.	1625	I-Fas, Camera del Granduca, f. 6b	5r, passim
Zanobi battezzato			1626	I-Fas, Camera del Granduca, f. 7b	2v, passim
Zanobi battezzato			1627	I-Fas, Camera del Granduca, f. 8b	4v, passim
Zanobi battezzato			1628	I-Fas, Camera del Granduca, f. 9c	6v, passim
Zanobi battezzato			1628	I-Fas, Camera del Granduca, f. 10b	2r, passim
Zanobi battezzato			1629	I-Fas, Camera del Granduca, f. 11b	4r, passim
Zanobi battezzato		Regular payments to Napoli for shoes for Zanobi Battezzato.	1630	I-Fas, Camera del Granduca, f. 12b	4v, passim
Zanobi battezzato			1632	I-Fas, Camera del Granduca, f. 14b	6r, passim

Reference (as given in document)	Baptismal name (if known)	Other descriptors in document	Year	Citation	Owner (if known)
Zanobi battezzato		Money for shoes each month.	1633	I-Fas, Camera del Granduca, f. 15b	6r, passim
Zanobi battezzato		Shoes each month.	1635	I-Fas, Camera del Granduca, f. 17b	9r, passim
Zanobi battezzato		Money each month to buy a pair of shoes.	1636	I-Fas, Camera del Granduca, f. 18b	10r, passim
Zanobi battezzato		Paid each month for a pair of shoes.	1637	I-Fas, Camera del Granduca, f. 19b	7r, passim
Zanobi battezzato		Reimbursed for 10 months' worth of new shoes.	1639	I-Fas, Camera del Granduca, f. 20b	35r
Zanobi battezzato		Payment for a new pair of shoes.	1639	I-Fas, Camera del Granduca, f. 21b	19v, passim
Zucherec Adem	Caterina	Turca, stiava, father Ali from Prevesa, approx. 13y.	1606	I-Fca, Pia Casa, 1	Niccola Capponi
Zucherec Adem	Caterina	6/25/1606.	1606	I-Fd, Battesimi f, reg. 247, fg. 137	
Zuffa di Mustaffa Chiecho		Turca, from Dalmatia.	1676	I-Fca, Pia Casa, 2	

Anonymous Individuals Who Can Be Strongly Linked to the Medici Family

Reference (as given in document)	Baptismal name (if known)	Other descriptors in document	Year	Citation		Owner (if known)
uno schiavo delle stalle		A barber is rewarded for having healed a slave who had been injured, 2 scudi.	1621	I-Fas, Camera del Granduca, f. 2b	20r	SAS
Al morino lavorante alla fabrica de Pitti			1621	I-Fas, Camera del Granduca, f. 2b	20v	SAS
Al Morino Cocchiero		Tipped at Christmas.	1621	I-Fas, Camera del Granduca, f. 2b	32v	SAS
Mezzo moro		Mezzo moro and Giovanannino, both lackeys, are tipped for having accompanied the Grand Duke's carriage to Pisa.	1622	I-Fas, Camera del Granduca, f. 2b	44v	
Mezzo moro			1622	I-Fas, Camera del Granduca, f. 3b	27r	
Morino Cocchiere		Tipped for Christmas.	1622	I-Fas, Camera del Granduca, f. 3b	37v	
Mezzomoro			1623	I-Fas, Camera del Granduca, f. 5b	19r, passim	
lo stiavo che tiene conto del Cammello il Morino che sta in Boboli			1624	I-Fas, Camera del Granduca, f. 5b	31r	
Mezzomoro			1624	I-Fas, Camera del Granduca, f. 5b	39r	
Mezzomoro		The father of Mezzomoro is also mentioned.	1625	I-Fas, Camera del Granduca, f. 6b	1r, passim	
Mezzomoro, padre di Mezzomoro			1626	I-Fas, Camera del Granduca, f. 7b	3r, passim	

Reference (as given in document)	Baptismal name (if known)	Other descriptors in document	Year	Citation		Owner (if known)
Mezzomoro, padre di Mezzomoro			1627	I-Fas Camera del Granduca, f. 8b	1r, passim	
Morino di Credenza			1627	I-Fas, Camera del Granduca, f. 8b	1v	
un Moro garzone di stalla			1627	I-Fas, Camera del Granduca, f. 8b	2v	
Morino di Credenza			1627	I-Fas, Camera del Granduca, f. 8b	10v	
Morino Credenziere		Rewarded for having presented "un'insalata bella."	1628	I-Fas, Camera del Granduca, f. 8b	21v	
Mezzomoro			1628	I-Fas, Camera del Granduca, f. 9b	5r, passim	
Morino lache'			1628	I-Fas, Camera del Granduca, f. 9c	5v	
il morino di credenza			1628	I-Fas, Camera del Granduca, f. 9c	6r	
il moro di camera del Sr. Cardinale			1628	I-Fas, Camera del Granduca, f. 9c	26v	
il pollachino del S. Don Pietro			1628	I-Fas, Camera del Granduca, f. 9c	26v	
Mezzomoro, padre di Mezzomoro			1628	I-Fas, Camera del Granduca, f. 10b	1v, passim	
il pollachino del Sr Principe Don Lorenzo			1628	I-Fas, Camera del Granduca, f. 10b	8r	
il morino			1628	I-Fas, Camera del Granduca, f. 10b	14v	
il Morino di Credenza			1629	I-Fas, Camera del Granduca, f. 10b	22r	
il Pollacchino			1629	I-Fas, Camera del Granduca, f. 10b	22r	

il Morino		Per la nuova di chi vinse il Palio.	1629	I-Fas, Camera del Granduca, f. 10b	39r	
Al morino		Che porta la nuova del Palio.	1629	I-Fas, Camera del Granduca, f. 10b	45v	
Al Morino			1629	I-Fas, Camera del Granduca, f. 10b	51r	
Mezzomoro, padre di Mezzomoro			1629	I-Fas, Camera del Granduca, f. 11b	3r, passim	
Morino		Tipped for participating in a boxing match.	1629	I-Fas, Camera del Granduca, f. 11b	5v	
Morino			1629	I-Fas, Camera del Granduca, f. 11b	7r	
Morino		Went to Pratolina to fetch "Lo Schiorina."	1629	I-Fas, Camera del Granduca, f. 11b	8v	
Morino		Tipped along with Jacopino, Mezomoro, Tramontano and il Rosso for regularly following SAS when he rides.	1629	I-Fas, Camera del Granduca, f. 11b	16v	
Morino		The jeweler is paid 5 lire for a pearl earing for Morino.	1629	I-Fas, Camera del Granduca, f. 11b	18r	
Morino		Tipped for participating in a boxing match with the nephew of Mencarone.	1629	I-Fas, Camera del Granduca, f. 11b	18r	
Morino		Participated in a boxing match with Pietro Nano and Marcuccio.	1629	I-Fas, Camera del Granduca, f. 11b	18v	
Morino		The cupmaker is paid for 4 cups for il Morino.	1629	I-Fas, Camera del Granduca, f. 11b	19r	
il turco, che ci serve alli stalli	Giovan Carlo	Records the prince's permission for baptism to take place and notes that afterward Giovan Carlo will be paid a salary of 30 lire a month.	1630	I-Fas, Mediceo del Principato, f. 5178	20r	Prince Giovan Carlo de' Medici
Morino			1630	I-Fas, Camera del Granduca, f. 11b	23r	
Morino			1630	I-Fas, Camera del Granduca, f. 11b	23v	

Reference (as given in document)	Baptismal name (if known)	Other descriptors in document	Year	Citation		Owner (if known)
Morino		Rewarded along with Pietro nano.	1630	I-Fas, Camera del Granduca, f. 11b	23v	
Morino			1630	I-Fas, Camera del Granduca, f. 11b	24r	
Morino			1630	I-Fas, Camera del Granduca, f. 11b	24r	
Morino		In this particularly dense passage of references to the Morino, the court is in Livorno, and the Morino is being tipped for the morning of this day, the evening of that, though it is not clear what activity he was doing to merit the payouts.	1630	I-Fas, Camera del Granduca, f. 11b	24r	
Morino			1630	I-Fas, Camera del Granduca, f. 11b	24r	
Morino			1630	I-Fas, Camera del Granduca, f. 11b	24v	
Morino			1630	I-Fas, Camera del Granduca, f. 11b	24v	
Morino		Boxed with the nephew of Menacarone.	1630	I-Fas, Camera del Granduca, f. 11b	25r	
Morino		The cabralaio was paid for a pair of shoes for the Morino.	1630	I-Fas, Camera del Granduca, f. 11b	25v	
Morino			1630	I-Fas, Camera del Granduca, f. 11b	26r	
Morino			1630	I-Fas, Camera del Granduca, f. 11b	26r	
Morino		Paid for having traveled to Livorno and back.	1630	I-Fas, Camera del Granduca, f. 11b	26r	
Morino			1630	I-Fas, Camera del Granduca, f. 11b	27r	
Morino			1630	I-Fas, Camera del Granduca, f. 11b	27r	
Morino			1630	I-Fas, Camera del Granduca, f. 11b	27v	
Morino			1630	I-Fas, Camera del Granduca, f. 11b	29r	

Morino		1630	I-Fas, Camera del Granduca, f. 11b	30r
Morino		1630	I-Fas, Camera del Granduca, f. 11b	31r
Morino	Given money for the fair.	1630	I-Fas, Camera del Granduca, f. 11b	31r
Morino		1630	I-Fas, Camera del Granduca, f. 11b	31r
Morino	Tipped along with the Nanino.	1630	I-Fas, Camera del Granduca, f. 11b	31v
Morino		1630	I-Fas, Camera del Granduca, f. 11b	33r
Morino		1630	I-Fas, Camera del Granduca, f. 11b	33r
Morino	A baron is given the equivalent of 2 lire after the Morino broke his head with a rock.	1630	I-Fas, Camera del Granduca, f. 11b	33v
Moro	Tipped along with Nanino.	1630	I-Fas, Camera del Granduca, f. 11b	34v
Moro	Hit 3 shots with the crossbow.	1630	I-Fas, Camera del Granduca, f. 11b	34v
Morino	Tipped along with Pietrino Nano.	1630	I-Fas, Camera del Granduca, f. 11b	35r
Moro	"A Pietrino nano ballò meglio del Nano Moro."	1630	I-Fas, Camera del Granduca, f. 11b	35v
Morino		1630	I-Fas, Camera del Granduca, f. 11b	35v
Morino		1630	I-Fas, Camera del Granduca, f. 11b	36r
Morino		1630	I-Fas, Camera del Granduca, f. 11b	42r
Moro	Tipped along with Nano.	1630	I-Fas, Camera del Granduca, f. 11b	46r
Moro	Tipped along with "un'altro Ragazzo."	1630	I-Fas, Camera del Granduca, f. 11b	46r
Morino	Paid 10 scudi on the occasion of his marriage.	1630	I-Fas, Camera del Granduca, f. 11b	50r
Mezzomoro		1630	I-Fas, Camera del Granduca, f. 11b	50r
Mora	"Alla Mora SA perse due testoni." Not entirely clear whether this "Mora" is a person or a game of chance.	1630	I-Fas, Camera del Granduca, f. 11b	50r
Morino		1630	I-Fas, Camera del Granduca, f. 11b	51r

Reference (as given in document)	Baptismal name (if known)	Other descriptors in document	Year	Citation		Owner (if known)
Morino di SA		"Al Moro del Sig. Staffa et al Morino di SA in due volte quattro testoni 1.1.-." This entry clearly distinguishes between two different Black men (one of whom is young).	1630	I-Fas, Camera del Granduca, f. 11b	53r	
Morino			1630	I-Fas, Camera del Granduca, f. 12b	2r	
Morino			1630	I-Fas, Camera del Granduca, f. 12b	4v	
Morino		Along with il Nano.	1630	I-Fas, Camera del Granduca, f. 12b	5r	
Morino			1630	I-Fas, Camera del Granduca, f. 12b	5v	
Morino			1630	I-Fas, Camera del Granduca, f. 12b	8r	
Morino			1630	I-Fas, Camera del Granduca, f. 12b	9r	
Morino		Along with il Nano.	1630	I-Fas, Camera del Granduca, f. 12b	9v	
Morino		"[C]he fece a correre"	1630	I-Fas, Camera del Granduca, f. 12b	9v	
Moro		Along with il Nano.	1630	I-Fas, Camera del Granduca, f. 12b	10r	
Moro		"A quella Donna che fece alle pugnia col Moro."	1630	I-Fas, Camera del Granduca, f. 12b	10r	
Morino		Rewarded for boxing along with the boy of Menacarne.	1630	I-Fas, Camera del Granduca, f. 12b	10r	
Mezzomoro			1630	I-Fas, Camera del Granduca, f. 12b	10r, passim	
il Moro manovale		Worked to dig out rocks.	1630	I-Fas, Camera del Granduca, f. 12b	10v	
Moro			1630	I-Fas, Camera del Granduca, f. 12b	10v	
Morino		3 individuals (Scaccia, Frega, Sandino Pierino) are tipped for having run with the Morino in the Boboli gardens.	1630	I-Fas, Camera del Granduca, f. 12b	10r	

Moro	Along with il Nano.	1630	I-Fas, Camera del Granduca, f. 12b	12r
Morino	"Al Portiere per saltarelli per il Morino"; Saltarelli could mean fast-moving dances involving energetic jumps or parts for a virginal (instrument).	1630	I-Fas, Camera del Granduca, f. 12b	13r
Moro	"[P]er temporare Razzi."	1630	I-Fas, Camera del Granduca, f. 12b	13r
Morino	Rewarded for boxing with Marcuccio.	1630	I-Fas, Camera del Granduca, f. 12b	13v
Morino		1630	I-Fas, Camera del Granduca, f. 12b	15r
Morino	Along with il Nano and Lombrico.	1630	I-Fas, Camera del Granduca, f. 12b	15r
Moro	Along with il Nano.	1630	I-Fas, Camera del Granduca, f. 12b	15v
il Turco nano	The boatman is tipped for having transported the "Turco nano."	1630	I-Fas, Camera del Granduca, f. 12b	17r
Nano turco		1630	I-Fas, Camera del Granduca, f. 12b	17r
Morino	Boxed with the nephew of Mencarone.	1630	I-Fas, Camera del Granduca, f. 12b	17r
Moro		1630	I-Fas, Camera del Granduca, f. 12b	17r
Moro		1630	I-Fas, Camera del Granduca, f. 12b	17v
Moro	Along with Lombrico and Pietro.	1630	I-Fas, Camera del Granduca, f. 12b	18r
Moro	Along with il Nano.	1630	I-Fas, Camera del Granduca, f. 12b	18v
Morino	Along with Lombrico and Nano.	1630	I-Fas, Camera del Granduca, f. 12b	18v
Morino	"[C]he si imbriaco." Tipped for getting intoxicated.	1630	I-Fas, Camera del Granduca, f. 12b	18v
Morino		1630	I-Fas, Camera del Granduca, f. 12b	19v
il Tiratore Turco Battezzato	A marksman.	1631	I-Fas, Camera del Granduca, f. 12b	23v
Turco nano	Tipped for having washed himself.	1631	I-Fas, Camera del Granduca, f. 12b	23v

Reference (as given in document)	Baptismal name (if known)	Other descriptors in document	Year	Citation		Owner (if known)
Morino		Captain Vett.o is tipped for having loaned horses to Buffone and the Morino when they went to the house of the Cardinal.	1631	I-Fas, Camera del Granduca, f. 12b	23v	
il Tiratore Turco Battezzato			1631	I-Fas, Camera del Granduca, f. 12b	23v	
il Tiratore Turco Battezzato		Reimbursed for gunpowder and amunition.	1631	I-Fas, Camera del Granduca, f. 12b	21r	
Morino		"Spense la Candela in Bocca."	1631	I-Fas, Camera del Granduca, f. 12b	25r	
Morino		Along with Nano, tipped for having had his hair cut.	1631	I-Fas, Camera del Granduca, f. 12b	25r	
Moro		Along with Nano and Lombrico.	1631	I-Fas, Camera del Granduca, f. 12b	26r	
Morino		Along with Lombrico.	1631	I-Fas, Camera del Granduca, f. 12b	26r	
Morino			1631	I-Fas, Camera del Granduca, f. 12b	27r	
Moro		Along with Nibbino, rewarded for an activity in the snow.	1631	I-Fas, Camera del Granduca, f. 12b	27v	
il Morino che serve all fabbrica			1631	I-Fas, Camera del Granduca, f. 12b	27v	
Moro		Along with Lombrico.	1631	I-Fas, Camera del Granduca, f. 12b	28r	
Il Turco nano		"Al Barbiere che rapo' il Turco nano."	1631	I-Fas, Camera del Granduca, f. 12b	28v	
Morino		Along with Lombrico and Nano.	1631	I-Fas, Camera del Granduca, f. 12b	28v	
Moro		Along with Lombrico and Nano.	1631	I-Fas, Camera del Granduca, f. 12b	31r	
Morino		Boxing with Marcuccio.	1631	I-Fas, Camera del Granduca, f. 12b	31r	
Moro		Along with Lombrico and Nano.	1631	I-Fas, Camera del Granduca, f. 12b	33v	

Moro	Jacopo Capolettino is paid for 2 beast costumes in which Moro and the Buffone are to be masked.	1631	I-Fas, Camera del Granduca, f. 12b	33v
Morino	"[C]he infarino' il Morino."	1631	I-Fas, Camera del Granduca, f. 12b	33r
Morino	Presumably his tip for having been covered in flour.	1631	I-Fas, Camera del Granduca, f. 12b	33r
Turco nano	Shoes are bought for the Turco nano and for the Morino.	1631	I-Fas, Camera del Granduca, f. 12b	33r
Morino	Shoes are bought for the Turco nano and for the Morino.	1631	I-Fas, Camera del Granduca, f. 12b	33r
Nano turco		1631	I-Fas, Camera del Granduca, f. 12b	34r
Turco nano		1631	I-Fas, Camera del Granduca, f. 12b	35r
Morino		1631	I-Fas, Camera del Granduca, f. 12b	35v
Morino		1631	I-Fas, Camera del Granduca, f. 12b	36r
Morino	Boxing with the son of Maestro Piero.	1631	I-Fas, Camera del Granduca, f. 12b	36r
Morino	Along with Lombrico and Nano.	1631	I-Fas, Camera del Granduca, f. 12b	37v
Moro	For having his hair cut.	1631	I-Fas, Camera del Granduca, f. 12b	40r
Moro	Moro and Lombrico are paid for having carried a basket.	1631	I-Fas, Camera del Granduca, f. 12b	41r
Moro	Along with Lombrico and Nano.	1631	I-Fas, Camera del Granduca, f. 12b	43r
Moro	Along with Nano.	1631	I-Fas, Camera del Granduca, f. 12b	43v
Moro	Was hit in the head with a crossbow bolt.	1631	I-Fas, Camera del Granduca, f. 12b	44r
Mezzomoro		1631	I-Fas, Camera del Granduca, f. 12b	44v
Moro	"Al Moro uno scudo per dare al Gonnella suo maestro." Gonnella was a commedia dell'arte actor named Caraffa.	1631	I-Fas, Camera del Granduca, f. 12b	45v

Reference (as given in document)	Baptismal name (if known)	Other descriptors in document	Year	Citation		Owner (if known)
Moro		"[S]i tuffò nell'acqua."	1631	I-Fas, Camera del Granduca, f. 12b	48r	
Morino		Given money to buy saltarelli.	1631	I-Fas, Camera del Granduca, f. 12b	48r	
Moro		Along with Lombrico and Nano.	1631	I-Fas, Camera del Granduca, f. 12b	49r	
Moro		Along with Catorcio is tipped for having done many salti (jumps).	1631	I-Fas, Camera del Granduca, f. 12b	51v	
Moro		Along with Catorcio.	1631	I-Fas, Camera del Granduca, f. 12b	52r	
Moro			1631	I-Fas, Camera del Granduca, f. 12b	52r	
Moro			1631	I-Fas, Camera del Granduca, f. 12b	52v	
Moro			1631	I-Fas, Camera del Granduca, f. 12b	53r	
Mora			1631	I-Fas, Camera del Granduca, f. 12b	54r	
Mora			1632	I-Fas, Camera del Granduca, f. 14b	5v	
Morino spagnolo	Filippo	Boxed along with Bosco.	1632	I-Fas, Camera del Granduca, f. 14b	7r	
Morino spagnolo	Filippo	The "stufaiolo" (worker in charge of the stove) tipped for sprucing up the Morino spagnolo.	1632	I-Fas, Camera del Granduca, f. 14b	8r	
Moro spagnolo	Filippo	Merlupo is given money for his food.	1632	I-Fas, Camera del Granduca, f. 14b	11v	
Morino spagnolo	Filippo	Chiociolino from Siena is given money to cover material taken from his store in order to clothe the Morino spagnolo; and a tailor in Siena is paid for his work.	1632	I-Fas, Camera del Granduca, f. 14b	12r	
Morino		Presumably the Morino spagnolo as Merlupo is given money for his food.	1632	I-Fas, Camera del Granduca, f. 14b	15r	
Moro		Along with Bosco.	1632	I-Fas, Camera del Granduca, f. 14b	15v	

Name	Name 2	Description	Year	Source	Folio
Moro		Swallowed 2 coins.	1632	I-Fas, Camera del Granduca, f. 14b	16v
Morino		Boxed along with Bosco.	1632	I-Fas, Camera del Granduca, f. 14b	21v
Moro		"[U]n testone perche possa andare a spasso per mare." Given money so that he can wander along the beach.	1633	I-Fas, Camera del Granduca, f. 14b	26v
Morino spagnolo	Filippo	Paolosanti is given money for his upkeep.	1633	I-Fas, Camera del Granduca, f. 14b	27r
Moro		Paid for a small red beret (il Berrettino Rosso).	1633	I-Fas, Camera del Granduca, f. 14b	30v
Morino spagnolo	Filippo	Paolosanti is paid for his upkeep.	1633	I-Fas, Camera del Granduca, f. 14b	37r
Morino spagnolo	Filippo	The stove keeper who bathed the Morino spagnolo is paid.	1633	I-Fas, Camera del Granduca, f. 14b	38r
Morino spagnolo	Filippo	Paolosanti is paid for his upkeep.	1633	I-Fas, Camera del Granduca, f. 14b	39r
Moro		Boxed with a ragazzo.	1633	I-Fas, Camera del Granduca, f. 14b	49r
Moro		Swallowed 12 coins.	1633	I-Fas, Camera del Granduca, f. 14b	49r
Moro		Along with Bosco (elsewhere described as Bosco buffone, or Bosco the clown/jester).	1633	I-Fas, Camera del Granduca, f. 14b	49v
Moro			1633	I-Fas, Camera del Granduca, f. 14b	43r
Morino spagnolo	Filippo	Paolosanti is paid for his upkeep.	1633	I-Fas, Camera del Granduca, f. 14b	43r
Moro			1633	I-Fas, Camera del Granduca, f. 14b	45r
Morino spagnolo	Filippo	Paolosanti is paid for his upkeep. Along with Vincenzo and Catorcio.	1633	I-Fas, Camera del Granduca, f. 14b	45v
Moro			1633	I-Fas, Camera del Granduca, f. 14b	46v
Moro		Along with Nocciola, Bosco, and Catorico	1633	I-Fas, Camera del Granduca, f. 14b	52r
Morino spagnolo	Filippo	Paolosanti is paid for his upkeep.	1633	I-Fas, Camera del Granduca, f. 14b	52r

Reference (as given in document)	Baptismal name (if known)	Other descriptors in document	Year	Citation		Owner (if known)
Morino		"A Girolamo Trombetto per una Tromba per il Morino che impara a sonare."	1633	I-Fas, Camera del Granduca, f. 14b	54r	
il moro che suona la Tromba		Given money to buy a "brachiere."	1633	I-Fas, Camera del Granduca, f. 15b	6r	
il moro che suona la Tromba			1633	I-Fas, Camera del Granduca, f. 15b	6v	
il Morino di Credenza			1633	I-Fas, Camera del Granduca, f. 15b	15r	
Moro		Along with Cataccio.	1634	I-Fas, Camera del Granduca, f. 15b	35r	
i due Mori		Along with Cataccio.	1634	I-Fas, Camera del Granduca, f. 15b	35v	
Moro		A shoemaker in Livorno is paid for shoes for the Moro; the Moro himself is reimbursed for a hat; and Bastiano d'Amelia is reimbursed for accompanying the Moro to Florence.	1634	I-Fas, Camera del Granduca, f. 15b	35v	
Moro		Along with Lumaghino.	1634	I-Fas, Camera del Granduca, f. 15b	38r	
Spagnolo Moro	Filippo		1634	I-Fas, Camera del Granduca, f. 15b	47v	
Moro Trombetto		"Allo stufaiolo che lavo' il Moro Trombetto." The stovekeeper is paid for bathing the Moro Trombetto.	1634	I-Fas, Camera del Granduca, f. 15b	47v	

Moro Trombetto	"Al Moro Trombetto un zecc.o sonò in Camera di SA." The Moro Trombetto is paid for having played in the chambers of the Grand Duke; presumably, he was bathed in honor of this occasion.	1634	I-Fas, Camera del Granduca, f. 15b	48v
Moro	"A Brancone, Tromba e Moro che tutti cantarono in concerto." Tipped for having sung together in harmony.	1634	I-Fas, Camera del Granduca, f. 15b	51v
Moro Trombetto	"[Q]uello che ha condotto di Livorno li due Turchetti." Presumably, the "due Turchetti" are Solofar and Rosoan.	1634 1635	I-Fas, Camera del Granduca, f. 15b I-Fas, Camera del Granduca, f. 17b	54v 5r
turchetti				
il moro delle stalle il Moro del S. Principe Don Lorenzo		1635 1635	I-Fas, Camera del Granduca, f. 17b I-Fas, Camera del Granduca, f. 17b	7v 8r
turchetto	"A Cosimo Trinchi scudi cinque per il mese di Novembre che ha tenuto un 'Turchetto in Casa." Possibly the "turchetto" here is Rosoan or Solefar.	1635	I-Fas, Camera del Granduca, f. 17b	17v
turchetto	Another payment to Cosimo 'Trichi for keeping a "turchetto" at home.	1636	I-Fas, Camera del Granduca, f. 17b	23r
turchetto	Payment to Cosimo Trinchi.	1636	I-Fas, Camera del Granduca, f. 17b	25v

Reference (as given in document)	Baptismal name (if known)	Other descriptors in document	Year	Citation		Owner (if known)
il Morino Credenziere			1636	I-Fas, Camera del Granduca, f. 17b	27v	
turchetto		Payment to Cosimo Trinchi.	1636	I-Fas, Camera del Granduca, f. 17b	28v	
turchetto		Payment to Cosimo Trinchi.	1636	I-Fas, Camera del Granduca, f. 17b	31v	
turchetto		Payment to Cosimo Trinchi.	1636	I-Fas, Camera del Granduca, f. 17b	41r	
il Morino di Credenza		"[C]he fa una Monaca."	1636	I-Fas, Camera del Granduca, f. 17b	41r	
Morino		"Al Morino e a Brancone che chantano avanti a SA due scudi."	1636	I-Fas, Camera del Granduca, f. 17b	41v	
turchetto		Payment to Cosimo Trinchi.	1636	I-Fas, Camera del Granduca, f. 17b	43v	
turchetto		Payment to Cosimo Trinchi.	1636	I-Fas, Camera del Granduca, f. 17b	47v	
turchetto		Payment to Cosimo Trinchi.	1636	I-Fas, Camera del Granduca, f. 17b	52r	
turchetto		Payment to Cosimo Trinchi.	1636	I-Fas, Camera del Granduca, f. 17b	55v	
Turchetto		Each month Cosimo Trinchi is paid 5 scudi for his upkeep. The payments go through until April of 1637, at which point he is given 10 scudi for having returned the Turchetto.	1636	I-Fas, Camera del Granduca, f. 18b	12v, passim	
il Morino di Credenza			1636	I-Fas, Camera del Granduca, f. 18b	20r	
il Morino di Credenza			1636	I-Fas, Camera del Granduca, f. 18b	25r	

mezzo moro	This is presumably a different person from the Mezzomoro who was regularly cited earlier, as the widow of Mezzomoro was given a handout on several occasions. This individual is tipped along with Tramentano and Todesco (German).	1637	I-Fas, Camera del Granduca, f. 18b	30r
Morino		1637	I-Fas, Camera del Granduca, f. 18b	44r
Morino Credenziere		1637	I-Fas, Camera del Granduca, f. 18b	44r
Morino	Payment for the refreshment given to the horses on a trip made by the Morino to fetch Nardi.	1637	I-Fas, Camera del Granduca, f. 18b	50r
Mezzo moro lacche		1637	I-Fas, Camera del Granduca, f. 18b	53v
Mezzo Moro	"[A]ndó' dal Galileo."	1638	I-Fas, Camera del Granduca, f. 19b	50r
il Morino della fabbrica		1638	I-Fas, Camera del Granduca, f. 19b	50v
il Morino della fabbrica		1639	I-Fas, Camera del Granduca, f. 20b	36v
due Mori del S. Principe Mattias		1639	I-Fas, Camera del Granduca, f. 20b	39v
il Morino della fabbrica	"[E] suoi compagni."	1639	I-Fas, Camera del Granduca, f. 21b	7v
il Moro del S. Principe Mattias		1639	I-Fas, Camera del Granduca, f. 21b	12v
il Moro Piccino		1639	I-Fas, Camera del Granduca, f. 21b	15v
il Moro del S. Principe Mattias		1640	I-Fas, Camera del Granduca, f. 21b	28r

Reference (as given in document)	Baptismal name (if known)	Other descriptors in document	Year	Citation		Owner (if known)
il Moro Piccino		"[C]he bevettero in Boboli un fiasco di Vino." Paid along with "Moro Grande" and Lupo.	1640	I-Fas, Camera del Granduca, f. 21b	40v	
il Moro Grande		"[C]he bevettero in Boboli un fiasco di Vino." Paid along with "Moro Piccino" and Lupo.	1640	I-Fas, Camera del Granduca, f. 21b	40v	
il Morino della fabbrica			1640	I-Fas, Camera del Granduca, f. 21b	55r	
il Morino del Gran Duca			1645	I-Fas, Depositeria generale, f. 1604	26v	Francesco II de' Medici
Il Moro		Palle (balls) are mentioned.	1645	I-Fas, Depositeria generale, f. 1604	28r	
Il Morino		Palle (balls) are mentioned	1646	I-Fas, Depositeria generale, f. 1604	38v	
il Morino di Credenza			1647	I-Fas, Depositeria generale, f. 1604	50r	Francesco II de' Medici
il Morino del Gran Duca			1649	I-Fas, Depositeria generale, f. 1604	92v	Francesco II de' Medici
il Morino di S.A.S.			1649	I-Fas, Depositeria generale, f. 1604	98r	Francesco II de' Medici
il Morino del Gran Duca			1649	I-Fas, Depositeria generale, f. 1604	98v	Francesco II de' Medici

il Moro di S.A.S.	1649	I-Fas, Depositeria generale, f. 1604	99v	Francesco II de' Medici	
Il Morino Navicellaio	1649	I-Fas, Depositeria generale, f. 1604	100v	Card. Gio:Carlo de' Medici	
il Morino di S.A.S.	1650	I-Fas, Depositeria generale, f. 1604	109r	Francesco II de' Medici	
il Morino del Gran Duca	1650	I-Fas, Depositeria generale, f. 1604	111v	Francesco II de' Medici	
Il Morino	1650	I-Fas, Camera del Granduca, f. 22b	6r	Francesco II de' Medici	
Al Moro	1650	I-Fas, Camera del Granduca, f. 22b	7+	Francesco II de' Medici	
Il Morino per Mandare il navicello	1650	I-Fas, Depositeria generale, f. 1604	116v	Card. Gio:Carlo de' Medici	
Al Moro	1650	I-Fas, Camera del Granduca, f. 22b	8r	Francesco II de' Medici	
Il Morino per nettare il navicello	1650	I-Fas, Depositeria generale, f. 1604	118r	Card. Gio:Carlo de' Medici	
il Morino	1650	I-Fas, Camera del Granduca, f. 22b	6r		
Moro	1650	I-Fas, Camera del Granduca, f. 22b	7r		Paid along with Piloso.

Reference (as given in document)	Baptismal name (if known)	Other descriptors in document	Year	Citation		Owner (if known)
Moro		Along with Mantovanino, "fecero La Spia."	1650	I-Fas, Camera del Granduca, f. 22b	8r	
Al Moro			1651	I-Fas, Camera del Granduca, f. 22b	18r	Francesco II de' Medici
Al Morino tiratore			1651	I-Fas, Camera del Granduca, f. 22b	20r	? Card. Gio:Carlo de' Medici
Morino			1651	I-Fas, Camera del Granduca, f. 22b	20r	Francesco II de' Medici
Al Morino staffieri			1651	I-Fas, Depositeria generale, f. 1604	121v	Card. Gio:Carlo de' Medici
Al Morino del Gran Duca			1651	I-Fas, Depositeria generale, f. 1604	122r	Francesco II de' Medici
Al Moro			1651	I-Fas, Camera del Granduca, f. 22b	24r	Francesco II de' Medici
Al Moro			1651	I-Fas, Camera del Granduca, f. 22b	24v	Francesco II de' Medici
Al Morino p rimpeciare il Navicello			1651	I-Fas, Depositeria generale, f. 1604	123r	Card. Gio:Carlo de' Medici

Description	Year	Archive	Folio	Patron	Notes
Al Morino staffieri p spese con il Navicello	1651	I-Fas, Depositeria generale, f. 1604	123v	Card. Gio:Carlo de' Medici	
Al Moro	1651	I-Fas, Camera del Granduca, f. 22b	24r	Francesco II de' Medici	
Al Moro di stalla di S.A.S.	1651	I-Fas, Depositeria generale, f. 1604	122v	Francesco II de' Medici	
Al moro	1651	I-Fas, Camera del Granduca, f. 22b	24r	Francesco II de' Medici	
Il Moro di S.A.S.	1651	I-Fas, Depositeria generale, f. 1604	122v	Francesco II de' Medici	
Al Morino p spese fatto p il Navicello	1651	I-Fas, Depositeria generale, f. 1604	124v	Card. Gio:Carlo de' Medici	
Al Moro	1651	I-Fas, Camera del Granduca, f. 22b	c.n.n. [between 25 and 26]	Francesco II de' Medici	
Al morino segnature del Pallincino	1651	I-Fas, Camera del Granduca, f. 22b	c.n.n. [between 25 and 26]		Palle (balls) are mentioned.
Al Moro che segna che trovo il maniglio	1651	I-Fas, Depositeria generale, f. 1604	124r		
Al Moro	1651	I-Fas, Camera del Granduca, f. 22b	29r	Francesco II de' Medici	

Reference (as given in document)	Baptismal name (if known)	Other descriptors in document	Year	Citation		Owner (if known)
Al Moro			1651	I-Fas, Camera del Granduca, f. 22b	29v	Francesco II de' Medici
Al Moro			1651	I-Fas, Camera del Granduca, f. 22b	33v	Francesco II de' Medici
Al moro			1651	I-Fas, Camera del Granduca, f. 22b	36r	Francesco II de' Medici
Il Morino di S.A.S.			1651	I-Fas, Depositeria generale, f. 1604	127r	Francesco II de' Medici
Al Morino p ser. S.A.			1651	I-Fas, Depositeria generale, f. 1604	127v	Francesco II de' Medici
Al Moro			1651	I-Fas, Camera del Granduca, f. 22b	37v	Francesco II de' Medici
Al Moro			1651	I-Fas, Camera del Granduca, f. 22b	43r	Francesco II de' Medici
Al Moro			1651	I-Fas, Camera del Granduca, f. 22b	46r	Francesco II de' Medici
Al Morino			1651	I-Fas, Camera del Granduca, f. 23b	3r	Francesco II de' Medici

Al Morino	1651	I-Fas, Camera del Granduca, f. 23b	3v	Francesco II de' Medici
Moro	1651	I-Fas, Camera del Granduca, f. 22b	18r	
il Morino tiratore	1651	I-Fas, Camera del Granduca, f. 22b	20r	
Morino	1651	I-Fas, Camera del Granduca, f. 22b	20r	Along with Barboccia and Pazzaglia.
Moro	1651	I-Fas, Camera del Granduca, f. 22b	24r	
Moro	1651	I-Fas, Camera del Granduca, f. 22b	24r	Along with Mazzolli.
Moro	1651	I-Fas, Camera del Granduca, f. 22b	24v	
Moro	1651	I-Fas, Camera del Granduca, f. 22b	25+	Along with Mazzolli.
il morino segnature del Palloncino	1651	I-Fas, Camera del Granduca, f. 22b	25+	
il Moro	1651	I-Fas, Camera del Granduca, f. 22b	29r	
il Moro	1651	I-Fas, Camera del Granduca, f. 22b	29v	
il Moro	1651	I-Fas, Camera del Granduca, f. 22b	33v	
il Moro	1651	I-Fas, Camera del Granduca, f. 22b	36r	
il Moro	1651	I-Fas, Camera del Granduca, f. 22b	37r	Delivered fish from the Arno.
il Morino	1651	I-Fas, Camera del Granduca, f. 22b	37r	Presented a crow.
il Moro	1651	I-Fas, Camera del Granduca, f. 22b	37v	
il Morino	1651	I-Fas, Camera del Granduca, f. 23b	3r	
il Morino	1651	I-Fas, Camera del Granduca, f. 23b	3v	
il Moro	1651	I-Fas, Camera del Granduca, f. 22b	43v	
il Moro	1651	I-Fas, Camera del Granduca, f. 22b	46r	
Al Moro	1652	I-Fas, Camera del Granduca, f. 23b	21v	Francesco II de' Medici
Al moro	1652	I-Fas, Camera del Granduca, f.23b	23r	Francesco II de' Medici

Reference (as given in document)	Baptismal name (if known)	Other descriptors in document	Year	Citation	Owner (if known)
Al Morino che condusse il Casse			1652	I-Fas, Camera del Granduca, f. 23b 27r	Francesco II de' Medici
Al moro			1652	I-Fas, Camera del Granduca, f. 23b 29v	Francesco II de' Medici
Al Moro che corse p le letter			1652	I-Fas, Camera del Granduca, f. 23b 29v	Francesco II de' Medici
Al Morino			1652	I-Fas, Camera del Granduca, f. 23b 33r	Francesco II de' Medici
Al Moro			1652	I-Fas, Camera del Granduca, f. 23b 33v	Francesco II de' Medici
Al Moro			1652	I-Fas, Camera del Granduca, f. 23b 37r	Francesco II de' Medici
Al Morino del Sr Card. Gio:Carlo			1652	I-Fas, Camera del Granduca, f. 23b 37r	Card. Gio:Carlo de' Medici
Al Moro			1652	I-Fas, Camera del Granduca, f. 23b 37v	Francesco II de' Medici
Al Moro			1652	I-Fas, Camera del Granduca, f. 23b 43v	Francesco II de' Medici

Name	Notes	Year	Source	Folio	Patron
Al Moro		1652	I-Fas, Camera del Granduca, f. 23b	46r	Francesco II de' Medici
il Morino		1652	I-Fas, Camera del Granduca, f. 23b	33r	
il Morino del S. Card. Gio: Carlo	[Buonaccorsi?]	1652	I-Fas, Camera del Granduca, f. 23b	37r	
il Moro		1652	I-Fas, Camera del Granduca, f. 23b	21v	
il Moro	Along with Cavallino.	1652	I-Fas, Camera del Granduca, f. 23b	23r	
il Moro		1652	I-Fas, Camera del Granduca, f. 23b	29v	
il Moro	Per il piccione (rent).	1652	I-Fas, Camera del Granduca, f. 23b	33v	
il Moro		1652	I-Fas, Camera del Granduca, f. 23b	37r	
il Moro		1652	I-Fas, Camera del Granduca, f. 23b	37v	
il Moro		1652	I-Fas, Camera del Granduca, f. 23b	43v	
il Moro		1652	I-Fas, Camera del Granduca, f. 23b	46r	
Al Moro		1653	I-Fas, Camera del Granduca, f. 25b	10r	
Al Moro del S. Card. Gio:Carlo		1653	I-Fas, Camera del Granduca, f. 25b	12v	Francesco II de' Medici Card. Gio:Carlo de' Medici
Al med. Moro		1653	I-Fas, Camera del Granduca, f. 25b	12v	Card. Gio:Carlo de' Medici
Al Moro del s. Card. Gio:Carlo		1653	I-Fas, Camera del Granduca, f. 25b	12v	Card. Gio:Carlo de' Medici
Al Moro		1653	I-Fas, Camera del Granduca, f. 25b	12v	Francesco II de' Medici
Al moro del S. Card. Gio Carlo	[Buonaccorsi?]	1653	I-Fas, Camera del Granduca, f. 25b	12v	

Reference (as given in document)	Baptismal name (if known)	Other descriptors in document	Year	Citation		Owner (if known)
il Morino del Buonaccorsi	[Buonaccorsi?]		1653	I-Fas, Camera del Granduca, f. 25b	9r	
il Moro			1653	I-Fas, Camera del Granduca, f. 24b	28r	
il Moro			1653	I-Fas, Camera del Granduca, f. 24b	29r	
il Moro			1653	I-Fas, Camera del Granduca, f. 24b	31r	
il Moro			1653	I-Fas, Camera del Granduca, f. 24b	35r	
il Moro			1653	I-Fas, Camera del Granduca, f. 24b	35v	
il Moro		Along with Maometto.	1653	I-Fas, Camera del Granduca, f. 24b	47r	
il Moro			1653	I-Fas, Camera del Granduca, f. 24b	47v	
il Moro			1653	I-Fas, Camera del Granduca, f. 25b	10r	
il Moro			1653	I-Fas, Camera del Granduca, f. 25b	12v	
il Moro del S. Card. Gio Carlo	[Buonaccorsi?]		1653	I-Fas, Camera del Granduca, f. 25b	12v	
il Turchetto del S. Principe Leopoldo			1653	I-Fas, Camera del Granduca, f. 24b	44r	
il Turco		Along with Stinchi, who boxed together.	1653	I-Fas, Camera del Granduca, f. 25b	10r	
Moro		Maestro Costantino Pinelli sarto, in Pisa, paid for clothing made for Todesco Buffone, Mazzelli, and Moro.	1653	I-Fas, Camera del Granduca, f. 24b	23r	
Moro	[Buonaccorsi?]	"Al med. Moro."	1653	I-Fas, Camera del Granduca, f. 25b	12v	
Al Moro del S. Card. Gio:Carlo	[Buonaccorsi?]		1654	I-Fas, Camera del Granduca, f. 25b	23r	Card. Gio:Carlo de' Medici

Al Moro			1654	I-Fas, Camera del Granduca, f. 25b	23v	Francesco II de' Medici
Al moro			1654	I-Fas, Camera del Granduca, f. 25b	30v	Francesco II de' Medici
Al moro			1654	I-Fas, Camera del Granduca, f. 25b	33r	Francesco II de' Medici
Al Moro			1654	I-Fas, Camera del Granduca, f. 26b	14r	Francesco II de' Medici
Al Moro			1654	I-Fas, Camera del Granduca, f. 26b	14v	Francesco II de' Medici
il Morino del S. Card. Gio: Carlo	[Buonaccorsi?]		1654	I-Fas, Camera del Granduca, f. 25b	42r	
Al moro p pagare l'Anello nuziale			1654	I-Fas, Camera del Granduca, f. 25b	34v	Francesco II de' Medici
Al Morino del Sig.r Card: GioCarlo	[Buonaccorsi?]		1654	I-Fas, Camera del Granduca, f. 25b	42r	Card. Gio:Carlo de' Medici
il Moro			1654	I-Fas, Camera del Granduca, f. 25b	23v	
il Moro			1654	I-Fas, Camera del Granduca, f. 25b	30v	
il Moro			1654	I-Fas, Camera del Granduca, f. 25b	33r	
il Moro		"Al Moro [lire] ventisette per pagare l'Anello nuziale."	1654	I-Fas, Camera del Granduca, f. 25b	34v	
il Moro			1654	I-Fas, Camera del Granduca, f. 26b	14r	
il Moro			1654	I-Fas, Camera del Granduca, f. 26b	14v	

Reference (as given in document)	Baptismal name (if known)	Other descriptors in document	Year	Citation		Owner (if known)
il Moro del S. Cardinale	[Buonaccorsi?]	Along with ": 'i 'Turchetti."	1654	I-Fas, Camera del Granduca, f. 25b	23r	
il Turco moro		Along with il Moro del S. Ipolito.	1654	I-Fas, Camera del Granduca, f. 25b	20v	
		Along with Mutolo and Chinan.	1654	I-Fas, Camera del Granduca, f. 25b	34v	
Al Moro			1655	I-Fas, Camera del Granduca, f. 26b	14v	Francesco II de' Medici
Al Moro			1655	I-Fas, Camera del Granduca, f. 26b	40v	Francesco II de' Medici
Al moro			1655	I-Fas, Camera del Granduca, f. 26b	45v	Francesco II de' Medici
Al moro del Sr. P. Mattias			1655	I-Fas, Camera del Granduca, f. 26b	45v	Mattias de' Medici
Il Morino			1655	I-Fas, Camera del Granduca, f. 26b	58r	Francesco II de' Medici
Il Morino			1655	I-Fas, Camera del Granduca, f. 26b	58r	Francesco II de' Medici
Il Morino			1655	I-Fas, Camera del Granduca, f. 26b	58r	Francesco II de' Medici
Il Morino			1655	I-Fas, Camera del Granduca, f. 26b	58r	Francesco II de' Medici

Il Morino		1655	I-Fas, Camera del Granduca, f. 26b	58r	Francesco II de' Medici
Il Morino		1655	I-Fas, Camera del Granduca, f. 27b	9r	Francesco II de' Medici
Il Morino		1655	I-Fas, Camera del Granduca, f. 27b	9r	Francesco II de' Medici
Il Morino		1655	I-Fas, Camera del Granduca, f. 27b	9r	Francesco II de' Medici
Il Morino		1655	I-Fas, Camera del Granduca, f. 27b	9r	Francesco II de' Medici
Il Morino		1655	I-Fas, Camera del Granduca, f. 27b	18r	Francesco II de' Medici
Al Moro staff.e		1655	I-Fas, Camera del Granduca, f. 27b	23r	Francesco II de' Medici
il Morino	"[C]he portò li due Cardinalini."	1655	I-Fas, Camera del Granduca, f. 26b	40r	
il Morino	5 instances on this page.	1655	I-Fas, Camera del Granduca, f. 26b	58r	
il Morino	Along with Marancio.	1655	I-Fas, Camera del Granduca, f. 27b	9r	
il Morino	3 instances.	1655	I-Fas, Camera del Granduca, f. 27b	9r	
il Moro		1655	I-Fas, Camera del Granduca, f. 26b	14v	
il Moro	Along with Paquino staffiere.	1655	I-Fas, Camera del Granduca, f. 26b	40v	
il Moro	Along with Chinan.	1655	I-Fas, Camera del Granduca, f. 26b	45r	
il Moro del S. Principe Mattias		1655	I-Fas, Camera del Granduca, f. 26b	45v	

Reference (as given in document)	Baptismal name (if known)	Other descriptors in document	Year	Citation		Owner (if known)
il Moro staffiere		"[A]ndo' a Firenze."	1655	I-Fas, Camera del Granduca, f. 27b	23r	
il Turco		"[C]he ha ricato l'Areo."	1655	I-Fas, Camera del Granduca, f. 27b	13v	
Morino		Along with Marancio and Baroni.	1655	I-Fas, Camera del Granduca, f. 27b	18r	
Il Morino			1656	I-Fas, Camera del Granduca, f. 27b	69r	Francesco II de' Medici
Al Morino			1656	I-Fas, Camera del Granduca, f. 27b	68r	Francesco II de' Medici
Al Morino			1656	I-Fas, Camera del Granduca, f. 27b	75r	Francesco II de' Medici
Al Morino			1656	I-Fas, Camera del Granduca, f. 27b	75r	Francesco II de' Medici
Al Morino			1656	I-Fas, Camera del Granduca, f. 27b	87r	Francesco II de' Medici
Al moro del Sr. Card. GioCarlo			1656	I-Fas, Camera del Granduca, f. 27b	83r	Card. Gio:Carlo de' Medici
Al Morino			1656	I-Fas, Camera del Granduca, f. 27b	85r	Francesco II de' Medici
Al Morino			1656	I-Fas, Camera del Granduca, f. 28b	4r	Francesco II de' Medici

Al Moro del S.r Card.le GioCarlo		1656	I-Fas, Camera del Granduca, f. 28b	17r	Card. Gio:Carlo de' Medici
Il Morino		1656	I-Fas, Camera del Granduca, f. 27b	68r	
il Morino	Along with Marancio. 2 instances.	1656	I-Fas, Camera del Granduca, f. 27b	69r	
il Morino		1656	I-Fas, Camera del Granduca, f. 27b	75r	
il Morino		1656	I-Fas, Camera del Granduca, f. 27b	85r	
il Morino		1656	I-Fas, Camera del Granduca, f. 27b	87r	
il Morino		1656	I-Fas, Camera del Granduca, f. 28b	4r	
il moro del S. Card. Gio Carlo	[Buonaccorsi?]	1656	I-Fas, Camera del Granduca, f. 27b	83r	
il Moro del S. Card. Gio Carlo	[Buonaccorsi?]	1656	I-Fas, Camera del Granduca, f. 28b	17r	
il Mutolo del S. Card. Gio Carlo	Gio: Antonio Gaeta	1656	I-Fas, Camera del Granduca, f. 28b	25r	
la nostra Morina	Tuffega/Maria Adelaide	1656	I-Fas, Mediceo del Principato, f. 5487	4v	Prince Mattias de' Medici
	"Pagati a Carlo Ballerini scudi 8 tanto se li fanno dare per il vitto della nostra Morina di due mesi, cioe d'Aprile e MagGio."				
Al Morino del Sig.r Card. Gio:Carlo	[Buonaccorsi?]	1657	I-Fas, Camera del Granduca, f. 28b	37r	Card. Gio:Carlo de' Medici
Al morino		1657	I-Fas, Camera del Granduca, f. 28b	40r	Francesco II de' Medici
Al Moro del S.r Card.le GioCarlo	[Buonaccorsi?]	1657	I-Fas, Camera del Granduca, f. 28b	43v	Card. Gio:Carlo de' Medici

Reference (as given in document)	Baptismal name (if known)	Other descriptors in document	Year	Citation		Owner (if known)
Al Morino Garzone di Stalla			1657	I-Fas, Camera del Granduca, f. 28b	59r	Francesco II de' Medici
A Cinque Nani e Mori del Ill. P. Mattias			1657	I-Fas, Camera del Granduca, f. 28b	63v	Mattias de' Medici
Al Moro del Card.le GioCarlo	[Buonaccorsi?]		1657	I-Fas, Camera del Granduca, f. 28b	64r	Card. Gio:Carlo de' Medici
Al Moro Garzone di Stalla			1657	I-Fas, Camera del Granduca, f. 28b	67v	Francesco II de' Medici
Al Morino Garzone di Stalla			1657	I-Fas, Camera del Granduca, f. 28b	71v	Francesco II de' Medici
Al Morino Tiratore del Ser.mo Sig.re Card.le GioCarlo			1657	I-Fas, Camera del Granduca, f. 28b	73r	Card. Gio:Carlo de' Medici
cinque Nani e Mori del Illustrissimo Principe Mattias			1657	I-Fas, Camera del Granduca, f. 28b	63v	
il morino			1657	I-Fas, Camera del Granduca, f. 28b	40r	
il Morino del S. Card. Gio: Carlo	[Buonaccorsi?]		1657	I-Fas, Camera del Granduca, f. 28b	37r	
il Morino Garzone di Stalla			1657	I-Fas, Camera del Granduca, f. 28b	59r	

il Morino Garzone di Stalla		1657	I-Fas, Camera del Granduca, f. 28b	71v
il Morino Tiratore del S. Card. Gio Carlo		1657	I-Fas, Camera del Granduca, f. 28b	73r
il Moro del S. Card. Gio Carlo	[Buonaccorsi?]	1657	I-Fas, Camera del Granduca, f. 28b	43r
il Moro del S. Card. Gio Carlo	[Buonaccorsi?]	1657	I-Fas, Camera del Granduca, f. 28b	64r
il Moro Garzone di Stalla		1657	I-Fas, Camera del Granduca, f. 28b	67v
il Mutolo		1657	I-Fas, Camera del Granduca, f. 28b	48r
il Mutolo		1657	I-Fas, Camera del Granduca, f. 28b	65r
il Mutolo del S. Card. Gio Carlo	Gio: Antonio Gaeta	1657	I-Fas, Camera del Granduca, f. 28b	63v
il Mutolo del SA		1657	I-Fas, Camera del Granduca, f. 28b	63v
il Turchetto del S. Principe Leopoldo		1657	I-Fas, Camera del Granduca, f. 28b	68r
Moro di SAS	[Buonaccorsi?]	1657	I-FImmobili, 1.7, ins. 1	12, 13

"Monello e suo abito da Giudone." Though these archive documents clearly state the Moro of SAS, the published libretto refers to the singer as belonging to Cardinal Gio: Carlo.

Moro di SAS	[Buonaccorsi?]	1657	I-FImmobili, 1.7, ins. 4	1v

"Monello, Moro di SAS, Abito da Monello buono sotto e soppra ^ ma Straccione."

Reference (as given in document)	Baptismal name (if known)	Other descriptors in document	Year	Citation		Owner (if known)
mori	Carali/Mattia and Ali/Ferdinando	Arrigo Vinter paid for their upkeep, along with several nani; several payments listed.	1658	I-Fas, Mediceo del Principato, f. 5487	108r	Prince Mattias de' Medici
mori	Carali/Mattia and Ali/Ferdinando	Arrigo Vinter paid for their upkeep, along with several nani; several payments listed.	1658	I-Fas, Mediceo del Principato, f. 5487	108v	Prince Mattias de' Medici
mori	Carali/Mattia and Ali/Ferdinando	Arrigo Vinter paid for their upkeep, along with several nani.	1658	I-Fas, Mediceo del Principato, f. 5487	109v	Prince Mattias de' Medici
mori	Carali/Mattia and Ali/Ferdinando	Arrigo Vinter paid for their upkeep, along with several nani.	1658	I-Fas, Mediceo del Principato, f. 5487	110r	Prince Mattias de' Medici
mori	Carali/Mattia and Ali/Ferdinando	Arrigo Vinter paid for their upkeep, along with several nani.	1658	I-Fas, Mediceo del Principato, f. 5487	110v	Prince Mattias de' Medici
mori	Carali/Mattia and Ali/Ferdinando	Arrigo Vinter paid for their upkeep, along with several nani; several payments listed.	1658	I-Fas, Mediceo del Principato, f. 5487	111r	Prince Mattias de' Medici
mori	Carali/Mattia and Ali/Ferdinando	Arrigo Vinter paid for their upkeep, along with several nani.	1658	I-Fas, Mediceo del Principato, f. 5487	111v	Prince Mattias de' Medici
nostri mori	Carali/Mattia and Ali/Ferdinando, possibly also Tuffega/Maria Adelaide	Clothes are made and paid for.	1658	I-Fas, Mediceo del Principato, f. 5487	29v	Prince Mattias de' Medici

mori	Carali/Mattia and Ali/Ferdinando	Arrigo Vinter paid for their upkeep, along with several nani.	1659	I-Fas, Mediceo del Principato, f. 5487	113r	Prince Mattias de' Medici
mori	Carali/Mattia and Ali/Ferdinando	Arrigo Vinter paid for their upkeep, along with several nani.	1659	I-Fas, Mediceo del Principato, f. 5487	113v	Prince Mattias de' Medici
Moro		"Pelle, et altre robe" purchased from a tailor for Fegatello and Moro.	1659	I-Fas, Mediceo del Principato, f. 5487	114r	Prince Mattias de' Medici
il Morino			1660	I-Fas, Camera del Granduca, f. 30b	45v	
il Moro del S. Card. Gio Carlo	[Buonaccorsi?]		1660	I-Fas, Camera del Granduca, f. 30b	44r	
il Moro del S. Card. Gio Carlo	[Buonaccorsi?]		1660	I-Fas, Camera del Granduca, f. 30b	45v	
il Moro del Serenissimo GranDuca			1660	I-Fas, Camera del Granduca, f. 30b	47r	
mori	Carali/Mattia and Ali/Ferdinando	Arrigo Vinter paid for their upkeep, along with several nani; the total number has been reduced to 5, but "mori" is still given in plural.	1660	I-Fas, Mediceo del Principato, f. 5487	114v	Prince Mattias de' Medici
mori	Carali/Mattia and Ali/Ferdinando	Arrigo Vinter now paid for 4 individuals, though "mori" remains in plural. Several payments.	1660	I-Fas, Mediceo del Principato, f. 5487	115r	Prince Mattias de' Medici
mori	Carali/Mattia and Ali/Ferdinando	Arrigo Vinter paid for their upkeep, along with several nani.	1660	I-Fas, Mediceo del Principato, f. 5487	116v	Prince Mattias de' Medici
mori	Carali/Mattia and Ali/Ferdinando	Arrigo Vinter paid for their upkeep, along with several nani.	1660	I-Fas, Mediceo del Principato, f. 5487	117r	Prince Mattias de' Medici

Reference (as given in document)	Baptismal name (if known)	Other descriptors in document	Year	Citation		Owner (if known)
mori	Carali/Mattia and Ali/Ferdinando	Arrigo Vinter paid for their upkeep, along with several nani.	1660	I-Fas, Mediceo del Principato, f. 5487	117v	Prince Mattias de' Medici
mori	Carali/Mattia and Ali/Ferdinando	Arrigo Vinter paid for their upkeep, along with several nani; several payments listed.	1660	I-Fas, Mediceo del Principato, f. 5487	118v	Prince Mattias de' Medici
mori	Carali/Mattia and Ali/Ferdinando	Arrigo Vinter paid for their upkeep, along with several nani; a second payment on the same page notes that 2 of his charges have been in Marseilles.	1660	I-Fas, Mediceo del Principato, f. 5487	119v	Prince Mattias de' Medici
Moro		Collars and shirts are purchased for Batistone and Moro.	1660	I-Fas, Mediceo del Principato, f. 5487	117v	Prince Mattias de' Medici
il Morino del S. Card. Gio: Carlo	[Buonaccorsi?]		1661	I-Fas, Camera del Granduca, f. 30b	163v	
il Moro		Boxed with "un altro ragazzo."	1661	I-Fas, Camera del Granduca, f. 30b	89r	
il Moro		"[P]er bere," 3 separate instances.	1661	I-Fas, Camera del Granduca, f. 30b	89r	
il Moro		"[P]er andare in maschera," 2 separate instances.	1661	I-Fas, Camera del Granduca, f. 30b	89v	
il Moro			1661	I-Fas, Camera del Granduca, f. 30b	106r	
il Moro			1661	I-Fas, Camera del Granduca, f. 30b	132r	
il Moro			1661	I-Fas, Camera del Granduca, f. 30b	158r	
il Moro			1661	I-Fas, Camera del Granduca, f. 30b	176r	
il Moro del Principe Mattias			1661	I-Fas, Camera del Granduca, f. 31b	48v	

Name	Associated	Description	Year	Archive	Folio	Patron
il Moro del S. Card. Gio Carlo	[Buonaccorsi?]		1661	I-Fas, Camera del Granduca, f. 30b	114r	
il Moro del S. Card. Gio Carlo	[Buonaccorsi?]		1661	I-Fas, Camera del Granduca, f. 30b	143r	
il Moro del S. Card. Gio Carlo sudetto	[Buonaccorsi?]		1661	I-Fas, Camera del Granduca, f. 30b	163v	
il Moro del Ser. Principe Mattias			1661	I-Fas, Camera del Granduca, f. 30b	180r	
il Moro di SAS			1661	I-Fas, Camera del Granduca, f. 31b	25v	
mori	Carali/Mattia and Ali/Ferdinando, possibly also Tuffega/Maria Adelaide	Clothes are made and paid for.	1661	I-Fas, Mediceo del Principato, f. 5487	48v	Prince Mattias de' Medici
mori	Carali/Mattia and Ali/Ferdinando	Arrigo Vinter paid for their upkeep, along with several nani.	1661	I-Fas, Mediceo del Principato, f. 5487	121r	Prince Mattias de' Medici
mori	Carali/Mattia and Ali/Ferdinando	Arrigo Vinter paid for their upkeep, along with several nani.	1661	I-Fas, Mediceo del Principato, f. 5487	122r	Prince Mattias de' Medici
Moro		Money is spent on medication for Paggio Falconierij, Batistone, Filippo, and Moro	1661	I-Fas, Mediceo del Principato, f. 5487	120r	Prince Mattias de' Medici
il Morino			1662	I-Fas, Camera del Granduca, f. 31b	164r	
il Morino del S. Card. [Gio: Carlo]	[Buonaccorsi?]		1662	I-Fas, Camera del Granduca, f. 31b	85v	
il Morino Pescatore			1662	I-Fas, Camera del Granduca, f. 31b	160r	

Reference (as given in document)	Baptismal name (if known)	Other descriptors in document	Year	Citation		Owner (if known)
il Moro del Principe Mattias			1662	I-Fas, Camera del Granduca, f. 31b	53v	
il Moro del S. Principe Mattias			1662	I-Fas, Camera del Granduca, f. 31b	140r	
il Moro del Ser. Card. [Gio Carlo]	[Buonaccorsi?]		1662	I-Fas, Camera del Granduca, f. 31b	126r	
il Moro del Ser. Principe Mattias			1662	I-Fas, Camera del Granduca, f. 31b	163r	
il Moro di Camera del Ser.mo S. Card. Gio Carlo	[Buonaccorsi?]	"[P]ortò ostriche di Venezia."	1662	I-Fas, Camera del Granduca, f. 31b	82r	
mori	Carali/Mattia and Ali/ Ferdinando	Arrigo Vinter paid for their upkeep, along with several nani; several payments listed.	1662	I-Fas, Mediceo del Principato, f. 5487	123r	Prince Mattias de' Medici
mori	Carali/Mattia and Ali/ Ferdinando	Arrigo Vinter paid for their upkeep, along with several nani.	1662	I-Fas, Mediceo del Principato, f. 5487	125v	Prince Mattias de' Medici
mori	Carali/Mattia and Ali/ Ferdinando	Arrigo Vinter paid for their upkeep, along with several nani.	1662	I-Fas, Mediceo del Principato, f. 5487	126v	Prince Mattias de' Medici
il Morino			1663	I-Fas, Camera del Granduca, f. 33b	15v	
il Morino			1663	I-Fas, Camera del Granduca, f. 33b	62v	
il Morino della Gondola		"[P]er portare gli Orioli al Pignione et scaricare a Pisa."	1663	I-Fas, Camera del Granduca, f. 33b	42r	
il Mutolo			1663	I-Fas, Camera del Granduca, f. 33b	24v	

Name	Person	Note	Year	Archive	Folio
il Mutolo del S. Card. [Gio Carlo]	Gio: Antonio Gaeta	"[U]n zecchino per dare alla donna che l'ha governato."	1663	I-Fas, Camera del Granduca, f. 33b	62r
due Mori		Along with Fegatello (a nano).	1664	I-Fas, Camera del Granduca, f. 34b	44r
il Morino			1664	I-Fas, Camera del Granduca, f. 33b	76r
il Morino		Delivered eels.	1664	I-Fas, Camera del Granduca, f. 33b	90v
il Morino della Gondola	[Agniolo Pandolfini?]		1664	I-Fas, Camera del Granduca, f. 33b	143r
il Morino della Gondola	[Agniolo Pandolfini?]		1664	I-Fas, Camera del Granduca, f. 33b	90v
il Morino della Gondola	[Agniolo Pandolfini?]		1664	I-Fas, Camera del Granduca, f. 33b	142r
il Morino della Gondola			1664	I-Fas, Camera del Granduca, f. 34b	45r
il Moro		Along with the "Garzone di Lazzero."	1664	I-Fas, Camera del Granduca, f. 34b	29v
il Muscovito del S. Lorenzo Strozzi			1664	I-Fas, Camera del Granduca, f. 33b	111r
il Mutolo			1664	I-Fas, Camera del Granduca, f. 33b	96r
il Mutolo			1664	I-Fas, Camera del Granduca, f. 33b	135r
il Mutolo del SA			1664	I-Fas, Camera del Granduca, f. 33b	111r
il Mutolo del Ser. Principe Leopoldo			1664	I-Fas, Camera del Granduca, f. 33b	133v
il Mutolo nuovo			1664	I-Fas, Camera del Granduca, f. 33b	95v
due mori		"[C]he uno ballò e l'altro suonò."	1665	I-Fas, Camera del Granduca, f. 34b	92r
due Mori		Along with Batistone and Fegatelle.	1665	I-Fas, Camera del Granduca, f. 35b	50r
i Mori del S. Principe Mattias		"[P]er haver sonato con Batistone."	1665	I-Fas, Camera del Granduca, f. 35b	11r
il Morino			1665	I-Fas, Camera del Granduca, f. 34b	130r
il Morino		"[C]he recò chiannotti"	1665	I-Fas, Camera del Granduca, f. 34b	132r

Reference (as given in document)	Baptismal name (if known)	Other descriptors in document	Year	Citation		Owner (if known)
il Morino		Gathers strawberries.	1665	I-Fas, Camera del Granduca, f. 34b	159r	
il Morino	[Agniolo Pandolfini?]	Delivered eels.	1665	I-Fas, Camera del Granduca, f. 34b	172r	
il Morino della Gondola	[Agniolo Pandolfini?]		1665	I-Fas, Camera del Granduca, f. 34b	56r	
il Morino Pandolfini	[Agniolo Pandolfini?]	"[C]he recò chiannotti."	1665	I-Fas, Camera del Granduca, f. 34b	140v	
il Moro del Principe Mattias			1665	I-Fas, Camera del Granduca, f. 34b	56r	
il Moro del Principe Mattias			1665	I-Fas, Camera del Granduca, f. 34b	56r	
il Moro del Principe Mattias			1665	I-Fas, Camera del Granduca, f. 34b	132v	
il Mutolo i Mori del S. Principe Mattias		"[M]arita la sorella."	1665	I-Fas, Camera del Granduca, f. 34b	169v	
Morino			1665	I-Fas, Camera del Granduca, f. 34b	170v	
Morino	[Agniolo Pandolfini?]		1665	I-Fas, Camera del Granduca, f. 35b	11r	
			1665	I-Fas, Camera del Granduca, f. 35b	11v	
il Morino			1666	I-Fas, Camera del Granduca, f. 35b	71r	
il Morino		"[P]orto' torli e merle."	1666	I-Fas, Camera del Granduca, f. 35b	75v	
il Morino		Maestro Constantino is paid for an outfit for the Morino.	1666	I-Fas, Camera del Granduca, f. 35b	75v	
il Morino			1666	I-Fas, Camera del Granduca, f. 35b	79r	
il Morino		"Al Morino scudo uno per la Serva dove sta."	1666	I-Fas, Camera del Granduca, f. 35b	107v	

il Morino			1666	I-Fas, Camera del Granduca, f. 35b	159r
il Morino Cacciatore			1666	I-Fas, Camera del Granduca, f. 35b	105r
il Morino cioe Ali	[Cosimo Maria?]		1666	I-Fas, Camera del Granduca, f. 35b	135r
il Morino di SAS	[Cosimo Maria?]	Bill for an outfit "alla morescha di panno verdano" for the Moro; includes a "cosachono."	1666	I-Fas, Camera del Granduca, f. 35b	86r
il Moro			1666	I-Fas, Camera del Granduca, f. 35b	77r
il Mutolo			1666	I-Fas, Camera del Granduca, f. 35b	108v
il Mutolo			1666	I-Fas, Camera del Granduca, f. 35b	133r
il Mutolo del Ser. Principe Leopoldo			1666	I-Fas, Camera del Granduca, f. 35b	133r
il Mutolo del Ser. Principe Leopoldo			1666	I-Fas, Camera del Granduca, f. 36b	34v
Mori		"Per i staffieri lacchi Mori, e Cocchi."	1666	I-Fas, Camera del Granduca, f. 36b	23r
Morino		Along with Pippos, Gasparo, and Copitano.	1666	I-Fas, Camera del Granduca, f. 35b	79r
Morino	[Cosimo Maria?]	The tailor is paid for an outfit for the Morino.	1666	I-Fas, Camera del Granduca, f. 35b	79v
Morino	[Cosimo Maria?]	More details from the tailor.	1666	I-Fas, Camera del Granduca, f. 35b	96r
il Morino del S. Principe Mattias			1667	I-Fas, Camera del Granduca, f. 37b	2v
il mutolino del S. Principe Carlo			1667	I-Fas, Camera del Granduca, f. 39b	15r
il Mutolo		"[P]er andare a Livorno."	1667	I-Fas, Camera del Granduca, f. 37b	1v

Reference (as given in document)	Baptismal name (if known)	Other descriptors in document	Year	Citation		Owner (if known)
il Mutolo		"[P]er un cavallo per andare a Pisa."	1667	I-Fas, Camera del Granduca, f. 37b	18r	
il Mutolo			1667	I-Fas, Camera del Granduca, f. 38b	1v	
il Mutolo			1667	I-Fas, Camera del Granduca, f. 38b	34r	
il Mutolo del SA			1667	I-Fas, Camera del Granduca, f. 37b	19v	
il Mutolo del Ser. Principe Leopoldo			1667	I-Fas, Camera del Granduca, f. 38b	34r	
il Morino			1668	I-Fas, Camera del Granduca, f. 39b	31r	
il Morino tiratore			1668	I-Fas, Camera del Granduca, f. 39b	20v	
il Morino tiratore			1668	I-Fas, Camera del Granduca, f. 39b	23v	
il Morino tiratore			1668	I-Fas, Camera del Granduca, f. 39b	188v	
il Mutolo			1668	I-Fas, Camera del Granduca, f. 40c	13r	
Morino			1668	I-Fas, Camera del Granduca, f. 40c	10v	
il Morino Cacciatore			1669	I-Fas, Camera del Granduca, f. 41c	14r	
il Morino Cacciatore			1669	I-Fas, Camera del Granduca, f. 41c	20r	
il Morino Cacciatore			1669	I-Fas, Camera del Granduca, f. 41c	40v	
il morino garzone di Stalla			1669	I-Fas, Camera del Granduca, f. 40c	68v	
il morino garzone di Stalla			1669	I-Fas, Camera del Granduca, f. 40c	76r	
il moro del S. Cardinale	[Buonaccorsi?]		1669	I-Fas, Camera del Granduca, f. 41c	13v	
il moro garzone di Stalla			1669	I-Fas, Camera del Granduca, f. 40c	55r	

Name	Person	Description	Year	Source	Folio
il Mutolo			1669	I-Fas, Camera del Granduca, f. 40c	21r
il mutolo		"[P]er la stufa."	1669	I-Fas, Camera del Granduca, f. 40c	26r
il Mutolo			1669	I-Fas, Camera del Granduca, f. 41c	6r
il Mutolo			1669	I-Fas, Camera del Granduca, f. 41c	14r
il mutolo			1670	I-Fas, Camera del Granduca, f. 41c	61v
il Morino	Cosimo Moro	Girolamo Miliotti paid for his vitto and upkeep, 5 scudi for a month.	1671	I-Fas, Camera del Granduca, f. 42	15l
il Morino			1671	I-Fas, Camera del Granduca, f. 42	28r
il Morino	Cosimo Moro	5 scudi paid to Girolamo Miliotti, portiere di SAS, for the Morino's upkeep.	1671	I-Fas, Camera del Granduca, f. 42	30r
il Morino		Payment to the Calzolaio for 2 pairs of white shoes for the Morino.	1671	I-Fas, Camera del Granduca, f. 42	46r
il Morino di SAS		Money for fabric intended for 2 outfits.	1671	I-Fas, Camera del Granduca, f. 42	12r
il Morino di SAS			1671	I-Fas, Camera del Granduca, f. 42	25l
il Moro		"[C]he teneva conto dei Cani grossi. . . per li piu per essere stato malato."	1671	I-Fas, Camera del Granduca, f. 42	14l
il Moro	Cosimo Moro	"Pagati a Girolam Miliotti scudi cinque moneta a conto del vitto del Moro che tiene in Casa, per tutto il sopradetto mese."	1671	I-Fas, Camera del Granduca, f. 42	23r
il moro	Cosimo Moro	Payment to Girolamo Miliotto portiere, 5 scudi.	1671	I-Fas, Camera del Granduca, f. 42	48r
il Moro		Along with 2 (unnamed) lackeys was given money for having "fatto a Civetta et piu per un fiasco di Birra."	1671	I-Fas, Camera del Granduca, f. 42	52r

Reference (as given in document)	Baptismal name (if known)	Other descriptors in document	Year	Citation	Owner (if known)
il Mutolo		Tipped for Christmas.	1671	I-Fas, Camera del Granduca, f. 42	50l
il Mutolo del SA		"[I]n occasione di maritare una sua sorella."	1671	I-Fas, Camera del Granduca, f. 42	24l
il Mutolo del Ser. Principe Cardinale		Tipped for Christmas.	1671	I-Fas, Camera del Granduca, f. 42	50l
il mutolo di SAS			1671	I-Fas, Camera del Granduca, f. 42	12r
il Morino		Along with Tonino nano.	1672	I-Fas, Camera del Granduca, f. 42	77l
il Morino	Cosimo Moro	5 scudi paid to Girolamo Miliotti for the Morino's upkeep.	1672	I-Fas, Camera del Granduca, f. 42	56l
il Morino		A shirt and a crossbow purchased for him.	1672	I-Fas, Camera del Granduca, f. 42	57r
il Morino		Payments for clothing for the Morino.	1672	I-Fas, Camera del Granduca, f. 42	57r
il Morino		Paid along with 2 other "ragazzi … Per haver fatto a Civetta alla presenza di SAS."	1672	I-Fas, Camera del Granduca, f. 42	58l
il Morino		"Pagati a Girolamo Miliotti e per detto a Ferdinando Medici detto Chioggia scudi cinque moneta per il Vitto del Morino."	1672	I-Fas, Camera del Granduca, f. 42	61l
il Morino			1672	I-Fas, Camera del Granduca, f. 42	71l
il Morino		Along with Tonino Nano.	1672	I-Fas, Camera del Granduca, f. 42	72l
il Morino		Paid along with Masselli for having their hair cut.	1672	I-Fas, Camera del Granduca, f. 42	74l
il Morino			1672	I-Fas, Camera del Granduca, f. 42	74r

il Morino	Cosimo Moro	5 scudi paid to Girolamo Miliotti for the Morino's upkeep.	1672	I-Fas, Camera del Granduca, f. 42	79r
il Morino		5 scudi paid to Girolamo Miliotti for the Morino's upkeep.	1672	I-Fas, Camera del Granduca, f. 42	90r
il Morino		Along with the "Gobbino," presumably "il Gobbino Cristofano" who has been mentioned a few other times.	1672	I-Fas, Camera del Granduca, f. 42	125l
il Morino di SAS	[Cosimo Moro?]		1672	I-Fas, Camera del Granduca, f. 42	113r
il Moro		Along with Masselli and Battistone.	1672	I-Fas, Camera del Granduca, f. 42	53r
il Moro			1672	I-Fas, Camera del Granduca, f. 42	55r
il Moro		Along with Tonino Nano,	1672	I-Fas, Camera del Granduca, f. 42	84l
il Moro	Cosimo Moro	35 scudi paid to Girolamo Miliotti for the upkeep of the "Moro che tiene in casa."	1672	I-Fas, Camera del Granduca, f. 42	96r
il Moro	Cosimo Moro	5 scudi to Girolamo Miliotti.	1672	I-Fas, Camera del Granduca, f. 42	107l
il Moro	Cosimo Moro	5 scudi to Girolamo Miliotti.	1672	I-Fas, Camera del Granduca, f. 42	123l
il Moro	Cosimo Moro	5 scudi to Girolamo Miliotti.	1672	I-Fas, Camera del Granduca, f. 42	130r
il Moro	Cosimo Moro	5 scudi to Girolamo Miliotti.	1672	I-Fas, Camera del Granduca, f. 42	139r
il Moro	Cosimo Moro	5 scudi to Girolamo Miliotti.	1672	I-Fas, Camera del Granduca, f. 42	146l
il Moro	Cosimo Moro	5 scudi to Girolamo Miliotti.	1672	I-Fas, Camera del Granduca, f. 42	155r
il Moro Cacciatore		Paid "di comandamento di SAS per conto dei canini nanti della Razza grossa d'Inghilterra."	1672	I-Fas, Camera del Granduca, f. 42	61l
il Moro di SAS	Cosimo Moro	Girolamo Miliotti paid 5 scudi "per l'Alimento del Moro di SAS che tiene in Casa."	1672	I-Fas, Camera del Granduca, f. 42	70l

Reference (as given in document)	Baptismal name (if known)	Other descriptors in document	Year	Citation		Owner (if known)
il Mutolo		Tipped for Christmas.	1672	I-Fas, Camera del Granduca, f. 42	157r	
il Mutolo del Ser. Principe Cardinale		Tipped for Christmas.	1672	I-Fas, Camera del Granduca, f. 42	157r	
il Morino		Along with Gobbo, "per andare in maschera."	1673	I-Fas, Camera del Granduca, f. 42	163r	
il Morino			1673	I-Fas, Camera del Granduca, f. 42	209l	
il Moro		"[P]er andare in maschera."	1673	I-Fas, Camera del Granduca, f. 42	163r	
il Moro		Payment to the Mascheraio for costumes for il Gobbino, Montino, and Moro.	1673	I-Fas, Camera del Granduca, f. 42	169r	
il Moro		Along with Gobbo.	1673	I-Fas, Camera del Granduca, f. 42	175l	
Il Moro	Cosimo Moro	5 scudi to Girolamo Miliotti.	1673	I-Fas, Camera del Granduca, f. 42	175l	
il Moro		Along with Tonino Nano "per fare alla Trottola."	1673	I-Fas, Camera del Granduca, f. 42	181r	
il Moro	Cosimo Moro	5 scudi to Girolamo Miliotti.	1673	I-Fas, Camera del Granduca, f. 42	184l	
il Moro			1673	I-Fas, Camera del Granduca, f. 42	185r	
Il Moro	Cosimo Moro	5 scudi to Girolamo Miliotti.	1673	I-Fas, Camera del Granduca, f. 42	192r	
il Moro	Cosimo Moro	5 scudi to Girolamo Miliotti.	1673	I-Fas, Camera del Granduca, f. 42	203l	
il Moro	Cosimo Moro	5 scudi to Girolamo Miliotti.	1673	I-Fas, Camera del Granduca, f. 42	211l	
il Moro			1673	I-Fas, Camera del Granduca, f. 42	222r	
il Moro di Camera di SAS	[Cosimo Moro?]		1673	I-Fas, Camera del Granduca, f. 42	169l	
il Moro di SAS	[Cosimo Moro?]	"[P]er andare in maschera."	1673	I-Fas, Camera del Granduca, f. 42	162l	
il Moro di SAS		"[D]ati al Moro di SAS . . . in piu volte."	1673	I-Fas, Camera del Granduca, f. 42	198l	

Reference (as given in document)	Baptismal name (if known)	Other descriptors in document	Year	Citation	Owner (if known)
il Morino di Camera			1674	I-Fas, Camera del Granduca, f. 43	16l
il Morino di Camera			1674	I-Fas, Camera del Granduca, f. 43	23l
il Morino di Camera	[Cosimo Moro?]	Tipped for the Grand Duke's birthday.	1674	I-Fas, Camera del Granduca, f. 43	24r
il Morino di Camera			1674	I-Fas, Camera del Granduca, f. 43	28r

Anonymous Individuals and Groups of People

Reference (as given in document)	Baptismal name (if known)	Other descriptors in document	Year	Citation	Owner (if known)
		Approx. 1y. Presumably the child of Cechere/Caterina.	1606	I-Fca, Pia Casa, 1	Raphaello de' Pazzi
schiavi		"Si mandano 32 Trombetti non se ne sendo piu nel bagno al proposito per serviver in simili occasione si mandano anchora 38 schiavi di ricatto non ve ne sendo maggior quantità di poter mandar al presente, Capo di questa Condotta sarà Consalvo Aurino Reale homo molto diligente al quale li s'è Conseg.ti 48 marinari li quali serviranno per Guardia et accompag,a et se occorerà potranno anche servire a qualcosa nella battaglia." 22 di Ott.e 1608.	1608	I-Fas, Guardaroba medicea, f. 245	100r

Reference (as given in document)	Baptismal name (if known)	Other descriptors in document	Year	Citation	Owner (if known)
schiavi		"Mandai alle stinche p piu sicureza e meglio capacite di luogho li n.o 32 stiavi forzati trombetti e li stiavi turchi li o messi tra gli altri."	1608	I-Fas, Guardaroba medicea, f. 245	101r
Un giovane Turcho che si vuole battezzare		Lives in Pistoia.	1621	I-Fas, Camera del Granduca, f. 2b	20v
uno schiavo che venne con gli Barberi		A slave sent to help with the horses that are a gift from the Viceroy of Tunis, rewarded with 6 scudi.	1621	I-Fas, Camera del Granduca, f. 2b	26r	Viceroy of Tunis
uno schiavo dello Biscotteria		Tipped when the Grand Duke visited the galleys and the bagno in Livorno. Several other amounts that were distributed more generally are also recorded.	1622	I-Fas, Camera del Granduca, f. 3b	1v
uno schiavo		Charity.	1622	I-Fas, Camera del Granduca, f. 3b	9r
14 xtiani liberati		14 Christians liberated by the Grand Duke's galleys from Ottoman ships, rewarded with 1 scudi each.	1622	I-Fas, Camera del Granduca, f. 3b	27r
uno morisco		Transported grain to Livorno and was rewarded with a gold chain worth 20 scudi.	1623	I-Fas, Camera del Granduca, f. 3b	39r
moro che haveva portato porci		Delivered food.	1623	I-Fas, Camera del Granduca, f. 3b	40r
centocinquanto stiavi		151 enslaved individuals who have been ransomed and are tipped 1 scudi each; a printer is paid to produce passports for them on their return home.	1623	I-Fas, Camera del Granduca, f. 5b	9v, 10r
altri novi stiavi		Another 9 who are also ransomed.	1623	I-Fas, Camera del Granduca, f. 5b	10r

un'altro stiavo ricattato	Pollacco (Polish).	1623	I-Fas, Camera del Granduca, f. 5b 12r
uno di quelli stiavi ricattati		1623	I-Fas, Camera del Granduca, f. 5b 12v
Alli stiavi della Caravana		1624	I-Fas, Camera del Granduca, f. 5b 28r
li stiavi che lavorano li diaspri		1624	I-Fas, Camera del Granduca, f.5b 28r
li stiavi di Bischotteria		1624	I-Fas, Camera del Granduca, f. 5b 28r
il Servitore del Prete Moretto	The servant of a priest "Moretto."	1625	I-Fas, Camera del Granduca, f. 6b 9v
il Turco del Sig. Capitano Piero		1626	I-Fas, Camera del Granduca, f. 6b 23v
una povera donna Turca Battezzata	Sta all'Arsanale.	1626	I-Fas, Camera del Granduca, f. 6b 25r
un'altra Donna Turca battezzata		1626	I-Fas, Camera del Granduca, f. 6b 26r
quel Persiano che fece alla lotta in Livorno		1626	I-Fas, Camera del Granduca, f. 6b 26r
un povero vecchio che haveva la moglie e figluolo stiavi		1626	I-Fas, Camera del Granduca, f. 6b 31r
due greci che sono stati stiavi		1626	I-Fas, Camera del Granduca, f. 6b 33r

Reference (as given in document)	Baptismal name (if known)	Other descriptors in document	Year	Citation	Owner (if known)
un Giannozzero che si e' fatto Cristiano tredici greci			1626	I-Fas, Camera del Granduca, f. 6b 33r	
un Greco che va a Roma		Hanno a servire a Livorno.	1626	I-Fas, Camera del Granduca, f. 6b 35r	
Cinque stiavi scappati di man di Turchi		5 Christians who have escaped from Ottoman slavery.	1626	I-Fas, Camera del Granduca, f. 6b 35r	
uno stiavo			1626	I-Fas, Camera del Granduca, f. 7b 7r	
un ragazzo che e' stato stiavo			1627	I-Fas, Camera del Granduca, f. 7b 17v	
li Tamburini e trombetti Turchesci			1627	I-Fas, Camera del Granduca, f.7b 17v	
Certi Turchi che fecero il Buffone			1627	I-Fas, Camera del Granduca, f. 7b 17v	
uno stiavo			1627	I-Fas, Camera del Granduca, f. 7b 18r	
quel moro che fa il Buffone			1627	I-Fas, Camera del Granduca, f. 7b 18r	
due Mori Turchi che fecero il Buffone			1627	I-Fas, Camera del Granduca, f. 7b 18r	
un moro che fece il Buffone			1627	I-Fas, Camera del Granduca, f. 7b 19r	
			1627	I-Fas, Camera del Granduca, f. 6b 19r	

li Tuchi che cantavano	E portavano il legno che la Galera era fornita.	1627	I-Fas, Camera del Granduca, f. 7b	19r
Diciannove Musici Turchesci che sonorano	Quando li var' la galera.	1627	I-Fas, Camera del Granduca, f. 7b	19v
dodici Turchi	Presi in Portoferraio.	1627	I-Fas, Camera del Granduca, f. 7b	21v
due Zingari	Along with a "garzone" from the stables, rewarded for having trained the camels.	1627	I-Fas, Camera del Granduca, f. 7b	23r
cinque donne e quattro huomini di Macedonia		1627	I-Fas, Camera del Granduca, f. 7b	23v
uno stiavo		1627	I-Fas, Camera del Granduca, f. 7b	25r
quattro Pollacchi che erano scappati delle mani di Turchi		1627	I-Fas, Camera del Granduca, f. 7b	25r
due Todeschi stiavi	Since these Germans are referred to as if they are still enslaved rather than once having been slaves, they may be Protestants enslaved by the Florentines.	1627	I-Fas, Camera del Granduca, f. 8b	4r
uno che e' stato stiavo nelle mani de Turchi		1628	I-Fas, Camera del Granduca, f. 8b	17r
quattro Mori che fecero alle bastonate la Mora di Pratolino	I'm not entirely sure what "bastonate" means in this context, possibly fought together with staves.	1628	I-Fas, Camera del Granduca, f. 8b	28r
		1628	I-Fas, Camera del Granduca, f. 9b	9r
15 Pollachi		1628	I-Fas, Camera del Granduca, f. 9c	6r

Reference (as given in document)	Baptismal name (if known)	Other descriptors in document	Year	Citation	Owner (if known)
il morino che insegna alla pilotta		The "pilotta" was a very fashionable ball game, imported from Spain (the "Pelota basca"); in Florence, a special court was built, and this particular Moor was integral to the upkeep of the balls and teaching the game to the Florentine elite.	1628	I-Fas, Camera del Granduca, f. 9c 26r	
il moro tornaio d'anni 100			1628	I-Fas, Camera del Granduca, f. 9c 26v	
il moro tornaio			1628	I-Fas, Camera del Granduca, f. 10b 3v	
il vecchio Moro Tornaio			1628	I-Fas, Camera del Granduca, f. 10b 5v	
il vecchio Torniaio		Presumably the 100-year-old Moro.	1628	I-Fas, Camera del Granduca, f. 10b 7r	
A un Cristiano ricattato dalle Galere			1628	I-Fas, Camera del Granduca, f. 10b 8v	
i Cristiani ricattati dalle Galere di SA		511 scudi were distributed on this occasion to the ransomed Christians and the mariners who accompanied them to Florence. It was presumably a considerable number of individuals.	1628	I-Fas, Camera del Granduca, f. 10b 8v	
un Cristiano ricattato			1628	I-Fas, Camera del Granduca, f. 10b 9v	
tre riscattati dalle galere		Che erano ammalati.	1628	I-Fas, Camera del Granduca, f. 10b 10v	
il morino			1628	I-Fas, Camera del Granduca, f. 10b 11v	

due cristiani che furono ricattati	1628	I-Fas, Camera del Granduca, f. 10b	11v
un Turco fatto Cristiano	1628	I-Fas, Camera del Granduca, f. 10b	13v
il Moro Torniaio	1628	I-Fas, Camera del Granduca, f. 10b	15v
la mora di Pratolino	1629	I-Fas, Camera del Granduca, f. 10b	20v
tre stiavi	1629	I-Fas, Camera del Granduca, f. 10b	22r
il Turchetto del S.r Generale	1629	I-Fas, Camera del Granduca, f. 10b	37r
due stiavi Che vennero all'audienza.	1629	I-Fas, Camera del Granduca, f. 10b	43v
una greca fatta Cristiana	1629	I-Fas, Camera del Granduca, f. 10b	44v
un Veneziano che e' stato stiavo	1629	I-Fas, Camera del Granduca, f. 10b	54v
uno che era stato stiavo a Scio	1629	I-Fas, Camera del Granduca, f. 11b	4v
La Mora di Pratolino "[P]resentò ravigioli."	1629	I-Fas, Camera del Granduca, f. 11b	7r
certe povere donne state stiave "[P]er ricondurse al loro paese." Presumably, these are poor Italian women who were enslaved and are returning to their town rather than foreign women who are returning to their country of origin, though it is not entirely clear.	1629	I-Fas, Camera del Granduca, f. 11b	9v

Reference (as given in document)	Baptismal name (if known)	Other descriptors in document	Year	Citation	Owner (if known)
un povero Cristiano ricattato delle mani del Turco			1629	I-Fas, Camera del Granduca, f. 11b 10r	
due Ebrei fatti Cristiani		Jacopo Sarto was paid for making new clothes for the converts.	1629	I-Fas, Camera del Granduca, f. 11b 13r	
un Moro del Arsanale			1629	I-Fas, Camera del Granduca, f. 11b 18r	
un Turco Battezzato del Arsanale			1629	I-Fas, Camera del Granduca, f. 11b 18v	
Certi stiavi			1630	I-Fas, Camera del Granduca, f. 11b 24r	
li stiavi che fecero alla lotta			1630	I-Fas, Camera del Granduca, f. 11b 24r	
li stiavi che gioccarano a Dama			1630	I-Fas, Camera del Granduca, f. 11b 24v	
un Persiano		Gave SAS a dozen razors.	1630	I-Fas, Camera del Granduca, f. 11b 24v	
Morino che predico'		Possibly the Prete Moretto or even Giovanni Moro (whom Jong describes as having predicato when he first arrived).	1630	I-Fas, Camera del Granduca, f. 11b 36v	
il Turco del Generale			1630	I-Fas, Camera del Granduca, f. 11b 36v	
il Moro che fa il Buffone in Livorno		Meno' un Cane.	1630	I-Fas, Camera del Granduca, f. 11b 38v	
un poveraccio che e' stato stiavo			1630	I-Fas, Camera del Granduca, f. 11b 39v	

Subject	Person	Description	Year	Reference
Moro del Sig. Staffa		"Al Moro del Sig. Staffa et al Morino di SA in due volte quattro testoni 1.1.–." This entry clearly distinguishes between 2 different Black men (one of whom is young).	1630	I-Fas, Camera del Granduca, f. 11b 53r
il Morino all'acqua		Possibly the court Moro who was down at the water with SA; possibly a Moro whom they encountered down by the water.	1630	I-Fas, Camera del Granduca, f. 11b 54r
un Ebreo		"[C]he voleva medicare l'appestati" ("who wants to treat plague victims").	1630	I-Fas, Camera del Granduca, f. 12b 2r
Mora di Pratolino			1630	I-Fas, Camera del Granduca, f. 12b 14v
il Morino del S. Cardinale		The Luchese who brought him is tipped.	1631	I-Fas, Camera del Granduca, f. 12b 23r
Turco battezzato	Ferdinando	Maestro Frediano is given 20 scudi for the upkeep of the baptized Turk he is keeping in his house.	1631	I-Fas, Camera del Granduca, f. 12b 44v
uno d'Aleppo			1631	I-Fas, Camera del Granduca, f. 12b 48r
Turco battezzato	Ferdinando	Again, Maestro Frediano is given money for the upkeep of the turco battezzato.	1631	I-Fas, Camera del Granduca, f. 12b 49r
Turco del Sig. Generale Montauti		Presented a wolf.	1632	I-Fas, Camera del Granduca, f. 14b 15r
un Turco			1633	I-Fas, Camera del Granduca, f. 14b 25r
un Turco		"[C]he leggeva una lettera Turchesca." Paid to read and translate a letter that was written in Turkish.	1633	I-Fas, Camera del Granduca, f. 14b 26v
tredici Pollacchi stati stiavi e ricattati		13 Poles who were enslaved.	1633	I-Fas, Camera del Granduca, f. 14b 29v
due Pollacchi ricatti dalle Galere di SA			1633	I-Fas, Camera del Granduca, f. 14b 30v

Reference (as given in document)	Baptismal name (if known)	Other descriptors in document	Year	Citation	Owner (if known)
Moro dell'Arsanale			1633	I-Fas, Camera del Granduca, f. 14b 34r	
due Pollacchi gia stiavi			1633	I-Fas, Camera del Granduca, f. 14b 34v	
Persiani		"Al Persiani che dedico' a SA alcune canzone."	1633	I-Fas, Camera del Granduca, f. 14b 42v	
un povvero huomo d'Aleppo			1633	I-Fas, Camera del Granduca, f. 14b 49r	
Moro del Lenzoni			1633	I-Fas, Camera del Granduca, f. 14b 49r	
Moro del S.r Duca di Ghisa			1633	I-Fas, Camera del Granduca, f. 14b 51r	
due Mori del S.r Bartolomeo della Staffa			1633	I-Fas, Camera del Granduca, f. 14b 52r	
Alli sonatori d'un barca inglese, o fiaminghi		The musicians from the foreign boat are tipped 10 scudi among them. Interestingly, the boat and its occupants are considered heathen (Protestant), but whether they are Flemish or English is unclear to the note taker.	1633	I-Fas, Camera del Granduca, f. 15b 18r	
il Morino che Cavaleo' il Cavallo per Mare		The Moor who rode a horse in the ocean.	1633	I-Fas, Camera del Granduca, f. 15b 18r	
stiavi		"A due Brache di stiavi che lavoravano allo Galeazza."	1633	I-Fas, Camera del Granduca, f. 15b 18r	

un turco stiavo		1634	I-Fas, Camera del Granduca, f. 15b 23v
un povero Turco Battezzato uno stiavo		1634	I-Fas, Camera del Granduca, f. 15b 27r
		1634	I-Fas, Camera del Granduca, f. 15b 31v
il Morino del S. Cav. re Cansacchi		1634	I-Fas, Camera del Granduca, f. 15b 33r
il Turco del S. Arcimboldo		1634	I-Fas, Camera del Granduca, f. 15b 43r
lo stiavo del S. Ainolfo de' Bardi		1634	I-Fas, Camera del Granduca, f. 15b 46r
lo stiavo	"Al Moroniat per le spese fatte allo stiavo che gli aiuta translatare le leggi Turchesche."	1634	I-Fas, Camera del Granduca, f. 15b 46r
un Mutolo dal Ponte a Signa		1634	I-Fas, Camera del Granduca, f. 15b 51v
Mutolo		1634	I-Fas, Camera del Granduca, f. 15b 52r
Mutolo della lastra		1634	I-Fas, Camera del Granduca, f. 15b 53v
Persiani	"[C]he presentò a SA un sonetto."	1634	I-Fas, Camera del Granduca, f. 15b 54r
stiavi	"[U]na cassa per li stiavi coperta di Vachetta."	1635	I-Fas, Camera del Granduca, f. 17b 5r
due ragazzi stiavi del S. Gonzaga		1635	I-Fas, Camera del Granduca, f. 17b 5r
la Moglie di Mezzomoro Anna		1635	I-Fas, Camera del Granduca, f. 17b 9v

Reference (as given in document)	Baptismal name (if known)	Other descriptors in document	Year	Citation	Owner (if known)
il Moro del Lenzoni			1635	I-Fas, Camera del Granduca, f. 17b 13r	
Mutolo della lastra			1635	I-Fas, Camera del Granduca, f. 17b 13v	
un Greco che va a Livorno per Marinaro			1635	I-Fas, Camera del Granduca, f. 17b 15r	
All'Indiano		"Per due Anelletti."	1636	I-Fas, Camera del Granduca, f. 17b 25r	
stiavo		"A una povera donna che ha il marito stiavo."	1636	I-Fas, Camera del Granduca, f. 17b 31v	
due Turchi		"[C]he caneggiavano vion al Magazzino."	1636	I-Fas, Camera del Granduca, f. 17b 31v	
la Musica delle Galere		Presumably the ensemble rather than an individual woman.	1636	I-Fas, Camera del Granduca, f. 17b 35r	
uno stiavo del Prov. re della Graccia		"Porto' Carciofi."	1636	I-Fas, Camera del Granduca, f. 17b 35v	
l'Indiano		"Per un'Anello con nove diamanti comprato dall'Indiano che SA lo dono' per fiera in Pisa al Paganino."	1636	I-Fas, Camera del Granduca, f. 17b 36v	
un Franzese venuto di Turchia			1636	I-Fas, Camera del Granduca, f. 17b 39v	
L'Indiano		"[P]er un Diamantino che SA dono' a Ma. Maria."	1636	I-Fas, Camera del Granduca, f. 17b 43v	
un Tucimanno che veniva di Jerusalem			1636	I-Fas, Camera del Granduca, f. 17b 49v	

Description	Year	Source	Folio	Notes
tredici greci Marinari	1636	I-Fas, Camera del Granduca, f. 17b	52r	
l'Ebreo che fece la Commedia	1636	I-Fas, Camera del Granduca, f. 17b	55v	Paid 20 scudi.
il Moro del S. Arcimboldo	1636	I-Fas, Camera del Granduca, f. 18b	11r	
un mutolo dalla La Stia	1636	I-Fas, Camera del Granduca, f. 18b	15v	
una donna stiavona	1636	I-Fas, Camera del Granduca, f. 18b	24r	Wording implies she is from eastern Europe and may or may not have been enslaved.
	1636	I-Fas, Mediceo del Principato, f. 5363	388–400	Copy of the constitutional orders and rules of the Casa de' Catecumeni di Firenze; this same volume contains several other documents about the Casa, including multiple lists of the governors of the house from various points in the seventeenth century. Occasionally, converts are mentioned; however, I did not transcribe (and thus have not listed here) all such mentions.
lo stiavo del Priore della Graccia	1637	I-Fas, Camera del Granduca, f. 18b	30r	
uno di Persia	1637	I-Fas, Camera del Granduca, f. 18b	30r	
la Musica Turchesca	1637	I-Fas, Camera del Granduca, f. 18b	38r	"Alla Musica Turchesca che fu' quando si varò' la Galera dieci [scudi]."
una Monaca Todesca delle Convertite	1637	I-Fas, Camera del Granduca, f. 18b	39r	
una povera convertita	1637	I-Fas, Camera del Granduca, f. 18b	40r	"[P]er vestirsi Monaca."

Reference (as given in document)	Baptismal name (if known)	Other descriptors in document	Year	Citation	Owner (if known)
Morino che sta sul Ponte Vecchio			1637	I-Fas, Camera del Granduca, f. 18b 44v	
un Tedesco che era stato stiavo			1637	I-Fas, Camera del Granduca, f. 18b 47r	
tre Pollacchi scappati delle Mani de Turchi			1637	I-Fas, Camera del Granduca, f. 18b 58r	
la Moglie di Mezzo moro gia' staffiere	Anna		1637	I-Fas, Camera del Granduca, f. 19b 5v	
Mutolo della lastra			1637	I-Fas, Camera del Granduca, f. 19b 9v	
undici Pollacchi liberati dalle Galere di SA			1638	I-Fas, Camera del Granduca, f. 19b 17r	
un Moro che serviva il S. Duca di Mantova			1638	I-Fas, Camera del Granduca, f. 19b 18v	
il Moro del S. Capitano Lenzoni			1638	I-Fas, Camera del Granduca, f. 19b 26v	
lo stiavo del Prov.re Mortosa			1638	I-Fas, Camera del Granduca, f. 19b 30r	
lo stiavo del Mortosa			1638	I-Fas, Camera del Granduca, f. 19b 39r	
li due Mori		"A Giulio staffiere che condusse di Livorno a Pisa li due Mori."	1638	I-Fas, Camera del Granduca, f. 19b 39r	

Alla moglie di *Mezzomoro* gia' staffiere di SA		1638	I-Fas, Camera del Granduca, f. 19b 46r
il Morino del S. Marchese Collaredo		1638	I-Fas, Camera del Granduca, f. 19b 50r
tre scappati dalle mani de Turchi		1638	I-Fas, Camera del Granduca, f. 20b 4v
un soldato che e' stato in mano de Turchi		1638	I-Fas, Camera del Granduca, f. 20b 11r
un vecchio stato stiavo		1638	I-Fas, Camera del Granduca, f. 20b 11v
la Moglie di Mezzo Moro	"[C]he sono' il 'Tamburo."	1638	I-Fas, Camera del Granduca, f. 20b 11v
il figlio del Prete Moretto		1638	I-Fas, Camera del Granduca, f. 20b 20r
la Moglie di Mezzomoro		1639	I-Fas, Camera del Granduca, f. 20b 39v
il Morino di Livorno		1639	I-Fas, Camera del Granduca, f. 20b 39v
un Cristiano ricattato dalle Galere di SA	"[O]tto scudi perche la faccia studiare Stefanino suo figlio."	1639	I-Fas, Camera del Granduca, f. 20b 40v
Un Veneziano stato stiavo		1639	I-Fas, Camera del Granduca, f. 20b 47r
quattro Pollacchi scappati dalle Mani de Turchi		1639	I-Fas, Camera del Granduca, f. 20b 48r

Reference (as given in document)	Baptismal name (if known)	Other descriptors in document	Year	Citation	Owner (if known)
un ragazzo Croatto			1639	I-Fas, Camera del Granduca, f. 20b 52v	
li due Morini che vanno a Mantova			1639	I-Fas, Camera del Granduca, f. 21b 7r	
quattro Russi scappati dalli Turchi			1639	I-Fas, Camera del Granduca, f. 21b 7r	
un pollacco scappato delle mani de Turchi			1639	I-Fas, Camera del Granduca, f. 21b 8r	
Alla moglie di Mezzo Moro	Anna		1639	I-Fas, Camera del Granduca, f. 21b 11r	
All'Indiano		"[P]er la Riffa dell'Anello."	1639	I-Fas, Camera del Granduca, f. 21b 15r	
una mora fatta Christiana			1639	I-Fas, Camera del Granduca, f. 21b 17r	
il Morino del Cancacchi			1640	I-Fas, Camera del Granduca, f. 21b 27r	
lo stiavo di Pellegrino Fedi			1640	I-Fas, Camera del Granduca, f. 21b 30r	
li stiavi che carreggiavno il vino del Magazzino			1640	I-Fas, Camera del Granduca, f. 21b 30r	
lo stiavo che bollo' tordo nel Braccio		Paid along with Corvatto.	1640	I-Fas, Camera del Granduca, f. 21b 32r	

Musici Turcheschi	"Ai Musici Turchieschi che varorno la Galera."	1640	I-Fas, Camera del Granduca, f. 21b 32r
alla moglie di Mezzo Moro	"[P]er il suo ragazzo"	1640	I-Fas, Camera del Granduca, f. 21b 35r
un povero stiavo ricattato Veneziano		1640	I-Fas, Camera del Granduca, f. 21b 35v
uno che scappo delle man de Turchi		1640	I-Fas, Camera del Granduca, f. 21b 51r
il Moro del S. Marchese Collaredo		1640	I-Fas, Camera del Granduca, f. 21b 52v
due Turchi	"[P]ortono le lepre ammallate all'Inprueneta dalli Cavalieri tornati dalle Galere."	1640	I-Fas, Camera del Granduca, f. 21b 53v
uno Cristiano scappato da 'Turchi		1640	I-Fas, Camera del Granduca, f. 21b 56v
uno stiavo porto' una lettera		1640	I-Fas, Camera del Granduca, f. 21b 56v
Il Moro del Sr. Duca Sforza		1645	I-Fas, Depositeria generale, f. 1604 27r	Sforza
Il Moro del Sr. Bali Gondi		1647	I-Fas, Depositeria generale, f. 1604 61v	Bali Gondi
Il Morino del Sr. Marchese Corsini		1650	I-Fas, Depositeria generale, f. 1604 112r	Corsini
Morino di Piano di Ripoli	[Gave a gift of food.]	1650	I-Fas, Camera del Granduca, f. 22b 4r
Il Morino de Buonaccorsi		1650	I-Fas, Depositeria generale, f. 1604 116r	Buonaccorsi
il Morino di Piano di Ripoli		1650	I-Fas, Camera del Granduca, f. 22b 4r

Reference (as given in document)	Baptismal name (if known)	Other descriptors in document	Year	Citation	Owner (if known)
Il Morino del S. Marchese Corsini			1651	I-Fas, Depositeria generale, f. 1604 120r	Corsini
A un Moro dell'Indie			1651	I-Fas, Depositeria generale, f. 1604 129r	
Al Moro presento Piesci d'Arno		[Gave a gift of food.]	1651	I-Fas, Camera del Granduca, f. 22b 37r	
Al Morino presento il Corvo		[Gave a gift of food.]	1651	I-Fas, Camera del Granduca, f. 22b 37r	
Turchi		Letter from Vicenzo Medici describing a victory that the Venetian armada has had against the Ottomans, taking 5 ships and sinking 16, taking many turchi into slavery and liberating enslaved Christians from the enemy ships.	1651	I-Fas, Mediceo del Principato, f. 5354 71rv	
quattro stiavi		"[P]er bere."	1651	I-Fas, Camera del Granduca, f. 22b 20r	
un Indiano			1651	I-Fas, Camera del Granduca, f. 22b 36r	
un schiavatore Romano		Paid 10 doble, equivalent to 28 scudi, 4 lire.	1651	I-Fas, Camera del Granduca, f. 22b 37v	
Family of Jews		This document details some of the pageantry that accompanied high-profile conversions (in this instance, of a whole family of Jews, minus the wife, who were baptized on the feast of S. Giovanni), including trumpets, guards, and bell ringing.	1651	I-Fas, Mediceo del Principato, f. 5363 426r	
due Turchi		"Al Domenico Trevisani Locandiere della Fiamma per le spese fatte alli due Turchi per l'allogio."	1652	I-Fas, Camera del Granduca, f. 23b 43v	

il Morino che condusse il casse d'Inghitera		1652	I-Fas, Camera del Granduca, f. 23b	27r
il Moro che corse per le lettere alla Porta		1652	I-Fas, Camera del Granduca, f. 23b	29v
Al Morino del Buonaccorsi		1653	I-Fas, Camera del Granduca, f. 25b	9r	Buonaccorsi
lo schiavo del Priore di Livorno		1653	I-Fas, Camera del Granduca, f. 25b	10v
schiavi	"Al Priore Francesco Di S. Lorenzo per riscattare schiavi."	1653	I-Fas, Camera del Granduca, f. 25b	10v
Al Moro del Sig. Ipolito		1654	I-Fas, Camera del Granduca, f. 25b	20v	Vichi
Al moro del Sig.r Ipolito de Vichi		1654	I-Fas, Camera del Granduca, f. 25b	33r	Vichi
Alla sorella del moro		1654	I-Fas, Camera del Granduca, f. 25b	42v
i Turchetti	Along with il Moro del S. Cardinale, possibly Buonaccorsi.	1654	I-Fas, Camera del Granduca, f. 25b	23r
il Moro del S. Ipolito	Along with "il Turco."	1654	I-Fas, Camera del Granduca, f. 25b	20v
il Moro del S. Ipolito de Vichi		1654	I-Fas, Camera del Granduca, f. 25b	33r
la Musica Turchesca	"Alla Musica Turchesca sei scudi."	1654	I-Fas, Camera del Granduca, f. 25b	18v
la sorella del moro		1654	I-Fas, Camera del Granduca, f. 25b	42v

Reference (as given in document)	Baptismal name (if known)	Other descriptors in document	Year	Citation	Owner (if known)
Al Morino che porto li due Cardinalini			1655	I-Fas, Camera del Granduca, f. 26b 40r	
Alla sorella del moro			1656	I-Fas, Camera del Granduca f. 27b 74v	
Alla moglie del Moro gia staff.e			1656	I-Fas, Camera del Granduca, f. 27b 83r	
certi schiavi liberati			1656	I-Fas, Camera del Granduca, f. 28b 10r	
due altri schiavi ricattati da Veneziani			1656	I-Fas, Camera del Granduca, f. 28b 9r	
due Cristiani liberati da Turchi dalle Galera di Malta			1656	I-Fas, Camera del Granduca, f. 28b 17v	
due schiavi ricattati da Veneziani			1656	I-Fas, Camera del Granduca, f. 28b 9r	
la moglie del Moro gia' staffiere			1656	I-Fas, Camera del Granduca, f. 27b 83r	
la sorella del moro			1656	I-Fas, Camera del Granduca, f. 27b 74v	

				Prince Mattias de' Medici
un Turco	"Pagati a Gio Piero Venturini orefice … tanti se li fanno dare per la valuta d'una collana d'oro, servita per donare a un Turco che haviamo tenuto a Battesimo fino di settembre passato. 47.3.-.-." This is possibly the Ali from Candia who had a file in the Pia Casa in Florence from 1655 (Prince Mattias is mentioned in those documents); no baptismal record was found, however.	1656	I-Fas, Mediceo del Principato, f. 5487	100v
A Morino che marita una figlia		1657	I-Fas, Camera del Granduca, f. 28b	57v
Alla Mora che si marita		1657	I-Fas, Camera del Granduca, f. 28b	63v
certi Cristiani ricattati dalle Galere di Malta		1657	I-Fas, Camera del Granduca, f. 28b	33r
certi schiavi liberati		1657	I-Fas, Camera del Granduca, f. 28b	68r
il Morino che marita una figlia		1657	I-Fas, Camera del Granduca, f. 28b	57v
la Mora che si marita		1657	I-Fas, Camera del Granduca, f. 28b	63v
il Moro che auitato tener Scavvi grossi a Livorno		1661	I-Fas, Camera del Granduca, f. 30b	147r
la Moglie dello schiavo batezzato Garzone di stalla di SAS		1661	I-Fas, Camera del Granduca, f. 31b	47v
li schavi		1661	I-Fas, Camera del Granduca, f. 30b	106r

Reference (as given in document)	Baptismal name (if known)	Other descriptors in document	Year	Citation	Owner (if known)
un offizziale francesce stato schiavo			1661	I-Fas, Camera del Granduca, f. 30b 112r	
turco (unnamed child of Gelsima, 1)		Turco. Was enslaved (possibly still enslaved), currently living in the house of the Arighetti.	1662	I-Fca, Pia Casa, 2	
turco (unnamed child of Gelsima, 2)		Turco. Was enslaved (possibly still enslaved), currently living in the house of the Bartolomei.	1662	I-Fca, Pia Casa, 2	
certi zingari			1662	I-Fas, Camera del Granduca, f. 31b 116r	
due Ebrei fatti Christiani Todeschi i schiavi dell'Arsenale			1662	I-Fas, Camera del Granduca, f. 31b 84v	
il Moro pescatore		Porto Anguilla.	1662	I-Fas, Camera del Granduca, f. 31b 116r	
la Mora sorella del Gio: Staffiere Turco			1662	I-Fas, Camera del Granduca, f. 31b 163v	
		Letter from Prince Gio: Carlo to Prince Mattias: "Dice SA che VA si pigli pentiero di far trattenere il mandato Turco…"	1662	I-Fas, Camera del Granduca, f. 31b 125r	
un marinaro domandato Gio Bat'a di Mecche di Tunisia			1662	I-Fas, Mediceo del Principato, f. 5487 153rv	
			1662	I-Fas, Camera del Granduca, f. 31b 160r	
un Turco batezzato			1662	I-Fas, Camera del Granduca, f. 31b 105r	

una Mora	1662	I-Fas, Camera del Granduca, f. 31b 119r
uno stiavo moro del S. Maurazzoni	1662	I-Fas, Camera del Granduca, f. 31b 158r
la Moglie del Turco battezato	1663	I-Fas, Camera del Granduca, f. 33b 15v
quello della Gondola	1663	I-Fas, Camera del Granduca, f. 33b 43r
un spagnolo stato schiavo	1663	I-Fas, Camera del Granduca, f. 33b 62v
una Mora batezzata a Pisa	1663	I-Fas, Camera del Granduca, f. 33b 43r
certi schiavi	1664	I-Fas, Camera del Granduca, f. 33b 80r
certi schiavi	1664	I-Fas, Camera del Granduca, f. 33b 107r
la Mora	1664	I-Fas, Camera del Granduca, f. 34b 10v
un Olandese stato schiavo in Algiere	1664	I-Fas, Camera del Granduca, f. 33b 76r
un Todesco stato schiavo	1664	I-Fas, Camera del Granduca, f. 34b 11v
un Turchetto dello Strozzi	1664	I-Fas, Camera del Granduca, f. 33b 94v
uno scappato di schiavitudine	1664	I-Fas, Camera del Granduca, f. 33b 112r
due schiavi ricattati da Veneziani	1665	I-Fas, Camera del Granduca, f. 34b 132r

"A due schiavi che hanno spazzato la fortezza di Livorno uno detto Pulcinella e l'altro Zibelleo, una *pezza per uno*."

Reference (as given in document)	Baptismal name (if known)	Other descriptors in document	Year	Citation	Owner (if known)
i schiavi dell'Arsenale			1665	I-Fas, Camera del Granduca, f. 34b 62v	
i schiavi dell'Arsenale			1665	I-Fas, Camera del Granduca, f. 34b 108r	
i turchi		"Ai turchi della tuba, e Trombetti che vennero di Livorno per Vassare la Gelera, che sonono piu volti."	1665	I-Fas, Camera del Granduca, f. 34b 92r	
il Capitano della Barca Morino	[Agniolo Pandolfini?]	Along with Pippo.	1665	I-Fas, Camera del Granduca, f. 34b 83v	
il Garzone del Morino			1665	I-Fas, Camera del Granduca, f. 34b 156r	
il Moretto e Mora del Capitano Ciaves		Delivered jams and candied fruits.	1665	I-Fas, Camera del Granduca, f. 34b 60r	
il Morino del Capitano Cianos		Delivered jams.	1665	I-Fas, Camera del Granduca, f. 34b 55v	
il turco batezzato che sta nelle stalle			1665	I-Fas, Camera del Granduca, f. 34b 148r	
la moglie del Turco Batezzato garzone			1665	I-Fas, Camera del Granduca, f. 35b 20v	
la Mora			1665	I-Fas, Camera del Granduca, f. 34b 140v	
un danese stato schiavo			1665	I-Fas, Camera del Granduca, f. 35b 19v	
un Pollacco scappato d'Turchia			1665	I-Fas, Camera del Granduca, f. 34b 170r	
un Pollacco stato schiavo			1665	I-Fas, Camera del Granduca, f. 35b 32v	

un schiavo del Bornù		1665	I-Fas, Camera del Granduca, f. 34b 76r
certi Turchi		1666	I-Fas, Camera del Granduca, f. 35b 79v
i Turchi del'Arsenale		1666	I-Fas, Camera del Granduca, f. 35b 67v
il Moro Indiano		1666	I-Fas, Camera del Granduca, f. 36b 1r
il Moro indiano		1666	I-Fas, Camera del Granduca, f. 36b 35r
il Moro indiano	A jacket is made for him.	1666	I-Fas, Camera del Granduca, f. 36b 35r
il Turco batezzato garzone di stalla		1666	I-Fas, Camera del Granduca, f. 35b 136v
un Indiano		1666	I-Fas, Camera del Granduca, f. 36b 1r
un Maltese che fuggi di Tunis e sta a Firenze		1666	I-Fas, Camera del Granduca, f. 36b 15r
un Pollacco scappato di schiavitudine		1666	I-Fas, Camera del Granduca, f. 35b 108v
un povero schiavo		1666	I-Fas, Camera del Granduca, f. 35b 123v
un Veronese scapato di schivitudine		1666	I-Fas, Camera del Granduca, f. 35b 159v
uno schiavetto	An outfit is paid for.	1666	I-Fas, Camera del Granduca, f. 35b 85r

Reference (as given in document)	Baptismal name (if known)	Other descriptors in document	Year	Citation	Owner (if known)
il Morino del Tempi cioe di Tommaso			1667	I-Fas, Camera del Granduca, f. 37b 19v	
il moro del Pandolfino		"[P]er aver presentato granelli in Cingialo."	1667	I-Fas, Camera del Granduca, f. 37b 46v	
li schiavi che tengono ripulito la Fortezza			1667	I-Fas, Camera del Granduca, f. 37b 38v	
lo schiavo del Mendes Ebreo che fa i sorbetti			1667	I-Fas, Camera del Granduca, f. 37b 20r	
schiavi			1667	I-Fas, Camera del Granduca, f. 37b 54r	
un Maronito			1667	I-Fas, Camera del Granduca, f. 39b 1v	
un schiavo della Serenissima			1667	I-Fas, Camera del Granduca, f. 39b 15r	
un turcho battezzato gia garzone di stalla			1667	I-Fas, Camera del Granduca, f. 38b 15v	
una mora			1667	I-Fas, Camera del Granduca, f. 38b 15v	
uno del Borgo a S. Sepulcro stato schiavo			1667	I-Fas, Camera del Granduca, f. 38b 2v	
uno del Borgo a S. Sepulcro tornato d'Aleppo			1667	I-Fas, Camera del Granduca, f. 38b 2v	

due turchi del Capitano della torra	"A un marinato che accompagno due turchi del Capitano della torra da Livorno a Firenze."	1668	I-Fas, Camera del Granduca, f. 39b 39v
due turchi del Capitano della torra	"A un timoniere che chondusse due turchi del Capitano della torra da Livorno a Firenze, per Carrozza e spese per i medesimi come per nota."	1668	I-Fas, Camera del Granduca, f. 40c 5r, 5v
i schiavi del Capitano della torra	"Al timoniere che condusse i schiavi del Capitano della torra spese per i med"; "Al medesimo per le spese dei medesimi turchi di ritorno da Firenze a Livorno."	1668	I-Fas, Camera del Granduca, f. 40c 6r
i schiavi di Livorno	"[C]he ripuliscano la fortezza."	1668	I-Fas, Camera del Granduca, f. 39b 25r
schiavi	"Al timoniere di SAS che accompagna i schiavi del Capitano della torra per spese per i medesimi schiavi, scudi due, lire quattro danari otto come per nota."	1668	I-Fas, Camera del Granduca, f. 40c 3v
un maltese stato schiavo		1668	I-Fas, Camera del Granduca, f. 40c 5v
un turcho battezzato		1668	I-Fas, Camera del Granduca, f. 40c 7v
un turcho battezzato		1668	I-Fas, Camera del Granduca, f. 40c 13r
un turcho fatto Christiano		1668	I-Fas, Camera del Granduca, f. 40c 10r
uno schiavo liberato		1668	I-Fas, Camera del Granduca, f. 39b
il Custode de' Turchi		1669	I-Fas, Camera del Granduca, f. 40c 17r
il figliolo del Morino servitore delle dame	"[V]enne di Tunisia col Dottor Pagni."	1669	I-Fas, Camera del Granduca, f. 40c 32v

Reference (as given in document)	Baptismal name (if known)	Other descriptors in document	Year	Citation	Owner (if known)
il figliolo di Santi detto il Moro del Imperiale		"[P]resentò' fichi e fece alla pugna."	1669	I-Fas, Camera del Granduca, f. 40c 186r	
il morino del Calabrese			1669	I-Fas, Camera del Granduca, f. 40c 147r	
il morino di Ottavio Tempi			1669	I-Fas, Camera del Granduca, f. 41c 13v	
il moro di Brucianesi			1669	I-Fas, Camera del Granduca, f. 40c 148v	
la Mora sorella del Moro, che era staffiere			1669	I-Fas, Camera del Granduca, f. 40c 76r	
turco Pauletti			1669	I-Fas, Camera del Granduca, f. 41c 20r	
un Moro del Bornù			1669	I-Fas, Camera del Granduca, f. 40c 21r	
un turcho battezzato dello Arsenale di Pisa			1669	I-Fas, Camera del Granduca, f. 40c 125r	
il Bianco Cacciatore		Listed here because this individual seems named to differentiate him from the "Morino Cacciatore."	1670	I-Fas, Camera del Granduca, f. 41c 46r	
il Moro de' Cani Grossi			1670	I-Fas, Camera del Granduca, f. 41c 58r	
li schiavi dal Arsenale			1670	I-Fas, Camera del Granduca, f. 41c 58r	

il Moro del S. Ottavio Tempi		Delivered bergamot pears.	1671	I-Fas, Camera del Granduca, f. 42	39r
il Moro del S. Ottavio Tempi		Delivered citrus fruit.	1672	I-Fas, Camera del Granduca, f. 42	107l
il Moro del S. Ottavio Tempi			1672	I-Fas, Camera del Granduca, f. 42	129l
il Turco battezzato che sta in spezieria	Cosimo/ Almansor	Payment for shoes made for the Turco and also for 3 "forestieri"—presumably Flemish, as 3 Flemish visitors who came to Florence to make baked goods are mentioned in close proximity.	1672	I-Fas, Camera del Granduca, f. 42	105r
le femmine Candiotte		"Pagati al S. Girolamo Migliorotti Proveditore di questa Dogana di Pisa … E sono per suo rimborso di spese fatte a conto delle femmine Candiotte, e per noli e vitto da Tuni a Livorno, come per i conti, e ricevuta."	1672	I-Fas, Camera del Granduca, f. 42	53l
un povero schiavo ricattato			1672	I-Fas, Camera del Granduca, f. 42	86l
un Turcho		"[A] un Turcho lire venti che pescha sotto l'acqua."	1672	I-Fas, Camera del Granduca, f. 42	80l
una Povera Donna Mora			1672	I-Fas, Camera del Granduca, f. 42	96r
uno che viene dell'Indie		"[S]tato altre volte."	1672	I-Fas, Camera del Granduca, f. 42	120l
il Moro del S. Ottavio Tempi		"[P]er havere portato … dell Pere."	1673	I-Fas, Camera del Granduca, f. 42	169l
il Moro del S. Tempi			1673	I-Fas, Camera del Granduca, f. 42	220r
schiavi		"Per limosina … fatta dare SAS a un Frate Spagnolo, che porta la Crocetta per il ricatto delli Schiavi." 6 scudi.	1673	I-Fas, Camera del Granduca, f. 42	207l

Reference (as given in document)	Baptismal name (if known)	Other descriptors in document	Year	Citation	Owner (if known)
quattro donne forestiere		"Pagato al Sig. Gio Batt. Amoni Priore di San Paolo … E sono per robe servite rivestire le quattro donne forestiere che SAS tiene in detto ospedale."	1674	I-Fas, Camera del Granduca, f. 43	161
Mora		Indiana, mora indiana, stiava. Details are given of Mora's arrival in England as a slave at the age of 6y and of her disposal in the last will and testament of her English owner, Agnes Manifesta, who had recently died.	1703	I-Fca, Pia Casa, 3	Andrea della Costa

Bibliography

Manuscript Archival Sources

Florence, Archivio di Stato (I-Fas)
 Arte di Medici e Speziali, Registro dei morti della città di Firenze, n. 258, n. 259, n. 260
 Camera del Granduca, f. 1–f. 43
 Depositeria generale, parte antica, f. 397, f. 605, f. 1604
 Guardaroba medicea, f. 245, f. 664
 Mediceo del Principato, f. 5178, f. 5279b, f. 5354, f. 5358, f. 5363, f. 5405, f. 5417, f. 5487, f. 6396, f. 6424
 Miscellanea medicea, f. 31 (ins.10)
 Raccolta Sebregondi, f. 819
Florence, Archivio Storico dell'Istituto degli Innocenti di Firenze (I-FAoi)
 Balie e bambini, 537 (Q), 538 (R), 539 (S), 556, 557, 573, 574
 Orbatello, 10452
 Exito di fanciulli, 1654
 Esito delli Allevati delli Innocenti, 1655
 Libro delle balie di casa dall'anno 1667 all'anno 1719, 1835
Florence, Archivio dell'Accademia degli Immobili (I-FImmobili)
 Archivio storico, 1.7–1.10, 1.12–1.20
Florence, Curia arcivescovile, Archivio (I-Fca)
 Pia Casa dei Catecumini, f. 1–f. 3
 S. Felice in Piazza, Morti dal 1627 al 1686, RPU 0025.13
Florence, Opera del Duomo, Archivio (I-Fd)
 Registri Battesimali, http://archivio.operaduomo.fi.it/battesimi/ricerca_carte.asp

Printed Sources

Abbate, Carolyn. *Unsung Voices: Opera and Musical Narrative in the Nineteenth Century*. Princeton, NJ: Princeton University Press, 1991.

Abramov-van Rijk, Elena. *Singing Dante: The Literary Origins of Cinquecento Monody*. Farnham, UK: Ashgate, 2014.

Ad-Dīn II al-Ma'n, Fakhr. *Viaggio in Italia (1613–1618): La Toscana dei Medici e il Mezzogiorno spagnolo nella descrizione di un viaggiatore orientale*. Edited by Maria Alberti. Milan: Jouvence, 2013.

Agostini, Anna. *Istantanee dal seicento: L'album di disegni del cavaliere pistoiese Ignazio Fabroni*. Florence: Polistampa, 2017.

Akhimie, Patricia. "Performance in the Periphery: Colonial Encounters and Entertainments." In *Acoustemologies in Contact: Sounding Subjects and Modes of*

Listening in Early Modernity, edited by Emily Wilbourne and Suzanne G. Cusick, 65–82. Cambridge: Open Book, 2021.

Alberti, Maria. "Battaglie navali, scorrerie corsare e politica dello spettacolo: Le naumachie medicee del 1589." *California Italian Studies* 1, no. 1 (2010): 1–33.

Alberti, Maria. "Un emiro alla corte dei granduchi: Feste e spettacoli a Firenze in onore di Faccardino, Gran signore de' Drusi (1613–1615)." *Medioevo e Rinascimento* 11, no. 8 (1997): 281–300.

Ames, Eric. "The Sound of Evolution." *Modernism/modernity* 10, no. 2 (2003): 297–325.

Andrea, Bernadette. "Elizabeth I and Persian Exchanges." In *The Foreign Relations of Elizabeth I*, edited by Charles Beem, 169–199. New York: Palgrave MacMillan, 2011.

Andreini, Giovan Battista. "La Ferza: Ragionamento secondo contra l'accuse date alla Commedia (Paris, 1625)." In *La commedia dell'arte e la società barocca: La professione del teatro*, edited by Ferruccio Marotti and Giovanna Romei, 489–534. Rome: Bulzoni, 1994.

Andreini, Giovan Battista. *La Sultana*. Paris: Nicolas Della Vigna, 1622.

Andreini, Giovan Battista. *Li due Lelii simili*. Paris: Nicolas Della Vigna, 1622.

Andreini, Giovan Battista. "Lo Schiavetto (1612)." In *Commedie dei comici dell'arte*, edited by Laura Falavolti, 57–213. Turin: UTET, 1982.

Andrews, Walter G., and Mehmet Kalpaklı. *The Age of Beloveds: Love and the Beloved in Early-Modern Ottoman and European Culture and Society*. Durham, NC: Duke University Press, 2005.

Angiolini, Franco. "Slaves and Slavery in Early Modern Tuscany." *Italian History and Culture* 3 (1997): 67–86.

Arfaioli, Maurizio, and Marta Caroscio, eds. *The Grand Ducal Medici and the Levant: Material Culture, Diplomacy, and Imagery in the Early Modern Mediterranean*. Medici Archive Project Series. Turnhout: Harvey Miller, 2015.

Atkinson, Niall. *The Noisy Renaissance: Sound, Architecture, and Florentine Urban Life*. University Park: Pennsylvania State University Press, 2016.

Aureli, Aurelio. *La Rosilena, drama per musica*. Venice: Francesco Nicolini in Spadaria, 1664.

Aureli, Aurelio. *Perseo, dramma per musica*. Venice: Francesco Nicolini, 1665.

Avci, Mustafa. "Köçek: A Genealogy of Cross-Dressed Male Belly Dancers (Dancing Boys) from Ottoman Empire to Contemporary Turkey." PhD diss., New York University, 2015.

Baker, Geoffrey. *Imposing Harmony: Music and Society in Colonial Cuzco*. Durham, NC: Duke University Press, 2008.

Baldinucci, Filippo. *Notizie de' professori del disegno da Cimabue in qua*. Florence, 1682.

Bamford, Paul Walden. "The Procurement of Oarsmen for French Galleys, 1660–1748." *American Historical Review* 65, no. 1 (1959): 31–48.

Barbieri, Patrizio. "Gli stumenti poliarmonici di G. B. Doni e il ripristino dell'antica musica greca (c. 1630–1650)." *Analecta Musicologica* 30 (1998): 79–114.

Bárcenas, Ireri Chávez. "Singing in the City of Angels: Race, Identity, and Devotion in Early Modern Puebla de los Ángeles." PhD diss., Princeton University, 2018.

Baricci, Erica. "La scena 'all'Ebraica' nel teatro del rinascimento." *Annali della Facoltà di Lettere e Filosofia dell'Università degli Studi di Milano* 63, no. 1 (2010): 135–163.

Barker, Shelia. *Artemisia Gentileschi*. Los Angeles: Getty Publications, 2022.

Barthes, Roland. "The Grain of the Voice." In *Image, Music, Text*, 179–189. London: Flamingo, 1977.

Bennett, Herman L. *African Kings and Black Slaves: Sovereignty and Dispossession in the Early Modern Atlantic*. The Early Modern Americas. Philadelphia: University of Pennsylvania Press, 2019.

Berns, Jörg Jochen. "Instrumental Sound and Ruling Spaces of Resonance in the Early Modern Period: On the Acoustic Setting of the Princely *Potestas* Claims within a Ceremonial Frame." Translated by Benjamin Carter. In *Instruments in Art and Science: On the Architectonics of Cultural Boundaries in the 17th Century*, edited by Helmar Schramm, Ludger Schwarte, and Jan Lazardzig, 479–503. Berlin: De Gruyter, 2008.

Bertoluzzi, Mario. "Bendinelli's *Entire Art of the Trumpet* of 1614: A Modern Edition." DMA diss., University of Northern Colorado, 2002.

Bindman, David, and Henry Louis Gates, eds. *The Image of the Black in Western Art*. 10 vols. Cambridge, MA: Harvard University Press, 2010–2014.

Bing, Rudolf. *5,000 Nights at the Opera*. London: Hamilton, 1972.

Bisceglia, Anna, Matteo Ceriana, and Simona Mammana, eds. *Buffoni, villani e giocatori alla corte dei Medici*. Livorno: Sillabe, 2016.

Bissell, R. Ward. *Artemisia Gentileschi and the Authority of Art: Critical Reading and Catalogue Raisonné*. University Park: Pennsylvania State University Press, 1999.

Bloechl, Olivia. *Native American Song at the Frontiers of Early Modern Music*. Cambridge: Cambridge University Press, 2008.

Bloechl, Olivia. "Race, Empire, and Early Music." In *Rethinking Difference in Music Scholarship*, edited by Olivia Bloechl, Melanie Lowe, and Jeffrey Kallberg, 77–107. Cambridge: Cambridge University Press, 2015.

Blumenthal, Arthur R. "Giulio Parigi's Stage Designs: Florence and the Early Baroque Spectacle." PhD diss., New York University, 1984.

Bonfil, Robert. *Jewish Life in Renaissance Italy*. Translated by Anthony Oldcorn. Berkeley: University of California Press, 1994.

Bono, Salvatore. "Schiavi in Europa nell'età moderna: Varietà di forme e di aspetti." In *Schiavitù e servaggio nell'economia europea secc. XI–XVIII/Serfdom and Slavery in the European Economy 11th–18th Centuries*, edited by Simonetta Cavaciocchi, 309–335. Florence: Firenze University Press, 2014.

Bono, Salvatore. "Slave Histories and Memoirs in the Mediterranean World." In *Trade and Cultural Exchange in the Early Modern Mediterranean: Braudel's Maritime Legacy*, edited by Maria Fusaro, Colin Heywood, and Mohamed-Salah Omri, 97–116. London: I.B. Taurus, 2010.

Boorman, Stanley. "The Musical Text." In *Rethinking Music*, edited by Nicholas Cook and Mark Everist, 403–423. Oxford: Oxford University Press, 1999.

Bouchard, Jean-Jacques. "Voyage de Paris à Rome." In *Oeuvres complètes*, edited by E. Kanceff, I:39–135. Turin: Giappichelli, 1976.

Brady, Erika. *A Spiral Way: How the Phonograph Changed Ethnography*. Jackson: University Press of Mississippi, 1999.

Braudel, Fernand. *La Méditerranée et le monde méditerranéen à l'époque de Philippe II*. Paris: Librairie Armand Colin, 1949.

Bray, William, ed. *The Diary of John Evelyn, Edited from the Original MSS by William Bray*. Washington, DC: M. Walter Dunne, 1901.

Brege, Brian. "Renaissance Florentines in the Tropics: Brazil, the Grand Duchy of Tuscany, and the Limits of Empire." In *The New World in Early Modern Italy, 1492–1750*, edited

by Elizabeth Horodowich and Lia Markey, 206–222. Cambridge: Cambridge University Press, 2017.
Brosius, Amy. "'Il Suon, lo Sguardo, il Canto': The Function of Portraits of Mid-Seventeenth-Century *Virtuose* In Rome." *Italian Studies* 63, no. 1 (2013): 17–39.
Brown, Alan, and Donna G. Cardamone. "Moresca." In Grove Music Online/Oxford Music Online. Oxford University Press. http://www.oxfordmusiconline.com.ezp-prod1.hul.harvard.edu/subscriber/article/grove/music/19125.
Budasz, Rogério. "Black Guitar-Players and Early African-Iberian Music in Portugal and Brazil." *Early Music* 35, no. 1 (2007): 3–21.
Budasz, Rogério. *Opera in the Tropics: Music and Theater in Early Modern Brazil.* Oxford: Oxford University Press, 2019.
Buonarroti, Michelangelo. *Il balletto della cortesia fatto in Firenze dalle SS.AA. di Toscana il di 11 di febbraio 1613 [more fiorentino] che fu introdotto da un'altro trattenimento rappresentato in'iscena.* Florence: Mariscotti, 1614.
Burattelli, Claudia. *Spettacoli di corte a Mantova tra cinque e seicento.* Florence: Le Lettere, 1999.
Burattelli, Claudia, Domenica Landolfi, and Anna Zinanni, eds. *Comici dell'arte: Corrispondenze, G. B. Andreini, N. Barbieri, P. M. Cecchini, S. Fiorillo, T. Martinelli, F. Scala.* Vol. 2. Florence: Le Lettere, 1993.
Busenello, Giovanni Francesco. *La Statira principessa di Persia: Drama per musica.* Venice: Appresso Andrea Giuliani, 1655.
Butler, Judith. "Bodily Confessions." In *Undoing Gender*, 161–173. New York: Routledge, 2004.
Butler, Judith. *Gender Trouble: Feminism and the Subversion of Identity.* New York: Routledge, 1990.
Caccini, Francesca. *Il primo libro delle musiche.* Florence: Zanobi Pignoni, 1618.
Caccini, Giulio. *Le nuove musiche.* Florence: Marescotti, 1602.
Calcagno, Mauro P. "Dramatizing Discourse in Seventeenth-Century Opera: Music as Illocutionary Force in Francesco Cavalli's Giasone (1649)." In *Word, Image, and Song*, Vol. 1: *Essays on Early Modern Italy*, edited by Rebecca Cypess, Beth Glixon, and Nathan Link, 318–343. Eastman Studies in Music. Rochester, NY: University of Rochester Press, 2013.
Calcagno, Mauro P. "'Imitar col canto chi parla': Monteverdi and the Creation of a Language for Musical Theater." *Journal of the American Musicological Society* 55, no. 3 (2002): 383–431.
Calmeta, Vincenzo. *Prose e lettere edite e inedite (con due appendici di altri inediti).* Edited by Cecil Grayson. Bologna: Commissione per i Testi di Lingua, 1959.
Camiz, Franca Trinchieri. "'La bella cantatrice': I ritratti di Leonora Barone e Barbara Strozzi a confronto." In *Musica, scienza e idee nella Serenissima durante il seicento: Atti del convengno internazionale di studi, Venezia, Palazzo Giustinian Lolin, 12–15 dicembre 1993*, edited by Francesco Passadore and Franco Rossi, 285–294. Venice: Fondazione Ugo e Olga Levi, 1996.
Campt, Tina M. *Listening to Images.* Durham, NC: Duke University Press, 2017.
Carali, P. Paolo. *Fakhr ad-Dīn II, Principe del Libano, e la corte di Toscana, 1605–1635.* Vol. 1, Rome: Reale Accademia d'Italia, 1936.
Carali, P. Paolo. "Soggiorno di Fakhr ad-dīn II al-Ma'nī in Toscana, Sicilia e Napoli e la sua visita a Malta (1613–1618)." *Annali del Istituto superiore orientale di Napoli* 7, fasc. IV (1936): 14–60.

Cardamone, Donna G. *The Canzone Villanesca alla Napolitana: Social, Cultural, and Historical Contexts.* Variorium/Collected Studies. Aldershot, UK: Ashgate, 2008.
Cardini, Franco. *Il turco a Vienna: Storia del grande assedio del 1683.* Rome: Laterza, 2011.
Carletti, Francesco. *Ragionamenti di Francesco Carletti Fiorentino sopra le cose da lui vedute ne' suoi viaggi, si delle'Indie Occidentali, e Orientali come d'altri paesi.* Florence: Giuseppe Manai, 1701.
Carlson, Julie A. "New Lows in Eighteenth-Century Theater: The Rise of Mungo." *European Romantic Review* 18, no. 2 (2007): 139–147.
Carter, Tim, ed. and trans. *Composing Opera: From "Dafne" to "Ulisse errante."* Kraków: Musica Iagellonica, 1994.
Carter, Tim. "Music and Patronage in Late Sixteenth-Century Florence: The Case of Jacopo Corsi (1561–1602)." *I Tatti Studies in the Italian Renaissance* 1 (1985): 57–104.
Carter, Tim. "Non Occorre Nominare Tanti Musici: Private Patronage and Public Ceremony in Late Sixteenth-Century Florence." *I Tatti Studies in the Italian Renaissance* 4 (1991): 89–104.
Casule, Francesca. "Un episodio esotico della scena fiorentina: La visita dell'emiro druso Fakhr ad-Din alla corte di Cosimo I de' Medici." *Levante* 28 (1986): 25–38.
Cavalli, Francesco. *Scipione affricano.* Edited by Jennifer Williams Brown. Forthcoming.
Cavallini, Ivano. "La musica turca nelle testimonianze dei viaggiatori e nelle trattatistica del sei-settecento." *Rivista Italiana Musicologia* 21 (1986): 144–169.
Cervantes Saavedra, Miguel de. "The Jealous Husband." Translated by Thomas Shelton. In *Instructive Novels: Viz. The Story of Two Damsels, The Lady Cornelia Bentivoglio, The Generous Lover, The Force of Blood, The Spanish Lady, The Jealous Husband,* 285–342. Glasgow: Robert Urie, 1750.
Chakravarty, Urvashi. "What Is the History of Actors of Color Performing in Shakespeare in the UK?" In *The Cambridge Companion to Shakespeare and Race,* edited by Ayanna Thompson, 190–207. Cambridge: Cambridge University Press, 2021.
Chiarini, Marco. "Anton Domenico Gabbiani e i Medici." In *Kunst des Barock in der Toskana: Studien zur Kunst unter den letzten Medici,* edited by Florence Kunsthistorisches Institut, 333–343. Munich: Bruckman, 1976.
Chiarini, Marco. "Quadro raffigurante famigli della Corte di Cosimo III de' Medici." In *Curiosità di una reggia: Vicende della guardaroba di Palazzo Pitti,* edited by Kirsten Aschengreen Piacenti and Sandra Pinto, 59. Florence: Centro Di, 1979.
Chrissochoidis, Ilias. "Senesino's Black Boy (1725)." *Handel Institue Newsletter* 21, no. 1 (2010): 7–8.
Christiansen, Keith. "Artemisia Gentileschi: Esther before Ahasuerus." Metropolitan Museum of Art. https://www.metmuseum.org/art/collection/search/436453 (accessed 2020).
Cicognini, Jacopo. *La finta mora.* Florence: I Giunti, 1626.
Cohen, Thomas V. "Furto di nano." 2018.
Cole, Janie. *Music, Spectacle and Cultural Brokerage in Early Modern Italy: Michelangelo Buonarroti il Giovane.* Florence: Olschki, 2011.
Concina, Ennio, ed. *Venezia e Istanbul: Incontri, confronti e scambi.* Udine: Forum, 2006.
Conforzi, Igino. "Girolamo Fantini 'monarca della tromba': Nuove acquisizioni biografiche." *Recercare* 2 (1990): 225–239.
Conforzi, Igino. "Girolamo Fantini, 'Monarch of the Trumpet': New Light on His Works." Translated by Alexandra Amati-Camperi. *Historic Brass Society Journal* 6 (1994): 32–60.

Cooley, Marianne. "An Early Representation of African-American English." In *Language Variety in the South Revisited*, edited by Robin Sabino and Cynthia Bernstein, 51–58. Tuscaloosa: University of Alabama Press, 1997.

Cortelazzo, Manlio. "Il linguaggio schiavonesco nel cinquecento veneziano." *Atti dell'Instituto Veneto di Scienze, Lettere ed Arti* 130 (1972): 113–160.

Cortelazzo, Manlio. "La figura e la lingua del 'todesco' nella letteratura veneziana rinascimentale." In *Scritti in onore di Giuliano Bonfante*, 173–182. Brescia: Paideia, 1976.

Costa, Margherita. *The Buffoons, A Ridiculous Comedy: A Bilingual Edition*. Translated by Sara Díaz and Jessica Goethals. Edited by Sara Díaz and Jessica Goethals. Toronto: Iter Press, 2018.

Crawford, Katherine. *Eunuchs and Castrati: Disability and Normativity in Early Modern Europe*. New York: Routledge, 2019.

Crimi, Giuseppe, and Cristiano Spila, eds. *Nanerie del Rinascimento: "La Nanea" di Michelangelo Serafini e altri versi di corte e d'accademia*. Rome: Vecchiarelli, 2006.

Currie, Elizabeth. "Clothing and Cross-Cultural Perspectives at the Medici Court, 1550–1650." Conference presentation at The Medici and the Perception of Sub-Saharan Africa, Medici Archive Project, Florence, June 2–3, 2022.

Cusick, Suzanne G. *Francesca Caccini at the Medici Court: Music and the Circulation of Power*. Chicago: University of Chicago Press, 2009.

Cusick, Suzanne G. "Gendering Modern Music: Thoughts on the Monteverdi-Artusi Controversy." *Journal of the American Musicological Society* 46 (1993): 1–25.

Cusick, Suzanne G. "'La Stiava Dolente in Suono di Canto': War, Slavery, and Difference in a Medici Court Entertainment." In *Acoustemologies in Contact: Sounding Subjects and Modes of Listening in Early Modernity*, edited by Emily Wilbourne and Suzanne G. Cusick, 201–237. Cambridge: Open Book, 2021.

Cusick, Suzanne G. "'Thinking from Women's Lives': Francesca Caccini after 1627." *Musical Quarterly* 77, no. 3 (1993): 484–507.

Daston, Lorraine, and Katharine Park, eds. *Wonders and the Order of Nature, 1150–1750*. New York: Zone Books, 1998.

Davies, Surekha. *Renaissance Ethnography and the Invention of the Human: New World, Maps and Monsters*. Cambridge: Cambridge University Press, 2016.

Davies, William. *True Relation of the Travails and Most Miserable Captivitie of William Davies, Barber-Surgion of London, under the Duke of Florence*. London: Nicholas Bourne, 1614.

Davis, Robert C. *Christian Slaves, Muslim Masters: White Slavery in the Mediterranean, the Barbary Coast, and Italy, 1500–1800*. New York: Palgrave Macmillan, 2003.

De Angelis, Marcello, Elvira Garbero Zorzi, Loredana Maccabruni, Piero Marchi, and Luigi Zangheri, eds. *Lo "spettacolo maraviglioso": Il Teatro della Pergola: l'Opera a Firenze*. Florence: Pagliai Polistampa, 2000.

Decroisette, Françoise. "I virtuosi del Cardinale, da Firenze all'Europa." In *Lo "spettacolo maraviglioso": Il Teatro della Pergola: l'Opera a Firenze*, edited by Marcello de Angelis, Elvira Garbero Zorzi, Loredana Maccabruni, Piero Marchi, and Luigi Zangheri, 83–89. Ufficio Centrale per i Beni Archivistici. Florence: Pagliai Polistampa, 2000.

Decroisette, Françoise. "Un exemple d'administration des theatres au XVIIème siecle: Le theatre de la Pergola a Florence (1652–1662)." In *Arts du spectacle et histoire des idées: Recueil offert en hommage à Jean Jacquot*, 73–90. Tours: Publications de la Société des Amis du Centre d'Études Supériures de la Renaissance, 1984.

Dei, Adele. "Gli eden corrotti di Francesco Carletti." In *Percorsi di arte e letteratura tra la Toscana e le Americhe: Atti della giornata di studi Biblioteca Nazionale Centrale di Firenze, 3 Ottobre 2014*, edited by Nicoletta Lepri, loc. 1372–1615. Raleigh, NC: Aonia, 2016.

Dei, Adele, ed. *Ragionamenti del mio viaggio intorno al mondo di Francesco Carletti*. Milan: Mursia, 1987.

Dell'Antonio, Andrew. *Listening as Spiritual Practice in Early Modern Italy*. Berkeley: University of California Press, 2011.

Della Valle, Pietro. *Viaggi di Pietro della Valle, detto il Pellegrino, descritti da lui medesimo in lettere familiari all'erudito suo amico Mario Schipano, divisi in tre parti, cioè la Turchia, la Persia e l'India*. [Gioseffo Longhi, 1672.] Rome: Vitale Mascardi, 1845.

De Lucca, Valeria. "Dressed to Impress: The Costumes for Antonio Cesti's *Orontea* in Rome (1661)." *Early Music* 41, no. 3 (2013): 461–473.

De Lucca, Valeria. "Patronage." In *The Oxford Handbook of Opera*, edited by Helen Greenwald, 648–665. Oxford: Oxford University Press, 2014.

Dentenbeck, Laurie. "Dramatised Madrigals and the *Commedia dell'Arte* Tradition." In *The Science of Buffoonery: Theory and History of the Commedia dell'Arte*, edited by Domenico Pietropaolo, 59–68. Toronto: University of Toronto, 1989.

Descrizione del corso degli'indiani senza testa al palio. Florence: Zanobi Pignoni, 1616.

DiAngelo, Robin. "White Fragility." *International Journal of Critical Pedagogy* 3, no. 3 (2011): 54–70.

Dibdin, Charles. *The Padlock: A Comic Opera as It Is Performed at the Theatre-Royal in Drury-Lane*. London: J. Johnston, 1769.

Donà, Giovanni Battista. *Della letteratura de' Turchi: Osservationi fatte da Gio. Battista Donado senator veneto, fu bailo in Constantinopoli*. Venice: Andrea Poletti, 1688.

D'Onghia, Luca. "Aspetti della lingua comica di Giovan Battista Andreini." *La Lingua Italiana: Storia, Strutture, Testi* 7 (2011): 57–80.

Douglass, Frederick. *Narrative of the Life of Frederick Douglass, an American Slave*. New York: Penguin Books, 1986.

Douglas, Robert. "The First Trumpet Method: Girolamo Fantini's *Modo per Imparare a Sonare la Tromba* (1638)." *Journal of Band Research* 7, no. 2 (1971): 18–22.

Downey, Peter. "Fantini and Mersenne: Some Additions to Recent Controversies." *Historica Brass Society Journal* 6 (1994): 355–362.

Dudley, Robert. *Arcano del mare*. 2nd ed. Florence: Giuseppe Cocchini, 1661.

Edwards, Paul N., Lisa Gitelman, Gabrielle Hecht, Adrian Johns, Brian Larkin, and Neil Safier. "AHR Conversation: Historical Perspectives on the Circulation of Information." *American Historical Review* 116, no. 5 (2011): 1393–1435.

Eidsheim, Nina Sun. *The Race of Sound: Listening, Timbre, and Vocality in African American Music*. Durham, NC: Duke University Press, 2019.

Einstein, Alfred. "The Greghesca and the Giustiniana of the Sixteenth Century." *Journal of Renaissance and Baroque Music* 1 (1946): 19–32.

El Bibas, Kaled. *L'emiro e il granduca: La vicenda dell'emiro Fakhr ad-Dīn II del Libano nel contesto delle relazioni fra la Toscana e l'Oriente*. Florence: Le Lettere, 2010.

Epstein, Stephen A. *Speaking of Slavery: Color, Ethnicity, and Human Bondage in Italy*. Ithaca, NY: Cornell University Press, 2001.

Ewald, Gerhard. "Appunti sulla Galleria Gerini e sugli affreschi di Anton Domenico Gabbiani." In *Kunst des Barock in der Toskana: Studien zur Kunst unter den letzten Medici*, edited by Florence Kunsthistorisches Institut, 344–358. Munich: Bruckmann, 1976.

Eyerly, Sarah. *Moravian Soundscapes: A Sonic History of the Moravian Missions in Early Pennsylvania*. Bloomington: Indiana University Press, 2020.

Fabbri, Maria Cecilia, Alessandro Grassi, and Riccardo Spinelli, eds. *Volterrano: Baldassarre Franceschini (1611-1690)*. Florence: Ente Cassa di Risparmio di Firenze, 2013.

Fabbri, Paolo. *Il secolo cantante: Per una storia del libretto d'opera in Italia nel seicento*. Bologna: Il Mulino, 1990.

Fahrner, Robert. "David Garrick Presents *The Padlock*: An 18th-Century 'Hit.'" *Theatre Survey* 13 (1972): 52–70.

Falavolti, Laura. "Introduzione allo Schiavetto di Giovan Battista Andreini." In *Commedie dei comici dell'arte*, edited by Laura Falavolti, 7–36. Turin: UTET, 1982.

Fantappiè, Francesca. "Girolamo Caraffa *detto* Gonnella." amati.fupress.net.

Fantappiè, Francesca. "Sale per lo Spettacolo a Pitti (1600-1650)." In *Vivere a Pitti: Una reggia dai Medici ai Savoia*, edited by Sergio Bertelli and Renato Pasta, 135–180. Florence: Olschki, 2003.

Fantappiè, Francesca. "Una primizia rinucciniana: La *Dafne* prima della 'miglior forma.'" *Il Saggiatore Musicale* 24, no. 2 (2018): 189–228.

Fantini, Girolamo. *Modo per imparare a sonare di tromba (1638)*. Edited by Ignio Conforzi Bologna: Ut Orpehus Edizioni, 1998.

Farahat, Martha. "On the Staging of Madrigal Comedies." *Early Music History* 10 (1991): 123–143.

Farahat, Martha. "Villanescas of the Virtuosi: Lasso and the Commedia dell'Arte." *Performance Practice Review* 3 (1990): 121–137.

Faustini, Giovanni. *L'Alciade*. Venice: Francesco Nicolini & Steffano Curti, 1667.

Favila, Cesar. "The Sound of Profession Ceremonies in Novohispanic Convents." *Journal of the Society for American Music* 13, no. 2 (2019): 143–170.

Feld, Steven. "Acoustemology." In *Keywords in Sound*, edited by David Novak and Matt Sakakeeny, 12–21. Durham, NC: Duke University Press, 2015.

Feld, Steven. "Voices of the Rainforest: Politics of Music." *Arena* 99–100 (1992): 164–177.

Feldman, Martha. "Castrato Acts." In *The Oxford Handbook of Opera*, edited by Helen Greenwald, 395–418. Oxford: Oxford University Press, 2014.

Feldman, Martha. *The Castrato: Reflections on Natures and Kinds*. Berkeley: University of California Press, 2015.

Ferrari-Barassi, Elena. "La tradizione della moresca e uno sconosciuto ballo del cinque-seicento." *Rivista Italiana di Musicologia* 5 (1970): 37–60.

Ferraro, Eleonora. "Ventura e sventura dei nani nelle corti del Seicento." *Rivista Internazionale di Filosofia Online* 12, no. 23 (2017): 201–214.

Ferrone, Siro. "Pose sceniche di una famiglia d'attori." In *Domenico Fetti (1588/89-1623)*, edited by Eduard A. Safarik, 51–58. Milan: Electra, 1996.

Finley, Sarah. *Hearing Voices: Aurality and New Spanish Sound Culture in Sor Juana Inés de la Cruz*. Lincoln: University of Nebraska Press, 2019.

Florio, John. *Queen Anna's New World of Words, or Dictionarie of the Italian and English Tongues*. London: Melch and Bradwood, 1611.

Follino, Federico. "Compendio delle sontuose feste fatte l'anno MDCVIII: Nella città di Mantova, per le reali nozze del serenissimo prencipe D. Francesco Gonzaga, con la serenissima infanta Margherita di Savoia; Facsimile." In *Cronache Mantovane (1597-1608)*, edited by Claudio Gallico, 103–257. Florence: Olschki, 2004.

Franko, Mark. *Dance as Text: Ideologies of the Baroque Body*. Cambridge: Cambridge University Press, 1993.
Frattarelli Fischer, Lucia. "Il bagno delle galere in 'Terra cristiana.'" *Nuovi Studi Livornesi* 8 (2000): 69–94.
Freitas, Roger. "The Eroticism of Emasculation: Confronting the Baroque Body of the Castrato." *Journal of Musicology* 20, no. 2 (2003): 196–249.
Freitas, Roger. *Portrait of a Castrato: Politics, Patronage, and Music in the Life of Atto Melani*. Cambridge: Cambridge University Press, 2009.
Garrard, Mary D. *Artemisia Gentileschi: The Image of the Female Hero in Italian Baroque Art*. Princeton, NJ: Princeton University Press, 1989.
Gates, Henry Louis. *Figures in Black: Words, Signs, and the "Racial" Self*. Oxford: Oxford University Press, 1987.
Gerbino, Giuseppe. *Music and the Myth of Arcadia in Renaissance Italy*. Cambridge: Cambridge University Press, 2009.
Gerbino, Giuseppe. "The Quest for the Soprano Voice: Castrati in Sixteenth-Century Italy." *Studi Musicali* 32, no. 2 (2004): 303–357.
Gerzina, Gretchen. *Black London: Life before Emancipation*. London: John Murray, 1995.
Ghadessi, Touba. *Portraits of Human Monsters in the Renaissance: Dwarves, Hirsutes, and Castrati as Idealized Anatomical Anomalies*. Monsters, Prodigies, and Demons: Medieval and Early Modern Constructions of Alterity. Kalamazoo, MI: Medieval Institute Publications, Western Michigan University, 2018.
Giovanetti, Antonio Domenico. *Descrizione allegorica della città di Firenze divisa in più canzoni*. Florence: Francesco Moücke, 1733.
Giusti, Annamaria, and Cristina Acidini Luchinat, eds. *Masters of Florence: Glory and Genius at the Court of the Medici*, exhibition catalogue. Memphis: Wonders, 2004.
Glass, Wayne Allen, Jr. "The Renaissance Italian Madrigal Comedy: A Handbook for Performance." PhD diss., University of Arizona, 2006.
Glissant, Édouard. *Poetics of Relation*. Translated by Betsy Wing. Ann Arbor: University of Michigan Press, 1997.
Glixon, Beth. "More on the Life and Death of Barbara Strozzi." *Musical Quarterly* 83, no. 1 (1999): 134–141.
Glixon, Beth. "New Light on the Life and Career of Barbara Strozzi." *Musical Quarterly* 81, no. 2 (1997): 311–335.
Glixon, Beth, and Jonathan Glixon. *Inventing the Business of Opera: The Impresario and His World in Seventeenth-Century Venice*. Oxford: Oxford University Press, 2008.
Goodman, Glenda. "Sounds Heard, Meanings Deferred: Music Transcription as Imperial Technology." *Eighteenth-Century Studies* 52, no. 1 (2018): 39–45.
Gordon, Bonnie. "The Castrato Meets the Cyborg." *Opera Quarterly* 27 (2011): 94–122.
Gordon, Bonnie. "Talking Back: The Female Voice in 'Il Ballo delle Ingrate.'" *Cambridge Opera Journal* 11, no. 1 (1999): 1–30.
Gorton, Ted J. *Renaissance Emir: A Druze Warlord at the Court of the Medici*. London: QuartetBooks, 2013.
Gough, Melinda J. "Marie de Medici's 1605 *Ballet de la Reine*: New Evidence and Analysis." *Early Theatre* 15, no. 1 (2012): 109–144.
Gough, Melinda J. "Marie de Medici's 1605 *Ballet de la Reine* and the Virtuosic Female Voice." *Early Modern Women: An Interdisciplinary Journal* 7 (2012): 127–156.

Green MacDonald, Joyce. "Acting Black: *Othello*, *Othello* Burlesques, and the Performance of Blackness." In *Ira Aldridge: The African Roscius*, edited by Bernth Lindfors, 135–156. Rochester, NY: University of Rochester Press, 2010.
Greene, Molly. "Beyond the Northern Invasion: The Mediterranean in the Seventeenth Century." *Past & Present* 174, no. 1 (2002): 42–71.
Greene, Molly. *Catholic Pirates and Greek Merchants: A Maritime History of the Early Modern Mediterranean*. Princeton, NJ: Princeton University Press, 2010.
Guerra d'amore, festa del Serenissimo Gran Duca di Toscana Cosimo secondo, fatta in Firenze il Carnevale del 1615. Florence: Stamperia di Zanobi Pignoi, 1616.
Guidi, Fabrizio. "Pitture fiorentine del seicento ritrovate." *Paragone* 25, no. 297 (1974): 58–62.
HaCohen, Ruth. *The Music Libel against the Jews*. New Haven, CT: Yale University Press, 2011.
Hair, Paul Edward Hedley, and Jonathan D. Davies. "Sierra Leone and the Grand Duchy of Tuscany." *History in Africa* 20 (1993): 61–69.
Harrán, Don. "'Barucaba' as an Emblem for Jewishness in Early Italian Art Music." *Jewish Quarterly Review* 98, no. 3 (2008): 328–354.
Harris, Ellen T. *Handel as Orpheus: Voice and Desire in the Chamber Cantatas*. Cambridge, MA: Harvard University Press, 2004.
Hartman, Saidiya V. *Scenes of Subjection: Terror, Slavery, and Self-Making in Nineteenth-Century America*. Oxford: Oxford University Press, 1997.
Hartman, Saidiya V. "Venus in Two Acts." *Small Axe* 12, no. 2 (2008): 1–14.
Head, Matthew. "Musicology on Safari: Orientalism and the Spectre of Postcolonial Theory." *Music Analysis* 22, nos. 1–2 (2003): 211–230.
Hegyi, Ottmar. *Cervantes and the Turks: Historical Reality versus Literary Fiction in La Gran Sultana and El Amante Liberal*. Newark, DE: Juan de la Cuesta, 1992.
Heller, Wendy. *Music in the Baroque: Western Music in Context*. New York: W. W. Norton, 2014.
Hershenzon, Daniel. *The Captive Sea: Slavery, Communication, and Commerce in Early Modern Spain and the Mediterranean*. Philadelphia: University of Pennsylvania Press, 2018.
Hershenzon, Daniel. "Towards a Connected History of Bondage in the Mediterranean: Recent Trends in the Field." *History Compass* 15 (2016): 1–13.
Herzig, Tamar. "Slavery and Interethnic Sexual Violence: A Multiple Perpetrator Rape in Seventeenth-Century Livorno," *American Historical Review* 127, no. 1 (2022): 194–222.
Hill, John Walter. "Le relazioni di Antonio Cesti con la corte e i teatri di Firenze." *Rivista Italiana di Musicologia* 11 (1976): 27–47.
Hill, John Walter. *Roman Monody, Cantata and Opera from the Circles around Cardinal Montalto*. 2 vols. Oxford: Clarendon Press, 1997.
Holmes, William C. "Comedy—Opera—Comic Opera." *Analecta Musicologica* 5 (1968): 92–103.
Hornback, Robert. *Racism and Early Blackface Comic Traditions: From the Old World to the New*. Palgrave Studies in Theatre and Performance History. Cham, Switzerland: Palgrave Macmillan, 2018.
Horodowich, Elizabeth, and Alexander Nagel. "Amerasia: European Reflections of an Emergent World, 1492–ca.1700." *Journal of Early Modern History* 23 (2019): 257–295.
Howard, Deborah, and Laura Moretti. *Sound and Space in Renaissance Venice*. New Haven, CT: Yale University Press, 2009.

Hugford, Ignatius. *Vita di Anton Domenico Gabbiani*. Florence: n.p., 1762.
Hunter, Mary. "The *Alla Turca* Style in the Late Eighteenth Century: Race and Gender in the Symphony and the Seraglio." In *The Exotic in Western Music*, edited by Jonathan Bellman, 43–73. Boston: Northeastern University Press, 1998.
Il corago, o vero alcune osservazioni per metter bene in scena le composizioni drammatiche. Edited by Paolo Fabbri and Angelo Pompilio. Studi e Testi per la Storia della Musica 4. Florence: Olschki, 1983.
Ioly Zorattini, Pietro. *I nomi degli altri: Conversioni a Venezia e nel Friuli Veneto in età moderna*. Florence: Olschki, 2008.
Jaffe-Berg, Erith. *Commedia dell'Arte and the Mediterranean: Charting Journeys and Mapping "Others."* Transculturalisms, 1400–1700. London: Routledge, 2016.
Jones, Nicholas. *Staging Habla de Negros: Radical Performances of the African Diaspora in Early Modern Spain*. University Park: Pennsylvania State University Press, 2019.
Kanakamedala, Prathiba. "Staging Atlantic Slavery." In *The Oxford Handbook of the Georgian Theatre, 1737–1832*, edited by Julia Swindells and David Francis Taylor, 673–686. Oxford: Oxford University Press, 2014.
Kaplan, Paul H. D. "Giovannino Moro: A Black African Servant, Musician, Actor and Poet at the Medici Court." Conference presentatin at Staging Africans: Race and Representation in Early Modern European Theaters, Columbia University, New York, 2015.
Kaplan, Paul H. D. "Titian's 'Laura Dianti' and the Origins of the Motif of the Black Page in Portraiture (1 and 2)." *Antichità Viva* 21, no. 1 (1982): 11–18, no. 4 (1982): 10–18.
Kirkendale, Warren. *The Court Musicians in Florence during the Principate of the Medici: With a Reconstruction of the Artistic Establishment*. Florence: Olschki, 1993.
Kirkendale, Warren. "Franceschina, Girometta, and Their Compaions in a Madrigal 'a Diversi Linguaggi' by Luca Marenzio and Orazio Vecchi." *Acta Musicologica* 44 (1972): 181–235.
Kirkendale, Warren. "The Myth of the 'Birth of Opera' in the Florentine Camerata Debunked by Emilio de' Cavalieri: A Commemorative Lecture." *Opera Quarterly* 19 (2003): 631–643.
Law, Hedy. "A Cannon-Shaped Man with an Amphibian Voice: Castrato and Disability in Eighteenth-Century France." In *The Oxford Handbook of Music and Disability Studies*, edited by Blake Howe, Stephanie Jensen-Moulton, Neil Lerner, and Joseph N. Straus. Oxford Handbooks Online, 2018. https://doi.org/10.1093/oxfordhb/9780199331444.013.11.
Lawrence, W. J. "An Old English Music Handkerchief." *Musical Quarterly* 3, no. 4 (1917): 503–508.
Lawson, Melinda. "Imagining Slavery: Representations of the Peculiar Institution on the Northern Stage, 1776–1860." *Journal of the Civil War Era* 1, no. 1 (2011): 25–55.
Levenstein, Anna. "Songs for the First Hebrew Play *Tsahut Bedihuta Dekidushin* by Leone de' Sommi (1527–1592)." DMA diss., Case Western University, 2006.
Lewis, Susan Gail. "*Chi Soffre Speri* and the Influence of the Commedia dell'Arte on the Development of Roman Opera." MMus thesis, University of Arizona, 1995.
Little, Arthur L., Jr. "Re-Historicizing Race, White Melancholia, and the Shakespearean Property." *Shakespeare Quarterly* 67, no. 1 (2016): 84–103.
Locke, Ralph P. *Music and the Exotic from the Renaissance to Mozart*. Cambridge: Cambridge University Press, 2015.
Locker, Jesse M. *Artemisia Gentileschi: The Language of Painting*. New Haven, CT: Yale University Press, 2015.

Locker, Jesse M. "Artemisia Gentileschi: The Literary Formation of an Unlearned Artist." In *Artemisia Gentileschi: Interpreting New Evidence, Assessing New Attributions*, edited by Shelia Barker, 89–101. Turnhout: Brepols, 2017.

Locker, Jesse M. "Gli anni dimenticati: Artemisia Gentileschi a Venezia, 1626–1629." In *Artemisia Gentileschi e il suo tempo, exh. cat. Palazzo Braschi, Rome*, edited by Nicola Spinosa and Francesca Baldassari, 43–46. Milan: Skira, 2016.

Lowe, Kate. "Black Africans' Religious and Cultural Assimilation to, or Appropriation of, Catholicism in Italy, 1470–1520." *Renaissance and Reformation/Renaissance et Réforme* 31, no. 2, special issue on Sub-Saharan Africa and Renaissance and Reformation Europe: New Findings and New Perspectives (2008): 67–86.

Lowe, Kate. "The Black Diaspora in Europe in the Fifteenth and Sixteenth Centuries, with a Special Reference to German-Speaking Areas." In *Germany and the Black Diaspora: Points of Contact, 1250–1914*, edited by Mischa Honeck, Martin Klimke, and Anne Kuhlmann, 38–56. New York: Berghahn, 2013.

Lowe, Kate. "Isabella d'Este and the Acquisition of Black Africans at the Mantuan Court." In *Mantova e il Rinascimento italiano: Studi in onore di David S. Chambers*, edited by Philippa Jackson and Guido Rebecchini, 65–76. Mantua: Editoriale Sometti, 2011.

Lowe, Kate. "The Stereotyping of Black Africans in Renaissance Europe." In *Black Africans in Renaissance Europe*, edited by T. F. Earle and K. J. P. Lowe, 17–47. Cambridge: Cambridge University Press, 2005.

Lowe, Kate. "Visible Lives: Black Gondoliers and Other Black Africans in Renaissance Venice." *Renaissance Quarterly* 66 (2013): 412–452.

Luzio, Alessandro, and Rodolfo Renier. "Buffoni, schiavi e nani alla corte dei Gonzaga ai tempi d'Isabella d'Este." *Nuova Anthologia* 19 (1891): 112–146.

Macy, Laura. "Speaking of Sex: Metaphor and Performance in the Italian Madrigal." *Journal of Musicology* 14, no. 1 (1996): 1–34.

Mamone, Sara, ed. *Mattias de' Medici serenissimo mecenate dei virtuosi: Notizie di spettacolo nei carteggi medicei: Carteggio di Mattias de' Medici (1629–1667)*. Florence: Le Lettere, 2013.

Mamone, Sara. "Most Serene Brothers-Princes-Impresarios: Theater in Florence under the Management and Protection of Mattias, Giovan Carlo, and Leopoldo de' Medici." *Journal of Seventeenth-Century Music* 9 (2003): 4–8.

Mamone, Sara, ed. *Serenissimi fratelli principi impresari: Notizie di spettacolo nei carteggi medicei: Carteggi di Giovan Carlo de' Medici e di Desiderio Montemagni suo segretario (1628–1664)*. Florence: Le Lettere, 2003.

Marconcini, Samuela. "Una presenza nascosta: Battesimi di 'turchi' a Firenze in età moderna." *Annali di Storia di Firenze* 7 (2012): 97–121.

Marino, Giambattista. *Galeria poetica*. Edited by Marzio Pieri. Padua: Liviana, 1979.

Markey, Lia. *Imagining the Americas in Medici Florence*. University Park: Pennsylvania State University Press, 2016.

Markey, Lia. "Mapping Brazil in Medici Florence: Dudley's *Arcano del Mare* (1646–1647)." In *Far from the Truth: Distance and Credibility in the Early Modern World*, edited by Michiel van Groesen and Johannes Müller. University Park: Pennsylvania State University Press, forthcoming.

Massar, Phyllis Dearborn. "Costume Drawings by Stefano della Bella for the Florentine Theater." *Master Drawings* 8, no. 3 (1970): 243–266.

Mayer Modena, Maria Luisa. "A proposito di una scena 'all'ebraica' nello Schiavetto dell'Andreini." *Annali della Facoltà di Lettere e Filosofia dell'Università degli Studi di Milano* 43, no. 3 (1990): 73–81.
McClary, Susan. "Soprano as Fetish: Professional Singers in Early Modern Italy." In *Desire and Pleasure in Seventeenth-Century Music*, 79–103. Berkeley: University of California Press, 2012.
Megale, Teresa. "Bernardino Ricci e il mestiere di buffone tra cinque e seicento." In *Il Tedeschino overo Difesa dell'Arte del Cavalier del Piacere*, 7–75. Florence: Le Lettere, 1995.
Megale, Teresa. "La commedia decifrata: Metamorfosi e rispecchianti in *Li buffoni* di Margherita Costa." *Il Castello di Elsinore* 2 (1988): 64–76.
Meizel, Katherine. *Multivocality: Singing on the Borders of Identity*. Oxford: Oxford University Press, 2020.
Melani, Jacopo. *Ercole in Tebe*. New York: Garland, 1978.
Melani, Jacopo. *Il potestà di Colognole*. Edited by James Leve. Middleton, WI: A-R Editions, 2005.
Miller, Monica L. *Slaves to Fashion: Black Dandyism and the Styling of Black Diasporic Identity*. Durham, NC: Duke University Press, 2009.
Monaldini, Sergio. "Leandro: Carlo Righenzi musico e comico." *Musicalia* 8 (2011): 75–111.
Monga, Luigi, ed. *Galee toscane e corsari barbareschi: Il diario di Aurelio Scetti galeotto fiorentino 1565–1577*. Fornacette: CDL, 1999.
Moniglia, Giovanni Andrea. *Delle poesie dramatiche di Giovann'Andrea Moniglia, Accademic della Crusca, Parte prima*. Florence: Vincenzio Vangelisti, 1689.
Moniglia, Giovanni Andrea. *Delle poesie dramatiche di Giovann'Andrea Moniglia, Accademic della Crusca, Parte terza*. Florence: Vincenzio Vangelisti, 1698.
Moniglia, Giovanni Andrea. *Ercole in Tebe*. Florence: Stamperia all'Insegna della Stella, 1661.
Moniglia, Giovanni Andrea. *Il pazzo per forza, Dramma civile rusticale, Fatto rappresentare in Musica, Da gl'illustriss. Sig. Accademici Immobili Nel loro Teatro, Sotto la protezione del Sereniss e Reverendiss. Principe Cardinale Gio: Carlo di Toscana*. Florence: Il Bonardi, 1659.
Moniglia, Giovanni Andrea. *Il potestà di Colognole, Dramma civile rusticale. A gl'illustrissimi signori academici Immobili*. Florence: Il Bonardi, 1657.
Moniglia, Giovanni Andrea. *Il vecchio balordo*. Edited by Françoise Decroisette. Biblioteca Pregoldoniana. Venice: Lineadacqua, 2014.
Moniglia, Giovanni Andrea. "La serva nobile". In *Delle poesie dramatiche di Giovann'Andrea Moniglia, Accademic della Crusca, Parte terza*, 185–298. Florence: Vincenzio Vangelisti, 1698.
Moniglia, Giovanni Andrea. "La vedova, ovvero Amore vuole ingegno." In *Delle poesie dramatiche di Giovann'Andrea Moniglia, Accademic della Crusca, Parte terza*, 299–403. Florence: Vincenzio Vangelisti, 1698.
Moniglia, Giovanni Andrea. *L'Hipermestra, festa teatrale, rappresentata dal Sereniss. Principe Cardinale Gio. Carlo di Toscana, per celebrare il giorno natalizio del Real Principe di Spagna*. Florence: Stamperia di S.A.S., 1658.
Montaigne, Michel de. *Viaggio in Italia*. Milan: Rizzoli, 2008.
Morgan, Jennifer L. *Reckoning with Slavery: Gender, Kinship, and Capitalism in the Early Black Atlantic*. Durham, NC: Duke University Press, 2021.

Morrison, Matthew D. "Race, Blacksound, and the (Re)Making of Musicological Discourse." *Journal of the American Musicological Society* 72, no. 3 (2019): 781–823.

Morrison, Matthew D. "The Sound(s) of Subjection: Constructing American Popular Music and Racial Identity through Blacksound." *Women & Performance: A Journal of Feminist Theory* 27, no. 1 (2017): 13–24.

Moten, Fred. *In the Break: The Aesthetics of the Black Radical Tradition*. Minneapolis: University of Minnesota Press, 2003.

Nadalo, Stephanie. "Negotiating Slavery in a Tolerant Frontier: Livorno's Turkish *Bagno* (1547–1747)." *Mediaevalia* 32 (2011): 275–324.

Nagler, Alois Maria. *Theatre Festivals of the Medici, 1539–1637*. New Haven, CT: Yale University Press, 1964.

Nathan, Hans. "Negro Impersonation in Eighteenth-Century England." *Notes* 2, no. 4 (1945): 245–254.

Neri, Algerina. *Uno schiavo inglese nella Livorno dei Medici*. Pisa: ETS, 2000.

Newcomb, Anthony. *The Madrigal at Ferrara, 1579–1597*. Princeton, NJ: Princeton University Press, 1980.

Nirenberg, David. *Neighboring Faiths: Christianity, Islam, and Judaism in the Middle Ages and Today*. Chicago: University of Chicago Press, 2014.

Nussbaum, Felicity. "'Mungo Here, Mungo There': Charles Dibdin and Racial Performance." In *Charles Dibdin and Late Georgian Culture*, edited by Oskar Cox Jensen, David Kennerley, and Ian Newman, 23–42. Oxford: Oxford University Press, 2018.

O'Brien, John. *Harlequin Britain: Pantomime and Entertainment, 1690–1760*. Baltimore: Johns Hopkins University Press, 2004.

"On Being Present: Recovering Blackness in the Uffizi Galleries." Uffizi Galleries. https://www.uffizi.it/en/online-exhibitions/on-being-present.

Operstein, Natalie. "Golden Age *Poesìa de Negros* and Orlando di Lasso's *Moresche*: A Possible Connection." *Romance Notes* 52, no. 1 (2012): 13–18.

Origo, Iris. "The Domestic Enemy: The Eastern Slaves in Tuscany in the Fourteenth and Fifteenth Centuries." *Speculum* 30 (1955): 321–366.

Orsini, Francesca, and Katherine Butler Schofield, eds. *Tellings and Texts: Music, Literature and Performance Cultures in North India*. Cambridge, UK: Open Book, 2015.

Ossi, Massimo. *Divining the Oracle: Monteverdi's Seconda Prattica*. Chicago: University of Chicago Press, 2003.

Palisca, Claude. "The Florentine Camerata." In *The Florentine Camerata: Documentary Studies and Translations*, 1–12. New Haven, CT: Yale University Press, 1989.

Palisca, Claude. "G. B. Doni, Musicological Activist and His *Lyra Barberina*." In *Modern Musical Scholarship*, edited by Edward Olleson, 180–205. Stocksfield, UK: Oriel Press, 1980.

Palisca, Claude, ed. *G. B. Doni's Lyra Barberina: Commentary and Iconographical Study, Facsimile Edition with Critical Notes*. Bologna: Antiquae Musicae Italicae Studiosi, 1981.

Paoli, Lucia. "Da Livorno a Nombre de Dios: Una dettagliata relazione inviata a Firenze e il progetto dei Medici per un possesso in Brasile." In *Percorsi di arte e letteratura tra la Toscana e le Americhe: Atti della giornata di studi Biblioteca Nazionale Centrale di Firenze, 3 Ottobre 2014*, edited by Nicoletta Lepri, loc. 2333–2930. Raleigh, NC: Aonia, 2016.

Paoli, Maria Pia. "Di madre in figlio: Per una storia dell'educazione alla corte dei Medici." *Annali di Storia di Firenze* 3 (2008): 65–145.

Pentzell, Raymond J. "Garrick's Costuming." *Theatre Survey* 10 (1969): 18–42.
Peritz, Jessica Gabriel. *The Lyric Myth of Voice: Civilizing Song in Enlightenment Italy*. Forthcoming.
Perrucci, Andrea. *Dell'arte rappresentativa premiditata ed all'improviso*. Naples: Michele Luigi Mutio, 1699.
Piasere, Leonardo. "L'invenzione di una diaspora: I nubiani d'Europa." In *Alle radici dell'Europa: Mori, giudei e zingari nei paesi del Mediterraneo occidentale*, Vol. 1: *Secoli XV–XVII*, edited by Felice Gambin, 185–199. Florence: Seid, 2008.
Pirrotta, Nino. "Early Opera and Aria." Translated by Karen Eales. In *Music and Theatre from Poliziano to Monteverdi*, 237–280. Cambridge: Cambridge University Press, 1982.
Price, Leontyne, Leo Dillon, and Diane Dillon. *Aida*. New York: Voyager Books, 1991.
Purciello, Maria Anne. "And Dionysus Laughed: Opera, Comedy and Carnival in Seventeenth-Century Venice and Rome." PhD diss, Princeton University, 2005.
Quaderni storici 42, no. 3, special issue on Slavery in the Mediterranean (2007).
Ramos-Kittrell, Jesús A. *Playing in the Cathedral: Music Race, and Status in New Spain*. Oxford: Oxford University Press, 2016.
Rath, Richard Cullen. *How Early America Sounded*. Ithaca, NY: Cornell University Press, 2003.
Reardon, Coleen. *A Sociable Moment: Opera and Festive Culture in Baroque Siena*. Oxford: Oxford University Press, 2016.
Reed, Sue Welsh. *Giovanni Battista Bracelli: Bizzarie di Varie Figure (Livorno, 1624)*. Evansville, IN: Octavo, 2000.
Reeves, Nathan. "The Oar, the Trumpet, the Drum: Music and Galley Servitude in Spanish Naples." 2018.
Rehding, Alexander. "The Quest for the Origins of Music in Germany circa 1900." *Journal of the American Musicological Society* 53, no. 2 (2000): 345–385.
Richardson, Brian. "Sixteenth-Century Italian Petrarchists and Musical Settings of Their Verse." In *Voices and Texts in Early Modern Italian Society*, edited by Stefano Dall'Aglio, Brian Richardson, and Massimo Rospocher, 124–138. Abingdon, UK: Routledge, 2017.
Rico Osés, Clara. *L'Espagne vue de France à travers les ballets de cour du XVIIe siècle*. Geneva: Éditions Papillon, 2012.
Ridolfi, Roberto. "Pensieri Medicei di colonizzare il Brazil." *Il Veltro* 6, no. 4 (1962): 705–720.
Rinuccini, Camillo. *Descrizione delle feste fatte nelle reali nozze de' Serenissimi Principi di Toscana D. Cosimo de' Medici e Maria Maddalena Archiduchessa d'Austria*. Florence: I Giunti, 1608.
Rosand, David, and Ellen Rosand. "Barbara di Santa Sofia and Il Prete Genovese: On the Identity of a Portrait by Bernardo Strozzi." *Art Bulletin* 63 (1981): 249–258.
Rosand, Ellen. "Barbara Strozzi, *Virtuosissima Cantatrice*: The Composer's Voice." *Journal of the American Musicological Society* 31 (1978): 241–281.
Rosand, Ellen. *Opera in Seventeenth-Century Venice: The Creation of a Genre*. Berkeley: University of California Press, 1991.
Rothman, E. Natalie. *Brokering Empire: Trans-Imperial Subjects between Venice and Istanbul*. Ithaca, NY: Cornell University Press, 2012.
Salvante, Raffaella. *Il "Pellegrino" in Oriente: La Turchia di Pietro della Valle (1614–1617)*. Florence: Edizioni Polistampa, 1997.

Salvatore, Gianfranco. "Il teatro musicale delle lingue: Parodie di stranieri e minoranze nel Rinascimento italiano, dispensa per il corso di etnomusicologia 'Minoranze etniche nella musica rinascimentale,' a.a. 2011–2012." Università del Salento, 2011.

Salvatore, Gianfranco. "Parodie realistiche: Africanismi, fraternità e sentimenti identitari nelle canzoni moresche del cinquecento." *Kronos* 14 (2011): 97–130.

Sanford, Sally A. "A Comparison of French and Italian Singing in the Seventeenth Century." *Journal of Seventeenth-Century Music* 1, no. 1 (1995). https://sscm-jscm.org/v1/no1/sanford.html.

Sardellaro, Enzo. "Forme, struttura e lingua delle commedie di Giancarli: Studi sulla lingua della commedia veneta del cinquecento." *Studi Linguistici e Filologici Online* 6 (2008): 275–343.

Scetti, Aurelio. *The Journal of Aurelio Scetti: A Florentine Galley Slave at Lepanto (1565–1577)*. Translated by Luigi Monga. Tempe: Arizona Center for Medieval and Renaissance Studies, 2004.

Schleuse, Paul. *Singing Games: The Music Books of Orazio Vecchi*. Bloomington: Indiana University Press, 2015.

Scipione in Cartagine, dramma musicale; Fatto rappresentare da gli Accademici Sorgenti, nel loro Teatro, sotto la protezzione del Sereniss. e Reverendiss. Princ. Card. Gio: Carlo di Toscana. Florence: Gio: Anton Bonardi, 1657.

Simonsohn, Shlomo. *History of the Jews in the Duchy of Mantua*. Jerusalem: Kiryath Sepher, 1977.

Skeehan, Danielle. "Black Atlantic Acoustemologies and the Maritime Archive." In *Acoustemologies in Contact: Sounding Subjects and Modes of Listening in Early Modernity*, edited by Emily Wilbourne and Suzanne G. Cusick, 107–133. Cambridge: Open Book, 2021.

Smith, Bruce R. *The Acoustic World of Early Modern England: Attending to the O-Factor*. Chicago: University of Chicago Press, 1999.

Smith, Cassander L. "'Candy No Witch in Her Country': What One Enslaved Woman's Testimony during the Salem Witch Trials Can Tell Us about Early American Literature." In *Early Modern Black Diaspora Studies: A Critical Anthology*, edited by Cassander L. Smith, Nicholas Jones, and Miles P. Grier, 107–134. Cham, Switzerland: Macmillan, 2018.

Smith, Cassander L., Nicholas R. Jones, and Miles P. Grier, eds. *Early Modern Black Diaspora Studies: A Critical Anthology*. Cham, Switzerland: Palgrave Macmillan, 2018.

Smith, Mark M. *How Race Is Made: Slavery, Segregation, and the Senses*. Chapel Hill: University of North Carolina Press, 2006.

Solerti, Angelo. *Musica, ballo e drammatica alla corte medicea dal 1600 al 1637: Notizie tratte da un diario con appendice di testi inediti e rari, ristampa anastatica dell'edizione di Firenze, 1905*. Bologna: Forni Editori, 1969.

Sorrentino, Giulio Cesare. *Ciro, drama per musica: Nel teatro a SS Gio: e Paolo l'anno 1665*. Venice: Per il Giuliani, 1665.

Spicer, Joaneath. "European Perceptions of Blackness as Reflected in the Visual Arts." In *Revealing the African Presence in Renaissance Europe*, edited by Joaneath Spicer, 35–60. Baltimore: Walters Art Museum, 2012.

Spicer, Joaneath, ed. *Revealing the African Presence in Renaissance Europe*. Baltimore: Walters Art Museum, 2012.

Spinelli, Riccardo. "Ritratto di suonatore di liuto con cantore moro (Panbollito e Giovannino moro)." In *Volterrano: Baldassarre Franceschini (1611–1690)*, edited by

Maria Cecilia Fabbri, Alessandro Grassi, and Riccardo Spinelli, 244–245. Florence: Ente Cassa di Risparmio di Firenze, 2013.

Spohr, Arne. "'Mohr und Tropeter': Blackness and Social Status in Early Modern Germany." *Journal of the American Musicological Society* 72, no. 3 (2019): 613–663.

Stoever, Jennifer Lynn. *The Sonic Color Line: Race and the Cultural Politics of Listening*. New York: New York University Press, 2016.

Stras, Laurie. *Women and Music in Sixteenth-Century Ferrara*. Cambridge: Cambridge University Press, 2018.

Swanson, Barbara. "Barbara Strozzi, *Appresso ai Molli Argenti* (1659)." In *Analytical Essays on Music by Women Composers*, edited by Laurel Parsons and Brenda Ravenscroft, 74–105. Oxford: Oxford University Press, 2018.

Swanson, Barbara. "Old Chant, New Songs: Plainchant and Monody in Sixteenth-Century Rome." In *Chant Old and New/Plain-chant: L'ancien et le nouveau*, edited by William Renwick, 215–224. Ottawa: Institute of Medieval Music, 2012.

Swanson, Barbara. "Plainchant Psalmody in the Prologues of Early Opera." In *Chant and Culture/Plain-chant et culture*, edited by Armin Karim and Barbara Swanson, 151–160. Ottawa: Institute of Medieval Music, 2014.

Takao, Makoto Harris. "'In Their Own Way': Contrafactal Practices in Japanese Christian Communities during the 16th Century." *Early Music* 47, no. 2 (2019): 183–198.

Terry, Esther J. "Choreographies of Trans-Atlantic Primitivity: Sub-Saharan Isolation in Black Dance Historiography." In *Early Modern Black Diaspora Studies: A Critical Anthology*, edited by Cassander L. Smith, Nicholas R. Jones, and Miles P. Grier, 65–82. Cham, Switzerland: Palgrave Macmillan, 2018.

Thompson, Ayanna. *Blackface*. Object Lessons. New York: Bloomsbury, 2021.

Thompson, Ayanna, ed. *The Cambridge Companion to Shakespeare and Race*. Cambridge: Cambridge University Press, 2021.

Thompson, Rosemarie Garland. *Extraordinary Bodies*. New York: Columbia University Press, 1997.

Toderini, Giambattista. *Letteratura turchesca*. Venice: Giacomo Storti, 1787.

Tomlinson, Gary. *Music in Renaissance Magic: Toward a Historiography of Others*. Chicago: University of Chicago Press, 1993.

Treadwell, Nina. *Music and Wonder at the Medici Court: The 1589 Interludes for "La Pellegrina."* Bloomington: Indiana University Press, 2009.

Treadwell, Nina. "She Descended on a Cloud 'from the Highest Spheres': Florentine Monody 'alla *Romanina*.'" *Cambridge Opera Journal* 16 (2004): 1–22.

Van Orden, Kate. "Hearing Franco-Ottoman Relations circa 1600: The Chansons Turquesques of Charles Tessier (1604)." In *Seachanges: Music in the Mediterranean and Atlantic Worlds, 1550–1800*," edited by Kate van Orden, 33–68. I Tatti Research Series 2. Cambridge, MA: Harvard University Press, 2022.

Van Orden, Kate. *Music, Discipline, and Arms in Early Modern France*. Chicago: University of Chicago Press, 2004.

Van Orden, Kate, ed. *Seachanges: Music in the Mediterranean and Atlantic Worlds, 1550–1800*. I Tatti Research Series 2. Cambridge, MA: Harvard University Press, 2022.

Weaver, Robert Lamar, and Norma Wright Weaver. *A Chronology of Music in the Florentine Theater 1590–1750*. Detroit Studies in Music Bibliography. Detroit: Information Coordinators, 1978.

Weheliye, Alexander G. *Habeas Viscus: Racializing Assemblages, Biopolitics, and Black Feminist Theories of the Human*. Durham, NC: Duke University Press, 2014.

Weidman, Amanda. "Anthropology and Voice." *Annual Review of Anthropology* 43 (2014): 37–51.

Whenham, John. "The Gonzagas Visit Venice." *Early Music* 21, no. 4 (1993): 525–546.

Wilbourne, Emily. "Affect and the Recording Devices of Seventeenth-Century Italy." In *Sound and Affect: Voice, Music, World*, edited by Stephen Decatur Smith, Judith Lochhead, and Eduardo Mendieta, 325–341. Chicago: University of Chicago Press, 2021.

Wilbourne, Emily. "Demo's Stutter, Subjectivity, and the Virtuosity of Vocal Failure." *Journal of the American Musicological Society* 68, no. 3 (2015): 659–663.

Wilbourne, Emily. "Four Servants of the Medici Court, Anton Domenico Gabbiani (1686)." *On Being Present: Images of Black Africans in the Galleria degli Uffizi.* https://www.uffizi.it/mostre-virtuali/on-being-present, March 2020.

Wilbourne, Emily. "Gio: Buonaccorsi 'the Moor': An Enslaved Black Singer at the Medici Court." In *Teaching Race in the European Renaissance: A Classroom Guide*, edited by Matthieu Chapman and Anna Wainwright, 267–287. Tempe: Arizona Center of Medieval and Renaissance Studies Press, 2023.

Wilbourne, Emily. "'. . . La Curiosità del Personaggio': 'Il Moro' on the Mid-Century Operatic Stage." In *Seachanges: Music in the Mediterranean and Atlantic Worlds, 1550–1880*, edited by Kate van Orden, 133–148. I Tatti Research Series 2. Cambridge, MA: Harvard University Press, 2022.

Wilbourne, Emily. "Little Black Giovanni's Dream: Black Authorship and the 'Turks, Dwarves, and Bad Christians' of the Medici Court." In *Acoustemologies in Contact: Sounding Subjects and Modes of Listening in Early Modernity*, edited by Emily Wilbourne and Suzanne G. Cusick, 135–165. Cambridge: Open Book, 2021.

Wilbourne, Emily. "*Lo Schiavetto* (1612): Travestied Sound, Ethnic Performance, and the Eloquence of the Body." *Journal of the American Musicological Society* 63, no. 1 (2010): 1–44.

Wilbourne, Emily. "Musicological Indecency: Breastmilk, the Body, and the Interpellated Listener." *Echo: A Music-Centered Journal* 14, no. 1 (2016). http://www.echo.ucla.edu/volume-14-1-2016/article-breastmilk-exposed-bodies-politics-indecent/.

Wilbourne, Emily. "Music, Race, Representation: Three Scenes of Performance at the Medici Court (1608–1616)." *Il Saggiatore Musicale* 27, no. 1 (2020): 5–45.

Wilbourne, Emily. "The Queer History of the Castrato." In *The Oxford Handbook of Music and Queerness*, edited by Fred Everett Maus and Sheila Whiteley. Oxford Handbooks Online, 2018. https://doi.org/10.1093/oxfordhb/9780199793525.013.14.

Wilbourne, Emily. "A Question of Character: Virginia Ramponi Andreini and Artemisia Gentileschi." *Italian Studies* 71, no. 3 (2016): 335–355.

Wilbourne, Emily. *Seventeenth-Century Opera and the Sound of the Commedia dell'Arte*. Chicago: University of Chicago Press, 2016.

Wilbourne, Emily, and Suzanne G. Cusick, eds. *Acoustemologies in Contact: Sounding Subjects and Modes of Listening in Early Modernity*. Cambridge: Open Book, 2021.

Wilson, Kathleen. "Introduction: Three Theses on Performance and History." *Eighteenth-Century Studies* 48, no. 4 (2015): 375–390.

Wipertus, Rudt De Collenberg. "Le baptême des musulmans esclaves à Rome aux XVIIe et XVIIIe siècles. I. Le XVIIe siècle." *Mélanges de l'Ecole Française de Rome. Italie et Méditerranée* 101, no. 1 (1989): 9–181.

Wistreich, Richard. *Warrior, Courtier, Singer: Giulio Cesare Brancaccio and the Performance of Identity in the Late Renaissance*. Aldershot, UK: Ashgate, 2007.

Wright, Owen. "Turning a Deaf Ear." In *The Renaissance and the Ottoman World*, edited by Anna Contadini and Claire Norton, 143–165. Farnham, UK: Ashgate, 2013.
Wunder, Amanda. "Western Travelers, Eastern Antiquities, and the Image of the Turk in Early Modern Europe." *Journal of Early Modern History* 7 (2003): 89–119.
Wynter, Sylvia. "Unsettling the Coloniality of Being/Power/Truth/Freedom: Towards the Human, after Man, Its Overrepresentation—An Argument." *CR: New Centennial Review* 3, no. 3 (2003): 257–337.

Index

For the benefit of digital users, indexed terms that span two pages (e.g., 52–53) may, on occasion, appear on only one of those pages.

Tables and figures are indicated by *t* and *f* following the page number

Accademia (Academy)
  degli Immobili, 187, 188*t*, 193, 194*t*
  degli Unisoni, 163–64
  dei Sorgenti, 196, 197*t*
  Filarmonica, 121, 132–33
adoption, 16, 25, 163–64, 166
affect, xviii–xix, 1–2, 4, 9, 61–62, 99, 151, 153–54, 225–26, 240–41, 243–47, 289, 311–12, 313, 315
Africa, 6, 11–12, 14, 15, 32, 71, 185–86, 197n.18, 269–72, 291–92
agency, 2, 4, 7–8, 23–24, 166–67, 249–50, 251–52, 293–94, 296–97
Agostini, Anna, 10–11n.29, 21–23
Akhimie, Patricia, 159
Albizzi, Pier Giovanni, 175*t*, 177–84, 186–87, 217, 284
Aldridge, Ira, 295–96
America(s), 6, 34–35, 39, 82, 84–90, 94–97, 95*f*, 96*f*, 102, 151, 250–51, 290, 291–92, 295–96. *See also* New World
Ames, Eric, 137
Anderson, Marian, 280–81
Andreini, Francesco, 15–16, 117
Andreini, Giovan Battista, xx, 15–16, 64–65, 74–75, 78n.49, 104–5, 111, 114–17, 155
Andreini, Virginia Ramponi, xviii–xx, xxiii, 64–65
aria, 55, 56, 152–53, 155–56, 203, 218, 235, 240–46, 262–63, 269
Aureli, Aurelio, 266–68, 273–74

bagno, 11–12, 18, 21, 22, 23–24, 92, 94, 101–2, 106–10, 113–14, 118, 124
Balletto (ballet)
  Il balletto della cortesia, 43–52, 55–57, 61, 158

  Il balletto delle donne turche, 50–51
  La stiava, 50–51, 158
Baritoli, Ugolino, 113
Barthes, Roland, 1, 249–50
Battistone (dwarf), 229
Bendinelli, Cesare, 121, 128, 132–33
Bernardi, Francesco, *aka* Senesino, 285–87, 300–2
Berns, Jörg Jochen, 124–25, 182–83
Bickerstaffe, Isaac, 39, 295–300, 301*f*, 304*f*, 307*f*, 314–15
blackface, 39, 64–65, 157, 199, 251–52, 264–66, 294–97, 314
Blackness, 25–26, 30, 38–39, 125–26, 171, 196, 199–201, 203, 239, 249–50, 269–72, 280, 292, 294–96
Boorman, Stanley, 143–44
Bracelli, Giovanni Battista, 106–10, 114–15
Brazil, 87, 88–91, 101–2, 299
Broschi, Carlo, *aka* Farinelli, 285–86, 286n.10
Brown, Jennifer Williams, 196, 269–72
Buccia, corporal, 228–29
Budasz, Rogério, 34–35, 157
buffoon, 30, 38, 149–52, 158, 206, 211, 214–15, 226–27, 229, 263, 273, 286–87, 289, 300–2, 314–15
Buonaccorsi (family), 178–79
Buonaccorsi, Giovanni or Giovannino
  as a chamber musician, 171, 182–83, 238–39, 247–48
  biography, 171, 177–79, 190–91
  in Venice, 171, 193–94, 254–81
  poetry, 171, 208–30, 236
  stock character, 193–96, 205, 251–52
Busenello, Giovanni Francesco, 263–64
Butler, Judith, 117–18

Caccini, Francesca, 43, 46–56, 60–62, 151–52, 158
Caccini, Giulio, 51–52
Calergi, Vettor Grimani, 254–56, 263–64, 265–67, 269–72, 273–74, 286–87
camel(s), 114–15, 154, 235–36
Caralì, *aka* Mattia Medici, 204–6, 232, 255, 285, 296–97
Caralì (character), 194–97, 194*t*, 201–4, 205–6, 216–17, 257
Carletti, Francesco, 92–93, 101–2
carnevale (carnival), 43, 45–46, 58–59, 71, 73, 84–87, 152–53, 158, 187, 194–96, 198–202, 273
castrato, castrati, xviii–xix, 38, 177, 232–33, 238–39, 247, 248–52, 254–55, 264–65, 269–72, 283–84, 285–86, 293–94, 298–99, 300–2, 303
Cavagna, Giovanni Antonio, 264–66, 286–87
Cavalli, Francesco, 163–64, 184–85, 196, 247, 263–64, 270*f*, 271*f*, 275*f*
Cervantes Saavedra, Miguel de, 15–16, 298–300, 302, 313
Chamber music, 38, 122, 125–26, 132, 163–64, 171, 175*t*, 179–84, 238–39, 247–48
Chiarelli, Francesca, 175*t*
chiusette, 240–41
Christine of Lorraine, 111, 146
Christofanino (dwarf), 228–29
Cicognini, Giacinto Andrea, 247
ciuffetto, 108–10, 124
class, 1–2, 31, 32–33, 60, 64, 164, 280, 289, 302
clothing. *See* dress
Colli, Vincenzo, *aka* il Calmeta, 152–53
Colloreto (or Colloredo), Fabbritio, Marquis, 128–32
commedia dell'arte, xvii–xxiii, 2–3, 15–16, 31, 64–65, 74–75, 82, 104, 177, 189, 193–94, 196–97, 232–33, 240–41, 273, 294–95
comedy, xviii–xix, 53–54, 77–78, 193–94, 234, 274
comedy, madrigal: *L'Amfiparnaso*, 78–82
Constantinople, 64–65, 137–38
convict(s). *See forzati*

Coppa, Lucia, 175*t*
Corsini, Bartolommeo, Marquis, 83, 188*t*, 256–57
Costa, Margherita, 211–15
costume(s). *See* dress
countertenor. *See* falsetto
courtesan, 163–64
Crawford, Katherine, 249
cross-dressing. *See travestimento*
Cusick, Suzanne G., 53–55, 56–57, 56n.40, 61–62

dance, 38, 44, 50–51, 52, 53–54, 56–57, 59–61, 84–87, 100, 116–17, 122–23, 132–33, 143, 145, 159, 199, 202–3, 232–35, 237, 248, 274–79, 284–85, 286–87, 315
Daston, Lorraine, 229
Davies, William, 9–12, 18–22, 90–91, 92, 94, 101–2, 156n.38
Davis, Robert, 30n.101
de' Bardi, Giovanni, 135–36
De Castris, Francesco, 283–84, 285–86
Decroisette, Françoise, 173–74, 187, 193, 201–3
dell'Armaiolo, Jacopo or Jacopino, 122–23
della Bella, Stefano, 184–85, 187–89, 194–96, 199, 247–48
della Valle, Pietro, 135–36, 137, 141–43
d'Este, Isabella, 30, 149–50, 151–52, 313
dialect, 39, 64, 71–73, 74, 78, 82, 104, 201–2, 210, 233, 296–99
Dibdin, Charles, 39, 295–315
di Pers, Ciro, 25–26, 211–12, 228
disability
  developmental, 147–48
  dwarfism, xxi, 7–8, 30, 53, 124, 145, 151, 175*t*, 179–82, 189, 205–6, 211, 212–15, 227–29, 284–85
  hunchback, 189, 196–97, 201, 218, 228–29, 247, 263, 274–79
  mute, 74–78, 80–82, 151, 175*t*, 177, 179–82, 189
  stutter, 189, 196–97, 201, 203, 218, 225–26, 247, 257, 263, 274
disguise. *See travestimento*
Donà (or Donado), Giovanni Battista, 137–44

Doni, Giovanni Battista, 135–36
Douglass, Frederick, 251–52
dress
   of performers offstage, 21–22, 108–10, 184–86, 228, 283–84
   of performers onstage, xvii, 31–32, 38, 52–53, 60, 74–75, 85*f*, 88, 97, 102, 150, 183–86, 187–89, 194–96, 199, 256–57, 272–73, 296–97, 312–13
Dudley, Robert, 90–92, 94–97, 101–2
dwarf (as character), 212

Eidsheim, Nina Sun, 34–35, 286–87
Enslavement
   domestic, 8, 11–12, 16, 23–24, 25–26, 155–56, 165–66
   enslaved people as luxury commodities, 53, 149, 159, 184, 186–87, 312–13
   enslaved people given as gifts, 16, 53–54, 154, 179
   entry into, xxiv, 9, 10–12, 13–16, 25, 92–94, 204–5
   freedom from, 15, 16–18, 23–24, 25, 90–91, 101–2, 110, 249–50, 264–65, 311
   galley, 8–12, 16, 18, 19–24, 26–27, 37, 63, 94, 104–14, 121, 196, 201–5, 216, 229
   work during, 22–24, 110
eunuch. *See* castrato
exoticism, 33–34, 44, 50–51, 60–61, 102, 116, 117–18, 171–72

Fakhr ad-Din II, 44–46, 57–58, 87, 291–92
Falbetti Nacci, Lisabetta, 175*t*
Falbetti Ballerini, Leonora, 175*t*
falsetto, 238–39
Fantappiè, Francesca, 113, 211–12
Fantini, Girolamo, *aka* Girolamo Trombetto, 121–23, 125–33
Faustini, Giovanni, 264–65
favola: *Il passatempo*, 43, 44–45, 52, 53–54, 58–59
Feldman, Martha, 249
fencing, 122–23, 286–87
Fontei, Nicolò, 163–64
food, 18–19, 21, 22, 69*f*, 99, 105–6, 110–11, 159, 172, 177, 202–3, 216–17, 251–52, 257–62, 284–85

foreign languages
   Arabic, 58–59, 61, 71–72, 73–74, 84–87, 202–3
   Gergo, 71–72, 201–3, 232–33, 235, 236, 257–62, 263–64, 274, 280, 298
   German, 68–71, 72–73, 82, 119, 132, 257–62
   Hebrew, 72–73, 74–81*f*, 77n.41
   Italian, 91–92, 236
   Kanuri, 71–74
   Sabir, 71–72, 201–2, 233, 298
   Spanish, 30, 71–72, 147–48, 155–57, 165, 215, 298–99, 313–14
   Turkish, 65, 71–72, 82, 104, 108–10, 113, 115–16, 137–38, 155–57
forzati (convicts), 9, 11–12, 104–5, 110, 111, 113, 114, 116
Franceschini, Baldessare, *aka* il Volterrano, 172–73, 177–78, 182–85, 186–87, 191, 208, 217, 238–39, 247–48, 312–13
Freitas, Roger, 249
Frescobaldi, Girolamo, 135–36
Freud, 248–49

Gabbiani, Anton Domenico, 227–29, 283–84, 286–87
Gaeta, Giovanni Antonio, *aka* Mutolo, 175*t*, 177, 180*t*
gardens, 13, 19, 183–84, 256–57, 284
Gentileschi, Artemisia, xvii–xxiii, 286–87
Gerbino, Giuseppe, 249
Germany, Germans, 19, 68–71, 82, 88, 120, 132, 257–62, 303
gift giving, 16, 53–54, 154, 179
Glissant, Édouard, 182
gobo. *See* disability: hunchback
gold, xix–xx, 53, 87, 90–91, 94, 99, 114–15, 204–5, 257, 262–64, 267, 274–79
Gordon, Bonnie, 249, 250–51
Grassi, Alessandro, 208
Greece (ancient), 2–3, 37, 70–71, 135–37
Greece (modern), 18, 72–73, 88, 165–66, 290
Grimani. *See* Calergi, Vettor Grimani
Grimani, Michele, 286n.10
Guinea, 94–98*t*

"Gypsy" characters, 193–96, 201–2, 211, 212–14, 217, 232–33, 235–36, 247, 257, 273–81. *See also* Rom (for people)

hair, 10–11, 19, 53, 98*t*, 108–10, 124, 199, 220*f*, 283–84
Hallam, Lewis, the younger, 297–98n.20
Harris, Ellen, 182–83
Hartman, Saidiya, 151, 186–87, 239, 249–50
Head, Matthew, 117–18, 148–49, 154
Hershenzon, Daniel, 13–16
historically informed performance practice, 37, 102, 117–18, 132–33, 141–43, 248–49
Hornback, Robert, 39, 67–68, 251–52, 294–95
Hornbostel, Erich Moritz von, 137
horse ballet: *Guerra d'amore*, 84–86*f*, 97–98, 101, 111
Hugford, Ignatius, 227, 228–29
humor. *See* comedy
hunger, 241–52, 262–63

India, 34–35, 135–36
Indians, 83, 84–102, 143, 207
inheritance, 28–29, 30–31, 32–33, 82, 97–98, 159, 164, 196–97, 273, 280, 289, 292–93
intermedio, intermedii, 87, 88–90, 89*f*, 97–98, 104, 234

Janissaries, 44–45, 116
Janissary music, 116, 132–33
jargon. *See* foreign languages: Gergo
jester. *See* buffoon
Jews, xvii, 7–8, 14, 16–18, 27–29, 30, 74–82, 231
Jones, Nicholas, 67–68, 299
Jong (or Young), Thomas (or Tommaso), 147–49, 154
Judaism, 78–80

Kaplan, Paul, 149, 150n.13, 173–74, 184–85, 206, 208–10

Labita, Maria, 285–86
lament, 44, 55–56, 152–53, 158, 235, 262–63

Lasso, Orlando di, 68–71, 72n.28
"Matona, mia cara", 68–71
Law, Hedy, 249
Leonardi, Francesco, 175*t*, 232–33, 238–39
Leve, James, 173–74
Livorno (Leghorn), 9–12, 13–14, 18–19, 22, 37, 44–45, 57–58, 59–60, 88–90, 91, 92, 101–2, 103, 104–14, 118, 121, 123–24, 147–48, 150, 204, 215–16, 228–29
Lowe, Kate, 24–25, 26–27, 28–29, 30, 120, 132

Mamone, Sara, 173–77
Maria Maddalena of Austria, 8, 87, 90*f*
Martelli, Simone, 247
Martinez, Gabriello, 212, 215, 217, 229–30
Masotti, Giulia, 269
Massai, Luisa, 175*t*
Mattioli, Andrea, 273–74, 275*f*
Mazzocchi, Domenico, 135–36
Medici, Cardinal Prince Giovan Carlo, 16–18, 23–24, 171, 172–82, 187, 189, 191, 193, 194*t*, 196–97, 229, 238–40, 254, 256–57, 273
Medici, Cosimo II, 8, 16–18, 53–54, 57–58, 113, 227
Medici, Ferdinando I, xvi, 8, 11–12, 18, 19, 57–58, 87, 88–90, 92, 111
Medici, Ferdinando II, 8, 105–6, 171, 184–85, 191, 215
Medici, Giuseppe Maria. (*See* Mehmet)
Medici, Mattia, convert. *See* Caralì
Medici, Mattias, Prince, 191, 204–5, 239–40, 254–55
Mehmet, *aka* Giuseppe Maria Medici, 228–29, 285
mehter. See Janissary music
Mei, Girolamo, 135–36
Melani, Atto, 254–55, 273–74
Melani, Bartolomeo, 175*t*, 238–39, 249–50
Melani, Jacopo, 173–74, 193, 194*t*, 200*f*, 220*f*, 235, 239–40, 242*f*, 244*f*, 256–57
Merlupo, Paolo da, 284–85
Mersenne, Marin, 125
military music, 116–17, 120–33, 291
Miller, Monica, 121–22, 159, 184, 300, 312–13

minstrelsy, 39, 294–97, 298, 315
Monaldini, Sergio, 173–74, 218
monasticism, 147–48, 166
Moniglia, Giovanni Andrea, 29, 177–78, 184–85, 190*f*, 193–202, 203–6, 218, 219*f*–20*f*, 225, 232, 235–36, 239–40, 241–52, 242*f*, 256–57, 258*f*, 269–72
Monteverdi, Claudio, 55–56, 154, 158, 289
Moody, John, 297–98
Mora (used as a name), 28, 273–74
moresche, 67–68, 69*f*, 71–72, 201–2
Morino (used as a name), 122, 128–31, 150, 170, 178–79, 184–85, 192, 203–6, 256–57, 262–63, 283–85
Moro (used as a name), 16, 28–29, 122, 145, 150, 173–74, 187–89, 194–96, 194*t*, 198–202, 212, 217, 232, 242*f*, 247–48, 255–57, 262–64, 283–85, 293–94
Moten, Fred, 149–50
Mungo (character), 39, 295–315
music education, 97–98, 121, 122–24, 125–26, 136, 148–49, 239–40, 248, 251–52
musical instrument(s)
 bass (lack of), 115–16, 137–38, 238–39
 basso continuo, 4, 51–52, 126, 128–31, 241–43
 cennamela (pipes or bagpipes), 114–17
 cymbal, 107*f*, 108–10, 114–15, 116–17, 202–3
 drum, drums, 84–87, 97–98, 104–6, 107*f*, 108–11, 109*f*, 113, 114–15, 116–17, 118, 120–33, 143, 268
 flute, 99, 100–1, 136, 152–53, 175*t*, 311–12
 guitar, 100–1, 122–23, 155, 157, 311–12
 lute, 100–1, 108–10, 172, 177–78, 182–84, 247–48
 nackers, 84–87, 99, 104–5, 108–10, 109*f*, 113, 114–15, 116–17
 trumpet, 38, 97–98, 104–6, 111, 113–14, 116–17, 118, 120–33, 136–37, 155–56, 247
 violin, 172, 175*t*, 177, 243, 283–84
musical notation, 2–3, 33, 115–17, 118, 137–38, 141–43, 157, 238–39, 291
mute. *See* disability: mute; Gaeta, Giovanni Antonio, *aka* Mutolo

Nadalo, Stephanie, 22, 110
nano (character), 212
Nano (used as a name), 175*t*, 182, 214–15
nano (dwarf). *See* disability: dwarf
New World, 84–88, 94–97, 292. *See also* America(s)
noise, 4–5, 39–40, 78, 82, 84–87, 97–98, 102, 104–5, 110–11, 113, 116, 118, 121, 137, 193, 284, 285
nuove musiche, 4, 51–52

Olivicciani, Vincenzo or Vincenzino, 238–39, 262–63
opera
 Amore vuole ingegno, 187, 194*t*, 198–202, 247, 255–56, 256*t*, 258*f*
 Ercole in Tebe, 185, 194*t*, 194–99, 200*f*, 218, 219*f*, 220*f*, 225–26, 240, 241–52, 244*f*, 256*t*, 257
 Il pazzo per forza, 29, 194*t*, 194–96, 201–2, 232–34, 256*t*, 262–63, 273–79
 Il potesta di Colognole, 173–74, 187–89, 190*f*, 194–97, 194*t*, 240, 241, 242*f*, 255–56, 256*t*, 262–63
 La Rosilena, 266–69
 La serva nobile, 29, 194*t*, 194–96
 La statira principessa di Persia, 263–64
 Scipione affricano, 269–72, 270*f*, 271*f*
 The Padlock, 39, 295–97, 298–99, 300, 301*f*, 302–3, 304*f*
opera (musical genre), xviii–xix, 2–4, 35–36, 100–1, 151–53, 189, 225–26, 249, 280–81, 286–87, 289, 294–95, 300–2, 315
orientalism, 50–51, 61, 148–49, 171–72
Ottoman Empire, 13–14, 57–58, 113, 116, 136n.4, 141, 239
Ottomans. *See* Turks

Palazzo Pitti (Pitti Palace), 11–12, 16, 43, 45–46, 111–13, 112*f*, 183–84, 191, 193
Parigi, Giulio, 84–87, 85*f*, 86*f*, 88, 89*f*, 100–1
Park, Katherine, 229
Paulsanti, Francesco, 113
Pavoni, Giuseppe, 113
peasant, 19, 53–54, 99, 100–1, 151–53, 177–78, 268, 284–85

Pergola Theater, 29, 173–74, 187, 193–96, 194*t*, 239–40, 247, 255, 256*t*, 269, 273
Persia, xvii, 18, 57, 99–100, 114–15, 135–36
Petrino (dwarf), 284–85
piracy, 8, 10–11, 13–14, 24, 104–5
Pisa, xxiv, 13–14, 15–16, 28, 88, 121, 158, 192
play(s)
    La Sultana, 64–67, 71–72, 104, 114–17, 154, 155–58
    Lo schiavetto, 74–75, 80–82, 155
poetry, xx, 25–26, 55–56, 71–72, 87, 152–54, 206, 208–18, 241–43, 311–12
Price, Leontyne, 272
Provenzale, Francesco, 273–74, 275*f*

race
    American Indians 7–8, 82, 83–87, 88–90*f*, 91–94, 97–99, 100–2, 108–10, 143, 151–52, 207
    Black African, xi–xii, xxi, 7–8, 32, 71–73, 82, 101–2, 104, 117–18, 120, 154, 178–79, 184–85, 204–5, 208–10, 228, 262–64, 285–86
ransom, 8, 12, 15, 16, 63, 113–14, 262–63
razza, 29–31, 32–33, 37, 61–62, 158–59, 160, 280, 285, 289, 292–93, 296–97, 314–15
recitative, 2–3, 51–52, 55, 56, 67, 151, 152–53, 203, 226, 246, 262–63, 269, 300–2
Reeves, Nathan, 34–35, 104–5, 110–11
refugee(s), 44–45, 56–57, 60–61, 101, 117–18, 151–52
religious conversion
    Islam to Christianity, 16–18, 24, 27–28, 131n.37, 146n.2, 160
    Judaism to Christianity, 18, 28
Righenzi, Carlo, 173–74, 175*t*, 177, 188*t*, 189, 196–99, 203, 218, 220*f*, 238–39, 240, 247, 257
ritornello, 68, 115–16, 240, 241–43
Rivani, Antonio, 175*t*, 177, 188*t*, 232–33, 238–39, 247, 249–50, 262–63
robbery, 30, 234, 235–36, 241–52, 274–79
Rom, Romani (people), 211n.5, 235–36
romanesca: "Io veggio", 44, 46–51, 47*f*, 48*f*, 53–56, 60–62, 101

Rome, 100–1, 135–37, 193–94
Rosand, Ellen, 164, 165, 264–65
Rossi, Luigi, 135–36
Rothman, E. Natalie, 67, 166

Salvatore, Gianfranco, 71–74, 201–2
Scatapocchio (dwarf), 212, 214–15, 217
seconda prattica, 4
Settimanni, Francesco, 104–5, 113
sexual activities, 25, 28, 163–64, 166–67, 212, 217, 228, 230, 250–51
Shakespeare, William, 5–6, 31–32, 295–96
silk, 22, 184–85, 228, 283–84, 312
silver, 53, 94, 114–15, 185–86, 257, 283–84
slave trade
    Mediterranean, 10–16, 26, 38–39, 101–2, 104–5, 155–56, 179
    transatlantic, 12, 14, 38–39, 292–93
Socii, Angela, 238–39
song (musical genre), 4, 51–52, 53, 55–56, 67–68, 115–16, 151–53, 157–58, 182–83, 186, 216, 235, 289, 297–98, 314–15
Sorrentino, Giulio Cesare, 273–79, 275*f*
sovereignty, xxi–xxii, 23–24, 30, 56, 61–62, 249–50, 265–66, 280, 285–86, 291–93
Spain, 13–14, 38–39, 87, 124–25, 147–48, 149–50, 151, 159–60, 183–84, 186, 249–50, 251–52, 257
Spicer, Joaneath, 32, 120
Spohr, Arne, 34–35, 120, 132
spy, 212, 215, 217, 229
stile recitativo. *See* recitative
stock character(s), 193–94, 196–97, 273, 296–97, 298
strophic, 67, 101, 116–17, 157, 162–63
Strozzi, Barbara, 162–67
Strozzi, Giulio, 163, 164, 165–66
Susier, Niccolò, 285–86
Sustermans, Justus, 149, 204–5, 283–84
Syria, 44–45, 56–58, 60, 82, 151–52

Tacca, Ferdinando, 200*f*, 219*f*
tenor, 175*t*, 177, 189, 196–97, 238–39, 247, 248–50
Tesi, Alessandro, *aka* Il Moretto, 285–86
Tesi, Vittoria, *aka* La Moretta, 285–86
Thompson, Ayanna, 5, 272

Toderini, Giambattista, 141–43
travel, xviii–xix, 9, 12, 14n.42, 15–16, 57–58, 90–91, 92, 94–97, 99–100, 101–2, 110, 116, 135–36, 141–44, 284–85, 290
travestimento, 31, 45–46n.10, 64–68, 74–75, 84–87, 100–1, 114–15, 157, 197n.19, 214, 232–33, 235–36, 262–63, 265–66, 274, 292–93
tuning, 108–10, 108*f*, 135–37
turban, xix–xx, 28–29, 124, 215–16
Turco (used as a name), 65–67, 84–87, 215–16
Turco, Maometto, 212, 215–16
Turco, Rosoan, 122–24, 151–52
Turco, Solefar, *aka* Solefar Trombetto, 122–24, 125–26, 128–31, 132–33, 151–52
Turk(s), 7–8, 9–11, 15–16, 18, 27–28, 65, 77–78, 82, 88, 105–6, 110, 117–18, 123–24, 137–38, 141–43, 150, 211, 212, 215–16

van Orden, Kate, 34–35, 71–73, 157
Venice, xx, 12, 38, 45–46, 163–64, 165–66, 171, 254–55, 269, 273
versi pari. *See* strophic

versi sciolti, 55–56, 212, 226, 246
Vespucci, Amerigo, 6, 87, 89*f*
Vinta, Paolo, 114
Violence, 21, 67, 77–78, 121–22, 125, 239, 249–51, 268, 293–94
voice, 1–5, 6–8, 31, 32–33, 36–40, 44, 56–57, 61–62, 64–82, 88, 125, 132, 148–54, 158–60, 166–67, 171, 177, 186–87, 201–2, 212, 233–35, 238–39, 247–52, 254, 286–87, 289, 293–94, 296–302, 314–15
Volpe, Giovanni Battista, *aka* Rovettino, 266–67

Weaver, Robert and Norma, 173–74
Weheliye, Alexander, 251–52
whiteness, 33, 172, 249–50, 265, 272, 292–93
word painting, 158, 241
Wynter, Sylvia, 6–7, 32–33

zanni, xxiii, 232–33
Ziani, Pietro Andrea, 264–65
zingara/o, zingari. *See* "gypsy" character; Rom (as people)
Zotti, Michele, 146, 147–48